R A P E

A History from 1860 to the Present Day

Joanna Bourke

virago

VIRAGO

First published in Great Britain in 2007 by Virago Press
This paperback edition published in 2008 by Virago Press
Reprinted 2008, 2010

The moral right of the author has been asserted

A CIP catalogue record for this book
is available from the British Library

ISBN 978-1-84408-155-4

Typeset in Perpetua by M Rules
Printed and bound in Great Britain by
Clays Ltd, St Ives plc
Printed and bound in Great Britain by Clays Ltd, St Ives plc

Papers used by Virago are natural, renewable and
recyclable products sourced from well-managed forests and certified
in accordance with the rules of the Forest Stewardship Council.

FSC
Mixed Sources
Product group from well-managed
forests and other controlled sources
www.fsc.org Cert no. SGS-COC-004081
© 1996 Forest Stewardship Council

Virago Press
An imprint of
Little, Brown Book Group
100 Victoria Embankment
London EC4Y 0DY

An Hachette UK Company
www.hachette.co.uk

www.virago.co.uk

Contents

Preface

On or about 30 February 2005 I became enraged. I am ashamed to admit it, but this book had been born of fear, not anger. Sexual violence was familiar to me. Like all women, I had been warned of sexual danger since childhood and I had seen marks of violence imprinted on the bodies and spirits of friends. On that day in February, however, I read a Home Office report that revealed that only 5 per cent of rapes reported to the police in the UK ever end in a conviction. My lifelong awareness of the harms caused by sexual violence suddenly crystallised into a political and intellectual project. Of course, I had known that things were bad. In the 1970s just one in three reported rapes resulted in a conviction. But I never imagined that, today, it would have dropped to one in twenty.

Who are these violent people? What can we do about them? Those are the questions I address in this book.

It is a question that has tormented every generation of feminists. Susan Brownmiller's powerful polemic, *Against Our Will* (1975), has been particularly influential in transforming our understanding of sexual violence. But I was a young child when her book was being written. The world that 1960s and 1970s feminists lived in was radically different from that facing my generation. Ironically, it was precisely the political and cultural achievements of second-wave feminists that created the environment that has led many women today to question the positions of some of our predecessors. More to the point, however, men are still getting away with rape, despite three decades of rigorous feminist lobbying and extensive law reform.

Should we despair? No. Sexual abusers have a history. By demystifying the category of rapist we can make him less frightening and more amenable to change. Through the invention of a new politics of masculinity, we can create a future in which sexual violence is no longer inevitable.

As every author knows, books can only be written with the help and encouragement of a community of colleagues, friends, and acquaintances, only a few of whom can be named. The people at Virago made this book possible: I am especially indebted to Lennie Goodings. I am grateful to my agent, Andrew Wylie, and to the patient labours of Katherine Marino and James Pullen. The research for this project could not have taken place without the generous financial support of Birkbeck College, the Arts and Humanities Research Council, the British Academy and the Humanities Research Centre and Research School of Social Sciences at the Australian National University. Thanks to my parents and siblings who, although bemused at why I would choose to write about such a distressing subject, were always encouraging. Special gratitude, though, must go to Efi Avdela, Alexandra Bakalaki, Sean Brady, Nicholas Brown, Ana Carden-Coyne, Roger Cooter, Phaedra Douzina-Balalaki, Nikos Douzinas, Marianne Elliott, Richard Evans, David Feldman, Alan Forth, Vanessa Harding, John Harwood, Robin Haines, Aglaia Komninos, Maria Komninos, Eric Leed, Christos Lyrintzis, Shaun McVeigh, Zoyi Ngaiboye, Akis Papataxiarchis, Dorothy Porter, Heather Prior, Robin Prior, Deborah Rae, Gregory Tychopoulos and Jay Winter. My source of inspiration, sparring companion and nurturer has been Costas Douzinas. His political engagement and sense that the impossible is always possible has taught me that it is never enough to simply *be* angry: I had to act on it.

Finally, converting my fear into political engagement could only have taken place with the help of dozens of women (and a few men) who shared their experiences of sexual abuse with me. They not only taught me a great deal, they also changed the way I look at the world. I dedicate this book to them.

RAPE

A History from 1860 to the Present Day

SECTION ONE

Introduction

For one, the sudden fantastic grimace
Above, the red clown's-grin ripping the chalk sad sky,
Hailstones hatched out of a midsummer, a face
Blanched with love's vile reversal.

CECIL DAY LEWIS, 'SEX-CRIME'[1]

CHAPTER ONE

Sexed Bodies

We are never told her name. None of the American soldiers encircling her would have been interested in such niceties. The only relevant considerations were that she was Vietnamese and a virgin. 'Guys are taking turns screwing her,' recalled one of the participants, adding, 'It was like an animal pack. Nobody was turning their back or nothing. We just stood in line and we screwed her.' While this soldier was 'taking her body by force', his heavily armed comrades stood and watched. Then, suddenly, unexpectedly, the unnamed woman turned towards him. 'Why are you doing this to me?' she said in English. 'Hey . . . why are you doing this to me?'[2]

This is the question I asked myself time and again while writing this book: why do some people set out to sexually humiliate and torture others? The rapist, not the victim, is at the centre of this book. Would you have picked up this book if it was called *Rapists* rather than *Rape*? Most of my friends were honest enough to say 'no'. Why not? It is because we are afraid.

But if we are to dissect the scourge of sexual violence in Britain, America and Australia from the mid-nineteenth century to the present, we must train a steely gaze on the guilty parties: those who carry out these acts. The vast majority of abusers are male. Victims, most of whom are female, tell their stories in this text, but it would be wrong to explore the violence carried out predominantly by men by studying the women they wound. To do otherwise is to contribute to a long-standing tradition of blaming women for their own violation. It is also to encourage the illusion that sexual danger loiters in social spaces, like some agentless germ that a woman can 'catch'. The rapist is not a 'social virus'. He is human.

Deep down, we all recognize this truth. Every one of us is vulnerable, and we all possess the capacity to be vindictive. A significant number of people, however, purposefully set out to exploit the human propensity to suffering. The infliction of cruelty is a choice. Who are these people who opt to deliberately inflict pain in sexual encounters? They may not be immediately recognizable, but their actions are disconcertingly familiar. Rape is a form of social performance. It is highly ritualized. It varies between countries; it changes over time. There is nothing timeless or random about it. Indeed, meaning has not been stripped bare from deeds of brutality, but has been generously bestowed. For perpetrators of sexual violence, it is never enough to merely inflict suffering: those causing injury insist that even victims give meaning to their anguish.

Although rape or sexual abuse may not be the worse thing that can happen to someone, it remains a terrifying and agonizing experience for victims. Rape is not a metaphor for the ruin of a city or nation ('The Rape of Nanking' or 'The Rape of Kuwait'). It is not an environmental disaster ('the rape of our planet'). It is the embodied violation of another person. In Jean Améry's description of being tortured by the Nazis, while the physical agony might fade away, the realization that the other people present are impervious to one's own suffering never wanes. This is what most destroys 'trust in the world'. 'Whoever has succumbed to torture can no longer feel at home in the world,' Améry concluded.[3] Inevitably, therefore, some parts of this book are distressing. I found the relentless talk of violence profoundly upsetting. There is no comforting tale of recovery or redemption to be told in a book that faces up to perpetrators of suffering. One school of thought contends that humans 'come to terms with' their experiences through narrative – that is, by telling stories, we make sense of our lives and rise above our confusion, pain and trauma. The accounts of violence narrated by rapists, however, never metamorphose into anything even remotely transcendent. Instead their stories circle endlessly around acts of transgression.

I can't deny that listening to rapists, and trying to make sense of their extreme experiences, has been a task fraught with anxiety. Focusing on perpetrators of sexual violence is risky. In innumerable subtle ways, misleading dichotomies of male-active and female-passive emerge within texts of violence. Might the focus on male agents of suffering reduce women to mere spectacles of victimization, thus contributing to cultural fantasies of female passivity? There is also the danger of strengthening the other side of the dichotomy: the purported natural link between masculinity and aggression. Man appears primed to rape. He is not.

Yet, in our society, we are frequently exposed to the aggressors' vernacular. Their words try to harm women. No amount of distancing oneself from their comments can negate the fact that simply repeating their distortions threatens to construct a female body that (once again) becomes little more than property, the object of trespass. Rapists literally invade and attempt to conquer the sexual terrain of their victims, and – through transforming her 'no' into his 'yes' – strive to triumph over their social territory too. It is crucial to repudiate the rapist's insistence on his agency, his power, over that of others. I use the word 'victim' in order to draw attention to the hurt of abuse; it is not a moral judgement, nor an identity. Many 'victims' are survivors.

I think there is another difficulty, though, in focusing on violent individuals. In seeking to counter the mindless, yet profoundly satisfying ('them' not 'us') dehumanization of sexual violators, we humanize them. This is both positive and troubling: positive because it removes them from the category of inhuman monsters, and thus makes their actions amenable to change; troubling because we risk becoming over-familiar and inured to the terrible harm they cause. Their rape narratives endeavour to force an intimacy, insist that we adopt their languages. It can seem that in the beginning were *their* words: the grunts, groans and obscenities of rapists made flesh despite the distance of time (history) and place (geography). But we have little to fear in the patois of the rapist. Those of us who have been hurt by him know that he is incapable of silencing us.

Most crucially, however, this book operates within an historical paradigm. It sets itself in opposition to essentialist explanations such as that of evolutionary psychology, which posits a continuity of sexually violent behaviour that can be traced back to our most distant ancestors and can even be located within (male) genes. There is also a constant skirmishing in these pages with those who wish to convert rape into an ahistorical phenomenon, as in the mantra that 'all men are either rapists, rape-fantasists, or beneficiaries of a rape-culture'.[4] On the contrary, rape and sexual violence are deeply rooted in *specific* political, economic and cultural environments.

Defining Rape

There is no single definition of 'rape' or 'sexual abuse'. In popular parlance, contradictory coinages and euphemisms are commonplace. Thus we hear terms such as 'consensual gang rape', 'involuntary brothel prostitution' and 'distorted loving'.[5] Some descriptions of rape nonchalantly acknowledge that the woman willingly 'agreed to' each and every 'sexual intimacy';[6] other accounts coolly concede that the victim desperately pleaded for the men to stop, yet still refuse to admit that the act was in any way forced. Articles on rape often slip casually between discussions of consensual and coerced encounters.[7]

Scholarly commentators hardly inspire more confidence. Does the designation 'rapist' require a stranger brandishing a knife or will a spouse who gradually wears down a 'no' meet the necessary conditions? The definition of sexual abuse as 'a sexual activity witnessed and/or experienced that is emotionally unsettling or disturbing'[8] may seem overly encompassing (when the definition is this broad, have any of us escaped abuse?), but requiring brutal physical force also clearly excludes a universe of cruelty (who can deny the suffering caused by emotional coercion?). Imprecision permeates much clinical and psychiatric literature. In many cases rapists are discussed in the same breath as gays, peeping Toms and verbal harassers. In conducting research for this book I sometimes found it impossible to distinguish analyses of violent rapists or paedophiles from studies focusing on consenting homosexuals (whose actions, these commentators believed, would inevitably degenerate into more serious forms of 'deviance' if not treated or punished). Rape is an 'essentially contested category',[9] infused through and through with political meaning.

What if we turn to the law? Legal definitions have an aura of meticulousness – until explored more carefully. Commentators often assume that legal statutes decree that rape involves the forced penetration of a vagina by a penis. But this is not the case. Rape sometimes must involve violence; other times, lack of consent alone suffices. Still other statutes refer to sexual acts committed 'against a woman's will'. In some jurisdictions proof of penile penetration of a vagina might be required, while others insist on evidence of emission of semen. Yet at other times the law accepts non-penile penetration as evidence of rape: fists, tongues, bottles and broom handles are some of the ways a person can be violated. And the vagina is not the only part of the body that can be forcibly entered. What about the anus or mouth? As I show later, at various times and in various jurisdictions, these p[illegible] included in the corporeal mapping of rape. Men have increa[illegible] allowed to make accusations of rape against other men or even a[illegible] women. Women have raped other women. Since rape legislation h[illegible] often been framed from a male perspective, the victim's unique identity has often been effaced in the legislation, making rape the act of having sex with a woman who does not 'belong' to the perpetrator. Thus married men have often been automatically spared prosecution under rape legislation if their actions were directed against their own 'property', that is, their wife.

The hurdles in prosecuting close friends and intimates for sexual assault have, in all practical ways, had a similar effect. Sexually active women become 'common property'. The ambivalent status of having sex with one's own children is another case in point. In England and Wales incest was not a crime under common law until 1908.[10] Before that incest could be heard in the Ecclesiastical Courts; it was treated as an offence against morals. Most cases of incest first occurred when the girl was under-aged, but the crime was defined as a crime against the family as opposed to child abuse. Before the mid-1970s incest was discussed as though it wasn't child abuse.[11] In many jurisdictions young boys were deemed incapable of rape altogether (in the UK, until the 1993 Sexual Offences Act, boys under the age of fourteen could not be charged with rape). As I will show, these are just a few of the shifts in defining rape that have taken place in British, American and Australian legal jurisdictions during the past 150 years.

Where does this definitional ambiguity leave us? What is rape? Refusing, and in defiance of institutional directives, to bestow primacy on any single, static definition, I have proceeded on the simple principle that sexual abuse is any act called such by a participant or third party. The definition of sexual abuse has two central components. First, a person has to identify a particular act as sexual, however the term 'sexual' is defined. Second, that person must also claim that the act is non-consensual, unwanted or coerced, however they may wish to define those terms. The person performing the act of classification may designate themselves as the victim, the perpetrator or a third party (the suffering of infants, very young children and the severely mentally impaired can only be described by third parties).[12] For the purposes of my analysis, so long as someone says that an act is 'rape' or 'sexual abuse', that claim is accepted.

This definition does not claim normative status. In other words, it does not prescribe what *ought to be adopted* as the correct definition for institutional or political purposes (although it forms the background against which normative statements may emerge). Nor does it set itself up as a truth statement: it remains neutral about the veracity of any specific claim. Rather, the definition is a heuristic device. It enables us to problematize and historicize every component of the complex interactions between sexed bodies.

In writing a history of rape, the advantages of my definition are many. Most importantly, it avoids universalizing and essentializing either sexuality or the body. According to this definition, if a person designates an act as 'sexual', it is. This approach accepts that the body is sexed through discursive practices. In other words: certain body parts or practices *become* sexual through classification and regulation. As legal philosopher Jeanne Schroeder astutely reminds us, there is no sexuality free from construction; no consent that is not constrained; no 'authentic sexuality that can be distorted'.[13] The parts of the body labelled and experienced as 'sexual' change over time. They also vary dramatically over geographical space, which is why I claim to deal with the construction of the rapist only in British, American and Australian societies. The discursive creation of the rapist in Bosnia, Rwanda and Russia awaits a history. As I show throughout this book, there is nothing natural or permanent about the body and its sexualization. The body is constructed as sexed by a host of discourses, including legal, penal, medical and psychological ones. Much of what follows examines how this takes place. Linguistic practices give meaning to bodies.

Nevertheless, this sexed being is not merely a blank slate on to which narratives of violence are inscribed. As I hope will become clearer as you read this book, human subjects *choose* their 'coming into being' from a range of discursive practices circulating within their historical time and place. Their choices don't simply 'represent' their experience; they constitute it. Through linguistic practices, the rapist constructs himself as a human subject. Agency remains important. After all, embodied narratives do not wholly determine the person. As the philosopher Ann J. Cahill expressed it (albeit in relation to rape victims, rather than perpetrators):

> That the embodied subject is understood . . . as constructed by her or his social, historical, and political situation does not necessarily imply that such a subject is wholly and relentlessly determined by the situation. The fact that forces of power act on bodies and affect their literal

> shape and habits does not indicate that those forces act identically or with equal force on every single body . . . [I]ndividual subjects . . . respond to the play of forces in radically different ways . . . the body on which political and social forces act [are not] an inert surface.[14]

The sexed body 'acts as an active and sometimes resistant factor', both in processes of subjection (the rape victims Cahill discusses) and those of subjugation (the perpetrators I scrutinize).

So far I have discussed my definition of rape as useful in the way it allows for a discursive sexing of the human subject, thus avoiding the perils of universalizing and essentializing sexuality or the body. However, more obviously, my definition also enables me to speak about divergent ways of viewing the act of rape and the identity of rapist. In particular, my definition can encompass a dramatic historical shift in the understanding of sexual violence: what was initially seen as an *act* involving sexual violation became eventually conceived as part of an *identity* ('the rapist'). The designation 'rapist' is modern, first used as late as 1883. There are parallels here with philosopher Michel Foucault's discussion of gays. In the course of the nineteenth century the homosexual and (I argue) the rapist 'became a personage, a past, a case history, and a childhood, in addition to being a type of life, a life form, and a morphology . . . Nothing that went into his total composition was unaffected by his sexuality.'[15] Medical and psychiatric literature first began propagating the idea that people engaged in sexually abusive practices were not simply expressing their 'tastes' but were a discrete category of human in the late nineteenth century. In the chapters in Section 3, 'Identities', I examine some of these processes.

If the construction of 'the rapist' as a persona is recent, so too is the notion of 'consent'. My definition merely states that a person can claim that a particular 'sexual' act is rape if it is non-consensual, unwanted or coerced, *however they defined those terms*. This definition deliberately avoids *exclusive* emphasis on liberal notions of consent. A definition of rape based on a male-who-acts and a female-who-reacts (through uttering a 'no' or 'yes') is highly problematic. Female sexuality is not merely reactive, just as male sexuality is not always driven by the need to take the initiative. As I have mentioned already, to assume otherwise is to adopt the rapist's view of the female body as nothing more than property upon which he trespasses.

It is important to note, too, that consent has a history. As historian Pamela Haag argues in her complex and highly insightful *Consent: Sexual*

Rights and the Transformation of American Culture (1999), the liberal notion of consent is a recent construction. According to classical nineteenth-century laissez-faire principles, sexual abuse was concerned no … sire or rejection … of economic co… omen could tak… seducer. As a c… nd Charlotte Gi… it violated a wo… ause it comm… simply ask, 'D… the concept 'co… d,

… course, is … e word as … ual power … onsent, or … ed today.[16]

I a… d extremely common) way to define rape, but it is not the sole definition.

Indeed, at various times in the past, greater importance might have been given to 'coercion' (however defined) in defining sexual abuse than the lack of consent. Coercion, like all the other components in my definition, is also given meaning within specific temporal and topographical spaces. It may include f…cing a sexual encounter through the use of violence, manipulation … blackmail or deceit. The harm of rape can be triggered … nt of brute force. Violence is often the *means* … rape may exist independently of the … instance, is often more eff… victim. In the period I hav… coer… o a fo… m not … ical viol… nore attention has been paid to the harm … tegies used to compel a person to engage in s…

Furthermore, in this book I will be spe… d bodies

and the ways in which violence is sexualized. Although my definition does not essentialize sexuality or sexual organs ('sex' is whatever a person says it is), it remains the case that my definition of rape requires that something be *identified* as 'sex'.

This may seem obvious to many readers. However, many feminists of the 1970s and 1980s radically insisted that rape was about 'power not sex'. Most famously, this has been the argument of the distinguished anti-rape campaigner Susan Brownmiller, but has become mainstream in much feminist writing.[17] Ruth Seifert, for instance, boldly asserted that rape studies 'unanimously came to the conclusion that rape is not a sexual but an aggressive act'.[18] Rape prosecutor Alice Vachss accused people who 'think rape is about sex' with confusing 'the weapon with the motivation'.[19] By focusing on rape as a crime of power, these feminists explicitly rejected the individualistic, psychopathological arguments that reinforced stereotypes of women. At a period when police routinely asked rape victims if they had experienced orgasm during the assault, the assertion that rape had nothing to do with sex but concerned systems of oppression was both psychologically astute and politically prudent.[20]

There are important pragmatic grounds for being sympathetic to this view, but I shall argue against it in the penultimate chapter. As I show throughout this book, rapists choose to attack their victims in a way that they, and often their victims, identify as sexual. As philosopher Catharine MacKinnon correctly observed, 'if it's violence not sex why didn't he just hit her?'[21]

Finally, my definition does not question the right of victims to name any act as 'rape' or 'sexual abuse'. Perpetrators and a male-biased legal system have retained that exclusive entitlement for too long. Every analysis of sexual abuse must involve interrogating the nature of sex: what is 'bad' sex? What do the victims of 'bad sex' say? Conversely (as I discuss in the last chapter), we cannot ignore the complementary question: what constitutes 'good' sex? A commitment to the link between sex and enjoyment remains central to the feminist project.

Masculinity

'Men' are not rapists. Some men are. A few women are. People choose their 'coming into being' from within a range of discursive practices circulating within their historical time and place. Their choices construct themselves as speaking subjects. This book is an exploration of some of the most common narratives of rape and sexual abuse, with an emphasis on how these stories have changed over time. Because of the huge discursive power wielded by professions like law, criminology, psychology and psychiatry, much of my analysis focuses on their languages of violation. In the conclusion I will be looking at alternative narratives available for (primarily male) human subjects – that is, narratives that place sexual aggression outside the threshold of the human.

It is not hard to locate aggressive narratives, though. Western society is deluged by a glossolalia of violence, particularly sexual violence. Nineteenth-century Penny Dreadfuls recounted stories of lust and violation in gruesome detail. Romances lovingly depict their heroines being 'ravished' against their will. One in every eight Hollywood movies includes a rape scene.[22] Indeed, no Western or Vietnam War film would be complete without at least one image of rape. Newspapers increasingly and routinely describe horrific sex attacks. From being located on the periphery of newspaper journalism, stories of rape and sexual assault edged their way to the centre of reportage from the 1980s.[23] The penis is commonly coded as a weapon. Discourses of pleasure and shame vie for attention in stories of sexual abuse.

Furthermore, I suggest, whichever narrative is espoused, they fulfil important functions for the rapist. Through recitation, act of sexual violation is given meaning, including pleasure and pain, guilt and shame. Rape narratives may ultimately always fail, but they are an attempt to grasp something profoundly significant for the perpetrator. The insistence on recitals of consent ('she was wearing a tight red dress') and pleasure ('she was begging for "it"'), for instance, are attempts by sexual abusers to integrate their actions into a bearable narrative of the self. They are integral to the process of enabling the perpetrator to assimilate his (or her) acts into a non-violating/non-traumatizing 'self'. Narrative or putting one's experience into words restores 'the social dimension of the self lost in the midst of violence'.[24] These stories are fundamentally situated in space and time. For example, with the development of a 'dating culture', rapists began attempting to fit their actions into romantic frameworks. In the words of a twenty-year-old coastguard who raped a young hitchhiker, 'You don't want to get hurt, baby – you want to get laid. You want it as much as I do.' Afterwards he offered to buy her dinner.[25] Typically, a rapist in the twentieth century would take the trouble to drive the victim to her home, dropping her off politely at her doorstep. As one police report of a rape described it, 'when the suspect was finished, suspect dressed himself, being very nonchalant about what had happened, making small talk as he dressed. Suspect then drove from scene to bus stop, gave complainant a dollar for bus fare, and left complainant there.'[26]

Such actions are an attempt not only to elicit 'approving' behaviour from the victim by translating forcible rape into romantic seduction, but are also an attempt to shore up his own identity as a man capable of giving as well as receiving sexual pleasure and companionship. The account of sexual violence not only frames cruelty, it enables it.

Prevalence

Rape and sexual abuse are common, even if we do not actually know how many women and men are raped every year. Sexual assault eludes statistical notation. It is not simply that the statistics are not collected in a consistent or reliable manner. They cannot exist. As well as the difficulties I mentioned earlier in defining sexual abuse, legal and societal definitions of sexual abuse can change abruptly. In Britain, for instance, the number of recorded rapes jumped dramatically in 1885 owing to the criminalization of sex with girls between the ages of thirteen and sixteen. Legislative change alone could not explain the increase, however. After all, there was also an increase in 1885 in the number of sexual abuse cases involving girls *under* the age of thirteen. In other words, definitional changes were a response to a broader moral panic about the 'white slavery' of English girls* and, in turn, the legislative changes encouraged greater reportage of abuse.[27] Similarly, the rapid increase in reports of rape since the 1960s was strongly influenced by improvements in the efficiency of reporting and recording these crimes, which were, in turn, partly a response to feminist-led awareness of the harm of such abuse and their encouragement of women to speak out against violation.[28]

But even if we agreed on a definition (let's say a specific legal one), most acts of sexual violence are neither reported nor recorded. For instance, in a national, representative sample of American women in the early 1990s, only 12 per cent of rape victims said that they had reported the crime to the authorities.[29] In that sample, 60 per cent of

*This is discussed in Chapter 3, '"No" Means "Yes"', and Chapter 5, Brutalizing Environments'.

the assaults occurred when the women were below the age of eighteen. But, even among girls and women who were abused since the age of twelve, less than nearly one-third reported the assault to a law enforcement agency, according to the National Crime Victimization Surveys of 1994 and 1995.[30] In Britain a Gallup Poll for 2000 found that one-quarter of people who claimed that either they or someone else in their household had been sexually assaulted or raped failed to report the assault to the police.[31]

The reasons for this failure to complain to authorities are many and varied. Members of minority groups might (rightly) fear that they will not be believed – or sometimes worse, they might be believed and thus find their communities subjected to increased policing. Formally accusing a father, husband or brother could trigger financial catastrophe. In addition, so-called 'secondary victimization' is common. The stigma of sexual victimization remains fierce. Courts often require rape victims literally to air their dirty linen in public. The embarrassment of a court case and the attendant publicity often leads victims of rape to support the downgrading of the offence from rape or sexual assault to simple assault. Offenders might be more likely to plead guilty in such circumstances, confident of receiving a lesser penalty. All in all, victims are correct to doubt their ability to gain sympathy, let alone reparation, from a justice system so weighted towards protecting perpetrators. Indeed, the anger underpinning my decision to write this book was stimulated by statistics revealing that less than 5 per cent of reported cases of rape in the UK ended in the conviction of the perpetrator. Men are getting away with rape. These issues are explored in greater detail in the penultimate chapter.

Rashly ignoring inconsistencies and incompleteness in the statistics, however, what can be deduced from police files, court records and surveys? In this book I focus primarily on the rape and sexual abuse of adults (there is a sophisticated literature on child sexual abuse).[32] In other chapters I present the most reliable estimates for male-on-male rape and female-on-male rape. However, for the largest proportion of rapes – that is, male-on-female attacks – the broad trend seems to be high levels of rape in the early-modern period, which dipped significantly in the period I start with (that is, from the mid-nineteenth century). Rape rates then rose steadily from around the 1910s, with the exception of the 1930s and 1950s (when they stabilized and even dropped). From the mid-1960s rape did not simply rise: it soared.

What about the specifics? The British Crime Survey of 2001 found that the prevalence rate of rape was 0.3 per cent for women over sixteen years. That is equivalent to an estimated 47,000 adult female victims of rape each year. Since the age of sixteen, 7 per cent of women (that is, one in every twenty-seven women) had suffered a serious sexual attack at least once in her lifetime.[33] In the United States the main statistics for rape rates come from the 1940s onwards. According to the Uniform Crime Reports (UCR), in the 1950s reports to the police of rape and attempted rape were about 25 per 100,000 Americans each year. This was almost four times the rate reported in the 1940s. By the 1980s the rate had climbed further, to about 70 per 100,000. Victimization studies generally revealed levels of sexual abuse about three or four times higher than these estimates. But victimization studies showed much less increase over time when compared with the UCR, suggesting that the increase in the UCR rate may be partly the result of increased reporting to the police.[34]

Given the incompleteness and ambiguities of the official statistics, some sociologists and criminologists have attempted to estimate how many men might be willing to *admit* to coercive sexual behaviour. Surveys of male college students in America found that around 25 per cent admitted to one or more forcible attempts at sexual intercourse since entering college.[35] In a study of 359 male college students in Rhode Island, 12 per cent said they would commit sexual assault if the chances of their being reported and punished were removed.[36] Neil Malamuth's startling survey of 1981 discovered that one in every three men attending college reported, hypothetically, that they would rape a woman if they could be sure that they would not be caught. Twenty-six per cent admitted to actually having made a forceful attempt at sexual intercourse that caused observable distress (crying, screaming, fighting or pleading) to the woman.[37]

Finally, the two most cited statistics of sexual abuse are those of Mary Koss and Diana Russell. Koss studied 3187 women and 2972 men at thirty-two American institutions of higher education. She found that over 27 per cent of college women experienced either rape or attempted rape since the age of fourteen. Fifteen per cent of these women had been raped, and 12 per cent experienced attempted rape. Nearly 8 per cent of the college men admitted to perpetrating an act that met the legal definition of rape.[38] In 1984 Diana Russell surveyed 930 randomly selected women over the age of eighteen in San Francisco. Again, 24 per cent of women claimed to have been raped.

This figure soared to 44 per cent when attempted rape was included. Clearly, deciding between such divergent estimates is a political act.

These statistics can seem frightening. As I point out in the last chapter, they are often used deliberately to make women take precautions against the risk of being the next person harmed. We should not be cowed, though. The person who sexually tortures others is a reasoning being who has made choices; those can change. By exposing those cultural tropes that he (and, occasionally, she) employs, we can hold them up to ridicule, and undercut them. We can provide alternatives. The narratives examined in this book were crucial in creating the sexual subject; but no person is relentlessly framed by these abusive scripts. They choose from a pool of circulating meaning. Rapists are not born; they become. By seeing the sexed body as always in the process of 'becoming', of being *rendered* meaningful, we can imagine a world in which different choices are made. We can forge a future without sexual violence.

SECTION TWO

Lies

A few raw souls accuse
Themselves of this felony and find not guilty –
Acquitted on a mere alibi or technical point.
Most see it as an island eruption, viewed
From the safe continent; not dreaming the same fire pent
Within their clay that warps
The night with fluent alarm, their own wrath spewed
Through the red craters of that undistinguished corpse.

CECIL DAY LEWIS, 'SEX-CRIME'[1]

CHAPTER TWO

Rape Myths

In 1880, a week before Christmas, a fourteen-year-old domestic servant called Harriet Stump dressed up in some old flour sacks, blackened her face and, with a doll she had made out of rags, danced at a party held in her employer's house. Her mistress had taught her a song about a 'sinker', that is, a miner who opens new shafts. She sang this risqué song at the party:

> My father is a sinker and a sinker was he
> He sinkered my mother before he had me.

With this song and dance, Harriet Stump destroyed her reputation: henceforth, no court of law would believe her account of having been raped by the master of the house only seven days earlier.

According to Harriet, at about 8.10 on the evening of 11 December 1880, she had been mending some curtains in the parlour at 88 Andover Road, Islington (London). Her mistress Mrs Burholt, had gone out for a stroll with her two daughters (aged thirteen and fourteen). Without warning, Henry Francis Burholt, a baker whose shop was beneath the family's residence, burst into the parlour and bolted the door behind him. In Harriet's words, 'he did not say anything but he came and pushed me down on the sofa and pulled up my clothes, and put a cushion over my face, so that I could not holloo. He then put his thing in me, he hurt me.'

Immediately after she managed to push him off her, Harriet ran across the room. Henry Burholt ran after her, but fell against the table, breaking it. Mrs Burholt returned a few minutes later to witness the hubbub. Her husband was frantically attempting to fix the table, while a tearful Harriet spluttered out the words: 'Mrs Burholt your husband has been and pushed me on the sofa, and pulled up my clothes and got on top of me.' While Henry Burholt yelled, 'I never did it', Mrs Burholt 'jawed' him. Henry Burholt responded by beating his wife with his hat. When calm was restored, Harriet was warned not to tell her mother what had happened since they 'did not want a war and a disgrace'. Harriet was given a 'hanky and Water' and sent to bed.

The following days were a trial for Harriet. Although her mother lived just across the road, Mrs Burholt made sure that she was unable to contact her. According to Harriet, she 'asked Mrs Burholt 5 or 6 times to let me go out and she said she wanted to go out herself'. As a bribe, Mrs Burholt promised to buy her a 'frock'. But instead of things improving, they got worse. Harriet found herself crying all the time and her work suffered. Relations between mistress and servant rapidly broke down. Harriet complained that her mistress

> did buy me a frock and gave it to me, and after that I wanted to tell my mother because she kept jawing me, and did not give me my money, she told me afterwards that she had bought my frock out of my money . . . Mrs Berholt 'jawed' me and said she would not keep me. She did not say why . . . Mrs Burholt began jawing me about a week after it happened. She had not jawed me before.

The day after Christmas, Harriet's mother went to the bakery for bread and, noticing that her daughter looked ill, asked her what was the matter. Overwhelmed by the events of the past few days, Harriet burst into tears. Believing that Harriet was about to 'complain of her place' and beg to be allowed to return home, Harriet's mother simply walked away.

By 5 January Mrs Burholt had tired of Harriet's 'slovenly conduct' and sent for her mother. This time, and in the presence of Mrs Burholt, Harriet once again accused her master of rape. Harriet's mother immediately went to the police and lodged a complaint. Harriet was medically examined and it was found that her hymen had been ruptured 'but not recently'. Later, when pressed in court, the police physician admitted that if the rape had taken place when alleged, any injury would have healed by the time of examination.

When Harriet and her mother returned from the police station, they found Henry Burholt waiting for them. Harriet's mother recalled what happened next:

> He said, 'Now then Mrs Stump what is all this about?'
> I said, 'It's best known to you. What have you been doing to my child?'
> He said, 'Oh! nothing only having a game the same as I would with my own.'
> I said, 'It's a curious way to have a game with a child and it must be seen into.'
> He said, 'It's no use for you to interfere in it, it's too long ago and you had better settle it and I'll give you any recompense you want.'
> I said, 'No, not under the circumstances, nothing would recompense me.'

Henry Burholt also promised that, if Harriet returned to his service, 'my missus and I will make her comfortable'. In the presence of Harriet's father (a labourer and father of twenty-four other children by two wives), Henry Burholt repeatedly boasted, 'It's too long ago. No doctor would be able to tell.' On 17 May 1881 Henry Burholt was arrested and charged with rape. He entered a plea of Not Guilty.

At the trial it was insinuated that fourteen-year-old Harriet had been drinking: hadn't she been sent to the Franchise Tavern to collect the 'Dinner Beer'? She denied it. Hadn't she been overly friendly with two youths called Joseph Attwater and 'Hoppy' Laurence Warki? No. Hadn't her schoolteacher accused her of 'untruthfulness'? No. A week after the rape, hadn't she dressed up for a party hosted by Mrs and Mr Burholt? Yes, but she had been ordered to do so. But, without being ordered, hadn't she also sung a vulgar song at that party? Yes. With that word, Harriet Stump sealed her fate.[2]

As Harriet Stump was to discover, there is no crime more difficult to prove than rape and no injured party more distrusted than the rape victim. People who wish to make their abuse known to the authorities are besieged on all sides by what anti-rape campaigners have branded 'rape myths'. Although frequently disparaged as mere 'cognitive distortions' (as though there existed some pure or undistorted truth existing somewhere in the ether), these myths are relentlessly recited whenever the topic of rape is mentioned. Rape myths take numerous forms, but the most common ones are 'it is impossible to rape a resisting woman', 'men risk being falsely accused of rape' and 'some categories of forced sex are not really rape'. In the following chapter I will be exposing an additional lie: 'no can mean yes'. These myths are pivotal to the meaning of modern sexuality.

Why are these falsehoods given the status of myths? The term does not simply connote 'untruth'. Rather, the use of the word 'myth' is a shorthand way of referring to a structure of meaning permeating a particular culture. As a group of beliefs or images that are imaginatively or viscerally apprehended, myths enable people to create a world of hierarchy and distinction. They create unified communities by clarifying positions and transforming commonplace assumptions into objective truths. As such, myths 'grip the mind'; they seem commonplace, unquestioned. Instead of being expressed as long, coherent narratives, myths survive as fragments – often contradictory and always delivered in sound-bite formats. According to the anthropologist Roland Barthes' famous characterization in *Mythologies* (1972), myths are a form of 'depoliticised speech', abolishing complexity for 'the simplicity of essences'.[3] Attempts to question these myths too stridently rapidly elicit accusations of political correctness – a charge that, ironically, strips political acumen from every form of critique.

In the context of rape, the myths I focus upon here are responsible for converting historical and geographical specificities into flaccid catchphrases that seem clear and self-evident, yet are profoundly damaging for people who suffer sexual abuse. Rape myths situate sexual torture in the realm of moral edification. They enable individuals (such as perpetrators) to place their actions in a framework that is recognizable by others (such as potential victims) while withdrawing legitimacy from people (actual victims, for instance) who wish to contest them. Only an appreciation of the suffering person is capable of exposing the underlying functions of rape myths: that is, attempts to reduce the lived experiences of specific individuals to undifferentiated bodies.

The Vibrating Sword

The first item in the rapists' charter: it is 'impossible to sheath a sword into a vibrating scabbard'.[4] It was a phrase that appeared time and again in textbooks of medical jurisprudence. Metaphorically, the penis was coded as a weapon; the vagina as its passive receptacle. Merely by 'vibrating', this receptacle could ward off attack. In the words of the most prominent jurist of the 1830s, it was 'almost impossible' to rape a resisting woman.[5] Allegations of assault by children like Harriet Stump needed to be probed particularly cautiously: was it even *possible* to rape a child? 'No,' maintained John Leeson, a member of the Royal College of Surgeons who had been troubled by the conviction and death sentence of Thomas Williams for the rape of a child in 1835. He had 'consulted many medical men of eminence and experience in the profession, and . . . they have declared almost the impossibility that the crime [of rape] could be committed upon girls below puberty'. It was 'impossible, under ordinary circumstances, and extremely improbable under any, for the crime of rape to be committed upon females of the tender age'. Even when the accuser was an adult woman, he went on, 'the nicest investigation of the surgeon cannot prove the offence'.[6]

This wasn't a mere fancy of the early nineteenth century. In the 1890s the authors of the textbook *Medical Jurisprudence, Forensic Medicine, and Toxicology* entitled one section of their textbook '*Can* a Woman be Violated Against Her Will?' The question had been 'debated with more or less acerbity since the infancy of medical jurisprudence', these distinguished authors observed, but the 'majority of writers' agreed that 'a fully matured woman, in full possession of her faculties, cannot be raped, contrary to her desire, by a single man'. Because 'light pressure in those parts of the female form' was 'often sufficient to determine an ecchy moss [sic]', they advised lawyers that if 'only slight traces of a struggle are found on the thighs and breasts', this should be taken as evidence that the woman had *failed* to use 'all her strength in her defence'. Indeed, a 'certain class of woman', they continued, were known to routinely 'make a point of a show of resistance before yielding'. For these authors even more serious injuries to a woman's genitals could be explained away: horse-riding, vulvitis or gangrene could cause injuries resembling sexual assault. They reminded jurists of a case fifty years earlier when a boy was accused of raping a four-year-old girl with whom he had been sleeping. Nine days after the alleged rape the child had died of inflammation of the vulva. Luckily for the defendant, the defence was able to show that several other young girls, unknown to the defendant, had died of a similar inflammation of the genitals. Rather than an epidemic of sexual violence, they concluded that the scourge of gangrene had ravaged these young girls.[7]

The metaphor of the vagina as a scabbard that, if agitated, prevented the sheathing of the penile sword continued to be invoked well into the twentieth century. In the words of Gurney Williams in a paper published in the highly respected *International Clinics* in 1913 and purportedly based (as the title proudly declared) on the 'Personal

Investigation of Several Hundred Cases of Rape and of Over Fourteen Thousand Vaginal Examinations', the 'mere crossing of the knees absolutely prevents penetration'. The female body was designed to defy assault. 'Taking into consideration the tremendous power of the pelvic and abductor thigh muscles', Williams argued, it was obvious that 'a man must struggle desperately to penetrate the vagina of a vigorous, virtue-protecting girl'.[8] As late as the mid-1920s a major forensic textbook concurred. The logistics of raping a woman were more difficult than might be imagined, the authors contended. The woman

> has to be overpowered, held on the ground and prevented from screaming, while at the same time her hands must be held or otherwise restricted, and her legs forced open after disposing of her clothes. This, coupled with the fact that she is still able to twist her body, renders the introduction of the penis extremely difficult, even in women used to coitus, and much more so in a virgin.[9]

This wasn't simply a theoretical issue: in police surgeries and courtrooms the myth legitimated distrust of any accuser. In *Practical Forensic Medicine. A Police-Surgeon's Emergency Guide* (1924) physicians who would be called to examine (alleged) rape victims were informed that rape was 'undoubtedly rare'. Despite many years of experience, this divisional surgeon (who had been involved in the Jack the Ripper case) reminded less-experienced police surgeons that he had seen only one case of rape and 'it took four men to do it'.[10] It was a position repeated as late as the 1970s in *Crimes of Violence* (1973), a book published by the Lawyers Co-Operative Publishing Company. The authors insisted that the 'average woman' was

> equipped to interpose effective obstacles to penetration by means of the hands, limbs, and pelvic muscles. Indeed many medical writers insist that these obstacles are practically insurmountable regardless of the usual relative disproportionate strength between men and women.[11]

By definition, all penetration by a sole man was consensual.

Who was this woman who merely had to apply the 'tremendous power' of her pelvic and abductor thigh muscles to evade her assailant? She was not Everywoman. She was not the delicate daughter of an aristocrat. Nor did she have the soft hands of the burgher's wife. The unrapable woman hailed from a more humble home. She was a domestic servant like Harriet Stump or a factory operative. From early childhood girls and women of the working classes were already said to be 'thoroughly conversant with the sexual life in its most bestial manifestations'.[12] Their familiarity with sex was assumed to have prepared them to rebuff its imposition. In the words of J. Dixon Mann in an influential forensic textbook of the 1890s, 'women of the lower classes' were 'accustomed to rough play with individuals both of their own and of the opposite sex', and thus had 'acquire[d] the habit of defending themselves against sportive violence'. Their 'capacity for defence' rendered them capable of frustrating the attempts of any 'ravisher'. In case the point was not clear enough, Mann candidly contrasted these sturdy working women with their more 'delicately nurtured' counterparts who might be 'so appalled by the unwonted violence that her faculties may be partially benumbed and her powers of resistance correspondingly enfeebled'.[13] Mann's opinions were echoed in innumerable other textbooks. Women of the lower classes were 'more used to roughness', echoed the author of *Forensic Medicine. A Text-Book for Students and Practitioners* (1925), and were thus less liable to be terrified than 'a more refined type of woman would be'.[14] Even the type of violence alleged to be directed at working-class women was disparaged – it was 'sportive violence' and thus should be gamely repelled.

With these assumptions in place, only gang rape was even theoretically feasible. Since it was impossible for one man to rape a (working-class) woman, any women from the lower classes who dared claim to have been assaulted was patently lying. Bodily signs of struggle could be dismissed as evidence of token opposition or proof of former misconduct (clumsy bodily comportment on a bicycle, poor hygiene or venereal disease). This myth placed women in an impossible situation. On the one hand, since resistance was said to be always successful, they could never cry rape. On the other hand, the very fact of resistance was used as evidence that they were loose women in the first place.

This fiction that it was impossible to 'sheath a sword into a vibrating scabbard' was gradually abandoned in forensic and legal texts but, in popular culture, it remained one of the most trenchant myths of rape throughout the twentieth century. Hugo Paul's populist *Cry Rape: Anatomy of the Rapist* (1967) confidently told his readers that it was simply not possible for a single man to rape a resisting woman. He went further, in fact, declaring that even *two* men could not succeed 'without such use of force and violence as to abolish the men's desire and potency'. He elaborated in an arithmetic fashion: rape required a minimum of three men to take place, he finally calculated, because 'the average rapist is repelled by violence, especially the marking of the victim'.[15]

Less surprisingly, rapists often concurred. As one group of rapists maintained in the 1970s, 'one man alone could not really rape a girl without using violence'.[16] Some women even found the myth that no woman who 'truly' resisted could be raped strangely appealing, since it held out the possibility of preventing victimization (while unjustly stigmatizing those women who somehow 'failed'). As rape-law reformer Katharine Whitehorn sighed in the 1970s: 'I wish I had a get-out-of-jail-free card for every time I have been told that "women with skirt up run faster than man with trousers down".'[17]

Women Lie

The second item in the rapists' charter: false accusations of rape are endemic. As *The Times* lamented on 16 July 1866, there was 'no small danger' that women 'may have at their absolute disposal the reputation of any man whom they may happen to meet'.[18] Gurney Williams in *International Clinics* believed every man should be wary. As he curtly expressed it in 1913, 'a girl who has had sexual intercourse is in possession of all the medical evidence necessary . . . all she has to do is to make a charge of assault against you to procure your arrest'.[19] Beware of the 'devious and capricious foibles of the female mind when she decides to become the aggressor, not the victim', echoed the author of *Cry Rape: Anatomy of the Rapist*.[20] It was a fear that permeated all sexual interactions between the sexes. As the naïve cockney soldier Edward Casey recalled during the First World War, his comrades advised him to 'be very careful, you may find a girl the [sic] urges you on, and when you try to force them, they cry rape, then it's a case for the coppers'. He decided that the best option was to safeguard his virginity. 'I could be one of the unlucky ones,' he mused, 'from then on no more Girls, no matter how much [I] was pempted [sic].'[21]

The myth about the pervasiveness of false allegations has no basis in fact. Although some women *do* lie, and the consequences for the men they accuse are ruinous, fear of being falsely charged with rape has been stoked up by the vastly disproportionate media attention given to instances of malicious accusations. It is also stirred up by anxiety about the sexual act itself, the exact meaning of 'consent' and how it is communicated, and disquiet about sexual difference. In the penultimate chapter I shall be presenting the evidence against this myth.

Nevertheless, the *belief* that women are prone to lie about rape wields significant political influence. According to the myth, who are these counterfeit victims? In the penultimate chapter I argue that African-American women were and continue to be routinely stigmatized with the accusation that they are liars. In the nineteenth century Irishwomen were commonly accused of being especially prone to dissembling. This slur on Irish womanhood was often tied to financial rewards. In the 1830s, for instance, *The Times* reported that women in the counties of Galway, Mayo and Carlow were making accusations of rape in order to blackmail men into marriage. It was alleged that this form of 'husband-hunting' was all too common. The Irish Poor Law Commissioners even warned that rape accusations, with an eye to marriage, were becoming more frequent. They fretted that 'some men have been lately executed (!!) for the offence'. In order to prevent men from marrying 'out of the dock', parish priests imposed a regulation prohibiting the marriage of couples while prosecution was pending. According to *The Times*, it was a uniquely Irish phenomenon: there was nothing in the parochial annals of England and Wales to match such 'depravity', they insisted. The newspaper did not deny that Englishwomen might commit perjury, influenced by 'a design upon the pockets of men whom they selected as the fathers for their children'. However, there was a vast difference between 'a woman swearing half-a-crown a-week out of a man's pocket' by claiming he impregnated her, and 'swearing away his life – in the event of his refusing to marry her'. 'Perjury for blood,' they thundered, 'has not, we believe, been alleged against the English frail ones . . . It is nevertheless a common crime with Irish women.'[22]

There were, however, some major shifts in the categories of people most commonly blamed for making malicious accusations. In the nineteenth century and then again from the 1980s, accusations made by children were strongly distrusted. In the 1980s the moral panic about deceitful children focused upon middle-class homes.* In contrast, during the nineteenth century it was working-class children (often said to be spurred on by their misguided mothers) who

*This is discussed later in this chapter.

experienced the full brunt of suspicion. The full extent of this panic over the dangerous nature of working-class sexuality and the suggestibility of ignorant mothers could be seen in Michael Ryan's lecture on rape, published in his *Manual of Medical Jurisprudence* (1831). Ryan was incensed by the fact that many of his fellow physicians were unnecessarily worrying working-class mothers about the risk that their child was infected with a venereal disease such as gonorrhoea. Many vaginal secretions, Ryan insisted, were nothing more than the everyday 'purulent discharges' physicians should expect in grimy children. According to Ryan, children could easily be made to accuse innocent men of the crime of rape: the consequences were literally murderous.[23]

Part of the problem for doctors like Ryan was uncertainty about distinguishing venereal infections from childhood vaginitis and vulvitis. While mothers tended to recognize infections as evidence that the child had been 'tampered with', physicians lecturing on the 'diseases of women' in the mid-nineteenth century warned that 'the disease is improperly imagined', particularly when the patients heralded from 'the lower orders'.[24] Although syphilitic discharges had been recognized from the middle of the nineteenth century and gonorrhoea had been identified in 1879, physicians continued to misdiagnose venereal infections as evidence of 'irritation' well into the twentieth century.[25] As late as the 1940s, physicians were reminded that 'in most cases of assault of this type the children come from the poorer classes of home, where the daily tub is not the rule'. Therefore signs of redness or irritation of the child's genitals were probably due to threadworm, not abuse.[26]

However, many physicians identified malice, as opposed to ignorance, behind allegations of rape by working-class children. In *Forensic Medicine and Toxicology* (1898), for instance, it was claimed that mothers deliberately harmed their children's genitals (by scrubbing them with a blackening brush, for instance) in order to make the story sound plausible.[27] The dilation of the vagina with any number of hard objects might also be performed in order to 'substantiate a false claim', cautioned *The Students' Hand-Book of Forensic Medicine and Medical Police* (1883).[28]

These fears of working-class children and their scheming mothers were linked both to class (middle-class children were not thought to be prone to this vice) and to the nature of childhood. In 1901 *The Alienist and Neurologist* attempted to explain the phenomenon by observing that 'much sentiment has been wasted on the frankness of childhood', when there was 'little if anything more false'. In a charge of rape, they continued,

> the child finds herself a center of attraction and it naturally increases her importance and makes her a heroine in her own eyes. Either she has learned her lesson by dint of her mother's inquiries repeated time and again or she has been taught . . . until she can repeat it, word for word.[29]

Physicians had to be particularly careful of this natural propensity of (working-class) girls to dissemble. According to Gurney Williams in 1913, young girls

> will use every means possible to mislead, and their endeavor to evade the truth is at times surprising, and even wonderful. To those unfamiliar with such examinations I would suggest that they listen carefully to the various stories, perhaps fables, which even very small girls will often relate with apparent truthfulness.

He advised physicians to 'be guided only by the physical conditions that present themselves to your eye and finger, and . . . forget what the sense of hearing has suggested. As a matter of fact, the girl's statements often amount to nothing.' A young girl – like her grown-up counterpart – will 'lie as easily as a morphine fiend'.[30]

To a large degree the anxieties of these physicians and jurists emerged from the fact that it was axiomatic to them that working-class girls were precocious. As one Chief Inspector admitted in 1924 after hearing evidence by an eight-year-old girl: 'I'm a married man with two children and [the victim] knows the names of the male organs better than I do.'[31] This sense of unease concerning the clued-up working-class child survived well into the middle of the twentieth century. Dr Letitia Fairfield, medical examiner of children for the London County Council in the 1940s, was one of many physicians who warned of the danger. According to her, it was 'well-known' that 'pathological liars' were extraordinarily difficult to identify. She 'could recall cases of innocent-looking little girls who had invented the whole story', while children who had been 'genuinely assaulted' might not be particularly upset by the experience because girls of the lower classes were 'accustomed to rough-and-tumble play'.[32]

According to a vast range of commentators, girls were 'natural' liars. Addressing a mixed audience of parents and police in 1947, Philip Piker announced that false accusations were most frequently made by children. The reason was simple:

> Youngsters, as you know, go through phases in their development when their imaginations are remarkably active and vivid – and they are apt to turn up with some exceedingly tall stories, some of which they more or less believe at the time. They may report in all seriousness that they have just barely escaped the onslaught of a lion, or that they performed some heroic deed, or even some long and complicated fabrication. And occasionally their phantasies, or their falsehoods, have to do with sexual matters.[33]

Alfred C. Kinsey and his fellow sex researchers concurred, arguing in the groundbreaking *Sexual Behavior in the Human Male* (1948) that children often accused elderly men of molesting them when, in reality, many of these men were impotent. These eminent sex researchers believed that

> Many small girls reflect the public hysteria over the prospect of 'being touched' by a strange person; and many a child, who has no idea at all of the mechanisms of intercourse, interprets affection and simple caressing, from anyone except her own parents, as attempts at rape.

It was regrettable, they concluded, that courts tended to disbelieve sworn testimony that these men were incapable of performing the sex act at all. Instead the 'usual professional interpretation' designated these men 'sexually thwarted, incapable of winning attention from older females, and reduced to vain attempts with children who are unable to defend themselves'.[34] In reality they were innocent and harmless old men.

By the 1960s such fears had grown exponentially. 'We seem to have in our midst a new kind of generation, sometimes described as sex kittens, young girls under the age of consent who seem to have a good deal more knowledge of sex than even a professional prostitute would be expected to have,' began Judge Travers in September 1963. These under-aged women were 'a menace to the youths of the community', he noted (assuming, of course, that all these 'youths' were male). Young girls were 'fully aware that they remain anonymous, while the male who has been a party to the offence with them has his name published and is often severely punished in one way or another, while they go merrily on their way looking for a new victim'. Judge Travers issued a passionate plea for greater powers to be given to the court to send sexually active young women to reformatories.[35]

Working-class girls were not the only people addicted to inventing their own ruin. Hysterical and neurotic women* were also said to be adept at playing this game.[36] As an alienist (the nineteenth-century term for physicians working inside insane asylums) from the New York City Asylums for the Insane noted in 1897, pubescent girls who came from 'neurotic stock' frequently made rape allegations.[37] In 1900 Bernard Sachs (the 'dean of American neurology'[38]) provided a detailed discussion of the link between hysteria and false charges of rape. According to him, hysterical women were liable to make these accusations when in a state of great excitement, such as during menstruation. At these times it was not uncommon for delusions of persecution to develop, causing even 'respectable women' to 'imagine themselves the victims of man's sexual passion'. To illustrate his point Sachs drew upon a case from 1873 in which an eighteen-year-old woman accused the vicar of the village of approaching her while she was praying. She claimed that the vicar invited her into the sacristy, where he violated her. It was only during the trial, when she was questioned about the particulars of the sexual encounter, that her 'childish details' aroused suspicion. Upon medical examination she was found to be nothing more than an hysterical virgin. In another case Sachs pointed to an unmarried woman of thirty-eight who accused her father of inviting a man into her bedroom and raping her and her sister. The woman claimed that, as a result, she had 'been pregnant by this man' for the past two years. The woman was confirmed insane and sent to an asylum.[39] The 'erotic delusions' of hysterical women threatened to diminish respect for religious faith and family.

Indeed, for physicians at the beginning of the twentieth century, one of the main proofs of hysteria in a woman was a propensity to throw about accusations of sexual immodesty. 'So frequent, and so well known to physicians, are such accusations,' argued a Chicago

*This section does not explore false accusations made by women under hypnosis. Because that version of the argument involves interesting reflections on the nature of free will, it is discussed in Chapter 3, '"No" means "Yes"'.

Professor of Preventive and Clinical Medicine in 1911, 'that a man trained in the traditions of the profession is obliged to regard any confession as to unchastity implicating a physician, and made by a woman, of being of a morbid origin.'[40] William Robinson, President of the Medical Board and Chief of the Department of Genito-Urinary Diseases and Dermatology in the Bronx Hospital, agreed. Writing in his popular *America's Sex and Marriage Problems* (1928), Robinson argued that women who made rape accusations were 'degenerate'. They were 'hysterical, psychopathic, notoriety-seeking or simply vicious'. The lies that women weaved were 'really remarkable in their ingenuity', especially since they often ended up believing their own tall tales. For Robinson, women crying rape were probably

> virgins, of a crabbed old-maid type, or they may be of the worn-out prostitute type, who had lived a very promiscuous life and have been finally discarded. Intellectually, these women may be ignorant and conservative, or they may be educated and radical, even ultra-radical. We have been told that even some female varietists [sic], denizens of Greenwich Village, are addicted to this delectable vice of pathologic accusation.

After sweeping so many women into the class of malicious accusers (virgins as well as whores; unschooled women and their educated sisters; conservatives in addition to radicals), Robinson went further. Rather than simply being addicted to lying, women who accused men of rape were labouring under a peculiar sexual perversion. If judges, lawyers and 'people in general' would only study the new science of sexology, they would become aware that 'there is a distinct type of woman that derives a peculiar sadistic pleasure from accusing men, and seeing them suffer'. In some women it was 'the only way in which they can experience sexual satisfaction'. He recalled a case where the rape situation was 'so cunningly contrived that the accused had absolutely no way of proving his innocence'. If he hadn't managed to persuade a physician to testify that the woman was diseased and a 'disreputable character' who had lived in sin with several men, the 'poor man might still be languishing in prison'. His conclusion? 'Accusations of rape should be taken not with a grain but with a pinch of salt.' The 'cunning and malice of some females' was 'beyond belief', he thundered.[41]

By the 1940s the myth of unbridled allegations by scheming women was emphasizing the role of psychic fantasy more than ever. Might women crying rape really be lamenting their lack of a penis? In 1943 Florence Clothier (who worked at the orphanage and child welfare organization called the New England Home for Little Wanderers) certainly thought so. According to Clothier, upon reaching adolescence girls realized with great bitterness that they were not men. To compensate for this lack they developed fantasies of rape, particularly against fathers or father-substitutes.[42]

According to other psychoanalytically inspired narratives, the neurosis that resulted in false rape charges arose out of witnessing the primal sex scene. In 1960 Narcyz Lukianowicz of the Bristol Mental Hospitals proffered the example of a sixteen-year-old girl who accused her father of rape. In taking down her history Lukianowicz found that she had begun masturbating at the age of six after she was allowed to join her parents in their bed when she had the measles. One night she was awakened by the sound of her parents making love. According to Lukianowicz's case notes,

> At first she was frightened and lay still holding her breath. After a while she saw her father getting up, completely naked. When he was passing her bed, she saw his penis. 'It was big and beautiful. I became very excited and subconsciously began to play with my privates, till I trembled with pleasure and could not go any more'.

Thereafter she masturbated to fantasies of her father every night and admitted that 'sometimes I was not sure if it all was real, or sort of a dream only'. At the age of ten she twice attempted to seduce her younger brother and, after he complained, received 'a good hiding' from her father. Feeling rejected, she attempted to make him jealous by staying out late at night. Finally she accused him of rape. According to Lukianowicz, she possessed a 'hysterical personality' which had originated in her 'great excitement' in witnessing the primal scene. This sensation went beyond her 'capacity for mastery as yet developed'. In his words, the primal scene had created a 'traumatic state' by 'flooding the organism with an inappropriate excitation'.[43]

Given this emphasis on acute female pathology, it is not surprising that the *result* of women's perfidiousness was also extreme: women were (literally) killing men with their lies. As one physician told members of the Chicago Academy of Medicine in 1911, women who made rape accusations ('migrainous neuropaths' who were either widowed or deserted by their husbands, he claimed) were capable of rousing their neighbourhood to murder 'by the unwritten law so much eulogized in the south'.[44] In other words, false accusations led to the lynching of innocent men. It was a claim made in pop-psychology books such as Hugo Paul's *Cry Rape: Anatomy of the Rapist*, in which women threatened to publicly accuse African-American men of rape if they did not engage in sexual intercourse with them. Paul recounted the story of a black barman who claimed that a white woman had told him that 'I've always heard you niggers are bigger than our men, let's see if that's right or not . . . Now warm me up, nigger, or you'll burn over a slow fire, so help me!' On another occasion a white woman insisted that this barman act as though he was raping her. 'I tried to beg off,' he recounted, adding that 'I told her that a black boy like me got lynched.' But the woman simply laughed and said, 'I'll make sure you get lynched if you don't do what I say, and you'll have to take your chances.'[45] Paul's purpose was twofold: he intended to both stigmatize white women as liable to make false accusations of rape and titillate his readers with perverted fantasies of black male sexual potency and formidable female nymphomania.

Female pathology and their super-active fantasy lives were two prominent explanations for the belief that women were prone to make false allegations. Other, more rationalistic, reasons were also put forward, however. First, it was claimed that making an allegation lay open the possibility of social or even financial gain; second, those making the allegation garnered psychological rewards.

Social benefits could be cited without difficulty. In many accounts the allegation of rape was made only once a woman became pregnant and the man refused marriage. False rape accusations were an attempt to force marriage. On the basis of the examination of 1500 inmates of state prisoners in the 1930s, the author of *Crime and Sexual Development* (1936) went so far as to urge that many rape charges should really read 'failure to contract marriage' rather than 'rape' because both the man and the woman were 'indulgers'.[46] Others pointed out that not all victims were women: for men raped within prison, there could be more to gain than simply attention and sympathy. Claiming to have been raped might sway a judge to be more lenient towards a prisoner when it came to sentencing.[47] Finally, some commentators observed that there was actual cash to be gained from securing a rape conviction. According to the British government's Criminal Injuries Compensation Board in 2001, a woman raped by one attacker could be given £11,000 as compensation, rising to £22,000 if the rape left her with 'serious bodily injuries' and £27,000 if she was left with 'permanently disabling mental illness confirmed by psychiatric prognosis'. This compared with £1000 for a broken nose, £4400 for a fractured hip ('substantial recovery'), £22,000 for the loss of sight in one eye and £55,000 for the loss of fertility.[48] As an Australian paper mused when the scheme was published in 1996, 'with rape victims now being paid at specific rates, it would hardly be surprising if the incident rate in Merrie Old England skyrockets as the news gets around'.[49] The piece was, of course, simply stoking up a wholly unwarranted panic.

From the 1980s, however, the benefits of making a rape allegation focused upon the mantle of victimhood that it wrapped around the accuser. This talk of the psychological benefits in lying about rape arose out of the dramatic rise in accusations of child sexual abuse that resulted from therapies claiming to be able to recover previously 'forgotten' memories. A range of therapists (mainly unregistered psychotherapists and self-proclaimed specialists in recovering memories of sexual trauma) propagated the notion that painful memories such as those of child sexual abuse were routinely 'repressed' or pushed into the unconscious. Others claimed that such memories became 'dis-associated' (that is, the thoughts or feelings were not integrated with other information and the mind detached itself from the traumatic experience as it occurred). In either case the person undergoing the traumatic event had no conscious recollection of what had happened to her. Later in life, however, these repressed or disassociated memories surfaced in the form of symptoms similar to those of Post-Traumatic Stress Disorder, including severe depression, social dysfunction, drug and alcohol abuse and low self-esteem, or as multiple personalities. The original trauma remained a secret to the suffering woman until it was brought into the conscious mind by therapy.[50]

Therapists, faced with patients exhibiting a bewildering range of symptoms, often sought to 'unlock' the unconscious through a range of therapies, in their belief that bringing the trauma into consciousness would cause their patients to recover. The entire movement was strongly influenced by the notion that remembering – and, in particular, 'talking about it' – was vital for 'recovery'. Many of these patients went on to bring legal suits against their abusers. They accused fathers of rape, mothers of complicity and neighbours and acquaintances with satanic practices.

The problem was that some of these recovered memories proved false. As Elizabeth Loftus, a fervent opponent of recovered memories, correctly observed, the use of questionable therapies only served to 'trivialize the genuine memories of abuse and increase the suffering of real victims'.[51] The phrase 'recovered memory' quickly changed to 'false memory syndrome', and was said to have reached epidemic proportions.[52] In 1992 a False Memory Syndrome Foundation was established, initially in Philadelphia, intent on defending parents being sued by their children for child abuse or satanic abuse. Within a couple of years more than 17,000 families had contacted the Foundation complaining of being falsely accused of sexual abuse.[53] Both the American Medical Association and the Canadian Psychiatric Association issued policy statements describing recovered memory therapies as unreliable.[54]

According to one perspective, then, 'recovered memories' were really false accusations. Unlike the nineteenth-century panic about false accusations in which working-class children were mendacious troublemakers, these accusations were made by adults claiming to have been molested years or decades earlier when they were growing up in comfortable middle-class homes.

But what was there to gain by claiming to having been sexually abused as a child? There were two main answers to this question: one focusing on therapists, the other on patients. Critics pointed out the ease with which therapists could manipulate (either consciously or unconsciously) the memories of patients. Hypnosis, age regression, guided visualization, dream analysis, free association, body massages and injections of sodium pentothal or sodium amytal ('truth drugs') had often been used, despite widespread concerns about their validity in recovering historically accurate memories.[55] Memory turned out to be even more unreliable than previously believed. It was influenced by misinformation and suggestion. Innumerable laboratory studies were able to show how memories were easily distorted at every stage – from the moment an event was perceived, to the way it was stored, to the process of retrieval.[56] The last phase was particularly important for the critics of recovered memories, in part because it was the process most amenable to examination but also because of the unique circumstances in which memories were recovered – that is, in a highly suggestible therapeutic encounter. On the one hand, therapists often held strong opinions about the extent of childhood sexual abuse and the way this had traumatized patients' lives. On the other hand, patients were often led into therapy with the expectation of uncovering such abuse. They were routinely given books and pamphlets encouraging them to associate feelings of unhappiness with the experience of sexual abuse. *The Courage to Heal* (1988) by Ellen Bass and Laura Davis was particularly influential. After informing readers that one in three girls and one in seven boys had been sexually abused, the authors went on to say that 'if you are unable to remember any specific instances . . . but still have a feeling that something abusive happened to you, it probably did'. In writing down the story of their abuse, women were told, 'Do not be reasonable.'[57] Very few critics of the 'recovered memory' movement actually believed that the therapists had acted in bad faith, but a vocal minority claimed that 'recovered memory' practitioners were naïve and incompetent zealots.[58] Worse, they accused these practitioners of greed. Whether unconsciously or consciously, recovering the memories of vulnerable middle-class women was remunerative. Both sides in the squabble rapidly became acrimonious, if not downright vicious.

A more delicate and nuanced debate developed around what the *accusers* might have to gain by claiming to have been sexually abused by their (former) loved ones. The most convincing explanation pointed out that grasping widely circulating trauma narratives* was a way these women (whether consciously or not) were able to 'make sense' of their unhappiness. Feminists (many of whom had been at the heart of recovering memories, giving their patients the 'gift' of being believed in a world in which their voices were routinely denigrated) observed that narratives of sexual abuse were a way some women used to speak publicly about dissatisfactions with their 'lot' in life. Authoritarian family structures, coupled with unfulfilled expectations of sexual pleasure and aggravated by the mass media's obsession with sexuality, had left many middle-class women with a feeling that their lives had been blighted by some force outside their comprehension. The victim trope was important for many women, the author of *The Mismeasure of Women* (1992) argued, because it served as 'a lightning rod for the inchoate feelings of victimization they have as a result of their status in society at large. It provides a clearer focus than such vague enemies as "the system", sexism, deadening work, welfare, or boredom.' For accusers, sexual abuse became 'a metaphor for all that is wrong in women's lives'.[59]

Psychoanalytic clinician Janice Haaken was influential in developing this argument. For her the rise of false memories in the 1980s

*This is discussed in greater depth in Chapter 15, 'Violence, Politics, Erotics'.

represented the way women rebelled against their fathers and families. Forbidden sexual fantasies could be expressed through making these accusations.[60] Trauma stories also helped to keep in check internal divisions within the feminist movement. Haaken pointed out that focusing on retrieving a traumatic memory situated in a woman's childhood positioned 'the perpetrator securely in the past'. She continued, suggesting that

> As some women achieve authority within public life, yet find themselves continuing to be subjugated to more powerful men, it may be less dangerous to confront the 'dead' fathers of early childhood than the living ones. The trauma model also unifies women in a common project that evades differences between those who have achieved authority – including authority over women – and those who are subject to that authority. It defends against the struggle to recognize the various and divergent grievances among women, including the ways in which women may be implicated in the suffering of other women.[61]

Recovering false memories contained an 'emotional truth', if not an historical one.

Furthermore, by recovering memories of sexual abuse women could locate their feelings of despondency within their individual families. This was politically useful in a period in which welfare programmes were being cut. It was a profoundly apolitical mechanism for dealing with misery. The language of victimhood (or survivorhood) 'soothe[s] women temporarily while allowing everyone else to go free', argued Carol Tavris in 'Beware the Incest-Survivor Machine' (1993). 'If the victim can fix herself, nothing has to change,' she added.[62] Individual dysfunctional families or pornography rather than poverty or patriarchy could be blamed for unhappiness.[63]

Finally, the furore over the recovery of historically inaccurate memories of child sexual abuse obscured two important facts. First, as implied above, it created a false dichotomy between 'true' and 'false' memories, as though memory itself was not *always* a creative and complex process. 'Remembering' sexual abuse was part and parcel of the coming-into-being of a person. What was noteworthy was that this *particular* narrative was chosen to frame a woman's life.

Second, and more important, the acrimonious nature of the debate often caused protagonists to ignore the historical context in which memories of abuse came to the fore (and then, from the 1990s, silently faded away). The memory-recovery movement arose in a period when the myth that women were inherently untrustworthy was particularly trenchant. As a result, many therapists felt impelled to go to the opposite extreme, accepting each and every account of abuse as historically true and encouraging women to read their symptoms according to the abuse paradigm. These therapists, and the entire feminist movement of the time, were patently aware that reports of sexual abuse were routinely belittled and dismissed. As one psychotherapist argued, the charge that psychotherapists were causing patients to 'remember' what never happened was 'not a controversy, it's a very large, stinking, red herring'.[64] An enormous proportion of sexual abuse was going unreported, and even highly verified cases were frequently trivialized not only by perpetrators but also the wider community. The crisis that arose out of the acrimonious brawl between 'recovered' and 'false' memory protagonists obscured the fact that the problem of sexual abuse within the family was not primarily an issue of false accusations but of silence about sexual, physical and emotional cruelty against women and children.

Rape is Not Serious

An additional item in the rapists' charter is that some acts of forced sex are not really rape. The only 'true' rapist is a stranger; he employs physical violence. Thus the staple comic image of a man chasing a fleeing woman around his desk is not a portrayal of attempted rape. In rape discourse the penis most typically became a weapon, but (the logic goes) since weapons leave wounds, if there is no wound, there is also no rape. The use of psychological coercion to persuade an unwilling person to engage in sex is also exempted from the tag 'sexual abuse' since any 'sensible woman' should be able to take care of herself. Husbands,* boyfriends and close acquaintances might get 'carried away', but to brand them rapists would be a gross abuse of the term. After all, where is the harm in a bit of sexual raunchiness? Doesn't widening the category of rape once again situate women as helpless pawns, vulnerable to subtle forms of coercion and incapable of independent and rational action? Isn't it wrong to chuck all forms of non-consensual sex into the same disgusting pile?

*See Chapter 11, 'The Home', for a lengthy examination of marital rape.

Other categories of humans were also set outside liberal notions of consenting subjects. In the next chapter I will be developing this argument in the context of issues of the consent of African-Americans and mentally ill women, as well as children. For the purposes of the present chapter, however, I want to point out a range of other ways in which forced intercourse becomes 'bad sex', not rape. Thus criminologist G. D. Woods launched an attack on the relevance of applying notions of consent when discussing an epidemic of violent sex within the deprived suburbs of west and south-west Sydney in the 1960s. Since the 'middle class prohibition against boys hitting girls' was 'meaningless' to these young men, Woods contended, the distinction between consent and coercion needed rethinking. Basing the criterion for consent in terms of 'an absolute distinction between a state of chaste non-contact and the violent laying on of hands' might not be appropriate, he urged. If pack rape simply arose out of 'the very common practice' of 'gang-bangs', then how could the two be distinguished, he asked? 'In most cases,' Woods concluded, 'the dividing line between group intercourse with consent and group intercourse without consent is extremely nebulous.' 'A girl may get into a car with a group of boys and agree that she will "have them on",' Woods noted. However,

> she willingly allows the first three, but changes her mind about the others. Or again, a second carload arrives at the scene and invites itself to partake. What should this be called? Pack rape? It should be remembered that the youths involved will probably have had previous experience of group intercourse in which there was no resistance at all from the girl, or at most only formal protestations and a certain amount of horseplay.[65]

Wood's point was a classic instance of blaming the victims: some 'girls' could not be harmed by gang rape because they had consented in the past.

The category of 'woman' exempted from the harm of rape simply went on expanding. If young women in deprived areas were to be excluded from the category of active agents, so too could their senior equivalents. This argument was made most starkly in 1928 by radical eugenicist William J. Robinson when he came to the defence of John Oliver. This eighteen-year-old man had been sentenced to eighteen months' imprisonment with hard labour for attempting to rape a fifty-eight-year-old woman. Robinson believed the harshness of the penalty was due to 'superstition and sadism'. 'Manifestly the woman was past child-bearing age,' he began, adding that there was

> no suggestion that the boy had venereal disease. If the boy had knocked out one of the woman's teeth, and thereby injured her for life, he would probably have been fined 5 shillings and warned to be more careful in the future. Yet for doing her a far smaller injury he is given the next thing to a sentence of death . . . If it were not unchivalrous to do so, we would like to ask the question whether the woman of 58 was really so shocked and horrified by the boy's attempt that a sentence of 18 months of hard labour was necessary to soothe and calm her maidenly feelings.[66]

Not surprisingly, Robinson also adhered to other rape myths, claiming that 99 per cent of rape accusations were lies. Even as late as 2001, evolutionary psychologists like Randy Thornhill and Craig Palmer in their *A Natural History of Rape* (2001) erroneously insisted that women past the age of childbirth were less harmed by sexual coercion when compared with their more fertile younger sisters.[67]

John Oliver had attacked an older stranger who was assumed to have been 'well used' already and therefore not likely to be physically or psychologically wounded by stranger rape. However, the myth that non-consensual sex might not always be 'so bad' was easily stretched further to exonerate men who sexually violated their girlfriends. Commonly held notions about male sexual needs and female seductiveness, together with problems associated with the amassing of evidence ('she said' versus 'he said'), made it almost impossible for a woman to successfully prosecute her boyfriend or date for rape. It was popularly assumed that if a woman had 'got herself into the situation' she deserved 'it'. Commonplace tendencies for people to regard the world as 'just' bolstered assumptions that a victim must have done something herself to 'deserve it'.

And what was so wrong about a man forcing his girlfriend to have sex if he really wanted 'it' and she had given him some encouragement? A classic statement rejecting the gravity of date rape was published in the *San Francisco Examiner* on 4 August 1991 when the right-wing popular advice columnist Ann Landers published a letter purporting to be 'A Male's Theory on Date Rape'. The letter writer informed readers that there was 'no hiding a man's arousal'. 'Usually', the woman

> enjoys bringing it on every bit as much as the man enjoys the experience. It is all part of human nature. The problem is that for many men, there is only one way to end arousal and that is ejaculation. At the height of ecstasy, does the female partner think the man is going to excuse himself, go . . . and take a cold shower? No way. He *wants the final act* . . . If the female partner has made up her mind that there is NOT going to be penetration, she should put a stop to the proceedings at the very first sign of male arousal. A female who doesn't want the total sexual experience should have healthy respect for a flashing warning light.

Landers concurred, echoing this correspondent's view that a woman who 'agrees to hours of petting but does not want to complete the sex act is asking for trouble and she will probably get it'.[68] In such accounts it was the woman's responsibility to act as gatekeeper to sex by ensuring that men act 'correctly'. The men themselves were excused as mere victims of their irrepressible male sex organs.* In addition there is some evidence to suggest that, with improvements in forensics making it more difficult for the accused to deny that intercourse has taken place, there was an increased tendency for rapists to deliberately set up date-like encounters.[69] From the late twentieth century the rise of a dating culture (without chaperones), the introduction of effective measures of birth control and the emphasis on the desirability of pre-marital sex merely exacerbated commonplace notions that a man could 'force' his girlfriend to have sex without actually 'raping' her.

It is not surprising, then, that rape by close (although non-familial) acquaintances increased from the mid-twentieth century. Although the *OED* states that the term 'date rape' was first used in 1975 by Susan Brownmiller in *Against Our Will*, there was awareness of the problem long before her book was published.[70] In 1957, for instance, sociologists Clifford Kirkpatrick and Eugene J. Kanin reported that 56 per cent of female university students had experienced 'an offensively aggressive episode' in the previous year.[71] In another survey Kanin reported that 62 per cent of the 262 first-year university women he questioned reported that they had experienced 'offensive male sexual aggression' in the year before university and 13 per cent had experienced attempted or completed

*This is discussed further in Chapter 15, 'Violence, Politics, Erotics'.

unwanted intercourse.[72] A vast array of surveys showed that between one-fifth and half of girls experienced physical violence during a date.[73]

Young men even owned up to acting in sexually aggressive ways. According to one famous study in the early 1980s, 26 per cent of college men surveyed admitted that they had made a forceful attempt at sexual intercourse that caused observable distress to the woman in the form of crying, screaming, fighting or pleading. Just over half admitted that they had been sexually aggressive without attempting penetration. Thirty per cent of these men admitted that they would rape a woman if they could be sure that they would never get caught.[74] Another survey found that 15 per cent of men admitted that they had forced or coerced a woman to engage in sexual intercourse against her will.[75] Alcohol and drugs were crucial props in such scenarios, with 39 per cent of male students in another survey claiming that it was 'all right' to force sex if a girl was 'stoned' or drunk.[76]

Clearly there was considerable confusion about where the line should be drawn between 'consensual sex' and 'rape'. For instance, in one survey of college men, 73 per cent of respondents believed that a woman should 'have the final say' when it came to sexual intercourse. Yet significant proportions of these same respondents believed that forced sex was acceptable under the following conditions: if the couple had been dating for a period of time (24 per cent said that made forced sex acceptable), if she had touched his genitals (29 per cent) or if either had performed oral sex on the other (34–5 per cent).[77] In case this gives the impression that such moral fuzziness was a problem unique to university culture, a study of 1700 middle-school children by the Rhode Island Rape Crisis Center found that 65 per cent of the boys and 57 per cent of the girls believed it was acceptable for a man to force a woman to have sex with him if they had been dating for more than six months.[78] A sizeable proportion of young people simply do not see certain acts of sexual coercion as morally wrong.

Why are there such high levels of violence in intimate relationships? Eugene Kanin blamed 'the lack of parental sex guidance and the absence of older siblings'. In particular he was struck by the 'significant correlation' between the presence of an older male sibling and a young woman's ability to *avoid* sexual aggression. Older brothers were responsible for instructing their sisters about male sexual exploitation and might also have given them 'an added insight and knowledge into the male subculture' and thus the ability to avoid it. Less positively,

Kanin mused that the presence of an older male sibling might simply have meant 'greater understanding of male expectations and consequently an increased tolerance of male aggressiveness, rendering the girls less prone to report such episodes as offensive'. Given that 70 per cent of the aggressive encounters Kanin examined took place in cars, he emphasized the 'role of the automobile in providing seclusion and escape from social controls'. He also observed that 'certain characteristics of the pair relationship also increased the probability of aggression'. In particular young women might not realize that their demeanour and body shape were provocative to young men. And young men might have been influenced by the 'stereotype of the moving picture and pulp-magazine heroine being forcefully embraced and kissed, momentarily resisting but soon to melt in the hero's arms and become overly receptive'.[79]

Kanin's emphasis on the dangerous nature of the dating culture was picked up by many other commentators. In the words of the authors of 'Victimology and Rape: The Case of the Legitimate Victim' (1973), the 'American dating system is a major contributing factor to the date rape scene' because it placed young men and women who had widely 'differing expectations regarding sex role behavior' in 'ambiguous situations with maximum privacy'.[80] These authors also identified cars as particularly perilous locations for women on a date, but also pointed the finger of blame at cinemas and fraternity houses.

Of all the types of rapists I examine in this book, date rapists were most prone to find ways to excuse their behaviour. Drink was a favourite excuse. Thus, in a survey of seventy-one date rapists in the 1980s, one-fifth claimed that the incident would not have occurred if they had not been drunk. An additional 41 per cent argued that alcohol had been a 'disinhibiting agent' that had facilitated 'the perception of their partners' coital receptivity'.[81] Interestingly, however, other surveys showed how the disinhibitory effect of alcohol was at least partly socially constructed. In an intriguing experiment by psychologists W. H. George and G. A. Marlatt entitled 'The Effects of Alcohol and Anger on Interest in Violence, Erotica, and Deviance' (1986), college students were given drinks while they looked at violent and violent-erotic slides. The students were given either alcohol, non-alcohol or an alcohol-placebo (that is, a liquid the researchers maintained was alcohol when it was not). These psychologists discovered that students who *believed* they were drinking alcohol (whether this was correct or incorrect) 'behaved as if actualizing the widespread belief that alcohol promotes violence and sexual responsiveness'. Indeed, the more the students *expected* a link between drinking alcohol and either acting violently or in sexually responsive ways, the more deviant their behaviour. The researchers concluded that men who believed they had consumed alcohol could 'attribute their deviant behavior to drunkenness rather than to the self'. In other words, drinking alcohol provided 'both the impetus and alibi for inappropriate behavior'.[82]

Shocked by its prevalence, feminists of the 1970s and 1980s decided to tell the world that date violence was unacceptable. To critics of the designation 'date rape' who argued that it demeaned women to imply that they were 'so vulnerable to coercion or manipulation that they must always be escorted by the strong arm of the law', these critics pointed out that it 'also demeans women to be raped and to be disbelieved because we *do not* hold men responsible for what they do with their penises'. As Lynne Henderson lamented in 'Rape and Responsibility' (1992), it was astounding 'how quickly the move is made away from male responsibility to focusing on female responsibility'.[83]

For such feminists, a woman had the right to withdraw consent at any time, and not just at her male partner's bidding. Feminists went on to point out that explanations for date rape that emphasize risky situations (like cars or fraternity halls) implied that danger was 'natural' to these locations, as opposed to deliberately chosen by coercive men in order to maximize their potential for abusing. Indeed, simply coining the words 'date rape' and 'acquaintance rape' was revolutionary, disrupting notions of what was normal and giving woman a language with which to speak about sexual violation in their everyday lives. As a result, possibilities for resistance and change were made available. They did not seek to trivialize stranger rape, but rather to '*end* the trivialization of those who had been nonforcibly raped'.[84]

Feminist campaigning against date and acquaintance rape had positive results. As a result of feminist educative schemes, date and acquaintance rape did become less accepted. Publicly acknowledged levels of acquaintance rape thus rose dramatically from the 1970s. In the United Kingdom, for instance, the proportion of rape convictions where the offender and victim were intimately known to each other increased from 14 per cent in 1973 to 30 per cent in 1985 while stranger rapes fell in the same period from 47 per cent of all rapes to 39 per cent.[85] In the 1990s, stranger rapes made up only 12 per cent of all reported rapes: 45 per cent of rapes were committed by acquaintances and 43 per cent by intimates.[86] Although a huge proportion of date and acquaintance rapes were still not reported (let alone reached court), public awareness of this new form of 'wrong' and the dismantling of the myth of the inoffensive nature of date rape were significant victories for the 1970s and 1980s feminist movement.

Rape myths are strategies by which less powerful members of a community could be even further marginalized. Children of the poor, hysterics, unmarried, menstruating or menopausal women and discontented wives: these groups needed to be put in their place lest they usurp some of the power of their (male) betters. As power regimes in society more generally shifted, so too did the rhetoric of false accusations, with fears about accusations by children and women in the working class gradually giving way to panic over the 'bolshy' women of the feminist movement and their wide band of supporters. These rape myths, and the way they permeated society, demonstrate the immense cultural sympathy for the sexual abuser. By creating a trauma aesthetic, sorting perpetrators, bystanders and victims into positions of hierarchy, abusers are able to justify inflicting pain.[87] Just as the pitiless actions of some perpetrators (boyfriends, for instance) are presented as more 'comprehensible' than others, so too victims are sorted into a hierarchy of suffering (African-American women or older women, for example, did not 'suffer' as much from rape as did young white women). Thus the rapist is judged by the moral status of his victim.[88] Even in law, certain kinds of violence are privileged over other: physical violence over invisible abuse. In this way the law not only prohibits but creates what is normal. Underlying languages and clichés of power are effectively employed to command other bodies.

I began this chapter with the rape of fourteen-year-old Harriet Stump. In 1880 Stump was doomed to lose her case in court after evidence emerged that she had sung a risqué song at a party. One important item in the rapists' charter is that evidence of sexual knowledge or experience renders a girl 'fair game' to sexual approaches from anyone. Unfortunately for Stump, a number of other rape myths could also be applied to her. She was a female child lobbing an accusation of rape against a respectable baker and family man. Delay in reporting the rape to the authorities meant that physical evidence of the attack was not forthcoming. There were suggestions (which she vigorously denied) that she had been seen in the Franchise Tavern collecting

'Dinner Beer' and was overly friendly with two local boys. When her alleged attacker was confronted, he claimed that he was 'only having a game the same as I would with my own [adolescent daughters]'. Harriet Stump was caught within a sexual script biased towards perpetrators of sexual violence.

The various items in the rapists' charter are so widely accepted within society that they attain the status of myths, or commonplace and unquestioned ways of looking at the world. Indeed, the myths are so accepted that even those men who willingly admit to having forced a woman to engage in sex with them remain resolutely opposed to their actions being labelled 'rape'.[89] When, from the 1970s, feminists began questioning the veracity of these myths, they were bombarded with accusations of political correctness. Rape myths thus serve to smear the characters and intelligence of people who dare to suggest that rape exists and sexual abuse is wrong, women are prone to making false accusations and rape is not harmful in all circumstances. As we shall see in the next chapter, though, the most potent item in the rapists' charter is that 'no' often does not mean 'no'.

CHAPTER THREE

'No' Means 'Yes'

On 15 August 1973 William Morgan, a senior non-commissioned officer in the Royal Air Force, went out drinking with three other RAF men, none of whom had met before that night. In the course of the evening he persuaded them that his wife Daphne was 'kinky', enjoyed group sex and 'the only way she could get "turned on" was by pretending to be raped. The men accepted his story. They went to his house, found Daphne Morgan sleeping in a room with her eleven-year-old son and dragged her screaming to another room, where all three men raped her. She cried and struggled throughout the assaults. When she yelled to her children to call the police, the men held her mouth and nose shut. When she finally managed to break free, she ran out of the house, drove to a hospital and told medical personnel that she had been raped.

Daphne Morgan appealed to the justice system. Her husband couldn't be prosecuted for rape because she was still married to him; instead he was tried for aiding and abetting a rape.* The other men faced rape charges. All three defendants admitted that Morgan had cried 'no' many times. Yes, she had screamed. She had struggled. But this, they claimed, did not make them rapists.

Their defence must have surprised Daphne Morgan. The defendants' counsel appealed to the well-established legal concept of *mens rea*, or 'guilty mind'. To be liable for conviction, a person must *intend*

*This is discussed in Chapter 11, 'The Home'.

to act illegally. At the very least, the person must have been reckless about committing an unlawful act. As the distinguished jurist H. L. A. Hart explained in *Punishment and Responsibility* (1968),

> All civilized penal systems make liability to punishment for at any rate serious crime dependent not merely on the fact that the person to be punished has done the outward act of a crime, but on his having done it in a certain state or frame of mind or will. These mental or intellectual elements are many and various and are collected together in the terminology of English jurists under the simple sounding description of mens rea, a guilty mind.[1]

To be found guilty of rape, therefore, a man must have *believed* that his victim was not consenting. If he sincerely believed that she was consenting to sexual intercourse, then he lacked the requisite *mens rea* to rape.[2] According to the lawyers defending the three men who attacked Daphne Morgan, the defendants had believed that she had consented when she had not. They had not *intended* to have sex with a non-consenting woman.

When the case came to trial, however, the trial judge instructed the jury that, to return a guilty verdict, they had to be convinced not only that the defendants believed that Mrs Morgan was consenting, but also that this belief was 'reasonable'. If 'a reasonable man . . . applied his mind and thought about the matter' would he conclude that Daphne Morgan's screams and struggles signalled non-consent, or would they believe her husband's assertion that resistance was the only way Daphne Morgan could get 'turned on'? The jury convicted the three accused men of rape and William Morgan of aiding and abetting the rape.

Was the trial judge correct, however, to tell the jury that these men's belief had to be 'reasonable'? Absolutely not, the defence continued to argue. The men were young and naïve; William Morgan had convinced them that his wife had this odd sexual proclivity to say 'no' when she meant 'yes'. Even if their belief that Daphne Morgan was consenting was 'unreasonable', the *sincerity* of the belief rendered them innocent.

When an appeal was made to the House of Lords, the majority of the Law Lords sided with the defence (although they upheld the conviction on the view that the jury would have convicted the men anyway). In a prominent statement Lord Hailsham argued that for an act to be classed as rape, the perpetrators should have *intended* to force non-consensual intercourse.

In his words,

> [o]nce one has accepted . . . that the guilty state of mind is an intention to commit [rape], it seems to me to follow as a matter of inexorable logic that there is no room either for a 'defence' of honest belief or mistake, or for a defence of honest and reasonable belief and mistake. Either the prosecution proves that the accused had the requisite intent, or it does not . . . Since honest belief clearly negates intent, the reasonableness or otherwise of that belief can only be evidence for or against the view that the belief and therefore the intent was actually held.[3]

Under the ruling of R. v. Morgan (1975), therefore, the subjective state of mind of the defendants could decide whether a rape 'really' had taken place; objective evidence of non-consent (crying, screaming, saying 'no') was no longer sufficient proof. What was important was what was going on in the defendants' minds. As the author of 'Twenty Years of *Morgan*' (1995) put it, the

> court stated that a man who had intercourse with a woman based on an inadequate belief in consent would not say that he had committed rape. This line of reasoning reflects a traditionally masculine perception of rape. While a man who acts on an unreasonable belief in consent will not believe that he has committed rape, a woman who is subjected to the act of sexual intercourse without her consent will believe that she has been raped, regardless of the mental state of the aggressor.[4]

A man's *mens rea* was more important than the victim's autonomy and bodily experience. Despite the fact that the only evidence of consent the defendants possessed came from her husband, its unreasonableness was irrelevant. No matter how loudly Daphne Morgan screamed 'no', the law's focus on the mind (*mens rea*) of the perpetrators was heard more clearly. The victim's clear 'no' became 'yes'.

Sexual intimacy between two or more people is predicated on the word 'yes', yet 'no' sounds erotic to many people, particularly men. Surveys from the last quarter of the twentieth century found that while only 3 per cent of women fantasized about forcing someone to have sex, between 13 and 33 per cent of men admitted to this fantasy.[5] Pornographic scenes in which a woman has to be subdued before becoming sexually excited are intensely arousing for many young men.

Indeed, studies have found that a significant minority of men find such scenes *more* arousing than portrayals of non-violent, consensual sex.[6] Men often find 'no' sexy. Worse, as the rapists of Daphne Morgan found, some men believe that 'no' *really* does mean 'yes'.

Law attempts (and fails) to regulate fantasies. As opposed to the actions of volatile bodies, the law lays down strict contracts. The premise that sexual intercourse is a contract between two or more consenting individuals forms the basis of most legal formulations of sexual abuse. It is no surprise, then, that the justification most frequently tripping off the rapist's tongue is 'she consented'. In the privacy of the home or in more public settings, such as the pub, club or court of law, assertions that the alleged victim actually 'wanted it' resound louder than any other plea. In examining rape, particularly in a legal setting, the most important question is: *did* a person consent to a particular act of sexual intercourse? And who decides the answer?

The Betraying Body

The body is an enigma. Might a woman's body betray a silent willingness to engage in sex, independently of any vocal exclamation of rejection? In particular, might any subsequent pregnancy provide evidence that a woman making an accusation of rape had not been averse to intercourse after all? Until the early nineteenth century many physicians and jurists would have answered in the affirmative. Onesipherous W. Bartley's widely read *A Treatise on Forensic Medicine or Medical Jurisprudence* (1815) observed that conception required a woman's orgasm. And female orgasm was impossible in rape. In his deliberately enigmatic prose, conception

> must depend on the exciting passion that predominates; to this effect, the *œstrum / veneris* must be excited to such a degree as to produce that mutual *orgasm* which is essentially necessary to impregnation; if any desponding or depressing passion presides, this will not be accomplished.

In case readers didn't grasp his point, Bartley drew a parallel with a man confined in a room enveloped in flames. Eventually the man escaped through a window 'of awful height from the ground'. What was the 'predominant passion' that enabled him to escape? It was not the 'impulse of fear', declared Bartley, because fear paralyses. Rather, his energies were animated only through the passion of hope. Equally, according to Bartley's logic, if a woman became pregnant as the result of a sexual assault, the conception was proof that she must have been under the 'cheering influence' of an 'exciting passion'.[7]

The notion that a woman 'under the control of depressing passions' such as terror or alarm could not get pregnant was increasingly ridiculed. Forensic textbooks, however, still found it necessary to mention the belief until the end of the century, if only to discredit it.[8] What other corporeal states could override questions of consent? A sleeping woman, for instance, might be thought to be incapable of saying 'yes' or 'no'. But was it plausible to believe that a man could have sex with a woman without awakening her? In classic texts such as H. Aubrey Husband's *The Student's Hand-Book of Forensic Medicine and Medical Police* (1883) and Charles Gilbert Chaddock's 'Sexual Crimes' in *A System of Legal Medicine* (1900), it was decreed that a sleeping virgin could not be raped but a woman 'accustomed to sexual intercourse' might be.[9] Indeed, in 1862, the *Edinburgh Medical Journal* described the case of a married woman who 'slept so heavily that her husband frequently had connection with her during sleep'.[10]

Other more intrusive means could be used to make the victim forfeit her ability to consent or not: sexual abusers could bypass a woman's right to permit intercourse by administering alcohol, drugs or strong anaesthetics. Nineteenth-century feminists and moral reformers on both the political right and left united in campaigning against men's use of 'stupefying draughts' to coerce vulnerable women into sexual debauchery generally and prostitution in particular. Indeed, one of the main planks of the temperance movement was the link between alcohol and sexual violence. Used to 'seduce' young women, alcohol and other drugs were said to be responsible for the corruption of innumerable innocent girls. The Reverend Edgar of Belfast, speaking in London in 1841, for instance, claimed personal knowledge of a species of 'gay girl' who were at risk. Typically, such girls were 'innocent as a lamb', yet were 'enticed away by an old satanic procuress in the hope of a pleasant party, and then besotted and drugged' until they 'fell an easy prey'. At other times the innocent girl might be 'lured' into vice by a 'tempting basilisk' professing his 'honourable love'. But when she 'awoke to consciousness from his stupefying draught', she found herself 'hopeless and ruined, and lost'.[11]

From the late nineteenth century the temperance campaign grew in political power, fuelled by sensational stories of 'innocents' being given alcohol or drugs, after which they would be sexually assaulted and cast from respectable society.[12] The only options for debauched women who refused to sink into 'total depravity' were madness or suicide. Even *The Times*, a normally restrained newspaper, spread such sensationalist stories. In 1877, for instance, it carried a lurid tale of 'criminal outrage', which 'has created the utmost indignation and has had the most deplorable results'. According to the reporter, two daughters of 'highly respectable' parents went for a walk along the Brixton Road (London) when two 'well-dressed, gentlemanly-looking' men approached them. Although the two women refused to accompany the men to a theatrical performance in the Strand, they agreed to a stroll. Thirst was their downfall: when they accompanied the men to a pub, their drinks were 'drugged'. The young women 'became stupefied, and while in that condition the scoundrels succeeded in outraging them' in a small lodging house. Then, as *The Times* put it,

> unseen by the landlady, the two men shortly after quitted the place together. Not suspecting what had happened, and being, of course, ignorant of the respectability of the poor girls, the landlady treated them as persons of questionable repute, and at about 11 o'clock at night ejected them from her house. Frenzied . . . and overwhelmed with a sense of disgrace, they had not the courage, nor had they probably the sense, to retrace their steps home. The poor creatures, therefore, wandered about all night in a distracted state.

The sisters were eventually found 'in a most deplorable state huddled together in one of the recesses on Blackfriars-Bridge'. One sister 'did not long survive her shame' and died; the other sister, reported *The Times*, was in a 'state of prostration'. Even if she survived, it was feared that 'her mind is likely in any case to be affected'. At the time of the report no one had been apprehended.[13]

Such tragic tales spread widely, forming the mainstay of the 'yellow press' (what we now call tabloid journalism) and fuelling major campaigns against the sale of alcohol. For these temperance reformers the poisonous cup inevitably led to the downfall of working-class girls, who would be preyed upon by equally drunk fathers, lovers and neighbours. Punishing these men was imperative. As leading reformer Francis William Newman (brother of Cardinal Newman) argued in 1889, any man who used alcohol to 'gain his end' should be found guilty of 'aggravated seduction'. He lamented the existence of 'omnipresent drink-shops' in which 'vile plebeians corrupt girls of their own order'. After calling for the closing down of these shops in order to 'extinguish this atrocity', Newman insisted that, irrespective of the woman's age, men who induced women to drink 'as an aid to his plot against her virtue' should be punished most severely. 'The fatal cup equalizes all ages, so that the woman of 30 becomes as defenceless as the child of 14,' he thundered. The crime 'should be simply called "Rape"'.[14] Although Newman was a staunch advocate of abstinence in tobacco and meat as well as alcohol, his proselytizing activities were highly class-based. He was less condemnatory of the wealthy consumers of the 'fatal cup' than he was of the 'vile plebeians' crowding the streets of the new industrial cities.

Although this late-nineteenth-century panic has a historical specificity and is linked to alarm about working-class men and women 'out of control', it has seen a revival in the late twentieth and early twenty-first centuries with fears that young women are being raped during alcohol- or drug-fuelled parties. The spread of the drugs Gamma-Hydroxybutyrate (GHB, also known as 'easy lay') and Flunitrazepam (Rohypnol or 'roofie') turned these fears into a moral panic.[15] Contrary to popular belief, GHB and roofie rarely cause women to lose consciousness. Rather, the drugs operate by sidestepping questions of consent by lowering anxiety and inhibitions in the victim. Because they induce anterograde amnesia, thus eroding the victim's ability to recollect events afterwards (creating a 'memory void' which the brain rationalizes as unconsciousness), these drugs are particularly dangerous.[16] In combination with alcohol, they hold particular terror. Thus the Roofie Foundation warned women to be 'afraid . . . very afraid!'.[17]

In another echo of the nineteenth-century panic, the use of alcohol to sidestep issues of consent continues to elicit concern. In 'Dirty Work in the Moral Maze' (2006), outspoken journalist Rod Liddle believed this was simply a moral scare. He was responding to a report by the Solicitor General pressing for clearer advice to be given to juries in rape cases where the victim was drunk. The courts, Liddle argued,

> believe that it is the individual's responsibility not to get drunk in the first place. This strikes me as entirely sensible . . . We know that imbibing alcohol makes us drunk, loosens our inhibitions and our tongues – and, you have to say, very often our clothing. It would be stretching the credulity of any jury to argue that on the night in question, m'lud, we downed pint after pint of fizzy lager, plus several chasers, not knowing the likely personality change that this action would engender and indeed the possible denouement: . . . having desultory sexual intercourse with that rather nice high-cheekboned chap in the tight jeans. Of course we knew.[18]

Such overblown rhetoric disguises the operation of a double standard in contemporary society. On the one hand, the consumption of alcohol is viewed as making women *more* responsible for their own rape: by choosing to get drunk, women are deliberately increasing their risk and should be prepared to face the consequences. On the other hand, male consumption of alcohol is viewed as making them *less* responsible for their actions: by choosing to get drunk, men increase the chance of inappropriate behaviour and should *not* therefore be required to pay the price for their actions.

Alcohol has a long history of being used to force sexual intercourse on an unwilling woman, but more technologically sophisticated ways may render a woman unconscious in order that sexual liberties may be taken. One of the most striking of these new techniques followed the invention of forms of anaesthetics from the mid-nineteenth century. Although discovered in 1831, chloroform was first used on a patient in 1847. As early as 1850 the press was already reporting cases of attempted rape using this new substance.[19]

The crime was not restricted to men. Women, too, used chloroform to sexually assault and rob men. On 10 January 1850, for example, a respectable young solicitor called Frederick Hardy Jewitt was returning home from his office in Lime Street in the City of London when, the court was later told, he was accosted by a 'corpulent middle-aged woman who rapidly pressed a handkerchief over his mouth, and he was immediately seized by a feeling of stupor, which was succeeded shortly afterwards by total insensibility'. He remembered nothing further, until he awoke and 'found himself stretched upon a wretched bed at a low lodging-house in Thrall-street, Spitalfields, completely stripped of nearly the whole of his clothing' and robbed of his watch, ring and money. Miss Elizabeth Smith, known as 'Fat Beth' and a 'woman of abandoned habits', was eventually arrested as she attempted to escape at the rear entrance to a 'notorious brothel' in George Street, Spitalfields. At the time of the trial Jewitt was still 'confined at home, under the care of a surgeon, from the effects of the treatment to which he had been subjected'. After giving evidence at the trial he relapsed into 'a delirious and very dangerous state'. The magistrate instructed the police to 'discover the persons who had supplied such characters as [Fat Beth] with ingredients capable of being applied to such nefarious purposes'.[20]

The case of 'Fat Beth' was sensational because the alleged perpetrator was a 'low-life' woman while her victim was a respectable solicitor.

In the vast majority of cases, however, the violator was a middle-class man. The use of chloroform to gain sexual access to an unwilling person came to widespread public knowledge in 1864 when Sir William Wilde was implicated in a sexual scandal as outrageous (and as avoidable) as the one that later ensnared his son, Oscar. The true story may never be known, but it began when Wilde attempted to terminate relations with his mistress, Mary Josephine Travers (the daughter of the Professor of Medical Jurisprudence at Trinity College, Dublin). Travers took revenge, distributing a pamphlet that claimed that Wilde had tried to rape her with the aid of chloroform. Tired of Travers's harassment of her husband, Lady Wilde sent a letter to Travers's father, informing him of his daughter's threats and mentioning his daughter's sexual 'intrigue' with her husband. Mary Travers found the letter and promptly sued Lady Wilde for libel. The jury upheld Mary Travers's charge that Lady Wilde had libelled her but, because they held Travers's virtue in low esteem, they awarded damages of only one farthing.[21]

Sir William's biographers have characterized Mary Travers in terms strikingly reminiscent of the way women who make false accusations were described in the previous chapter. In Terence De Vere White's biography of Sir William and Lady Wilde, Travers was described as having 'haunted eyes, stringy looks, uncontrolled garrulity and hysterical malice'. She 'belonged to a familiar type', he continued, being

> intense, with a great deal to say for herself, and looks of the sort that soon go, leaving haggardness in their wake. Girls of this type tend to become involved in 'movements', to have literary and artistic ambitions not always in proportion to their natural endowments. Their sexual life does not flow in conventional channels. An uncomplicated urge, or generous disposition to please, is not theirs. Not kept in its proper place, given as it were, the run of the house, sex in these cases tends to make for the attic storeys.[22]

Even Eric Lambert's more restrained biography of Oscar Wilde's parents wondered whether the 'crazed creature' was 'a genuine nymphomaniac'. Lambert concluded that she 'displayed all the nymphomaniac's desperate fury at being deprived of regular sexual intercourse'.[23] As I argued in the previous chapter, slurs on the character of the (alleged) rape victim were easy to make, hard to refute.

Sir William Wilde's troubles were a media sensation at the time, highlighting the potentially perilous uses of the drug chloroform. After all, chloroform was freely available in shops and from street hawkers at the time. People purchased it for many ailments, including hysteria, asthma and chronic pain. Once restrictions on its sale began to be applied, accusations of rape increasingly focused on the one group who retained access to the powerful drug: physicians.

From the 1870s anxieties about the erotic imaginings of young women (even middle-class ones) under the spell of chloroform began to plague doctors.* Doctors used the courts to prove their innocence. In 1877, for instance, a respectable woman named Fanny Harriet Child accused George Howard, a surgeon's assistant, of raping her after she had been administered chloroform before an operation. Child told her husband that she had been 'quite conscious' when the surgeon's assistant was having sex with her, but had been 'speechless and powerless' to move. The courts called Dr Benjamin Richardson, an expert witness and Fellow of the Royal Society. Confident that Child was mistaken about what had taken place, Richardson gave evidence on behalf of the defence. He informed the court that chloroform made patients notoriously 'subject to delusions'. 'In the case of the fair sex', Richardson stated under oath, these delusions 'sometimes assumed quite a scandalous form'. Indeed, Richardson proffered evidence of a case in which a female patient had accused her surgeon of sexual improprieties, despite the fact that both her parents and an assistant had been present throughout the operation. Child's case collapsed.[24]

Even though the court decided that Fanny Harriet Child had wrongly accused her physician of committing a lewd attack on her unconscious body, the judge pointed out that 'such a verdict would not be the slightest imputation upon the absolute sincerity of the prosecutrix, who, no doubt, firmly believed every word she said'. Indeed, it was not unusual for 'modest, virtuous and refined gentlewomen' to make such accusations, observed Dudley Wilmot Buxton, the author of *Anaesthetics. Their Uses and Administration* (1888). 'The cause for this remarkable and deplorable state of things,' he added, was

> fortunately not far to seek. Chloroform, ether, nitrous oxide, gas, cocaine and possibly the other carbon compounds employed in producing anaesthesia possess the property of exciting sexual emotions and in many cases produce erotic hallucinations . . . Women, especially

*These debates were also linked to fears of false accusations, as discussed in the previous chapter.

> when suffering from ovarian or uterine irritation, are prone to such hallucinations, and it is almost impossible to convince them after their recovery to consciousness that the subjective sexual sensation is not of objective existence.[25]

As this author and many others reiterated, even orgasm could occur under anaesthetic. None of these experts explained why the delusions experienced under chloroform took an 'erotic' tinge only for female patients.

The defence of the medical profession could be even more extreme. Surgical textbooks insisted that it was actually *impossible* for a physician or other medical personnel to rape a woman under such circumstances. As Buxton put it, while chloroform and other anaesthetics did render an individual unable to protect herself, her body would be rendered 'utterly flaccid', a 'dead weight'. Consequently it would be 'exceedingly difficult' to move such a body to and from a dental chair, for instance, and such actions could 'hardly be accomplished without causing much disarrangement of clothing'. Furthermore, Buxton went on, if the agent used was nitrous oxide gas, the woman's 'muscular rigidity and subsequent violent jactitation' would make rape impossible. The speed with which the assault would have to take place (unconsciousness could last for less than one minute) also made assault unlikely.[26] But there was another reason to doubt women who claimed to have been raped under the influence of chloroform: unless a man had accomplices, was rape in these circumstances feasible? No, insisted the author of the standard textbook *Forensic Medicine and Toxicology* (1898). Even in a surgical setting, an assistant was often needed to help 'restrain the struggles of a patient who voluntarily submits' to being anaesthetized. In a woman who did not consent to be rendered unconscious, it would be 'no easy matter to administer chloroform single handed'.[27]

However, as Stephen Rogers, the President of the New York Medico-Legal Society, acknowledged in 1871, the problem remained that the 'growth of human knowledge does not advance beyond the reach of corresponding developments of the original propensity to sin'. The invention of chloroform was an example of the 'long and proud stride' of science 'in its race in the interests of humanity'. But, 'with the glories of the discovery of the anaesthetics . . . arose the idea, among the ignorant and wicked, that the state of insensibility they produced offered the most agreeable facility for all manner of unlawful acts which the instincts of self-respect and preservation would oppose'. Only three years after its introduction, Rogers observed, the British Parliament had started debating whether it should be made a felony to unlawfully administer chloroform or other 'stupefying agents'. Lord Campbell, the chief proposer of the Prevention of Offences Bill, believed it should be made a felony, especially since chloroform had (allegedly) been used to commit serious crimes such as rape. Rogers was not convinced that such a law was necessary. The 'sensation of pungency' given off by chloroform was unmistakable. Criminals would be much more liable to injure themselves than any struggling victim.

Furthermore, Rogers reminded readers, administering chloroform was a slow process and, during its administration, the patient 'becomes excited, often very violent and turbulent, with an irrepressible propensity to sing and shout, which is often so loud as to alarm the inmates of a whole house'. Chloroformed women were often in 'a state of wild, chloroformic intoxication'. There were, he coolly declared, better ways for a man to 'win' the maiden. To prove his point Rogers drew attention to an article published in the *London Medical Gazette* in November 1850 in which a young man induced his dancing companion (his 'sweet heart') to go with him into a stable-yard where he attempted to anaesthetize her with chloroform. The woman

> at once tore the handkerchief away, and called out in such a manner as to bring a policeman to her assistance, and also secured the offender, who is reported to have subsequently soothed and finally subdued the rebellious propensities of this maiden by other influences less anæsthetic, but more agreeable and charming, than villainous chloroform.

In fact, the 'sweet heart' then rescued her attempted rapist from the noose by marrying him.[28] 'Seduction' could be a delicate business.

The Unconscious

According to the commentators I have examined so far, the body is an unreliable defence against assault: it could be rendered vulnerable and passive through sleep, intoxication and oblivion caused by the administration of a range of anaesthetics and other drugs. But there is another reason why free will was an unstable concept upon which to base agency. *Unconscious* forces could also cause the faculties of reason to dissipate with startling rapidity. According to this view, to be human is to be possessed of an inner psychological self which is profoundly suggestible.

The rise of hypnosis in the nineteenth century threatened the entire theological and legal edifice of free-will doctrine.[29] Hypnosis raised two fundamental questions. First, if a woman did not want to engage in sexual intercourse with a particular person, could hypnotism make her change her mind? Second, if it *was* possible to achieve this result, did this outcome prove that the woman was being less than honest about her sexual proclivities in the first place?[30] The answer to these questions had a profound impact on the responsibility assigned to the hypnotist: was he seducer or rapist?

One school of thought argued that hypnosis could induce 'distorted perceptions', tricking the hypnotized person into acting in ways that she would otherwise find abhorrent.[31] Accordingly, the hypnotist who made a woman have sex with someone she would normally have rebuffed was a rapist. In 1891 Hippolyte M. Bernheim published *New Studies in Hypnotism*, a passionately argued defence of this position, although he was reluctant to point a finger of blame at male perpetrators. He began by observing that while some individuals resisted immoral suggestions made to them by hypnotists, others did not. It was wrong, however, to imply that those who succumbed were wicked to start with. Indeed, they could be as innocent as children, their subconscious having temporarily 'annihilated' their conscious being. In this state 'true conscience no longer exists'. In other words, the hypnotized person was in a state similar to dreaming. Some dreams could be 'seen without being lived', while others rocked the foundation of an individual's identity. These latter dreams were 'lived' in the sense that the dreamer became 'body and soul, the person that imagination suggest[ed] us to be'. In such cases the individual would awaken from his dream in a state replicating the emotions of the dream. In similar fashion, immoralities committed in a somnambulistic state were a form of 'active dream' or examples of offences 'committed without responsibility'.

Bernheim also drew upon ideas about 'the crowd' and mass suggestion. He argued that an 'honest man' could commit a crime if 'carried away by an impulsive intoxication or led by a delusion or hallucination'. This 'psychologic mechanism', he pointed out, was the 'generating mechanism' of many crimes, including those committed by 'nihilists, anarchists, socialists, revolutionaries, and political and religious fanatics'. Suggestion, especially in the midst of a crowd, was profoundly influential. Many had observed an 'excited mob' suddenly turn and 'furiously and bloodthirstily thrash some poor inoffensive devil who has been denounced'. Wasn't this a form of collective suggestion, he asked? An 'idea spreads through the mob, a single word – spy, traitor, exploiter of the people. Brains become excited. One is carried away and becomes a fanatic! No one imagines controlling it! This is the blind passion which carried the masses away! The beast is unchained!' For Bernheim the suggestibility of the mob was merely the suggestibility of each individual multiplied.

It was relatively simple, therefore, for Bernheim to explain how a woman might be coerced, without her consent or even conscious knowledge, into sexual intercourse with a man she would normally have shunned with every ounce of strength in her body. He illustrated his explanation by telling the heartbreaking story of the rape and murder of Mrs Grille. Grille was a young married woman 'of good background and of perfect morality'. She adored her husband and children. One tragic day, however, she was found naked, lying in her isolated garden pavilion with a single bullet to her head. At her side was a severely injured young guest, called Chambige. When Chambige was able to speak he claimed that Grille had thrown herself at him, proclaiming love. She made it a condition of 'giving herself' to him that neither of them survived her 'dishonour'. Chambige agreed, promising to kill her after sexual intercourse. He would then kill himself. He had nearly succeeded in carrying out both parts of the pact.

What did Bernheim make of this story? He disbelieved Chambige's version of events. Grille had been 'perfectly tranquil' immediately before her death. She had given no indication of any penchant to clan destine debauchery. Grille was 'guilelessness itself. Raised with severe moral principles which her family exemplified for her, this was a woman who was devoted to her husband and children. She was gentle, timid, good, affectionate, and not at all impassionate.' She did, however, possess one weakness: she was a highly sensitive, and therefore suggestible, woman.

In contrast with Grille's virtue, Chambige had 'a perverted imagination' and was one of the decadent generation who 'substitute sensation for sentiment'. He was arrogant, possessed 'little or no moral sense' and was 'thirsty for sensation'. Impatient to 'possess' the young wife, Chambige 'did not wait to grasp her feeble mind with his strange influence'. Rather, he 'acted strongly on her pliable imagination' and 'suggested an unhealthy passion in her; he suggested a sensual excitement'. Bernheim guessed that 'in the presence of Chambige, profoundly disturbed by his gaze, his manner, and perhaps his declarations, she fell into a somnambulistic ecstasy; she lost her personality and was in an altered state of consciousness.' Grille's 'faculties of reason were overthrown, and she could not resist' his advances.

Nevertheless, Bernheim warned readers it would be wrong to conclude that Chambige was a rapist. Indeed, he excused the young man, declaring that he could not be fully responsible for Grille's defilement since Chambige

> made suggestions without knowing it; he was capable of believing that she loved him from her heart. He did not know that this insane suggested love existed only as a result of the new state of consciousness that his influence (without his knowledge) had induced in her delirious imagination. The normal conscious being did not love him; the subconscious being loved him falsely.

Even on the night of her downfall Grille 'did not know what was going to happen'. Chambige simply 'suggested' to her that she follow him to the pavilion, where he 'implanted a crazy passion in her imagination and an irresistible excitation in her senses'.

How could we explain the death pact, however? 'If the poor woman did make her seducer promise to kill her so as not to survive her dishonor,' Bernheim hypothesized,

> it was as a result of the remaining moral sense in her new state of consciousness. It survived as a former suggestion, hereditary or educated, which could not be eradicated. It was her true and indestructible moral conscience which could be dominated, but not extinguished, in her somnambulistic state. But the suggestion possessed her physical and mental being; the suggested passion carried her away irresistibly. She was no longer herself.

To be sure, this could not explain why the 'decadent' Chambige would go along with the murder-suicide plot. But Bernheim was interested only in explaining the woman's actions. The 'mysterious drama' of suggestion in combination with the 'imaginative faculties and ideodynamic automatism' removed free will. Grille was literally 'no longer herself'. Echoing the words of Grille's husband, Bernheim concluded that 'Alive or conscious, she had never been with Chambige!'

Bernheim refused to accuse Chambige of taking advantage of a hypnotized woman. Instead he portrayed Chambige as nothing more than a feckless young man who used the power of suggestion to sexually abuse an otherwise chaste woman. In another example, however, Bernheim's failure to apportion blame was even more remarkable. Once again, the victim (a Mrs de B.) was a 'gentle and affectionate' young woman 'from a good family'. Suffering from hysteria, she was sent to a young physician who regularly hypnotized her. During one hypnotic session de B. admitted that she was unhappily married and was in love with her physician. Henceforth, every time she entered the somnambulistic state her doctor had sex with her. When conscious de B remembered nothing of these encounters. Tragedy came when she discovered that she had become pregnant. Knowing that she had not had sexual relations with her husband, she panicked. She 'lost her head and believed in spirits and devils'. After giving birth she had to be sent to an insane asylum.

Bernheim was unruffled. Mrs de B. was 'always innocent; only the somnambule was guilty'. Yet, the physician-hypnotist was not held accountable for forcing de B. to have sex without her conscious consent, even though it (literally) drove her mad. According to Bernheim, several years later, after de B. was released from the asylum, they met again. Bernheim calmly observed that de B. 'never suspected that he had been the hero of the adventure in which she had been the victim'.[32]

Not everyone accepted Bernheim's view that actions committed under hypnosis were separate from the individual's 'will'. Even when hypnotized, the President of the Medico-Legal Congress insisted in the 1890s, individuals were not absolutely under the domination of the will of the hypnotist.[33] Truly virtuous women – such as Mrs Grille and Mrs de B. – should have been able to resist 'seduction', whether conscious or not. According to this school of thought, hypnosis was merely 'a license for the hypnotized person to act out pre-existing desires'.[34] The hypnotist was doing nothing more than seducing a woman to act on her desires. How did this happen? According to this school of thought, from infancy onwards people were subjected to forms of 'suggestion'. Parents, for example, repeated the mantra 'you will not steal' to their children. Similarly, hypnotists might say 'if I suggest to you to steal and to commit some evil act, you will not do it'. In both cases the suggestions would be etched on the person's brain. There was a difference, however. Parental suggestions 'derived from education' and were therefore 'strongly enough rooted in [the person's] conscience to prevail against criminal ideas that are suggested later on'. In contrast, suggestions given to individuals in a somnambulistic state would prevail only if the woman's 'moral sense' was 'naturally weak' in the first place. A hypnotist who planted the suggestion 'you will desire me and have sex with me' in a woman's mind would prevail only if she already, albeit unconsciously, desired to have sex with him.

Chicago physician Xavier Suddeth developed this point in an article published in the *Medico-Legal Journal* in 1895. Hypnosis, he explained, was a mental state. Under its influence the individual was possessed by 'dual consciousness'. Accordingly, virtuous women could not be hypnotized and then sexually molested. They could, however, be hypnotized in order to allow physicians to undertake examination or operations on their 'generative organs'. If the operation was 'for the acknowledged good of the subject' and was 'performed under circumstances calculated to secure her confidence', a virtuous woman would be able 'expose her person' under hypnosis. Clearly Suddeth didn't have in mind the physician responsible for Mrs de B.'s 'treatment' for hysteria.

Moreover, Suddeth was not convinced by European experiments purporting to show that virtuous women could be made to act immorally under hypnosis. The women chosen for such experiments were courtesans, already 'susceptible . . . not adverse to the [sexual] act'. Many were also peasants, a class of woman 'notorious' for their 'lack of virtue'. Such women could easily be made to forget under hypnosis what had happened upon awakening ('provided amnesia had been suggested during the hypnotic state'). In contrast, any 'truly virtuous woman would resent the least approach towards familiarity in the hypnotic state, even as she would in the waking condition'. If the hypnotist persisted in making 'immoral suggestions', the virtuous woman would swiftly wake up. 'Woe betide the [hypnotist] who had the temerity to attempt improper advances,' Suddeth warned. The implications of Suddeth's argument were significant – and not only for peasants and prostitutes. To his way of thinking, *any* woman who claimed to have been 'seduced' under hypnosis was automatically proclaiming herself to be an 'immoral person'.[35] Women who claimed rape under hypnosis were therefore either immoral in the first place or maliciously lying.

It was a warning echoed by Charles Chaddock, Professor of Diseases of the Nervous System in St Louis, only a few years later. False allegations of rape under hypnosis were extremely common, he pointed out, particularly if the woman was a hysteric (like Mrs de B.). In part, this was because the hypnotic state was 'an abnormal state of consciousness'. As a hallucinatory state, hysteria also made women 'prone to originate false ideas'. All accusations by women who had been hypnotized needed to be 'scrutinized with the greatest caution', Chaddock insisted: they had to be 'corroborated by more objective evidence than alleged perceptions of events during such an abnormal state of consciousness'.[36] The myth that women are easily 'seduced' through hypnosis and other manipulations of the unconscious persisted throughout the century. As late as 1979 the International Society of Hypnosis and the Society for Clinical and Experimental Hypnosis issued a 'resolution' restricting the use and teaching of hypnosis to qualified professionals.[37]

'No' Means 'Yes'

So far in this chapter I have looked at a number of ingenious ways a person's consent to sexual intercourse could be evaded (the victim was asleep, drugged or anaesthetized) or overridden (through suggestion or hypnosis). There is a broader problem with consent, however: many men claim to hear 'yes' when a woman says 'no'.

As we saw in the case of Daphne Morgan, women have been accused of deliberately confusing 'no' and 'yes'. This claim was repeated in the 1860s as keenly as in the 1960s. Thus leading Boston physician and vice-president of the American Medical Association Horatio Robinson Storer maintained in 'The Law of Rape' (1868) that women 'coquet and dally', giving an 'appearance of refusal', so that they might 'thereby add still greater value to the favors finally granted'.[38] One hundred years later the author of the widely read *Sexual Behavior and the Law* (1965) made a similar assertion, stating categorically that it was 'customary' for a woman to say 'no, no, no' when she means 'yes, yes, yes'. The 'desideratum is an aggressive male', he proclaimed.[39] [See cartoon, p. 68.]

The driving force behind this myth is the belief that women generally want 'it', and the more 'passionate' the man, the better. An article in the *Yale Law Journal* in the early 1950s expressed this position clearly, insisting that 'many women' required 'aggressive overtures by the man' as part of their 'love play'. Often, the anonymous authors continued, 'their erotic pleasure may be enhanced by, or even depend upon, an accompanying physical struggle. The 'love bite' is a common, if mild, sign of the aggressive component in the sex act.'

'If all women secretly want to be raped'

They warned that these 'tangible signs of struggle' might 'survive to support a subsequent accusation by the woman'.[40]

As might be expected, an evolutionary spin was added to this argument. In the words of a sexologist in the 1960s, the

> sex act is basically an act of violence by the male. Our remote ancestors – for it seems safe to presume that this animalistic trait was dominant in our original forbearers – pursued the female they wanted, the female offered resistance, or pretended to do so; she was overcome and taken by force . . . It is probable that the female's reluctance is simply a device to intensify man's aggressiveness and thereby enhance the ardour of his wooing. It may well be that Nature invested humankind with this challenge and this aggressiveness for the purpose of ensuring only the procreation of the strongest specimens.

In case readers were not making the leap from earliest origins of humanity to the twentieth century by themselves, this author insisted that 'though we may not like these thoughts, this primitive feature still clings to heterosexual behaviour in our own day . . . Rape is the result'.[41]

From music-hall sketches to operas, the theme that women, either secretly or unconsciously, want to be raped is popular. The author of *Cry Rape: Anatomy of the Rapist* (1967) for instance, claimed that it was 'symptomatic and significant' that

> many women who work in isolated areas and keep late hours are not more cautious in their goings and comings and will often shun public transportation in favour of walking along lonely, dark streets. If we may speak of the 'accident-prone' individual, we must surely regard such behaviour as 'rape-prone'; we must always remember the psychological premise that when a person is compelled against his or her will, submission exonerates guilt. And the 'rape-prone' female who consciously or unconsciously exposes herself by dress, behaviour, itinerary, or other means to potential sexual assault is surely motivated by that kind of rationalization.[42]

In films, too, the theme of a woman hankering after sexual violation appears time and again. Most notoriously, harlequin romantic novels routinely depict women keenly desiring to be ravished by the hero. Films are equally complicit in propagating the idea that women always consent because they long for sex. In the Western *Little Big Man* (1970) the hero's sister was deeply disappointed when the Indians failed to act according to her (longed-for) expectations; in *Curtains* (1983) rape became just another form of foreplay between lovers. Going back in time still further, in the 1899 film *The Disappointed Old Maid*, a man dressed in black is shown sneaking through a window into a bedroom. A caricatured image of an ageing spinster enters the bedroom and, in the course of undressing, spies the man hiding beneath her bed. With delight, she claps her hands and skips over to the window, firmly locking it shut. She then reaches under the bed to drag the man out, only to grasp a large doll. The Old Maid burst into tears.[43]

The Disappointed Old Maid is a crude sketch of a psychodynamic thesis that became increasingly popular in the twentieth century. Sigmund Freud instigated the debate about the ways in which the unconscious 'muddied' clear-cut cognition. He had been struck by the large numbers of patients who claimed to have been sexually violated as children. Initially Freud had believed these accounts. However, in a letter to his friend Wilhelm Fliess in 1897, he admitted to having changed his mind. 'I no longer believe in my neurotica [theory of the neuroses],' he admitted, citing as reason for his scepticism, his

> continual disappointments in my attempts at bringing my analysis to a real conclusion, the running-away of people who had for a time seemed most in my grasp, the absence of the complete success on which I had reckoned, the possibility of explaining the partial successes in other ways, or ordinary lines.

Hysteria, Freud argued, arose only 'where there has been an accumulation of events and where a factor that weakens defence has supervened'. If hysteria was the result of childhood sexual abuse, then such abuse would have to be extremely common. Indeed, 'in every case the father, not excluding my own, had to be blamed as a pervert'. This could not be the case.

Freud also observed that the unconscious could not distinguish between 'truth and fiction that is cathected [sic] with affect'. Perhaps the 'theme of the parents' was mere phantasy, Freud mused. Finally, he observed that in the 'most deep-going psychosis the unconscious memory does not break through, so that the secret of the childhood experiences is not betrayed even in the most confused delirium'.[44] In other words, Freud abandoned his seduction theory because uncovering and discussing childhood sexual abuse did not relieve the patient's symptoms, there were 'no indications of reality in the unconsciousness' and psychotic patients (believed to be incapable of repression) did not claim to have been sexually abused. Although Freud acknowledged that some of his female patients had been sexually abused as children, he came to accept that many memories of abuse were symptoms of other underlying complexes, in particular the accuser's Oedipal desires for her father.

In *The Psychopathology of Everyday Life* (1914) Freud went even further, arguing that a woman might find it difficult to use her 'full muscular strength' to ward off a sexual attack because 'a portion of the unconscious feelings of the one attacked meets it with ready acceptance'. He then related a tale from *Don Quixote* in which a woman prosecuted a man 'who was supposed to have robbed her of her honour by force of violence'. Sancho Panza, the judge,

> indemnified her with a full purse which he took from the accused, but after the departure of the woman he gave the accused permission to follow her and snatch the purse from her. Both returned wrestling, the woman priding herself that the villain was unable to possess himself of the purse. Thereupon Sancho spoke: 'Had you shown yourself so stout and valiant to defend your body (nay, but half so much) as you have done to defend your purse, the strength of Hercules could not have forced you.[45]

The woman's conscious assertion of 'no' was undone by her unconscious desire for violation.

It was a position embraced by many psychoanalysts. According to the influential psychoanalyst and feminist Helene Deutsch, author of *The Psychology of Women* (1944), women needed to be overpowered by men in order to experience sexual pleasure. Deutsch located female masochism at the centre of what it meant to be a woman. 'Women's entire psychologic preparation for the sexual and reproductive functions is connected with masochistic ideas,' she insisted. Coitus was 'closely related with the act of defloration, and defloration with rape and painful penetration of the body . . . Actually, a certain amount of masochism as psychologic preparation for adjustment to sexual functions is necessary in women.'[46]

This position had a pre-echo three-quarters of a century earlier, when the vice-president of the American Medical Association argued that, 'as every one knows', it was not uncommon

> for a fully consenting woman to experience in the first, or even subsequent acts of coitus, such suffering as to extort from her an unwilling groan of anguish, which might well deceive a listening ear; and for women fully consenting at first, under these circumstances of pain to strive to get free.[47]

Women's bodies were considered to be inherently painful; sexual suffering is woman's lot.[48] Cries of 'no!' could never be relied upon.

Between the 1940s and early 1970s the psychodynamics of sexual assault was refined in more invidious ways. Rather than *all* women's speech acts being treated as untrustworthy, particular types of women were singled out for disbelief. Rape was christened a 'victim-precipitated' crime. 'If there are criminals,' argued Hans von Hentig (one of the founding fathers of the newly invented field of victimology), 'it is evident that there are [also] born victims, self-harming and self-destroying.' According to von Hentig, the typical rape victim was a middle-aged woman at the onset of menopause. Such a woman, he believed, easily found herself a victim of 'an aggressor and her own critical condition'.[49] An author in the 1957 issue of the *International Journal of Psycho-Analysis* even claimed that female rape victims were partially 'on the side of the rapist'.[50] A woman might 'unconsciously tempt the offender' into carrying out an attack precisely in order to 'rid herself of the fear' of rape, observed the author of *Sexual Behavior and the Law* (1965), adding that a woman might 'allow herself to be raped in actuality in order to deal with it [in fantasy]'.[51] Or, as forensic psychiatrist Seymour Halleck put it less obliquely in 1972, the rape victim 'frequently' played 'as large a role in precipitating the offense as the offender. Many rapes, particularly where the victim is known to the offender, might never have taken place had the "victim" not been both flirtatious and ambivalent as to her desire for a sexual experience.'[52]

By placing the word 'victim' in inverted commas, Halleck implicitly queried her accusation of assault. It was not surprising that incarcerated rapists obsessively repeated the fiction that victims of rape actually triggered their own violation. Indeed, interviews with these felons had provided most of the evidence psychiatrists used for their charge of 'victim precipitation'.

To be sure, the victims who 'precipitated' their own violation, and were thus (unknown to themselves) consenting, hailed from particular areas and classes. The nonchalant conviction that sexual violation was a 'natural hazard' for girls and women living within certain areas (or 'subcultures')* was maintained even in the face of evidence of extreme violence. In a particularly vicious account in the early 1960s, Vincent Riccio reported talking to gang members, including one called Freddi, about 'gangbangs'. As a sign of respect, Riccio was offered first place in raping a woman. He admitted that 'technically' the action was 'mass rape'. However, he explained,

> [i]n cold fact, it is very rarely rape. Far from it . . . I have seen the fellows pick up these gangbang girls. The girls are delinquents, of course. And frequently mentally slow or worse. They can stop the line at will. One scream and everybody runs . . . The knowing and compassionate Freddi explained to me. 'First of all, Rick, they like to get laid. And then they have the same problems at home the guys have. Instead of going out and busting heads, like the guys do when they get fed up, they stand still for a gangbang'.

According to Freddi, these women did not want 'one man'. He swore that although he had 'heard a million whistles, and a hundred uncouth questions', he had never 'seen a girl touched who didn't want to be touched'.[53] Explicit consent was irrelevant.

Acceptance of the rationalizations proffered by rapists is only one support for this belief. As already noted, arguments about women's

*This is discussed in Chapter 5, 'Brutalizing Environments'.

'unconscious complicity' in their own violation were strongly influenced by psychoanalytical principles. Women often found that their 'sexual desire and superego' were 'in conflict', argued the anonymous authors of an article in the *Yale Law Journal* of 1952–3. It was normal, they continued, for a woman to feel an 'unconscious desire for forceful penetration' (as a way of alleviating guilty feelings, for instance) while at the same time her superego vigorously opposed the uncivilized use of aggression. Yet there was 'no explicit provision in the law for the woman's attitude of ambivalence', they lamented.[54] It was axiomatic for such commentators that, in the 'struggle to deal with the forbidden pleasure of sexuality', some women actually courted rape. As David Abrahamsen, criminologist and former director of scientific research at Sing Sing Prison in New York, put it in his influential *The Psychology of Crime* (1960):

> the victim herself unconsciously also may tempt the offender. The conscious or unconscious biological and psychological attraction between man and woman does not exist only on the part of the offender toward the woman but also on her part toward him, which in many instances may to some extent be the impetus for his sexual attack. Often a woman unconsciously wishes to be taken by force . . . We sometimes find this seductive inclination even in young girls.[55]

This appeal to shared biological and psychological drives was used to explain why rape victims often felt guilty for what had happened: they *were* guilty.[56]

Of course, criminologists and psychiatrists did not apply the notion of victim precipitation only to accusations of rape. Victims of other crimes could also be blamed for acting in ways that 'triggered' the crimes against them. Even murder victims could be held accountable for their own slaying. Twenty-two per cent of homicides showed discernible signs of victim precipitation, according to the National Commission on the Causes and Prevention of Violence in 1969. In contrast, the Commission concluded that only 4 per cent of forcible rapes showed such signs.[57] Nevertheless, only in rape cases was the idea of victim precipitation so widely *believed* – not only as a way of explaining why 'it' happened to a particular person, but also in helping to dilute the responsibility of the criminal. Only in rape cases did victim precipitation become victim liability.

Victim precipitation serves to exonerate perpetrators of rape and denigrate victims. A diluted, but equally pernicious, version of this myth simply stated that the victim had acted imprudently: she *seemed* (to the man) to be consenting, when she was not. In an extreme form, this is seen in the Morgan case that opens this chapter.

As I show throughout this book, signs of a woman's immoral character could encompass everything from subtle informality in demeanour to evidence of raucous sexual licentiousness. [See image, below.] A woman's complicity in her own sexual abuse was a staple in reportage in the mass media, so that a 'no-good girl of 15½, who slept with black men promiscuously' in 1960 could not expect even a charge of statutory rape to be made out.[58] This invidious defence could even apply to cases of gang rape. In an article entitled 'Forcible Rape by Multiple Offenders' (1971) sociologist Gilbert Geis and criminologist Duncan Chappell quoted one fifteen-year-old girl's account of being raped. The unnamed girl began by admitting that she and a girlfriend had 'ditched school' that day and accepted a lift from men in a red car. She admitted that they had gone into a house with the men and she had consented to sex with one of them.

'If a Girl's a Tease', from *Adventure for Men*, 1967

Afterwards, however, another man confronted her. In her words, he

> grabbed me by the arm, twisted it, pushed me into the bedroom and slammed the door. He forced me on the bed and had an act of sexual intercourse with me. Then he got up and opened the door and let the

> other two boys into the room. They held me down and when one finished having intercourse with me the other one got on top before I got up. All three of them forced me to have intercourse against my will. I was afraid because they said they would hurt me if I didn't have intercourse with them.

Geis and Chappell treated the account with profound scepticism. They denounced the victim's story as confirming 'the uncertainty that often surrounds that issue of victim-precipitation and consent'. Additionally, the 'problem' with this girl's story was that she admitted to the police that she had engaged (initially) in consensual sex. This was information she might be 'well-advised not to notify the police about'. Women's body has been considered for long periods as a form of property: prior consent to sexual intercourse implied longer-term surrender of bodily possession and integrity to the man.* Indeed, the police responded to the rape accusation by placing both girls in custody, booking them as juveniles 'in danger of becoming delinquent'.[59]

With anxieties about permissiveness growing, the denigration of 'no-good girls' and the claim that rape victims had 'asked for it' became particularly shrill. Was it any surprise that the increasing candour, if not sensual abandonment, of young women might be construed as invitations to sexual intercourse, some people asked? In particular the 'Liberation of Women' was largely responsible for the increase in rape, one commentator asserted, because 'many women and girls have put themselves in more dangerous positions; for example being alone on streets and in bars at night, and have acted more provocatively, especially in matters of (un)dress'.[60] Drinking alcohol, accepting lifts home in cars containing a number of men and not being a virgin were all 'strong evidence' that the victim was responsible 'for both the position in which she finds herself and the outcome of the evening's excursion', concluded Ross Barber in his study of an 'epidemic' of pack rape in Australia during the 1970s. The 'conduct of many "pack" victims is such as to strongly encourage, if not invite, the members of these packs to fulfil their ambitions', he maintained.[61] Birth control and abortion were also thought to encourage rape, because they allowed the perpetrators to evade one of the possible consequences of their actions. Indeed, rape could even be put forward as a reason why

*This is also seen in cases of date rape and marital rape, discussed in Chapter 2, 'Rape Myths', and Chapter 11, 'The Home'.

abortion should be banned. After all, reasoned a woman in *The Times*, the 'very young girl' who had been raped should *not* be allowed an abortion lest men 'come to regard such conduct even more lightly than they do at present'.[62] Victims were to be severely punished in order to deter potential perpetrators.

In response to the growing rejection of this suggestion that women were to blame for their own violation, some commentators even suggested that feminists possessed a *particularly* strong unconscious desire to be raped. For instance, Sheldon H. Kardener, an influential California-based psychiatrist, published an article entitled 'Rape Fantasies' (1975). He criticized feminists who, on the one hand, shrilly insisted that 'all men are rapists' while, on the other hand, behaved and dressed in 'a seductively provocative way'. According to Kardener, by acting in this way feminists were able to fulfil their 'worst expectations by demanding that the man force his attention upon her'. She might then 'self-righteously scream "rape".'[63] According to this rape myth, feminists secretly desired violation: they deserved what they got.

As with the victim precipitation myth, this emphasis on women's solicitation of rape effectively altered the balance of blame and responsibility. It was the responsibility of female rape victims to ensure that they were not attacked: no heed was paid to the men who purposefully carried out the rape. By this sleight of hand, male sexual violence was normalized.

Humans Incapable of Consenting

Finally, some types of people are deemed to be unable to consent to sexual intercourse in the first place. For them consent does not apply. Slaves, for instance, were simply not human enough for the concept of 'consent' to be relevant. Slave women were regarded as the absolute property of another person and were incapable of acting as individual agents. Concepts of consent or resistance were inappropriate. They were inherently rapable.

Indeed, the tension between the slave as property and as person was at its strongest when it came to sexual violence. Because slaves were not autonomous agents, they were not conceived as possessing a meaningful 'free will', rendering any notion of 'consent' meaningless. When men *were* prosecuted for raping slave women, the person bringing the case was not the victim but her owner. The law treated rape of a slave woman as trespass on the (valuable) property of the woman's master.[64]

As Saidiya Hartman put it in 'Seduction and the Ruses of Power' (1996), 'the enslaved existed only as an extension or embodiment of the owner's rights of property'.[65] According to Thomas Cobb's *Inquiry into the Law of Negro Slavery* (1858), the law 'by recognizing the existence of the slave or person, thereby confers no rights or privileges except such as are necessary to protect that existence'. Thus slaves must be protected by law from being murdered, but 'all other rights should be granted specially'. Because rape did not affect the physical existence of the slave woman, Cobb asserted, the penalties for rape should not be applied to the man accused of violating her. Although Cobb admitted some concern about this anomaly in the law, he did not think it should cause undue worry because 'the occurrence of such an offense is almost unheard of; and the known lasciviousness of the negro renders the possibility of its occurrence very remote'.[66] He was, of course, wrong: 18 per cent of former slaves described either experiencing or witnessing sexual coercion by whites on the plantation.[67]

Cobb's statement also drew attention to another reason why requiring consent for sex with one's own slave women was barely conceivable. Slave women were regarded as lascivious, and therefore *always* consenting. The rape victim was thus presented as the seducer of white men.

This legacy of slavery continued well into the twentieth century in the form of the myth that even free African-American women could not be raped because they were 'naturally' promiscuous.* Gurney Williams, author of 'Rape in Children and Young Girls' (1913), put it curtly when he claimed that the 'young colored girl . . . do[es] not appear to have any moral sense'.[68] As the Florida Supreme Court decreed in 1918,

> What has been said by some of our courts about an unchaste female being a comparatively rare exception is no doubt true where the population is composed largely of the Caucasian race, but we would blind ourselves to actual conditions if we adopted this rule where another race that is largely immoral constitutes an appreciable part of the population.[69]

*As I argued in the previous chapter, one effect was the assumption that when an African-American woman did claim to have been raped, it was probably a false allegation.

It was a characterization that was strongly resisted, especially by the National Association of Colored Women's Clubs, which, with over 50,000 members by 1914, was the largest African-American protest organization.[70]

Activists recognized that, in court, racist prejudices against black women effectively wrecked any hope of justice. Defendants appealed to such myths throughout the century. As late as 2000 a prominent British barrister freely bragged to a legal researcher about the way he had demolished the case against a prisoner accused of raping an Afro-Caribbean woman. After luring the accuser into denying that she was an exhibitionist, the barrister produced a video of her dancing in a club. In the words of this barrister, 'We had a video of her dancing in a club in a very flamboyant and suggestive Afro-Caribbean way. And you could see the jury, once I'd played the tape . . .'

In other words, despite the fact that the video had been filmed on a different occasion to the alleged rape, and ignoring the fact that on the occasion of the rape the accuser had jumped out of a window and broken her ankle in an attempt to evade her attacker, the man was acquitted.[71] The barrister had effectively employed two myths: that a woman who displayed sexual traits 'deserved it', and that black women in particular were promiscuous.

In such a way blackness was reduced to an extreme form of corporeality. As I will reveal in the next chapter, rapists who targeted black women were generally given significantly lighter sentences. Indeed, at times, the rape of black women in America was so commonplace that it excited no legal qualms. Thus 'institutional access' to African-American women actually increased after the Civil War. The rise of the Ku Klux Klan and the increased propensity of white males to turn to mob violence during Reconstruction, as well as black women's increased vulnerability within the workforce, put African-American women in a vulnerable position. Even when the rape of black women was acknowledged, it was in the context of the harm done to the *black* man's pride: lynching (of men) rather than rape (of women) became the symbol of African-American subjugation.

African-American women were not the only group for whom notions of consent or its lack were irrelevant. As with black women, mentally ill women were thought to be always 'ready for it'. Thus, the author of *The Students' Handbook of Forensic Medicine and Medical Police* (1883) noted, juries ought to ask if the 'idiot girl' yielded to the man 'from animal instinct'.[72] This notion surfaced regularly in certain mass media. As the magazine *Slam* advised its male teenage readers in the 1970s, if accused of having sex with a mentally subnormal woman, they should not panic because a 'retarded' woman 'certainly won't be believed'. *Slam* continued, asserting that

> retarded people are always claiming one preposterous thing or another, so one more allegation won't cause any stir. Simply say 'No I didn't do that' and you'll be cleared completely, assuming anyone would actually press an inquiry on the claims of a scrunch face.[73]

It was a point emphasized by Hugo Paul in 1967 when he also maintained that forced sex with a 'mentally retarded' woman could not be called 'real rape', since such women were 'notoriously ill-controlled and loose in the face of a sexual stimulus. Customarily they acquiesce . . . and even may return for more "rape" if they are at large and unsupervised.'[74] Perhaps not surprisingly, such women were seen as easy targets by both opportunistic and serial sexual predators. An Australian study showed that women with intellectual disabilities were ten times more likely to be sexually assaulted than non-disabled persons.[75]

Children below a certain age were often equated with mentally subnormal women in the sense that they were also assumed to be incapable of giving consent. Below a particular age it was irrelevant whether or not the girl consented; the defendant could be accused of rape merely because sexual intercourse had taken place. Originally the age of consent in England and Wales was twelve. This was confirmed in the Offences Against the Person Act of 1861, in which having sex with a girl of under twelve was deemed to be a felony. Sex with a girl aged between ten and twelve became a misdemeanour. In 1875 the Offences Against the Person Act raised the age of consent to thirteen and then, scarcely ten years later, the Criminal Law Amendment Act raised the age again, this time to the present age of sixteen. In 1885 it was seen as a risky move, with judges warning that the new law on the age of consent 'might be used for the purposes of extortion' and 'might suggest to females of impure mind to bring unfounded charges'.[76]

The ability of a child to consent to sexual intercourse is more confusing in the USA, where the age of consent varies widely by state. In most states the age of consent in the 1880s was ten years. In 1889, after Congress revised the statutory age in the District of Columbia to sixteen years, other states began to raise the age. The result was startling:

by the end of the nineteenth century the difference between the ages at which a girl's 'yes' was legally deemed to be meaningful was as much as eight years, with an age of consent of ten in Mississippi and Alabama while it was as high as eighteen in Kansas and Wyoming.[77] This variation was popularly attributed to (mistaken) notions that girls reached puberty earlier in Southern states. In reality it was due to different expectations about childhood and the relative strength of feminist lobbying within each state.

Should there even be an age restriction on sexual intercourse? Some commentators say 'no': stipulating an age of consent denies children 'agency'. This was an argument strongly posited by groups such as the P.I.E. (Pedophile Information Exchange), P.A.L. (Pedophile Action[78] for Liberation) and the René Guyan Society. Crucially, they insisted, children were not necessarily hurt by sex. After all, sexual development was determined by a host of highly individual circumstances. As one psychiatrist observed in 1945, some women over the age of eighteen were 'infantile'. But equally, he went on, some women under the age of eighteen were 'sexually mature and aggressive'. He believed that it was wrong to punish men who slept with under-aged yet 'aggressive' girls: would it not be better to allow men to act freely and according to good conscience and (if some 'problem' did arise) place the girl in some kind of reforming institution?[79]

Statutory rape legislation, however, set a clear point of demarcation. As a result, in common law there were two defences most typically used by defendants accused of statutory rape: the girl looked older than her years or she was 'promiscuous'. The 'mistake of age' defence was not accepted in American courts until 1964 and, even after then, it was a difficult case to argue. In contrast, the 'promiscuity defence' was frequently accepted, largely because it was in harmony with the notion that statutory rape laws reflected notions of young girls as 'undamaged property'. Non-virgins were already 'spoiled' and therefore could be harmed no more by intercourse. Prior sexual experience threatened the complainant's credibility, it questioned her claim that she had not consented and it physically reduced the likelihood of finding evidence of intercourse. The legislation was to protect virginity and guard its cultural power. It protected only 'good girls'. As one lawyer observed, the

> result of this age-based construction of the law, which only perceives as victims those girls who have not yet been 'violated', is that the male who has intercourse with a seventeen-year-old female virgin commits

> a crime, even if he reasonably believed her to be an adult. But if that man has sex with a thirteen-year-old non-virgin, who could not possibly be mistaken for an adult, he has not broken the law.[80]

Yet, since many young girls with sexual experience had been victims of sexual abuse, surely her lack of virginity should be a sign of vulnerability, not 'promiscuity'?

The final point to note about age-of-consent arguments is that their enforcement was inextricably tied into fiscal priorities and political reflections. Thus statutory rape legislation fell into abeyance between the 1970s and the 1990s, partly as a response to a general liberalization of sexual mores and partly because prominent sections of the feminist movement promoted the sexual rights of young women. Even though there was significant concern about 'teen pregnancy' in these years, statutory rape was rarely invoked as a response to pregnancy. As one Justice observed, in the late 1970s approximately 50,000 women aged between thirteen and seventeen became pregnant in California, yet only an average of 413 boys or men were arrested for statutory rape per year.[81] In some states statutory rape was abolished altogether. States retaining the offence made it gender-neutral, thus allowing it to be used against older women who had sex with under-age boys.

From the mid-1990s this toleration changed. Laws against statutory rape in the USA began to be increasingly used as a mechanism for reducing welfare costs. The most important signal of this shift came in 1996 with the passing of the Personal Responsibility and Work Opportunity Reconciliation Act, which started the process of ending centralized welfare. Although teen pregnancies had actually been declining and did not represent a significant proportion of the people receiving direct cash assistance, aid to young mothers was curtailed. This was happening at a time when evidence was emerging that many teenage mothers may be in highly unequal relationships. A Californian-based study, for example, revealed that two-thirds of babies born to school-age mothers were fathered by men of post-high-school age.[82] A nationwide survey found that half of all the fathers of babies born to girls aged between fifteen and seventeen were twenty or older.[83] The possibility that substantial coercive elements existed in these relationships generated concern. From the 'promiscuous girl', attention shifted to the 'predatory male'. Statutory rape legislation also came to be used to prosecute cases where there was insufficient evidence to prosecute under rape laws.

As a consequence, many states decided to 'get tough' on statutory rape. In an insightful analysis of statutory rape law Rigel Oliveri argued that states adopted three types of policies. In several states the age of consent was increased. Georgia raised it from fourteen to sixteen years, for instance. In other states offenders were prosecuted more vigorously and penalties were stiffened. Thus Delaware introduced the Sexual Predator Act, increasing maximum prison sentences. In Florida a man over twenty-one who impregnated a girl under sixteen could be prosecuted for a third-degree felony, and if he was twenty-four or older and the girl was sixteen or seventeen, he could be prosecuted for a second-degree felony. Significant budgets were given to encourage the prosecution of cases. Finally, awareness of statutory rape and its seriousness led states to engage in wholesale educational campaigns. In Georgia, for instance, over 400,000 'Sex Cards' were distributed to churches, courts and health agencies. As Oliveri maintained, all these initiatives were a response to financial considerations about the cost of welfare due to the sexual activities of young women, rather than the danger of the activities of young men.[84] The laws were more concerned with reducing welfare bills than protecting vulnerable girls from sexual exploitation. As Jack Doyle, politician from Monroe County (New York), unashamedly commented when talking about Monroe County's energetic policing of statutory rape: 'We will no longer sit back and wait for the welfare bills to roll in. We're going to be pro-active.'[85]

The tension between protecting minors and reducing welfare bills could also be seen in cases where the victim of statutory rape was a young man. In such cases the minor could be forced to pay child support to the older woman who, under law, statutorily raped him. In the case of State ex re. Hermesmann v. Seyer, the Kansas Supreme Court decreed that a thirteen-year-old boy who had impregnated his older babysitter was still liable to pay child support. The court declared that it was the State's interest to require 'minor parents to support their children'. In an action of the State against a minor, 'the fault or wrongdoing of the mother at the time of conception, even if criminal, has no bearing on the father's duty to support such child'.[86]

Young men who engaged in *consensual* relationships with under-aged women could be imprisoned and forced to register as a sex offender for life. Such convictions count as a 'strike' in states with 'Three Strikes' laws. Although the sexual relationship might have been coercive or forced in some cases, a large proportion of teenage girls were capable of giving meaningful consent. Nevertheless, the decision whether to prosecute was taken not by the girl but by the prosecuting authority. These policies introduced significant state intervention into the private sphere, a situation particularly intrusive for black and Latino women, who are much more likely to find law-enforcement intervention oppressive.[87]

Certain adults also are deemed to be unable to freely consent to sexual intercourse with other adults. This was most notable in the case of members of the same family – even if they were adult and willing. In the USA incestuous relationships were criminalized at different periods in the various jurisdictions. The Mormon community of Utah, for instance, ensured that sexual intercourse between family members did not become a criminal offence until 1892. States also prohibited intercourse between different degrees of 'family', with almost half of the states prohibiting intercourse between first cousins, while others prohibited sexual relations between grandmothers and grandsons and between uncles and nieces. The decree of consent required also varied. Thus in some states incest and rape were mutually exclusive in the sense that a conviction for incest required proof of consent.[88] In England incest became a crime only in 1908, under the Punishment of Incest Act.[89]

Finally, for much of the past two centuries men were forbidden to consent to sexual intercourse with other men. (There had never been any specific legislation regulating lesbian sex, including no formal age of consent.) In many jurisdictions until very recently, buggery was a crime even if the woman or, indeed, man had consented. Consensual homosexual acts committed in private by men over twenty-one were not legalized in England and Wales until the Sexual Offences Act of 1967. Scotland and Northern Ireland only came into line with the 1967 legislation in 1980 and 1982 respectively. Strangely, the Acts did not change the legal status of buggery of a woman, which remained punishable by life imprisonment irrespective of the age of the participants and any evidence of consent until the Criminal Justice and Public Order Act of 1994. Under that law consensual buggery of a woman over eighteen became legal, and the age of consent for male homosexual acts was lowered from twenty-one to eighteen. The age of consent for same-sex couples differed from that for heterosexual couples until 2000.[90]

So who is human? Debates about who is allowed to engage in consensual sexual intercourse are fundamentally about the point at which a person becomes a full subject under the law. Slaves, racial minorities, children, family members and homosexuals were ruled out of the matrix of 'willing' subjects. Even assertions of will by white heterosexual women, however, could be erased. Daphne Morgan's 'no' was subordinate to her attackers' desires. At the very least, 'no' could be bypassed through the administration of drugs, anaesthetics or hypnosis. Perpetrators of sexual abuse experienced little guilt (they lacked the *mens rea*) because they accepted the full range of justifications or myths discussed in this and the previous chapter. Women really wanted 'it'; refusal was token. There was no need to appeal to any external standard or idea of reasonableness. Permission for sexual intercourse was already decided along lines decreed by white heterosexual males. In their hands, consent – the basis of rape law – proved to be an extraordinarily malleable concept. Although the uproar over the decision of the House of Lords in the case of Daphne Morgan was important in the passing of the Sexual Offences (Amendment) Act of 1976, which placed some curbs on the use of evidence about a victim's sexual past, such evidence was routinely bypassed in court. A short skirt, previous sexual relationships and 'foolish behaviour', although irrelevant to the question of consent to a particular act of intercourse, were routinely used to discredit any rape accuser.

So long as the courts emphasize consent (an undefined concept) as the benchmark for rape, the need for explicit verbal affirmation will be emphasized. Some critics have maintained that it is unrealistic, if not impossible, to insist on a definite agreement to each and every act of sexual intercourse. Accepting the notion that sexuality is an irrepressible force and that male sexuality in particular is impetuous, these critics doubt whether requiring an unequivocal 'yes' is practical. Ilene Seidman and Susan Vickers, in an article entitled 'The Second Wave' (2004–5), disagree, pointing to the highly effective public health campaign to promote condom use in response to the AIDS epidemic. Before this campaign it was assumed that getting sexually aroused people to 'stop and think about safe sex' was impossible. But safe sex did become 'part of the everyday landscape of sex'. Insisting upon 'an affirmative "yes" before engaging in sexual intercourse is no more an imposition of sexual expression than condom use'.[91] Or, as Stephen Schulhofer put it in 'The Gender Question in Criminal Law' (1990), the argument that 'no' means 'no'

> does not go far enough . . . When there is no question that her partner can enforce his will if he has to, why should silence be taken as the

> equivalent to consent? Why should the law in effect presume the existence of consent in the absence of an explicit 'no'? . . . citizens may not presume a privilege to intrude upon the rights of others, but rather must respect the autonomy of each person and stand clear in the absence of a direct, affirmative manifestation of consent.[92]

A person should not be presumed to have consented to sexual intercourse if she or he agreed to it under 'coercion, including . . . economic deprivation, abuse of authority, deception, or threat to the welfare or security of a child'.[93] More to the point (and I return to this issue in the penultimate chapter), why should there have to be a 'no'?

SECTION THREE

Identities

The spirit died
First – such blank amazement took away its breath,
And let the body cry
Through the short scuffle and infamy of death.
For the other, who knows what nice proportion of loathing
And lust conjured the deep devil, created
That chance of incandescence? Figures here prove nothing.

CECIL DAY LEWIS, 'SEX-CRIME'.[1]

CHAPTER FOUR

Rapacious Bodies

Yuba County is located in the Northern Sacramento Valley, California. On 24 April 1906 a white woman called Miss Ocea Taylor accused John Walker, a twenty-one-year-old African-American cook and teamster from Louisiana, of attempting to rape her. At five o'clock that morning Taylor, who was employed looking after the young children of John Schonlan, had been woken by Walker and asked to check that he was correctly weighing some hay. According to the official report, when she entered the barn, 'the negro struck her in the face with his fist, breaking her glasses and knocking her down'. Taylor

> fought and scuffled with him and endeavored in every way to get away from his embrace. After a severe scuffle she broke away and ran from the barn, but was caught and carried back again. Then the Negro tried to stuff a handkerchief down her throat to keep her from calling for help, and although Walker is a powerfully built man the little woman of but about 20 years managed to fight him off until he finally gave up his purpose.

It later emerged that there was a question mark over the last part of Taylor's testimony. Walker's attorney believed that the rape had not been 'attempted' but completed. According to him, Ocea Taylor had 'withheld the facts for the reason that her pride forbade her telling the whole truth'.

When Taylor's near or actual rape 'became noised about', men in the local community 'all became highly indignant and a search was commenced for the brute'. One man, believing the 'brute' was hiding in the barn, took a pitchfork and began poking it down into the bales of hay. When his efforts were 'rewarded by a loud scream', the barn was surrounded by armed men and the sheriff was called.

John Walker almost died on the spot – and not only by being speared with the pitchfork. While waiting for the sheriff and his guards to arrive, Ocea Taylor's employer raised his rifle to shoot him, only to be physically restrained by some other men. Walker welcomed the arrival of the sheriff, observing that another of the men surrounding him 'kept fingering his gun while it was pointed in his direction'.

Walker protested his innocence. He even proffered the fact that he had served in the US Army as proof of good character. Unfortunately the police rapidly discovered that he had been dishonourably discharged and was unemployed. Worse, one of his workmates testified that Walker had spoken about robbing Schonlan's house. The sheriff also found some looted clothes and a razor on him. His fate was decided once Miss Ocea Taylor positively identified him as her assailant. The local newspaper reported that 'the desperate colored man confined in County Jail on a charge of assault with intent to commit rape' had been photographed and his picture hung 'in the rogues' gallery'. [See photograph, below.]

Walker's attorney admitted to having 'used a great amount of persuasion' to convince Walker to plead guilty. Walker was told that 'he had not one chance in a thousand of getting anything less than the limit of fourteen years for his crime if he held to his purpose of standing trial,

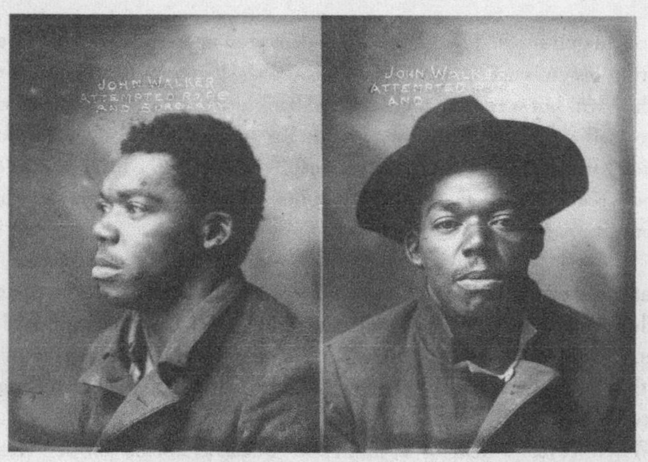

John Walker's prison photograph, 1906

and that he will stand a better show of pleading guilty'. In the end this proved false. Walker pleaded guilty but was still sent to the notorious Folsom Prison (California), sentenced to serve the full fourteen years. The judge regretted that he could not impose a life sentence.

Five years later Walker applied for parole. His half-sister was tracked down and wrote a letter of testimonial to the warden. In this, she admitted that she was 'indeed surprised to hear of Johney [sic] been alive' since they had 'lost trace of him'. Her half-brother had received very little schooling, she admitted, but 'he had a good Christen [sic] mother' who had died three years earlier. Walker was 'the only child she had on earth, and she loved the very ground he stood on. She died worrying about Johney.' She concluded her letter with the 'hope to hear from you that Johney is out'.

This favourable testimonial was undercut by Walker's own attorney at the parole hearings. 'He no doubt would be a very good man if he was casterated [sic] before leaving prison,' the attorney wrote. Surgical castration would make Walker 'harmless', even turn him into a 'good citizen'. However, the attorney continued, Walker was 'one of those unfortunate men, like many of his race, and not a few white men, who have trouble controlling their passions for the gentle sex, and while all strong men have strong passions in that direction, yet, they can be managed by the most of men'.

He went on, saying that he had a duty not only to Walker and society in general, but also to himself as a citizen. Walker

> is a Southern negro, and I am a Southern man, and every incentive of my nature is prejudiced in favour of the negro, they have been my childhood companions, they have played with me, they have cared for me, and I love them, I know their weakness, and their ability, while I have had trouble with innumerable whitemen, and some of them, are meaner than any negro, worse than John Walker, I could name some of them prominent, but the trouble is with Walker, he is weak in that particular. He is unbalanced. Unbalanced in the fact, that his passions for women are greater than his self control, greater than his fear for the prison, greater than his discretion.

He could not recommend setting Walker free. Walker was not paroled for another two years, on 14 May 1913. He was released only on condition that he never return to Yuba County.[2]

*

Whether guilty or innocent, Walker conformed to popular prejudices about rapists: he was a poor, itinerant African-American man without any nearby family or friends to provide him with an alibi or support. The white community of Yuba County had no doubt that he was a victim of his race's 'strong passions' for the 'gentler sex'. They were perfectly happy to lynch him on the spot, as a warning to other 'desperate colored men'. Walker's own attorney believed that he was 'unbalanced' and the only real way to protect white women from his irrepressible lusts was to attack the fundamentals of his degenerate body through castration. These ideas were most commonly applied to African-American men and other minorities, but other types of men were also regarded as belonging in the lower reaches of humanity.

In this chapter I address the question: who is 'the rapist'? Do sexual aggressors share certain physical or psychological characteristics? Over the past 150 years these questions have intrigued and obsessed people concerned with the scourge of sexual violence in their society. The most commonly debated question is: what biological or environmental forces have forged the sex offender? Of course, practically no theorist believes that biology exists outside of the social; they all agree that there is an interaction between the two. However, the degeneration theorists and evolutionary psychologists I examine in this chapter prioritize biology. It is followed by a chapter in which I discuss the parallel discourse that emphasizes the effect of environment in creating aggressive men. At times ideas about the nature of rapists are illuminating; at other times they are ludicrous, racist and profoundly offensive. Where did such ideas come from?

The 'Science' of Degeneracy

Nineteenth-century criminality conjured up images of physical corruption. For commentators anxious about levels of crime, the rapacious man was a degenerate, a fact that could be seen literally 'at a glance'. According to these theories, the corporeal surface told the 'truth' about the person's inner nature. The body itself was the index of interior states and dispositions.

Although developed within a European (and specifically Italian) context, notions of the degenerate body of the violent criminal were popularized in Britain and America by the influential sexologist Henry Havelock Ellis. Ellis was not a naïve observer of these debates. In particular he warned against confusing 'expression' (an appearance of elation or alarm, for instance) with anatomical physiognomy (the shape of the jaw or cut of the ears). To illustrate the difference Ellis reported on the ways a journalist and a prison chaplain described the same nineteen-year-old man, who had raped and killed a young girl. The journalist wrote:

> Imagine a sort of abortion, bent and wrinkled, with earthy complexion, stealthy eyes, a face gnawed by scrofula, of cunning, dissipated, and cruel aspect. The forehead is low, the beard sparse and slovenly; the hair black and thrown backwards, reaching to the shoulders; it is a head absolutely repulsive.

In contrast, the prison chaplain claimed that the same man was 'far from being repulsive'. He had 'a sympathetic and prepossessing physiognomy, the air of a young man who has been well brought up, a gentle, honest, *naïve* face; he looked to me, like a page in a good house', observed the chaplain. According to Ellis, both men had confused expression with physiognomy. The journalist knew the man's crime and witnessed him in a hostile courtroom, while the chaplain saw a broken man in his cell, in an 'attitude of respectful humility'. For the science of physiognomy to work, attention had to be fixed entirely on the 'strictly organic' aspects of a person's appearance – aspects that could 'safely be called congenital'.

Ellis asserted that, if physiognomy was to be used to identify sex criminals, it had to be transformed into a 'very exact science'. What did scientific research reveal about the sex offender's body? Anomalies of genitals had 'no small diagnostic importance', reported Ellis, 'especially when united to other characters which distinguish them [sex criminals] from the honest and from criminals in general'. These other characteristics included the greater likelihood of having malformed ears and noses, either blue eyes or differently coloured irises, asymmetrical faces and voluminous lower jaws. Hair was also important, with sex offenders more liable to sport an 'abundance of hair' (a trait correlated with animal vigour), which was more likely to be fair, especially red. They were more likely to suffer from epilepsy, the most common mark of degeneracy. Finally, Ellis pointed out that alcoholism was 'a symptom as well as a cause of degeneration'. The danger of alcohol lay 'not in any mysterious prompting to crime', but 'in the manner in which the poison lets loose the individual's natural or morbid impulses'. Indeed, the 'action of the poison may be slow, and carried on from generation to generation. The fathers eat sour grapes; the children's teeth are set on edge'.[3]

Discussions about the degenerate bodies of sex criminals were particularly popular in the years leading up to the First World War. These 'broken-down' and mentally weak people unmistakably displayed the 'stigmata of degeneracy', most obviously a tiny penis or monorchidia, argued Henri Colin, author of 'Mental and Physical State of Criminals Convicted of Sexual Crime' (1898). Their 'infantile' sexual organs were only one sign of degeneracy. They also had 'imperfect' teeth and jaws, 'marked cranial and facial asymmetry' and were 'weak-minded'.[4] Such 'degenerates' had been born into families with a history of neuroses, added Martin W. Barr, Chief Physician at the Pennsylvania Training School for Feeble-Minded Children. Indeed, they were often the 'offspring of exaggerated lust'. The stigmata of degeneracy could be seen in their irregular spines, asymmetrical heads, and ears with adherent lobules. 'Defect, unlike disease, knows no cure,' Barr gloomily intoned.[5]

Degeneracy was generally considered to be a hereditary condition and therefore 'congenital' to the person. The one main exception appeared in discussions about the abuse of children by elderly men. The noticeable lengthening of life expectancy (coinciding with a declining birth rate, making the elderly a larger proportion of the population) fuelled these debates. In the mid-nineteenth century the average male life expectancy was forty years, compared with fifty-two by 1911. As men lived longer and were assumed to retain sexual urges, anxiety about (male) geriatric sexual practices came to the fore. Throughout the nineteenth and twentieth centuries commentators insisted that the main reason for the propensity of elderly men to attack children was that younger girls and boys proved easier to 'seduce'.[6] In the words of the author of a book on forensic psychiatry, children represented 'the only available market for the shoddy, libidinous wares of the worn-out old man'.[7] However, others claimed that elderly men were also in the process of degeneration. Senile dementia was a form of 'reverse evolution' that manifested itself in 'indecent exposure, urination in public, indecent assaults upon children, and libidinous loquaciousness', announced the consultant physician to the Manhattan State Hospital for the Insane in 1900.[8] By weakening inhibitory mechanisms, senility led directly to 'infantile forms' of sexual behaviour.[9] Man degenerated into child.

These fears about debauched elderly male bodies were trivial when compared with racial anxieties underpinning debates about the dangers of degeneration. According to late-nineteenth-century recapitulation theory, the individual's body and mind 'recapitulated' the life of the species. Some people failed to 'develop', and so were stuck at a lower level of evolution. These developmental failures were believed to be most common among non-white races. According to George E. Dawson, psychologist at Clark University and author of 'Psychic Rudiments and Morality' (1900), the rapist illustrated the 'persistence of a very primitive sex diathesis in the midst of civilization'. 'Among savage peoples', he explained, force was 'often employed in sexual union'. It did not surprise him therefore that 'the crime of rape should be so common among our Negro and Indian populations.' For Dawson evidence of rape within these populations proved the persistence of savagery into modernity. He believed that the savage tendency in African-Americans had been suppressed under slavery because, being 'placed under white taskmasters they were obliged to work somewhat after the manner of the civilization surrounding them'. Emancipation, however, unleashed the 'race instinct of carelessness and improvidence'. The result was an increase in sexual attacks by blacks.[10] [See image, below.]

The scientific veneer of the racist rhetoric about the primitive nature of the rapist was embraced by the mob menacing John Walker, with which episode I started this chapter. It was also eagerly co-opted by the mass media. Indeed, throughout the nineteenth and twentieth centuries reports of rape were infused with fears of blacks, immigrants and

'The Black Plague', from *The Thunderbolt*. Newspaper of the National States' Rights Party, Marietta, Georgia, October 1969

racial 'outsiders' – and not just in the USA. Thus Antony Lucas (born Antony Lugas Surgy) was convicted in 1928 of raping twenty-five-year-old Marion Greig of Gilliant (Queensland, Australia). Although he was a naturalized British citizen who had lived in Australia for fourteen years, the language of race permeated reportage. According to the headline in the Brisbane *Truth*, Lucas was a 'Mediterranean Moron . . . Degenerate'. He was a 'degraded and despicable Greek' who violated an 'Australian mother' (in fact, his victim was of French descent). In a single article he was described as 'gross and animalistic . . . a mentally and morally greasy Greek . . . a vile Greek beast . . . dirty dog . . . lying foreigner . . . human monster . . . scum of the Mediterranean'. When a physician examined 'the Greek satyr' he was found to be suffering from a 'loathsome disease'. This 'disgusting specimen of humanity' thought he could 'indulge his appetites' upon 'defenceless Australian womanhood'. The judge sentenced this 'low and lecherous son of the Levant' to seven years' imprisonment.

The *Truth* lamented the 'laxity of an administration that allows the inflow of his degraded type'. It was 'a shocking commentary on our social laws, or their administration', the paper continued, 'that lecherous morons from the Southern Mediterranean shore, by virtue of the opportunities which the amassing of a little money gives them, can lay traps, snare & subject to unnameable degradation Australian womanhood'.[11] The monster in the midst of civilized society was a racial 'other', a degenerate throwback to more primitive times.

Rapacious Instincts

Commentators who characterized rapists as degenerate or as relics from an archaic past were drawing on ideas developed within Darwinian theories of evolution. An alternative version identified man's 'natural' rapaciousness with certain innate instincts, once again inherited from humanity's primordial past. For these social psychologists an instinct was

> an inherited or innate psycho-physical disposition which determines its possessor to perceive, and to pay attention to, objects of a certain class, to experience an emotional excitement of a particular quality upon perceiving such an object, and to act in regard to it in a particular manner, or, at least, to experience an impulse to such action.[12]

The sexual and the pugnacious were the two important instincts. The latter had arisen out of the ancient and perpetual feud between the patriarch and his sons for possession of the women of the tribe. According to these theories, survival depended upon the outcome of this struggle and, as a result, a sexually driven humanity retained the instinct of pugnacity as part of what it meant to be human.[13] The fact that this formulation of instinct theory ignores the female half of humanity (generally not seen as possessing strong aggressive sexual appetites) was not seen as problematic.

In practical terms, how was instinct theory employed to explain sexual violence? In the next chapter I will be exploring explanations that emphasized environmental factors. Instinct theorists stressed the overriding character of evolutionary processes upon the body. The relative influence of instincts and environment was evaluated in the work of the prominent criminologist William Adrian Bonger, writing in *Criminality and Economic Conditions* (1916). 'Every normally constituted man would be a born rapist if the sexual appetite could find no other means of satisfaction,' he insisted. Reassuringly, he added that, thankfully, there were 'women for the ugliest and the poorest'. However, since 'famine may come', it was important to remember that 'opportunity' and 'many devils' were 'capable of leading into temptation the brute that every man is at his birth'. Man became a 'brute' with beguiling ease within certain environments. Rapists emanated from those 'strata of society' where (because of their 'living conditions') 'sexual life is considered from a purely animal point of view'. Poor housing and exposure to immoral scenes bred children who were 'thoroughly conversant with the sexual life in its most bestial manifestations'. Since children learned ethics and moral restraint within their family unit, how could anyone expect civilized sexual behaviour to be 'awakened in the offspring of the lowest ranks of the proletariat', Bonger asked? After all, the 'undisguised sexual intercourse of parents, other adults, and prostitutes' would obviously suppress even any latent moral sense.

Bonger did not stop there. He observed that working-class men regarded their womenfolk as inferior (a prejudice he regarded as particularly strong among the poor). This unrefined attitude encouraged them to act as though women were 'designed to submit' to male sexual desires. Of course, Bonger hastened to add, not all underprivileged men ended up raping women. The 'sexual instincts' vary with age, and some men 'naturally' possessed stronger instincts than others. In his words,

> There are individuals who have very pronounced sexual propensities, others who are almost indifferent in this respect, and between the two extremes lives the great majority. It is only for the first class that the danger of a crime against morals is great, for the others it is less so. If the opportunity . . . presents itself to persons already predisposed, the moral check to restrain them is lacking. If they had lived in another environment, this act would be repugnant.

The emphasis on 'moral check' was important, because, Bonger believed, better nutrition actually *strengthened* the sexual instincts. According to Bonger, the fact that rape was a crime 'not committed by persons of the other [more privileged] classes, although there are naturally proportionately more persons with strong sexual instincts among them' could be explained by stronger environmental checks. If you were 'to take a well-born child from a distinguished European family and isolate him from his birth from all the influences of environment except those strictly necessary for the preservation of his life, we do not know what strange beast he would turn into', Bonger hypothesized. After all, a man 'becomes a brute only under certain fixed circumstances, and commits then acts that would be repugnant to him if he live[d] in a different environment'. All men contained within their breast the 'human beast', but he emerged only under certain environmental conditions.[14]

It was an immensely popular view, adhered to by the political left as well as the right. Thus in 1920 the famous trial lawyer and socialist Clarence Seward Darrow was equally forthright, insisting that rape was 'almost always the crime of the poor, the hardworking, the uneducated and the abnormal'. He continued, arguing that in such a man

> sex hunger is strong; he has little money, generally no family; he is poorly fed and clothed and possesses few if any attractions. He may be a sailor away from women and their society for months, or in some other remote occupation making his means of gratifying this hunger just as impossible. There is no opportunity for him except the one he adopts. It is a question of gratifying this deep and primal instinct as against the weakness of his mentality and the few barriers that a meagre education and picked-up habits can furnish; and when the instinct overbalances he is lost.[15]

Darrow attributed immense power to an omnipotent yet strangely ill-defined 'Nature' that inadvertently forged sex criminals from among the 'wretched and the plainly defective' members of society. Like Bonger's, Darrow's 'man' and 'mankind' was utterly masculine. 'In her determination to preserve the species,' Darrow noted,

> Nature . . . has planted sex hunger very deep in the constitution of man. The fact that it is necessary for the preservation of life, and that Nature is always eliminating those whose sex hunger is not strong enough to preserve the race, has outweighed man and perhaps all animal life with this hunger. At least it has endowed many men with instincts too powerful for the conventions and laws that hedge him about.[16]

In this conception, 'conventions and laws' existed in order to rein in men's natural rapaciousness.

Such attitudes had significant implications for the punishment of rapists. According to its logic, if a man was brutalized enough to rape he could probably only respond to violence. In other words, rapists needed a good flogging. In 1898 the anonymous author of an article in the *Albany Law Journal* put it succinctly when he argued that 'acute physical pain' was probably 'the only thing' a molester could 'really feel', the 'one punishment he really dreads'. It was 'ridiculous' to worry about whether the punishment might 'degrade' the prisoner since he was obviously already 'as low in the moral scale as he can be'.[17] Around the same time the Chief Justice of the Supreme Court of Delaware agreed, noting that while he strongly believed 'in the reforming influences and power of love and of gentle treatment, rather than of fear and harsh punishment', there were 'certain natures, some it may be irreclaimable, whose conscience and conduct can be best governed by the application of the rod'.[18] It was an added benefit that the man who had been 'stripped and put under the lash' was dishonoured within the criminal community, claimed Simeon Baldwin of the Supreme Court of Errors and Appeals of Connecticut in 1899. Furthermore, the punishment was not really cruel, Baldwin claimed. At most 'the same degree of suffering is inflicted, for the purpose in one respect not dissimilar, on half of our larger domestic animals'. Yet 'We do not deem it cruelty to them.'[19] The 'rod' effectively attacked the 'conscience and conduct' of evil men.

In a speech given to members of the Kansas State Bar Association in January 1901, Lucius H. Perkins elaborated on the value of flogging sex offenders. Like Baldwin, he stressed that vicious men responded only to fierce pain. Of course, Perkins reminded his listeners, he was not advocating 'the reinstatement of the lash, in the savage cruelty of other days, when the flesh was cut in ribbons by the cruel cat-o'-nine-tails'. Rather, he was proposing the civilized infliction of pain. He was calling for nothing more than the 'reasonable castigation with a rod or strip intended only to produce sharp pain, but no laceration of the flesh or skin'. The integrity of the flesh was to be respected so that it could better violate the spirit.

Perkins did express some scruples. He did not 'advocate the lash at all for the man of refined instincts and sensitive soul'. The 'prison brand' would 'bring far keener torture' to the 'refined' rapist than anything that could be 'done upon his body'. In case the distinction he was making between middle- and working-class sexual abusers was not clear enough, Perkins repeated that corporal punishment ought to be reserved for the 'hardened criminal' who had been a 'companion of criminals from his youth' since such a man was disdainful of 'modern sentimentalism'. In contrast, imprisonment alone was effective in rehabilitating the 'educated, sensitive, [and] refined' sex criminal. In other words, punishments should be tailored to fit the criminal, not the crime. On an almost evangelical note, Perkins concluded his plea. If 'brutal man' was going to

> trample under foot the closest ties of blood, outrage the holiest instincts of humanity, and bring unutterable misery and shame on those who should deserve their tenderest care, before high heaven they do deserve such chastisement as will appeal to their dull faculties, and, failing all things else, it may be that the lash, revived in christian hands, in this new century, may prove an instrument of mercy.[20]

'Scientific Racism' and Retribution

At this point I am going to take a slight detour, because racist myths had a significant impact on some men accused of rape. We have just heard how Perkins (and others) differentiated the middle-class sex offender (who could be reformed) from his working-class brother (innately degenerate). Much more frequently distinctions were being made by race. Indeed, class was often used as a code for race. I began this chapter with the example of John Walker, a rapist who was almost lynched by the white mob who captured him. Degenerate sexual aggressors were deemed worthy of lynching, particularly in the USA, although isolated incidents occurred in the United Kingdom, mainly in the context of meting out 'rough music' which got out of control.[21] In the USA, however, lynching was a fairly modern phenomenon. As many historians have noted, lynching was rare in the USA before the Civil War. Indeed, so long as certain discretion was observed (in particular the racial lines were not blurred through the birth of a child), sexual intercourse between white women and black men tended to be tolerated before the war. After the Reconstruction, however, this changed as African-American demands for political rights threatened white male supremacy, in bed and boardroom.[22]

The most common justification for lynching was that white women had to be protected from black men intent on corrupting their virtue. The language of bestiality permeated all these discussions. As Rebecca Felton, leader of the Georgia Chapter of the Women's Christian Temperance Union and first woman elected to the US Senate argued in the late 1890s, 'If it needs lynching to protect woman's dearest possession from human beasts, then I say lynch a thousand times a week if necessary. The poor girl would choose death in preference to such ignominy, and I say a quick rope to assaulters!'[23] Such attitudes almost got John Walker summarily shot.

It is important to note, however, that lynching was not reserved for (alleged) rapists and other violent criminals. Between 1889 and 1929 only one-sixth of lynching victims were accused of rape. In contrast, 38 per cent were charged with murder.[24] 'Neck-tie parties' were held for striking workers; African-American women were also lynched.

Nevertheless, racist accusations of sexual assault were the most common *excuse* for the practice of lynching. The author of 'The Remedy for Lynch Law' (1889) counselled his readers in the prestigious *Yale Law Journal* to 'consider how profoundly humiliated any woman must feel who has been the victim of an outrage of this character, and how, under existing social conditions, this humiliation must be greatly intensified by the wrong having been committed by a negro'.[25] The 'any woman' he referred to in this article was, of course, white: African-American women were not regarded as harmed by rape since they were portrayed as being innately promiscuous.* In contrast, as the Georgia Supreme Court stated in 1964, white women were 'soil[ed] for life' after the 'forcible sexual invasion of her body, the temple of her soul' by a black man.[26] In this way lynching also served

*This is discussed in Chapter 2, 'Rape Myths'.

to remind (white) women of their dependence upon (white) men for protection. While African-American men were portrayed as bestial degenerates, white women were purified and desexualized, even though their status depended upon the precarious authority of white men.

The central function of lynching was to enforce racial and class hierarchies. Even a latent threat could be effective. As the *Afro-American* lamented in 1907,

> [s]uch is the condition of affairs in some communities that a Negro is almost afraid to meet a woman on the streets or in a road after dark for fear that he will in some way be incriminated and possibly lynched for no reason in the world save that he met the woman on the street or in the road.

This state of affairs was 'unreasonable and to say the least outrageous', they concluded.[27]

The threat of lynching, therefore, was explicitly meant to keep *all* black men in line. As Haywood Patterson, one of the so-called Scottsboro boys who had been sentenced to death for a rape that didn't happen (and was lucky to have escaped being lynched),* reflected,

> It was never in me to rape, not a black and not a white woman. Only a Negro who is a fool or a crazy man, he would chance his life for anything like that. A Negro with sound judgment and common sense is not going to do it. They are going to take his life away from him if he does. Every Negro man in the South knows that. No, most Negroes run away from that sort of thing, fear in their hearts.[28]

Historian Lisa Lindquist Dorr's research on Virginian mores confirms Patterson's analysis. It was precisely the 'arbitrariness . . . unpredictability' of lynching that upheld segregation. 'Whose life was sacrificed for racial transgressions, and whose was not, was largely random', Dorr discovered. Yet, at the same time,

> the willingness of white elites to show mercy to black men accused and convicted of crimes was also a means of control over the black community. The terror of lynching combined with the hope of court-mandated mercy, either through acquittal, short sentence, or pardon,

*This case is discussed in Chapter 12, 'The Prison'.

> created a subtle and effective system of control that policed interracial boundaries while simultaneously maintaining class and gender norms.[29]

The fear inspired by lynching affected even highly educated, upwardly socially mobile men, tarnished by the belief among white elites that their 'good behaviour' was simply an attempt to get close to white women. Attempts to refute that myth merely exposed these Americans to accusations of condoning black violence.

Proponents of lynching vigorously defended the practice. On 2 September 1921 Luther Rosser addressed the American Bar Association, seeking to explain the practice of lynching in racial terms. According to Rosser, white Americans lacked confidence that the legal system would deal efficiently with 'bestial' criminals. Using the language of 'scientific racism' that I discussed earlier in this chapter, Rosser observed that in all life there was a tendency to 'revert to original primitive types'. Unless provided with adequate moral and mental training, every individual was capable of reverting 'backward to his cave ancestor'. Nevertheless, it was uncommon for white Americans to regress in this fashion, he contended, even if, under certain circumstances, they could be roused by 'some great temptation or obsessed by some primeval passion' to strike out with hatred and vengefulness. Base crimes committed by African-Americans were precisely the spark igniting the inferno. According to him, black Americans had been 'removed from the ignorance and dependency of slavery' for under fifty years and their 'poise and self-control' remained 'near zero'. Furthermore, the era of reconstruction had transformed African-Americans' image of themselves and their worth. 'Troublemakers' had 'destroyed the negro's confidence in and reliance on his old master', encouraging the 'ignorant negro' to dream of social equality and even intermarriage with white American women. These agitators had propagated the doctrine that the black man was the 'equal of any white man, socially, mentally and morally, and that he had but to assert himself to become his superior and his master'. These militants had

> robbed him of his every stay, his every comfort and hope; and they gave him instead an imagination diseased and distorted, and developed in him a malignant hatred for the only friend he had ever had . . . They found him simple, trusting, polite, goodnatured and hopeful; they

> bereft him, so far as they were able, of all these simple, lovable qualities and, in their stead, they gave him unrest, suspicion, hate, a diseased and inflamed ego, an ill-balanced ambition to strut and bluster in place and position for which he had no aptitude by mental or moral equipment or by tradition or training.

The tragic result could have been predicted, Rosser continued. The typical African-American man became lazy, disgruntled and determined to 'gratify his lust' with any white woman he chose.

In such circumstances, Rosser ranted, was it any wonder that the white American population became 'beguiled . . . into lynching'? It was merely 'thoughtlessness' on their part. Since white American men made the laws, elected the judges and sat on juries, they were 'very sure that the whole machinery of government' belonged to them. Why should they throw out the 'form of procedure that they themselves have made' to 'dispense justice speedily'? Lynching promised a rapid application of white majority rule. Naturally the rape of one of their own race was the crime most likely to stir the 'Anglo-Saxon' into action. The

> equilibrium of a community may successfully stand the shock of murder, even cowardly, brutal murder; and may even withstand, though most unlikely, the shock of rape when the woman is defiled by one of her own race, without murder or mutilation; but when a woman, innocent and of good repute, is ravished, mutilated and murdered, and especially by a brutal, ignorant member of an inferior and socially ostracized race, then nothing but Divine Providence . . . can hold the fury of the mob.

It was of little avail to argue that justice could be found within the courts, Rosser noted. Black rapists were not deterred. In fact, the courthouse was nothing more than a stage upon which the black offender 'struts as the leading actor; the gallows is but a gateway to martyrdom and a martyr's crown'. The law was 'too calm in its procedure' to terrify the black potential rapist. It was 'not equal' to 'Judge Lynch in striking terror'.[30]

Rosser's vicious diatribe was not exceptional, although most commentators adopted more subtle language. In 1903 unnamed academics at Yale University, for instance, observed that (white) Americans had a peculiar attitude towards justice. In 'older countries', these men pointed out, the justice system was 'regarded as a sacred authority from a superior source'. In contrast, American law 'lacks long practice and the growth of tradition'. Democratic ideals had encouraged the belief that citizens were 'a law unto themselves', so it was simply a small step to see lynching as a way to 'terrorize the lawless'. Male and female perpetrators of lynch violence against alleged rapists and other villains acted according to the motto 'let a past crime be met with a present crime to prevent a future crime'.[31]

This individualistic approach to the law coexisted with a curious calculus for apportioning blame. Members of lynch mobs were especially enraged by (alleged) offenders who proffered *reasons* for their violence. In other words, African-Americans who raped white women with personal or political revenge motives were considered more deserving of the noose than those who raped out of lust. According to the surgeon F. E. Daniel, speaking at the International Medico-Legal Congress in Chicago in 1893, it was 'less abhorrent to a just mind' to kill a 'stout negro man' who had raped a small child if there was evidence that the rapist had committed the act out of 'revenge for an offense or injury done the negro by the child's father'. The attack was 'more atrocious' if there were 'reasons assigned for the act'.[32] Rape was much more than an attack on a woman; it was an assault on the entire structure of white power and authority.

Defenders of extra-judicial application of the death penalty increasingly faced tough opposition, however, especially from groups as diverse as the Commission on Interracial Cooperation and the Association of Southern Women for the Prevention of Lynching. Their primary objections were that lynching was racist and a form of community pathology. The author of *Rope and Faggot* (1929) went so far as to claim that the practice emerged out of a society 'stunted' in 'mental and moral growth'. Lynchers led dull lives, devoid of 'excitement' and 'diversions such as theatres'.[33]

Nevertheless, the 'wrong' of lynching also lay in the way it hurt white Americans. Lynching reflected badly upon local white communities, exposing them as uncivilized. As State Attorney Farrior admitted after the lynching of Robert Johnson in Tampa in 1934, lynching was 'deplorable; it reflects on the County and State . . . we must not tolerate such happening that spreads a blot on Tampa's history'.[34] Lynching gave the city 'a black eye', agreed Doyle E. Carlton, former Governor of the State, adding that it 'will draw no people to Florida or the west coast'.[35] Mob violence was a threat to economic prosperity and social stability.

Finally, commentators who deplored lynching did not necessarily have the same objections towards judicially imposed death sentences. Again there was a strong racial dimension to this penalty, especially in the USA (in Britain, the death penalty for rape was abolished in 1841).[36] Until recently most American states that impose the death penalty include rape as a capital crime. Given the long history of extra-judicial killing of rapists, it is not surprising that one of the justifications for state-sanctioned execution was that it was an effective substitute for lynching. Discussions always referred to blacks in code. The anonymous author of an 1899 article in the *Yale Law Journal* coyly noted that there was 'a certain crime of which one seldom speaks'. Yet

> the thought of it is a daily terror to every woman in the South, and brings a sense of uneasiness and constraint into the life of her Northern sisters. It is the cause of most of those lynching cases which disgrace our civilization. It is to be kept down only by the severest methods. Is it too much to say that if the courts are not ready to apply these, the people will?

These citizens who 'may thus bring some ruffian to his death' were not 'the best people in the community', he admitted, and they might 'occasionally seize the wrong man', but no court of law has ever convicted a member of a 'mob of lynchers for hanging a man accused of rape'. It was the duty of the law to punish with the greatest severity those men who trespassed against the virtue of the 'weaker sex'.[37]

Given this link with lynching, it is hardly surprising that African-Americans risked execution more than their white fellow convicts. In the words of a district attorney for State v. Petit (1907),

> During the reconstruction days, when we had negro domination in this state, the Kuklux [sic] Klans were organized and the best people of the state shouldered their guns for the protection of our white people. During those days white people were thrown into jail and tried by negro justices of the peace and negro juries. Now we have no more negro domination, but a government by the white people, and hence no necessity for lynching.[38]

It was a view sarcastically noted by Oliver Hill, an African-American attorney for the National Association for the Advancement of Colored People, who defended black men accused of rape: 'We don't need to lynch the niggers,' he cynically reported, because 'We can try them and hang them.'[39]

Discriminatory sentencing was not just conventional practice; it was law. In Alabama (1823), Georgia (1837), Louisiana (1841) and Texas (1859), for instance, a black man who attempted to rape a white woman could be sentenced to death, but a white man convicted of the same offence could get anything from a few months to seven years' imprisonment.[40] The 1860 Code of Virginia decreed that a white man convicted of 'carnally knowing' a child under the age of twelve should be sentenced to between ten and twenty years in prison. If a 'free negro' committed the same offence, he could be sentenced to death.[41] Although penal codes were made race-neutral after the Civil War, in practice black men who raped white women continued to be treated more harshly than their white counterparts. In fact, some historians convincingly argue that slaves accused of rape were given 'relatively fair trials', with significant attention paid to due process (albeit with harsher penalties if a conviction followed), in comparison with the situation after the Civil War.[42] After emancipation, when white men could no longer rely upon bondage to maintain racial hierarchies, they were more likely to employ lynching or demand the death penalty for black offenders. In particular, when deciding guilt or innocence, juries were allowed to consider the race of the defendant and victim. In the 1950s, for instance, a court trying an African-American man determined that when the jury was considering 'the question of intention', they could take into account 'social conditions and customs founded upon racial differences, such as that the prosecutrix was a white woman and defendant was a Negro man'. In this particular case the prisoner had been accused of walking within six feet of a white woman and saying something that no one heard, but prejudices about the 'conditions and customs' of African-American men meant that he was found guilty of an 'attempt to commit an assault with intent to rape'.[43]

If convicted, black offenders in many cases paid for their crime with their life. A study carried out in the mid-1960s found that all of the forty-one men executed for rape or attempted rape in Virginia since the electric chair was installed in 1908 were African-American,[44] Indeed, in Hampton v. Commonwealth (1960) it was contended that 'it was the policy, practice and custom of the Commonwealth of Virginia, to inflict the death penalty upon Negroes because of their race and color'. The Supreme Court of Appeals in Virginia was affronted by this accusation. 'There is not a scintilla of evidence,' it retorted, 'to support this statement . . . This contention is an abortive attempt to inject into the proceedings racial prejudice.'[45] In reality the evidence pointed in exactly the opposite direction. According to a detailed examination of rape convictions, not only was 'rape by a Negro man' in Virginia a crime that 'has been treated as meriting an extreme punishment', but judges and juries proved more than willing to impose this punishment.[46]

This discriminatory practice was not restricted to Virginia. Elmer Johnson, of the Center for the Study of Crime, Delinquency and Corrections at Southern Illinois University, revealed major racial inequities in the proportion of death-row inmates convicted of rape actually executed between 1909 and 1953. If the victim was a white adult woman, three-quarters of the rapists were executed, but if the victim was an African-American adult woman, the proportion fell to only 14 per cent. Only one-third of white rapists were executed between 1909 and 1933, compared with 54 per cent of black rapists. The proportion of black and white rapists executed moved closer in the period 1935 to 1954, but still half of all white rapists were executed, compared with 58 per cent of black rapists.[47] Innumerable other studies exposed similar discrepancies. In those states that had the death penalty for rape, between 1930 and 1962 90 per cent of such penalties were imposed against African Americans. In six jurisdictions no white defendants had ever been executed for rape.[48] Might these discrepancies be due less to racial prejudice and more to an unacknowledged third factor (for instance, black offenders might be more liable to be in possession of a weapon or have more prior convictions)? This was not the case. When researchers examined capital sentences of 1265 rapists in eleven Southern and border states between 1945 and 1965, out of thirty-five variables that might have increased the risk of a capital sentence, race was the only significant one. Seven times more black rapists than white rapists were sentenced to death. In addition, blacks who raped whites received the death penalty in 36 per cent of cases, while blacks who raped blacks or whites who raped whites received the death penalty in only 2 per cent of cases.[49]

Although these discriminatory practices are indisputable, they should not be exaggerated. Although black rape defendants were disproportionately sent to their death, not all suffered this fate. In one detailed examination of 230 black-on-white sexual assaults in Virginia between 1900 and 1945, three-quarters of the black defendants were neither lynched nor executed. In fact, nearly 80 per cent of those not sentenced to death received custodial sentences shorter than the permitted maximum.[50] The reason? Racist societies were also misogynistic. Male jurors and judges regarded many white women with suspicion. White female complainants who failed to observe certain middle-class norms could find themselves shunned by their community, their rape accusations dismissed. By their actions such women had compromised their right to protection from white men. Indeed, in certain circumstances, white men chose to defend their black tenants or neighbours against rape charges. False accusations threatened to destabilize masculine privilege, white and black.

Nevertheless, after the Second World War the rise of the Civil Rights movement turned the clear evidence of bias against African-Americans in sentencing into an explosive political issue. Even popular novels began to depict judicial injustices – most famously, Harper Lee's novel *To Kill a Mockingbird* was published in 1960 and made into a film two years later. As the nine-year-old narrator put it, the black defendant was 'a dead man the minute [white accuser] Mayella Ewell opened her mouth and screamed'.[51] Of course, objections to discriminatory sentencing within African-American communities started well before 1960. As the *Afro-American Ledger* had protested over fifty years earlier, it was outrageous that black rapists were likely to receive the death penalty while white rapists received sentences ranging between six months and twenty years. It was almost as if the courts believed that 'the Negroes of this country' were 'scarcely anything else but a race of brutes, waiting only the opportunity to lay violent hands on every white woman that came their way'. They reminded readers that the wave of sex crimes sweeping New York was the work of white men. Yet 'the white man has the daring impudence to place the great bulk of these crimes upon the shoulders of the Negro'. They concluded that it was 'time that the white man should shoulder his own responsibilities for crime'.[52] In fact, the *Afro-American Ledger* insisted that it was not opposed to the death penalty for rape and believed that 'no guilty man should escape'. But 'let there be one law for all irrespective of color or condition'.[53]

If execution, with its bias towards African-American convicts, was too brutal a way to get dangerous men off the streets, then incarceration would have to suffice. Gradations of seriousness could be taken account of, as could other so-called mitigating circumstances (generally distinguishing between the *victims*, in the sense that sexual assault was thought to harm some women – that is, white women – more than others).* Most notably, length of incarceration depended on the race of both perpetrator and victim. Thus, according to one detailed analysis of 881 'forcible sex' offences in a large Midwestern city between 1970 and 1975, 45 per cent of all rapes involved black men assaulting black women, yet they represented 26 per cent of all men sentenced to the state penitentiary and only 17 per cent of all men who received sentences of six or more years. In contrast, nearly a quarter of rapes involved black men accused of assaulting white woman, but they represented 45 per cent of all men sent to the state penitentiary and half of all men who received sentences of six or more years. For cases involving white victims and defendants, the discrepancies were small. A study of rape in Dallas in 1988 showed similar inequities. According to this study, when a man was convicted of raping a black woman he could generally be expected to be sent to prison for two years. This increased to five years if the victim was Latino and ten years if she was white.[54] Race affected judicial perceptions of the seriousness of the offence.[55]

Evolutionary Psychology

I want to conclude this chapter by turning to a more modern 'take' on instincts and humanity's evolutionary history. Stripped of the non-scientific racist ideology (there is more difference within so-called 'races' than between them), the evolutionary history of rape has seen a revival in the twentieth century with the development of the schools of socio-biology and (more recently) evolutionary psychology. In 1931, for instance, Gerrit Miller, author of 'The Primate Basis of Human Sexual Behavior', observed that, although there was 'nothing very exceptional' in human sexuality when compared with that of other mammals, single-mate bonding and rape were unique to human culture. Only humans possessed 'both the psychological and physical specializations' that made rape an 'always present possibility', he argued. Rape was a

> by-product of human ingenuity seconded by the upright human posture with its specially human remodelling of the primate pelvic region. This remodelling has brought the vaginal orifice into a position relative to

*This is discussed in Chapter 2, 'Rape Myths', and Chapter 3, '"No" Means "Yes"'.

> the adjacent parts that renders sexual intercourse possible with a resisting or unconscious female forced to lie – or lying helpless – on her back.

Unlike in quadrupedal and 'imperfectly bipedal' mammals, where the female had to cooperate in order to 'affect conjunction of the sexual organs', man's 'superior intelligence and favorable anatomy' made it possible for a male human to force a female human to mate against her will. (Bizarrely, Miller's use of the phrase 'favorable anatomy' can only mean 'favorable for potential rapists'.) Miller went further, however, insisting that this unique characteristic helped explain the 'exact forms of many social institutions'. Indeed, the male ability to 'take sexual advantage' had 'made an indelible impression on the thinking and acting of the species as a whole'. Since in humans alone 'sexual decision has passed from the female to the male', marriage evolved as a way of containing sexual violence.[56] It was a common argument in socio-biological circles.

Other socio-biologists drew opposite conclusions. According to these scientists, male humans *shared* the propensity to rape with other animals. Practices described as rape could be found in other species, including scorpion flies and ducks. Species closer to humans were also observed engaging in forced sex. Thus chimpanzees carried out 'search and destroy' missions, during which they frequently forced rival female chimpanzees to copulate. Orang-utans who were unable to acquire their own mates could also be seen to use violence to copulate.[57]

Was it right to name these acts of forced sex within the non-human animal kingdom 'rape'? The attribution of human characteristics to non-humans is always problematic. Anthropomorphizing reached extraordinary heights in David Barash's classic 1979 textbook on sociobiology (subtitled *The Whisperings Within*), in which he explained that rape was 'epidemic' among mallard ducks. [See photograph, p. 112.] Rapacious ducks were described as 'bachelors' who committed 'adultery' when they realized that they had been 'excluded from normal reproduction'. Therefore they adopted the 'next best strategy: raping someone else's female'. When that female mallard's 'husband' realized what had happened 'we would expect him to do something about it' – so he

> does a most remarkable – and ungentlemanly – thing. He proceeds to rape the just-raped female himself! . . . the male simply forces himself upon his hapless and exhausted mate, without even the by-your-leave of 'head-pumping', *de rigueur* in mallard boudoir etiquette.

Rape by mallard ducks. Photograph by P. Johnsgard in David P. Barash's *Sociobiology and Behaviour*, 1977

Barash was not shy of claiming that duck behaviour applied directly to humans. 'Rape in humans is by no means as simple', he acknowledged, because it was influenced by cultural attitudes. 'Nevertheless,' he continued,

> mallard duck and bluebird adultery may have a degree of relevance to human behavior. Perhaps human rapists, in their own criminally misguided way, are doing the best they can to maximise their fitness. If so, they are not that different from the sexually excluded bachelor mallards. Another point: Whether they like to admit it or not, many human males are stimulated by the idea of rape. This does not make them rapists, but it does give them something else in common with mallards.[58]

Recently more sophisticated versions of these evolutionary explanations have become popular again.[59] The publication of Randy Thornhill and Craig Palmer's *A Natural History of Rape: Biological Bases of Sexual Coercion* (2000) set out the most systematic case for rape as an adaptive act within animal and human cultures.[60] Thornhill and Palmer put forward two hypotheses: the 'direct selection' and 'by-product' propositions. According to the first, rape was a reproductive act, an adaptation produced by natural selection. In contrast, the by-product hypothesis (which tended to be favoured by most evolutionary psychologists) posited that rape was only a by-product of other evolved mechanisms. As Donald Symon explained in *The Evolution of Human Sexuality* (1979), these other mechanisms included

> the male's greater visual arousal, greater autonomous 'sex drive', a lesser ability to abstain from sexual activity, much greater desire for sexual variety *per se*, a greater willingness to engage in impersonal sex, and a less discriminatory criteria of sexual partners.[61]

The result? The sexual violation by the male of the female of the species.

It was not necessary for rapists themselves to conceive of what they were doing in reproductive terms. The basic assumption was that rapists were 'overwhelmingly men of lower class and status' who had 'very dim prospects to gain legitimate reproductive access to women', in the words of the authors of 'Why Men Commit Crimes (And Why They Desist)' (2000). These criminals 'do not cite reproductive success as a motive for their crimes' because 'psychological mechanisms usually operate at the unconscious level'. An irresistible force 'compels them' to commit crimes and is 'the evolved psychological mechanism that predisposes all men to seek reproductive success'. Rapists are 'completely unaware of the evolutionary logic behind their motives'.[62]

This fashionable genealogy of violence has been expanded to explain female sexual aggression. Women, too, it turned out, inherited their aggression from a primordial past. While male-on-female rape evolved out of a struggle to reproduce the man's genes, a feminist version of this argument adjusted the scenario to include women in the active frame. These commentators presented a vast array of evidence revealing that non-human female primates and other animals often acted in sexually aggressive ways.[63] Just like their male counterparts, female primates actively sought out their genetic advantages.[64] They didn't just wait to engage in sexual intercourse: they cajoled, coerced and sexually attacked potential male mates. As Anne Campbell argued in *Men, Women, and Aggression* (1993), female insistence on intercourse was just as 'hard-wired' as male persistence. However, unlike the male, whose evolutionary success was determined by the quantity of successful mating, female success was about *quality* or finding a high-status mate who would supply superior material goods for any offspring. This interpretation was highly compatible with the observation that much female sexual aggression was directed against other women (as opposed to against men). Three out of every four violent female offenders, for instance, targeted a female victim.[65] According to this interpretation, mate selection for women was primarily intrasexual, with women competing with other women for the most desired (in evolutionary terms) males.[66]

Of all the theories I examine in this chapter, the evolutionary one has generated the most vigorous rebuttals. Most scientists see little merit in it. Thornhill and Palmer's book has stirred up a huge media frenzy, leading many scientists to feel that they could not let it go unrefuted. Thornhill and Palmer are accused of seriously distorting the arguments of other scientists.[67] More typically, they are said to be peddling bad science.[68] As many critics note, drawing direct parallels between flies or ducks and humans is simply unconvincing. Even drawing links between our ancient ancestors and modern society is dubious. In his devastating attack on evolutionary approaches to rape in 'Of Vice and Men' (2003), Jerry Coyne points out that

> if natural selection built the human 'rape module', this almost certainly occurred in our distant evolutionary past, when society differed from our own in unknown and unknowable ways. Human civilization, after all, arose in only the last 1/10th of one percent of the interval since we branched off from our primate ancestors. All that we can say, therefore, is that the reproductive benefits of ancestral rapists may have been lower than those of modern rapists (because of a lack of contraception, it is possible that females were pregnant far more often than they are now, and subsequent nursing of a child usually suppresses ovulation); and the costs may well have been higher (given the lack of jails, punishment for rape was probably more severe, and the chances of getting caught higher in small social groups).

In other words, evolutionary psychology is nothing more (or less) than speculation or 'mere stories about our unrecoverable past'.[69]

But there are other problems with the evolutionary account. The assumption that sex is primarily about reproduction is false: after all, many primatologists have shown that sexual encounters among our nearest evolutionary neighbours (the bonobo chimpanzee) are more acts of 'social exchange and a basis for cohesion' rather than the violent, reproductive strategies assumed by Thornhill and Palmer.[70] More to the point, rape does not increase reproductive chances in human cultures. Many raped women are either too young or too old to reproduce. Even Thornhill and Palmer accept that 29 per cent of rape victims were below the age of eleven. And how does the theory explain the prevalence of homosexual rape, gang rape (competing sperm complicates reproductive strategies, to put it mildly), rape that does not involve vaginal penetration or the fact that a significant proportion of rapists fail to ejaculate? In the end, as Coyne abruptly puts it, the evolutionary-psychological narrative about rape as a by-product of other evolved human traits (such as aggression and male promiscuity) is simply banal. 'Since we have an evolutionary history,' Coyne observes,

> everything that we are and do can be furnished with an evolutionary explanation. There is no behavior, for example, that does not originate in our having a brain that is the product of natural selection. And this opens the evolutionary floodgates. Playing the violin? A by-product of creativity, manual dexterity, and the ability to learn. Collecting stamps? A by-product of our evolved desires to acquire resources and to categorize our environment.

Not only is this ridiculous, Coyne insists, but the 'by-product' hypothesis lacks 'the defining property of any scientific theory – falsifiability, that is, the ability to be disproven by some possible observation'.[71] The care and exactitude applied when evolutionary psychologists study non-human animals is not followed when studying humans. Evidence contrary to that predicted by the theory is simply dismissed as evolutionary aberrations.[72] Thus, when evolutionary psychologists are reminded of the prevalence of paedophilia (an act that could not be a reproductive strategy), they simply dismiss it as a 'dysfunction of the male sexual preference system'.[73]

Evolutionary-type arguments have certain attractions. Their simple logic and aura of scientific certitude are appealing. But they do not actually explain any of the shifts I examine in this book. By reducing the complexity of human society and history to a primordial connection with our primate ancestors, these explanations fail to account for individual motivations or cultural trends in sexual violence in a historical context. Evolutionary arguments provide no insights to account for shifts in sexual violence over time.

The interesting question, therefore, becomes: why has the evolutionary narrative proven so popular? In part its esteem is directly related to its status as 'science'. The scientific mantle provides moral validity in an increasingly complex and confusing world. The cultural readiness to believe in the priority of biology over culture should not be underestimated. In the context of rape, evolutionary views tie into Christian beliefs of sex as sinful and violent. The evolutionary argument is another way of saying that 'all men are rapists', because they are genetically predisposed to rape. It meets the desire to attribute irrational behaviours and acts to biological laws. As Pauline Bart expresses it in 'Theories of Rape' (1991):

> Were a radical feminist to propose a theory that included the 'evolutionary fact' that the 'fittest' men are rapists because they historically have been able to impregnate as many women as possible, and the fittest women are rape resisters because they want men who will help them care for their offspring (which presumably rapists don't), the woman would be denounced as an essentialist and a man hater.

Worse, 'Men would be insulted, feminists embarrassed'.[74]

The various ways of characterizing rapists that I have examined in this chapter share a basic pessimism about eradicating the scourge of rape. In the 1860s Horatio Robinson Storer, leading Boston physician and vice-president of the American Medical Association, believed that 'chronic satyriasis' was 'wholly dependent upon physical causes' and therefore as 'easily removed, as constipation, haemorrhoids, vesical calculus, enlarged prostate, and the like', but most commentators discussed here struggled to present any remedy for rape.[75]

Since these biological and evolutionary theories generally portrayed rape as inevitable or, at the very least, likely to be with us for many generations to come, its proponents sought to solve the problem of rape through targeting female behaviour, education or providing men with 'legitimate' sexual outlets. The first option was the most common. Despairing over notions of enforcing non-sexually abusive male behaviour, most commentators shifted emphasis on to the female victims. If the problem of rape was 'in the blood or genes' (whether in the sense employed by evolutionary psychologists or in the chromosomal explanation focusing on the 'exaggerated maleness, aggressiveness, and violence' typical of men with an extra Y chromosome), wasn't it sensible to simply teach women to fear and avoid men?[76] I find this argument abhorrent for a reason similar to why I believe studying rape exclusively through an analysis of rape victims is wrong: it lets men off the hook. There are other reasons to avoid this approach, however, as I shall discuss in the final chapter.

The education of young adults was a second, and related, solution to male rapacity. It was strongly supported by evolutionary psychologists. Thus Thornhill and Palmer argued that teaching young men about the evolutionary bases of human actions would enable them to 'avoid behaving in an "adaptive" fashion that is damaging to others'. They explicitly suggested that boys should be told 'the evolutionary reasons why a young man can get an erection just by looking at a photograph of a naked woman'. They also proposed teaching girls about 'the costs associated with attractiveness', once again implying female responsibility for their own violation.[77] As one critic sneered, 'Does anyone imagine that young men will be less inclined to rape when they hear that it is in their genes? Or that rape victims will be consoled by understanding the supposed evolutionary roots of their trauma and depression?'[78]

Thirdly, however, the implication behind many of these explanations (as well as the ones discussed next) is that rape was the result of unsatisfied sexual yearnings. The solution therefore could be as simple as advising men to masturbate. Indeed, masturbation was (in the words of Wilhelm Stekel in his 1951 classic *Auto-Erotism*), 'man's best defensive measure against the outbreak of his paraphilic . . . so long as he masturbates he abstains from acting out his forbidden phantasies'.[79] If masturbation did not satisfy every man, then why not introduce policies that would give men easier access to female sexual bodies. Reducing the age of consent (thus increasing the 'pool' of sexually available girls) was one 'solution'.* Proposals to liberalize laws against prostitution fulfilled a similar function. Making it difficult for prostitutes to ply their trade simply 'deprived' men 'of easy and accessible sexual satisfaction' and therefore 'drove men with strong sexual impulses, but weak moral fibre' to rape 'innocent, trusting girls and children' (in the words of one politician in 1961).[80]

The extremely popular book *Everything You Always Wanted to Know About Sex But Were Afraid to Ask* (1969) was even more direct. 'Peeping, exhibitionism, child molestation, incest, all feed on undischarged sexual tensions,' David Reuben reasoned. Inadequate wifely actions were to blame if men could not 'discharge' their 'sexual tensions'. Most customers of prostitutes, he claimed, were married, so 'they have access to complete sexual gratification with their wives'. But

*This is discussed in Chapter 3, '"No" Means "Yes"'.

these wives were not fulfilling their husbands. 'At least seventy-five to eighty-five percent of clients want to have their penises sucked,' Reuben claimed, but their wives 'refused'. 'If a dollar or so buys a willing companion,' he concluded, 'raping a stranger doesn't make sense.'[81] Even more radically, in the context of the so-called sexual revolution of the 1960s and 1970s, neither prostitution nor rape should be necessary. As late as 1976 sociologist Murray Straus insisted that women needed to 'escape the culturally stereotyped role of disinterest in and resistance to sex'. If they took 'an assertive role in expressing their own sexuality, rather than leaving it to the assertiveness of men', rape would be reduced. Why? 'Most obviously,' he contended, 'voluntary sex would be available to more men, thus reducing the "need" for rape'. If women took the initiative it would also 'help to reduce the confounding of sex and aggression'.[82] It was a view highly compatible with an individualized notion of the sexual abuser.

Are there more convincing explanations, and solutions, for rape if we turn to arguments placing greater stress upon environmental factors? That is the question I address in the next chapter.

CHAPTER FIVE

Brutalizing Environments

Amos was a friendly young man who was always smiling. In the late 1970s, he walked into the interview room of the Green Haven Correctional Facility in New York State, tidily dressed in a black-and-brown sweater. He sat down with his hands neatly folded on his lap and began reciting a host of reasons why he had raped twenty or more women.

Forced incest was his first serious crime. 'I raped her, I literally raped her,' he mused, referring to his sister. Why did he do it? Amos scattered blame at everyone except himself. 'I think overall why I raped my sister and continued to rape people,' he explained,

> was 'cause of the fact that I guess I was lonely and I wanted attention. I wanted a mother image, right, 'cause I hated my own mother – someone else I could have loved 'cause she would have treated me nice, spoiled me and did what I wanted her to do.

According to Amos, his mother was responsible for his sexual rages. She had been inadequate. She had abandoned him as an infant, then when she reappeared, removed him from his middle-class foster home and dumped him in a life of poverty in upstate New York. His mother and 'uncle' used to beat him 'for absolutely nothing'. He recalled seeing his brothers also being beaten 'with chickens – frozen chickens – like they [mother and uncle] were orientated to a down-South atmosphere, right? They brought it to New York.'

Amos claimed that he became involved in violence 'in order to survive'. Gang life, with its drugs, alcohol and 'fast girls', attracted him. Even within this vicious milieu Amos claimed that he raped to punish his mother. In his words,

> The women I raped, I had it in my mind that it was the image of my mother. The slightest little thing, the slightest little thing that triggered a nerve in me and a spark in my mind, was reflected in my mother, and I would rape . . . when she [his victim] asks me why I done it, I tell her, 'Because you remind me of my mother, and I *hate* my mother'.

Amos became a violent pimp. Whenever he believed a woman was 'humiliating' him or acting 'high-class', he would rape her or a substitute. He described himself as 'kinda shy with words', so when a woman rebuffed his advances he would 'squat her', or wait until he caught her alone and rape or sodomize her. He always had a knife ready.

Amos expressed neither remorse nor guilt about any of his victims. 'I didn't get no trouble' from most of them, he claimed. Then he added: 'I was rapin' them, right, and then actually sittin' down holdin' a conversation with them. And I'm sayin', "I just raped this woman. What the hell is wrong with them?"'

Amos believed he was the one to be pitied. He characterized himself as a victim of poverty, a subculture of violence and a disorganized family life. He kept repeating that he was 'so lonely, you know, with the family problems, et cetera'. He was 'used to being institutionalized', having spent most of his youth from the age of nine in prisons, state hospitals and shelters. Although he had been 'treated for various nervous disorders' since he was a child, he had received 'virtually no psychiatric care' in recent years. In his narrative his female victims were to blame for their own victimization: their confidence threw his sense of manliness into doubt. By raping them he was simply reasserting his own masculinity and placing women in their correct 'place'.

As the interview with Amos came to an end, he reiterated the excuse he felt was most persuasive for his many rapes: his mother. 'I really hate her to this day,' he lamely explained as he stood up and quietly left the interview room. A few days later, he was released from prison, after serving six years of a sentence of ten to twenty-five years for rape in the first degree.[1]

Amos's story was packed with rationalizations and justifications for his sadistic behaviour. He was scheduled to sit his college exams immediately after the interview and he hoped to walk out of the Green Haven Correctional Facility with a degree in his hands. Amos was perhaps deliberately using social-scientific explanations for violence that he had picked up from his college education. Or he was simply drawing on popular rationalizations of rape that he had heard in prison. Either way the social and psychological explanations he proffered have been decisive in forming the rapist's identity. As I discuss in this chapter, at various periods of history many of Amos's justifications for his sprees of sexual aggression had been espoused by social scientists. Psychiatric and psychoanalytical discourses are explored later in this book,* primarily because those narratives were framed principally in terms of therapeutic regimes. In contrast, the languages I discuss here are less concerned with treatment and more with simple categorization. Unlike the explanations I presented in the previous chapter, which assign a disordered body to rapists, here I examine those explanations that situate rapists such as Amos within defective urban cultures that espouse perverse ideals of masculinity.

Social Explanations

As I mentioned earlier, no theorist believes that biology exists outside of culture. There is always an interaction between the two. Degeneration theorists and evolutionary psychologists prioritized biology; but there is a parallel discourse about the rapist that prioritized environment. According to this alternative characterization of sexual abusers, sexual crime must be attributed not to degenerate bodies or evolutionary processes but to the pernicious influence of corrupt societies. In the eighteenth century villains were identified as self-aggrandizing aristocratic men who raped less-privileged women and acted as though they were above the law.[2] By the period I discuss in this book, this focus on the aristocracy had abated. In their place wealthy middle-class men and, in the case of America, big businessmen, were presented as potentially rapacious. This new capitalist elite used their riches to purchase and violate working-class girls.

This type of critique took off in the 1880s, fired by the emergence of 'yellow journalism'. It all started in 1885 when the radical journalist William T. Stead published 'The Maiden Tribute of Modern

*See Chapter 7, 'The Couch'.

Babylon' in the *Pall Mall Gazette*. Stead went undercover for four 'terrible weeks' to expose the extent of forcible child prostitution in the cities of England. In the resulting series of newspaper reports London was transformed into the Cretan labyrinth of Greek myth, into which, every nine years, the ancient Athenians sent seven virgin maids as a sacrifice to the Minotaur. The only difference was that nineteenth-century wealthy professionals were demanding 'not seven maidens only, but many times seven . . . served up as dainty morsels to minister to the passions of the rich'. In grisly prose Stead described young girls who had been 'snared, trapped and outraged either when under the influence of drugs or after a prolonged struggle in a locked room'. These girls' 'shriek of torture is the essence of [rich men's] delight, and they would not silence by a single note the cry of agony over which they gloat'. Stead then described how he posed as an 'immoral man' and bought, took to a locked room in a brothel and pretended to rape a thirteen-year-old girl named Lily Armstrong. Lily was never in any real danger of a sexual attack, but the alarmist account published in the *Pall Mall Gazette* told readers that after Lily had been locked in the room, 'there rose a wild and piteous cry . . . like the bleat of a frightened lamb . . . "There's a man in the room! Take me home; oh, take me home!"'[3] The resulting international furore forced Parliament to raise the age of consent for girls from twelve to sixteen.*

Stead achieved his aim, although at the cost of three months imprisonment in Coldbath-in-the-Fields and then Holloway on charges of abduction and indecent assault (he had failed to ensure that Lily's father consented). Stead was far from alone in battling men who used money to abuse vulnerable working-class girls. Feminist and temperance activists had long shared his concerns. The literature of the feminist-inspired Women's Christian Temperance Union, for instance, resounded with stories of young naïve girls 'seduced' by their middle-class employers who used their power to 'ruin' them and force them into a life of prostitution. No one doubted that this form of seduction (often pointedly said to be carried out by Jewish 'kaftans')[4] was little more than rape. Urban spaces were risky places for women.

The dangers posed by moneyed sexual abusers were restricted to periods of heightened alarm and were linked to forms of abuse surrounding prostitution and the 'corruption' of young native girls. These

*This incident is discussed in Chapter 8, 'Female Perpetrators; Male Victims'.

attacks on sexual violence were inextricably related to a critique of financial shenanigans in capitalism. There was another seam of concern, however, in which sexual abuse was portrayed as more blunt and more physically violent. The guilty men according to this discourse were factory workers or unemployed itinerants jostling on the pavements of the new industrial cities. These violent men had been identified as part of broader social investigations by middle-class philanthropists into the lives of the poor. As one lawyer informed members of the Kansas State Bar Association on 31 January 1901, it was

> into the world by vicious, drunken, dissolute parents . . . that he knows of God only by the picturesque forms of criminal blasphemy; that from his earliest remembrance he is kicked and cuffed and cursed; not for what he has done but because he is in the way and must be fed; that the very air he breathes is poisoned with the miasma of vice and crime.[5]

In other words, the violence of inner cities spawned further violence. It was no wonder that the (male) child raised in poverty thought little of forcing an unwilling woman to have sex.

Of course, the inclination to act in sexually aggressive ways distinguished the respectable from the unrespectable poor. It also distinguished the so-called civilized from the so-called savage. Environmental explanations for male sexual aggression were as racially vicious as their biological counterparts. Dread of vagrant African-Americans in times of economic crisis was particularly strong. In the words of 'A Southern Lawyer' writing in 1900, most rapes of white women were 'committed by the more worthless blacks – ordinarily "strange niggers", or members of that vagrant class of black proletariat that has sprung up since the great economic changes of recent years'. These men lacked 'steady employment' and so roamed the countryside, 'a prey to every brutal propensity'.[6] It was a form of racism that saturated the mass media throughout the period examined in this book. From *Birth of a Nation* (1915) to Westerns such as *The Searchers* (1956) and *Little Big Man* (1970), African-Americans and native Indians were portrayed as sexually voracious and 'wild'.[7] The racist smear was not dented when faced with evidence of white violence: white rapists were simply characterized as non-white. Thus a gang rape by Lancashire miners of a vagrant woman in 1874 prompted the *Daily Telegraph* to lament that the 'most brutal, the most cowardly, the most pitiless, the most barbarous deeds done in the world' were 'being perpetrated by the lower classes of the English people'. Some Englishmen resembled African 'savages'.[8]

The prominence given to the threat of sexual violence arising out of poor households echoed broader fears of working-class disorder in society. For many middle-class commentators trade unionism, suffrage campaigns (fighting for votes for plebeian men as well as women) and an increasingly vocal working-class community had increased the need for more effective surveillance of the poor within cities. In this context the working-class family was not seen as a natural institution that emerged out of conjugal love and paternal duties, but as something that required significant middle-class intervention to achieve.

In this role, no institution was more influential than the National Society for the Prevention of Cruelty to Children, an organization that was almost exclusively concerned with the abuse (physical as well as sexual) of the children of the poor, as opposed to children living in more prosperous homes. The Society regarded incest as endemic within working-class homes, and resolved to stamp it out. When critics objected to the ways in which it intervened into the inner sanctum of plebeian families, the Society retorted that 'the sacredness of parental rights' had limits. It was a misconception, its members reasoned, to assume that the 'instinct of affection for offspring' could be 'found everywhere'. 'No one doubts the sacredness of parental rights', they conceded, but surely these rights had to be 'exercised under the overruling law of parental duty imposed by Him who has constituted the law'? It would be

> honouring the *letter* to the disparagement of the *spirit* if the Good Samaritan should be required to follow the lead of the Pharisee and the Levite, and to pass by on the other side, leaving the children to suffer and die rather than to interfere with the liberty of the father or mother to ill-treat and neglect them while they indulged their violent propensities.[9]

In their conception, however, only the liberty of parents in humble households required curbing. Very little was said about incest and sexual abuse within the homes of their own social peers. Furthermore, the 'liberty' referred to was primarily the liberty to be allowed to act as parents. Although the father-perpetrator needed to be morally rehabilitated (primarily through swearing a pledge of temperance), by and large, he was sidelined by the reformers, who focused on the child.

Abused children had to be removed from their sullied families. Wider economic issues were generally ignored, even though the Society implicitly recognized that raising the entire family, from the (presumed) violent unrespectable class to the (presumed) serene respectable class, was a matter of employment and the provision of social services in health and education. Rather than advocating any sweeping restructuring of society, its concern was to 'rescue' individual abused children who could be returned to a state of wholesomeness (if not quite purity) through contact with 'ladies'. These ladies' 'example of refinement and delicacy of manner, speech and habits unconsciously sets before them a higher ideal of living than they have been accustomed to'.[10] Attention was thus diverted from structural inequality to individual human weakness, and from the father-perpetrator to the female child.

Perhaps proposals aimed at overhauling major societal institutions and norms was just too daunting. After all, these commentators generally assumed that sexual abuse was inevitable within the urban-industrial complex – at least this was what the Cologne criminologist Gustav Aschaffenburg believed. In 1913 his influential *Crime and Its Repression* (originally published in 1903) was translated into English. Aschaffenburg placed the blame for sex crimes firmly in the lap of industrial workers in the large cities, who, while constituting only 17 per cent of the population, committed over 43 per cent of rapes. Even in times of prosperity, Aschaffenburg claimed, industrial workers were prone to sexually attack women – indeed, because prosperity was linked to increased indulgence in alcohol, rape would increase at those times, he predicted.[11]

Drawing a connection between increases in sexual offences and the availability of alcohol in urban slums was commonplace. Many studies suggested that alcohol consumption figured prominently in between one-third and half of forcible rapes.[12] As the historian Martin J. Wiener put it, in the second half of the nineteenth century 'it became a judicial cliché to blame the easy availability of drink for violent (and often non-violent) crime'. Drunken violence became increasingly intolerable in Victorian society as much because it represented a 'fundamental affront to the ideal of personal reasonableness and self-command' as because of the violence it promoted.[13]

Again it was the working-class or unemployed man who was portrayed as particularly prone to alcohol-fuelled sexual abuse. American social reformers of the nineteenth and early twentieth centuries singled out African-Americans and immigrants as the major offenders. In 1890 Frances E. Willard, president of the National Women's Christian Temperance Union and leading campaigner against white slavery (the term for white women who were sold to men who then forced them to have sex), argued that the 'safety of women, of childhood, [and] the home' was 'menaced' by the proliferation of 'grogshops'. The 'grogshop' was 'the Negro's center of power. Better whiskey and more of it is the rallying cry of great, dark-faced mobs. The colored race multiply like locusts of Egypt.'[14]

In *The White Slave Hell; or, With Christ at Midnight in the Slums of Chicago* (1910), the Reverend F. M. Lehman focused his wrath on immigrants more generally. According to him, the 'evil' of white slavery was due to the laziness of foreigners. 'They come from countries where the highest good is just to lie in the sun and sleep,' Lehman claimed. Such men were incapable of understanding the 'dignity of labor'. Indeed, such creatures did even more harm than the owners of black slaves. Wasn't it the case that 'white girls were enslaved even more than the black ones' had been before the Civil War? 'How long would slavery have lasted,' he asked rhetorically,

> if every white man knew that his own daughter was in danger of being bought and sold? It is far worse than African slavery, for many of the black slaves were happy and many of them were good, even deeply religious, while no woman, though she be deceived and made an innocent victim, can be happy after she has been ruined, can live happily in sin, or when surrounded by vice.[15]

According to this historically absurd formulation, foreigners were even more dangerous than former slave owners since they stripped their victims of their last vestiges of dignity and humanity.

Freely available alcohol and the mixing of the races were only two explanations for the sexual dangers prowling urban streets. According to Gurney Williams, author of 'Rape in Children and in Young Girls' (1913), high and rising levels of urban sexual violence could be explained by the entire culture of the city. 'Moving-picture shows and the environment of the patrons' were 'provocative of sexual thoughts', he lamented. Furthermore, the 'high cost of living tends to overcrowding and underfeeding', and this 'brings out the animal qualities on both old and young'. Insufficient 'food and fuel drives men to drunkenness, which in turn is a common cause for attempted assaults',

Williams asserted. He failed to observe that economic privation was triggering sexual violence only in urban *men*.

Williams did have something to say about women, however. He condemned plebeian mothers for failing to protect their daughters. He deplored the fact that children were being 'allowed the utmost freedom' to go on picnics and excursions. Even sending young girls to local shops 'alone and unprotected' was 'a potent factor in multiplying the opportunity for assault'. Williams did admit that mothers could not safeguard their daughters 'against the brute which attacks while the child is coming home from school', but they could 'minimize the danger by not allowing the child to go out unattended except when absolutely necessary'. The 'laxity of mothers' was compounded by risks inherent in being poor, particularly the need to take in boarders. At the time Williams was writing, the majority of working-class homes would have included boarders; they were an essential part of the families' income. In his curiously passive formulation, when parents invited boarders into the sanctum of their home 'there develops a condition which often ends in the rape of the daughter'.[16]

This emphasis on the inevitability of female victimization within deprived inner-city neighbourhoods was not only held by medical men like Williams. The police agreed. In 1908, for instance, the Metropolitan Police debated the extent of incest in London. Most commentators were convinced that incest was a common vice among the lower orders. There was only one dissenting voice. Various superintendents insisted that incest was inescapable 'in neighbourhoods where the very poorer [sic] classes live, and, from want of means, are huddled together and many of both sexes have to sleep in same room'. Overcrowding obviously 'blunts all feelings of delicacy and respect for the female sex', contended another superintendent.[17] For some this also explained why foreigners featured disproportionately in rape and incest cases. Their 'low cultural level' was exacerbated by 'living conditions which are such as to furnish unusual hazards', alleged the Commissioner of Correction for Massachusetts in the early 1930s.[18] Overcrowding was the assumption behind much discussion of incest in Ireland as late as the 1970s.[19]

In the interwar years, as sex crimes seemed to be increasing, the heightened visibility of itinerant men seeking work intensified these middle-class anxieties. 'What is at fault?' one fraught sexologist asked.[20] Certainly economic distress could be blamed. In both England and Scotland major governmental reports on sex offences pointed the finger at 'appalling housing conditions' and unemployment as increasing men's propensity to offend in sexual ways.[21] Marie E. Kopp, writing in the *Journal of Law, Criminology, and Police Science* in the 1930s, was even more direct. 'Unattached persons' in the cities were responsible for the increased level of threat to women, she blandly stated. These men were 'restless and unstable', migrating 'from place to place in search of work'. They would have been less of a danger if they had remained in rural areas, where the police were especially vigilant, social support systems better organized and the effects of notoriety more inhibiting. In contrast, potentially violent men were anonymous and increasingly desperate in the cities. Sex crimes were part and parcel of criminality more generally.[22]

In America this view was clearly held by the formidable couple Jacob and Rosamond Goldberg, also writing in the 1930s. For them 'standards of decency' were 'notoriously difficult to maintain in congested tenement homes'. While admitting that 'a similar environment can mean different things for different persons', they accepted that the need to take in lodgers, lack of beds for all members of the family, and mothers 'distracted by the presence of man children [sic]' meant that sexual violation was almost inevitable. Environment 'outweighed' inheritance since 'hereditary possibilities' remained 'latent and undeveloped unless they were stimulated into activity by the environment', they hypothesized. Furthermore, in these deprived environments, men were 'sex starved'. Unmarried and lacking permanent familial ties, they preyed on vulnerable women in their communities.

Who were these sexual aggressors? According to the Goldbergs, they were typically stepfathers, boarders and 'janitorial assistants'. They also included adolescent boys who had never been given proper moral or religious training, let along sex instruction. These young men had their 'sex feelings prematurely and abnormally aroused'. Is it any wonder that they would 'seek a way out' of their 'emotional state' through sexual aggression? Men had sexual needs that had to be 'served': if legitimate channels were not open, they would seize illegitimate ones. For the Goldbergs the rapist was the man who

> under the influence and stimulation of alcohol, seizes upon his young daughter as a readily accessible female to give vent to his overstimulated senses; the passionate father whose wife is ailing, or is in a hospital, or perhaps is dead, seeking through the person of his daughter satisfaction for a normal urge which is deflected into an abnormal channel; the adolescent brother who foists his early sex drive upon a younger sister.[23]

Gender positions were clearly inscribed for the Goldbergs. Pernicious environments transformed men into natural predators and turned women into permanent victims.

Like many commentators of the time, the Goldbergs placed temperance at the heart of their proposed solution. Rapists acted 'under the influence and stimulation of alcohol'. In the previous chapter I mentioned the fact that nineteenth-century reformers also blamed drunkenness for sexual violence. In the mid and late nineteenth century, I argued, excessive alcohol consumption tended to be portrayed as a *symptom* of something else – disease or hereditary defect, for instance. Thus physicians like Havelock Ellis believed that drunkenness and degeneracy were inextricably linked: sexual violence was simply one expression of infirmity.[24]

In contrast, from the 1920s onwards, commentators began placing the emphasis on alcohol abuse *in itself* as a sufficient explanation for sexual assault. As the formidable Medical Inspector of HM Prisons W. Norwood East alleged in 1924, sexual offences were 'much commoner when liquor was cheaper and restrictions absent'. This was due to the 'aphrodisiac action of alcohol' and the way it caused a 'loss of higher control'.[25] East stuck by this position, writing over twenty years later that alcohol was a 'sexual excitant' which strengthened the 'life instinct' and consequently also bolstered the 'sexual instinct'.[26] A prominent prison medical officer in the mid-1950s concurred, observing that in most cases of rape it was not necessary to look for psychiatric abnormality. The rape could simply be explained in terms of a 'fairly typical concatenation of events', such as 'encouraging and stimulating company earlier in the evening, a lonely road and/or darkness, opportunity and alcohol, often a lot of alcohol'.[27] Alcohol reduced inhibitions.

Later in the century this emphasis on the social, as opposed to pharmacological, effect of alcohol was bolstered by a study in which a group of young men were tricked into believing that they were being given alcohol to drink, when in reality they were imbibing a non-alcoholic substance. In these studies the men who either *had*, or *believed they had*, drunk alcohol became more aroused by violent rape pornography than men who believed they were sober.[28] In other words, the social meaning ascribed to alcohol as an inhibitor was more important than its chemical effects.*

*This is also discussed in Chapter 2, 'Rape Myths'

Subcultures of Violence

By the late 1960s fears about young men raised on city streets took a new form – anxieties about 'subcultures of violence'. These subcultures were portrayed as teaching men aggressive 'scripts', which they then enacted. Amos, the young multiple rapist with whom I opened this chapter, clearly saw himself as acting within a subculture conducive to sexual aggression.

Clifford R. Shaw and Maurice E. Moore, sociologists and authors of *The Natural History of a Delinquent Career* (1968), were prominent promoters of this theory. Their analysis of sixteen-year-old rapist Sidney Blatzman pointed out that the 'social and cultural situations in which his delinquent behavior occurred' was crucial. Blatzman had grown up in 'one of the most deteriorated and disorganized sections' of Chicago. In this urban wasteland 'the conventional traditions, neighborhood institutions, and public opinion through which neighbourhoods usually effect a control over the behavior [of a] child' had disintegrated. As a consequence, Blatzman neither had access to the 'cultural heritages of conventional society' nor was subjected to 'the constructive and restraining influences' that cosseted children growing up in 'the more highly integrated and conventional residential areas of the city'. His criminality was exacerbated by the extreme disorganization of his family life. Blatzman's father continually deserted his responsibilities, forcing his mother to take paid employment. Growing up without close parental supervision, Blatzman had his attitudes shaped by older delinquents and prostitutes. Rape was simply a way of life within the subculture of violence in which he was immersed.[29] As Professor Ernest W. Burgess argued in his epilogue to Shaw and Moore's book, the 'complex, impersonal, anonymous life of the city' favoured the 'separation of the satisfaction of human impulses from their organic unity within the personality', making it easy for sexual cravings to detach themselves with ease from 'sentiments of love and respect'.[30]

American commentators such as Shaw and Moore tended to place emphasis on the dangers of inner-city slums. In other contexts, however, the suburbs were seen as breeding grounds for rapists. This was certainly the case in Australia. Criminologist G. D. Woods observed that an epidemic of 'pack rapes' occurred predominantly in the fringe urban areas of the new working-class housing settlements to the west and south-west of Sydney. Areas such as Blacktown, Green Valley and Cabramatta had experienced dramatic population growth since the war, and the result was severe social disorganization. Interestingly, however, Woods admitted that rapid population growth was also characteristic of the (more middle-class) northern and north-western suburbs, where rape was not a serious problem. How could this be explained? Woods correctly observed that it was not enough to simply declare that the middle classes were 'naturally' less prone to crime ('there are probably more defalcating solicitors in Killara than in Bankstown and Liverpool together', he sniped). Nor, he believed, could the difference be explained in terms of middle-class reluctance to report sexual violence.

Rather, Woods drew attention to unequal resources available to ease the inevitably disruptive process of suburbanization. 'When working-class people move,' he brusquely explained, 'there is a maximum of disorder.' Council and commission rehousing schemes were notoriously bureaucratic and intimidating, making poorer supplicants feel both sullen and resentful. The areas where working families were relocated lacked basic facilities, such as adequate schools. Furthermore, these fringe suburbs offered many opportunities to engage in violent sex. In Woods's words, gang rape was 'a crime the execution of which requires some degree of isolation'. High wages meant that practically every youth possessed a car: wasteland was less than five minutes' drive away from these suburban centres. In these deprived suburbs not only sex but 'almost all social interaction' took place in a violent atmosphere. He alleged that among working-class communities 'scuffling, jostling and hitting' were 'natural and acceptable modes of behavior'. Pack rapists were acting according to the norms of their culture: they 'may be cruel, brutal and senseless' but they were 'not psychotic'. They might be characterized as 'emotionally abnormal' but they were not ('for the most part') 'mentally abnormal'. For this subculture gang rape was as insignificant as a 'sneeze in the loins'.[31]

This approach had much in common with earlier theories about the innately corrupting nature of urban poverty. Poor men were presented as compelled to act according to the violent sexual narratives freely circulating in their everyday environments. Accordingly, drunkenness was neither a *symptom* of degeneracy, nor a *facilitator* of violence through its effects in lessening inhibition. It was simply a part of the broader cultural routines habitual among young men.[32] These men were violent when inebriated; they were also violent when sober. Aggression was a subcultural norm.

This 'subculture of violence' theme was frequently given a racial slant.[33] Sociologists and criminologists uniformly agreed that over 90 per cent of rapes were intra-racial.[34] But, unlike the approach used for exploring white-on-white rape, rapes and all forms of violence within the black community were frequently ascribed to ghetto culture. Thus the authors of *Sex, Crime, and the Law* (1977) argued that sexual aggression was 'taught, admired, [and] institutionalized' in African-American subcultures. In the ghettos black men had 'only limited opportunities to be breadwinners' or otherwise 'assert their dominance in a normative manner'. Rape was simply an expression of 'their general alienation and anger, their desire to display assertiveness, aggression, and dominance'.[35] Similarly the eminent criminologist Menachem Amir argued in 'Sociocultural Factors in Forcible Rape' (1974) that 'lower class people' tended to 'show more freedom in sexual experimentation' and acted more sexually aggressively. According to him, the

> Negro lower class subculture embodies all the characteristics of a lower class subculture but has some of its features in a more pronounced form. The Negro subculture is characterized by the revolving of life around some basic 'focal concerns', which include a search for thrills through aggressive actions and sexual exploits. The emphasis is given by males to masculinity, and their need to display and defend it through brief and transitory relations with women.

These needs, he went on, and the 'subsequent concern with sex' arose from being raised by 'dominant' mothers and 'marginal' fathers.[36]

Of course, African-American men were not the only group believed to be immersed in subcultures that encouraged sexual violence. Male immigrants were also said to be driven by cultural forces to rape women. As Professor Ernest Burgess argued in relation to Chicago, in the 'demoralized area of first settlement' (meaning those areas of the cities where new immigrants initially settled) the 'so-called gang-shag' was a 'more or less established pattern'. He claimed that victims generally hailed from a different 'national group' to the rapists. It would be 'outrageous' and probably 'unthinkable' for assailants to attack women from their own ethnic group, he claimed, since such women were 'held in high repute'. Gang rape – or what Burgess dubbed 'unconventional behavior' – within one's own group would 'entail obligations', unlike sexual attacks on 'other' women.[37] In such a way the cultures of minority groups were branded 'sub'cultures, existing in some lower form in which violence was endemic.

A more radical version of the 'subcultures of violence' argument also appeared. Black Power leader Eldridge Cleaver put an insurrectionary spin on it. In *Soul on Ice* (1968) he claimed that rape arose out of the frustration experienced by young black men. African-American males from the inner city were intensely resentful of the economic and political oppression exerted by white society. Cleaver described how he found rape 'an insurrectionist act'. In his words,

> It delighted me that I was defying and trampling upon the white man's law, upon his system of values, and that I was defiling his women – and this point, I believe, was the most satisfying to me because I felt very resentful over the historical fact of how the white man had used the black women. I felt I was getting revenge.[38]

In other words, poverty bred a violent subculture which, in combination with black politicization, encouraged black men to take out their aggression against whites, especially white women (the most highly prized 'property' of white men).

Although Cleaver and other commentators appealing to cultures of violence did not directly allude to it, their arguments were closely in line with contemporary psychological experiments which identified links between frustration and aggression. John Dollard (from the 1930s) and Leonard Berkowitz (from the 1960s) were influential social scientists arguing that aggression was the consequence of frustration. Concerned with explaining wartime aggression rather than rape, they claimed that the larger and more frequent the frustrating impulse, the greater the aggressive response.[39] Although they did acknowledge that aggression could be inhibited (by fear of punishment, for instance), they did not explain why men didn't respond to frustration by regression, substitution, sublimation or resignation. Indeed, as other psychologists were able to show, frustration resulted in aggression only in situations where the person already possessed 'a habit of being aggressive'.[40]

Furthermore, it was patently obvious that the most economically frustrated men were not necessarily the most aggressive. Indeed, the frustration-aggression hypothesis merely labelled all poor (and especially poor black) men as rapists. It did worse, in fact, since it forged a link between African-American sexual aggression and political movements. As Lynn Curtis blatantly explained in *Violence, Race, and Culture* (1975),

> Black-white sexual attacks can be related to a new emerging sense of identity and confidence in the black community that originated in the Civil Rights and black power movements and has filtered down to the street-corner level. One result may be reduced inhibitions against attacking whites – whether or not frustration-aggression is attached to the framework . . . The average street-corner male may not be able to pimp a white woman, but he can combine physical overtness and sexual exploitation to rape her.[41]

In such a way Civil Rights and Black Power were conceptualized as being infused through and through with sexual violence. Ironically, Curtis's ideological position mirrored that of Eldridge Cleaver. For both, African-American political movements were signs of frustration; aggression against women was part and parcel of the radical project.

There were other problems with the 'subcultures of violence' argument. Its proponents acknowledged that women as well as men were immersed in these subcultures, yet none questioned the fact that it was only *men* who turned into sexual aggressors. Furthermore, there was an insidious tendency to deflect blame from the (male) perpetrators to the (female) victims.* Indeed, derogatory terms such as 'promiscuous', 'mental defective' and 'severely disturbed' were frequently applied to girls and women who were raped.[42] Woods, for instance, casually noted that most of the 'girls' raped by west Sydney gangs were 'of low intelligence, plain or unattractive appearance'.[43] Since gang rape was a 'natural hazard' for young women living in the slums and run-down suburbs of the cities, it was disingenuous for women to complain about it.[44] In subcultures of violence male individuals were impelled to sexual violence by a blind obedience to the norms of their (adolescent) communities. Their female counterparts were pictured as prepared to 'stand still for a gangbang'.

Developmental Failures

Immersion in rough communities was not necessarily decisive in the process of turning innocuous male adolescents into sexual aggressors. Their familial context had to be defective, too. In the words of Lewis

*This theme was elaborated in Chapter 2, 'Rape Myths'.

J. Doshay and George W. Henry, psychiatrists for the Children's Court and Department of Correction in New York City and authors of *The Boy Sex Offender and His Later Career* (1969), growing up in a tough neighbourhood had a destructive impact on children 'only when the home standards and controls break down', exposing them to 'the morbid elements of the street'. In their study half of the delinquents lacked one or both parents or had at least one parent who was seriously disabled physically or mentally. Common forms of familial pathology included parents who were divorced or separated, as well as homes characterized by drunkenness, cruelty, immorality and domestic neglect.[45]

Although this focus on dysfunctional families was used to explain crime in general, it was seen as particularly pertinent in explaining why young men engaged in crimes of a sexual nature. Thus, according to one study in the 1930s, the parents of sex offenders had been less affectionate towards their sons than had the parents of murderers. For these researchers it was significant that sex offenders were much more liable than murderers or non-criminals to have been 'subject[ed] to a foreign culture' in terms of having a mother or a wife who was of a different nationality.[46] Miscegenation was made to share some culpability for sex crime.

According to these commentators, what were parents doing wrong? The wartime economy had resulted in households in which fathers were absent while mothers flocked into paid employment outside the home. The situation was scarcely improved when the war ended. Broken marriages and 'clingy' mothers became the norm.[47] These mothers were failing to provide their male offspring with adequate sex education. Quick to pick up the unspoken fears of their parents regarding sex, boys were failing to develop 'sound and consistent' attitudes to intercourse. Their 'twisted ideas about bodies' were driving them to commit sexual offences, blandly noted the author of 'A Psychiatrist Looks at Sex Offenses' (1947).[48]

General domestic mayhem was even more important than the lack of accurate sex education in socializing boys into sexual aggressors. In a survey published in *The Nervous Child* in 1951 the author found that, in contrast with just over 60 per cent of non-sexual criminals, over 90 per cent of sex criminals had been severely and frequently beaten as children. Razor strops, sewing-machine straps, electric cords, broomsticks and iron bars were just some of the instruments used to attack these children.[49] Another survey of 102 sex offenders in the late 1950s found that nearly all had experienced a difficult childhood: their parents had been 'unstable', even cruel. A large proportion of these men had grown up in orphanages or been 'cared for by unloving stepfathers or stepmothers'. According to this researcher, rape was simply a way these scarred young men were able to 'express their hostilities and rebellion against the authority of their parents'.[50] It was a behaviourist-inspired version of the more psychoanalytically infused 'cycle of abuse' arguments.*

The households in which future rapists were reared were also notable for sexual shamelessness and indiscipline. Boys raised in these homes had been repeatedly fondled, given alcohol to drink and made to share a bed with an adult. Although these boys had become intensely sensitive to sexual stimulation, they were categorically denied access to accurate sexual knowledge. Their mothers were said to be 'sadistic and castrating'; their fathers 'passive-dependent, ego-weak individuals who went into moral hiding or actually had abandoned the home'. Thus, in the words of Renatus Hartogs, author of 'Discipline in the Early Life of Sex-Delinquents and Sex-Criminals' (1951), a boy who was humiliated by his mother as a child would grow up to seek sexual revenge against 'strange women, mostly older than the offender himself' in order to 'satisfy his early aroused vindictiveness'. 'Malignant early discipline' meant that these men were forever unable to limit their primitive sexual urges, rendering sexual violence inevitable. For society the only solution was early intervention into such homes. Hartogs called for 'an intense public warning against malignant parental discipline'.[51] As the eminent developmental psychologist John Bowlby argued in *Attachment and Loss* (1969), the quality of attachment in childhood affected relationships throughout life. Those who failed to achieve attachment bonds in childhood were unable to develop relationship skills. As a consequence, they adopted 'inappropriate' ways to pursue intimacy.[52] Rape was caused by a developmental failure.

Warren Wille, the director of the psychiatric clinic that served the entire prison population of Michigan, believed that thirty-one-year-old 'Robert' was emblematic of this type of offender. Wille's analysis could be firmly placed within a developmental model. Robert was a serial offender who had been sentenced to thirty to sixty years' imprisonment for kidnapping and repeatedly raping a woman. He felt 'very bad' about

*These arguments are discussed in Chapter 8, 'Female Perpetrators; Male Victims'.

his crimes and begged Wille to castrate him to 'rid [me] of this strange quirk'. However, Robert was incapable of explaining his actions, blaming 'something wrong with my head'. He had not even wanted to have sex with his victim, confessing that he had been 'hardly able to get an erection and was unable to get a discharge' during the rape.

Although Robert was confused about his motivations, Wille was not. Robert's behaviour could be traced to his youth, this prominent psychiatrist argued. His parents had abandoned Robert when he was eighteen months old and he had been adopted by an unmarried schoolteacher. Wille noted disapprovingly that the foster mother was

> a woman of very high principles and well educated. She has an intellectual interest in children and pursued courses in psychology, sociology and education with the feeling that she would be better fitted to care for her family. She seems to take life very seriously and has very little sense of humor. She is rather restrained and reserved in outward displays of affection.

To make matters worse Robert had slept in the same room as his foster mother during childhood and she had joined him in the bath until he was 'quite a big boy'. Robert believed that women – particularly his foster mother, but also someone he described as an aggressive female supervisor who was constantly 'nagging' him – were persecuting him. According to Wille, these two women 'drove [Robert] to his later pathological behavior'. It was no coincidence that Robert chose to rape women who were 'mother figures'. In Wille's words,

> An overly close relationship with the foster mother was promoted by her seductive behavior when he was a young boy. On the job . . . he was working under a woman supervisor with some personality characteristics similar to those of his foster mother . . . The wife's pregnancy at this same period was probably an added factor in reactivating incestuous and aggressive conflicts previously held toward the foster mother.

Wille speculated about the 'hostile feelings he may have had during early childhood towards his true mother for having abandoned him and to what extent these feelings were carried over toward the adopting mother'. By this stage in Wille's analysis of Robert, and in case readers had not shifted all the blame for the rape on to the women in

Robert's life, Wille added that 'as often happens in these cases, the victim revealed some features in her behavior that hint at unconscious desires to be the victim of a sexual assault'.[53]

The lengths to which many of these developmental theorists went to blame people other than the rapist for his actions is noteworthy. Parents – and predominantly mothers – were made responsible for their sons' sexual aggressiveness. Alternative accounts could have been employed. For instance, it is striking that relatively little was said about the Oedipal conflict (the son's relationship with the father) as stimulating sexual rage against women. Rather, pre-Oedipal conflicts (or mother-son relationships) were seen to hold the clue to explaining the crimes of these men.[54] In some of these accounts culpability for rape was diverted almost entirely away from the perpetrator.

Crisis of Masculinity

From the 1970s the habit of finding fault in (some) women for the sexual assaults committed by (some) men underwent a dramatic class and generational shift. Instead of promiscuous young slum girls being blamed for implicitly whipping up sexual aggression in their male companions (as 'subcultures of violence' theorists did) or mothers accused for the crimes of their sons (as did developmental theorists), a new discourse emerged in which the rapist was portrayed as someone forged within a crucible created by unmarried, white and educated women.

What were these women doing that could so seriously corrupt young men, spurring them to act in sexually abusive ways? According to some commentators, these women were demanding equality with men, particularly in the workplace and education, but also in the home. They were insisting on their right to rule their own lives – to talk, dress, work and move as they chose. What came to be known as 'second-wave feminism' empowered women and, according to this line, disempowered men and turned some to sexual violence.

According to one influential theme of the 1970s onwards, the rapist was a young man whose identity had been threatened by the 'new women' who were usurping male social and economic standing within society. Frustrated by their inability to achieve the stereotypical image of what it meant to be a man, men were collectively going through an identity crisis. Was it any wonder (this argument went) that a subset of men sought mastery over their lives by forcibly compelling women to have sex with them?[55] It was an excuse that Amos (the young rapist with whom I began this chapter) employed: his fury at 'uppity' women made him lash out and rape as many as he could. As Chaplain H. Rex Lewy (a physician at the University of Chicago) put it, men no longer had clear ways to 'attain individual recognition and sexual identity'. Gender roles had become confused and traditional coming-of-age rituals for young men had been swept away. Rape was 'a frustrated coming-of-age syndrome in a society that no longer has a definable way of recognizing the achievement of manhood, a status once associated with physical maturity, physical competition and marriage', he concluded.[56]

Faced with the rise of a generation of strong, confident women, men felt 'desperate'. Like frustration, desperation led men to act in sexually aggressive ways. Thus, for the authors of the widely read *Understanding Sexual Attacks* (1978), men who attacked women were experiencing 'a chronic feeling of dissatisfaction, real or imagined, with their own masculine performance, social or sexual'. They also harboured 'strong and ambivalent emotions towards women, who tended to be perceived as agents of frustration and guilt'.[57] Typically these men developed violent sexual fantasies as a response to anxieties that rape was (as one rapist put it) 'the only way I would ever be able to have intercourse'.[58] Unsurprisingly the crisis was portrayed as particularly severe within African American communities. As poet and activist bell hooks pointed out, black males were 'utterly disenfranchised in almost every arena of life'. The 'assertion of sexist domination' was their 'only expressive access to the patriarchal power they are told all men should possess as their gendered birthright'. In case responsibility for rape was too heavy for perpetrators to bear by themselves, black women were complicit in their 'dick-thing masculinity', she added.[59]

Many historians and social theorists agreed with some aspects of the 'crisis of masculinity' explanation for male rape. Eminent historian Roy Porter, for instance, pointed out that the 'strident and successful women's movement' in the USA had destabilized gender relations, reaping a 'vicious male backlash'. He concluded that 'in these circumstances rape does indeed become male vengeance'. Unlike the pre-industrial world, when sexual abuse was relatively low, during the twentieth century rape reached crisis levels. Particularly in North American, 'cults of glamourized women and macho men' competed with a vigorous feminist movement. This meant that 'contradictions in sex roles' were 'uniquely naked' there.[60] The great explosion in pornography from the 1970s was similarly interpreted as an 'attempt to recoup in the domain of sexual fantasy what is denied to men in production and politics', the founder of the Society for the Philosophy of Sex and Love claimed in the 1970s.[61] Although this emphasis upon a crisis of masculinity in the late twentieth century was profoundly ahistorical and solidified a peculiarly modern conception of what constitutes 'stability' in gender relations, it remains a common narrative within mass culture.

Feminist Model

Those feminists accused by 'crisis of masculinity' theorists of being instrumental in destabilizing gender relations (and thus goading men into becoming sexual aggressors as the only way of asserting their 'stolen' virility) were profoundly successful in propagating an alternative narrative of sexual abuse. From the 1960s, but especially from the 1970s, a revolution in ways of understanding rapists took place: women – the social group predominantly at risk of *being* raped – successfully demanded that their narratives of sexual violation take precedence over those of the perpetrators. This is not to imply that women had been silenced before the 1960s. Quite the opposite. Nineteenth-century feminist activists had been influential in 'naming' abuses such as white slavery and rape within marriage.* They had also sought to relocate the danger from the vicious criminal (the pimp who sexually coerced women into prostitution, for instance) to the everyday abuser within the home and among respectable society.[62] However, from the 1970s the narrative of rape formulated by feminists soared in popularity.

According to this model, rape was a deliberate by-product of male domination. [See cartoon, p. 141.] As a commentator in the feminist journal *Signs* expressed it in 1980, it was no longer possible to believe that 'widespread violence' against women's bodies could only be 'the responsibility of a small lunatic fringe of psychopathic men'. The pervasiveness of sexual violence was proof that 'the locus of violence against women rests squarely in the middle of what our culture defines as "normal" interaction between men and women'.[63] Florence Rush, a prominent feminist activist, observed that sexual abuse fulfilled a cultural function. It was part of the way young girls were socialized into their female role. Sexual abuse was 'a process of education which prepares them to become the wives and mothers of America', she famously claimed.[64] In the deservedly classic

*Some of these feminists are discussed in Chapter 11, 'The Home'.

'Viagra Sex Offenders', by Pat Bagley, 2005

book *Against Our Will: Men, Women, and Rape* (1975), Susan Brownmiller agreed. For Brownmiller rape was the means by which all men intimidated all women. She drew an analogy with the American South, where *some* white men lynched *some* black men but the entire African-American community was held in intimidation and fear. For her the same was the case with rape: some men did it but all men accrued the benefits.[65] Although often frowned upon as representing a kind of feminist functionalism (in which all evils could be traced to patriarchal structures of domination), this was a profoundly influential discourse.

Second-wave feminists also drew attention to the way pornography provided men with what they called 'rape scripts' that promoted sexual aggression. Again concern about the link between widely circulating narratives of sexual violence and the occurrence of sexual aggression had been registered well before this period. At the turn of the twentieth century, for instance, many commentators were anxious about the popularity of the 'yellow press', which glamourized sexual violence and thus reduced inhibitions about acting in aggressive ways. In the words of the Chief Constable in Glasgow in 1908, real-life stories of criminals 'warp the minds of our youth, and lead them to regard criminals as heroes'. Even worse, 'the publication of the details of crimes leads to the imitation of those crimes'.[66] In 1938 the Commissioner of Correction for New York City put it even more strongly, claiming that 'sex murders almost always come in cycles'. Once a newspaper gives a rape-murder a 'play-up', it was

> almost certain to cause from two to a half-dozen more, within a short period . . . people who commit the worst types of sex crime are highly suggestible, are keeping themselves under control with the greatest difficulty, and very often are impelled by an uncontrollable urge after they have dwelt on the details of the crime and have feasted on the newspaper pictures long enough.[67]

FBI director J. Edgar Hoover put it strongest when he argued that 'We know that in an overwhelmingly large number of cases sex crime is associated with pornography. We know that sex criminals read it, are clearly influenced by it. I believe pornography is a major cause of sex violence.' Eliminating the 'distribution of such items among impressionable children', he believed, would cause America's 'frightening sex-crime rate' to drop.[68]

The critique of second-wave feminists differed, however, from the views of these predecessors. Their concern was not only with the obscene effect of pornography on male consumers (although that also incensed them), but on the dehumanization and objectification of women. They insisted that violent sexual images were 'not only fictionally *depicted*' but '*enacted* on the bodies of women'.[69] This view was succinctly expressed by Robin Morgan in her famous axiom 'pornography is the theory; rape the practice'.[70]

It was not a line that was uniformly accepted, even within the feminist community. Feminist 'sex radicals' saw danger lurking beneath attempts by 'regulatory feminists' to restrict or eradicate the circulation of pornography. As Ellen Willis observed in 'Feminism, Moralism, and Pornography' (1983),

> The basic purpose of obscenity laws is and always has been to reinforce cultural taboos on sexuality and suppress feminism, homosexuality, and other forms of sexual dissidence. No pornographer has ever been punished for being a woman-hater, but not too long ago information about female sexuality, contraception, and abortion were assumed to be obscene. In a male supremacist society, the only obscenity law that will not be used against women is no law at all.[71]

Others pointed out that pornography could be liberating. Many women use pornography as ways of exploring their own sexual fantasies and enhancing their pleasure. While agreeing that the sexual abuse of models and other women depicted in pornography ought to be made illegal, sex radicals accused anti-pornography feminists of denying female agency, treating women as universally victimized, and exerting a repressive power over other women.

Nevertheless, the 'pornography debate' *within* feminist circles was mild in comparison with the general anti-feminist backlash. The viciousness of these attacks was itself evidence that the feminist critique of male-dominated society was seriously threatening dominant power structures. Much criticism appealed to what right-wing critics claimed was a 'commonsensical' understanding of rape, which they saw feminists as expanding.* It had been 'always understood', erroneously argued Norman Podhoretz, editor of *Commentary*, that rape involved a man wielding a weapon or threatening to use physical violence. He asserted that attempts to 'broaden' the category so that it included 'verbal and psychological' means to overcome a woman's resistance was to confuse rape with what 'has in the past been universally known as seduction'. Podhoretz accused feminist thinkers of engaging in 'a brazen campaign to redefine seduction as a form of rape, and more slyly to identify practically all men as rapists'. He lambasted feminists for attempting to 'delegitimize any instance of heterosexual coupling that starts with male initiative and involves even the slightest degree of female resistance at any stage along the way'.[72] Typically Neil Gregory, Professor of Social Welfare at the University of California (Berkeley), informed his students that 'Comparing real rape to date rape is like comparing cancer to the common cold.'[73] Such attacks were not restricted to panicky men. In *The Morning After: Sex, Fear, and Feminism on Campus* (1993), Katie Roiphe sneered at women she christened 'rape crisis feminists' who acted as sex police, dictating not only what intercourse '*shouldn't* be, but also the way it *should* be'.[74] The sense of outrage was palpable: how dare these feminists criticize the collective view (*vox populi*) exonerating date or acquaintance rapists.

The hostility quickly became personalized, with a few individual feminists standing in for a host of fiends. Susan Brownmiller was an obvious target. Theologian and former US ambassador Michael Novak was one of many men who launched an assault on *Against Our Will*, claiming that Brownmiller's classic text 'cannot be taken seriously either as history or journalism'. The book disseminated 'myths in the

*In particular critics were incensed about the introduction of date and acquaintance rape. This is discussed in Chapter 2, 'Rape Myths'.

service of propaganda', he went on. It was 'nothing more or less than a propagandistic attack on heterosexuality and marriage (and by extension the family) in the guise of an attack on rape'. 'Its implicit logic makes it a tract in celebration of lesbianism and/or masturbation,' he ludicrously asserted.[75]

New York-based psychoanalyst Gerald Schoenewolf was even more vitriolic. He was particularly incensed by Brownmiller's line that 'all men keep all women in a state of fear'. Schoenewolf dubbed this statement a 'manifestation of female hysteria'. He went on to claim that Brownmiller was suffering from a particularly severe form of castration envy. Indeed, he continued, the 'state of fear' that Brownmiller wrote about

> might be seen as an ontogenetic reference to the infantile discovery of the difference in sexual anatomy. When a little girl first discovers a penis, it probably is a frightening event, due to the talion principle; the immediate desire to pull it off and take it for herself arouses the counterfear [sic] that the male will penetrate and destroy her with his penis.

Feminists like this, he believed, suffered from 'narcissistic projective identifications typical of women with multiple pregenital fixations, particularly those who have not resolved the narcissistic blow of lacking a particularly visible organ'. This rebellion against the primal father was really about castrating all men. Their narcissism and penis envy imprisoned them at the Oedipal stage of development, always defending the mother-as-victim against the father-as-oppressor. Like Novak, Schoenewolf believed that a 'latent or actual homosexual orientation' lurked behind feminist ideology. They were trying to 'lure' other women into 'an actual or symbolic form of lesbianism'.

Female feminists took the brunt of the attack, but Schoenewolf also castigated male fellow travellers. These men had clearly been unable to maintain their 'critical faculties' and were suffering a severe case of male narcissism and castration anxiety. In the past, Schoenewolf maintained, men coped with their underlying fear of women by bonding together in men's fraternities and by 'suppressing women'. Indeed, he believed that 'a certain amount of male bonding and a certain amount of freedom in voicing complaints about women' was a healthy thing not only for society but also for women themselves. Conversely, feminist attempts to 'intrude on male bonding and muffle men's complaints about women' was culturally damaging, because

> when men cannot freely verbalize critical feelings about women, they will more readily act them out. On an unconscious level this is what the psychopathological feminist wants. She wants men to act out their feelings, wants them to be sexual abusers, in order to have all the more reason for the rage at the root of her gender narcissism.

As he explicitly noted, the modern women possessed 'power over men in the personal realm as well as in other aspects of society' and this power had corrupted the female sex, encouraging the 'acting out of collective hysteria'. Men had been rendered passive creatures, threatened by the creation of a 'feminist state with an increasingly perverse value system'.[76]

In the concluding chapter a lot more will be said about feminists' discourse on rape. Their diagnosis of the harm done by a male-dominated society that encourages sexual aggression has been more compelling than their critique of pornography. Indeed, the jury is still 'out' on the link between pornography and sexual violence. Some surveys found that sex offenders had *less* exposure to erotic stimulation than other men.[77] Other studies concluded that the artistic production of violent images actually served as a kind of catharsis, relieving men of the emotions that would otherwise be channelled into sexual abuse. As the filmmaker John Waters advised young boys in a hospital for the 'criminally insane' in the 1990s: 'I teach them that everybody has the same rage you had when you committed these crimes, that they have to use their rage in a different way. Make a movie. Do a painting. Don't do the rape, do a painting of the rape.'[78] Finally, critics of the 'pornography leads to rape' narrative suggest that it confuses cause and effect. Rapists and other sexual aggressors were not spurred to rape through pornography, these critics argued, although rapists often used pornographic scripts to justify their acts. In other words, pornography provided a vocabulary of motive.

For our purposes, however, the feminist naming of the sexual abuser was significant in one important way. It relocated the rapist away from the tough world of the streets and into white, middle-class and seemingly placid environs. The typical rapist was not a 'low-browed apish creature, with little intelligence and education', as one commentator believed in 1950, but could be 'tall, handsome . . . with a mild look on his fresh face. One could imagine him in flannels on a cricket field, or at tennis in any middle-class suburb; the pride of doting parents and the quarry of pretty women'.[79] Until the feminist critique rape was portrayed as flourishing on the margins of society, among young men who had not yet been acculturated into 'normal patriarchal sex', with its 'classic rules of husband and father' (what Roy Porter famously dubbed the 'permanent erections of mature patriarchy – wealth, property, office, "standing".').[80] Instead second-wave feminists exposed the violence sustaining the most secure and respected patriarchal bastions. Rape flourished in the marital bedroom. It took place against the boardroom table. It was an everyday practice in schools, universities, offices and factories. Although there has been a furious backlash against this narrative,[81] it was a narrative that left a deep mark on definitions of rape and sexual abuse.

In this chapter and the last one I argue that rape discourses produce the subjects they claim to describe. Social agents constitute social reality. Through the range of languages and narratives explored in these two chapters, a man *becomes* someone who rapes. The chief question shared by all these narratives is: how is human criminality fashioned? Does it arise from a degenerate or chaotic body, as alienists believed? Or does environment (particularly unruly urban spaces and dysfunctional families) make all the difference?

Echoing what I observed in the previous chapter, most commentators were gloomy about the possibility of eradicating rape. Education, providing men with other sexual 'outlets' and encouragement of female self-policing were the main solutions. What is particularly notable in these explanations is the avoidance of radical socio-economic change. With the exception of feminism (to which I shall return in the final chapter), both the biological and the environmental explanations for male aggression avoided proposing widespread reorganization of societal norms, institutions and political structures. Even arguments that stressed the role of endemic poverty and inequality in creating sexually violent men resolutely remained focused on individuals when turning to ways to prevent offending. Only the feminist narrative provided an account of the rapist that situated him within a gendered material reality, insisting that rapists were made, not born.

CHAPTER SIX

The Knife (and Other Invasive Therapies)

Dr Lionel L. Westrope castrated at least one boy and two young men at the Poor Law Hospital in Gateshead County Borough (Durham) in the 1920s and 1930s. All three had been sexually aggressive. The eldest of these men was twenty-two-year-old William George Wilson, notorious for public displays of masturbation. He was so addicted to masturbation that he sometimes haemorrhaged from his penis. Wilson's mother begged Westrope: 'For God's sake, Doctor, will you do something to this boy of mine?' Fifteen-year-old Richard Pegram practised a similar habit, but was brought to Westrope after 'pushing up' against a woman, insisting that he was 'horny' and 'had the "horn"'. Westrope's third patient was nine-year-old Henry Lawton, whose head had been 'much crushed' by forceps when he was born. He was 'an epileptic, imbecile, unable to talk', who generated alarm after he began attacking his five-year-old sister. At the hospital he used to 'lie on his face and work his body as though having sexual connection' and, when turned over, was found to have an erection. Henry Lawton's mother pleaded with Westrope to castrate the boy because she was 'afraid that if he recovered sufficiently to leave the Institution he might cause his parents endless anxiety by attacking females'. Westrope went ahead with the operations, removing the testes of all three boys.

Given that Westrope claimed that the behaviour of the boys improved after the operation (although we only have Westrope's word for it), the boys' mothers must have been pleased with the result.

Some of his colleagues, however, were not at all happy. Westrope had not followed correct legal procedures. Sir George Newman, Chief Medical Officer, was informed that the castrations were illegal: 'Consent or no consent, the surgeon is guilty of unlawful wounding,' complained the whistle-blower. The crisis was exacerbated when it was found that neither Pegram nor Lawson had even been certified insane. Another physician marshalled a defence of Westrope's actions on the grounds that Westrope was a 'thoroughly honest man' who had carried out the operations with therapeutic, rather than 'sociological', intentions. Westrope was right to castrate, rather than sterilize these boys, he argued. Sterilization would have been 'particularly useless' in all three cases because it would simply have 'let loose' these boys into the community 'with undiminished sexual appetites which they were too feeble-minded to control, and, possibly, [with] the *knowledge that no woman could become pregnant by them*'. In the end Westrope was merely chastised for 'mix[ing] up the therapeutic and sociological aspects of these cases'.[1]

Dr Westrope's extra-legal surgical indiscretion is not surprising, given the popularity of radical responses to sex crime. What if the root cause of sex crime is simply that piece of flesh lolling between the legs of nearly half of all humans? If the penis is the problem, then surely the solution also resides in men's biology. With a single caress of the knife the thorn in humanity's social flesh could be eliminated. According to this narrative, the solution to sex crime lay in the hands of physicians such as Westrope. Sterilization and castration attacked the fundamentals of male sexual performance, with the added advantage of fusing a progressive therapeutic imaginary with a more satisfying retributive imperative. The body is a crafty operator, however. Which component of the male sex organs is blameworthy? What if the problematic penis had active lines of communication with the white brain cells? If so, an equally radical response involved a different class of surgeon, with neurologists replacing general surgeons in the surgical management of rapists. By severing the delicate fibres in the brain, aggressive urges could be placated. As I will show, however, the knife was not the only radical intervention into the lives of rapists and other sexual abusers. Competing scientific knowledges led to a swing away from ideas of the innately rapacious male body. New ways of disciplining the sex criminal came to the fore, replacing the knife with equally radical behavioural modification procedures.

Sterilization

Male sterilization may seem a bizarre way to eradicate sexually violent behaviour in male offenders. Severing the seminal duct – running from the epididymis to the ejaculatory duct – of the testis does not, at first sight, seem a promising solution to sex crime. At the turn of the twentieth century, however, it appealed to legislators and physicians alike. The virtues of compulsory sterilization arose initially out of nineteenth-century evolutionary thought. Most compellingly, Francis Galton (Charles Darwin's cousin) coined the term 'eugenics' to refer to attempts to improve the human stock in positive ways (by encouraging 'superior' individuals to breed) and negative ways (by preventing 'degenerate' individuals from reproducing). Inspired by Shakespeare's *The Tempest*, in which Prospero lamented that his slave Caliban was 'A devil, a born devil, on whose nature/Nurture can never stick', Galton popularized the phrase 'nature versus nurture'. There was no question in his mind that the balance of power lay with nature.

The 'nature' part of the equation also enthused prison reformers, physicians and others concerned with crime abatement from the early years of the twentieth century. America led the way in the spring of 1907, with Indiana introducing the first laws enabling certain designated individuals to be compulsorily sterilized. Within thirty years, thirty-one states had followed its lead[2] and within fifty years around 60,000 people had been forcibly sterilized.[3] The majority of these operations were not carried out on sex offenders. Instead proponents of sterilization primarily targeted the mentally deficient, insane or epileptic. Three-quarters were women, who had their fallopian tubes cut, sewn or burnt. They were rendered barren in order to regulate their consensual sexual relationships. Largely poor immigrants or African-Americans, these 'unfit' women were sterilized to ensure that they never became mothers.

Most states also, however, allowed the sterilization of sex offenders, particularly of men convicted of rape or the 'carnal abuse of a female person' under a particular age. In some states it was enough for a man to be pronounced a 'habitual criminal' to be brought under the knife. Many therapeutic reasons were put forward for subjecting sex criminals to sterilization or vasectomy. In terms of the individual criminal, sterilization was believed to curb the scourge of masturbation within prisons and to make convicts less violent. After all, the argument went, since male deviancy was the result of excessive sex drives, sterilization should alleviate manly aggressiveness.[4] More broadly, however, it was also essential that sex criminals did not pass on their defective genes to the next generation. In the words of one commentator, if released from prison and allowed to reproduce, the criminal would inoculate 'that new life with the very germs of theft and murder already stirring in the blood of its progenitors ages back'[5] The stability and prosperity of American society depended upon ensuring that 'criminal defects' did not duplicate themselves.

But punishment was the main reason for sterilizing sex criminals. After all, most rapists and sexual aggressors who ended up being sterilized would remain in prison for a very long time. Reproduction was unlikely. Sterilization, therefore, was imposed on the violent man as an additional punishment for his crime. It also sent a clear message to the public that the 'crime wave' was being tackled in a robust and scientifically progressive fashion. The fact that African-American convicts were twice as likely to be sterilized as their white counterparts[6] not only confirmed prejudices about the danger of 'Negro rapists', but reassured white commentators that this tough stance was necessary.

Opposition to the policy of sterilizing sex criminals was strident, nevertheless. Indeed, from the early twentieth century there was increasing disquiet about imposing it as a punishment. Most famously, its legitimacy was debated in the appeal court of the State of Washington in 1912. Peter Feilen, a defendant who had been convicted of raping a young girl, petitioned against being vasectomized on the grounds that sterilization constituted cruel punishment and was therefore unconstitutional. The sentence had been passed under a State of Washington statute which provided that 'whenever any person shall be adjudged guilty of a carnal abuse of a female under ten years, or of rape, or shall be adjudged to be a habitual criminal, this operation [vasectomy] may be directed to be performed'. The judge sentenced Feilen to life imprisonment and sterilization.

Feilen lost his appeal against sterilization. The court ruled that because the vasectomy would be carried out by a skilled surgeon and would be painless, it could not be said to be cruel. Furthermore, the crime for which Feilen had been convicted was 'brutal, heinous, and revolting'. If the state legislature had willed it, Feilen could even have been executed for his crime without infringement of any of his constitutional rights. If the death penalty ('devoid of physical torture') was not considered cruel, why should sterilization be any different, the judges reasoned? Finally, the court drew attention to a range of so-called experts who endorsed the irreversible operation.[7] Peter Feilen was sterilized against his will. A few years later he was found innocent of the original crime. He was pardoned and released from prison, but the sterilization was irreversible.[8]

Feilen's losses were many and his case excited wide debate. Surely, an unnamed commentator asked in a 1914 article in the *Yale Law Journal*,

> to take from one who has committed the crime of rape but once, all hope of future progeny, when he may go forth from confinement at some future time a reformed man, seems as cruel and unusual punishment as can well be conceived of. It is a punishment which lasts beyond the term of imprisonment, even to the grave.[9]

Other state assemblies agreed. In 1915, for instance, the *Virginia Law Register* had also pointed out that the 'question of cruelty does not depend on physical discomfort alone, but also on the shame and humiliation attendant on loss of virile powers and inability to enter rightly into the marriage relation'.[10]

Was it right that none of the 'authorities' cited by the Washington court hearing Feilen's appeal were knowledgeable in scientific and hereditary matters? asked Charles Boston, writing in the *Journal of the American Institute of Criminal Law and Criminology* in 1913. The physicians who had given evidence had spoken only about what they knew: 'the painlessness of the operation'. '[A]re we to understand that with the introduction of anaesthetics mutilation became constitutional?' Boston enquired.

Furthermore, the very basis of the legislation allowing for compulsory sterilization of sex criminals was flawed: genetic transmission of criminality lacked any scientific foundation. 'I defy anyone to prove that the fact that a man committed rape' was 'any indication that there will be transmitted to his offspring any undersirable [sic] hereditary trait', Boston maintained. The idea of hereditability came from 'sociologists and amateur reformers' rather than biologists. Boston continued his attack. 'If criminal traits were hereditary,' he reasoned,

> there are some parts of the civilized world to which we could look with certainty for a depraved population obviously inferior to the rest of mankind, namely, those places which have in time past been used as penal colonies, or to which criminals have been banished. It would perhaps be invidious to name them, but they will readily occur to the

> reader. As they pass before me in reflection . . . they appear, on the contrary, to have produced an unusually high grade of citizenship.

Boston shrugged off critics who claimed that convicts sent to penal colonies such as Australia had (by and large) not committed crimes of 'real moral turpitude' but were merely 'independent spirit[s]' protesting against 'the legally established order of things'. While this was true enough, Boston conceded, there were 'enough crimes of moral turpitude' to 'afford a fair test of the theory'. Not only was there no proof that criminal tendencies were hereditary, but even if there *was* evidence, 'there would be more substantial reason for sterilizing reckless chauffeurs' rather than rapists since many more people were injured or killed in car accidents than during sexual attacks.

In the end the chief problem for Boston was that sterilization was being imposed as a vindictive form of punishment. Laws allowing for the operation were simply a kind of 'raw pseudo-reform'. Contrary to the decision of the Washington court, sterilization could, in fact, be classified as a cruel and unusual punishment. Boston drew a comparison with torture. 'Just as France, Germany and Spain, and occasionally English sovereigns, justified torture, in the interest of public safety,' he began, so now

> the sponsors of the sterilization laws justify mutilation in the fancied interest of the public welfare. But my thesis is that the public welfare requires neither torture nor sterilization, and that it weakens our sense of respect for the rights of each individual man.

If people were to be sterilized for being a 'menace to the peace and welfare of the community', then, he proposed (tongue in cheek), enormously wealthy men should be forcibly sterilized since it could be proved without a shadow of a doubt that 'inordinate individual wealth' was 'damaging to society'. Their wealth was evidence of the 'over development' of the impulse of 'inquisitive greed'. It could also be shown that 'undesirable civic tendencies' were 'transmissible by heredity' as easily as criminal ones.[11]

Boston's radical critique echoed criticisms increasingly circulating within judicial and penal circles. Eventually criminals could be sterilized for eugenic purposes, but after 1925 no statute allowed convicts to be sterilised simply as a form of punishment. By this stage even proponents of the operation were admitting that they harboured reservations. The most obvious objection to the sterilization laws was that the operation did not make men incapable of sexual abuse. As Clarence Ruddy, founder and first editor of the *Notre Dame Lawyer*, candidly asked in the 1920s, 'is to be supposed for an instance that a rapist will be deterred from his beastly designs merely because he can never beget children?' Indeed, the opposite might be the case: a vasectomy might 'secure to a rapist his eroticism and uninhibited lust' while releasing him from 'any responsibility for offspring'.[12] And, as another critic of the Feilen ruling pointed out, sterilization removed the 'only existing deterrent' to forced sex. By relieving rapists 'of the fear of possible bastardy proceedings', the operation reduced the 'danger attending the gratification of such immoral desires'.[13] Worse: the operation could spread the moral pollution even further, since the vasectomized offender, once released from prison, was liable to become 'a moral libertine, a menace and a most dangerous individual to even the most virtuous, the moment it became known that he is not a dangerous one to cohabit with so far as causing conception is concerned'.[14]

In other words, once ordinarily virtuous women became aware that the sex offender was infertile, they might be willing to submit to his embraces, thus increasing his danger to the community. 'What is the essence of the crime of rape?' asked a commentator in the *Yale Law Journal* in 1914: it was 'dishonour by violence, not by impregnation', yet sterilization did nothing to 'protect women from this crime'.[15]

Surgical Castration

While sterilization came to be seen as unjustly punitive (especially since it could not achieve its stated purpose), calls for even more extreme procedures paradoxically seemed more palatable. Might surgical castration or orchidectomy be an acceptable substitute?

The operation is straightforward surgically: it requires a physician to make an incision in the offender's scrotum (preferably near the pubis in order to hide the scar) and then cut and remove the testes. In some cases the testes are replaced with prostheses made from marble, ivory, aluminium, silver, celluloid or even petroleum jelly. From 1942, glass prostheses weighing around 12 grams were used and from the 1970s plastic testes proved popular.[16] Castration did more than simply sever the seminal duct. It was a much more radical operation than sterilization, and fulfilled a different function. As Marie E. Kopp, who had toured Germany studying the Nazi sterilization laws for the American Eugenics Society, explained, while sterilization was primarily intended to prevent 'defective social individuals' from passing on their moral flaws to another generation, castration was a 'crime prevention measure' that served *both* 'the existing generation and indirectly posterity'.[17] It was an attractive two-in-one deal.

The compulsory castration or 'asexualization' of criminals – particularly murderers and rapists – has a long history. Lobbying in favour of the procedure was particularly vociferous in America. Lynch mobs frequently carried out extra-judiciary castration on African-American men accused or convicted of raping white women. Defenders of compulsory castration also existed within the formal justice system. Their arguments were simple. As Lucius H. Perkins told members of the Kansas State Bar Association in January 1901, 'if this morbid and unbridled passion is disease, then treat it like appendicitis, remove the cause'. Rape was 'the one crime for which the *jus talionis* ['eye for an eye'] is the only proper punishment' and castration was

> the one punishment that will deter. It is the one that will satisfy the public mind. Given a reasonable assurance of its prompt infliction, and add to it the lash, and three things are sure: This offender will so offend no more; the law will take its course, with no infraction by impatient mobs; and the fear of a like visitation will deter more evil-minded men than burning at the stake, or eternal torment in hell fire.[18]

At the International Medico-Legal Congress in Chicago in 1893, F. E. Daniel launched a typical vindication of legalized castration. Daniel was a surgeon and the first editor of the *Texas Medical Journal*. Like proponents of sterilization, he was as interested in the eugenic consequences of castration as in its punitive and therapeutic effects. Even the lower animals 'limit production, and eliminate the weaker by battles between the males for the possession of the female', he argued. The 'degrading effects of hereditary transmission' of criminal traits was something to be taken very seriously indeed. Some people, he admitted, had proposed castrating *all* criminals, 'thus arresting the descent of their respective vices', but Daniel admitted that this posed the serious risk that 'we might *cut the wrong man*'. Instead he proposed limiting compulsory castration to men who committed sex crimes (implying that the possibility of convicting and cutting the wrong testicles was negligible in the case of men accused of sex crimes).

There was more to the operation than preventing reproduction, though. Castration would act as a deterrent, Daniel predicted. The threat of castration would have a greater 'restraining effect' on rapists than 'hanging, burning at the stake, or electrocution'. Daniel regarded it as remarkable that a society was willing to 'break a criminal's neck' but would 'respect his testicles'.

At this point Daniel's racist ideology, always implicit in his work, abruptly came to the surface. Castration was the only effective way to deal with the evil of 'so much rape by negroes in the South', he asserted. There was an advantage in castrating the rapist. Castration would not only render the sex offender incapable of repeating his crime, but 'turn[ing] him loose' into the black community like a 'singed rat' would make him 'a warning to others'. It was a sorry fact, Daniel added, that 'a hanging, or even a burning, is soon forgotten; but a negro buck at large amongst the ewes of his flock, minus the element of his manhood, would be a standing terror to those of similar propensities'.[19]

Daniel fought for decades for the legalization of castration. In 1907, fourteen years after his first defence, he was still promoting surgical castration. In commenting on a Bill before the Texas House of Representatives that would allow courts to castrate rapists, Daniel dismissed the same constitutional objection that had been used to attack sterilization: that it was a cruel and unusual punishment. Not true, he insisted. Castration was to be inflicted 'not as a punishment, but as a sanitary or hygienic measure' to prevent the rapist from reoffending and to preclude 'the propagation of a race of sexual perverts'. The operation was 'in the interest of public morals and race integrity'. Once again racist ideology underpinned his argument: surgical castration would 'act as a powerful restraint on the evil-inclined, for a negro values those possessions more than life'. Even 'burning by a mob' did not 'restrain . . . negroes'. It would be 'a big step in the advance of civilization if we can get such a law in every state', he reminded the House.[20]

A number of states including Texas could garner support for the compulsory castration of convicted sex offenders because, like sterilization, it was a relative easy, cheap and quick way to lash out at this class of criminal. The theory behind the procedure also appealed to commonsensical thinking about the rapacious male body. To put it in the medical terminology of a later period, by removing the testes the hormonal production of plasma testosterone (an androgen or sex hormone) was eradicated. As a consequence, the castrato's sex drive should plummet.

Given the heinous nature of sex crimes, the direct attack on the sex offender's genitals was also seen as appropriate punishment. As Simeon E. Baldwin (long-time Chief Justice of the Connecticut Supreme Court and President of the American Bar Association) noted in 1899, castration 'reforms his body if it does not his soul'. It was a fitting punishment for rape and sexual assault because it 'dishonors and degrades, as he has dishonored and degraded. It would be dreaded by most men, little less than capital punishment.'[21]

Half a century later similar sentiments were being expressed. In September 1951, for instance, the *British Medical Journal* published letters from readers in response to a public outcry over a lenient sentence given to a man convicted of assaulting five young boys. G. Orisra Taylor of Winchester argued that castration and corporal punishment together would act as an effective deterrent to homosexual sex crimes. As the parents of five boys he and his wife 'always hoped and prayed they and we might be spared the horrors of sodomy'. He lamented the fact that evidence from the theatre and literature revealed that society was becoming more 'condoning' of this 'moral disease'. Taylor believed that harsh punishment of homosexual sex offenders would be an effective deterrent: such punishment could not be called a 'vindictive act' because it was 'administered for the good of the community' as well as the culprit. Taylor was man enough to admit that harsh retribution would deter *him* from raping young boys. As he put it, 'I fancy if I were tempted to yield in this direction I should hesitate if I knew I should lose my income, go to gaol, and especially if I might expect a good thrashing for each boy whose outlook on life I had so smirched.'

Harrow Burrows agreed, telling fellow readers of the *British Medical Journal* that he would be happy with nothing less than the removal of the offender's testicles. 'This treatment would be cheaper than imprisonment, would cure the criminal of his evil propensity, and would protect the public,' he insisted.[22]

But did castration work? Many rapists believed so. Castration was perfectly in line with their view that they were victims of their penises. Some even attempted to castrate themselves out of self-disgust.[23] More fastidious abusers pleaded with surgeons to do the dirty deed for them. In the words of a thirty-one-year-old rapist in 1961,

> I am of the opinion that I am abnormal sexually because I did the same thing in 1951, and under practically the same conditions. I realize fully what I am up against now; I have no one to blame but myself, and of

> how I messed up my opportunity and probably that of my wife and unborn baby.

He swore that if castration would help rid him of 'this strange quirk', he would willingly submit to the operation.[24]

For criminals like this rapist, castration seemed a less invasive procedure when compared with the chemical or behavioural treatments that I will be turning to later in this chapter. Sex criminals might beg to 'undergo orchidectomy', as Californian psychiatrists with extensive experience with men committed for indefinite prison terms under legislation dealing with 'sexual predators' pointed out in 2005. These prisoners believed that castration would 'enable them to maintain better self-control over deviant sexual impulses' as well as increasing the likelihood that mental health professionals and courts would consider them safe to release from confinement.[25] A radical surgical option was their only hope of ever being set free.

The effectiveness of castration was addressed in studies carried out in European centres for sex offenders, particularly in Denmark. The Asylum for Psychopathic Criminals at Herstedvester was established in 1935 to treat psychiatrically abnormal individuals who were 'neither psychotic nor feeble-minded'. Many of the institution's inmates were surgically castrated – often for activities that would not be punished today, such as homosexuality.[26] Nearly half of the thirty-eight rapists housed there between 1935 and 1961 were surgically castrated, and follow-up reports found that most did not reoffend sexually after release, although six were rearrested for non-sexual crimes.[27]

The studies carried out in Herstedvester were based on very small samples, but they were systematic. Other evidence for the effect of surgical castration is much less conclusive. Asexualization 'completely changes the character of the individual', a proponent argued in the early 1890s. It relieved 'some, if not all, of the disturbance of the mind'.[28] Another supporter noted that before the operation these criminals were constantly struggling with 'sexualism' and their life could be described as a constant shuffling to and from prison, coupled with 'destroyed family life, broken means of livelihood, disaster upon disaster, sorrow and destitution'. After the operation, 'quite apart from the disappearance of criminality', most castrated men became 'so pacified, balanced and concentrated upon their family life and work' that life became 'sedate and respectable', concluded an expert on castration in Denmark.[29]

The *British Medical Journal* claimed that castration was particularly suitable for mentally subnormal men who had been raised in poor households where early training in social skills had been neglected.[30] It was uniformly agreed that sterilization, one of the side effects of the operation, was also not altogether a bad thing since 'in the majority of cases' the men being castrated were either 'tainted psychopath[s]' or other 'inferior' individuals 'whose descendants one dare not assume would be of any value to the community'.[31] Not only would the offender be 'rendered incapable of a repetition of the offence' but 'the propagation of his kind' would be 'inhibited in the interests of civilization and the well-being of future generations'.[32] As late as 1947 a physician wrote to the *British Medical Journal* to support this argument, calling for the routine and immediate castration of men convicted of sex offences so that 'at the end of his incarceration, impotence and loss of desire would render him incapable of harm'.[33]

Just as importantly, the operation was cheap. Lifelong segregation of persons not amenable to treatment and unable to control their sexual urges is expensive. Castration offers to cut through the cost of repeated court proceedings and detention.[34] It is, in the words of a consultant psychiatrist at the Metropolitan Hospital (London) in 1975, a 'surgical cure for a social illness and no more inhumane than cutting a troublesome ulcer from a man's stomach'.[35]

There were critics, however. As early as the late-1880s, law journals protested that castration was 'barbarous and disgraceful'. Such measures were 'suited to Feejee [sic] Indians, not to civilized and dignified communities', huffed the *Albany Law Journal*.[36] Like sterilization, wasn't castration simply retributive? Wasn't it based upon 'the idea of retaliation – the thought of revenge which is deeply rooted in human nature . . . but which has always had a harmful effect on penal law?', queried a reader of the *British Medical Journal* in 1946. Others, in the same journal, went still further, asking whether supporters of compulsory castration also proposed to exterminate sufferers of tuberculosis or cut off the hands of shoplifters.[37]

The extra-legal aspects of some operations also caused concern. It was felt that judicially enforced castration could encourage mobs to follow suit in extra-judicial lynching. Even professional physicians might be inspired to take the law into their own hands and castrate men without court approval. This fear was confirmed by the illegal sterilizations carried out by Dr Lionel L. Westrope in England (as discussed at the start of this chapter). In the USA, from 1889 Dr Harry O. Sharp of Jeffersonville (Indiana) had sterilized inmates in the State Institution for Delinquent Boys, as had Dr Isaak N. Kerlin, superintendent of the State Training School for Delinquent Boys in Elwyn (Pennsylvania), in every case without legal authority.[38]

Disapproval began to mount. The views of most men who had been forcibly castrated were never heard. Those few whose views are recorded often complained of distressing side effects. They sweated profusely. Like 'women during menopause', they blushed a great deal.[39] Body hair thinned; head hair thickened; skin became softer. Some men grew breasts. Depression was common.

Public opinion started turning against the operation as social and political reservations grew. The legitimacy of giving defendants in sex-crime cases suspended sentences if they consented to the operation periodically created outrage.[40] In 1983 a high-profile case was reported around the world. It involved three men, aged nineteen, twenty-one and twenty-seven, convicted in Anderson (South Carolina) of prolonged rape and torture of a woman. The judge allowed them to choose between thirty years in jail or surgical castration followed by five years' probation. While the youngest rapist whimpered about wanting to have children in the future, the eldest opted for castration. 'Either way I could be destroyed,' he complained, but 'to be isolated and not able to contribute to the world would be more damaging to me than to undergo castration.' Critics were appalled by both the judge's decision and the callous self-centred attitude of the prisoners. Wouldn't castration followed by probation simply throw these men, who had been extraordinarily violent towards women, back onto the streets? The refrain of 'will our courts be giving thieves the option of having their hands cut off?' was heard yet again.[41]

There were other, more political, objections to surgical castration. F. E. Daniel, the vigorous advocate of castration mentioned earlier, was unabashed about his racist agenda. In the end around half of all judicial mutilations were performed on African-American men (that is, twice their proportion in the population).[42] For many this was a stark return to the days when African-American men were routinely castrated if even *accused* of rape or attempted rape (as was allowed by law in Kansas in 1855, for instance).[43] African-American organizations drew attention to this particularly visceral form of discrimination.

From the late-1930s Nazism silenced many supporters of compulsory surgical castration. In 1934 *The Times* could calmly recount the benefits of 'penal castration' of sex criminals; by 1945 this was profanity.[44] In 1951 a highly respected authority on the treatment of sex offenders put it bluntly when he noted that castration was

> a nonreversible procedure subject to serious abuses as Nazi experience has thoroughly proved. What with the hysteria so easily provoked in the United States relative to sex criminality, there is a very real danger that the castration technique, if it were adopted here, would too easily be misapplied.[45]

For diehard supporters of the operation the irresolvable problem was the same as that faced by supporters of sterilization: 'desexing' seemed not to be achieving the required outcome. In fact, evidence began emerging that a man's libido could persist for years after the operation.[46] In some cases it would never decline. As early as 1897 a physician who had been employed at the New York City Asylums for the Insane testified that men who were castrated ended up 'mental wrecks with the old desire remaining'.[47] Even the positive results reported about castration at the Asylum for Psychopathic Criminals at Herstedvester in Denmark were ambiguous. Yes, most castrati did not reoffend, but they were 'still able to perform the sexual act on occasion'.[48] Surgical castration at Herstedvester was discontinued in 1970, to be replaced with psychotherapy and, from 1989, anti-hormonal medicines combined with psychotherapy.[49] Another survey, published in the *Archives of Sexual Behavior* in the early 1980s, discovered that nearly one-third of castrated sex offenders were still able to engage in sexual intercourse. In fact, of the three groups of criminals studied – rapists, paedophiles and homosexuals – rapists proved to be the ones most likely to remain sexually active after the operation.[50] In those cases where reduced potency could be observed, it was more plausible to conclude that it was due to advancing age rather than the operation.[51] As the author of *Asexualization: A Follow-Up Study of 244 Cases* (1958) glumly concluded, 'no general effect of pacification has been encountered at all'. The operation had 'no sedative influence on exaggerated affections, no harmonization of emotional life, no "resocializing" influence on asocial or anti-social behaviour beyond the sexual sphere'.[52]

So what was happening? Human sex hormones are also produced outside of the testes; removing them does not automatically eradicate sexual urges or performance. Nor is the capacity to develop an erection in response to sexual stimulation eliminated.[53] Even more disturbing, a man's sexual activities could actually increase after castration.[54]

Women in rape crisis centres observed that rape is a crime of violence.[55] If a man was motivated to rape by an urge to humiliate or cause pain, castration would not prevent him from carrying out his mission. Indeed, it might encourage him to employ weapons potentially even more damaging than the penis. The implication that sexual offending was a problem of the scrotum seemed to have been theoretically and politically undercut.

Chemical Castration

Although the *surgical* removal of the genitals of sex offenders declined from thc 1940s, castration, rathcr than disappearing, was actually refined. Chemical equivalents of the knife provided the way ahead. According to its proponents, sex was just another 'biological drive', susceptible to pharmacological treatment. As two researchers blandly observed, sexual sadism was comparable to eating disorders. In eating disorders the biological drive is hunger. If it is put out of balance the result is obesity or anorexia. Similarly, if a man's sexual drive is disturbed he is liable to lash out and rape someone. So what is the solution? Physicians had to find ways to reduce the sexual drive and redirect it 'away from deviant sexual interests'. Since the biological components of the sexual drive were hormones and neurotransmitters, possible solutions included using anti-androgens to reduce plasma testosterone; prescribing hormonal agents such as medroxyprogesterone acetate (MPA) to reduce the secretion of gonadotropins (or hormones that stimulate gonads, such as testes); or increasing serotonin levels.[56]

The first option was developed from the 1940s and was promoted as superior to both surgical castration and psychotherapy.[57] In the 1940s F. L. Golla, the first director of the Burden Neurological Institute in Bristol, argued that the use of stilboestrol, or large doses of a synthetic oestrogen, effectively eradicated a man's libido.[58] Typically, after a short period of treatment with stilboestrol, a man's penis and testes would have 'diminished to approximately two-thirds of the pre-therapeutic size' and he would be unable to ejaculate when masturbating.[59]

Dosing a sexual aggressor with MPA was another means of chemical castration. John Money and his colleagues at the Johns Hopkins Hospital in Baltimore first employed it in 1966.[60] Initially developed as an injectable contraceptive for women and marketed as Depo-Provera,

MPA was soon observed to also lower 'sexual precocity in girls and boys'.[61] Giving sex offenders forty times the dosage prescribed to women as a contraceptive had a 'predictable effect'. Money observed that 'the penis is unable to erect, semen is not produced, and orgasms do not occur'. However, he warned that it was important to distinguish between 'loss of feeling of lust' and 'loss of ability to be attentive to stimuli formerly associated with sexual arousal'. MPA simply diminished 'attentiveness' to previously arousing sexual cues, thus inhibiting 'carry-through behaviour'. A great deal depended upon the type of sexual behaviour involved. Money noted that behaviour 'requiring an erect penis, as in oral, anal, or vaginal penetration, obviously disappears if the penis no longer becomes erect', but 'other activities of lovemaking are not lost, but are optional'. Whether they were 'put into practice or not' depended on the 'ratio of apathy to interest in sexual opportunities and circumstances'. In terms of halting sexual aggression, however, it was a good sign that patients tended to become sexually apathetic as their potency waned. The side effects of the drug and the violation of patients' rights could be justified on the grounds that the alternative was often 'sexual homicide, life imprisonment, death in the gas chamber, or a masochistic stage-management of one's own murder', Money argued.[62]

Cyproterone acetate (CPA) was another powerful synthetic anti-androgen or substance that inhibited the action of the endogenous androgens produced by the testes and adrenals. Even medium doses of CPA led to 'reduced or inhibited libido and potency as well as the incidence and intensity of sexual activity'. Typically men being treated would first lose their libido, then potency. If treatment continued they would find themselves unable to have an orgasm. An associated effect included the inhibition of spermatogenesis, of production of sperm.[63]

What did it mean to be treated with an anti-androgen like CPA? In the early 1970s a group of Edinburgh-based psychiatrists and endocrinologists published an article in the *British Journal of Psychiatry* in which they described a typical treatment regime. These physicians believed that CPA was the most effective anti-androgen for treating men with 'deviant hypersexuality'. One of their patients was a forty-year-old man who had sexually assaulted his fifteen-year-old daughter. He admitted that he had 'lost self-control' on previous occasions as well, confessing to indecent exposure, homosexuality, transvestism, fetishism and 'interfering with' other adolescent girls. He also grumbled about 'unresolved heterosexual tension due to his wife's refusal to accommodate his coital needs', which he estimated should be between five and seven times per week. According to these doctors, their patient was a psychopath who 'lacked a conscience and had extremely poor impulse control'. When sexually aroused he was unable to prevent himself from seeking 'an immediate outlet, irrespective of surroundings or circumstances and without concern for the consequences'. Feelings of remorse or guilt were outside his emotional range.

The seriousness of his behaviour made him an ideal candidate for a three-week therapeutic trial with CPA. After admission and for the next few weeks samples of his blood were taken every morning and evening. Some days, at 3.30 p.m., he was encouraged to masturbate. The patient was 'instructed to employ optimal stimulation and reach orgasm and ejaculation as quickly as possible'. After each of these sessions his blood was tested again for plasma testosterone levels.

During the first four days in the hospital the patient's testosterone levels were fairly normal. Once the CPA treatment started, however, his levels fell off rapidly, dropping by nearly 50 per cent almost immediately. Even more significantly, the patient was no longer troubled by erections in the morning, nor did he have spontaneous daytime erections. After seven days of receiving 100 mg of CPA a day, the patient found that he was incapable of masturbating to orgasm and ejaculation. 'Despite 15 minutes of vigorous manipulation,' the physicians observed, 'he remained virtually unaroused, with an extremely poor erection'.

The doctors concluded that the treatment was a success. Its effects were reversible: three weeks after stopping the drug the patient was experiencing 'powerful erections' and masturbation to orgasm and ejaculation was yet again 'accomplished easily'. His plasma testosterone levels had returned to normal. There was no evidence of 'feminization' (a 'serious drawback' of oestrogens). The physicians also noted that the effect of treatment was primarily physiological since the psychological manifestations of sexuality (sexual desire) remained 'intact'. They continued: 'It might have been expected that "desire:" without "capacity" would result in frustration or depression or both', but this was not the case. On the contrary, this patient (and their other patients, many of whom were hospitalized in order to be 'cured' of homosexuality) frequently reported 'feelings of considerable relief'.[64]

Plasma testosterone was not the only chemical capable of dramatically altering male sexual behaviour. Serotonin levels were also important: the higher the level, the lower the sex-drive.

Pharmacological treatment, therefore, also included serotonin reuptake inhibitors.[65] As a form of obsessive-compulsive disorder, deviant sexual behaviours and compulsions responded to medications that raised central serotonin metabolism.[66]

This treatment was suitable for female abusers too. Ms A., for instance, was a twenty-three-year-old woman who had separately sexually assaulted two four-year-old girls while babysitting. In each case she had become sexually aroused while bathing the girl and had licked her genitals. Deeply ashamed, Ms A. had confessed her actions to the minister of her church, who then escorted her to the police. Because she had sought help and turned herself in, she was sentenced to three years' probation and sent for treatment at a Sexual Behaviours Clinic. Psychiatrists at the clinic diagnosed her as meeting the American Psychiatric Association's criteria for paedophilia (as set out in the DSM-IV, the fourth edition of its *Diagnostic and Statistical Manual of Mental Disorders*) and proposed treating her in the same way they treated men, that is, with 50 mg daily of the selective serotonin reuptake inhibitor sertraline. The treatment worked: she virtually ceased fantasizing about young girls. During her rare lapses she was easily able to stop herself acting on her daydreams. Whether the improvement was the result of a direct effect of sertraline or whether the effect was indirect (in that the treatment reduced her tendency to act impulsively), the psychiatrists were pleased with the result.[67]

The various methods of chemical castration were relatively inexpensive and easily monitored.[68] Even more importantly, they proved particularly effective when used alongside other treatments, such as behaviourist-orientated programmes (which I shall discuss later) or psychotherapy.* As physicians quickly discovered, even if the hormones failed to cure the sexual offender of his (or, more rarely, her) inappropriate or aggressive behaviour, they did give a 'breathing space' within which other treatments could begin to take effect.[69] After all, some sexual offenders were so obsessed with sadistic sexual fantasies that it was literally impossible to talk to them in any depth. Only when their obsessions were reduced through hormonal treatment could other forms of therapy progress.[70] Freed (even temporarily) from the 'distraction of the paraphilic fantasies and urges', the patient could start to 'realign the lovemap of sexual interests and develop self-governance of

*This is discussed in Chapter Seven, 'The Couch'.

his/her sexual behaviour'.[71] Today chemical castration remains an important way of managing the sexual impulses of abusers.

The drawbacks, however, are similar to those of surgical castration. Treatments focusing on reducing testosterone levels came unstuck when so much scientific evidence linking high testosterone levels with sexual aggressiveness proved to be contradictory. Although the authors of 'Plasma Testosterone Levels in the Rapist' (1976) found that violent rapists had higher testosterone levels than non-violent rapists and child molesters (whose testosterone levels were normal), they concluded that it was 'unlikely that the aggressive act of rape is determined largely by high levels of testosterone'.[72] Other studies revealed that rapists, child molesters and prisoners incarcerated for non-sexual offences had fairly average testosterone levels,[73] while still other researchers found that sexual offenders actually had lower levels of testosterone.[74]

Furthermore, all forms of chemical castration had negative side effects. Weight gain, nausea, osteoporosis and an increased risk of deep vein thrombosis and diabetes were significant risks. Degeneration of the testicles and 'marked gynaecomastic development' (the growth of breasts) was common.[75] Men who found themselves growing breasts might be allowed to have them amputated. At Dartmoor Prison in the 1970s, for instance, prisoners who grew breasts after oestrogen treatment were allowed to have them amputated either at the clinic at Grendon Underwood Prison in Buckinghamshire or at the small hospital at Tavistock in Devon.[76] Many seemed not to be comforted by this offer to remove their 'embarrassment'.[77] Most conspicuously, many hormonal treatments required the offender's cooperation. Hormonal treatments that relied on regular swallowing of pills were of little practical use: the 'good' patients who took their tablets were precisely those who probably would not have reoffended in the first place, while 'bad' patients stopped the treatment as soon as they were able to evade close surveillance. Even the use of implants (which reduced nausea as well as ensuring that doses remained constant) could last only a few weeks.[78]

There was another problem with the treatments. Because many rapists' actions were motivated by hatred, anger and fear, any medication that merely curbed sexual desire bore 'no reasonable relationship to the offender's criminal behaviour'.[79] Without shifts in the underlying *meaning* given to sexual intercourse, hormonal castration failed. Castrated sex offenders relished boasting about their irrepressible potency. They took extreme measures to ensure that their manliness was still assured.[80] When they observed that their 'main interest in life' (that is, sexual prowess) was waning, they evaded all drugs, noted psychiatrists with experience gained at Wormwood Scrubs Prison.[81] 'Demasculinization' was simply too awful a fate to countenanced.[82] Furthermore, because castration did not abolish sexual desire or fantasy, sexual abusers would continue to indecently assault their chosen victims, as a former HM Commissioner of Prisons in England and Wales observed.[83] In fact, already feeling sexually inadequate, many offenders responded to treatment with ever more exaggerated acts of sexual bravado. Castration produced personality changes, including feelings of resentment and inadequacy, which actually increased these men's dangerousness.[84]

Nevertheless, the unpopularity of surgical and chemical castration saw a reversal in the more punitive environment of the 1990s. The argument for 'incapacitating' the male sex organ was made most emphatically by Steven S. Kan in the 1996 edition of the *Journal of Legal Studies*. According to Kan, biological, medical or other technological ways of temporarily incapacitating the penis were a better and cheaper option than imprisonment. He pointed out that the mere fact of incapacitation should not worry people since this was common practice in both medicine (anaesthesia during operations, for instance) and law enforcement (handcuffs and shackles, for instance). It was 'our limited imagination', he argued, 'that makes us think that only the bloody sanctions of whipping, mutilation, and castration can deliver incapacitative effects on organs'. Instead, recent advances provided other ways to 'temporarily incapacitate some organs by way of injection or electric shock without creating long-term side effects'. In particular he proposed using a 'high-voltage electric shock' to 'treat a rapist's offending organ in order to curb the incidence of rape'. An added advantage was that such 'incapacitating measures' would have a deterrent effect as well. Reforming criminal punishment did not require more prisons to be built, nor was there any need to 'revert to bloody corporal punishment'. Instead, he concluded, a utilitarian analysis pointed to the advantages of adopting

> temporary incapacitative [sic] measures that can target particular organs at fault . . . After all, from the standpoint of economic analysis bodily organs are resources, just as money and time are, and how a criminal justice system can utilize this resource is worth careful examination.[85]

Kan's punitive response was exceptional, but was in harmony with the New Disciplinary focus of law enforcement more generally. From the 1990s state intervention into the corporeal lives of people dramatically expanded. Under many Sexually Violent Predator Acts or Sexually Dangerous Person Acts, persons designated 'rapist' or 'sexual abuser' could be forcibly sent to prison indefinitely.* Physical pain and pleasure were the only absolutes worthy of consideration. To bring the greatest happiness to the greatest number of people, a sacrifice was needed: the mutilation and incarceration of sexual offenders trumped any rehabilitative impulse. Politics increasingly operates upon the body.

Lobotomy

Castration tackled the scrotum and other hormonal hotbeds; other radical treatments trained the spotlight on a man's cranium. Lobotomy, leucotomy, fractional surgery and psychosurgery (terms for a range of similar procedures) represented a shift away from chemicals and a return to the knife. In the 1950s and again in the 1970s lobotomists, or psychosurgeons applied their minds to the issue of sexual aggression.[86] According to Harvard neurologists Vernon H. Mark and Frank R. Ervin, authors of the influential but controversial *Violence and the Brain* (1970), lobotomy was based on the assumption that human behaviour, including violent assault, was an expression of the functioning brain.[87] Rapists suffered from a 'lack of balance between primitive drives, probably originating in the hypothalamus and other lower brain centres, and the inhibitory effect of the cerebral cortex which normally regulated them'.[88] Psychosurgeons did not deny the cognitive or emotional components of sexual desire, but pointed out the crucial role played by neuro-physical aspects. Through surgery, neurosurgeons like Roy G. Spece (see a drawing by him of a lobotomy, p. 168) claimed to be able to close down a man's 'sex-switchboard'.[89]

A variety of surgical techniques was employed, but all aimed at destroying targeted areas of the brain with cuts or burns.[90] Most commonly an instrument resembling an ice pick would be inserted into the orbital roof of the brain, severing the fibres linking the thalamus and prefrontal areas. As a result, anti-social habits, aggressive urges and

*This is discussed in Chapter 10, 'Sexual Psychopaths'.

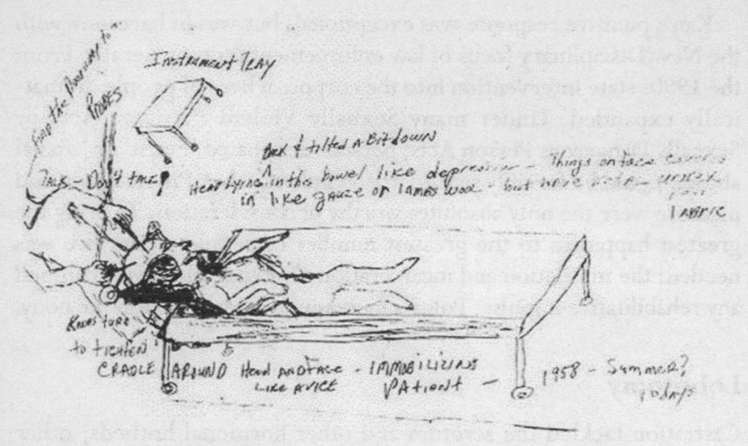

Roy G. Spence performing a lobotomy: self-portrait

cruel fantasies would be permanently banished. In particular the obsessive components of the crime would shrink, if not be eradicated altogether.[91] A man's sex drive, as well as the 'intensity of pleasure accompanying the sex act', would be gone for ever.[92] Even better, as a Californian psychosurgeon bragged at an international congress of psychosurgeons, by reducing prison time, 'psychosurgical pacification' would save taxpayers nearly £100,000 per criminal.[93] Psychosurgery was the cheap man's version of psychotherapy.

Did it work? Harry Howard (see photograph, p.169) was a serial sex offender who was operated on in the late 1950s. He was persuaded to undergo a prefrontal leucotomy because, in his words, he was 'afraid of finishing up on a capital charge'. The operation was explained to him in simple, if misleading, terms. 'We bore a hole in each side of your head,' the surgeon told him, 'and a nerve is severed. We won't know the results exactly, but you're supposed to have a childish mind for a while and then gradually work yourself back to your normal age.' The operation was not what Howard expected. In his words,

> I had all the hair shaved off my head till it was like a billiard ball. I was wheeled to the theatre and strapped down, because the sister said I might kick out.
>
> 'But you put me to sleep, don't you?'
>
> 'No, we just numb you. Your mind has to be clear for this operation.'

Harry Howard in Venice, 1960

> They marked a blue cross of either side of my head, and the surgeon took his electric drill and started to bore the holes. As soon as he touched me I kicked like hell, and smashed the table, even though I was strapped. 'Sister,' I said, 'give me something to put me to sleep, it's terrible, I can feel it.' She said they couldn't, and the surgeon carried on boring, while four male nurses held me down as best they could. I couldn't see, because they'd covered my eyes, but I could feel him shove an instrument through the holes and cut something.

The doctors admitted that 'We don't really know what's wrong with you, we can't understand it', yet they promised that he would feel the effects of the operation within the year. The operation failed. The next time Harry Howard was in court, the judge told him that 'the best psychological treatment for some people is to send them to prison', as he duly sentenced him to four years' incarceration.[94]

Harry Howard preyed on young women and was widely believed to be a psychopath with little (if any) conscience. The operation was probably not the best form of treatment for someone like him. After all, some psychiatrists believed that lobotomizing men with psychopathic tendencies was actually 'liable to increase those tendencies'. Since the operation removed 'the last shreds of conscience', it could be the worst possible treatment for psychopaths.[95]

In contrast, there was one type of sex offender believed to benefit particularly by lobotomy: the man who molested young boys. This was hardly surprising since psychosurgery was widely practised on homosexuals who engaged in *consensual* sex acts. Homosexuals who assaulted boys – in other words, men doubly guilty from this standpoint – could scarcely expect to be exempted. In a typical example from the early 1970s a team of neurologists speaking at the Second International Conference on Psychosurgery in 1972 forcefully contended that 'degenerate, perverse sexual drives' (by which they meant homosexuality) were linked to cerebral structures. Lobotomy would weaken if not abolish altogether the 'persistent distressing pressure of the sexual drive' and, unlike either surgical or chemical castration, it had no depressive side effects.

Thirty-year-old 'J.' was one of their patients. J. was a long-standing child molester, claiming to have had sex with over one hundred boys over the previous decade. He had been imprisoned twice for his activities but prison only seemed to make his abusive sexual urges worse (the neurologists observed that his 'homosexual drives were stimulated through seduction by other prisoners').* Psychoanalysis had failed, and chemical castration with the anti-androgen CPA had lessened his sexual drive but failed to eradicate desire. On 4 June 1970 the three neurologists lobotomized J. They claimed that the result was 'one of the quickest returns from perversion to normal sexual adjustment' they had witnessed. Within five months, they could report, J.'s 'pedophilic sexual drive seems to be extinguished'. Indeed, he had actually developed a phobia of male children. Given the fact that J. relished violence, their bland observation that the operation had radically altered his attitude to adult females was more disturbing: the presence of women now 'excites him sexually', they trumpeted. Normality had returned.[96]

J. had undoubtedly abused many young boys and if that was brought to a halt, then the lobotomy 'worked'. But, as with castration, evidence of success was highly problematic. In most cases sexual desire and behaviour either did not change at all after the operation (as with Howard) or actually worsened. Even the two most strident advocates of lobotomy,

*This is discussed in Chapter 12, 'The Prison'.

Walter Jackson Freeman and James Winston Watts (authors of major textbooks on psychosurgery), gave examples of patients who were adversely affected by the procedure. In one case the patient began demanding frequent sexual relations with his wife and, when she refused, beat her mercilessly. In another case the patient's behaviour became more sexually erratic after lobotomy. He masturbated continually in public and would 'slap the nurse on the rump every time she got within reach'. He seemed incapable of understanding why the nurses became upset, insisting that he whacked them because they were 'so soft and nice and pudgy'.[97] Opponents of the operation sneered that surgeons might as well leave the brain alone and simply cut off a criminal's penis since this would be even more efficacious in reducing his capacity for mischief.[98]

Civil libertarians also attacked the procedure. In Michigan, for example, lobotomy was introduced as part of an experiment to see whether it was more effective than anti-androgen therapy in reducing sexual compulsions in sexually violent criminals. Since these men had been committed for an indefinite period under sexual-psychopathology statutes, their consent could hardly have been freely given.[99] The meaning ascribed to the effects of lobotomy was also under dispute. Lobotomy had been a favourite way to 'cure' homosexuality: the burgeoning Gay Pride movement stopped such abhorrent practices.[100] Indeed (again, like the other treatments I look at in this chapter), an important question was whether psychosurgery was a form of treatment at all. Lobotomy was simply another form of punishment. More to the point, there was simply no evidence that criminal behaviour was the result of cerebral dysfunction in the first place.[101]

These critiques were not universally shared. The author of *The Limits of the Criminal Sanction* (1968) maintained that lobotomy could be considered a form of rehabilitation because one of its effects was the reduction of those 'aggressive drives that impel one toward criminal activity'. He admitted that it was 'not a very selective procedure' because it was incapable of discriminating between the drives. As a consequence, a lobotomized man was 'as unlikely to do anything useful as he is to do anything destructive'. Nonetheless, if lobotomy reduced an individual's 'drive toward criminality', it constituted rehabilitation. The fact that the rehabilitation was 'not invited' and was 'accomplished at the cost of a profound alteration in the patient's personality' was 'irrelevant', the author maintained, so long as the 'immediate goal' of pacification had been achieved.[102]

Some physicians went further; the fact that the individual 'preferred not to undergo' the operation was actually a *positive* feature. For lawyer Richard Delgado one of the benefits of lobotomy was that it deterred others from following in their criminal footsteps. Because radical organic treatments like lobotomy caused dramatic changes in an individual's personality, it was 'a form of mini-death, in which the pre-treatment (offender) personality ceased to exist and a new identity arose in his place'. The fear of this 'mini-death' might 'prove as effective as incarceration in deterring individuals from committing violent crimes', he maintained.[103] It was an argument taken a step further by inmates who underwent invasive treatments in order to cure them of uncontrollable rage. The operations apparently being successful, they claimed that they were literally new men. Each demanded release from prison on the grounds that 'he' had not committed any crime.[104] Important ontological questions are involved here: where does 'the individual' reside? If all traces of violent behaviour could be eradicated by organic therapies, is there anyone who could be called a 'rapist'? Are criminal or pathological acts separate from an individual's identity? If this is the case, punishing this individual served no purpose in terms of either retribution or deterrence. The 'new man' of this biomedical dream could be rendered innocent, his slate wiped clean.

The Behaviourist Revolution

Invasive techniques such as sterilization, castration and lobotomy, presupposed that sexual violence was the result of physical pathology rather than cultural practice. Not everyone agreed. Instead of a physical malfunctioning, could sexual aggression be a form of social conditioning and malfunctioning? The influential behaviourist school answered 'yes'. Their ways of attacking the problem turned out to be as invasive as those who turned to knives and chemicals.

The behaviourist revolution was sparked by the work of psychologists, notably John B. Watson, who argued, from the 1920s onwards, that people were creations of their environment rather than their genes. From infancy onwards individuals responded to signals and stimuli that subtly conditioned them to act in particular ways. Behaviourist ideology was in harmony with the democratic Zeitgeist: discriminatory environments corrupted the basic equality of all individuals.[105]

It was not until the 1960s that behaviourist insights began to be systematically applied to the treatment of sex offenders. According to behaviourists, men who commit acts of sexual aggression have been conditioned to respond erotically to violence in their fantasy life. Actual sexual experiences, as well as exposure to pornography and violence in films, are 'incorporated in the masturbatory fantasies of a subset of individuals', gradually becoming 'closely associated with sexual excitement, pleasure, and orgasm'. Because a link is forged between violent fantasies and the attainment of certain 'rewards' (such as orgasm), these men became conditioned to aggressive sexual behaviour.[106] Anti-social sexual interests either develop as a form of positive conditioning (that is, a chance association between sexual arousal and a deviant object of desire) or arise out of repeated masturbation to a deviant fantasy which serves to build up and maintain that particular sexual interest. In other words, sexually violent fantasies that were conceived and reinforced in masturbation eventually lead to the 'acting out' of rape. These men were so conditioned to associate sexual pleasure with violence that they could get 'turned on' in no other way. Incarceration made the situation worse. As one person observed in relation to the Glenthorpe Centre in Birmingham (England) for serious adolescent sex offenders, 'many boys, deprived of access to the usual kinds of sexually arousing situations to which most adolescents are exposed, masturbate to fantasies surrounding their offence, which in some cases is their only experience of sexual contact'.

According to classical conditioning theory, this is how sexually deviant fantasies become 'set' in an individual's psyche.[107] In other words, the main motivation for rape is sexual arousal in the presence of rape cues. Fantasy and performance are inextricably intertwined.

The purpose of treatment therefore is to correct this distorted thinking or 'cognitive distortion', thus changing the pattern of deviant arousal. Since all forms of behaviour are learned, they can be unlearned. Obviously learning took place most effectively during and immediately after initial arousal.

So, before therapy could commence, the psychologist had to discover the sexually exciting 'cue'. Once again the male sexual body was the source of all truth. Sexual arousal was most commonly measured through changes in skin temperature, variations in blood pressure or (most popularly) changes in penile length or circumference.[108] Technology played a main role. The penile plethysmograph, for instance, was a much-loved instrument. It had been invented in 1908 for use in animal research. After being adapted for studying male impotence, it crossed over into human criminological studies in the 1970s.[109] The instrument was a pressure-sensitive ring or tube filled with mercury. After this was placed around the penis the male subject would be shown images or recorded accounts of sexual situations while a computerized monitor recorded changes in the circumference of the penis. In most cases arousal would be analysed in terms of ratios: the level of arousal to 'inappropriate material' (such as rape) would be compared with the level of arousal when the subject was shown 'appropriate material' (consensual adult sexual activity). In the 1990s nearly one-third of programmes for adult sex offenders used some version of a phallometric test.[110] There was a version for female offenders: a vaginal photoplethysmograph measured 'arousal-dependent measures', such as the blood pressure, pulse rate and pulse amplitude of the vagina and how long arousal lasted.[111]

Once the person's pattern of arousal had been identified, an attempt was made to either dampen down levels of arousal or change its focus. The most dramatic technique employed was aversion therapy, a form of conditioning that attempted to unhitch sexual pleasure from its link with deviant fantasies through employing noxious stimuli (such as painful electric shocks) or malodorous substances (valeric acid or rotting tissue extract), in association with images or recordings of the prohibited sexual activity.[112] In some regimes patients were encouraged to imagine distressing images (of being arrested or stabbed while attempting a rape, for instance). The patient would be gradually taught to pair the urge to rape with these aversive stimuli and images.

This could be done in many ways. The simplest form of aversion therapy involved wearing an elastic band around the wrist. Whenever the offender had a deviant sexual thought, he was to pull the band taut and then release it, stinging his skin.[113] But such a method was largely ineffective with serious offenders, especially if they lacked a powerful desire to eradicate their sexual fantasies.

In most cases a tougher approach was required. In a typical case the patient chose three fantasies from those that produced the largest penile response. Each fantasy would be divided into segments, moving from thinking about engaging in the deviant behaviour to approaching a situation in which such behaviour usually occurred, seeking out the object, approaching it, engaging in the behaviour, and finally reaching orgasm. Images of each segment would be mounted on a screen in front of the patient and the fantasies taped, with a three-second pause between each of the segments. The patient would then be led through each segment. Immediately before the pauses the therapist would be heard saying 'stop', then the patient would receive an electric shock. It was hoped that this 'stop' would become a 'conditioned punisher'. At first shocks were given at each segment, but gradually the shocks would occur less frequently, although the therapist's 'stop' would still be heard.

In other cases the patient would be taught relaxing exercises and encouraged to imagine various scenes, including those stimulating or relating to the offending behaviour, at which point the therapist would hold an uncapped bottle of valeric acid or other foul extract under the patient's nose. As one therapist boasted, 'valeric acid seemed appropriate for it not only assaults the olfactory senses with an odor benignly termed foul, but it adds a certain human decaying property'. Practitioners of this technique claimed to have great success. The treatment was cheap and efficient. A bottle of valeric acid could be purchased cheaply from any chemical supply firm and the therapist did not even need to be present for much of the therapy since up to 80 per cent of the 'scene presentations' could be pre-recorded.[114]

Another therapy went even further. The drug anectine produced total muscle paralysis and suspended respiration. When it was given to patients they remained aware of what was going on around them but could not respond in any way. In an experiment at the California Medical Facility (a 'medical-penal complex' in Vacaville) patients were placed on a trolley and injected with 20–40 mg of anectine. While the patient was under the influence of the drug yet unable to respond the physician would repeatedly remind him that his behaviour was 'dangerous to others or to himself'. He would be told that he had to 'stop the behaviour in question' or he would be repeatedly subjected to aversion treatments. During this berating, which lasted about two minutes, the patient would be unable to breathe. When it was over, an oxygen mask would be applied, to reiterate the 'symbolic aspects' of the procedure, with the physician as the 'omnipotent, benevolent parent figure who holds the power of life and death'. It was, as one psychiatrist admitted, a procedure that 'perhaps borders on torture and threat of torture'.[115]

Anectine treatment was not the only one based on the principle 'no pain, no gain'. Shocks were also used as negative reinforcements, and were particularly effective when paired with positive reinforcements. An illustration of this approach can be seen in the case of homosexual paedophiles. Until the 1970s behaviourists had targeted the 'homosexual' part of the diagnosis 'homosexual paedophile': in other words, they attempted to 'cure' men of their liking for other men. In that decade, however, more 'progressive' programmes began to emerge that stressed the coercive nature of these men's activities (the 'paedophile' part) rather than the choice of partner. Radically, behavourists instigated programmes that attempted to persuade these men to engage in *consensual* activities with adult men, as opposed to attempting to shift their sexual orientation towards women. In the words of Robert Kohlenberg, employed in the 1970s by the Center for Psychological Services and Research at the University of Washington (Seattle), adult males were 'chosen as the positive sex object because the patient's social contacts were all homosexual and heterosexual sex was not one of the therapeutic goals requested by the patient'. Kohlenberg's report on treating a thirty-four-year-old man (Mr M.) who had been arrested twice for molesting young male children was published in the *Journal of Abnormal Psychology*. The first phase of the treatment involved reducing the sexual arousal value of children by pairing imagined stimuli with electric shocks. Kohlenberg used a Lehigh Valley 551-12 finger shocker, with the 'shock intensity' set at 'a level judged to be painful by Mr M.'. Sessions were arranged in which Mr M. was asked to imagine a sexual scene with a male child and, when Mr M. indicated that the imaginative scene was especially vivid, the therapist would depress a button and deliver a shock.

This form of aversive conditioning seemed to be progressing slowly, so Kohlenberg refocused attention to redirecting sexual arousal towards consenting adult males. This was done by procuring a 'suitable', adult partner who would be willing to commit himself to at least ten weeks of therapy sessions involving at least two sexual 'encounters' with Mr M. each week. Eventually a thirty-two-year-old friend of Mr M. was recruited. This friend was instructed to caress Mr M. in bed and, in order to relieve any 'performance anxiety' in Mr M., to proceed to genital touching only after weeks of this non-genital stroking. The treatment was pronounced a success within thirteen weeks as Mr M. gradually transferred his sexual arousal response from children to the adult male friend.[116]

Aversion reconditioning – such as giving Mr M. painful shocks – was a severe approach; a desperate measure for desperate men. The second form of treatment used on Mr M. was gentler, seeking not to suppress deviant behaviour so much as to induce desirable behaviour. Procuring a living sex partner was not always necessary. In other forms of orgasmic reconditioning patients could be encouraged to masturbate to pornographic material and encouraged to gradually substitute pornography depicting 'legitimate' fantasies for those depicting their deviant fantasies.[117] In some clinics patients were taught to substitute 'normal heterosexual fantasies in place of [their] sexually aggressive fantasies during masturbation', while in others there was a gradual 'fading' of the 'source of a patient's erection response' from a deviant object (arousal to a young child, for example) to a non-deviant one (an adult woman).[118] For ethical reasons the deviant fantasies were often presented in audio, rather than visual, media: some abuses were too sensitive to photograph (although audiotapes could also be extremely graphic, in some cases including depictions of the rape of actual previous victims).[119] The success or otherwise of these behavioural modification techniques was measured with a phallometric instrument.[120] The penis thus took on a life of its own as the truth-telling organ. It was a construction of men as split selves, with their mind in charge of rationality but always at risk of being overruled by the penis.[121]

In conjunction with behaviourist approaches to sexual violence, the focus on malformed masculinity encouraged the introduction of 'social skills training' and its innumerable variants (such as 'life management skills training', 'intimacy training' and 'impression management'). These schemes were all designed to give men who had sexually offended some basic tips about conducting relationships in a healthy manner.[122] If, as one forensic psychiatrist diagnosed it, rape was a 'courtship disorder', that is, a flawed performance of 'normal' courtship behaviour, then men could be trained out of it.[123] Social skills training threw together a hotchpotch of elements, including sex instruction, sensitivity and empathy training, lessons in communicating more effectively and exercises in dealing with emotions such as anger, frustration and anxiety.[124] In some institutions offenders were required to 'go out' on informal dates within the prison with (often understandably reluctant) female employees of the prison.[125] As 'John', imprisoned for his part in a gang rape, explained it,

> I've had social skills where they show you how to communicate with people and get away from your shyness and try to be more outward instead of inward. There's female therapists that teach you different skills. They have games that you play . . . And then sometimes you're filmed, and they show the films back on you, and they show you how you done, whether you had any hand movement, whether you had good eye contact, whether the volume of your voice was well enough.

He was also taught how to 'pick up' women and how to 'communicate with them, how to make that first approach'. Dating itself was co-opted as a new form of disciplinary power.

The schemes had its critics, however. Subjecting rapists to personality tests led to contradictory results, with some showing that rapists possessed poor social skills, while others showed the opposite.[126] Furthermore, critics queried, wasn't social-skills training based on a dubious premise? Didn't it imply that unless rapists were about to 'carry out the preliminary conversation, flirting, and other dating skills antecedent to a relationship', they would not have 'the opportunity to become involved sexually with the female (except by rape)'?[127] Most pertinently, as I showed in the previous chapter, a powerful feminist critique insisted that rape was linked with the pleasures of exerting power.[128] Might men who underwent such training simply use their newly honed social skills to augment their repertoire of ways to abuse women?[129]

Invasive procedures like sterilization, castration and lobotomy assumed that rape arose primarily as a result of uncontrollable sexual urges. The behaviourist revolution focused on the instrumentally calibrated rise and fall of the penis, albeit dictated by a culturally constructed fantasy life. Sexual desire itself remained sacrosanct: sex offenders simply needed to find legitimate ways to express it and thus gain access to compliant sexual partners.

Throughout the nineteenth and twentieth centuries the sarcastic quip that excising the entire male genitalia was the only truly effective way of rendering the rapist harmless was repeated. In contrast with dualistic conceptions of Woman as Body and Man as Mind, these narratives conceived of men as weighed down by a capricious body, an independent penis requiring disciplinary interventions. Invasive techniques that fell just short of drastic mutilation arose precisely because they seemed modern, rational, calculable ways of reducing suffering. When these therapies were carried out without overt physical pain, they were regarded as even more progressive. Edward De Grazia, writing in the *University of Chicago Law Review* in the mid-1950s, was not impressed. These therapies, he reminded readers, had been presented as the 'humanistic, scientific, psychiatric answer to inhuman, barbaric, legal punishment by imprisonment'. However, if they were efficacious, wasn't it because the 'patient' experienced them as simply alternative types of physical and psychological punishment? De Grazia mused that defendants might wish to think twice before submitting an insanity plea: the 'certain austerity of the prison' might be preferable to the risk of psychologically painful as well as physically distressing treatment within psychiatric hospitals.[130] Sterilization, castration, lobotomy and behaviourist interventions were forms of disguised punishment. In the name of treatment and for the good of civilization, physicians and psychologists were co-opted into the penal system, becoming the chief experts in creating a hierarchy of humanity, with African-Americans, immigrants and homosexuals labelled the most 'suitable' criminal subjects for radical intervention.

It was no wonder that there was considerable resistance from within the prison system. Men accused or convicted of sex crimes refused to cooperate. In one major survey, less than half of all sex offenders wanted treatment and the most frequently used therapy – aversion therapy – was regarded as least acceptable by these criminals.[131] As the 'Credo' for the group Prisoners Against Rape stated in the mid-1970s, 'we are against chemotherapy, psychosurgery, and aversion therapy, and all methods that falsely change the mental attitudes of human beings by making them mechanical robots *forced* to do the "right" thing'. They insisted that the only legitimate treatment was 're-education of the self, true evaluation of the causes of rape, group discussion among the individuals affected by or effecting rape'.[132] Such statements were partly a reflection of a shift in discourse from the medicalized languages of effectiveness towards the legal languages of rights. However, as I shall be arguing in the next chapter, on psychiatry, it also represented an alternative vision of the integral self.

CHAPTER SEVEN

The Couch (and Other Interior Therapies)

The deeply impoverished and morally upright parents of one of the most infamous sex criminals in mid-twentieth-century America christened their son Carol. As soon as he was able, Carol Chessman jettisoned his Danish-inspired name,* adopted the name Caryl and threw

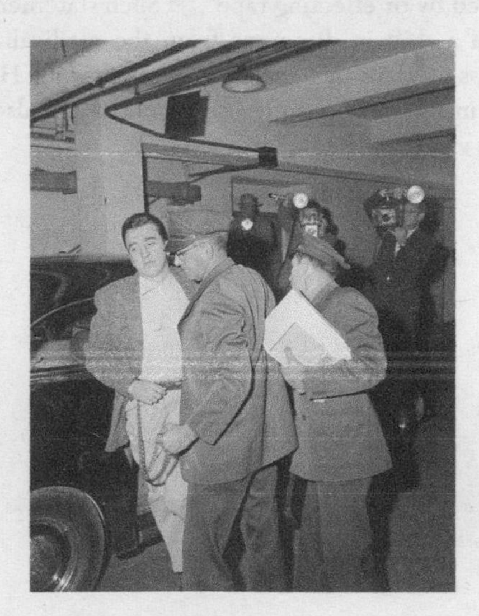

Caryl Chessman

*In Denmark it would have been spelt 'Karil'.

himself enthusiastically into petty crime. [See photograph, p. 180.] Six feet tall, with a permanent sneer, hooked nose and thick black hair that rapidly receded into a prominent widow's peak, Chessman unfortunately looked like a villain. In the guise of the 'red light bandit', he terrorized Los Angeles in 1948, attacking young couples in lonely areas, robbing them and sometimes forcing the women to perform fellatio on him. For these crimes he was sentenced to death.

Although he always proclaimed his innocence, in a number of autobiographies he eloquently made the case that people who endangered society did not 'spring full grown from Hell'. Sexual aggressors 'hunger emotionally', he wrote. They

> need love. They need to feel wanted; they want to belong. But reality can treat them harshly, cruelly. Fear can enter their lives, a fear that is ugly and unreasonable. They can develop terrible feelings of guilt, of inadequacy, of being unloved, unwanted, rejected, alone.

Inevitably they rebelled and this rebellion transported them 'into a jungle world' where they embraced 'a cause – crime'. This 'jungle world' distorted their minds, making them 'sick'. Yes, Chessman admitted, rapists 'commit terrible crimes', but they were

> abnormal men and their abnormality is a sickness, not a revolting mystery of the soul. Society is reluctant to recognize this fact . . . for such an attitude, it is felt mistakenly, would relieve the individual of responsibility and undermine society's power to punish.

Just as it was wrong to argue that because the hand holds the gun 'the robber's hand is the reason for the robbery', so too it was not the 'generative organs' themselves that 'determine[d] the manner in which our sex drives [were] overtly expressed', but those 'psychological-environmental laws'.[1]

Chessman sold over half a million copies of his autobiographical *Cell 2455 Death Row* (1954) and it was translated into eighteen languages. He wrote another two memoirs and one novel, and his life was immortalized in a Lenny Bruce stage routine, a 1955 feature film (named after his first memoir), the television film 'Kill Me If You Can' (1977) and a popular song by Ronnie Hawkins entitled 'The Ballad of Caryl Chessman (Let Him Live, Let Him Live)'.[2] [See photograph, p. 182, of the advertisement for the 1955 film.] Chessman's stark

Caryl Chessman's 'Cell 2455, Death Row', poster of the film

exposition of how the criminal mind was forged swayed many influential commentators to speak out against capital punishment. Eleanor Roosevelt, Billy Graham, Pablo Casals, Aldous Huxley, Ray Bradbury, William Inge, Norman Mailer, Dwight MacDonald, Christopher Isherwood, Carey McWilliams and Robert Frost supported his appeal not to be put to death. However, Chessman's insistence that something called 'society' was responsible for creating sex fiends infuriated other critics, who saw the argument as an attempt by criminals to evade responsibility. After eight stays of execution the Governor of California (ironically, an avowed opponent of capital punishment) eventually allowed the death sentence against Chessman to be carried out. He was executed in the pale-green basement gas chamber of San Quentin on 2 May 1960. [See image, below.]

The execution of Caryl Chessman

Rapists are bad men, evil even. But might they also be mad? More controversially, might insanity excuse their actions? Chessman's books were autobiographical meditations on such questions. But these questions have been increasingly debated in courtrooms, mental asylums and doctors' surgeries from the nineteenth century. Alienists as well as people within the burgeoning professions of psychiatry and neurology started claiming to have knowledge superior to that of jurists and penologists in understanding sexually aggressive men. They were also progressively more likely to insist on their right to dictate the fate of this class of criminal. It was now the responsibility of the 'medical expert to enlighten the jurists', observed a prominent neurologist in 1905. Medical authorities were uniquely capable of deciding whether 'immorality or abnormality occasioned a certain sexual act'. Analysis of 'the perpetrator and not the crime' would eventually reveal the causes and cures for sexual violence.[3] Henceforth these authorities argued, the rapist was to be defined by an inner identity or personality ('a rapist'), not an outward act.

Moral Insanity

In order to distinguish between the 'mad' and the 'bad', there had to be some criteria for separating normal from abnormal. Late-eighteenth-century jurists embraced a Lockean philosophical framework in which humanity was defined in terms of reason. When individuals lost the ability to think rationally – when they exhibited delusions, for instance – they could be designated as insane. This definition of insanity was condensed in English law in M'Naghten's Rules of 1843. The rules were named after Daniel M'Naghten, who, while under the delusion that the government was persecuting him, killed the Prime Minister's Secretary, whom he mistook for the Prime Minister.[4] One of the Rules stipulated that

> To establish a defence on the ground of insanity it must be clearly proved that at the time of committing the act, the accused was labouring under such a defect of reason, from disease of the mind, as not to know the nature and quality of the act he was doing, or if he did know it, that he did not know he was doing what was wrong.[5]

Not knowing what one was doing and being unable to distinguish between right and wrong were the hallmarks of insanity.

For some commentators this was a particularly narrow definition of insanity. Didn't it simply generalize from the symptoms of one class of mental disorder (delusional states, for instance) to all classes?[6] Even before the M'Naghten Rules had been established, alternative definitions had been discussed, all of which had long-term implications for dealing with sex offenders. The most important of these definitions was that of 'moral insanity'. The term was coined by the physician and ethnologist James Cowles Prichard in *A Treatise on Insanity, and Other Disorders Affecting the Mind* (1835). It was defended by some of the most eminent psychiatrists of the time, including the leading English alienist Henry Maudsley. Prichard defined moral insanity as

> madness consisting in a morbid perversion of the natural feelings, affections, inclinations, temper, habits, moral dispositions, and natural impulses, without any remarkable disorder or defect of the intellect or knowing and reasoning faculties, and particularly without any insane illusion or hallucination.[7]

It was a widely employed concept. In 1890, for instance, Havelock Ellis described the morally insane as characterized by

> an incapacity to feel, or to act in accordance with, the moral conditions of social life. Such persons . . . are morally blind; the psychic retina has become anæsthetic. The egoistic impulses have become supreme; the moral imbecile is indifferent to the misfortunes of others, and to the opinions of others; with cold logic he calmly goes on his way, satisfying his personal interest and treading under foot the rights of other.

Although such men were morally 'defective', they were often intelligent and capable of thinking in abstract terms. As a consequence, they were able to 'maintain anti-social theories with much skill'.[8]

Under such a definition of insanity, alienists were able to argue that a particular individual was suffering from *diminished* responsibility, that is, he or she recognized the distinction between right and wrong but was unable to choose between them. This was a dramatic departure from conceptions of insanity that emphasized the loss of intellectual reasoning powers. Indeed, in Prichard's reformulation, reason as the supreme arbiter of humanity was jettisoned. Instead the brain was conceived as possessing several components, one dealing with reason and another with morality or emotion. As a consequence, an individual could be both intellectually sane and morally or emotionally insane.

Some elements of insanity, in other words, could coexist with other elements of sanity.

It was a controversial view. Critics worried that the term 'moral insanity' could become an expedient substitute for words like vice or depravity.[9] Were concepts such as moral culpability and free will to be recklessly jettisoned? Writing in 1900, New York neurologist B. Sachs asked whether it was possible to separate moral and intellectual spheres? If the term 'moral insanity' was to be employed, he continued, it should be reserved for patients whose most prominent symptom was a 'defective moral sense'. Sachs presented as an example the case of a young man who had sexually assaulted and attempted to murder his mother. When asked to explain himself, the man had replied: 'you might as well kill your mother as anyone else'. Sachs was willing to diagnose this young man as suffering from moral insanity because he 'had received no intellectual or moral training, had received no religious instruction, had grown up among the most degenerate of mankind, and had never received the most ordinary moral teachings. Naturally the moral sense was deficient.'[10] In extreme cases only, Sachs argued, moral insanity might be diagnosed: the vast majority of sex offenders exhibited no such inner defects.

Critics were also anxious lest the principle of just retribution was going to be replaced by a diagnosis of moral insanity. The eminent American medico-legal theorist Francis Wharton, made the point strongly in *A Treatise on Mental Unsoundness* (1873). He argued that even 'moral lunatics' possessed some 'flickering of conscience' which education could either 'develop or pervert'. In most insane criminals there still existed 'such an amount of responsibility as to require the infliction of a degree of punishment which, though different from that imposed on the sane, will yet be accompanied with a corrective as well as a preventive discipline'. Wharton reminded his readers that one of the functions of law was to 'educate reason and give it supremacy, by penalty'. 'Sin is to be punished because it is Sin,' he thundered.[11]

The Psychoanalytic Contribution

If critics of the notion of 'moral insanity' thought they had triumphed, they were wrong. General medical practitioners as well as the newly established profession of psychiatry enthusiastically applied Prichard's very specific use of the term to a vast range of aberrant behaviours.

Although its later uses would have appalled Prichard, a version of moral insanity was revived in the form of 'psychopathy' later in the century.*

Both Locke's and Prichard's methods of distinguishing sanity from insanity were anathema to Freudian psychoanalysts. Instead of focusing on insanity, psychoanalytical approaches drew attention to the influence of normal processes of the unconscious and infantile sexuality in creating individuals whose sexual practices were aberrant. The sexual pervert (a definition which covered a range of individuals from exhibitionists to violent rapists) displays residues of infantile sexuality that have failed to be integrated into the adult self, Sigmund Freud argued in *Three Essays on the Theory of Sexuality* (1905). As a result, all the savagery of infantile fantasy is enacted in sexual relations.[12] This helped to explain the ambivalence many people felt about sex crimes: rape or sexual assault evoked (in the words of one psychiatrist) 'an echo, albeit a grotesquely distorted one, from the infantile depths of the unconscious mind of everyone'.[13]

In contrast with the keenness with which psychiatrists adopted Freudian ideas about child sexuality, paedophilia and incest, it took half a century for Freudian understanding of sexuality and crime to be applied to rapists of *adults*. When applied, it was revolutionary. The most significant probe into the usefulness of Freudian concepts for the understanding of sex crimes was carried out by Benjamin Karpman, chief psychotherapist at Saint Elizabeth's Hospital in Washington DC and author of *The Sexual Offender and his Offenses* (1954). According to Karpman, sex offenders were neither criminals nor perverts. In fact, most were not mental defectives either (although those who were mentally subnormal were much more likely to be caught).[14] Karpman insisted that these individuals, when looked at scientifically, could only be described as psychiatrically ill. Sexual offenders were 'victims of a disease from which many of them suffer more than their victims', he controversially claimed.[15]

For Karpman the central mystery was the criminal's motivation, not the nature of the crime. Instead of distinguishing criminals on the basis of whether their offence had been committed against property, the person or morals, he urged that criminals be classified according to whether they acted in a predatory (in which case they might be

*This is discussed at greater length in Chapter 10, 'Sexual Psychopaths'.

psychopathic) or an emotional manner (in which case the psychiatrist should look for psychoneurotic tendencies). Crime was 'a disease at the psycho-social level'. It was not something 'detachable or independent of the criminal', but was 'entirely a part and parcel of him'. In this way Karpman was influential in creating a discrete human category, a unique personage – 'the rapist'.

Since the important factor in crime was the 'doer and not the deed' psychiatric intervention was essential. Rapists were neurotics who could be cured in much the same way as physicians cured anxiety, depression or gastric ulcers.[16] Like other neurotics, rapists were desperate men, plagued by numerous insecurities at emotional, economic and environmental levels. In seeking to 'obtain mastery' over their lives, they lashed out at 'society' (Karpman did not specify 'females') in the hope of 'freeing themselves from tension and regaining self-esteem'. This meant that their repetitive and perverse sexual acts served to 'reduce tension' by enabling them to regress to 'less complex, earlier, outmoded but previously satisfying' patterns of sexual behaviour.[17] According to this model, rehabilitation had to take priority over retribution. Just as 'no sensible physician would think of punishing a typhoid carrier for having infected others', Karpman reasoned, so too criminals should be provided with treatment and care until cured of their 'germ'.[18]

This was a profoundly influential philosophy, and one that rapidly informed both psychiatric as well as civic discussions. In the psychiatric field men like Nathan Roth (Senior Psychiatrist to the New York State Research Project on the Sexual Offender) echoed, although perhaps not consciously, Karpman's view that rapists were inflicted with a disease that made them 'suffer more than their victims'. Writing in the early 1950s, Roth portrayed the sexual abuser as a man who was powerless in the face of emotional conflicts. It was not simply that these individuals failed to exercise self-control: sex offenders underwent 'the most painful and distressing emotional conflicts' before engaging in activities that even they regarded as 'most reprehensible'. The sex offender was 'not master in his own home'; he was 'powerless before the onslaught of forces within himself which make him disregard even the rules of self-preservation'. What was driving him? In Roth's words, the aggressive sex attack was

> a desperate, ill-considered and frantic attempt to overcome wounded pride, to repair injured self-esteem and to escape mortification. The

> rapist who overpowers a woman unfamiliar to him is symbolically trying to force warmth and acceptance from the woman who has held herself aloof in her contempt for him.

The aim in molesting women therefore was not sexual gratification, but an 'irrational' demonstration that he could 'win acceptance'. In order to 'muster the courage and aggressiveness to engage in such behavior', the sex offender had 'to borrow from the lessons of harshness and insensitivity to which he was exposed as a child'.[19] Rape was therefore attributed to aloof, contemptuous women and mothers who failed in their duty of love to protect the boy-child from a ruthless world.

In civic discussions, too, these psychoanalytical insights were increasingly used to explain sex crimes. Here, too, Karpman's comparison with typhoid victims proved popular. Thus, speaking to a group of parents and policemen in 1947, psychiatrist Philip Piker emphasized time and again that the sex offender was 'sick'. 'I am not recommending that sex offenders be coddled,' he hastened to add, 'any more than I would recommend that a patient with typhoid fever be coddled'. However, the 'typhoid fever victim needs to be treated and cured for his own sake, because he is a sick human being; and – please note this – he also needs to be cured so that he will not infect others, and not remain a menace to society'.[20] The unspoken assumption behind the typhoid metaphor was that the man labelled 'sex offender' could be *forcibly* 'treated' – a problematic proposition within psychoanalytical thought, introducing an authoritarian twist into analytical practice.

Some psychiatrists sought to delve deeper than this, and interrogate the very assumptions underpinning Freudian ideas. In the 1950s, for instance, E. F. Hammer, Senior Research Scientist at the Psychiatric Institute, New York, set out to test the psychoanalytical notion that rape represented a response to severe castration anxiety. According to this hypothesis, rapists may be seeking to mask their fears of castration by employing their penises in aggressive ways, thus reassuring themselves of their continued phallic mastery. In a different conceptualization rape could be a way of 'identifying with the aggressor'. As Otto Fenichel put it in *The Psychoanalytic Theory of Neurosis* (1946), sexual sadism was 'a reassurance against castration fear . . . If sexual pleasure is disturbed by anxiety, it is comprehensible that an "identification with the aggressor" can be a relief. If a person is able to do to others what he fears may be done to him, he no longer has to be afraid.'[21]

Hammer decided to test these explanations. Eighty men incarcerated in Sing Sing Prison were to serve as his experimental subjects. Sixty had been convicted of rape or paedophilia and twenty (the 'control group') had been convicted of non-sexual offences. All were given 'projective tests' such as the Rorschach Test and the House-Tree-Person (H-T-P) Test, designed to see how they 'projected' their personality or psychopathology when presented with ambiguous objects. Since, if his theory was correct, rapists should express greater castration anxiety than other men, Hammer then employed a number of clinical psychologists to rate the intensity of castration anxiety reflected in the results.

The outcome was striking. Ninety per cent of the sex offenders were found to express marked or moderate castration feelings, compared with 55 per cent of the control group. For instance, in the H-T-P Test, sex offenders frequently portrayed tree branches, arms, noses, legs and feet as severed, broken or withered. Typical responses to the Rorschach Test (in which the men were shown symmetrical ink blots and asked to describe what they saw) included comments such as 'dog looks back at his mutilated tail', 'bent and distorted penis', 'withered finger' and 'fish with sharp teeth, wowie, dangerous looking'. To explain why just over half of the *non*-sexual offenders also revealed castration fears, Hammer argued that 'this is a group of persons whose actions, frequently with a gun or knife, also suggest the use of compensation to cloak feelings of inadequacy as men'. Nevertheless, the much higher level of castration anxiety of the sex offenders was proof for Hammer that castration feelings were the 'motivational mainspring behind the sex offences'. Rape was the rapist's attempt to 'rid himself of the intolerable inner tension'. The fact that most of the sex offenders claimed that they obtained little or no sexual pleasure from their actions was further evidence that the act of rape was 'in the service of the reduction of anxiety rather than aimed predominantly towards sexual gratification and enjoyment'.[22]

Hammer was intrigued by another finding: not all sex offenders responded the same way to their underlying castration conflicts. Men who raped adults could be distinguished from those who attacked children. In raping adults, Hammer concluded, men attempted to cloak castration feelings by overriding them, while paedophiles submitted to castration feelings by choosing non-threatening sexual partners.[23] Furthermore, it was possible to use the H-T-P Test to demonstrate 'degrees' of psychopathology. This time he tested eighty-four sex offenders in Sing Sing, some of whom he called 'normal rapists' (that is, men who raped adult women) while others he classified as either heterosexual or homosexual paedophiles. Hammer assumed that individuals were more likely to attribute emotionally disturbing negative traits to the Tree than to the Person, because when drawing a tree there was less need for 'ego-defensive maneuvers' (put another way, drawing a scarred tree with truncated branches was psychologically easier than drawing a mutilated person with truncated arms). After asking these sex offenders to draw, on separate sheets of paper (each of 8.5 × 7 inches), a House, a Tree, and a Person, Hammer went on to analyse their tree drawings. Just over 6 per cent of rapists claimed to have drawn a dead tree, compared with 15 per cent of heterosexual paedophiles and 30 per cent of homosexual paedophiles. For Hammer this was proof of increasingly more serious psychopathology in the progression from the rapist, at the one end, to the homosexual paedophile at the other extreme. As he put it, his findings suggested that

> an increasing distance from an appropriate sex object goes hand-in-hand with an increase of the likelihood of serious psychopathology. The homosexual pedophiles, who deviate from the norm in *both* age and sex of the partner chosen, are then to be viewed as the most emotionally crippled.[24]

Hammer's work distinguished sex offenders by level of psychopathology. Other psychiatrists believed it was more accurate to distinguish them by degree of psychosexual immaturity. This model, too, took much of its inspiration from Karpman, who had argued that sexual perversion represented 'not a new phenomenon' but a 'fixation at a lower stage of psychosexual development; a stunting of growth'.[25] Karpman was not by any means the first commentator to make this leap. The notion that sex criminals were 'fixated at a lower stage of psycho-sexual development', as one author put it in 1939, had been around a long time.[26] It was also an explanation that tied neatly into early-twentieth-century fears of the aggressive adolescent. For these commentators sexual aggression by adolescents might simply be a 'developmental step on the road to heterosexual normality'.[27]

Writing in the 1950s, George E. Gardner (Director of the Judge Baker Guidance Center in Boston) was a prominent proponent of the developmental theory. In his writings he included rapists in the same category as homosexuals and exhibitionists. Their 'problem' was the same: at some stage in their development their sexual urges had been diverted from the 'normal' path. In terms of psychic structures the belligerent young man was reverting to the oral aggressiveness typical of young children. He simply had not 'grown out of it'. Sexual violence was a 'disastrous error in the expected maturation process'.

Gardner went one step further than most developmental theorists, however. He linked male aggression to the development of the species. In his words, biologists and psychologists had shown that in the evolutionary history of humanity, from 'the simpler organisms upwards to man', there has been a progressive tendency to separate destructive tendencies from sexual activities. 'Man alone' has succeeded in making this separation. Gardner saw this as an important instance in which 'ontogeny, or the development of the *individual*, to some extent repeats phylogeny, or the history of the *race*'. In the 'aggressive-destructive sexual deviate', however, there was a breakdown in the development of self-control, so that 'the child enters puberty still deriving pleasure from the *actual expression in behaviour* of *person-directed* killing and mutilative impulses'. In other words, in adolescents there persisted 'some of the unresolved, pleasurable, murderous-mutilative components of the aggressive-destructive impulse' left over from an earlier evolutionary stage.[28] Of course, Gardner's description of the evolution of humanity was thoroughly male. The pleasures of aggression he waxed so lucidly about were possessed by only one half of the species.

The other main psychiatric trend that contributed to this shift from act to actor involved the identification of a 'raping personality'. This approach drew substantially from work that had been done in the 1950s onwards exploring the rapist's 'personality'. T. W. Adorno's *The Authoritarian Personality* (1950) was highly influential in this context, involving an analysis of all 110 inmates convicted of sexually violent offences in San Quentin Prison. These men, Adorno concluded, possessed 'authoritarian personalities': they were aggressive, lazy, sexually uninhibited and they lacked moral scruples as well as social control.[29]

This approach – and the range of schemes and inventories generated – exploded in the 1970s. The traits found in rapists varied according to the inventory. Thus, while some found authoritarian personality components, others found precisely the opposite. The Edwards Personal Preference Schedule, for instance, found that, when compared with 'normal males', rapists were 'less aggressive, less independent and self-motivated, and less self-assured and dominant'. When compared with non-sexual criminals, they tended to be 'less achievement orientated, less self-assured and aggressive, less independent and self-directed, to have less need for change, and a greater need to endure, a lower heterosexual drive, a greater self-criticism and a greater need to nurture others and to be dependent upon others'. For these researchers this confirmed their view that the act of rape was an 'expression of hostility' by men who felt 'weak, inadequate and dependent'.[30] Nothing could have been further from Adorno's aggressive criminals.

Treatment

The diagnosis of a specific 'rapist psychopathology' was the easiest part. Once designated as suffering from castration anxiety, developmental immaturity or personality defects, how should rapists be treated? Psychoanalytically informed commentators almost universally agreed that imprisonment was unhelpful and probably counterproductive. Because the sex criminal was often seeking punishment because of a sense of guilt for some 'imaginary crime of childhood', imprisonment simply played into this fantasy. Incarceration also placed the offender in 'a position of utter childlike dependence' which promoted 'the very infantile drives, the immaturity, from which the crime arose'. In many instances the very harshness of society's punitive response to criminals actually risked promoting further violence, because 'excessive punishment, in doing violence to the offender's "sense of justice", which in his Unconscious took the form of a *lex talionis*, is interpreted by him as advanced payment for future violations, a credit on future crimes'.[31]

So what was to be done? Ideally each rapist needed extensive psychotherapy. This meant timetabling regular fifty-minute sessions between each prisoner and a trained psychoanalyst. Provision would need to span years, if not decades.

Obviously this was not practicable in a penal setting. Instead psychiatrists of an analytical bent experimented with hypnosis and group therapy. Typical hypnosis programmes of the early 1980s were based on relatively few hypnotic sessions with a trained therapist followed by twice-daily auto-hypnotic practice (such as taking a few deep breaths while introducing safe imagery). The aim was to teach the offender to master his castration anxiety.[32] Advantages included the fact that it was easily learned and 'economical in therapist'.[33]

Group therapy was much more successful as well as more popular among psychiatrists. It was used at Wormwood Scrubs from 1949, but the range of programmes accelerated after 1953. Psychodrama, or encouraging patients to act out emotionally charged situations in their lives, and abstract painting (which patients and their therapists then analysed) were two techniques employed in these group settings.[34] Similarly, at the Treatment Unit of the New Jersey Program for Sex Offenders, opened in 1967, a programme called ROARE, or Re-Education of Attitudes and Repressed Emotions, was instituted to encourage sexual offenders along with therapists (a rule that created a problem recruiting staff) to vigorously express anger and 'unmanly hurt' in an attempt to achieve total abreaction.[35] As I point out later, the treatment regimes constantly faced funding constraints and the needs of the penal complex – all problematic, particularly when both diagnosis and the possibilities of cure became increasingly questioned.

Impact

Psychiatric analyses of rapists initially found favour with the general public, even if it was less enthusiastic about the tax bill for the requisite treatment regimes. By the middle of the twentieth century the belief that rapists and other sex offenders were more mad than bad had made headway. 'Which do you think is the best thing to do with sex criminals: send them to hospital or a jail?' the citizens of Louisville were asked in the summer of 1950. Despite extensive publicity given to a recent vicious sex attack, less than a quarter of respondents opted for the punitive response. Men over the age of sixty-five supported imprisonment most vigorously, while men and women with a college education were most prone to favour hospitalization.[36]

Similar attitudes could be seen in Britain by the mid-century. A survey of adults from twenty-three towns and villages in England and Wales in May 1960 established that 66 per cent believed that people who sexually assaulted women and children should 'be given medical treatment and advice rather than punishment alone'. Less than one-third believed they should be 'severely punished'. Once again there were dramatic differences by age and class. Over 70 per cent of respondents in their twenties and thirties endorsed treatment as opposed to punishment alone, compared with just half of respondents over the age of sixty. Middle-class respondents were also more likely than working-class respondents to advocate treatment.[37]

Legally, too, sex offenders were increasingly regarded as having an automatic *right* to treatment. This trend began in the 1930s. By 1943 Wormwood Scrubs and Wakefield had psychiatric units. Provision accelerated from the late 1940s. In Britain the 1948 Criminal Justice

Act emphasized the duty of legal authorities to provide treatment for habitual sex offenders. Within fourteen years Grendon Underwood, Britain's first therapeutic community for sex offenders, had been opened. As Lady Wootton put it succinctly in 1963, this new prison near Aylesbury would 'put the churches and the moralists out of business'. 'Today,' she bravely declaimed, 'Freud and Marx might fairly compete for the title of the biggest popular success since Jesus Christ: and Freud, I think, would win.'[38]

Like most of these initiatives, prisons like Grendon Underwood were directed towards the psychiatric treatment of sex offenders, none of whom could be technically certified as insane.[39] In the words of R. A. ('Rab') Butler, the Home Secretary in 1960, such prisons were to cater for a new understanding of sex criminals. 'It is beyond doubt,' he said, that

> among those who have offended against the law are some who, although they are a danger to society, are very far from being cold, completely sane, deliberate doers of evil . . . The people I am thinking of are not those who are certifiably insane or mentally deficient, but they are, in various ways, mentally abnormal or disturbed and they are not easily amenable to treatment by the ordinary penal methods.

He went on to insist that Grendon Underwood's inmates were to be chosen not by their crime but by their 'personal symptoms of maladjustment'.[40] The shift from crime (act) to criminal personality (identity) was thus institutionalized.

Outside such places, however, theory and practice diverged. Thus Wilfred Johnson, a fifty-eight-year-old man convicted of indecently assaulting young boys between 1945 and 1965, sought help from the prison psychologist (Johnson described him as a 'great big man he was, more like a publican than anything else, very loud-voiced and rude'), who bluntly told him that 'there's no treatment we can give you, so you're wasting my time'.[41] In most prisons, treatment regimes remained meagre. This was not because of lack of attention. The League for Penal Reform had long been lobbying for more effective treatment of offenders. In the same year that the Criminal Justice Act was passed, they sponsored a questionnaire into prison conditions. One prison visitor told them that he had

> met several men convicted for sexual offences – and made a point of checking (unbeknown to them) as to what mental treatment might

> have been attempted. Each admitted *not having seen a Dr for any reason whatsoever*, despite (in at least one case of a man convicted for indecent assault) having pleaded for help.[42]

A year after the legislation, however, there had been little change. The Home Secretary was even forced to admit in Parliament that no drugs aimed at reducing sexual impulses were being administered to sex offenders.[43] The problem was partly financial. As early as 1938, reformers pushing for psychiatric treatment of offenders acknowledged that they had to 'face the facts': 'our desire to hospitalize rather than to imprison sex offenders runs us bump into the fact that there is not room enough in the hospitals for them', pointed out the Commissioner of Correction in New York City.[44] However, scepticism about the efficacy of psychiatric intervention served to discourage any full assault on the punitive model of dealing with rapists, the development I examine next.

Critique

Even though a decisive shift in favour of a psychiatric, as opposed to penal, understanding of sex crimes occurred between the 1950s and the 1980s, opposition to the psychiatric model remained vigorous. The main difficulty facing psychiatrists attempting to convince jurists and penologists to transfer responsibility for sex criminals into their hands was that there was both a bewildering proliferation of diagnoses and a vast array of symptoms that were being lumped together under a limited number of headings. On the one hand, the range of illnesses suffered by rapists seemed never-ending. 'Nearly every variety of mental disorder may have this type of misconduct as a symptom,' grumbled a couple of legal experts in the 1950s: paedophiles could be classified as senile arterio-sclerotics; rapists as post-encephalitics or schizophrenics; exhibitionists as manics.[45] This was probably inevitable given that the 'experts' making the diagnoses were often overworked and often not even trained in psychiatry.[46] According to one review of sex-offender programmes in American institutions in the 1980s, in the seventy-three programmes examined there were 785 different therapies in operation.[47]

On the other hand, sadistic rapists could find themselves placed in the same diagnostic category as masturbators or homosexuals. In books and articles claiming to address the problem of sex crime, I sometimes found it difficult to know if, for instance, the psychiatrist was referring to an adolescent boy ashamed about spontaneous nocturnal emissions or a man mortified by his compulsive habit of prowling the street in search of vulnerable women to rape.

Even more worryingly, psychiatrists' close examination (as opposed to theoretical musings) of rapists often failed to unearth any pathology at all. Of the first one hundred sex offenders sent to Bellevue Hospital in New York for psychiatric evaluation, only fifteen were found to be psychotic while another seven were pronounced mentally defective.[48] Such findings forced Ralph Brancale, the director of the New Jersey Diagnostic Center, and Albert Ellis, the chief psychologist there, to risk the censure of their colleagues by suggesting that rapists were sexually and psychiatrically *normal*. Unlike those of men who exhibited themselves or engaged in consensual homosexual conduct (men that such experts regarded as 'true' sexual deviants), rapists' actions were simply 'an offshoot of their general antisocial behavioural patterns'.[49]

Why were there such diverging views about the psychiatric status of rapists? Perhaps sexually aggressive men really were not different from their non-aggressive brothers. In a nationwide American sample of more than 6100 college students, one in twelve college men admitted to committing rape.[50] In another random sample of 1846 college men, 23 per cent responded 'yes' to the question: 'Have you ever been in a situation where you became so sexually aroused that you could not stop yourself even though the woman didn't want to?'[51]

But even in cases of stranger rapists using violence, finding conclusive evidence of psychiatric pathology was difficult. Part of the problem was that offenders had a great incentive to fake mental illness in order to escape punishment.[52] As a deputy district attorney in Los Angeles argued in the early 1960s, 'Since psychiatric opinions are based entirely on what a prisoner tells the doctor, and because clever prisoners could lie and fool the doctor, reliance upon the work of the psychiatrist is dangerous and a threat to the cause of justice'.[53] Cheating was widespread and relatively easy, especially since 'everyone is, in a sense, an amateur psychiatrist' now, the attorney lamented.[54] Truth was elusive. Popular measuring devices like the penile plethysomograph purported to be able to tell the truth about a man's sexual preferences (for violent sex, for instance) simply by measuring levels of penile arousal while he was watching sexually explicit films. However, as one study revealed, 80 per cent of rapists and child molesters were able to 'voluntarily and completely inhibit arousal in the presence of stimuli that had previously elicited their highest level of arousal'.[55] Of course, the technique was flawed in other ways, too, confusing fantasy and action, and treating the penis as an autonomous agent.

More to the point, did psychotherapeutic interventions cure rapists of their violent propensities? Increasingly, the answer seemed to be 'no', although the risks of carrying out double-blind placebo studies of sexually deviant men meant that no one was really certain.[56] Obviously, however, if most offenders were not suffering from psychiatric problems in the first place, programmes designed to deal with 'deep underlying conflict' were bound to be pointless.[57] But even in cases where there might be evidence of compulsion, therapy often did not help. Harry Mills was a serial offender who had 'every possible treatment that there is: imprisonment, drugs, aversion therapy, group therapy, psycho-therapy – whatever you can think of, you name it and I've had it', but nothing worked. His conclusion about the psychological treatment he received in mental hospitals was 'they work too, they do a lot for me. But it's only while I'm there'. Mills spoke highly of the hospitals he had been sent to, saying that therapy had helped him understand the psychological importance of the fact that he was the result of an incestuous relationship between his mother and her brother and therefore harboured a strong resentment against women. 'I think there's a lot in that,' he admitted, adding, 'but understanding it and learning what it's all about still doesn't seem to make a blind bit of difference you know, when I get outside.'[58]

These were not the only difficulties. Family-based therapies were found to be highly problematic, since it was in the interests of the family that the offender was permanently separated from them rather than reintegrated.[59] As the result of an attempt to adapt treatments to a penal situation, the usefulness of psychotherapy was significantly diluted. For reasons of 'economy and convenience', group therapy was substituted for individual psychotherapy, but many psychiatrists felt that this substitute lacked any 'clear theoretical focus or explicit treatment goals'.[60]

Psychiatrists were also involved in political controversy. Psychotherapeutic responses to sexually violent criminals were highly correlated to race and class. The treatment offered to sexual psychopaths in the USA was rarely given to African-American offenders, for instance*.

*This bias is explored in Chapter 10, 'Sexual Psychopaths'.

Additionally, the provision of psychotherapeutic treatment was biased by socio-economic class. Middle-class sex offenders were considered more suitable for psychotherapeutic treatments. This was potentially problematic. On the one hand, as a prominent prison medical officer in Britain mused in 1955, there was a risk that psychotherapy would be offered to educated criminals while the 'less fortunate' were dumped in prison or labour colonies. Although he admitted that the 'lightest restriction' might have a 'salutary effect on an intelligent man' while a 'duller man may require sterner action', it was dangerous to have one law for the rich and another for the poor.[61] On the other hand, some psychiatrists attempted to justify inequality, arguing that many prisoners 'had neither the requisite level of intelligence nor the verbal facility to make psychotherapy meaningful'. These prisoners were embarrassed by intimate discussions and often 'felt compelled to constantly justify and rationalise [their] past behavior'. Even the rare offender who managed to grasp simplified psychoanalytic principles questioned how 'this knowledge alone' was going to give him 'sufficient control over his impulses to avoid the next offence'.[62] Psychotherapy might have been an appropriate treatment for intelligent, highly motivated offenders with a 'capacity for abstract thinking and self-observation'. But 'none of these qualities' was 'prominent among the majority of men who rape', observed the Director of the Sex Offender Program in the State of Connecticut Department of Corrections.[63]

Referring to group psychotherapy carried out at the outpatient Clinic of the Philadelphia General Hospital in the 1960s, therapists concluded that most offenders failed to understand the relationship between their inner feelings and their crime. They could not 'relate their current behavior to intrapsychic patterns', the therapists complained, but insisted on attributing their difficulties to their everyday victimization. Thus a typical paedophile would 'attribute his act to rejection by his wife', but remained unable to 'recognize that his unconscious fear of women keeps him at home'.[64] Less intelligent offenders, particularly those serving indeterminate sentences in prison, tended to 'eagerly grasp' the 'psychological or moralistic formula' of psychotherapy in order to provide a superficial rationalization for their behaviour.[65] [See photograph, p. 199, for a sex offender taking an intelligence test.]

The exasperation many psychiatrists must have felt when asked to psychiatrically evaluate some of these men was palatable in the testimony given by Alan Austin Bartholomew, the psychiatrist superintendent at Pentridge Gaol and the Alexandra Clinic in 1961. The court

A sex criminal takes an intelligence test, from Bertram Pollen's *The Sex Criminal* (1939)

had asked his opinion on Walter Russell Deathe, convicted of having carnal knowledge with Doris Elsie Bradbury against her consent after creeping into her bedroom late at night on 4 January 1961 at Ivanhoe (State of Victoria, Australia). Bartholomew told the court that it was 'impossible to get anything from him' because he 'refused to answer questions in the ordinary way'. He treated the psychiatrist as if he was a defense lawyer, he 'rambled' and refused to cooperate with an IQ test. As a 'dull average man', Deathe was simply not 'up to' psychotherapy.[66]

The mix-and-match strategies of offenders and their tendency to employ psychoanalytical tenets to absolve themselves of responsibility was not surprising given that – as offenders immediately recognized – therapy itself was an 'extension of police and court action'.[67] This presented psychiatrists with a host of ethical dilemmas. As early as 1927 distinguished psychiatrist Herman M. Adler was complaining that in court the psychiatrist found himself in a position that violated 'all his professional principles': he was forced to be partisan, for instance. When testifying for the prosecution, psychiatrists risked being accused of being a 'tool of the officials', yet when testifying for the defence they were taunted for being 'venal'. It was a no-win situation.[68] In 'The Therapeutic Encounter' (1972), Seymour Halleck made a similar observation. The prisoner-patient could not trust his psychiatrist. 'If the patient does not know this and relates to the psychiatrist as though the latter were solely his agent,' Halleck continued,

> such cooperativeness might result in the loss of his freedom or other privileges . . . The psychiatrist's main allegiance in diagnosing sexual psychopathy is to the state. He may feel that in the long run a recommendation for specialized treatment may be good for the offender, but this attitude is based upon a kind of benevolent paternalism that is alien to almost any other medical role.[69]

In the counselling of sex offenders, the patient's interest was often secondary to the interests of third parties. What was the therapist to do when, in the course of therapy, the patient confessed to previously undetected offences? For social workers such disclosures were important since they suggested that the offender remained a danger to children or women. In contrast, for therapists such disclosures were an important part of 'clinical management'.[70] It was no wonder that lawyers acting for sex offenders often warned their clients against seeking psychiatrist help, fearful that the analyst might obtain information that might weaken any appeal.[71]

As a result, both lawyers and offenders responded to possible therapeutic intervention with one question in mind: would it reduce the court's punitive reaction to the crime? If that was the chief consideration, how could a psychiatrist 'obtain free and informed consent from individuals who have lost their liberty?' David Crawford of Broadmoor Hospital (Crowthorne, England), nervously enquired.[72] Offenders keen to avoid extended incarceration might be too willing to agree to psychotherapy, unaware of the psychological suffering (depression and suicidal feelings, for instance) it might cause them.[73] Castration might even be willingly agreed to if the alternative was believed to be worse.[74] For many sex offenders standing before the court or already behind bars, informed consent was a luxury they could not afford.

Damning critiques stemming from practical issues of legal process augmented this ethical angst. If the rapist could be 'cured' and released from prison, might not his victims feel that they had 'not been sufficiently avenged'? Was the possibility of cure to override the deterrent effect of incarceration?[75] As we saw in the previous chapter, was the rehabilitated prisoner literally a 'new man', and therefore of no further interest to the law? This was taking the separation of act from identity to its logical extreme.

The main problem with psychiatric interventions in the courtroom, however, was that they were often irrelevant. Henry Alexander Davidson, author of *Forensic Psychiatry* (1952), put it most bluntly when he disputed the basic tenet of psychiatry as it related to criminality – that is, the notion that crime was only a symptom that had to be 'judged in terms of the offender's total personality and treated as a form of illness'. According to Davidson, any physician who made such an argument forfeited his 'usefulness to the courts'. Except in the case of severe psychosis, the notion of sickness was 'so much at variance with public thinking that the psychiatrist will be of no use in the administration of justice if he insists on it'.[76]

Davidson went further, pouring scorn on physicians who dared to mention psychoanalytical explanations in the courtroom. The 'average judge simply will not believe the doctor who tells him that a voyeur has an unconscious wish to be struck blind or that the mouth is an erogenous zone', Davidson sneered. Psychoanalytic interpretations

> belong in the classroom and in the conference room, but never in the courtroom. They clutter up the record with legally irrelevant testimony, they confuse the court, and the jury, and they tend either to discredit the psychiatrist or to make him sound like someone living in a dream world which has no contact with social reality.

The psychiatrist should 'spare himself the embarrassment of ill-informed cross-examination before a frankly incredulous jury', and stick to questions of insanity, psychiatric diagnosis and the criminal's awareness of right and wrong.[77]

It was a view strongly promoted by prominent sex-crimes prosecutor Alice Vachss. She was infuriated by the invention of the diagnosis 'rapism', defined (by Gregory Lehne) as a rare psychosexual disorder 'where the primary source of sexual arousal is the real or imagined act of forcing a person to engage in sexual relations'.[78] In Vachss's words, it was time to return focus upon the crime rather than the criminal. 'We know that he has some disorder,' she insisted, adding

> There is something wrong with anybody who rapes. There is certainly something wrong with anybody who rapes over and over again. That doesn't mean that he is insane . . . There is no dispute that there is something wrong with this man, but it is something criminally wrong with him. He commits crimes. He commits offensive, obscene crimes. We're here to try him not for his personality, not for his whole life . . . We're here to try him for specific crimes . . . he is raping because he wants to.[79]

This retreat from the therapeutic ideal from the 1980s was also driven by the increasing conservatism of British and American political administrations, keen to show themselves as 'tough on crime' and wary of any accusations of being 'soft' on criminals, especially sex criminals. These men were criminals who deserved harsh prison sentences, not 'mollycoddling' in psychiatric institutions. In 1995, for instance, a survey by the US Bureau of Justice revealed that only half of all states had treatment programmes for sex offenders. Even in these states the average programme had a capacity for only 11 per cent of all incarcerated sex offenders.[80] In this context, on those occasions when psychiatric languages were employed, they were totally co-opted by penal ideologies. Thus 'socio-shock treatment' or 'milieu therapy' were pseudo-psychiatric terms used to describe 'the impact felt by the inmate when transplanted from the free community' to the prison, where, 'for the first time they realize the seriousness of their behaviour and . . . the direction in which their lives were heading'.[81] 'Milieu therapy' *was* incarceration, nothing more or less.

The retreat of psychiatric discourses coincided with the withdrawal of psychiatrists from the criminal system. They turned their attention to the more lucrative job of treating the depressed and the 'worried well'.[82] Social workers, psychologists and criminologists took their place. The resulting tension between psychiatrists and criminologists can be illustrated by the shifting status of the diagnosis of 'Sexual Sadism' in the American Psychiatric Association's 'bible' – the DSM. The DSM-III-R (1986) had included a description of 'Sadistic Personality Disorder' in a section entitled 'proposed diagnostic categories needing further study'. The essential feature of this new diagnosis was 'a pervasive pattern of cruel, demeaning, and aggressive behavior, beginning by early adulthood'. Nathanial Pallone, author of 'Sadistic Criminal Aggression' (1996), believed that this diagnosis resonated well 'with conceptualizations drawn from criminological data'. However, he complained that 'the "proposed category" has utterly disappeared in DSM-IV'. This was

> a cause of wonderment but not surprise to criminologists, who are often baffled by the 'here today, gone tomorrow' fashions in mental health nosology under which, within a space of years, the same set of behaviors is at one point litanized as a mental disorder but at another totally invisible.

There was 'little mystery', Pallone continued, that there was 'but indifferent intercourse' between psychiatrists and criminologists.[83] The disciplines had radically divergent ways of conceiving of human subjectivity: one focusing on the act, the other on the actor.

Finally, the psychiatric model was fundamentally altered by the interventions of two movements, feminism and self-help. From the 1970s feminists turned a critical gaze on psychiatry, insisting that there was no pathology to be found in rapists. Rapists were 'normal men' acting out a masculine ideal.*

The second important intervention came from the introduction of a more personalized regulatory politics. At the same time that crime prevention was being privatized and individualized, treatment regimes were also taken over by the offenders themselves. At the end of the previous chapter I quoted from the 'Credo' of Prisoners Against Rape, in which they spurned professional intervention in favour of 're-education of the self, true evaluation of the causes of rape, group discussion among the individuals affected by or effecting rape'.[84]

Other popular self-help groups modelled themselves on programmes originally developed to deal with narcotics abuse. 'Sexual recovery programs' were set up by private organizations for men who sought to 'deal with' their sexual urges. Examples included Healing Together, the National Council on Sexual Addiction and Compulsivity, Sexual Deviates Anonymous, Sexual Recovery Anonymous and the Sexual Recovery Institute, among many others.[85] Many of these groups adopted the '12-step recovery program'. Others brought together abusers and victims.[86] In a typical example, Sexual Recovery Anonymous even adopted the language of alcoholism. 'Our primary purpose,' it stated at the top of its web page,

> is to stay sexually sober and help others achieve sobriety. Sobriety is the release from all compulsive and destructive sexual behaviors. We have found through our experience that sobriety includes freedom from masturbation and sex outside a mutually-committed relationship. We believe that spirituality and self-love are antidotes to the addiction. We are walking towards a healthy sexuality.[87]

Responsibility could be easily blunted. 'As with contracting the flu,' one commentator noted, 'feeling too much . . . desire is nobody's

*Such feminist interventions are evaluated in Chapter 5, 'Brutalizing Environments'.

fault'.[88] The problem was located within an individual's body – literally his or her chemistry – internalizing disease models. If the problem was chemical, there was no need for social or political reform. Perpetrators of sexual aggression and abuse were thus positioned as masters of their own fate, defining their desires and policing them in a new panopticon project of self-surveillance and self-fashioning.

From the mid-twentieth century the influence of psychology and psychiatry in constructing narratives of sexual violence dramatically grew in importance. It was a growth reflected in these disciplines more generally. In 1940, for instance, the American Psychological Association had only 2739 members, yet by 1970 it could boast a membership of 30,839 and this had surpassed 75,000 by the early 1990s. Similarly the American Psychiatric Association in 1940 had fewer than 2500 members but more than 18,000 in 1970 and 38,000 by 1993.[89]

More importantly, their languages had permeated modern society – so much so that even detractors found it helpful to adopt their narratives. Thus, in the 1980s and early 1990, Kaye-Lee Pantony and Paula Caplan decided that it was time that male sexual aggression was properly pathologized – and that for this to be done it was crucial that the DSM recognized it as a psychological disorder. After all, the traditional 'good wife' pattern had been pathologized in the context of SDPD (self-defeating personality disorder) and LLPDD (late luteal phase dysphoric disorder, which was later renamed premenstrual dysphoric disorder). Why shouldn't equivalent masculine disorders also enter the lexicon of psychological disorders? They proposed introducing Macho Personality Disorder, John Wayne Syndrome, Delusional Dominating Personality Disorder (DDPD), or even acknowledgement of Testosterone-Based Aggression (as the equivalent of LLPDD). Although the proposals partly had a satirical purpose, Caplan submitted DDPD to the American Psychiatric Association for consideration for the DSM-IV. Her proposal was summarily dismissed.[90] As political satire, however, it was a masterstroke. After all, how *do* we decide who is normal?

Psychological and psychoanalytical theories focused attention on individual pathology rather than on larger cultural influences. Rapists were 'mad'; like typhoid sufferers, they needed treatment (even if they had to be coerced into seeking help). They effectively drew attention away from social, political and economic forces that might have facilitated the violence. Lady Wootton's succinct statement in 1963 that

'Freud and Marx might fairly compete for the title of the biggest popular success since Jesus Christ' was correct for her time. Until the feminist revolution of the 1970s to 1990s, individualized psychopathologies triumphed over theories based on broader socio-economic factors.[91] Even more influential was the psychotherapeutic insistence that the rapist was defined by an inner identity or personality, rather than by his or her acts. As such, it was possible to 'be' a rapist without ever having committed any act of rape. In Benjamin Karpman's words, criminality was 'entirely a part and parcel' of the offender. The rapist was a discrete category of human.

It was a view that was compatible with many rapists' accounts of their lives. Russell George, for instance, was a serial molester of young girls. It wasn't until very late in his life that, as part of his parole, he began seeing a psychiatrist. 'To someone like myself,' he recalled years later, 'it wasn't easy by God; it wasn't easy at all.' He was a quiet, introspective man who had lived his entire life 'not being talkative with anyone', and suddenly he was required to talk to a psychiatrist (who generally remained silent) most days of the week. 'There were days when I couldn't get a word out, not a thing,' he recalled, and he would

> sit wriggling about in downright misery, not knowing why I'd come or what I was supposed to be doing or anything. So I'd just talk about that, tell him all about that, how confused I was and scared . . . But I always managed to bring myself to tell the doctor about it [his near-relapses] at the next session; I went over and over it in detail, talking it out of myself, talking it out all the time. Till eventually I got to the stage of not wanted to do it much at all, just wanting to talk about it instead; and that was how it went on then, and the worst was over.

Gradually his sexual urges disappeared – the talking cure, or old age, it was impossible to know. His remorse for 'the children . . . the dreadful things it must do to them' was sincere. At the end of the interview George was speaking about paedophiles like himself in the third person, 'If only you could, you know, get them to see there is something the matter with them,' he began, adding the wish that other paedophiles would realize that

> it's something there's treatment for, that it can be cured. So they don't have to go on all through their lives, bringing misery to those who are near and dear to them, and all the shame. It doesn't have to

> be a complete waste for everyone, like my life was. They don't have to end up at seventy like me, looking back knowing it was all thrown away and when they're gone they're gone, and there's nothing anyone will ever remember them by.[92]

In the past four chapters I have examined the main historically specific ways of conceptualizing the rapist. The most startling conclusion is that the community of sexually violent individuals is extremely heterogeneous. As the authors of 'Cognition in Rapists', published in *Aggression and Violent Behavior*, correctly observed in 2001, while it may be 'necessary for research purposes to categorize sexual offenders into broad generic groupings', these categories ignored 'the wide range of individual differences exhibited within such groupings'. Indeed, most commentators were forced to acknowledge the dramatic variability in all assessments and descriptions of rapists.[93] Their sexual preferences were dramatically different; they did not share any identifiable personality traits; they exhibited different degrees of empathy towards victims; they suffered different mental disorders; and they might or might not abuse alcohol or drugs. Furthermore, they did not share the same *modus operandi*. Some rapists employed violence while others bombarded victims with romantic bluff. Some assaulted companions while others turned to strangers. Penetration was not always the aim. The fundamental problem was that none of the responses provided an effective 'cure' – and many offenders were reluctant to seek a cure since their sexual pleasures were tightly linked to abusive acts. As one therapist admitted, 'It is no easy task to induce a person to give up what to him is exquisite pleasure.'[94]

In all cases, however, these professional narratives about 'the rapist' were attempts to contain the perpetrator's violence within a framework that could 'make sense' of the chaotic nature of aggressive sexuality. Whether this was understood as an inheritance from the evolutionary past, evidence of a pathological faultline, a sign of psychiatric abnormality or proof of a perverse situational adaptation, the great clash between different forms of truth or competing visions of what it means to be human exposed crucial shifts in the accommodation of sexual violence within British and American societies.

SECTION FOUR

Case Studies

One step took him through the roaring waterfall
That closed like a bead-curtain, left him alone with the writhing
Of what he loved or hated.
His hands leapt out: they took vengeance for all
Denials and soft answers. There was one who said
Long since, 'rough play will end in tears'.

CECIL DAY LEWIS, 'SEX-CRIME'[1]

CHAPTER EIGHT

Female Perpetrators; Male Victims

On 28 April 2004 the CBS television network broadcast photographs taken by American soldiers at the Baghdad Correctional Facility (Abu Ghraib). They showed Iraqi prisoners stripped and piled up to form human pyramids. Prisoners were naked and hooded. Many had clearly been tortured. Some photographs showed men forced to simulate fellatio. The perpetrators were not just young American men, but female soldiers as well. A photograph of Private Lynndie England holding a naked man on a leash was to become the most iconic image of the war in Iraq and of the decadence of American womanhood.

Soon afterwards evidence of sexual abuse and other forms of torture carried out by American women as well as men began appearing. Nori Samir Gunbar Al-Yasseri, for instance, was one of many prisoners who gave a sworn statement about his treatment. 'As soon as we arrived,' he recalled,

> they put sandbags over our heads and they kept beating us and called us bad names. After they removed the sandbags they stripped us naked as a newborn baby. Then they ordered us to hold our penises and stroke it . . . They started to take photographs as if it was a porn movie. And they treated us like animals not humans. They kept doing this for a long time. No one showed us mercy. Nothing but cursing and beating . . . He [Specialist Charles Graner] and the two short female soldiers and the black soldier . . . When we were naked he order us to stroke, acting like we're masturbating and when we start to do that he would bring another inmate and sit him down on his knees in front of the penis

> and take photos which looked like this inmate was putting his penis in his mouth. Before that, I felt that someone was playing with my penis with a pen . . . 3 men and 2 women.[2]

Reports of sexual torture had been circulating for months before this exposé, but the photographic evidence of female and male abusers stunned the world. Although most of the abusers were men, the mass media were spellbound by the sexual abuse and torture carried out by the female participants: Private Lynndie England, Private Megan Ambuhl and Specialist Sabrina Harman.

For many principled feminist, pacifist and human rights campaigners, incorporating the existence of female perpetrators into their analyses of sexual abuse has been hard. Female perpetrators of sexual abuse in earlier conflicts – from Buchenwald to the Balkans – are known to exist. But they are easily marginalized, both descriptively and theoretically. In the context of the twenty-first-century conflict in Iraq, however, some of the most visible architects of suffering have been women. These women were regarded as much worse than their male comrades-in-atrocity: they were not merely inhuman, but monstrous. Even when women were engaging in not explicitly sexual abuses, the very womanliness of the perpetrators sexualized their actions. By definition, female performance was pornographic. Lynndie England became intriguingly attractive as the dominatrix of the American dream.[3] The photographs emerging from Guantánamo Bay, and even those of the Basra abuses, had none of the power of the images from Abu Ghraib. Sexual abuse, with female perpetrators standing alongside male, provided a frightening vista for the future. One hundred years from now, will the early twenty-first century be defined by monstrous acts of sexual abuse and torture carried out by women?

It is easy to exaggerate the stunned response, however. After all, when the scandal first broke, members of Congress were shown some 1800 more photographs and videos, some of which were – and still are – considered far too revolting to be publicly broadcast.[4] When a selection of further photographs *was* released in 2006, the response was tepid at best.

The torture images – and particularly those associated with the female perpetrators – were rapidly assimilated into a society already saturated with spectacle. [See cartoon, p. 211.] Thus one of the most popular radio show hosts could say,

> You know, if you look at – if you, really, if you look at these pictures, I mean, I don't know if it's just me, but it looks like anything you'd see Madonna or Britney Spears do onstage. Maybe I'm – yeah. And get a NEA [National Endowment for the Arts] grant for something like this. I mean, this is something that you see onstage at Lincoln Center from an NEA grant. Maybe on *Sex and the City* – the movie.[5]

On the internet, civilian men and women posted photographs of themselves 'doing a Lynndie'. Detailed internet instructions on 'doing a Lynndie' start with the phrase: 'Find a victim who deserves to be "Lynndied"', 'Make sure you have a friend nearby with a camera ready to capture the "Lynndie"', 'Stick a cigarette (or pen) in your mouth and allow it to hang slightly below the horizontal . . . tilt your upper body slightly forward but lean back on your right leg. Make a hitchhiking gesture with your right hand and extend your right arm so that it's in roughly the same position as if you were holding a rifle. Keeping your left arm slightly bent, point in the direction of the victim and smile.'[6] The smile was important: it bestowed individuality and agency in contrast with the degraded and objectified 'victim'.

The gender of the female perpetrators of sexual (and other) torture was only one factor that incited outrage. The other was the fact that the most widely publicized victims of sexual abuses in Abu Ghraib, Basra and elsewhere in the 'War on Terror' were not the 'usual victims' (women), but men. The photographs were a stark reminder of an uncomfortable

'Helmut Newton', by Mike Lester, 2004

observation: not only the female body, but the male body as well, is violable, penetrable. For many heterosexual men it is a hard admission to accept, particularly in wartime, when the military encourages the notion of the invulnerable male body. However, as I will be arguing, the sexual victimization of men within civilian contexts is more common than is generally assumed.*

Female Abusers

If all sexually aggressive individuals were gathered together in a great Dantean circle of hell, the vast majority would be men. Men commit practically every rape: only 1 per cent of incarcerated rapists are women.[7] Men's greater propensity to sexual violence mirrors higher levels of male criminality generally. In the early 1990s around 95 per cent of all new court committals for violent offences in Britain and America involved male defendants.[8] The association of masculinity with aggressiveness has tainted the entire male gender.

Nevertheless, the number of violent women is higher than most people believe. Statistically it is increasing. According to the US Federal Bureau of Investigation, in the decade after 1985 the number of juvenile women arrested for committing the entire range of violent offences rose by 250 per cent.[9] This growth rate was nearly twice that for young males.[10] Even more worryingly, in the sixteen years since 1981 the number of juvenile women arrested for weapons violations in America tripled.[11] Annie is getting her gun.

When we turn to *sexual* violence, however, girls and women often slip under the radar. A significant proportion of female perpetration fails to be registered in judicial statistics. For instance, women who sexually molest men or other women are likely to be charged with lewd and obscene conduct rather than indecent assault, thus muddling statistical comparisons between male and female offending.[12] In law-enforcement and legal precept, women are assumed to be passive as sexual subjects, in contrast with the active male. As early as 1952 a report in the *Yale Law Review* observed that the 'role of the man as the initiator of sexual relations and the active partner in the act . . . contributes to the assumption that man cannot be "raped" by a woman'.[13]

*Chapter 13, 'The Military', examines the sexual abuse of men in wartime. Here the focus is on peacetime abuses.

In most jurisdictions throughout the past two centuries, rape was simply defined as 'the carnal knowledge of a female forcibly and against her will' and required penetration of a vagina by a penis. Lacking that male appendage, women could not legally be rapists, although they could be convicted of being accomplices to male offenders. In effect, most female rapists were convicted for holding down or otherwise incapacitating another woman who was being raped, as in the case of R. v. Ram and Ram (1893), in which a wife forced her servant to drink whisky and then forcibly took her to her husband's bedroom, where he raped her.[14]

In recent years even the United Kingdom's allegedly 'gender-free' Sexual Offences Act of 2003 has failed to excise the penis altogether from its definition of rape. This much-lauded Act retained the requirement of penile penetration for a rape conviction. The Home Office admitted that it had debated removing this precondition, but in the end decided that rape 'as commonly understood' involves the penis. It accepted, however, that the penis does not necessarily have to penetrate the vagina or anus, but could forcibly enter the mouth too. As a consequence, forced fellatio was added to the rape statute. This was justified on the grounds that coerced oral penetration was 'as horrible, as demeaning, and as traumatising as other forms of forced penile penetration'.

Admitting that the inclusion of forced fellatio in the rape statute was a radical alteration to 'commonly understood' definitions of rape, the Home Office concluded, however, that the effect of a *woman* forcing a man to have sex with her or taking advantage of him by fraud (pretending she was someone else, for instance) or while he was incapacitated (say, unconscious) was not as 'horrible', 'demeaning' or 'traumatising' for the victim. In contrast with the male body, the female body is regarded as especially violable: the 'offence of penile penetration was of a particularly personal kind', the Home Office observed, because it 'carried risks of pregnancy and disease transmission'. Yet, presumably, the harm of forced fellatio did not include the risk of pregnancy. And wasn't a female assailant just as capable of transmitting a disease to her (male) victim as was her male counterpart?[15] Female assailants could be prosecuted under the revised statute, to be sure. A woman who forced a man to have sex with her could be indicted under Section 4, which related to the new offence of 'causing someone to engage in sexual activity without consent'. In emotional terms, as well as regards sentencing guidelines, this offence was hardly the same as being convicted of rape.

In this book I do not shrink from using the word 'rape'. I have adopted much broader definitions of rape and sexual abuse than those established by law, on the grounds that judicial definitions fail to encompass the full range of sexual acts that have been constituted as abusive (non-consensual or forced) over time and in geographical place. As I have argued in earlier chapters when attempting to estimate the extent of male-on-female sexual violence,* survey evidence provides a more nuanced indication of what actions have been classed as sexually abusive at any particular time. It also enables us to locate female perpetrators.

Until the 1970s it was rare for investigators to even ask men if a woman had ever sexually assaulted them. When the question began to be posed, however, the results were startling. In surveys of college students carried out in the late 1970s and early 1980s a significant proportion of people who claimed to have been sexually abused pointed the finger of blame at a female aggressor. Sociologist David Finkelhor was active in bringing the problem of the female perpetrator to public attention. In a series of studies he conducted in the late 1970s he established that one-fifth of boys and 5 per cent of girls who had been sexually abused named a female perpetrator.[16] In the early 1980s the American Humane Association and the National Center for Child Abuse and Neglect estimated that between 14 and 24 per cent of boys and between 6 and 14 per cent of girls who had been molested were assaulted by females.[17] A nationwide, random telephone survey in 1985 found that 22 per cent of the 2627 Americans interviewed had been sexually abused as a child: in 7 per cent of these cases the aggressor was female.[18] The US Department of Health and Human Services Administration on Children, Youth, and Families discovered that of the children who had been sexually abused in 1998, the perpetrator was female in 12 per cent of cases.[19] Although rape crisis centres in the 1990s admitted that females had abused just over 6 per cent of the victims coming to them, only half of these agencies offered male victims any kind of help.[20]

In most surveys, therefore, female perpetrators made up between 6 and 24 per cent of all abusers. However, some vastly higher estimates

*Survey evidence about the extent of sexual violence is presented in Chapter 1, 'Sexed Bodies' (for male-on-female rape), and Chapter 12, 'The Prison' (for male-on-male rape).

have also emerged. By some reckonings female perpetrators constituted 60 per cent of all aggressors,[21] but most of these higher estimates hovered around the halfway mark. For instance, a survey of 2474 men in England found that 3 per cent of men had experienced non-consensual sex since they were sixteen years of age and, of these men, nearly half reported having had non-consensual sex with a woman.[22] Another survey, involving 224 men attending a genito-urinary clinic in London, uncovered the fact that 18 per cent had been sexually molested *as an adult*. In 48 per cent of these cases the perpetrator was female. These men were usually made to perform cunnilingus (38 per cent) or vaginal intercourse (44 per cent). In 63 per cent of the cases the female perpetrator fellated the victim and in nearly one-third of the cases she masturbated him. When the men were asked whether they had been molested *as a child*, the proportion of female perpetrators dropped to 28 per cent and the sexual activities were more likely to involve touching.[23]

The momentous discrepancies between these studies are troubling. They arise out of commonplace problems in social science research. In particular the wording of the questions influenced the answers. Responses differed wildly according to whether the individual was asked if they had 'ever had sexual intercourse that they didn't want' or if they had been 'forced' or 'coerced' into sexual intercourse. Some surveys did not even invoke the issue of consent or violence, simply assuming that if individuals reported having had sex under the legal age of consent then they had, by definition, been sexually abused ('statutory rape'). The pool of respondents used by researchers also affected the outcome. While some surveys were based on random telephone calls, others focused on specific high-risk groups, such as men attending clinics for venereal diseases. Disproportionate reliance on American college students and, within that subset, students attending psychology courses, also created an image of the sex offender refracted through the lens of white, middle-class, psychologically aware and politically more rebellious youth.

Translating human suffering into bald percentages will always be problematic. When the perpetrators of misery are women, additional difficulties emerge. Women's customary identity as nurturers inhibits discussion of female belligerence. Although female aggression has generated considerable anxiety at various times in the past, by and large there is a deliberate avoidance of this highly sensitive problem. Even judges might feign ignorance about what constitutes female sexual aggression. As late as 1975, in a case involving lesbian violence at the California Rehabilitation Center, the court report noted that 'we must confess a certain naïveté as to just what kind of exotic erotica is involved in the gang rape of the victim by a group of lesbians and a total ignorance of just who is forced to do what to whom'.[24] This reduction of sexual assault to 'exotic erotica' is not uncommon in male-on-female rape, but acknowledgement of female aggressors tends to be especially coy.

At least the court trying the case of lesbian sexual violence admitted that it deemed it a 'reasonable assumption' that lesbian gang rape involved 'as much physical and psychological insult to and degradation of a fellow human being' as did 'forcible sodomy'. After all, being assaulted by a woman could be just as agonizing as being attacked by a man. In addition to physical injuries, victims typically suffered nightmares, panic attacks, depression, anxiety and difficulty in maintaining intimate relationships. Like many male victims,* female victims of female sexual aggression were also sometimes confused by the involuntary responses of their own bodies. As one female prisoner confessed:

> She told me I wasn't her friend if I didn't agree then started kissing me locked the door pushed me on the bed and ripped my panties off she then pulled up her nightgown. She didn't have underwear on and started fucking me putting her pussy on mine moving up & down all over. I actually had an orgasium [sic]. But I was horrified, ashamed and bruised and battered. I wanted to kill her.[25]

Victims were highly stigmatized. Judy Jacobs, for instance, was assaulted by a fellow inmate while serving a two-year sentence in the York County Jail in rural Pennsylvania for the assault and battery of a man. 'It's to the point now where I almost don't wanna go back [home],' she fretted. 'What are we gonna be called when we go out? Sluts, criminals, homosexuals?' She was apprehensive that her friends and neighbours would say, 'Wow, you've just gotten out of prison, I know what you've been doing!'[26] The effects of coerced sex are traumatic, irrespective of the sex of the perpetrator.

Despite the suffering caused by female perpetrators of sexual violence, their actions are routinely belittled. Female sexual abusers often

*Male sexual responses during rape are discussed later in the chapter.

appear not in person but in metaphorical guises. Female self-confidence is often likened to rape. 'The women of America raped the men,' Philip Wylie famously declaimed in his best-selling *Generation of Vipers* (1942): 'I give you mom. I give you the destroying mom,' he proclaimed.[27] The psychiatrist Sheldon H. Kardener used a similar analogy in 1975, when he blandly informed readers that 'the mother who forces her children to eat or demands bowel regularity through imposed enemas may be raping the child orally or anally'. He believed that women who played an active role in lovemaking were actually using fantasies about raping men to boost their own sexual potency. Kardener even characterized everyday 'henpecking' as a form of female-on-male rape.[28] Such metaphorical use of the words 'female rapist' diminishes the real brutality of acts of female sexual violence.

This cheapening of the harm of female-on-male rape is even more pervasive in the mass media. There are some exceptions, such as in the film *Jaded* (1996), in which two women brutally rape another woman, or in the television movie *Born Innocent* (1974). This movie was one of the most controversial programmes aired on American television, in part because of its graphic female-on-female rape scenes (using a toilet plunger handle) in a state home for delinquent girls.[29] More typically, however, female-on-male rape is presented as the source of envy or wry humour. Thus the depiction of older women having sex with young men under the age of consent in films such as *The Graduate* (1967) and *The Summer of '42* (1971) are not characterized as abuse narratives ('statutory rape') but as initiation fantasies. In comedies like *Forty Days and Forty Nights* (2002) and *Wedding Crashers* (2005), male characters are forced to have sex with a woman against their will, yet no critic named these acts sexual assault.

In popular psychology books and autobiographies, female-on-male sexual abuse is also generally treated as a joke. Hugo Paul's popular book *Cry Rape: Anatomy of the Rapist* (1967), for instance, depicted the gang rape of adolescent schoolboys by a group of four women as an opportunity to make sardonic comments about masculine virility. 'None of these boys approved of the situation,' Paul quipped, before adding, 'but none approved of his inability to service the last two matrons, either.'[30] Two myths permeate such stories: first, as in Paul's account, that male sexual performance is imperative in all circumstances, but, second, that certain types of women need to be approached with caution. Thus, in the British autobiographical tradition, working women (particularly in street markets and the fishing industry) were caricatured for being sexually aggressive. 'Before we knowed [sic] what was happening,' began one account, 'the women'd got our gaffer down, got his legs, pulled his cock out – it was stiff and all! – and plastered it with lard! He yelled! He said after: "You two stood there! Never offered to defend me!"'[31]

The story was meant to entertain by making working-class neighbourhoods sound exotic, sexually electrifying even. In such accounts female aggression actually stood for a more honest and sexually robust femininity. It was portrayed as nostalgia for a mythical 'community' in which men and women tumbled about together more freely.

More frequently, however, descriptions of female abusers are deliberately used to titillate audiences, as in pornographic texts like Moira Lines's *Victim of a Female Rapist* (1971).[32] A troubling example of this can be observed in the film *Ilsa, She-Wolf of the SS* (1974), set in a Nazi concentration camp run by Ilsa, a sexually insatiable, pornographically clad, blonde camp commandant. She regularly rapes attractive male prisoners, castrating those who fail to meet her elevated standards. The film climaxes when Ilsa began sexually abusing a prisoner who could 'keep it up' indefinitely. Dyanne Thorne, the actress playing Ilsa, claimed that raping men actually empowered women. According to her, the commandant and the other sadistic female guards in the films were actually heroines. Ilsa was 'on top . . . we want to make that very clear', Thorne maintained, adding that the film was 'the first one where they had a female villain. She was like the leader of the feminists, if you will . . . the victim was the male and the three females are standing there with total control.'[33] As an exploitation film, *Ilsa, She-Wolf of the SS* (and its innumerable spin-offs and imitations) used the rape of men in order to eroticize the Holocaust and sexual violence.

Non-Aggressive Femininity

What about real female offenders, as opposed to fictive representations? Until recently the female sexual perpetrator's voice has been muffled under the deafening patois of and about the male perpetrator. This denial of female perpetrators of sexual violence came to an abrupt end in the late 1970s. Increased willingness to tackle issues of sexuality and the acute attention being paid to sexual abuse in general were partly responsible for this shift. A more gloomy explanation for the explosion of interest in female perpetrators points to a backlash against feminist thought. I address this problem at the end of this chapter.

This is not to claim that, before the 1970s, female perpetrators were *totally* excluded from serious criminological or psychiatric accounts. Quite the contrary: some of the most prominent cases of sexual abuse in early psychiatric literatures involved female aggressors. Many of Freud's case studies included descriptions of mothers sexually coercing their children. Similarly, in *Final Contributions to the Problems and Methods of Psycho-Analysis* (1933), Sándor Ferenczi casually mentioned the rape of young boys by 'mature women' alongside the 'rape of girls who have grown out of the age of infants' and 'enforced homosexual acts'. These acts were 'more frequent occurrences than has hitherto been assumed', this psychoanalyst coolly remarked.[34]

Nevertheless, it was rare for the *gendered* aspect of sexual violence to be explicitly analysed. Female perpetrators tended to be simply listed alongside their male counterparts, with little (if any) distinguishing comments made about any significance that might be attached to their femininity.

In fact, when gender was explicitly discussed in early criminological studies, it was used in order to explain the *absence* of women from the ranks of violent criminals. When women transgressed, these criminologists observed, they turned to prostitution, petty stealing and general 'delinquency', rather than sexual belligerence. Why?

A favourite explanation was that women lacked the 'body build' required to bend men to their will.[35] Thus the Italian physician and early criminologist Cesare Lombroso stated in the 1890s that women's 'piety, maternity, want of passion, sexual coldness, weakness, and undeveloped intelligence' debarred them from the fraternity of serious criminality.[36] The highly respected criminologist William Bonger, writing in 1916, concurred. He claimed that women possessed 'less strength and courage' than men. They were naturally submissive. As Bonger put it, 'the role of women in sexual life (and thus in the criminal sexual life) is rather passive than active'.[37]

Other criminologists observed that when women did act criminally, they did not fit the profile typical of male aggressors. Male sexual violence is common within gangs, for instance, but women are less likely to be involved in such groups and pregnancy and child-rearing often cause women initiated into gangs to drop out earlier than their male counterparts.[38] Sexually, too, women were described as possessing needs different from those of men. They had lower sex drives, for instance, and found it much easier to find sexual mates (the assumption that rape was stirred by excessive sex drives and that men were always sexually available lingered in the background of most of these studies). Even exhibitionism was portrayed as not psychologically necessary for women because they were allowed to disrobe in public to a much greater degree than men.

Perhaps there is an evolutionary explanation for women's lower criminality, other commentators speculated. This possibility was explored by the feminist Frances Alice Kellor, writing in 1898. According to her, both the male and the female organisms started their existence in a bisexual state ('parturition not being confined to either sex'), but as the environment became more specialized, so did the sexes. 'The greater amount of criminality in man' was 'remotely due to his more katabolic nature', she alleged. In her words: 'The male was carried farther away from the anabolic existence, to which the female is more closely allied, and in him was developed a stronger physique, greater passion, and larger brain capacity.' Thus women did

> not develop into crime because the psychic centres in women are less active, and the irritation consequent upon degenerative processes in her is neither so intense nor so constant . . . while excesses of passion in man, not directed into proper channels, lead to assaults and sexual perversion, in woman its existence more frequently culminates in mental degeneracy or physical disease.[39]

Men rape; women rave.

Finally, some commentators pointed out that women had simply not been socialized into cultures promoting sexual violence. From early childhood girls are discouraged from acting sexually and expressing their needs violently. Their subordination to boys is made clear. If the coercion of other girls is frowned upon, the idea of a girl physically forcing a boy to act against his desires is an even more extreme sign of waywardness. Female socialization into passivity and dependency are exactly the opposite of male socialization to aggressiveness and toughness – and the latter pattern is conducive to rape. If, as many commentators asserted, rape was carried out by men feeling angry and aggressive, then it is significant that when women experience these emotions they are more like to withhold, rather than force, sex.

The Pathological Individual and Family

Proponents of these explanations for why women are severely underrepresented in rape statistics eventually had to face up to the fact that some women *did* act in sexually aggressive ways. This position has been resisted by many criminologists, psychologists and legal commentators. Indisputably the most common approach was simply to deny any particular significance to the presence of women among perpetrators. At best many writers on sexual abuse acknowledged in a footnote that women did act in sexually abusive ways, before proceeding to develop a theory premised entirely on heterosexual male perpetrators. But, when pressed, every serious commentator had to admit that women could also be sexually aggressive toward children, boyfriends and husbands, as well as towards strangers. Women molest other women. They rape men. Confronted with evidence of female perpetrators, theories premised on the assumption that it was exclusively the male of our species who were 'rapists, rape fantasists, or beneficiaries of a rape culture'[40] became (at best) wishful thinking.

Given the existence of female perpetrators of sexual violence, what theories have been employed? Candid observers confronted female perpetration directly. They either suggested that women's violence was fairly contained, arising from individual needs or immediate familial dynamics, or else they drew attention to a wider social malaise driving an aesthetic of sexual violence. This aesthetic was presented as shared with violent men or as independent from men. In the first category, explanations that individualized female sexual aggression can be grouped under four headings: financial needs, pathological desires, sexual frustration and cycles of abuse.

In the rare cases where female-on-male sexual abuse was openly discussed before the 1970s, it was linked to the financial needs of working-class mothers and fathers. This explanation for female offending reached its peak in the late decades of the nineteenth century. During a panic about child abuse the media honed in on the role working-class parents played in forcibly prostituting their daughters. Thus, in the infamous case of the 'Maiden Tribute of Modern Babylon' (1886), the journalist W. T. Stead exposed the extent of forcible child prostitution in the cities of England.* Although most historians did not draw attention to it, Stead's exposé placed mothers at the centre of the

*This case is discussed in Chapter 5, 'Brutalizing Environments'

abuse of their daughters. When Stead interviewed an 'evergreen old gentleman to whom the brothels of Europe were as familiar as Notre Dame and St. Paul's', for instance, he was informed that men were able to 'buy little girls from their mothers in order to abuse them'. A brothel keeper actually promised to procure some virgins for Stead. 'After champagne and liquors', a mother

> agreed to hand over her own child, a pretty girl of eleven, for £5 if she could get no more. The child was virgo intacta, so far as her mother knew. I then went to Mrs. N——, of B——street, Dalston, (B—— street is a street of brothels from end to end). Mrs. N—— required little persuasion, but her price was higher. She would not part with her daughter under £5 or £10, as she was pretty and attractive, and a virgin, aged thirteen, who would probably fetch more in the open market.

Indeed, the climax of Stead's exposé occurred when he managed to buy thirteen-year-old Lily Armstrong for £5 from her mother (in fact, Lily's mother had overheard discussions about the sale of another young girl and had offered Lily instead, whispering eagerly to the seller, 'Don't you think she would take our Lily? I think she would suit'). Throughout Stead's report, mothers were engaged in plotting to have their daughters sexually abused.[41]

Financial need was particularly popular in reforming circles at the end of the nineteenth century as an explanation for why mothers sexually abused their daughters by selling them to men who physically carried out the assault. It was not simply that poverty forced mothers to extreme measures; rather, poverty had actually corrupted women utterly, putting them beyond hope of redemption. Lily's mother, for instance, was described as 'poor, dissolute, and indifferent to everything but drink'. This view of working-class women re-emerged in discussions of rape of daughters within poor, inner-city gang and drug culture in America in the late twentieth and early twenty-first centuries, as the economic crisis in these communities spun out of control.[42] The problem was that this explanation could be applied only to a limited number of female offenders. It worked for some female offenders who targeted their own children or other dependent young women, but not for the much wider community of female aggressors for whom no financial motivations for abuse existed.

As a result, commentators abandoned the claim that financial pressures produced female abusers, turning instead to explanations based on pathological bodies. This change was welcomed. Most people believed, like the feminist Frances Alice Kellor whom I quoted above, that women's bodies differed significantly from male ones but they had one thing in common: wickedness sprung from both male and female bodies. Nineteenth- and early-twentieth-century commentators repeatedly observed that women's bodies were 'irregular' and prone to 'imbalance', particularly during menstruation, childbirth and menopause. As Hans Gross argued in his widely read *Criminal Psychology: A Manual for Judges, Practitioners, and Students* (1912), menstruation 'may bring women to the most terrible crimes'. Under its influence even 'sensible women' might be 'driven to do the most inconceivable things – in many cases to murder'.[43]

This nonchalant link between femininity and madness was significant. Wasn't it obvious that the sexually aggressive woman was insane? The Italian positivist criminologist Cesare Lombroso put it even more starkly in *The Female Offender* (1895): when women commit violent crimes, they are grotesque. Writing about female offenders generally, Lombroso observed that a violent woman was untrue to her gender. Consequently,

> the criminal woman is . . . a monster. Her normal sister is kept in the paths of virtue by many causes, such as maternity, piety, weakness, and when these counter influences fail, and a woman commits a crime, we may conclude that her wickedness must have been enormous before it could triumph over so many obstacles.[44]

This interpretation was not confined to the reports of criminologists in learned journals. It entered popular accounts of sex offending and was present as late as the 1960s. Thus the author of *The Psychology of Rape* (1966), evoking Freud, argued that 'these aggressive females resent their sex; they secretly wish they were males'. Normally, the author continued, when a girl reaches adolescence she realizes that 'femaleness, like maleness, has its own exclusive benefits', and her yearning to be a boy vanishes. The problem with sexually aggressive women is that they botched this transition, thus condemning themselves to 'emotional immaturity'.[45]

Some physicians gave these women a name: nymphomaniacs. Other nineteenth-century terms, all with different intonations, were used, such as erotomaniacs, ovariomaniacs or hystero-epileptics. This diagnosis was assigned to women with excessive sexual appetites. Some of these women would attempt to force or coerce unwilling men to have sex. Because women were supposed to have lower sexual drives than men, those who were sexually voracious were regarded as more pathological than their male counterparts. Thus nymphomania was considered more serious and less easily controlled than male satyriasis.*

What caused such depravity? Mid-nineteenth-century physicians expounded on this question at great length. Diseased ovaries or even an enlarged ('engorged') clitoris might cause the disorder, they suggested. If so, the solution was readily at hand: ovaries could be removed; the clitoris and/or labia incized. In addition, sufferers were subjected to bloodletting, cold baths and diets (they had to forswear red meat, for instance). These radical responses were promoted by some of the most eminent physicians of the day. Removal of the clitoris would eliminate the 'peripheral excitement of the pudic nerve', urged Isaac Baker Brown, Fellow of the Royal College of Surgeons and author of the influential although controversial *On the Curability of Certain Forms of Insanity, Epilepsy, Catalepsy, and Hysteria in Females* (1866).[46] The clitoris, from being rarely mentioned in textbooks of the early 1800s, had become the source of a vast array of mental disorders.

Clitorectomy was pretty effective in curing women of the desire to masturbate. Removing their ovaries had less success. As in the debates over the use of sterilization and castration to cure male sexual offenders of their rampant sexual urges,† the operations failed to stop women from making excessive sexual demands. Rufus Hall, for instance, reported to the American Association of Obstetricians and Gynecologists in 1897 that, after examining more than 400 women who had had their ovaries removed, he could not find a single one reporting 'a total loss of sexual feeling'. Indeed, only three of those women even noticed 'any marked diminution in the sexual feeling' when questioned three years after the operation.[47] Moral considerations were also raised. Echoing concerns about the castration of male sex offenders, the president of the Royal College of Surgeons argued in 1886 against the operation's legitimacy as a means of curbing the desires

*Male satyriasis is discussed in Chapter 4, 'Rapacious Bodies'.
†This is discussed in Chapter 6, 'The Knife'.

of sexually enthusiastic women, asking: 'would anyone strip off the penis for a stricture or a gonorrhoea, or castrate a man because he . . . was a moral delinquent?'[48] Indeed, the most audacious physicians even admitted that while male sufferers of satyriasis could legitimately, albeit secretly, go to prostitutes to work off an excess of sexual desire, nymphomaniacs had no such option. As one physician conceded before the Boston Gynecological Society in 1869, speaking about a women suffering from 'obstinate erotomania', 'If this woman could go masked . . . to a house of prostitution, and spend every night for a fortnight at sexual labor, it might prove her salvation; such a course, however, the physician cannot advise.'[49]

The diagnosis was discredited by the end of the nineteenth century. The sexually voracious nymphomaniac, who refused to accept that 'no meant no', virtually vanished from the psychiatric manuals, appearing only occasionally under labels such as 'psychotics', 'maniacs' and 'epileptics'. More recently the term 'hypersexuality' has been applied, implying that female offenders' sexual mania is caused by especially sensitive androgen receptors and is therefore treatable with the anti-androgen drug cyproterone acetate*.[50]

Furthermore, claims that female sexual perpetrators were psychiatrically disordered were being questioned on two grounds.[51] First, the highly biased nature of the samples was pointed out. Most of these studies had been carried out on women who had been sent to clinics for psychiatric help in the first place. They were scarcely representative of female sexual aggressors generally. Second, and more importantly, it was difficult to detect whether the link between female sexual abusers and insanity was the result of cultural bias. Probation officers and psychiatrists were much more likely to probe into the family lives of women offenders compared with those of males.[52] Legal and medical authorities often regarded women who transgressed sexually as 'obviously' psychiatrically disturbed. The myth of female sexual purity determined that all exceptions were lunatics.

An alternative view posited the question: what if women were not innately reserved sexually? Was it too far-fetched to imagine that some 'normal' women (like some men) could be consumed with an irrepressible sexual fever? Failing to find a legitimate 'outlet', they turned to the illegitimate.

*The same drug was also used to treat male rapists, as is discussed in Chapter 6.

According to this argument, sexual frustration could have many origins. Physical incapacity, for instance, was used to explain why one eighteen-year-old girl raped two younger boys: she had 'an unnatural contradiction [sic] of the vagina which prevented intercourse with adult males', observed Richard Laur in his tawdry account of the psychology of rape, published in 1966.[53] More frequently frustration was portrayed as emanating from social restrictions. The war had resulted in a 'lack of men', Laur also pointed out. The shortage of men on the home front meant that 'the rape of men was not an infrequent occurrence'.[54] Incarceration in a woman's prison also reduced the possibility of intercourse, driving some highly sexed women to sexual violence against fellow inmates. As one young female prisoner recalled in the 1970s, she had managed to talk an aggressive woman into only 'suck[ing] my tits' as opposed to raping her with a root-beer bottle. 'I figured, why not,' the young prisoner said, 'the poor woman'd [sic] probably been in here a hundred years without seeing nobody half my age.'[55]

The belief that forced sex by women is a response to sexual frustration is flawed for the same reasons that it is dismissed as an explanation for male perpetration. It implies that sexual violence is primarily about sexual contact and assumes that aggressors have no alternative options. The notion that rape is primarily about sex has been often criticized, as have assumptions that forcing sex is the only way to 'get it'. After all, even within prisons many women formed nurturing consensual relationships. Sexual 'urges' are never impossible to restrain or divert.

Many commentators who resisted the idea that abuse arose out of the need to dampen down sexual desires turned to a more obvious explanation for violence: the need to dominate or to express strong emotions like anger. Was there evidence that both female and male perpetrators were trapped within a dizzying orbit of aggression or 'cycle of abuse'? Alice Vachss, the tough sex-crimes prosecutor who generally dismissed psychological explanations for rape on the grounds that they excused the perpetrators, put it plainly: 'no-one is born to rape – they are tortured into it'.[56] In other words, perpetrators of sexual abuse had been similarly molested as children.

This compelling explanation arose out of early psychoanalytical thought. The idea of 'identification with the aggressor' was established by Sándor Ferencz. In 'Confusion of Tongues Between Adults and the Child' (1933) he disputed Freud's theory that a child's emotional problems were a result of the struggle with his or her own instincts. Instead, he argued, the child's problems were caused by early sexual trauma inflicted by adults. As a result, the child developed a fragmented sense of the self, one part of which identified with the aggressor.[57] Another version of this argument insisted that the child became aggressive in order to master the violence he or she experienced at the hands of adults when young.[58] In the words of Anna Freud in 1937, '[b]y impersonating the aggressor, the child transforms himself from the person threatening into one who makes the threat'.[59] Abused children learnt to identify with the male figure inflicting pain; they sought mastery by repeating the abuse.

Not everyone espousing this view depended upon the psychoanalytical idea of identification with the aggressor. It was suggested that simpler psychological mechanisms could be operating. The abused child could have been psychologically conditioned to link sexual acts with violence; as an adult, he or she could feel that sexual cruelty was the only way to express the anger or hurt stemming from his or her childhood abuse.[60] A less common interpretation was that individuals who had experienced sexual abuse in childhood developed faulty communication strategies. As children, they had been relatively powerless to prevent what was happening to them. They responded by employing token resistance strategies (saying 'no' but meaning 'yes') and compliance strategies (saying 'yes' when meaning 'no'). As adults, they assumed that their partner was also drawing on similar tactics: when their child or partner said 'no', they continued to hear 'yes'. As one proponent of this interpretation argued in *Sex Roles* (2003), both token resistance and compliance behaviour were 'potentially conducive to sexual aggression because women who do not communicate their sexual intentions in an unambiguous way may be less likely to take a partner's rejection of their sexual advances at face value, thus showing a "false consensus bias"'.[61]

Irrespective of the different versions of 'cycle of abuse' arguments, the theory that 'abused child becomes abuser' has some evidence to support it. For instance, a study in the 1980s showed that 76 per cent of convicted serial rapists reported having been sexually abused in childhood, in comparison with 16 per cent of males in the general population and 7 per cent of males at college.[62] Furthermore, researchers were often impressed by the way the cycle of abuse operated not only in familial contexts, but also in substitute families, such as gangs. In recent years this argument was revived with the rise of female gangsters, living in poor, inner-city areas, deprived of positive role models and dependent on their gang for power, status and surrogate kin.[63] Rape was only one of many kinds of carnage inflicted on and by female gangsters.[64] Girls who were gang-raped by male gang members proved willing to attack other girls in turn. Thus a twelve-year-old gang member in San Antonio felt no compunction about luring her thirteen-year-old friend to a trailer to be raped by nine male gang members. She 'showed no remorse – the same had been done to her'.[65] The injured child harmed others.

Although frequently applied to male rapists, this explanation was particularly well suited to explaining female aggressors. Indeed, there was some evidence that girls (as opposed to boys) actually *were* much more likely to be stuck in this destructive cycle. Criminological studies of adolescents often uncovered a link between female aggressiveness and prior abuse. In one influential study one-fifth of violent girls had been either physically or sexually abused at home compared with only between 6 and 10 per cent of violent boys and non-violent girls. When *sexual* abuse was separated out, the pattern was even starker: one out of every four violent girls had been sexually abused, compared with only one in ten non-violent girls. Interviews with girls who had been sexually abused further revealed that they had learned the lesson that 'might makes right'.[66]

'Cycle of abuse' arguments provide a powerful explanation for sexual violence and do have minority application. The concept was rapidly politicized in the context of the 'battered women syndrome'. Girls and women who had been 'battered' turned into abusers themselves. They were literally victims of patriarchal rule and should be absolved of responsibility for their actions. According to this reasoning, the perpetrator-victim dichotomy simply did not (and should not) apply.

Nevertheless, this argument was influential in explaining female abusers partly because it conformed to assumptions about passive femininity and women's pervasive victimization. The problem is that many (if not most) women who commit crimes of sexual aggression are raised in loving homes. Equally, many (if not most) women who were abused as children respond in precisely the opposite way to that predicted by the 'cycle of abuse' argument: instead of turning violent, they become committed to not repeating the abuse.[67] Refuges and rape trauma centres are run by many people – men and women – who, according to this hypothesis, should have become assailants, not rescuers. The argument also does not explain why, since girls are much more likely than boys to be sexually victimized, sex offenders are predominantly male. Finally, there are questions over the use of self-reporting. Sex offenders are likely to over-report their history of childhood sexual abuse for many reasons, including eliciting sympathy, absolving themselves of responsibility and hoping for some remission in punishment.[68]

There were good reasons, however, why this explanation was so readily adopted. Many psychiatrists embraced the concept because some of the most difficult and therefore memorable patients had indeed been sexually abused when young, and such cases stick in the mind. More generally, the explanation is both intellectually and emotional satisfying. Children who have been sexually abused often do react aggressively in the immediate aftermath of the abuse. The explanation projects this short-term reaction into the future. Most importantly, however, the explanation makes emotional sense. Psychiatrist Judith Lewis Herman expressed this most cogently when she observed that the concept permitted clinicians to 'empathize with offenders' as well as offering the latter 'a comforting assurance that their behavior is an understandable result of a pathological history'. Perpetrators sometimes *were* victims. More cynically, she observed that the explanation made it easier for clinicians to argue for increased expenditure from 'a punitive and economy-minded public': it enabled them to claim that treatment would 'break the cycle' and thus help guarantee the safety of the next generation.[69] Finally, the model is in harmony with common ideas about the impact of *specific* negative events on the psyche. It is significant, in other words, that the model was not used to suggest that environmental factors, such as poverty within the home, would eventually spiral out of the contained domestic sphere and cause future abuse.

The Aesthetics of Abuse

What about those arguments that assumed that sexual violence was part of a wider social malaise driven by an aesthetic of sexual violence? These explanations situated female abusers in the context of their subordinate status within the home and patriarchal society. While these arguments most frequently identified a male-led aesthetics of sexual violence which aggressive women adopted, space was created for an explanation that emphasizes a form of female desire that is both routine in imagination and monstrous in performance.

Male perpetrators are sometimes said to abuse women as normal gender practice in patriarchal culture. Similarly, sexual abuse by women can be explained in terms of a continuation of other female tasks, especially those associated with the domestic sphere. According to an early version of this explanation, the female perpetrator was typically a stranger embedded within a middle-class home; she was, in short, a domestic servant. A strong social purity and class element coloured this argument. Thus in the early decades of the twentieth century feminists arguing that men needed to become socially pure and discard the double-standard (whereby they were allowed to indulge sexually while maintaining that 'their' women remain chaste) were concerned that young, middle-class boys were being sexually corrupted by servants from early youth. In 1920 the feminist author and headmistress Catherine Gasquoine Hartley maintained that mothers had been 'so occupied in safeguarding our girls from sexual hurt, that we forget the much greater dangers surrounding boys in this direction'. The chief threat was the boys' primary care-givers, that is, female servants. In her words, it was

> very rarely that young girls are placed in any position of necessary intimacy with an adult male, except their fathers or their brothers. The very reverse is the case with boys. They are tended by women servants; at school their clothes are looked after by women; in sickness they are nursed by women; they are brought in innumerable cases into much more personal and intimate relations with women than girls ever need be with men. It is folly to close our eyes to the evils that too often arise. I would trust growing boys with no servant, and with very few women.

In an atypical overturning of stereotypes of male agency and female passivity,* Hartley claimed that the lower-class servants were actually the aggressors, 'seducing' naïve middle-class boys. She admitted that this 'may seem a hard saying', but claimed that it was based on her expansive knowledge of 'what has happened, and is still happening to uncounted boys'. Servants were largely responsible for the 'sexual initiation of boys', but 'many boys of tender years have been seduced by women who often would be the least suspected of the committal of such an act'.[70]

*Not coincidentally, this switch is also seen in discussions of African-American men being accused of rape by white women: see Chapter 2, 'Rape Myths'.

Hartley was writing in the aftermath of the First World War, when servants were haemorrhaging out of the middle-class home, largely as a result of more attractive alternative employment opportunities but also because their job was made redundant because of technological changes and the increased domestic labour by middle-class mothers. Not surprisingly, as servants were elbowed out of the home, they disappeared from the sexual abuse canon. Mothers replaced them. Nearly all surveys in the twentieth century found that mothers were significantly over-represented in any cluster of female perpetrators of sexual violence.[71] This tendency was explained in many ways, including the fact that mothers had intimate access to children, notions that mothers somehow 'owned' their children and in terms of the relative powers of carers and children. The idea that such abuse constituted a form of 'distorted nurturing' was widely commented upon.[72] Sex abusers themselves often agreed. 'Fondling, just touching, sleeping with, touching, sort of a nurturing thing', was the way one women described her abuse of her two younger brothers.[73] Or, as another female abuser of her three-year-old daughter argued, she was merely 'educating the child by exposing her to loving sex rather than the violent variety she [herself] had experienced before'.[74] This was transgression in the name of love.

A related argument situated these deviant mothers in the context of patriarchal households. Perhaps these women were actually submitting to the desires of their abusive menfolk, either through some 'natural' response to dominant males or through socialization. In this way responsibility for female perpetration was deflected from the woman towards the men in her life. In fact, detailed research into the actual crimes committed by these women made one startling discovery: female sex criminals typically acted in cahoots with at least one man. In contrast, around 90 per cent of male sexual abusers undertook their abuse alone. In a large study carried out in a British prison, female sex offenders were found to have acted with a male co-defendant in 36 per cent of cases.[75] Other studies showed even greater percentages, sometimes soaring as high as two-thirds.[76] Women were simply playing 'follow the (male) leader'.

This was a popular interpretation, in both psychological manuals[77] and the genre of 'true crime classics'. Carlton Smith's *Hunting Evil* (2000) fell into the second category. In agonizing detail the book documented the kidnapping, sexual assault and eventual murder of young women and men by Michelle ('Mickie') Michaud and her male companion James Daveggio. [See their photograph, p. 232.]

Court photograph of Michelle Michaud and James Daveggio

Throughout the book Mickie's motivations were described as 'really' emanating from the men in her life. As Smith put it, Mickie lived in a world

> in which it soon became impossible to distinguish between the boundaries of herself and the wants of another. Her entire life she had survived by fitting chameleon-like into whatever surroundings she found herself in, and in trying hard to make the unacceptable become acceptable; and to Mickie, that way was power, the only kind of power she had ever known.

But the author went further in assigning blame. After all, Michelle Michaud was not only in thrall to James Daveggio. In fact, she possessed other fantasies, which emanated from another (male) source. 'In women, just as with men,' Smith informed his readers, 'fantasy plays an important role in thinking and feeling about reality.' Yet women who involved themselves in criminal activities were driven by 'powerful feelings of negative self-worth reaching far back into childhood, and which are very frequently associated with early sexual abuse by older, more powerful figures, usually males'. Elaborating on this 'cycle of abuse' argument, Smith explained:

> a woman may build a destructive fantasy around the notion that if she pleases a man with subservience, she may somehow gain control of him. Thus, while the male sex murderers may commit violence to validate control over women, female enablers such as Michelle Michaud may assist in the violence, and endure it themselves, to achieve the same over men . . . She may best be categorized . . . as a rebellious submissive – rebelling against authority in order to gain the attentions of a dominator.

Michelle Michaud's 'incorrigibility', according to Smith, stemmed from her 'difficult relationship with her father'. Unlike accounts of male rapists, in which the mother is generally held responsible, readers were told that the 'most powerful figure in Mickie's early life was "Daddy"' and it became 'Mickie's most urgent goal in life to make her father pleased with her'. Both 'Daddy' and his substitute, James Daveggio, were to blame for her sexual crimes. Michelle Michaud was merely 'the slavish assistant who would stop at nothing to serve her master's desires'.[78] In this way readers were pushed towards the recognition that the female perpetrator was actually a victim.

In violence between men and women the balance of power favours the male participants. But to deny the female perpetrators any significant agency is surely to go too far. After all, around half of female aggressors act alone, and when they abuse in the company of another person, they are not passive onlookers. Michelle Michaud actively tortured and raped her victims. In cases of parents abusing their children, mothers 'did not watch their husbands perform it', two researchers observed, but 'they touched the children themselves'.[79] The fact that women used weapons *more* frequently in perpetrating their offences also suggests that there is some degree of forethought in female perpetration.[80] Most significantly, female aggressors clearly take immense pleasure in their actions. Vaginal photoplethysmography* of female sex offenders reveals considerable arousal in the presence of paedophilic and other deviant images.[81] At the very least, female sex offenders speak about the satisfaction of relieving unbearable tension. Female aggressors devise elaborate, creative and highly individualistic ways to abuse.

The belief that, among perpetrators, women are just as likely as their men to be purposeful agents in carrying out cruel acts led some commentators to argue that the problem may actually be deeply embedded in patriarchal society. In other words, in a world that deprecates femininity (and the so-called female traits of compassion and care) and views bodies (particularly female ones) as commodities, it is inevitable that women, in emulation of men, would progressively turn aggressive. To put it slightly differently, as women become similar to men in social, economic and cultural terms, the inhuman within the female gender is sure to rise.

*The equivalent instrument for males (the penile plethysomograph) and the way it was regarded as capable of 'telling the truth' about desire is discussed in Chapter 7, 'The Couch'.

Since the upheavals in sexual and social mores in the 1960s, this argument has become one of the dominant explanations for female sexual perpetration. On a practical level, there is a great deal to be said for it. After all, the rise in female perpetration has coincided with major societal changes. For one, it has reduced the potential costs of abusing to women. Greater control over fertility, for instance, meant that forms of abuse involving penetration no longer ran the risk of pregnancy. Women coming into adulthood in the 1970s were the first generation of women for whom sex was not inevitably linked to the risk of pregnancy. Furthermore, as women increasingly felt able to initiate sexual intercourse, they became more liable to forcefully demand it. Indeed, many rape cases involving women aggressors arose from dates in which the woman decided not to take 'no as meaning no'. Female sexual aggression has been increasingly lauded: sexual assertiveness gradually became a positive trait, rather than something transgressive. Finally, in American inner-city culture, the increased involvement of adolescent girls and women in gangs and drug culture also increased levels of female-initiated abuse.[82]

However, most commentators employing this explanation for female offending have the problems of 'permissiveness' in mind. Hugo Paul's 'anatomy of the rapist' in 1967, for instance, blamed the increase in the number of 'deviant' women who sexually assault men on the 'sacrifice of masculinity' and the 'symbolic augmentation of the female's superior status' that accompanied the sexual upheavals of the 1960s.[83] Many agreed. 'The female of the species has become so sexually aggressive these last few years', lamented the author of an article on the difficulties inherent in defining rape in the early 1970s. While 'rape' may be 'too strong a word' for female sexual assertiveness, the author continued, 'it describes rather well what goes on in today's society'.[84] Freda Adler, in *Sisters in Crime* (1975), went further, predicting that as women moved into areas of employment conventionally occupied by men, they would leave behind 'traditional female roles', including nurturing ones. She forecast that 'as egalitarian forces expand, so too will the crime rate of the female young set.'[85]

More recently this assessment of female aggressors has dominated explanations of female abuses in Abu Ghraib and elsewhere in the 'War on Terror'. In an increasingly democratic military 'the American woman is given the phallus', noted one author in *Hypatia* (2006); she is 'invited to participate in the militarized masculine aesthetic along with the men, to become the one who penetrates the racialized other'.[86] Or, in the words of Barbara Ehrenreich, the women involved in the Abu Ghraib torture were 'working class women who wanted to go to college and knew the military was the quickest way in that direction. Once they got in, they wanted to fit in.'[87] 'A Uterus is not a substitute for a conscience,' she insisted elsewhere.[88] According to this view, the shared militarization and masculinization of feeling has been dissolving conventional gender divisions.

For the political elite and moral Right, there is a convenient response, serving as further fodder for the moral crusade of 'family values'. In churches throughout the West, fears about rampant female sexuality and increasing female-perpetrated violence were used to call the flock back to a more conservative morality. The National Coalition for the Protection of Children and Families put it bluntly when it declared that the torture photographs were 'liberalism taken to its natural and logical conclusion', drawing attention particularly to the 'tangled web of licentious behavior, sexual perversion, infidelity, and promiscuity' within the military. It should 'serve as a warning to those who continue to advance so-called sexual freedom beyond its intended boundaries of life-long, natural, and monogamous marriage'.[89] In this line of argument, responsibility was neatly diffused. 'It Was Porn That Made Them Do It', Frank Rich mockingly entitled his analysis of the Abu Ghraib abuses in the *New York Times*. He explained that

> [i]f porn or MTV or Howard Stern can be said to have induced a 'few bad apples' in one prison to misbehave, then everyone else in the chain of command, from the commander-in-chief down, is off the hook. If the culture war can be cross-wired with the actual war, then the buck will stop not at the Pentagon or the White House but at the Paris Hilton video, or 'Mean Girls', or maybe 'Queer Eye for the Straight Guy'.[90]

This is an argument usefully employed by critics of contemporary feminism. As notorious anti-feminist Phyllis Schlafly claimed, the photograph of Lynndie England holding a naked man on a leash would 'soon show up on the bulletin boards of women's studies centers . . . that picture is the radical feminists' ultimate fantasy of how they dream of treating men'.[91]

Schlafly's polemic is ludicrous. The 'public sphere' which allegedly created the opportunity for greater mixing of the sexes and the corruption of the nurturing woman ideal long pre-dated the sexual crime wave. More to the point, the 'new freedoms' allowed to women from the 1960s were not shared by those women most liable to be acting in sexually violent ways. Female perpetrators tended to hail from homes where husbands or fathers were both financially and morally dominant. As one researcher commented, the 'equality theory' (one of the shorthand terms for this position) failed because

> [W]omen's Liberation never occurred in the poor inner city – the location for the majority of crimes. Female offenders, largely lower income, minority women with little education and truncated employment opportunities, were not the beneficiaries of the 1970's women's liberation movement. Instead, only white middle-class women reaped the spoils.[92]

The problem lies not simply with the white, middle-class bias of the argument; more significantly, it implies a male norm, into which women are assumed to passively fall. Yet, in a culture permeated with assumptions of compulsory heterosexuality, men and women stand in different relations to sexual intercourse. After all, for many people one of the most distressing aspects of female-on-male rape is that the (penis-less) women trump male power, not only in the sense that these women claim omnipotence in relation to their male victims, but also because they have no need to use the penis to do so. For, the argument goes, the penis is a deeply flawed instrument of power and one with none of the resilience and fortitude that the fist or (fire-)arm have. In talking about weapons of torture in her classic *The Body in Pain* (1985), literary theorist Elaine Scarry referred to the way in which 'in converting the other person's pain into his own power, the torturer experiences the entire occurrence exclusively from the nonvulnerable end of the weapon'. But in forms of sexual abuse involving the penis, the perpetrator's attention begins to 'slip down the weapon toward the vulnerable end', contesting its power.[93] The cruel triumph of the female perpetrators resides in the fact that they employ sexual torture and abuse without experiencing that vulnerability.

Conscious of the limitations of the 'equality theory', some commentators attempted to inject a subtler gendered dimension. According to them, sexual violence 'masculinized' perpetrators who happened to be biologically female, while 'feminizing' victims who happened to be biologically male. This is a common argument among people commenting on rape in prisons or the military. Feminist psychologist Monique Plaza put it most succinctly when she stated that it is '*social sexing*' which is 'latent in rape'. She went on to argue that when men raped women they did so 'precisely because they [were] women in a social sense' and when men were raped, they were raped 'as a woman'.[94] Male victims became 'social women'; male perpetrators had their masculinity enhanced; female perpetrators became 'social men'. The female abuser was 'really' a man. Thus female abusers were said to be 'male identified'.[95] In the context of the abuse at Abu Ghraib, Lynndie England was described as a 'phallic female', 'tomboyish', a 'leash-girl', who turned out to be 'something other than a natural lady'.[96]

At first sight this seems like a simple way out of the problem of explaining female perpetrators: nothing much changes – just a few labels. The Female is erased and coded as Male. The argument follows an easy logic. Undoubtedly both male and female perpetrators taunt victims with degraded words used to refer to femaleness. There is also no question that perpetrators of both sexes take strength and power, as well as pleasure, from their actions. But to say that this turns female perpetrators into 'social men' is both to imply an essential link between manliness and violence, and to reinforce the dichotomies male-active and female-passive. The gendered notion of masculinity and femininity as respectively active and passive confuses the social imaginary with lived history, placing women at the margins of the symbolic order.

Indeed, many female abusers were not merely participating in masculine rituals. They were using conventional tropes of their gender to shame and subjugate. Abu Ghraib provides many examples of this phenomenon. While male guards stomped on male prisoners with boots, threatened to bugger the men in the showers and poked phosphoric lights up their rectums, the women threw menstrual fluid and slowly stripteased. The sexualization of abuse carried out by women had distinctive characteristics, drawn from the arsenal of feminine strategies of romance and seduction.[97] We must take seriously the idea that female perpetrators are not simply imitating men, but living out their own feminine fantasies about power and sexuality.

Male Victims

So far in this chapter I have addressed explanations for the actions of women who sexually abuse children, men and other women. No distinction has been made between types of victim. Since the majority of rape and sexual abuse cases involve men abusing women, most of my book emphasizes female victims.*

It cannot be ignored, however, that one influential 'rape myth' is that men cannot be raped – at least not by a woman. Women, it is assumed, are physically incapable of forcing a man to have intercourse with them. Not only does this imply that men always want 'it', but it also ignores a vast array of ways in which a woman may sexually abuse a man – such as by wielding a weapon, employing modes of psychologically manipulation or abusing him while he is asleep or drugged. It also implies that all women are weaker than all men (and that they would not 'gang up' on a single man). Men may respond to sexual threat in similar ways to many women, that is, by 'freezing'. When a man is face to face with abusers of men (who could be either male or female), it is clear that it is not only the female body 'whose borders cannot be defended'.[98] Consider the use of a broom handle by NYPD officers to sodomise Abner Louima, a Haitian immigrant; or the naked skirmishing and sodomization forming part of the 'hazing' incidents in the navy, air force and army which are periodically publicized. The tortured body transcends 'straight' gendered inscriptions.

The humiliation of sexual assault is not restricted to one gender; it is shared by both. Similar insults are used. As an unnamed man recalled, 'He called me a bitch and a cunt – then called me filthy for sucking his penis – which he had forced me to do . . . He repeatedly said I wanted it.'[99] For this victim the anguish of rape included the assault on his manliness. Until recently men like him were silenced in public fora. This has severely distorted analyses of sexual violence, such as debates about the relationship between pornography and male sexual violence. In an otherwise sophisticated analysis of pornography, Linda Williams's 'Power, Pleasure, and Perversion: Sadomasochistic Film Pornography' (1989) ignored violence against men in both gay and heterosexual pornography. As a consequence, she was able to develop a theory of sexual violence that stressed 'the sexual perversion' (that is, sadism and domination) that 'haunts masculine sexual identity'. At one stage she admits that 'in gay male pornography . . . where there is no heterosexual identity to maintain, male submissiveness occurs frequently'. Nevertheless, Williams proposed to simply ignore these 'examples of male submission in heterosexual

*The exception, of course, is Chapter 12, 'The Prison', which deals with one common form of male-on-male violence.

hard core . . . in order to concentrate on the problem that most concerns feminists: the domination of women proffered as a form of pleasure to both the women depicted and to viewers'.[100] By her own admission, she deliberately excluded those instances of male masochism that could challenge her conclusion that sadism and domination reside at the core of masculinity.

Until recent years the myth that men could not be raped was even inscribed in law. Forced buggery was not recognized as rape, but was dealt with under statutes dealing with intercourse with animals. As late as the UK Sexual Offences Act of 1956, the law stated that it was 'an offence for a person to commit buggery with another person or an animal'. Under this statute even *consensual* buggery was a crime. Although persons who sexually abused men could be prosecuted under legislation dealing with indecent assault[101] (and thus attracting a lesser penalty), they were not covered by *rape* legislation until the 1990s, when the UK Sexual Offences Act was widened to include anal as well as vaginal penetration. The 1994 Act made non-consensual buggery by a man of a man or woman an act of rape for the first time. It took nearly another decade before forced fellatio was recognized as rape.[102] Furthermore, the law treated male rape as less harmful than the rape of women. Penalties were lower, for example. Thus, according to the Sexual Offences Act of 1967, if the male victim was over sixteen years of age and the male assailant over twenty-one, the maximum penalty for the perpetrator was only ten years, while the buggery of a woman of any age carried a maximum sentence of life (regardless, incidentally, of whether or not she had consented).

Public reticence to discuss male rape and legal reluctance to prosecute it ignore the fact that the male body is as vulnerable as the female. According to the UK Crown Prosecution Service in 2002, 7 per cent of complaints of rape were made by men. Between April 2000 and March 2001, 664 men were reported to have been raped.[103] Surveys showed much higher levels, suggesting that between 3 and 16 per cent of men experienced forced sex and between 6 and 24 per cent of the perpetrators of this abuse were women.[104] The US National Crime Victimization Survey, which is based not on reports to the police but random survey of Americans, found in 1999 that over 39,000 men were either raped or sexually assaulted that year.[105] As with women, however, there is some evidence that men are increasingly likely to report abuse. Thus a major United Kingdom Home Office research project published in 2005 found a large increase in reports of rape by men to rape crisis centres, although men still account for only 8 per cent of all people using the centres.[106]

Distressingly for the gay liberation movement, evidence emerged in the 1990s that sexual violence was as common within their community as it was between heterosexuals. In a study of 930 male homosexuals living in England and Wales in the early 1990s, 27 per cent claimed to have been sexually assaulted and one-third of these men accused a previous or current sexual partner. Not only did very few of these men report the sexual assault to the police,[107] but the male gay community was also keen to hush it up. In part this was because of justifiable fears that evidence of sexual violence within their community would be annexed to homophobic agendas. They were also anxious lest one crucial fact would be forgotten: the majority of men who raped other men were heterosexual. To people who queried why 'a straight man would rape another man', Fred Pelka, in 'Raped: A Male Survivor Breaks His Silence' (1995), advised readers to 'see rape as a way of exerting control, of confirming your own power by disempowering others'. If a man could 'feel powerful and macho to force sex on a woman or child, think of how much more powerful you feel raping another man', he maintained.[108]

Gagging public discussion about sexual assaults on male bodies is not restricted to the male gay community.[109] Until recently, for instance, rape within religious establishments was covered up at the highest levels.[110] [See cartoon, p. 241.] More frequently evidence of male sexual abuse was brazenly overlooked. Thus nineteenth-century societies established to 'rescue' young women from white-slave traders intent on forcing them to have sex, often (although not always) failed to observe the market for adolescent boys coerced into prostitution. Because a woman's character was dependent upon her sexual purity, she could 'fall', unlike her coerced male equivalent.[111] When the existence of young male victims was acknowledged, late nineteenth-century feminists tended to argue that the harm was less for the male of the species. As the newsletter for the Women's Christian Temperance Union (the leading feminist organization) observed in 1886, while 'almost all girls are brought up in ignorance of the wiles of men . . . almost all boys are fully equipped with knowledge, and in the majority of cases, commit the sin with their eyes wide open'. Unlike the 'damning' effect of sexual abuse on women, the 'social penalty for boys and men' was 'almost nothing', they insisted. 'When old women of eighty, and married and unmarried women of

'Pope Covers Up', by Bob Englehart, 2005

middle age, in good society and of fine social standing, go about ruining boys of ten and twelve and sixteen,' they lectured, 'it will be time to sound the alarm for boys as we are now sounding it for girls.'[112] They had a point: old women of eighty and married women of 'fine social standing' were under-represented in the annals of rapists – but that was not where the danger lurked.

At other times male sexual abuse is simply discounted: obvious examples include rape within prisons and the so-called 'rough and tumble' of 'hazing' within the armed forces, fraternities and sports teams. Just as significantly, little notice is taken of the fact that male genitals were regularly and deliberately molested in street and bar-room brawls. In 1859, for instance, 'John W.', a father of three and a publican, got into a fight while attempting to quell a disturbance in his pub. The *Dublin Quarterly Journal of Medical Science* reported what occurred under the heading 'Fiendish Attempt at Castration in the Human Subject'. According to the report,

> a fiendish attempt was made . . . to drag away [John W.'s] testicles by sudden and brutal force. The testicles, probably from the violence of the grasp, and just before the hellish drag was made, slipped from within the hand of the scoundrel, who, however, tore away the greater part of the scrotum, with a corresponding portion of the trowsers [sic], the latter being of substantial and recent manufacture.

The narrator assigned blame for the nasty attack on John W.'s genitals to foreign influences: the culprit was 'an Irishman, who, having been abroad for some years, learned this diabolical practice far away from his native land'.[113] Setting aside the curious assignation of such violence to un-English influences, it is noteworthy that deliberate acts of brutality to men's sex organs during brawls were not categorized as sexual abuse. It was just violence. Despite widespread agreement that anger and aggression (as opposed to pleasure) drive people to act in sexually abusive ways, male-on-male abuse of genitals is coded differently from male-on-female abuse of genitals.

The violence done to John W.'s testicles may not have been classified as *sexual* (and therefore not 'rape' according to my definition), but it was definitely a case for the courts. When the violation could be identified as something even vaguely resembling conventional modes of consensual sex, the abused man was often denied even the pretence of sympathy. Thus the experiences of under-aged boys who had sex are actually very similar (in terms of the levels of coercion and force used) to the experiences of girls except that their female abusers are much more likely to make a pretence of 'asking'. In addition, young male victims have an alternative sexual narrative within which they could slot their experiences: they could appeal to 'an alternative and status-enhancing interpretation of their experience, an option that was largely unavailable for girls in similar circumstances'.[114]

This indifference to male sexual abuse is exacerbated by the belief that men always want sex with women. Given the opportunity and a reasonably attractive offer, it would be a queer man indeed whose 'no' meant 'no', went this fiction. The fact that nearly half of all men fantasized about *being* raped by a woman was sometimes used as evidence that the occasional accuser was being disingenuous.[115]

It is no wonder that many male victims are reluctant to report being sexually harmed. According to the London Rape Centre, in the early 1990s almost 90 per cent of male victims kept their abuse a secret.[116] Men from ethnic minorities were particularly prone to silence, anxious that their victimization would not be taken seriously or even that it would rebound on them.[117] There was evidence that African-American victims were much more likely to be blamed for their own victimization, particularly if they were gay.[118] The fact that many male victims (like their female counterparts) froze rather than fought back further inhibited them from reporting the attack to friends, let alone to the police. Indeed, most victims only reported the rape if they suffered injuries severe enough to require medical help: even then, hospital staff discovered that many attempted to conceal the sexual context of their assault.[119]

Female victims, too, are reluctant to admit being raped. Shame, the fear of being disbelieved and trepidation about facing their attacker in a hostile courtroom setting are just some of the reasons why both female and male victims may decide to remain silent about their experience.

In a number of ways, however, the sexual abuse of men significantly diverges from the canon established with female victims in mind. For example, when the victim is a man a different inflection is given to the term 'victim precipitation'. While female rape victims were caricatured as foolish girls who had acted in ways that any 'virile' man could hardly be expected to resist, male rape victims were assumed to have triggered their abuse by being homosexual. Male victims 'really wanted' to engage in sexual intercourse with other men and unconsciously set up situations in which they could 'cry rape' while still getting what they secretly desired. Even victims sometimes accepted this logic. According to one survey, over 80 per cent of male rape victims admitted to feeling profoundly guilty for their own violation.[120]

The resilience of the fiction that male victims are partially, if not wholly, responsible for their rape (they 'really wanted it') was most forcefully demonstrated in a study carried out in the early 1990s by Cindy Struckman-Johnson and David Struckman-Johnson. They questioned 315 white college students from a psychology class at a Midwestern university about whether they agreed with some of the classic 'rape myths'. Do you think that victims make false allegations of rape? they asked. Was it true that some victims wanted to be raped? Did the victims of rape 'deserve it' because they acted or dressed inappropriately? Was rape really harmful?

Encouragingly, these researchers discovered that many of these psychology students were sceptical about the truth of the main rape myths. Less happily, they found that the one exception to the students' fairly liberal attitudes occurred when they were questioned about male victims. At that point students abruptly shifted positions, agreeing that *male* victims could be making false allegations, were responsible for their own sexual assault and were less likely to be traumatized by the experience anyway. Twenty per cent of the male students believed that a man who was raped by another man was somewhat to blame for the attack (he was careless or should have been able to flee, for instance): when the perpetrator was a woman, the proportion of male students blaming the victim soared to almost 40 per cent. Nearly all of the students recognized that a man who was raped by another man would be upset. However, if the aggressor was a woman, over one-third believed that the victim would not be upset. They seemed to believe that heterosexual men would want to have sex with any woman: even if forced, the man was deemed to be getting pleasure from 'it'. These researchers also discovered that a woman who raped a man was assumed to be motivated by 'strong sexual attraction or an intent for romantic seduction', rather than aggression. Presumably, this reinforced the students' belief that the male victim would not be harmed by her actions.[121]

A 1988 article in the *Journal of Sex Research* drew similar conclusions. Presenting students with a number of sexual scenarios including male-on-female, male-on-male and female-on-male rape, the authors also found that the scenario depicting a woman sexually assaulting a man was much more likely to elicit rape myths. When presented with a setting in which a woman sexually coerced a man, students claimed that the male victim contributed to the attack, experienced pleasure in the course of it and would be less distressed afterwards. When asked to sentence to prison the perpetrators in all three scenarios, female assailants were given shorter terms than male assailants.[122] Although AIDS and other sexually transmitted diseases are as much a threat to male victims as to their female counterparts, and there is abundant evidence that sexual coercion is distressful, many people assume that the male victim will be delighted if the assailant is a woman.

Finally, the male body in pain was constructed differently from his female counterpart. Although male victims frequently spoke about being stunned by the betrayal of their own bodies – erections, even ejaculations, during the rape, for instance – for many outsiders these biological reactions offered irrefutable evidence that the victim had 'really wanted it' after all. While the logic of purposefully ejaculating in order to 'get it over with' might be understood by the wider public,[123] *involuntary* erections or ejaculations disrupted commonly understood rape scripts. Victims, too, were bewildered. As one heterosexual man admitted after his rape by another man:

> If I really thought that the sexual acts I was subjected to during the assault were so degrading and perverse, why did I ejaculate? For a long time I thought I must have really enjoyed it, therefore, I must have homosexual tendencies. I was very confused for a very long time.[124]

Yet around a quarter of male victims ejaculated while being raped.[125] In fact, many assailants regarded it as absolutely necessary to force their male victims to ejaculate. Because they confused ejaculation and orgasm, assailants believed that ejaculation symbolized their total sexual domination over the victim. Some assailants also expressed pragmatic concerns: victims who ejaculated during the assault were much less likely to report the crime. If the case ever came to court, ejaculation by the victim dramatically strengthened the assailant's position. Faced with such evidence, jurors rarely returned a guilty verdict.[126] In the words of *A Psychology of Rape* (1966), an 'unwilling male would not, and could not have the necessary erection'.[127]

He is wrong. Numerous studies have established that the emotional turmoil of a sexual attack sometimes triggered an erectile response, independent of sexual desire.[128] According to the Director of the Kinsey Institute and author of 'Psychophysiology of Sexual Dysfunction' (1980), 'although peripheral sexual responses' were 'influenced by the brain', they were 'mediated through centers in the spinal cord'. They could therefore 'function independently, as seen among spinal-cord-injured patients'. Thus men who claimed that they were 'paralyzed with fear' may have been experiencing 'a sexual response determined by spinal cord discharge without full cerebral control'.[129]

Nevertheless, the *belief* that the reactions of a man's penis provide irrefutable proof of pleasure (as opposed to being an expression of a host of other emotional responses) is widespread. As Alan Hyde put it in *Bodies of Law*, an assumption exists that the penis is able to communicate 'a kind of truth of which the man is unaware or wishes to keep secret'. Indeed, in criminology and law, the independence of the penis was central to practices tested by the penile plethysmograph, in which the desires of sex offenders were judged according to the size and volume of their erections.* As Hyde argued, if law

> were to contract bodies with agency, bodies that acted without minds, without 'our leave', bodies that had their own civil and criminal responsibility, I am confident that the penis would become that body part par excellence to which independent agency would be attributed.[130]

*Examples of the use of the penile plethysmograph are given in Chapter 6, 'The Knife', and Chapter 7, 'The Couch'.

Commonplace assumptions about the independent nature of a man's penis did not blunt the sense of shame experienced by male victims when 'betrayed' by their own bodies. Misunderstandings about penile response patterns effectively stifled male protest against their abusers.

Indeed, in many ways the abused male body has always been portrayed as lacking. On the one hand, if the male victim does not 'perform' (erections, ejaculations even) during sexual abuse, he is laughed at as deficient. Female abusers, in particular, frequently taunt men for their sexual inadequacies. On the other hand, *involuntary* erections also confirm a defect in the individual man: a lack of masculine will, coupled with the suggestion of homosexuality. Tumescence and detumescence, not a display of patriarchy, a show of weakness.

Politically, the argument that 'women do it too' and that 'men can also be victimized' is difficult to make. The proportion of female to male perpetrators is small. Nearly all accounts of rape start with the statement that almost all victims of rape are women and nearly all perpetrators are men. As I have shown in this chapter, however, this is true only if statistics referring to conviction rates are used. It also requires adopting a particularly narrow definition of sexual abuse. I argue that for an act to be called 'sexual abuse' two central components must be present. First, a person has to identity a particular act as sexual, however they may wish to define the term 'sexual'. Second, a person must also claim that the act was non-consensual, unwanted or coerced, however they may wish to define those terms. If we use this definition, the fact that women have been sexual aggressors, as well as victims, is patently obvious.

Talking theory, this is fine; doing activism, it may be dangerous.[131] In recent decades shrill arguments that 'women do it too' have arisen as part of a vicious backlash against feminist understandings and conceptions of the world. At a time when social welfare schemes are being slashed, insisting that some women violate other people not only undermines female solidarity in the face of continued inequality, but also threatens radical proposals to reallocate certain resources *from* men *to* women. Indeed, recognizing the existence of male victims of female abuse opens the floodgates for a diversion of resources in the opposite direction. Feminists are right to be wary. We have faced similar threats before, especially in connection to refuges for 'battered' women. Evidence from the 1980s that some wives beat their husbands risked a shift in funding priorities.[132] In a highly competitive funding culture male victims are still more powerful than female victims. In the late twentieth and early twenty-first centuries, the argument that 'women do it too' has been co-opted by some father advocacy groups and used in highly charged courtroom battles.[133] At the very least, male victims are able to marshal more sympathy precisely because of their anomalous position in the imaginary of suffering.

In addition, propagating the idea that some women are sexual aggressors could have a more invidious effect, undermining arguments that women are discriminated against in innumerable ways. Although feminists have consistently argued against the 'defenceless little woman' stereotype, exchanging this myth for one that portrays women as aggressive brutes risks expunging recognition of women's continued subordination. For these reasons, arguments that 'women do it too' have become highly acrimonious, with feminists researching female aggressiveness being dubbed 'pseudo-feminists' or 'male-identified feminists'.[134]

The so-called 'rape crisis feminists' are correct: there is no 'gender symmetry' in sexual violence. Men act in sexually aggressive ways much more frequently than women and the risk for women is higher in heterosexual than in lesbian contexts. Nevertheless, as Lisa D. Brush has put it in her research on violence within the home, 'the needs of women and men who are targets of abuse from their intimate partners need not be zero-sum'.[135] Arguing that 'women do it too' need not be part of a feminist backlash, but an engagement within feminism about the nature of sexual violence. After all, each and every body is permeable and appropriable. The tortured body transcends common gendered inscriptions. Although most rape victims are women, the exclusive association of 'woman' with 'victim' relegates another group of victims – men – to a dismissive footnote. Creating a hierarchy of suffering endorses some kinds of abuse.

Earlier in this chapter I showed how female perpetrators of sexual violence have 'fallen out of history', despite the role they have played in inflicting sexual suffering. Their victims are regarded as not having been harmed as much as the victims of male rapists. When commentators attempt to understand the actions of female aggressors, they turn to myths of pathological female bodies or to some kind of perversion in the homes of individual female abusers. When notions of a violent aesthetic are evoked, there is considerable disquiet about identifying this aesthetic as feminine. After all, the bipolarity of male perpetrator and female victim is particularly powerful (I develop this theme in the last chapter). The suggestion that there are not simply two categories of perpetrator and victim, but a range of subject positions between which a person might move within relatively short periods of time is disturbing. Nurturing housewife and child abuser may be the same person; caring father-provider and child abuser may be one and the same. In the face of suffering, sexually aggressive women and distressed men must become a feminist issue.

CHAPTER NINE

Exhibitionists

'I am a bundle of nerves. I have been worried a lot . . . I scarcely know what day it is,' stammered John Pettitt, a driver for the Post Office in Canberra (Australia), when questioned by Detective Sergeant Bernard Alphonsous Rochford in 1950. He had been accused of an act of lewdness. His nerves were shattered. Three young boys claimed that he masturbated in front of them while they read comics in his small room at the Narellan Guest House. 'Yes, I have done that,' Pettitt admitted, 'but have done nothing more.' He insisted that 'I have never interfered with a boy in my life . . . I have been suffering dreadfully. I have laid awake at night fighting against temptation. I have not had any boys near the room, I wont [sic] allow them to come here now.'

Excuses began piling up. 'You wouldn't understand,' he stammered,

> I am a single man, I was to have been married, but another chap came between us, ever since then I have longed for someone on whom to place my affections. I know how wrong it is to do what I have done, and it has worried me. I have taken dope, I have been to a doctor, I am on sick leave now. I want to get to Sydney to see a doctor I know well and to whom I can tell everything.

But 'telling everything' proved difficult. 'I am not a criminal,' he lamely repeated, 'I have never interfered with a boy in my life.' But 'interfering' was not the accusation: Pettitt's crime was indecent exposure. He was charged with having uncovered his 'naked private parts' in the presence of three adolescent boys and of placing his 'hand upon and against his naked parts', where he did a 'lewd and beastly act then and there'.[1]

Although he was not aware of it, John Pettitt's plea to the detective sergeant touched on arguments that had intrigued jurists and psychiatrists for decades. Why does a book on rape contain a chapter on exhibitionists? The acts performed by exhibitionists are often described as sexual. The people they expose themselves to do not consent. This makes exhibitionists sexually abusive according to my definition. Even though I follow this chapter with one on sexual psychopaths – surely at the opposite extreme to exhibitionists of 'unwanted sex' – it is legitimate to ask whether the stigma attached to indecent exposure is proportionate to its dangerousness. Related questions include: should exhibitionists be treated as sex criminals or psychiatric patients? What is the nature of free will: *could* Pettitt have 'controlled himself'? Exhibitionists, of course, claim that they deserve sympathy, but should we fear or should we pity the man who could find no legitimate partner on whom to 'place [his] affections'?

Indecent Exposure v. Exhibitionism

Understanding, as opposed to simply condemning, men who indecently exposed their penises, had interested legal experts and psychiatrists for decades. Indeed, it was precisely the shift in language from the legal term of 'indecent exposure' to the psychiatric one of 'exhibitionism' that represented a shift from a punitive response to the *act* of exposure to a medical response that focused on the *person* carrying out the act, the exhibitionist. This shift was relatively new. The act of exposing one's genitals to a non-consenting stranger was a crime, punishable under a vast array of legislation, including the common-law offence of outraging public decency, public-order law proscribing acts that caused an 'obstruction, annoyance or danger, of the residents or passengers' (the Town Police Clauses Act of 1847, for instance) and vagrancy law. This remains the case in British[2] and American legal jurisdictions today. In 1987, for instance, nearly one-third of the 171 people prosecuted under the 1824 Vagrancy Act were prosecuted for indecent exposure. The rest were prosecuted for sleeping out, begging and being on enclosed premises for an unlawful purpose.[3]

However, as I shall show, this legal insistence on illegal *acts* was increasingly overlaid with an emphasis on unlawful *identities* – in this case, the persona 'exhibitionist'. Before the 1870s the category called (in French) 'les exhibitionnistes' did not even exist. The term was first used by Charles Lasègue in 1877, and in the English language the word 'exhibitionist' first appeared in print in 1893 in Charles Gilbert Chaddock's translation of Richard von Krafft-Ebing's *Psychopathia Sexualis*.[4]

This increased emphasis on the status of the entire person – the exhibitionist – was mirrored in the legal sexualization of the crime. Thus, under nineteenth-century legislation, men who exhibited their genitals were placed in the same category as men who begged, slept outside, loitered or solicited prostitutes. Laws typically focused upon persons who were 'idle and disorderly', 'incorrigible rogues' or 'rogues and vagabonds'. Exhibitionists were lumped together with people telling fortunes, displaying obscene prints or pictures, or 'wandering abroad and lodging in any barn or outhouse, or in any deserted or unoccupied building, or in the open air' without 'having any visible means of subsistence and not given a good account of himself or herself'. The assumption was that the man who exposed his genitals was a drifter, a vagabond.

By the end of the nineteenth century, however, men were increasingly criminalized under laws dealing with sexual morals. Vagrancy took second place to indecency.[5] Increasingly, public order offences were sexualized. The drafters of the Model Penal Code's 'Comments' on exhibitionism in 1961 observed that 'genital exposure for sexual gratification' was a 'special case' which should be punished 'more severely than ordinary open lewdness'. They explained that such behaviour 'amounts to . . . threatening sexual aggression'. Therefore the offence was rightly 'placed in the article of the Code dealing with other types of sexual aggression' while 'open lewdness' was 'included in the article that encompasses obscenity and prostitution'.[6]

Furthermore, the crime of indecent exposure shifted from being defined in terms of the *victim* to being defined in terms of the *criminal*. In the earlier period indecent exposure had been an act that could only be committed against a female. Thus, under Section 4 of the 1824 Vagrancy Act, an offender could be charged with being a Rogue and Vagabond in that he 'did wilfully, openly, lewdly and obscenely expose his person with intent to insult *a female*'. It was explicitly an insult against women, not men. By the twenty-first century the offence is increasingly generalized, placing ever-greater emphasis on the *offender* and his or her identity as an exhibitionist, rather than the exposee's experience as victim. This reached its logical conclusion in the UK Sexual Offences Act 2003, which repealed sections of the Vagrancy Act 1824, the Town Police Clauses Act 1847 and the Vagrancy Act 1898 (all of which criminalized indecent exposure) and created a new offence of 'Exposure' to replace that of 'Indecent Exposure'. According to Section 66 of the 2003 Act, a person commits this offence by intentionally exposing his or her genitals. It is a gender-neutral law. By changing 'exposes his person' to 'exposes genitals', the 2003 Act covers the exposure of female as well as male genitalia. A conviction can be obtained even if there is no victim and no one is alarmed or distressed. The Act increases the penalty from a maximum of three months' imprisonment (which in the past was sometimes accompanied by a flogging) to a maximum of two years' imprisonment.

Who is the Exhibitionist?

Exhibitionism is legally difficult to define. The range of activities proscribed in 'indecent exposure' legislation differed dramatically over time and between geographical jurisdictions. Sometimes exposure referred only to the penis; at other times buttocks, anuses or breasts were also proscribed. The 'indecent' body was either explicitly named or was euphemistically referred to as 'the body', 'the person', 'intimate parts' or 'private parts'. Some laws required that the exposure occurred in a public place; others simply required the act to be carried out in the presence of another person; still others stipulated the sex of the witnesses (the victim had to be a woman, for instance, thus dictating gender differences in susceptibility to sexual horror and fear). In the USA more than two dozen states insisted that there had to be evidence of 'lewdness or sexual arousal'.[7] Agency was often, but not always, invoked. Thus in some but not all jurisdictions exposure had to be intentional or wilful. It was no wonder that naturists were often concerned that the indecency legislation criminalized their activities.

Nevertheless, most commentators estimate that around one-third of all sexual criminals are exhibitionists,[8] but this is a highly unreliable statistic. Until recently it was not possible to know what proportion of criminals charged under vagrancy laws had actually exposed the penis. Even more than in relation to other sex crimes, victims did not bother reporting exhibitionism to the police, although changing norms may have influenced the level of reporting. As a London prison medical officer claimed in the mid-1950s, the rise in this offence in the previous few decades could have been due to mounting female sensitivities to sexual insults coupled with an increased willingness to turn to legal authorities for redress. Two hundred years ago, he mused, a man who exposed his genitals to a female stranger risked having 'some robust measures applied to him by the crowd'. 'I doubt if the exhibitionist was ever charged with insulting a female,' he continued, 'unless he performed his antics before the lady of the manor.' In contrast, 'to-day, with improvements in education, culture and social conditions, there is no woman so humble that she does not feel herself entitled to be protected against that sort of misbehaviour'. As a result, the police were more liable to become involved in cases of exposure.[9]

This prison medical officer was evoking myths of community and community solidarity (albeit, highly hierarchical) that supposedly existed in the past and could enforce respectable behaviour even before the creation of police forces (as late as 1829 in the UK). He did recognize, however, that the chief handicap to preventing indecency was less female chagrin than male insensitivity. After all, denying the commission of the offence was characteristic of this class of sex criminal. Men accused of indecency often claimed to have forgotten to fasten their trousers after dressing. Or they had merely been observed while urinating, they tediously exclaimed: they suffered from an enlarged prostate or a sensitive and small bladder. Enuresis, nephritis, urethral stricture and scabies were all proffered as excuses. More simply, men accused of exhibiting themselves simply pleaded guilty to drinking too much and remembering too little.[10]

After all, was indecent exposure such a serious offence anyway? they queried. Religious scruples convinced some men that exhibitionism was a lesser sin than 'having relations with a woman to whom you are not married'. 'You go to hell for that,' explained one unabashed forty-five-year-old virgin addicted to exhibiting himself to young girls.[11] Treatment might even be seen as a form of 'martyrdom', since it deprived the individual of his sexual pleasures.[12] It was no wonder that, from a psychoanalytic perspective, exhibitionists were lambasted for being stubborn, even hostile, men. The exhibitionist was 'always a sick person', argued Benjamin Karpman. He was 'rigid, isolated, sheltered, orderly, all for one purpose, protection'. Shyness and extremely conscientious behaviour masked his inward rebellion. Compulsive rituals dominated his life; he was plagued by a bewildering range of pathological symptoms, including 'complete abstinence, excessive masturbation, frequent emission dreams, priapism, absolute or relative impotence, ejaculation at the sight of women, *ejaculatio praecox*, or sexual incompetence'. Karpman observed that such men preferred the 'comparative safety of compulsive defenses to the ordeal of facing their unconscious drives'. 'Once an exhibitionist, always an exhibitionist,' Karpman grumbled.[13]

The question of responsibility was furiously disputed by legal and psychiatric experts. A great deal depended on whether men who engaged in indecent exposure were considered as dangerous. In courts exhibitionists were often harshly treated, indicating that there was considerable fear about their activities. They could be sentenced to anything from one to twenty years' imprisonment. In California indecent exposure was punished more harshly than the 'wilful infliction of pain on a child under circumstances likely to produce death'. Until a 1972 decision by the California Supreme Court, the courts could sentence repeat offenders to an indeterminate term of imprisonment.[14]

Some psychiatrists agreed with legal experts about the risks posed by this category of offender. Was there a tendency for the seriousness of crimes committed by exhibitionists to escalate? According to psychiatrist Graham Rooth, writing in the early 1970s, one in ten men convicted of exhibitionist activities had previously attempted rape and one in five had prior convictions for sexual offences in which force had been used.[15] Although Rooth regarded these statistics as evidence that exhibitionists were *not* dangerous, I am tempted to draw the opposite conclusion. Some observers saw sadistic elements in certain acts of exhibitionism. Was it possible that some exhibitionists were actually suppressing a wish to rape women?[16] As was asked in 1939 by the senior psychologist in charge of the sex clinic responsible for evaluating sex offenders committed to the penitentiary on Rikers Island (New York): could the men who committed this misdemeanour today become 'the rapists and murderers of tomorrow'? This psychologist had no doubt that the answer was affirmative. As evidence he gave the case of a twenty-eight-year-old prisoner. Having been arrested five times for exhibiting his penis on the subway, this prisoner admitted that he got his greatest pleasure 'not from the act of exhibiting himself, but from the look of horror on the women's faces when they suddenly come upon him in the act'. 'It is quite safe to predict,' the psychologist concluded, that 'sooner or later, if his condition remains untreated, this sadistic urge may no longer remain satisfied merely from the look of horror on women's faces . . . but may translate itself into stronger and more potent sadistic drives, such as rape, assault or murder.' This was why the penal authorities ('indecent exposure') should cooperate with the psychiatrists ('exhibitionism'): the *motive* was as important as the *act*.[17]

Nevertheless, as I observed in Chapter 7, 'The Couch', most psychological experts advocated compassion rather than chastisement. There is no point in punishing the exhibitionist simply because he has 'temporarily lost normal mental functioning', Karpman pointed out. There could be 'no question of responsibility', he believed.[18] Because the most common age for a man to start exposing was fifteen,[19] some researchers concluded that exhibitionism was a form of adolescent sexual experimentation, which (paradoxically) is a 'safe strategy' for the exhibitionist since it avoids 'the twin perils of intimacy and rejection'. In this view exhibitionism is simply a 'courtship disorder'.[20] Men who expose themselves do 'little harm to society', claimed legal experts for the UK National Council for Civil Liberties.[21] Psychoanalytic approaches went even further, pointing out that many people dream of being naked in a public space. Such dreams revealed 'what we ought in the interests of human sympathy to recognise', lectured a neurologist in 1921, that 'between ourselves and those whom we stigmatise as exhibitionists, and therefore criminals, the difference . . . is one of degree alone'.[22] In the 1930s the psychiatric director of Bellevue Hospital in New York even accused individuals who treated exhibitionists and 'peeping Toms' as 'terrible sex criminals' of being hypocrites. The same people who condemned exhibitionists were willing to spend large sums of money in nightclubs, enjoying the sight of 'nude or almost nude women dancing about in a very suggestive fashion'.[23] Striptease, fan dances and 'bubble dances' were simply legitimized forms of exhibitionism, carried out by women rather than men.[24]

This link between sexual emancipation and tendencies to exhibitionism continued to be made into the 1950s and 1960s. Exhibitionism was the way men who were denied access to free and fulfilling means of sexual expression coped with deprivation. It should be seen as the heartfelt cry of 'a cornered human being, in need of a social relationship he is not able to make', claimed the author of 'Sex-Crime and its Socio-Historical Background' (1964).[25] Others wanted to put an even more positive gloss on indecent displays. As David Thomson Maclay, a psychiatrist at Brentwood Mental Hospital in the UK, observed in 1952, the 'potential exhibitionist' found himself in a difficult position. On the one hand, he was impelled to commit an act that was legally and socially prohibited, yet, on the other hand, he was living in a culture permeated by suggestive displays. If only children could be given 'freer rein' to express themselves, Maclay bemoaned, they would not feel the need later in their lives to 'revolt against suppression . . . of childish and youthful desires and acts'. The adult exhibitionist was 'another manifestation of their revolt against mishandled childhood urges'.[26] In a slightly more radical version of this argument, exhibitionists were not simply scared and desperate: they were proto-revolutionaries – at least the psychiatric adviser to the medical department of the US Office of the Surgeon General thought so. For him exhibitionism was a 'revolt against the moral shackles which our civilization has set upon itself'. Exhibitionists were asserting a principled opposition to those 'moral laws' that had been 'artificially superimposed on natural instincts'.[27]

This romantic notion of the benefits of unrestrained sexual expression met with much opposition, even from within psychiatric circles. As the author of 'Sexual Pervert Impulses and Obsessions' (1900) warned, the 'irresistible tendency to exhibit in public' was dangerous to the entire social fabric.[28] Experts were concerned about the dramatic rise in cases of indecent exposure coming before the courts between the 1940s and the late 1960s. More conservative commentators thought it significant that this rise was particularly marked among men aged under twenty-one. Was it just a coincidence that this increase in 'sexual difficulties among young people' occurred in a society 'dedicated to the removal of those inhibitions and barriers supposedly responsible for the sexual perversions and neuroses'? Were changes in sexual and social mores 'exercising an adverse effect on psychosexual development', making it more difficult for young men to establish adult relationships?[29] If these men were mentally ill, society as a whole was placing itself at risk.

Pathological Exhibitionism

Once the idea that exhibitionists were psychiatrically ill ('mad') as opposed to simply vagrants ('bad') began gaining support, the precise nature of their pathology became the main issue. In 1900 Charles Gilbert Chaddock (Professor of the Nervous System at Marion-Sims College of Medicine in St Louis) insisted that the act was 'so obviously silly and purposeless' that it had to be the result of 'anomalous mental factors'.[30] Were exhibitionists 'degenerate'? Could they be epileptics, as many influential psychiatrists believed, including Richard von Krafft-Ebing, author of the highly respected study of sexual perversions *Psychopathia Sexualis* (1886)?[31] Or could the purported link between exhibitionism and degeneracy be an illusion? Writing in the early 1920s, W. Norwood East, the influential Medical Inspector of HM Prisons, disputed any link between exhibitionism and epilepsy, arguing that the label 'degenerate' simply tended to 'thwart clear thinking' and inhibit meticulous investigation.[32] Epileptics exhibited their genitals in the process of losing consciousness; they lacked the deliberate motive that made the exhibitionist 'deviant'.[33]

In the early years of the twentieth century a new generation of psychiatrists argued that exhibitionists were suffering from an obsessive or compulsive disorder instead of degeneracy. The impulsive, obsessive feature of exhibitionism was what made exhibitionism dangerous. Thus a speaker to the International Medical Congress in 1900 lamented the 'irresistibility of the need, the anguished struggle between the morbid pleasure which commended it and the consciousness which appreciated and resisted it'. The exhibitionist's 'irresistible tendency to exhibit in public' condemned him to a life that alternated relentlessly between 'remissions and paroxysms'.[34]

There was another kind of compulsive pathology that could have been responsible for these men's affliction: 'satyriasis', a male form of nymphomania. I have already discussed this prognosis in Chapter 4, 'Rapacious Bodies', and Chapter 8, 'Female Perpetrators; Male Victims'. The 'victim of satyriasis' suffered from a compulsive urge to 'expose his person in public', even if it ruined his reputation as a 'clergyman or dignified banker', concluded the author of 'Insanity in Medico-Legal Bearings' (1900).[35] David S. Booth (neurologist to the Missouri Pacific Railway) pondered the same question, but he wanted to make a distinction between satyriasis and erotomania. For Booth satyriasis (and nymphomania) were neuroses while erotomania was a psychosis. As a result, persons afflicted with satyriasis attempted to satisfy their 'inordinate sexual desire', while sufferers of erotomania were plagued with the need to perform impulsive acts that had very little to do with sexual intercourse or orgasm (indeed, their actions were often accompanied by flaccidity of the sexual organ). Either way this medicalization of a sexual act was important. The terms 'satyriasis' and 'erotomania' served as both symptom and cause of disease.

Booth illustrated his understanding of the pathological (erotomanic) nature of exhibitionism by drawing on his examination and treatment of 'Mr G. A. R.' who sought help in February 1904. Mr G. A. R., a machinist of German descent, had a long history of indecent exposure. The security of his marriage and family were threatened by his urges. Despite knowing that the newspapers had published warnings of his activities, he simply could not restrain himself from exhibiting his penis in public. Even worse, he was obsessed with exhibiting himself in the same place and at the same time of day as he had in the past. It was a compulsion: Mr G. A. R. described the urge as feeling like a 'wave passing over him'. During these attacks his mind went 'blank'. He was not even aware of being in a crowded public place. Sexual desire did not seem to be the motivating factor. Indeed, Mr G. A. R. was unable to say whether or not he had an erection at those times.

Booth was intrigued by his patient. He ruled out any hereditary predisposition to exhibitionism, and observed that although Mr G. A. R. often worked overtime, his way of life was otherwise healthy. Pulse and temperature? Normal. Tongue? Clear. Bowels? Regular. However, there were some indications of a general neuropathic condition. Mr G. A. R. suffered from slight loss of sensation on his left side (especially of his hand and foot), his knee jerks were exaggerated and some skin reflexes, including the cremasteric reflex,* were lost. In Booth's words: 'Exaggerated knee jerks occur in all functional and most organic cerebral diseases . . . skin reflexes are usually lost in those diseases in which the tendon reflexes are exaggerated [and] are also lost in brain diseases, but never in hysteria'. Booth diagnosed erotomania. When Mr G. A. R. was brought before the courts on an indecency charge, Booth recommended that the jury acquit him on the grounds of insanity.

There was a problem, however. Judges and jurors found it difficult to accept that men of good character could be psychologically compelled to carry out depraved actions. In the case of Mr G. A. R., it took three trials before Booth could persuade a jury that the defendant was insane. The first two juries could not make up their minds. The previous good character of the defendant militated against the diagnosis of a long-term mental illness like erotomania. But, as Booth insisted, 'to punish as criminals those unfortunates who happen to be diseased in a

*This reflex is elicited by stroking the superior and medial part of the thigh in a downward direction; in males, this will normally cause the cremasteric muscle to contract and pull up the scrotum and testis.

manner which forces them to criminal acts, is a sad commentary on 20th century civilization'.[36]

Psychiatrists had to convince jurists that civilization rested upon both differentiating clearly the sane from the insane and treating the latter with the kind consideration that flawed specimens of a common humanity deserved. To do so, psychiatrists developed detailed nosologies, or elaborate classification schemes, which could distinguish the 'voluntarily vulgar and depraved sensualist' from the 'involuntary exposure propensities and acts of the naturally continent and virtuous'. The fundamental purpose of such classification was to enable medical personnel to evaluate the health of a person's inner mental world through an examination of outward signs, many of which related to class, race and gender. In the early years of the twentieth century, for example, C. H. Hughes published an article in *The Alienist and Neurologist* which presented the tribulations of Charles K. Cannon, a widower of about sixty who was a prominent local lawyer and an active member of the Trinity P. E. Church in Hoboken (New Jersey). Unfortunately, Cannon's reputation had been destroyed when seventeen girls aged between eight and fourteen accused him of exposing his penis to them. He was found guilty, fined $1000 and sentenced to a prison term of fifteen years. Hughes brooded over whether it was even *possible* that such a prominent figure in the community was guilty of such a debased crime. Perhaps, he speculated, Cannon had been the latest victim of 'feminine morbid erotism' (that is, false accusations). Even if the exposures had taken place, Hughes claimed that Cannon could not have been responsible for his actions, saying:

> the age of the man, his life history, and the record of the fact suggest to the expert in psychiatry the possibility of a doubt of voluntary moral guilt. The presumption of mental decay and aberration would, *prima facie*, appear to be a more rational conclusion in this case.

Economic respectability, white skin colour and conformity to dominant middle-aged masculine norms were sufficient to authenticate Cannon's moral innocence. The only explanation left to Hughes was to claim that Cannon must have exposed his penis under delusions arising out of the 'erotopathic perversions of neurone disease degeneration'.[37] Psychiatric diagnosis fulfilled an important function in maintaining social stability.

Compensatory Exhibitionism

This labelling of indecent exposure as a degenerative pathology had become less fashionable by the 1920s. Like Hughes, new commentators noted that exhibitionists were frequently highly intelligent men. The psychiatrist could not assume therefore that such men were depraved, psychopathic or mentally deficient.[38] Could indecent exposure arise out of something far simpler: a man's lack of alternative ways to express his sexuality? In the 1920s the commentator on sex crimes and Medical Inspector of HM Prisons W. Norwood East explicitly argued that many (although, he was careful to point out, not all) acts of exhibitionism were normal responses to sexual frustration. A lot of exhibitionists were simply depraved, hastily attempting to attract the attention of a woman. These cases might be 'revolting' but, East explained, they resembled 'courtships of the farmyard' or the 'love antics and "showing off" indulged in by certain animals to arouse sexual desire in the females of their species'.

Women may reject these 'antics' or they may actively incite such behaviour. As an example, East recalled the case of a middle-aged man whose wife had abruptly announced that, despite 'several years of happily married life', she would no longer engage in sexual relations with him. The effect was catastrophic. Within eighteen months this man had been convicted three times of exposing himself on an outdoor seat (although East wryly observed that the man's 'enormous pendulous abdomen must have partially, if not entirely, concealed his genitals'). The man was devastated by his own actions, realizing that he was 'ruining himself', but claimed to be unable to control himself. In East's view a significant portion of responsibility for criminal exposure could be neatly shifted into the laps of 'frigid' women.[39]

The assumption that the closing off of men's legitimate sexual outlets was the cause of the development of a psychopathology was frequently applied in the service of imperial endeavours.[40] In the 1920s, for instance, Martin Peck of the Psychopathic Hospital in Boston recounted the lengthy treatment of a missionary who had become an exhibitionist. This missionary had suffered 'sexual trauma' as a six-year-old when an older girl exposed herself to him. He endured anguish in his attempts to rein in his masturbatory urges. His 'exceptionally strong sexual drive' had been subdued by 'old-fashioned religious repression' rather than by 'any real adjustment', Peck believed. It was not unexpected, therefore, that the crisis would come to a head when the missionary was thrown into a 'primitive Oriental environment'. 'Deprived of social outlet', he was no longer able to repress his sexual drives and began exhibiting his penis in public. Despite the fact that it cost him his job, the missionary regarded his acts as a 'normal masculine weakness of a minor order' and would have been more upset and embarrassed if his errors had 'involved ordinary illicit sex with other women'.

What was the solution to this missionary's dilemma? Peck admitted that, in addition to the provision of a lengthy course of psychoanalysis, 'it seemed wise to the physician to use rather heroic measures in order to jolt the patient from [his] complacency'. 'Dire pictures' were painted of the possible consequences of his continuing to exhibit himself. Peck admitted that this scaremongering was 'opposed to all theories of suggestive therapies' and risked throwing the patient into a 'reactionary depression' once he became aware of the 'enormity of his psychopathology'. Nevertheless, Peck still felt that such a blunt approach was appropriate in this case. According to him, the treatment worked. Three years after treatment stopped, the man had still not reoffended. Peck did warn, though, that the compulsion might recur 'in the event of some external deprivation of his love-life'.[41]

By the 1950s this 'compensatory' explanation for exhibitionism had gained popularity. Men exhibited their genitals to compensate themselves for the lack of alternative, socially acceptable ways of expressing their sexuality. The exhibitionist discussed by East had been impelled to expose himself by the frosty refusal of his wife to accommodate his sexual needs and Peck's missionary had been driven to his actions by the clash between a lascivious Orientalism and the absence of white 'outlets'. Still other men were said to have turned to exhibitionism simply because their wives were incapable of giving valid consent to intercourse. Thus, in a case discussed by psychiatrist David Thomson Maclay of Brentwood Mental Hospital, the exhibitionist's wife had not actually refused her husband sexually. Rather, she had been rendered incapable of sexual response because she had become senile. Deprived of his wife's companionship, her sixty-four-year-old husband began exposing himself to girls at the entrance to a lavatory.

Maclay drew extensive conclusions from this single case study. He pointed out that exposing one's genitals to strangers gave satisfaction. It was a substitute for 'more acceptable forms of love-making' and, for lonely sixty-four-year-olds, was preferable to visiting prostitutes or embarking on the tedious process of courting other women. After all, the psychiatrist continued, exhibitionists were typically timid and prudish. They feared rejection as much as they dreaded contracting venereal diseases. Many were also emotionally and psychosexually immature. Given these handicaps, they lacked the ability to restrain their 'natural' masculine drives. Wasn't it obvious, Maclay insisted, that *all* men were polygamous and this 'streak' was only held in check if the monogamous ideal was coupled with a 'love-match'? Men who were unfortunate in being denied a 'sterling and enduring' sexual match had to find other ways to discharge their mounting sexual tension. This was a view of male sexuality as a pressure pump. In times of mounting inflammation, indecent exposure was a natural and (according to Maclay) relatively harmless moral response. Obviously, imprisonment was counterproductive for these exhibitionists and could even exacerbate the problem by weakening what little stability and self-confidence they possessed.

Equally, although castration might be necessary in 'desperate cases', any 'free resort' to this operation would be 'a step towards undermining the fundamental values of the inviolability of human personality that we in this country hold dear'. It would be much better to encourage exhibitionists to channel their sexual energies into other spheres (Maclay urged them to develop a 'love of animals, an athletic instinct, [or] a constructive bent').[42] What few psychiatrists mentioned, however, was the chief drawback of the 'compensatory argument'. The most obvious cure – vigorous attempts by exhibitionists to 'exhaust' themselves sexually 'by frequent intercourse' – inevitably failed.[43]

This mid-century emphasis on exhibitionism as 'compensating' men for women's failure to satisfy them sexually was used to explain what many commentators found puzzling: the absence of exhibitionism among those they designated as 'primitive races'. Maclay reflected on this surprising discovery. While working as a medical missionary in Natal he had noted that exhibitionism was absent among Zulus. Perhaps, he ruminated, this was because their communities took it as natural that young people required sexual expression. Youth in this culture 'suffered less repression than among some western races' because they were reared 'more closely to nature', he concluded.[44] The author of a 1947 article in the *Journal of Mental Science* concurred: exhibitionism was absent among 'naked savages'. The perversion was clearly a 'product of civilization'.[45]

This racial argument was applied closer to home. Some commentators were mystified as to why so few African-American men turned to exhibitionism, when 'everyone knew' they were profligate sexual abusers in other ways. Two psychiatrists advising courts in Chicago in the early 1940s thought they could explain the paradox. It was their belief that 'the negroes' early heterosexual adjustment' acted as a prophylaxis to indecent exposure.[46] Manfred Guttmacher, leading psychiatrist and Chief Medical Officer to the Supreme Bench of Baltimore, went even further. According to him, the low incidence of exhibitionism and paedophilia among African-Americans was due to the physical superiority of the black man's penis. Exhibitionists tended to be 'passive-dependent individuals, with marked feelings of general and penile inferiority'. Because African-American penises were 'considerably longer than that of the [white] man's' – as was 'fully confirmed by Kinsey's actual measurements', Guttmacher brashly went on – they were spared this inferiority complex. Guttmacher also acknowledged that the 'compensatory' explanation was credible. After all, the 'low frequency of sexual exhibitionism among Negros may in part be due to the free rein that many males at certain socio-economic levels give to exhibitionism in other ways – with their gaudy-colored zoot suits and their flashy automobiles'.[47] As I will be arguing later, this last explanation feminized African-American men. Women's bright clothing and accoutrements were the main arguments used to explain why women did not need to exhibit their genitals: African-American men enjoyed similar latitude in self-expression.

Psychoanalytical Approaches

While the 'compensatory' explanation derived some of its impetus from Freudian concepts, a more rigorously psychoanalytical interpretation starting gaining popularity around the middle of the twentieth century. These analysts, like earlier commentators, drew a clear distinction between perverts and exhibitionists. While perverts acted in pursuit of hedonistic pleasures, exhibitionists were driven by unconscious and compulsive drives. Exhorting exhibitionists to 'control themselves' was therefore ridiculous. Their acts were not aimed at sexual gratification – indeed, orgasm was of little concern to them. Rather, this explanation went, exhibitionists were preoccupied with relieving much more fundamental frustrations – those arising out of buried incestuous desires and the subsequent fear of castration. Accordingly, the young boy, in rivalry with his father for his mother's affection, becomes terrified that his father may retaliate by castrating him. In order to dispel this unconscious fear, certain men respond by publicly exposing 'the integrity of their genitals' to female strangers.[48] It did not surprise these analysts that the parents of exhibitionists were severe disciplinarians. Despite the fact that their mothers tended to be 'oral-sadistic' and 'narcissistically dominating', exhibitionists were

> strongly attached to their phallic mothers with whom they shared unconscious incestual strivings, while they felt deeply humiliated by the rejecting and infantalizing attitude of the 'too masculine' father. Through their exhibitionist acts, they proved to themselves and to the world that the mother did not succeed in possessing and castrating them and that they remained as manly as the father.[49]

In the words of one leading Freudian, the exhibitionist was unconsciously sending out a message to his audience: 'Reassure me that I have a penis by reacting to the sight of it.' The exhibitionist also wanted to broadcast the message: 'Reassure me that you are *afraid* of my penis, that is, that you fear me; then I do not need to be afraid myself.' It was 'a kind of magical gesture'.[50] Of course, these castration-fearing men were sensible enough to ensure that they exhibited themselves only to young girls: lurking behind male defiance was the recognition of women's castrating powers.[51]

Nathan King Rickles's article 'Exhibitionism' (1942) and his 1950 book of the same title were influential examples of this approach. As the Director of the Psychiatric Center in Seattle, Rickles was well placed to promote the argument that exhibitionists suffered because of their distorted processes of repression. The exhibitionist was generally a timid, unassertive man dominated by his wife or mother, Rickles insisted. Through exhibitionism this individual sought to prove that he was virile and attractive, possessing at least one thing that his mother or wife lacked. The exhibitionist's highly honed form of auto-eroticism or narcissism meant that his sexual emotions were 'entirely lost in self-admiration'. Rickles explained that, according to Freudian analysis, narcissism was a stage in the development of masculine sexual inversion in which the individual was 'supposed to identify himself with a woman (usually his mother) and so to acquire self-love'. In the case of exhibitionists this son–mother love became exaggerated. The 'self love stage of sexual inversion' failed to 'give satisfaction' and rapidly became intolerable. As a result, the 'exposure of the sexual organ symbolically represent[ed] a revolt from repression; an attempt to prove the masculinity of the subject and an unconscious striving for a real love object'. In time this need to assert his 'masculine superiority' would become so great that it could not be controlled. However, women remained the 'giant, engulfing figures before whom the grown-up little boy was helpless'. The exhibitionist was paralysed by the fear of being castrated or swallowed up by the female. In order to seek release from this overwhelming dread, he acted out childhood fears with female strangers (or substitutes for the mother). He required a strong reaction from the women to whom he exhibited himself, because he was motivated by 'an overwhelming need to find an outlet for the frustration set up by his forbidden goal: incest'.

Rickles placed much of the blame for this unhappy state of affairs on the exhibitionists' mothers, whose faults were legion. He castigated them for being both 'aggressive' and 'clinging vines'. They were 'masculine' in appearance; they tended to marry passive men. Rickles accused these mothers of being 'extremely narcissistic women, unconsciously motivated by strong penis-envy'. The great enemy was the 'phallic mother'. For Rickles 'all women, and consequently all mothers' were narcissistic. Indeed, within certain limits, this was a 'normal female attribute'. After all, Rickles believed, *all* female children felt ('more or less consciously') that they had been 'discriminated against because they have no penis'. Normally, he continued,

> this feeling is outgrown as the girl begins to recognize that femininity has its own special advantages and assets. But immature women, those whose libido has remained largely attached to themselves, are apt to retain this 'masculine protest' for the rest of their lives. The advent of a male child seems to them a solution and a compensation for their own dilemma.

As a result of her excitement that 'here – actual, tangible, and in her own possession – is the male organ of which she was originally deprived', the mother of the exhibitionist snapped apart proper bounds. Her 'masculine protest' became 'a demand to achieve superiority, or at least equality with men'. What better way to achieve this than through producing male offspring ('as a means of producing the lost penis') and retaining an 'emotional hold' on her son throughout her life?

For Rickles this psychoanalytic theory not only explained why mothers of exhibitionists were so attached to their sons, but also why sons had such an overwhelming need to exhibit their genitals to female strangers. Through exposure the son made 'an unconscious effort to break this identification with his mother, to cut the cord that binds him to her so tightly and to affirm himself as a separate, *masculine* individual'. By exposing his 'overvalued, envied, all-powerful organ' he was attempting to 'break away from the engulfing mother, to assert that his penis belongs to him and him only'. It was an act of barefaced defiance. So great was the urge to defy convention that the exposer was often relieved, if not downright delighted, when arrested: 'It seems to give him satisfaction to know that he is capable of doing something which will classify him as a criminal,' Rickles reckoned. Punishment was welcomed as a 'means of reducing the guilt which he feels because of his incestuous drive. The policeman or the jail represents his superego or father, and he gladly pays the penalty for his offence in order that he may be better able to forgive himself.' The message to society was clear: 'See, I am a man.' Exhibitionists were shouting, 'I show myself so that all can see me and I welcome arrest as proof that I have a male organ and am like other men.'

In contrast, the exhibitionist's cry to his mother was swollen with mute reproach. Rickles placed himself in the position of the exhibitionist. 'I have tried to convey to you in so many ways that I wanted to share things with you, particularly my body which you have made me feel is wonderful', Rickles imagined the exhibitionist silently telling his mother. However,

> when I wished to share my new sex experience, I was always frustrated by your attitude. You made me feel that this was wrong and sinful . . . I tried to be all the things that you demanded of me: a superior, healthy child, clever, neat, clean, morally firm and upright. To do this, I had to suppress the normal desires that all children have . . . I stayed away from girls. More and more, I was thrown on my own devices and limited to my own company, with the result that my body became the center of my attention and I glorified it to the same degree that I strove to be your ideal. It is all for you. I can no longer dam back the strong tide within me that demands release.

In this narrative punishment was also welcomed: 'It will be worthwhile if I can get relief from my tension and in some way convey to you that I am exposing myself to you and for you.'

Psychotherapy provided the only escape from this torturous situation. According to Rickles, the exhibitionist must be helped to assert his superiority over his wife while at the same time renounce his mother. If he was married, it was crucial that his wife also received therapy. In part this was because treatment of the exhibitionist would inevitably lead to changes in the couple's sex life (for instance, because the exhibitionist had to be informed of the ruinous effects of the 'infantile act of masturbation' and coitus interruptus, proper contraceptive information had to be given so that 'coitus could be completed'). But treatment of the wife was also necessary to ensure that she did not hamper the entire curative process by continuing to refuse sexual intercourse. She must be 'made aware that completion of the sex act is an important part of her husband's cure'.

If asserting superiority over the wife was a gruelling challenge, separation from the mother was even harder. 'Hell has no fury like a woman scorned,' Rickles quipped, so the therapist had to be prepared to go to extremes to enforce the break. A court order might be required. The struggle would not stop at that point. Once the two had been separated, the exhibitionist's 'distorted' attachment to his mother had to be tackled. Breaking the patient's unconscious resistance to an in-depth analysis of his past might require the use of a 'truth serum' (sodium pentothal). In such circumstances, Rickles continued, it was imperative that the therapist was a man. Exhibitionists needed to be taught to 'respect authority . . . If the male therapist can partially but effectively supplant the mother, the key to the solution is close at hand'.[52]

As psychiatrists like Rickles repeatedly contended, 'effectively supplanting the mother' was difficult. Analysts like Thomas Hackett, who had been offering psychotherapeutic treatments to men convicted of indecent exposure at the Court Clinic in East Cambridge (Massachusetts) since 1954, agreed, observing, however, that exhibitionists typically went through three phases in the torturous route towards cure. Initially they enthusiastically embraced the analytical regime. Professing keenness to attend the fifty-minute sessions, they often insisted that they had been thinking of obtaining psychiatric help before being apprehended by the police. (Hackett, however, claimed to have never met an exhibitionist who had sought help without the persuasive edict of the constabulary or court.) In this phase the urge to exhibit generally subsided and the patient believed that simply talking about his problems ('although no insight has been gained') was sufficient to cure his problems. Therapists were exhorted to resist any hint of complacency and persevere to the second phase: that is, dealing with the inevitable relapses.

How was the patient to foil temptation when the urge returned? Initially Hackett believed that encouraging masturbation would prove efficacious. He was rapidly disillusioned: indeed, many exhibitionists 'regarded masturbation as more heinous an act than exposing'. Might pain be a restraining force? Just as people trying to give up smoking were advised to burn themselves with lighted cigarettes, Hackett encouraged the exhibitionist to harm himself in some way when faced with the illicit urge. This advice had drastic consequences for one of his patients, a hod carrier. When 'tormented' by the desire to expose, this man 'emptied the entire hod of bricks upon his foot breaking a metatarsal'. 'Needless to say,' Hackett dryly observed, 'the resulting pain precluded exhibitionism.'

Identifying what led a man to exhibit himself was the next challenge for both therapist and patient. Exhibitionists generally attempted to persuade the therapist that their actions were sexual. Exposure was a 'prelude to seduction', patients wished to believe, insisting that they expected women to marvel at the sight of their penis. This was nonsense, the therapist was required to point out: 'There are far better ways of approaching a woman for sex than affronting her with a naked penis.' Rather than sex, the therapist had to convince patients that exhibitionism was about aggression. But what was the source of patients' anger? Once this was identified (through the talking cure), patients had to find alternative ways of coping with this destructive emotion. Hackett believed that sublimation was unlikely to work. Exhibitionists tended to be sexually inhibited men: they were generally incapable of exposing themselves in front of mirrors, let alone baring themselves to girlfriends or wives. 'Socially acceptable' ways to express anger had to be found – and Hackett took for granted that it was socially acceptable to vent anger against women within the domestic context. In his words,

> I encouraged patients to express anger at their wives when this was called for by shouting, talking back, pounding the table, or even simulating anger that wasn't felt. The last, like method acting, sometimes worked beautifully. It was of great help when the wife of the exhibitionist was also in treatment with our social service department because she, too, could be taught to encourage rather than thwart nascent attempts at the expression of anger on the part of her spouse.[53]

In this way Hackett (who boasted about his impressive 'cure' record) managed to prevent men from exhibiting themselves to female strangers by redirecting their aggressive energies towards female intimates. Anger management – in a form that encouraged the abuse of female relatives and lovers, as opposed to simply bashing a pillow or punch bag, for instance – became a way of managing men who, until this time, had focused their sexual abuse on female strangers.

Hackett was not atypical in his approach. It was a recommendation proposed by many other analysts frustrated by what they saw as the domineering, over-assertive, over-protective, sexually ignorant and prudish personalities of exhibitionists' wives and mothers. In 1976 Arnold Veraa strongly advised probation officers to ensure that wives and mothers understood 'how they are contributing to the stress which triggers the exposures'. In order to prevent reoffending, the exhibitionist had to be encouraged to become 'more active and assertive in the family environment' and gain 'an increased recognition of his masculinity'. His wife had to 'lose some of her own inhibitions about sexuality, so developing a more satisfying sexual relationship'. If improvement was too slow, Veraa recommended 'environmental manipulation', such as encouraging the exhibitionist to leave home and live elsewhere. It was important that the man was encouraged to express his aggression in order to develop a 'more stable and more satisfying male identity (in accordance with his cultural expectations)'.[54] Although psychoanalytical approaches were too time-consuming and expensive[55] for most criminal jurisdictions, the emphasis upon male sexual needs which women were responsible for nurturing and accommodating was in harmony with the Zeitgeist of the 1950s to the 1970s.

The Mystery of the Absent Women Exhibitionists

Both 'compensatory' and psychoanalytical explanations of male exhibitionists pointed the finger of blame at the female sex. Given this magical reversal of responsibility from the (active-male) exhibitionist to his (passive-female) spouse or mother, it is perhaps surprising that this sex crime is committed almost exclusively by men.[56] This exclusivity is unique to the human species: in public spaces female apes regularly exhibit their genitals to their male counterpart, for instance.[57] Leaving aside the anthropomorphic fallacy of this comparison (as well as the problem of talking about 'public versus private' in relation to apes), why do women refrain from openly displaying their genitals to non-consenting men? The obvious explanation was the one given by sociologists: women possessed far greater opportunities than men for adorning and displaying their body. Women were licensed to undress in public to a much greater degree than men.[58] Rather than impelled by an urge to shock or frighten, female sexual display to male strangers was performed in the interests of seduction.[59]

The psychoanalytic community, however, regarded this explanation as superficial. According to some analysts, women did not expose their genitals because 'they have nothing to expose'.[60] Not possessing a penis, they had no need to find mechanisms to deal with castration anxiety. 'Consciously or unconsciously, they are ashamed because they do not have a penis and they seek to hide that lack,' Rickles maintained. Instead women coped with their 'narcissism' and 'penis-envy' by having male children – whom they promptly turned into exhibitionists.[61]

The most-cited elaboration of this theory was put forward by Berlin psychoanalyst Jeno Hárnik in an article published in the 1924 issue of the *International Journal of Psycho-Analysis*. Employing principles laid down by Sigmund Freud and Sándor Ferenczi, Hárnik premised his argument on the view that puberty represented a major crisis for girls. With the onset of menstruation, clitoral masturbation ('which is very frequently practised up to puberty') suddenly ceased. Unconsciously for the young woman, the flow of blood represented castration and, along with that other flow of blood caused by defloration, helped prepare her for the 'transition of the libido from the clitoris to the vagina'. It was a momentous change because, before puberty, the girl's sexual life had 'a masculine trend, expressed in excitability and masturbation of the clitoris'. Puberty caused a 'reinforcement of sexual inhibitions, the appearance of secondary sex characteristics, the development of "beauty" and an intensification of narcissism'. In Hárnik's words,

> before the onset of repression at puberty the little girl virtually possesses a penis; at puberty her 'beauty' develops, accompanied by those 'charms' which are destined sexually and æsthetically to excite the desire of men. These charms are now the object of the narcissistic self-love which compensates the woman not only for the social restrictions imposed upon her object-choice . . . but also for the renunciation of her infantile masculinity – the loss of her penis. Thus her physical beauty, and especially the beauty of her face, makes up for the lost penis.

For the female sex, he argued, puberty was characterized by the onset of sexual inhibition. In contrast, masturbation increased dramatically at puberty for males. As a consequence, men retained 'the narcissistic estimation of his own penis to a great extent all his life long, whilst the woman, on reaching maturity at puberty, [was] obliged to renounce this high valuation and instead to prize the beauty of her figure and face'. Incidentally, Hárnik argued that girls who failed to repudiate clitoral masturbation at puberty would also fail to develop female 'charms': they would be condemned to possess boyish figures and an 'uncomeliness of face which is permanent'. The normal woman, however, 'replaces her infantile wish to show her genitals by a wish to show all the rest of her body *except* the genitals'. For women the 'whole body becomes genital'.[62] Hárnik held, however, that the face was particularly important. The narcissistic significance of women's faces, in particular, helped explain why the evolutionary history of women meant that they lost their facial hair. The evolutionary disappearance of women's facial hair was due to that sex's 'narcissistic desire' to expose the face. The female version of exhibitionism 'has reference to other parts of the body, above all, to the face', while the male version of exhibitionism remained genital.[63]

This explanation was approved by the radical left-wing psychoanalyst Otto Fenichel in *The Psychoanalytic Theory of Neurosis* (1945). Fenichel agreed that both sexes had an 'instinct' to exhibit themselves, but 'whereas the man, who fears the possibility that he might lose the penis, can reassure himself by showing that the penis is still present, the woman, who actually has no penis and feels this as a narcissistic injury, tries to conceal this lack'. Thus men showed off their 'potency', while women were reduced to merely displaying their 'attractiveness'.[64]

Fenichel was aware, however, that a very rare breed of women did become exhibitionists. What could explain their psychology? According to him, most female exhibitionists were able to displace their castration anxiety. Instead of genital display, they displaced their castration anxieties to their feet, for example. Thus one of his patients 'liked to go barefoot and to show photographs of herself barefoot. She also had the neurotic symptom of feeling a need to stretch and spread her toes during sexual intercourse'. There was a more dangerous type of female exhibitionist, though. These women showed 'a preference for cunnilingus', a practice that allowed 'an especially intense display of the genitals to the man'. For illustration Fenichel discussed a patient of his whose masturbatory fantasy was

> to expose her genitals; this exhibitionism was combined with a predilection for cunnilingus. She had the unconscious idea of taking

> revenge on men by charming them into dependence on and fright of the very organ they once 'despised'. Showing herself as being castrated was a magical gesture aimed at castrating the spectator.

At another level this woman 'unconsciously believed that she had a penis. Her perversion demanded that men should "look more carefully" – then they would find the penis'. There was another side to her preference for cunnilingus. In Fenichel's words, exhibiting the 'ugly' female genitals 'has the unconscious attitude of humiliating men by threatening them stubbornly: "I am castrated; very well, by showing this, I am going to castrate you, too!"'[65]

Behavioural Modification

Behaviourists from the interwar years onwards regarded such speculations as highly fanciful. Wasn't it simpler to assume that exhibitionist acts were learned rather than instinctual? Children were regularly stimulated and touched by other people; they often found themselves naked in the presence of strangers. As a consequence, for some men 'the sight of others, or the removal of clothing' turned into a lifelong 'substitute' for sexual excitement.[66] Of course, this account could not explain why only men become exhibitionists, nor did it account for the fact that men almost always chose female victims, but these minor difficulties were brushed aside with the comment that women had learned alternative ways of self-display and men were accustomed to addressing their sexual needs to women rather than to other men.

As I discussed in Chapter 6, 'The Knife', behaviourist treatments of exhibitionists involved the full range of techniques. Because exhibitionists achieved their gratification from witnessing the disgust and horror on their victims' faces, some treatments aimed at replicating exhibitionist behaviour while eliminating all positive reinforcements. As a result, some effective treatments required the exhibitionist to undress in front of a group of both male and female medical staff for progressively longer periods. The audience would show no emotion while asking him intimate questions. The anxiety created by repeatedly being forced to display himself was believed to suppress the urge to exhibit in the future. Because exhibitionists tended to be less anxious when watched by women-only groups, it was deemed 'therapeutically undesirable'. In this form of negative conditioning, anxiety was precisely what had to be encouraged.[67]

A similar technique, Aversive Behaviour Rehearsal, involved the exhibitionist, his wife or parents, lawyer and medical staff. In the company of these witnesses, the exposer was asked to stand naked in front of a mirror, pull out his penis and 'go through his usual masturbation ritual'. At the same time the witnesses would ask him 'pointed questions' about his thoughts and feelings during masturbation. For instance, he would be asked 'what he thinks about the sight of his body in the mirror, what he imagines the observers are thinking about him, and so forth'. The sessions lasted forty minutes, after which the patient was usually 'in tears, trembling and nauseous'. Patients unwilling to go through the therapy themselves were shown video recordings of other cases in order to experience the treatment 'vicariously'.[68]

Finally, another behaviourist treatment involved applying systematic desensitization. In this approach the compulsive exhibitionist would be taught to relax, then exposed to stimuli referring to the place of exposure, the type of female and her physical attributes. Gradually he would become less and less aroused by the stimuli and his sexual fantasies would consequently lose their impact.[69] All such treatments had to be accompanied by attention to alcohol abuse, courtship behaviour and marital relationships.

Was the indecent exposer a vagrant or a sex criminal? Was the *act* of exposure criminalized or the *actor*? Criminologists and psychiatrists alike were interested in developing classification schemes that would enable them to judge a person's inner life according to outward signs. The middle-class, white male was most easily slotted into the role of exhibitionist; his working-class black counterpart was much more likely to be classed as an indecent exposer.

In either case, for the police and jurists exhibitionism fitted the psychiatric model much better than other sexual crimes. Courts were more likely to refer exhibitionists to psychiatric services than other sex offenders, despite the fact that the prognosis was poor.[70] It was easier to imagine these men as acting according to a broader masculinity: indecent exposure was constructed as an (active) violation of the (passive) visual field of women and children. The shift of emphasis from men who acted in particular ways (men who indecently exposed their penis) to men who possessed an exhibitionist identity was in place from the late nineteenth century. Most notably, however, in the discussions about exhibitionism the primacy given to the male sex organ by analysts mirrored that of the (male) exhibitionist. This approach of the analyst and that of the exhibitionist were not mutually exclusive. Both infused the act of genital exhibitionism (psychiatry) or indecent exposure (law) with an 'aura of mysticism and magical significance'.[71] It was a way of saying, 'This is divine. You may look and adore, but you must not touch.'[72]

The male sex organ was seen as so potent and undeniable that men actively sought castration as the only way to resist its compulsion to exhibit itself to people assumed to be endowed with lesser sex organs.[73] Neither exhaustion through sexual athleticism nor the threat of lengthy incarceration had much effect in restraining the independent, rapacious penis.[74] The penis *was* the man; phallus and penis became conflated into the one organ, clearly excluding women from the symbolic order. In the caustic language of the author of *Sexual Deviation* (1964), men are often comforted by the belief that they have 'large impressive genitals' and 'it is natural for him to think that women will be impressed by them too'. Regrettably, he continued, women 'seldom are' impressed because women tend to 'treat the penis as an organ for use rather than for aesthetic admiration, and are seldom as impressed by its magnificence as men would like them to be'.[75]

In response to female incomprehension, therefore, the exhibitionist was attempting to confirm himself as 'a separate, *masculine* individual'. He 'symbolically shakes his penis at women as he might shake his fist'.[76] Although the exhibitionist was identifying himself as permanently split from women (particularly from those intimate ties with mother and wife), he must always remain alert, 'shaking his fist' at possible encroachments and potential humiliation.

CHAPTER TEN

Sexual Psychopaths

The attacks of 26 July 1957 took place in one of the largest municipal parks in New England, the D. W. Field Park in the north-western section of Brockton, Massachusetts. John and Paul Logan were twelve and ten years of age when their father drove them beside the Ellis Brett Pond and watched them set up their blanket near the edge of the water. His last words to them were, 'Have fun, kids. I'll be back to pick you up here at 3.30.' When he returned six hours later they had disappeared.

The police were immediately called and the pond dragged. More than a hundred policemen, firemen and volunteers scoured the unspoiled woodland around the area where the boys had last been seen. Shortly after nine o'clock the following morning the bodies of John and Paul were found. They had been sexually assaulted, strangled and stabbed to death. An attempt had been made to burn the bodies.

In tabloid fashion *True Detective* magazine took up the story of tracking down their killer. Obviously the person responsible had to be a 'homicidal sex fiend', it asserted, warning that 'somewhere in the city of 60,000 population lurked a homicidal maniac'. Panicking mothers and fathers asked, 'where was he skulking now?' Some parents reported that their children had recently been molested ('now they see the wisdom of reporting such things', a police captain grumbled). The police hauled in 'known offenders' – described as 'furtive characters, some terrified, some sullen and defiant'. The discovery of a house key under the bodies, and the similarities of the crime to one that had happened years earlier, led the police to the culprit: Raymond Ohlson (see photograph, below). A seven-and-a-half-inch, stiletto-like knife, inscribed in Spanish with the words 'I am a hunter', was found under his pillow. The brownish stains on the hilt and blade turned out to be blood. After Ohlson confessed, the other convicts in Plymouth jail nearly 'tore him apart'.

Raymond Ohlson, from Charles Green, 'This Man is Dangerous!', *True Detective*, March 1958

But that wasn't the end of the story. Twenty-one-year-old Ohlson had a lengthy criminal history. At the age of twelve he had sexually attacked a three-year-old boy and beat him unconscious. Two years later he had knifed, strangled and attempted to strip another young boy – also in D. W. Field Park. For this crime Ohlson had been ordered to undergo a thirty-five-day psychiatric examination at the Metropolitan State Hospital in Waltham. After being pronounced legally sane he had been sentenced to serve ten years at the Concord Reformatory. In fact, he had been released from the reformatory only seven weeks before the murderous sex attack on the Logan brothers.

Ohlson's lengthy history of sexual violence provoked outrage: 'Why was a sexual psychopath and potential killer like Raymond Ohlson released from prison without even any supervision?' residents asked. The answer was that Massachusetts had 'no clear-cut, enforceable law that could have kept Ohlson out of circulation'. The State Parole Board had advised the District Attorney that, as a sexual psychopath, Ohlson should be committed to some kind of secure institution for an indefinite period, but, since no certified centre existed, the reformatory had no option but to release him. The brothers had been assaulted and killed at the end of July 1957. By 14 August that year the Governor of Massachusetts had introduced a special bill to safeguard the public from men like Ohlson who had been designated 'psychopaths'. Ohlson was eventually committed for an indefinite term at the Bridgewater State Farm. In the words of *True Detective*, it was a pity and tragedy that the State 'had to learn the hard way that men like Ohlson are dangerous'.[1]

Psychiatrists and clinical psychologists Harry Kozol, Murray Cohen and Ralph Garofalo were given the responsibility for treating Ohlson. They worked at the Center for the Diagnosis and Treatment of Sexually Dangerous Persons at Bridgewater State Farm. They were right in crediting the furore over Ohlson's crimes with the passing of sexual psychopathic legislation and the creation of their Center. As I shall show, throughout America panicky media attention to a rare number of sex crimes (particularly those involving children) led legislatures to introduce special provisions for the incarceration and treatment of this class of offender. At Bridgewater Ohlson was treated by a mixture of individual and group psychotherapy. It was, as the psychiatrists openly acknowledged, an experimental enterprise. As they admitted in the *New England Journal of Medicine* in 1960, the 'magnitude of the burden assumed by the Center in attempting to implement this new law [dealing with sexual psychopaths] is not difficult to appreciate. We had no precedents to guide us. There was no consistent literature on the subject.' As a consequence, they claimed 'no dogmatic bias' and they had 'no therapeutic ax to grind'. Everything they did was experimental. Ultimately, the only test would be 'how well our patients do after they are paroled back into the community'. That would not have been a comfort to the good citizens of New England.

The problem these psychiatrists faced was that men like Ohlson generally showed such high levels of 'developmental retardation or psychologic regression' that therapy was 'hopeless'. Although psychiatrists remained optimistic about the possibility of rehabilitating a small proportion of psychopaths, they confessed that evaluating patients for parole was 'one of our most difficult tasks'. 'We are constantly struggling to avoid fooling ourselves,' they admitted, but 'articulate, communicative patients possess the tools for artful manipulation of their environments, and their prime target is bound to be the therapists who hold the keys to their release.'[2] Given the pressure to ensure that psychopaths like Ohlson must never be released only to reoffend, the safest course would be to convert 'indefinite' to 'enduring'. The diagnosis of 'psychopath' would thus be indistinguishable from the judicial sentence of life imprisonment.

*

The psychopath is the direct descendant of the 'morally insane' individual as defined in the early nineteenth century by the ethnologist and physician James Cowles Prichard and discussed near the beginning of Chapter 7 'The Couch'. For Prichard moral insanity was a 'morbid perversion of the natural feelings, affections, inclination, temper, habits, moral dispositions, and natural impulses' and could be present in an individual who was otherwise an intellectually reasoning being.[3] The diagnosis turned its back on notions of hereditary weakness (as epitomized by the diagnosis of 'constitutional psycho-pathic inferior'), in favour of a concept of a separate personality structure that inexorably impelled individuals towards anti-social activities. As the influential author of 'Psychopathic Personality and Crime' (1945) observed, Prichard's definition of moral insanity in the 1830s could be directly translated into that of a 'psychopathic personality', a term espoused almost exactly one hundred years later.[4]

According to twentieth-century psychiatrists, psychopaths were neither certifiably insane nor mentally deficient, but lived in a no man's land between these two extremes. They were men 'lacking in the balance of fundamental instincts, emotions and sentiments common to mankind' and therefore were incapable of acting socially responsibly.[5] There was no place for them in the traditional lexicon of insanity. After all, psychopaths realized 'only too well the implications of their various acts' but were 'impelled towards their dangerous behavior by a desire or passion against which they struggle in vain'.[6] They lacked conscience or a 'super-ego' and thus rarely felt guilt; they were excessively aggressive against others; they experienced great difficulties in forming affectionate attachments; they failed to respect other people; they sought immediate gratification ('often in primitive forms of behavior', such as in the sexual realm).[7]

To put it in psychoanalytical language, the psychopath's Ego (or conscience) was too weak to resist the sexual and aggressive impulses of the Id (the source of 'animalistic drives'). His aggressive acts always seemed to him to come from outside himself: his reasoning was not disturbed and he could distinguish right from wrong – but he was simply incapable of *feeling* the difference.[8] Psychopaths possessed a 'mask of sanity'.[9] As sociologist Harrison Gould put it in 1948, the psychopath could 'verbalize all the moral and social rules, but he does not seem to understand them in the way that others do'. It was a form of 'semantic dementia'. Unlike normal criminals and other categories of the insane (psychoneurotic or psychotic men, for instance), the psychopathic personality exhibited 'no signs of incongruity, of anxiety, or of self-doubting'. It was 'almost as if the person were a robot of indescribable ingenuity, able to do anything a healthy personality could do except to participate in a social group'.[10] This psychiatric diagnosis provided jurists with a category for criminals who seemed to be mentally normal and capable of distinguishing right from wrong, yet persisted in acting in seriously anti-social ways.

The most repellent aspect of the psychopathic personality, however, was their 'individualism': they lacked any 'community conscience'.[11] They were unable to identify with another person's point of view. They did not possess social emotions such as loyalty, contrition, embarrassment and discomfort, and were barely capable of role-playing.[12] In the words of W. Norwood East, prominent Medical Inspector of HM Prisons, psychopaths were 'ethical aberrant personalities' who possessed

> an unusual forcefulness of several instinctive urges, an exaggerated emotional instability, an abnormal deficiency of will-power, together with a lack of ethical understanding and an inability to profit from experience, so great that in spite of normal or superior intelligence, the individual is a danger to society and sometimes to himself.

The psychopath always showed 'a callous indifference to the rights and feelings of others, and an absence of affection accompanied by a lack of forethought or wisdom, together with a permanent inability to appreciate the importance of reality and the value of communal rights and conventions'.[13] Writing in the early 1940s, at a time of worldwide military emergency, East was sickened by psychopathic personalities. But those psychopathic traits were precisely what made some people wonder whether such men might be ideally suited to war. As the Physician Superintendent at the Royal Edinburgh Hospital for Nervous and Mental Disorders lamented in 1942, many parents of psychopaths

> regarded the war as a godsend. Here at last, they thought, would be a method whereby their difficult sons and daughters would be made to conform, and in any case they would rather have them die in a burst of glory on a foreign field than burden the home front, which otherwise they were almost sure to do.

This psychiatrist wished to disabuse parents and the military of the myth that: psychopaths simply did not make effective soldiers.[14] Not every person who committed a sex crime was a psychopath. Those who were, however, were particularly dangerous to a community struggling at a time of war and national insecurity.

The daunting proliferation of definitions and myths concerning the 'psychopath' masked significant shifts in the application of the label. The term was initially applied to habitual criminals in general, rather than to violent *sex* criminals. Indeed, until the 1930s, the main contenders for the label were male vagabonds and alcoholics, young delinquents of both sexes and 'hypersexed' women. The first specialist institution for psychopathic criminals in America was established at the Bedford Hills Reformatory for Women between 1916 and 1918, and its mission was to eliminate female prostitution.[15]

This changed quite abruptly in 1930s America when the term 'psychopath' was increasingly prefaced with the word 'sexual' or simply assumed to refer to sexual criminals. Male sexual dangerousness and the failure of prisons to deal with these men had sparked a nationwide panic. The rise of the sexual psychopath was partly the result of anxieties about the way economic depression had disrupted family life, triggering concerns about the changing nature of modern manliness. In the words of the historian Estelle Freedman,

> Unemployed men and vagabonds populated the depression-era landscape, signaling actual family dissolution and symbolizing potential social and political disruption . . . the psychopath could represent the threat of anarchy, of the individual unbounded by either social rules or individual conscience. The apparent 'sexualization' of the drifter reflected, in part, a merging of economic and psychological identities in modern America.[16]

From the 1930s the mass media played a significant role in the sexualization of the psychopathic diagnosis. They began to pay deliberate and often painstaking attention to sexual crimes, said to be committed by 'beasts' within previously cosseted local communities.[17] In particular the media focused inordinate attention on sexual assaults (often followed by murder) of young children. These men must possess no conscience, journalists asserted, since they chose victims who were so obviously innocent. Most vociferously, J. Edgar Hoover informed readers of the *American Magazine* in 1947 that 'degenerate sex offenders' were responsible for a wave of crimes. 'Should wild beasts break out of circus cages', the FBI

"The nation's women and children
will never be secure . . . so long
as degenerates run wild"

Illustration for J. Edgar Hoover's article, 'How Safe is Your Daughter?', 1947

director argued, 'a whole city would be mobilized instantly. But depraved human beings, more savage than beasts, are permitted to rove America almost at will.'[18] [See image, above, and 'Never Play Alone', below.]

By the 1950s this scaremongering had reached even greater heights. 'There is probably no criminal today that constitutes a greater danger to the American public than the sexual psychopath', declared the author of an article in the *U.C.L.A. Intramural Law Review* in the middle of that decade.[19] The *Saturday Evening Post* reported in 1948 that 'tens of thousands' of 'so-called sex killers' were 'loose in the country

alone in alleys,
or in deserted
buildings. Keep

NEVER wait
around toilets.
Always leave

The sex crime panic: a 1950s pamphlet

today'.[20] Although some commentators pleaded for calm ('However rational and cool we humans may be when considering securities legislation or revised Sales Acts, when sex rears its head, reasoning and detachment fly off and emotion is likely to fly in,' one expert observed, to deafening silence),[21] political and social concern about this new category of 'sexual psychopaths' regularly soared and then just as quickly plummeted between the 1930s and the 1970s.

It was no coincidence that anxieties about psychopaths concentrated as much on the *sexual* as on the *violent* aspects of their crimes. The psychopath was not simply a murderer; it was significant that his pathology was sexual. It was precisely his uncontrollable sexual urges that constituted the main definition of the psychopath from the 1930s onwards. The psychopath was the man who regarded sex as 'an itch that is scratched when the opportunity arises, without any compassion or identification with the impact on his "sexual object"'. He experienced 'no emotional relatedness, except the physical or fantasy manipulation of another'.[22] Even worse, as the author of 'The Sexual Psychopath' observed in 1951, in such men the urge to have sex took the form of 'a compulsive, insatiable, unremitting, unbridled (one might say inexorable), unrelenting drive that gives the man no rest or peace'. It was as if 'the man had consecrated his life to sex . . . Whatever other kind of life he leads appears to be purely incidental.'[23] This also helped explain why nearly all sexual psychopaths were men. In the words of the author of 'The Concept of the Psychopath' (1948), the 'primitive drives' were 'so weak in some girls and so faint in some women' that the 'task of controlling these drives' was 'not particularly burdensome'. This was unfortunately not the case with a large proportion of men.[24]

Explosive primitive drives were only one putative explanation for the development of a psychopathic personality. Although a minority of psychiatrists believed that psychopathy was caused by brain lesions,[25] most identified the cause of the illness in early childhood trauma and distorted sex education. For instance, according to the psychoanalytical framework adopted by Robert Lindener in *Stone Walls and Men* (1946), the psychopath had never worked through his early Oedipal conflict. In consequence, he lived his entire life burdened by guilt for his incestuous and parricidal fantasies. His acts of purposeless violence were an attempt to incur the wrath of his father and, by extension, society.[26]

Childhood sexuality was responsible in other ways as well. For the psychiatrist Ralph D. Rabinovitch, speaking at a symposium on sexual psychopaths in the early 1950s, blame could be placed on the 'overly restrictive and inhibiting' families in which such men had been raised. He believed that he could trace the personality disturbance to a 'severely punitive attitude towards casual and exploratory genital manipulation as early as the first year of life', with the result that sex was infused through and through with guilt.[27] A distorted childhood also helped explain to these psychiatrists why a boy from a wealthy family was just as liable to become a psychopath. Indeed, as one New York attorney commented, the wealthy child who was brought up by a professional nurse instead of loving parents was just as liable to experience a distorted upbringing leading to psychopathy as a child raised in an orphanage.[28]

Irrespective of class, the end result was a distorted sexuality, often exacerbated by unconscious feminine tendencies that the psychopath attempted to mask by engaging in exaggerated masculine behaviour. In the words of the Senior Psychiatrist at New York's Bellevue Psychiatric Hospital in 1948, the psychopathic rapist had a 'concealed fear of the usual masculine sentiments and attitudes surrounding sexual contact with women. Ruthless, egocentric attitudes toward women as sexual objects mask the disinclination to accept social standards of masculinity because of a fear of sexual inadequacy.'

According to this psychiatrist, 'aggressive sexual psychopaths' were 'driven to repeated sexual conquests in pursuit of the emotional security that successful masculine sexual dominance brings'.[29] It was a vision of relations between the sexes that presupposed 'masculine sexual dominance' as the norm to which these inadequate men aspired. The so-called immaturity of psychopaths was evidence that they had never 'grown out of' the adolescent 'crush' on members of their own sex. As Benjamin Karpman, psychotherapist and author of the much-cited *The Sexual Offender and his Offenses* (1954) expressed it, sexual psychopaths had never 'matured sexually'. They represented 'a kind of sex life that at an early period of development . . . detoured into aberrant channels leading to an abortive aim-inhibited sexual activity'. This explained why their victims were often young, and also why the strength of their desires was so powerful. In other words, by remaining at an infantile stage closer to the instincts, psychopaths lacked the controlling force of repression that would normally lead to mature sexuality.[30]

All promoters of the psychopathic diagnosis agreed that this class of criminal was psychiatrically ill. Karpman, as a tireless promoter of the psychopathic diagnosis, observed that the District of Columbia defined a psychopath as

> a person, not insane, who by a course of repeated misconduct in sexual matters has evidenced such lack of power to control his sexual impulses as to be dangerous to other persons because he is likely to attack or otherwise inflict injury, loss, pain, or other evil on the objects of his desire.

But, Karpman asked, 'what sort of person . . . is it who is not to be regarded as insane yet whose repeated misconduct in sexual matters reveals an utter lack of power to control his impulses, an irresistible desire to attack other people without regard for social or personal considerations?' Surely such men were as insane as schizophrenics. 'Sexual psychopaths', he insisted, were 'a sexual menace' but they were 'not conscious agents deliberately and viciously perpetuating these acts'. Indeed, their 'disease' often drove them to suicide. Because 'uncontrollable instinct' was 'beyond any punishment', treatment, not imprisonment, was required.[31] Bertram Pollens, author of *The Sex Criminal* (1939) agreed, observing that the sex criminal was 'not possessed by the devil and sending him to the electric chair or imprisoning him will not cure him nor will it deter others from becoming sexual psychopaths'. He was 'suffering from an illness – a distorted mental state' which might not be as 'tangible or visible as a broken arm' but was 'just as real'. 'Science must come to the rescue!' he exclaimed.[32]

Psychopathic Laws

Psychiatry and other sciences did manage to exert influence on the legal handling of men diagnosed (by them) as sexual psychopaths. Indeed, the concept of psychopathy gained influence less because of medical certainty than because it was rapidly inscribed in law. Legal appropriations of psychopathy took place in many countries, including Britain and the USA, but were immeasurably more powerful in the second. In Britain psychopathy was less tightly linked to sexual offences and, since the law required evidence of a long-term disorder, it remained linked with notions of a person's physical 'constitution'. Thus an article on 'Recent Trends in the Management of Psychopathic Offenders' (1951) simply defined psychopathy as 'a condition of distorted or incomplete development of mind existing before the age of

18 years coupled with strongly vicious or criminal propensities'.[33] Psychopaths were dealt with under legislation dealing more generally with mental health. They could be detained at criminal lunatic asylums such as Broadmoor, under Section 26 of the 1959 Mental Health Act. All that was needed was for two psychiatrists to state that the person was a danger either to himself or to others and had 'violent, criminal, or dangerous propensities'. Men could be diagnosed as psychopathic even if they had not committed any illegal act.

In contrast, American states began in the 1930s to pass laws specifically addressed to a species of humans labelled psychopaths. The first sexual psychopath law was passed in Michigan in mid-decade but, because it was declared unconstitutional, credit for the first valid statute went to Illinois in 1938. California, followed by other states, passed similar laws. Within thirty years sexual psychopathic statutes were operating in thirty-three states and the District of Columbia.[34]

These statutes differed from state to state, but most fell into one of two categories. The first effectively extended legislation dealing with persistent or violent offenders. In these cases an offender would be given a hearing before jury and if psychiatrists testified that he suffered from a 'criminal sexual psychopathic perversion' he could be committed to the psychiatric wing of the prison before conviction. Once psychiatrists at the hospital were willing to claim that he was 'cured', the offender could be either placed on probation and released or returned to court and sentenced for the original crime. Raymond Ohlson was committed under this type of statute. The second type of legislation did away with the requirement of a criminal act before committal. Any person – whether charged with an offence or not – could be brought before the court and, if designated a psychopath by expert witnesses, committed to a mental hospital until other experts could swear that he was no longer a danger to the health and safety of others. In both versions of the law a person committed to a mental institution as a psychopath had to stay there 'indefinitely' – that is, for any length of time ranging from one day to an entire life.

As with the case of Raymond Ohlson in Massachusetts, these Acts were typically passed as a result of a media-fuelled panics over sex attacks, particularly on children. At times of sensitive political climate, sexual psychopathic laws dramatically increased the courts' powers over sexual offenders. In periods of relative calm just over one-third of sex offenders were sent for evaluation and (if necessary) treatment in specialist programmes, while, just a few years later and in the aftermath of a sex scandal, the proportion of offenders sent for evaluation could rocket up to nearly two-thirds.[35] As the authors of *Characteristics and Management of Committed Sexual Offenders in the State of Washington* (1971) observed, psychopath laws allowed courts to increase their 'control over the offender' by the 'unique requirement of judicial review before the offender [could] be released'. In this way the law placed the court 'in a more knowledgeable and powerful position to fulfil its duty of protecting society'.[36]

According to this model, protecting society required that this category of offender be *treated*, rather than simply imprisoned. As already mentioned, these laws reflected psychiatric power, but also the belief that psychopaths were not deterred by the threat of imprisonment. After all, psychopaths could be identified only according to those characteristics that set them apart from 'normal' criminals: they lacked judgement, failed to learn from experience and were remarkably deficient in emotions such as guilt, grief and fear.[37] In fact, not only did prisons fail to deter psychopathic criminals, but imprisonment could even exacerbate their dangerousness by encouraging them to turn to 'sexual perversions' in order to relieve their 'stronger than average sexual propensities'. In such cases psychopaths threatened to corrupt the entire prison population.[38]

But was it possible to prevent this corruption? Could psychopaths be cured? Proponents of the psychopathy diagnosis admitted that treatment was slow and difficult, but possible. Individual or group psychotherapy was the most commonly proposed therapy, but psychopaths were treated with the full range of therapies.* As proponents loved to point out, treatment could be cheaper than incarceration. In the State of Washington, for instance, the cost of diagnosing and treating an offender for sexual psychopathy was $5.97 a day, compared with $13.46 if he was thrown into prison. Admittedly treatment was cheaper than in other states because Washington employed a 'guided self-help model' of treatment which did not call for a large clinical staff. In addition to this saving, however, the average length of hospitalization for sexual offenders was seventeen months, compared with an average length of imprisonment of twenty-nine months. Since half of the offenders were married and most of their families had to rely on public assistance while the offender was either in prison or undergoing treatment, the economic cost saved by shorter incarceration was

*These therapies are examined in Chapter 6, 'The Knife' and Chapter 7, 'The Couch'.

significant.[39] The question remained, however: was the prime purpose of the criminal justice system to deter future crimes? Or did they have a duty to impose retribution on the victims' behalf? Or did they have a duty to attempt to alleviate the symptoms of a mental affliction that the psychopath might be unable to control by himself? As proponents of the psychopathic diagnosis and laws argued, cure was possible and not too costly. The price tag was important, and not simply for society as a whole. As psychiatrist Edwin H. Sutherland imprudently admitted in his 'The Diffusion of Sexual Psychopath Laws' (1950), psychiatrists had 'an economic interest' in the extension of the laws.[40] But the real question remained, was cure ever possible?

Psychiatric Reservations

Belief in the benefits of separating criminals with sexual psychopathic tendencies from the rest of the criminal population peaked in the 1960s. The management of sex criminals under psychopathic legislation proved particularly popular in states such as California, where approximately 1000 sex offenders were confined under its statute each year between 1949 and 1980. But this approach was not universally accepted. In comparison with California, for instance, courts in Illinois were much more reluctant to apply psychopathic laws, confining only sixteen people under the state's statute in the first decade after its enactment in 1938. Similarly, in Washington DC between 1948 and 1949, 636 sex crimes reached the courts but only twenty individuals were committed under the state's psychopathic statute.[41] In all states, the laws had started to be repealed by the 1970s, although, as I discuss at the end of this chapter, they were gradually reinstated from the 1990s in the guise of Sexual Predators Acts.

The gradual repeal of sexual-psychopathic laws was due to a number of criticisms directed at the psychiatric diagnosis, the authoritarian uses made of the laws and the doubtful constitutional legality of the statutes. These critics had dramatically different conceptions of the meaning of citizenship and of the obligations a shared humanity placed upon people.

Psychiatrists found themselves at the forefront of attacks upon the psychopathic diagnosis. Their main concern was about the absence of an agreed definition of the psychopath, although many claimed that they could identify people who were *not* psychopaths.[42] Indeed, the diagnosis of psychopathy was often made on the grounds that the observed symptoms did not fit into any of the common psychiatric categories. As two physicians told attendees at the annual American Psychiatric Association meeting in Atlantic City in May 1952, the term 'sexual psychopathy' was really a 'descriptive label' useful in 'certain administrative and teaching situations'. It could be distinguished from other mental disorders only on the grounds that the disorder could not 'be classified as one of the traditional so-called psychoses or psychoneuroses or as mental deficiency', yet was clearly 'odd' behaviour which was inimical to the interests of society.

The psychopathic diagnosis was the 'waste basket' of psychiatric classification.[43] In the words of one leading criminological text that was reprinted many times between the 1950s and the 1970s, the terms 'psychopath', 'psychopathic personality', and 'constitutional psychopathic inferior' were 'used with little or no differentiation to refer to persons who are regarded as emotionally abnormal but who do not manifest the break with reality that characterizes psychotics . . . The method of diagnosing psychopathic personality is not at all standardized or objective.' The label could 'be applied to almost anyone'. They repeated the accusation that it was a 'wastebasket category' into which 'not-otherwise-explicable criminal behavior' could be 'tossed'.[44] The diagnosis was purely one of convenience. 'Psychopathic personality satisfies the necessity which is felt to give to each patient a label diagnosis,' the authors of *Psychiatry and the Law* (1952) concluded, adding that psychiatrists, like other physicians were reluctant to label a patient 'undiagnosed'.[45] Defining a 'psychopath' was like defining 'a hippopotamus': a psychiatrist only 'knew one when he saw it'.[46]

Finally, some psychiatrists questioned the assumption that sex offenders were not like 'other criminals' but possessed a particular psychology, were more likely to repeat their offence despite punishment and were especially dangerous for society.[47] Since many crimes (including burglary and murder) were committed by men under the sway of a sexual impulse, why not extend psychopathic laws to encompass all felons? they asked.[48] Either way circular reasoning characterized the entire approach: psychopaths were people who carried out violent crimes and they carried out these crimes because they were psychopaths.

The vagueness of the psychiatric definition of 'psychopath' can be illustrated by examining Massachusetts's Act of 1958, under which Raymond Ohlson was indefinitely detained. According to this Act, a 'sexually dangerous person' was someone

> whose misconduct in sexual matters indicates a general lack of power to control his sexual impulses, as evidenced by repetitive or compulsive behavior and either violence or aggression by an adult against a victim under the age of sixteen years, and who as a result is likely to attack or otherwise inflict injury on the objects of his uncontrolled or uncontrollable desires.[49]

But, psychiatrists pointed out, the term 'sexually dangerous' could be understood only in social terms and had no etiological resonance. It referred to no symptoms. It targeted future behaviour. As such, it imposed 'a relatively unfamiliar demand and a responsibility' on psychiatrists – that is, the ability to predict future actions. This was too heavy a responsibility, insisted the psychiatrists from Bridgewater who had treated Ohlson.[50] In addition, there was no obvious reason why such draconian statutes should apply only to sex criminals. Other violent criminals were dangerous, yet were not threatened with indeterminate detention. Clearly, distinguishing sexually dangerous individuals from socially dangerous ones was a reflection of social priorities, rather than psychiatric ones.[51]

From another angle commentators observed that, although the diagnosis of sexual psychopath was supposed to be medical, the physicians making it often confused medical judgements with legal considerations. Often the assessment that someone was a sexual psychopath was made without any of the usual diagnostic tools: psychological, projective and neurological tests, for instance, were not employed, nor were any of the other examinations that would ordinarily form a part of psychiatric assessment.[52] Even more worryingly, committing a particular crime could in itself be proffered as evidence of illness. One physician was reported to have made a diagnosis of psychopathy by stating that simply being 'guilty of incestuous relations' fulfilled 'the requirements of the sexual psychopath law'.[53]

The tensions between the legal or punitive aspects of the law and the psychiatric or diagnostic elements were exposed most starkly in debates about whether men committed under the psychopathic laws were entitled to disability pensions under the Social Security Act. In the 1967–8 issue of the *Stanford Law Review*, for instance, Sallyanne Payton argued that committal for 'insanity' under a psychopath statute was not automatically evidence of mental impairment. Confinement under the statutes was 'more closely related to the penal laws than to the provisions for civil commitment of the "mentally ill".' It was important to recognize the 'political realities' behind the statutes: they were a 'means of incarcerating persons for potentially longer periods of time than would be possible through normal criminal process', she conceded. Criminals 'must bear the economic consequences of their occupational incapacitations', otherwise there was the risk of rewarding 'a substantial portion of the criminal population', many of whom might be characterized as 'irresponsible and emotionally shallow'. 'To reward persons financially for behavior defined as culpable on the articulated basis that they are disposed to such behavior,' she concluded, 'is to commit a serious error in communicating standards.' In other words, committal to a mental institution did not by itself imply mental illness.[54]

Payton was at least honest in acknowledging that the diagnosis of madness was a legal rather than psychiatric judgement.[55] The use of psychiatry to deal with criminals became even more problematic if its main aim – that is, treatment – was subverted. After all, what was the point of committing these criminals to a mental institution or ward instead of a prison if they were not receiving any form of therapy? Diagnosis occurred quite independently of any pledge of treatment. In Nebraska, for instance, 63 per cent of psychopaths were being 'treated' by institutionalization alone.[56] Public mental hospitals were severely understaffed. Indeed, in 1958 only fifteen states had more than half the number of physicians decreed as adequate by the American Psychiatric Association.[57] In many mental institutions there were not even sufficient staff to report on each patient once a year, let alone provide any semblance of treatment.[58] It was no wonder that the former superintendent of the Hastings State Hospital informed the chairman of the Board of Control that the situation was in crisis. He admitted that 'we do not have sufficient doctors to give the extensive therapy' that patients needed. Although they were 'doing our best', the fact remained that the hospital had six doctors to look after 1700 patients. The treatment of psychopaths required extensive and long-term therapy, but resources simply made this impossible.[59]

Many commentators asked an even more basic question: are psychopaths treatable in the first place? Some psychiatrists bluntly maintained they were not. In the 'interests of the economic disposition of limited therapeutic resources', society should let psychopaths 'rot in custodial and incapacitative detention because of their unamenability [sic] to ordinary methods of control', they contended.[60] Therapies inevitably failed because the 'complexes derived from hostilities projected by society and the psychopath's natural defense reactions' undermined any cure.[61] In a study of men committed to the Massachusetts Correctional Institution at Bridgewater (where Raymond Ohlson was incarcerated) in the late 1960s, only 36 per cent of the patients were found to be responsive to psychotherapy.[62] Perhaps those patients who responded to therapy were not 'truly' psychopathic in the first place, some psychiatrists mused.[63] In 'true' psychopathy signs of improvement could simply be the outcome of normal processes of maturation. As psychopaths aged, their passions and hostilities petered away.[64] Pessimism over treatment outcomes even led some physicians at state hospitals to argue that psychopaths should be segregated in work colonies where they could at least be partially self-supporting. The establishment of psychopathic colonies would not only rid society of these dangerous men (perhaps for life) but would also 'give psychiatrists a chance to study these individuals at close range and over a sufficient period of time to learn something about them'.[65]

Social Critiques

Psychiatric critiques of the concept of the sexual psychopath were strengthened by concerns about the uses of the legislation. Commentators began noticing a disturbing trend: sex criminals being incarcerated under 'one day to life' indefinite prison terms were frequently the most minor offenders. Thus, while the public believed they were being safeguarded from extremely violent sex offenders, in reality courts were using the extensive powers under the Acts to monitor and discipline men who had committed relatively trivial crimes. For instance, over half of the sex offenders hospitalized under the Illinois Sexually Dangerous Persons Act were non-violent offenders.[66] A similar situation was observed at the New Jersey State Diagnostic Center at Menlo Park. Ralph Brancale, Albert Ellis and Ruth R. Doorbar examined the first 300 men sent to the Center to be examined for psychopathy under the Sex Offender Act. They found that most of the offenders were 'rather innocuous, inadequate, passive, and minor offenders rather than violent, sadistic sex fiends'. Fifty-eight per cent had carried out what they described as minor offences such as exhibitionism, dissemination of obscene material, verbal sex acts, 'mild sexual attacks' and statutory rape, while 42 per cent had committed what they described as major offences like forcible rape, 'serious sexual assault' and (significantly) homosexuality. In total a quarter of all the offenders sent for evaluation had used force or duress. Furthermore, these researchers found no correction between the seriousness of an offence and a person's degree of mental disturbance. In the end only 3 per cent of the men sent for evaluation were eventually diagnosed as sexual psychopaths.[67]

It was not surprising that many of the men incarcerated under the laws were homosexuals. For one thing, psychopathic statutes were passed at a time of severe sexual repression. In the early 1950s, for instance, thirty-eight states had laws that made extra-marital intercourse illegal – imprisonment for adultery was 'not infrequent'.[68] In such a repressive environment homosexuals were routinely classified as psychopathic, whatever their behaviour. Indeed, historians like Estelle Freedman have convincingly argued that the invention and promotion of sexual psychopathology fulfilled an important function in pathologizing homosexual males and presenting them as violent child molesters. She even suggested that the term 'psychopath' was 'code for homosexual'.[69] Although this point may be exaggerated, it was the case that many men were labelled psychopaths because of their homosexuality rather than any act of overt violence.

More broadly, the diagnosis of psychopath lumped together sadistic rapists and voyeurs. And since there were more peeping Toms than rapists (and voyeurs and exhibitionists had significantly higher recidivism rates), hospitals were filling up with non-violent men diagnosed as psychopaths.[70] In fact, some psychiatrists revealed that violent rapists were *less* liable to be incarcerated under the Acts. In one study of men charged with rape in 1961 it was found that rapists were very different from other sex offenders: they were less likely to show signs of psychiatric disorder and less likely to have a previous record of offending. In contrast with men convicted of exhibitionism or homosexuality, rapists tended to be 'sexually and psychiatrically normal individuals whose offences are partly an offshoot of their general antisocial behavioral patterns'.[71]

Psychopathic legislation was therefore applied much more widely than originally intended. 'Such legislation permits experimenting with new procedures in a limited area,' observed a couple of psychiatrists, adding that these procedures 'would be considered too radical for general acceptance'.[72] The Minnesota Psychopathic Personality Act was, in the view of one author, nothing more than 'a disingenuous use of the legislative power to define insanity as a means of incarcerating persons for potentially longer periods of time than would be possible under normal criminal process'.[73] This has led the medical historian Simon A. Cole to persuasively argue that the statutes were really a 'pretext to repress . . . nonviolent or consensual sexual activity'.[74] The effect, however, was to cause serious congestion in treatment facilities, further reducing provision for violent offenders.[75]

The lumping together of men with enormously different criminal histories was one of many anomalies. Depending under which legal jurisdiction they were processed, sex criminals experienced dramatically different risk of being held under the Acts. Thus 16 per cent of sex delinquents diagnosed by the Psychiatric Clinic of the Court of General Sessions in New York were said to be psychopathic, while of the sex offenders diagnosed by psychiatrists at the city's Bellevue Hospital, 53 per cent were judged to be psychopaths.[76] Furthermore, the law was applied differently even *within* states. In Nebraska, for instance, some counties included consenting homosexuals within the purview of the laws, while others did not; some regarded exhibitionism as a form of 'sexual misconduct' which might be psychopathic, while others required that the criminal act violently.[77]

There were also major discrepancies by class and ethnicity. Psychotherapists dealing with criminals tended to apply the diagnosis 'sexual psychopath' to people they were not used to dealing with: that is, educated, middle-class offenders who lacked a history of sexual offending. As a consequence, there was a strong class aspect to the treatment. As the author of 'The Therapeutic Encounter' (1972) spotted, therapists tended

> to designate as sexual psychopaths those who come from middle-class backgrounds, those who are more intelligent and those who do not have a long history of criminal behavior outside of their sexual transgressions. It is this group that therapy tends to help the most (or at least the group that therapists are most willing to work with); however, the 'sickest' or the most dangerous offenders are not always included.[78]

Furthermore, conceptions of race were at the heart of these characterizations. Psychopathic statutes were rarely applied to African-Americans. In the State of Washington, 90 per cent of the men committed under the sexual psychopathic law were white. Of all offenders, nearly three-quarters of white offenders were sent to the specialized treatment programme, compared with just over one-third of minority-race offenders.[79] As a result of these discriminatory practices, there was a strong racial profile in therapeutic establishments specializing in sex offenders. While in the general prison population there was a much higher number of black offenders to white ones (in proportion to their numbers in the general population), in institutions for sex offenders the racial profile more closely matched that of the general population. This 'perverse egalitarianism' reflects the fact that black sexual offenders remain much more likely to be regarded as criminals while their white equivalents are categorized as deviant.[80]

Legal procedures contributed to these discriminatory practices. Black offenders were less liable to have counsel and hence less likely to enter a plea under the statutes.[81] In addition, it was assumed that the black sex offender was psychologically constructed differently from his white counterpart. In the words of three employees of the State of Jersey's Diagnostic Center, writing in 1954,

> whereas the white offender tends to be a severely emotionally disturbed individual, with several serious psychiatric symptoms, the convicted Negro offender tends to be undisturbed emotionally, to be socially adjusted, to be young, to be a non-deviational offender, and to have committed his sex offense under extenuating circumstances.

Indeed, statutory rape was 'virtually a normal and expected part of the culture of many New Jersey Negroes'. Feeling 'less guilt, shame, and self-deprecation' for their crimes, black rapists were less emotionally disturbed by them, they claimed.[82] The author of an article in the *Indiana Law Review*, for example, suggested in 1957 that African-American sexual mores were 'such that fewer complaints are lodged against Negroes by Negroes than would be the case among white persons'.[83] The black sexual offender exhibited traits common to his race: that is, immature sexuality rather than *arrested* sexual development. Thus psychiatric treatments simply would not 'work'. For these offenders the mantra was 'discipline, not therapy'.[84]

Legal and Constitutional Reservations

Psychopathic laws were attacked on psychiatric grounds; they were accused of discriminating between individuals merely on social grounds. However, the most powerful critique came from within the law itself. In most jurisdictions psychopathic proceedings were civil, not criminal, in nature. A man could be committed to indefinite detention in a state mental institution not because he had been convicted of any crime, but simply because he had been diagnosed as a sexual psychopath. Although he could still be liable to prosecution for the original criminal charge once released,[85] in effect the laws allowed authorities to punish individuals for their status, not their actions.

Legal opponents, like psychiatric critics, attacked psychopathic legislation for lack of clarity. Many of the laws had a clause on recidivism (men could be committed for an indefinite term only if they were repeat offenders), but just how long a record of criminal misconduct was long enough? Equally, statutes that included a clause on 'dangerousness' failed to define the concept: when was 'dangerous' dangerous enough? Who would predict which sex offender was liable to reoffend and which not? Were psychiatrists supposed to be able to predict the future? Who could reliably testify that a particular offender exhibited 'an *utter* lack of power to control his sexual impulses', as required by the law in Nebraska, for instance?[86] Since no timeframe was given, courts were left to wonder whether an offender might reoffend in the course of his entire life. Since it was impossible to predict whether or when an individual would reoffend, a man could find himself sentenced to what was in effect life imprisonment. Many mental hospitals closely resembled prisons.[87] According to one study, the laws even failed in the basic aim of keeping sex offenders segregated from 'free' society, since almost 15 per cent of those committed to hospitals under the laws were able to escape.[88]

There were also concerns about the constitutionality of the laws. Most statutes were accused of contradicting constitutional guarantees against cruel and unusual punishment.[89] Psychopathic legislation was used to impose long sentences on criminals who would have been given much shorter sentences if they had been processed by the usual justice system. In Maryland, for instance, nearly half of all men detained under the statutes were held past the statutory maximum sentence for their crime.[90] The lack of proportion between the seriousness of the offence and the length of institutional confinement could be startling.

A vast array of basic legal rights was denied to men under psychopathic legislation. In some states the designation 'sexual psychopath' did not require any conviction for a crime, or even a criminal charge, yet under the legislation a person could be forcibly removed to a prison cell for an indefinite period of time without even a pretence of treatment.[91] In many states psychopaths did not have the right to an attorney, nor were they allowed the privilege against self-incrimination. Double jeopardy was common, with men being incarcerated on two separate occasions and in two different institutions for the same crime.[92] In the words of an expert on the Illinois Sexually Dangerous Persons Act in the late 1960s, the State's attorneys would file a petition under Sexually Dangerous Persons Acts only if they believed that they did not possess 'enough evidence to establish their criminal case beyond a reasonable doubt'. They could do this because the procedure to send a prisoner to hospital was a *civil* hearing, not a criminal one, and did not require anything resembling definite proof.[93] Critics of the Acts found this particularly odious because they believed that false accusations were especially prevalent in sexual cases. 'Scrupulous care will be needed to prevent the sexual psychopath law from being used as a wastebasket for unwanted family members or as an instrument for blackmail or fantasy,' decreed a legal commentators in Iowa in the mid-1950s.[94]

Psychiatrists proved to be even more 'tough on crime' than other prosecutors. Tensions centred on the question of whether incarceration itself was a form of therapy. This was the issue addressed in the legal case *In re Maddox* in 1958. Maddox had been civilly committed under the Michigan Sexual Psychopath Statute yet had been sent to a state prison. He claimed that he had not received any treatment other than a medical review every six months. In fact, he pointed out, he had been given *fewer* privileges than other prisoners. Four psychiatrists gave evidence, testifying that incarceration 'was on and of itself a form of treatment which, at least on some occasions, helped to make obdurate criminal psychopaths more ready to accept the treatment and assistance toward recovery'. The court disagreed, ruling that confinement in a prison did not constitute treatment: 'incarceration in a penitentiary designed and used for the confinement of convicted criminals is not a prescription available upon medical diagnosis'.[95]

The position was untenable. In a lively article entitled 'The Distinction of Being Mad' (1954–5) and published in the *University of Chicago Law Review*, Edward de Grazia objected to the idea that someone who had committed a crime or been otherwise 'irresponsible' was better off 'transported into the arms of the psychiatrists'. De Grazia was appalled by the way in which psychiatry had intervened so radically within the legal system, proving willing to 'incarcerate even the minor criminal offender for life unless "cured"' even though a psychiatrist could rarely promise a sex criminal that he could get better – indeed, an honest psychiatrist was much more likely to warn a criminal that he could never be cured. Yet these same psychiatrists went ahead and administered painful treatments (such as electric shocks) to men who had been neither charged nor convicted of any crime. In psychiatric confinement it was easy to forget that imprisonment 'may last for life. Forget that it may become at times rather painful. Forget that habeas corpus offers no freedom at all to one unable to prove himself "cured". And forget that it all may be unjust.'[96] An increasingly vocal radical psychiatric movement lamented this co-option of what they viewed as their duty of care.

The Modern Laws of Psychopathy

Panic about sexual psychopathy receded from the 1970s. In part the attacks on the concept had discredited it. Legal opponents disputed its constitutionality; legal proponents, keen to use the concept in increasingly punitive ways, found themselves burdened by the concept's clinical history. The Group for the Advancement of Psychiatry sounded the death knell in 1977 when they described the laws as 'social experiments that have failed', claiming that they lacked 'redeeming social value'. The idea that psychopaths could be treated and cured was as ludicrous as creating 'special categories of burglary offender statutes or white collar offender statutes and then provide for special commitments, such as to burglary psychopath hospitals', they scoffed.[97] It did not help that there was evidence that the recidivism rates for men who had been 'treated' under the schemes were no lower than for those who had gone through the more usual penal route.[98]

However, neither the legal nor the psychiatric tensions inherent in sexual-psychopathic diagnosis and punishment would have had such a dramatic effect if not accompanied by a reduction of concerns about sexual psychopaths supposedly stalking urban communities. From these psychiatrically distorted 'monsters' anxiety shifted to common forms of sexual abuse and rape: that is, violence within the domestic sphere and attacks carried out by friends, neighbours and acquaintances. Second-wave feminists were effective in channelling the mass media's attention away from the rare stranger rapist towards the much more common acquaintance rapist. In particular there was a renewed panic about child sexual abuse – not by strangers, but by intimates, such as fathers.* In America annual estimates of such abuse ranged from an

*This is discussed at greater length in Chapter 11 of my *Fear: A Cultural History* (London: Virago, 2006).

unbelievably low 2000 to an incredible 210,000.[99] In 1977 the topic even merited its own specialist journal, *Child Abuse and Neglect*, and in the 1980s popular films and television programmes joined the frenzy. Emmy-nominated *Fallen Angel* (1981), as well as *Something About Amelia* (1984), *Nightmare on Elm Street* (1984), *When a Bough Breaks* (1986) and *A Child's Cry* (1986) brought anxieties about child abuse to a wider public. The mass media designated child abuse, usually by people known to the child, an 'epidemic'.[100]

The emphasis on stranger rape returned in the 1990s, however. Many people seemed to think that the feminists' concern about the everyday rapist had gone too far, and there were renewed demands for a more punitive approach to sexual offending. Once again stranger rape – now erroneously dubbed 'real rape' – came to the fore as part of a wider concern with violent crime. In a vast range of legislation, there was a 'crackdown' on crime. This led to increased sentencing, laws which established life prison sentences for repeat offenders ('Two Strikes' or 'Three Strikes' laws) and 'repeat offender' statutes.

The 1990s also saw a return to a modified version of psychopathy laws, although that term was no longer used. Instead penal-inspired categories like 'dangerousness', 'violence', or 'predation' were adopted. Washington State started this new trend, passing the Sexually Violent Predators Act (1990) making provision for certain types of sexual offenders to be committed indefinitely to an institution. Within seven years eight other states[101] had followed Washington's example. Although there were slight variations, these laws allowed involuntary psychiatric treatment, which could be imposed for anything from one day to a lifetime. The diagnosis of a 'personality disorder' was so wide that it gave immense power to the courts to detain any individual who committed a violent sexual crime. Instead of a focus on mental disorder, the laws looked towards assessments of dangerousness generally. Their purpose was 'preventative detention' rather than treatment.

These new laws were also more punitive than their predecessors. While the older psychopathic statutes 'used civil commitment in lieu of criminal sentencing', the new statutes used 'civil commitment to add an indefinite period of preventive detention at the expiration of the criminal sentence'.[102] In other words, in the modern Acts, therapy and treatment took place *after* the prison term had been served rather than before or in its place. But, like the earlier Acts, they were the response to a wave of publicity about particularly violent sex crimes. Many of these laws made no pretence of being therapeutic, but focused on social control and incapacitation. Furthermore, the psychiatrists who had played such a dominant role in the earlier legislation were largely absent from the management and enforcement of these new laws. Other professional groups, such as social workers and psychologists, took their place. The sexual predators laws that swept America in the 1990s relocated the danger away from the 1970s feminist emphasis upon the threat residing within the home and other intimate networks to 'stranger danger'.

Not surprisingly, critics of the psychopath statutes were not silenced. The same constitutional concerns were raised. Critics insisted that the new laws also punished people twice for the same crime. They claimed that evidence that these offenders were mentally ill was simply not forthcoming. Dangerousness could not be predicted. Because offenders incarcerated under the Acts were those least likely to benefit from treatment, their continued incarceration was simply punitive. Indeed, sex offenders were almost never freed. Washington and Minnesota, for instance, operated commitment programmes from 1990 but, according to one study in 2000, 'no individuals have been discharged from commitment' and 'only a handful' had been sent to 'transitional placements'.[103]

These laws also represented an important shift in the power of psychiatric discourses. In contrast with the mid-century psychopathic laws that were profoundly influenced by psychiatric languages and knowledges, this new legislation retained the *language* of psychiatry but removed from the *profession* of psychiatry. Indeed, the main professional psychiatric bodies were opposed to these revised types of psychopathic legislation. As the Washington State Psychiatric Association argued, the term 'mental abnormality' was 'hopelessly vague' and possessed 'no clinically significant meaning as applied to sex offenders'. The New Jersey Psychiatric Association agreed, arguing that the legislature was simply putting a 'medical spin on a criminal justice problem'.[104]

The issue came to a head in 1993 when Andre Young brought a case before the Washington State Supreme Court. Young, a violent serial rapist, appealed against his indefinite detention on the grounds that being held against his will constituted punishment, not therapy. He also claimed that it violated the constitutional ban against being punished twice for the same crime. The court disagreed, not only holding that his incarceration was constitutional but also adding that psychiatric diagnoses could be divorced entirely from the psychiatric sciences: indeed, the legal profession could entirely co-opt medical discourse within its institutional structures. 'The fact that pathologically driven rape, for example, is not yet listed in the DSM-III-R', the Court decreed, in no way invalidated the clinical diagnosis of Sexually Violent Predator. The DSM was, it went on in an enlightened tone,

> an evolving and imperfect document. Nor is it sacrosanct. Furthermore, it is in some areas a political document whose diagnoses are based, in some cases, on what American Psychiatric Association leaders consider to be practical realities. What is critical for our purposes is that psychiatric and psychological clinicians who testify in good faith as to mental abnormality are able to identify sexual pathologies that are as real and meaningful as other pathologies already listed in DSM.[105]

In a different context a legal adviser to the New Jersey joint legislative task force blandly insisted that the 'mental abnormality' language was 'not intended to be a psychiatric term. The fact that it is not listed in the DSM-III-R is irrelevant. It is a legal term, intended to convey a form of pathology that leads to violent sexual offenses'.[106] In other words, the fact that the DSM-III-R did not list rape as a pathological condition did not mean that legislative bodies could not pass laws degreeing a condition as psychiatrically abnormal. All that the court needed was a few 'psychiatric and psychological clinicians' who could testify 'in good faith' and against the ambit of the professional body, the American Psychiatric Association. Psychiatry might have invented the term 'psychopath', but law controlled its application. As medical historian Simon A. Cole argued, this represented a major shift from the earlier situation. He astutely observed that although psychopathic statutes in the mid-twentieth century blatantly 'molded and distorted psychiatric ideas to fit their political objectives', they

> did at least feel the need to cloak the laws with references to psychiatry and medical expertise. Today, however, such obligatory references to medical knowledge are not longer even necessary. Instead, the heinousness of the crimes is enough to support the civil commitment of sex offenders.[107]

Deviance became the crime. Pathology was equated with the repetition of an offence. Psychiatric languages had become so much a part of everyday knowledges that psychiatrists and physicians were no longer required to provide the diagnosis. The result was a late-twentieth-century shift from a medical discourse to a penal one, albeit one that incorporated everyday languages of the psychological self.

Rapists who were diagnosed as psychopaths found the emphasis on pathology congenial. It did, after all, separate them from 'common criminals' and landed them in hospitals (where 15 per cent were able to escape)[108] rather than prisons. The term 'psychopath' was gratifyingly menacing, and it provided an escape from their obsessive, self-conscious assertion of agency frequently revealed in the rape itself.

But the psychopathic diagnosis also performed an important function for men who were *not* directly subject to its authority. The term 'psychopath' not only created the sex offender as a fixed category of sexual identity, different in kind from both 'normal' men and other violent criminals (particularly black rapists), it also forged a concept of the ideal desiring subject. This was not primarily intended to safeguard the home (since the rapist was still conceived of as separate from the domestic sphere), but attempted to shield a notion of manliness in the face of rising feminist critique. The focus on personality or type of identity rather than acts initially empowered psychiatric disciplines over criminological ones, but gradually was co-opted fully into the legal system. Even its critics within the legal system ended up debating questions of desire and agency. This shift away from the commission of crime and towards the structure of the perpetrator's desire was fundamentally about the boundaries of the 'human' part of 'human rights'. The psychopath was individualized and set outside the community in which his deeds were forged: the removal of his legal rights strengthened, rather than threatened, the rule of law.

SECTION FIVE

Violent Institutions

You, Judge, strip off! Show us the abscess boiling
Beneath your scarlet. Oh point, someone, to where it spreads
On every hand – the red, collusive stain . . .
All too well you have done your work: for one is dead,
And the other will not be whole again.

CECIL DAY LEWIS, 'SEX-CRIME'.[1]

CHAPTER ELEVEN

The Home

'I do': two words generally murmured to indicate consent. In exchanging marriage vows, however, those words are potentially perilous for the female. After repeating them wives may find that they have surrendered all *future* rights to say 'no' to their husbands. Their consent is fixed and inalienable for all time.

Are married women entitled to withdraw their consent to sexual intercourse with their spouses? This question was as furiously debated in marital-advice literature as it was in the courts. In answering it, sexologists (self-styled experts on all matters concerning bedroom comportment) commanded a degree of influence out of proportion to their credentials. Their books and articles were keenly read by courting couples and newlyweds anxious to ensure that their early days of wedded bliss would not be marred by sexual strife. Don James's *The Sexual Side of Life* is fairly representative of this genre. Published as a cheap paperback in 1957, it set out to provide solutions for some of the main complications of matrimony.

James presented the case of 'John' and 'Clara' as an example of some potential snags that newly wedded couples might face. They had been married for three weeks, but Clara was still a virgin. James pictured John 'sitting on the side of the bed, his face in his hands as he tried to contain his frustration and anger'. Prostrate on the bed, Clara was 'sobbing wildly'. 'But Clara,' John exclaimed, 'Clara . . . it *isn't* dirty! It *isn't* wrong . . .' John exclaimed. Hadn't Clara read the sex education books he had given her? Clara admitted that she had 'tried to . . . honestly', but she 'couldn't read them. The things they said men and women do. Some of them are awful . . .' At this point John lost his temper. 'I *will* shout at you!' he yelled, adding,

> You're my wife. I've tried everything. I've been gentle. I've been kind. I've done all the things they said to do in the book . . . What do you think I am, Clara? Stone? Wood? Dirt? Well, I'm not! I'm a man! Do you understand that? A *man*! . . . You're a woman. *Be* one!'

As Clara 'shook her head hopelessly, eyes closed, her sobs still muffled by the pillow', John took violent action. 'Oh, yes, you will [be a woman]!' he said abruptly, vowing that he would '*make*' her into one. Clara 'screamed once' before John's hand 'clamped over her mouth'. 'You're my wife,' he said angrily. 'Now be my wife, damn it!'

According to James, John felt remorseful after raping his wife, muttering, 'Please. I didn't mean to be so rough. To do it that way. Only it's been almost three weeks. I'm *sorry*. Honest, I am . . . please don't cry.' The message for readers seeking advice from this marriage manual was unmistakable: admittedly, John had not acted in a gentlemanly way (although he had tried valiantly to do so), but his expectations of sexual intercourse with his wife were perfectly understandable. No husband could be expected to 'wait' for three weeks simply to have intercourse with his lawfully wedded wife. John's remorsefulness only confirmed his innate decency in contrast with Clara's abnormal frigidity.

James's parable did not end with rape. Since Clara seemed incapable of assimilating sexual knowledge from books, she was dispatched to the family physician. 'With careful explanation, patience, sensible sex education and intelligent treatment,' readers were informed, 'Clara eventually adjusted to a happy sexual relationship with her husband.'[2] And so the marriage that started amid tension was happily resolved through sexual assault and the intervention of the medical profession. For Don James and (presumably) his readers, it was a satisfactory outcome. They might presume that, like Scarlett O'Hara in *Gone with the Wind* (novel, 1936; film, 1939) after she had been raped by Rhett Butler, Clara would be aglow. As Margaret Mitchell put it in her novel, O'Hara's husband had 'humbled her, hurt her, used her brutally through a wild mad night and she had gloried in it'.[3] In other words, sexual violation might be necessary if a couple were to finally attain marital bliss. Rape within marriage is the most common and most frequently excused form of sexual violation. In the guise of offering sanctuary and contentment, holy matrimony might bring only suffering for the wife.*

The (Contested) Meaning of Conjugal Love

The sexual abuse of wives like Clara by their husbands was not simply encoded in the everyday mores of modern society; it was also set in law. In Britain, America and Australia until the last decade of the twentieth century, a married woman was legally assumed to have consented to each and every act of vaginal intercourse with her husband. As in *Gone with the Wind*, a husband who forced his wife to have sex was not considered to have 'raped' her – even if (as in the case of Clara's husband) considerable violence was used. By definition a husband could not rape his wife.

This 'marital rape exemption' was commonly attributed to a ruling by Sir Matthew Hale in 1736.[4] [See image of Hale, below.] According to Hale, a wife gave lifelong consent to sexual intercourse with her husband. Under the marriage vows husband and wife became 'one person under the law'. It was a contract that 'she cannot retract'.[5] Thereafter, as *A Treatise on the Law of Domestic Relations* (1870) put it, 'wilfully declining matrimonial intimacy and companionship' was

Sir Matthew Hale

*Chapter 3, '"No" Means "Yes"', examines child abuse within the home and Chapter 8, 'Female Perpetrators; Male Victims', looks at female abusers, many of whom are mothers of their victims. This chapter focuses exclusively on husbands and wives.

nothing short of a 'breach of duty, tending to subvert the true ends of marriage'.[6]

This did not mean that a husband was granted absolute rights over his wife's body. He was prohibited from murdering her, for instance. A wife could charge her spouse with assault and battery. An analysis of assault charges brought by wives against their husbands in the nineteenth century has revealed that many of these assaults were described as having taken place in bed 'with no explanation of precipitating arguments'. It is a reasonable assumption that many wives were probably using evidence of physical assault to punish sexually abusive husbands.[7] Furthermore, a husband's protected status applied only to acts that violated his wife's vagina; a wife could charge her husband with sodomy. Judges were likely to be sympathetic to evidence of forcible buggery because, as one judge put it in the 1860s, the crime was 'so heinous and so contrary to experience'.[8]

A husband may not have absolute rights over his wife's entire body, but her vagina was legally assumed to be at his beck and call. Although this assumption was widely accepted, it came under attack from the middle of the nineteenth century. If marriage was based on coercion rather than conjugal love, what was the standing of a wife? The philosopher John Stuart Mill answered that question in no uncertain terms: a married woman was little more than a 'personal body-servant of a despot'. In 'The Subjection of Women' (1859) Mill railed against the fact that a wife could be 'made the instrument of an animal function contrary to her inclination'. This placed a married woman in a worse situation than a female slave, who at least possessed 'an admitted right', if not 'a moral obligation', to 'refuse to her master the last familiarity'. Not so the wife. No matter how

> brutal a tyrant she may unfortunately be chained to, though she may know that he hates her, though it may be his daily pleasure to torture her, and though she may feel it impossible not to loathe him – he can claim from her and enforce the lowest degradation of a human being.

Mill provocatively concluded that marriage was 'the only actual bondage known to our law. There remain no legal slaves, except the mistress of every house.'[9]

The wife's virtual slavery increasingly troubled a range of political commentators, from progressive feminists like Mill to conservative moralists. By employing the slave motif, the movement for reform could be tied to broader campaigns against the slavery of African-Americans and against the 'white-slave trade' associated with prostitution. As leading American suffragist Victoria Woodhull declared in 1873, she 'would rather be the labor slave of a master, with his whip cracking continually about my ears, than the forced sex slave of any man a single hour'.[10] The analogy with slavery was very popular with these early feminists, many of whom were also abolitionists. Thus Elizabeth Cady Stanton and Susan B. Anthony referred to married women forced to flee their violent husbands as 'fugitive wives: running to Indiana and Connecticut divorce mills, like slaves to their Canada, from marriages worse than plantation slavery'.[11] They proposed introducing the right to divorce and the right to 'voluntary motherhood' as measures aimed at rescuing wives from their sexually sadistic husbands.

Some feminists went further, agreeing with Mill that the wife's status was significantly *lower* than that of slaves. According to this line of thought, wives were not simply second-class humans because of their slave-like position vis-à-vis their husbands; they were actually set outside the category of the human altogether because they possessed fewer privileges than animals. In the animal world, noted one observer at the end of the 1870s, it was the female of the species who initiated sex. Why should female humans be refused this exclusive prerogative?[12] In the words of Russell Thacher Trall, mid-nineteenth-century founder of the Hygeo-Therapeutic College in New York and self-proclaimed expert on treatments for women,

> No male animal offers violence to the female . . . [He] never compels her to submit to the sexual embrace against her desire, nor forces her to bear offspring against her inclination or will. But, when she is in condition to propagate her kind, and desires the co-operation of her male partner, she informs him of it.[13]

How could marital sexual relations be improved? Mill's passionate plea for companionate marriages, based on mutual respect and love, was confined mainly to feminist circles. By the 1870s, however, reformers from a much broader range of philosophical and political perspectives began imploring husbands to change their marital behaviour. For many of these commentators, forcing a wife to have sex was wrong because it harmed the *husband*. Aggressive husbands were in danger of suffering from a 'general weakness of the nervous system', a 'weakening of the joints', a 'softening of the muscles' and a 'want of strength, according to John Cowan in *The Science of a New Life* (1869).[14] Nearly two decades later a similar catalogue of woes was reeled off by the widely read author of *The Transmission of Life* (1884). Forcing sex on an unwilling wife risked giving the husband heart palpitations, impairing his digestion and causing dyspepsia. The sexually abusive husband would literally observe his strength seeping away. Even worse, he would suffer spermatorrhoea (that is, the involuntary drooling of semen without erection) and his 'genetic powers' would 'lose their vigor'.[15] The offspring of forced sex within marriage would also inherit their father's weakness, having been endowed even before birth with 'lustful passions and morbid appetites'.[16] Indeed, the effects of forcing sex on a wife were similar to those of self-abuse or masturbation. According to this perspective, male bodies were a closed system, sapped by ordinary sexual intercourse but doubly drained if the husband had to use force to attain what he hankered after.

Emphasis on forced sex focused upon the husband's well-being, as opposed to the wife's, partly because it tied into a new cult of masculinity gradually emerging at the time.[17] This 'male domesticity' approach was not concerned with equality between the sexes (as John Stuart Mill had called for), nor was it bothered by the unequal distribution of domestic labour. It saw the home as a restful location where husbands could forge congenial and companionate relationships with their wives. Male dominance in the home was unquestioned, but 'modern' husbands professed to be happy to discuss their decisions with wives.

This new manly domesticity drew attention away from the marketplace and towards the home. The notion of a husband spending time relaxing at home, as opposed to spending all his leisure time with his colleagues, was crucial. It was a middle-class ideal, one that flourished most strongly in the suburbs. It signified a decisive shift in the way many husbands related to their wives. Obedience and discipline were jettisoned; companionship and friendship were embraced. This ideal affected every aspect of domestic interaction, but was particularly significant in reducing tolerance of cruelty within marriage. In America between 1867 and 1871 and 1902 and 1906, for instance, the number of divorces granted to wives on the grounds of cruelty increased by 900 per cent. In the years 1867 to 1871, 18 per cent of divorces granted to wives were based on accusations of cruelty: for 1902 to 1906 this jumped to 29 per cent.[18] Both husbands and wives were expecting more emotional succour from their marriages. Individual fulfilment and affection became the bedrock of modern matrimony, not gratifying extras. Even domestic architecture changed subtly in response to this companionate ideal. The typical upper-working-class and middle-class Victorian house with all its rigid separations (a discrete parlour, study and sitting room, for example) gradually gave way to more open, family-orientated spaces, such as the 'living room'.[19] Of course, the new ideal remained just that – an aspiration. Marital rape did take place within the reformed home, but it became less tolerated and significantly more private, a guilty secret. If the household was to retain its respectable position within upper-working-class and middle-class society, rape could only take place out of sight. Good wives cry silently.

The post-1870s rise of the male domestic ideal differed from the 'equality' arguments of feminists like John Stuart Mill in another way too. While earlier commentators focused on the equal status of men and women and therefore the need for each spouse to respect the other's desires, commentators from the 1870s onwards premised their attack on marital brutality upon the *separate* nature of men and women. Husbands had to respect the sexual integrity of their wives, not because of a shared humanity, but because women were different from men. For instance, women were seen as more pure. Such commentators cautioned against the imposition of male lusts upon innocent womanhood. This view led the charismatic public speaker Andrew Jackson Davis to warn against marriages that originated 'in the heat of the blood, and in the blind ignorance of passion'. Such unions were doomed to misery. In *The Genesis and Ethics of Conjugal Love* (1874) Davis reminded his readers that in the 'rage of an uncontrollable sexual attraction' rape was inevitable. He insisted on defining sexual violence within marriage as rape, 'notwithstanding its legal recognition by the State and the solemn sanction of the Supervising Church'. The domestic sphere had been corrupted by male lusts, he lamented. 'In the home,' Davis wrote,

> woman has been imprisoned, scourged, branded with the red-hot irons of cruelty, and for what? Because, sometimes she *dared* to claim her body and her soul as *her own property* – denying to the male-master the liberties he sought with her inalienable private rights and this with her own person.

When the wife resisted her husband's 'hot impulses and lawless usurpation', he punished her

> with unaccountable cruelties, perpetual dependence, imprisonment in her own home . . . all, because man has not been educated, and thus morally organized, to perceive and tenderly respect his wife's spiritual and physical rights, which are as irrepealable and inextinguishable as his own.

Radically, Davis went on to promote a 'bill of rights'. Legislation was required in order to give every wife rights over the property of the home, as well as providing her with an entitlement to an 'apartment exclusively and sacredly her own, the same as if she were yet a maiden, wherein she may sleep and make her toilet unmolested and alone'. Separate bedrooms and separate beds would allow each party to 'retire from and approach each other with polite defence and affectionate regard; avoiding every form of intrusion and indecorous familiarity, remembering the holy relation in which you live under the observation of innumerable angels'. This 'restoration of Eve to her garden of sacred maidenhood and graceful independence' would end 'all troubles of a sexual origin'.

Critics wondered whether Davis's solution would exacerbate rather than ameliorate ungratified sexual impulses. But Davis was uncompromising. Sexual frustration was a problem for only one half of the married couple, he pointed out. Women, he argued, were fortunate in that menstruation provided 'infallible and periodical relief' from sexual urges. Women's 'enlarged centres of conjugal vital essences' were 'soothed into tranquillity with every moon'. In contrast, men were 'charged to repletion, even to the verge of uncontrollable violence' by their sexual urges. Under no circumstances should this biological fact be used by husbands to 'invade the sacredness' of his wife's bedroom uninvited. 'Man is constituted to *conquer* all impulses of the subservient blood,' Davis thundered. 'When his spirit speaks,' he continued, 'his passion is essentially allayed, and his wild rage for sexual intercourse is gone; for thus, in all realms of higher being, matter is over-shadowed and mastered by Mind.' If 'your frenzy continues', he hastily advised his male readers, dietary routines should be changed and drinking habits moderated. Husbands needed to 'fix upon nobler physical habits' in order that their 'salvation shall be sure, beautiful, and sublime'.[20]

Davis became known as the 'John the Baptist of modern spiritualism'. The spiritualist movement of his time was egalitarian, rationalistic and actively involved in political and social reform in America. In late-nineteenth-century Britain, too, reformers from a range of religious and secular backgrounds attacked the myth that male health depended upon regular sexual intercourse. After all, as the moral reformer Francis William Newman lectured in the 1880s, 'a ship-crew of young men, chiefly under the age of twenty-five, picked for masculine vigour, may go to Arctic regions for a year or two, and return in splendid condition without seeing a woman's face'.[21] If the individual man's well-being could be assured within a celibate state, it was even more the case that the healthiness of society – nay, civilization itself – could be preserved only if the weaker sex was respected. In Newman's words,

> A married man is bound sternly to act the celibate during long months; and in some cases totally, through the weak health of his wife. (Not but that even here our law most cruelly treats a wife, stripping her of that self-defence against a brutal sensual husband which every female dog and cat retains and exercises) . . . self-restraint is necessary and salutary for every man.[22]

British moralists argued, like their American counterparts, that conjugal love within marriage was the ideal to be pursued. In *The Morality of Marriage* (1897) novelist and social commentator Alice Mona Caird railed against the 'tyrannical spirit' ruling over some marriages. She argued that the most abusive 'tyrant' was the husband who based his pleas on 'love and devotion', yet demanded sexual favours in order to retain that same devotion. Such tyranny

> expresses itself profitably by appeals to the pity and the conscience of the victims; by threats of the suffering that will ensue to the despot, if his wishes are heartlessly disregarded. Should these measures fail, more drastic methods are adopted. These are stern or pathetic reminders of indisputable claims, accusations of selfishness, of failing duty, and so forth.[23]

They were the strategies of a despot, not a devoted husband.

These commentators were particularly sensitive to the fact that a wife was most vulnerable to cruelty on her wedding night. Presuming that the new wife was a virgin, everything depended upon the husband's ability to exercise self-control and avoid carrying out an act that was, in everything but law, rape. As one advice book, frankly entitled *Satan in Society* (1880), warned, at the 'slightest intimation of pain or fear' the new husband must stop any sexual overtures. Sex that was not 'obviously invited and *shared*' was equivalent to 'committing a veritable outrage on the person of her whom God has given you for a companion'. The 'first conjugal act' should never become 'little else than legalized *rape*'.[24]

This emphasis on mutuality meant that the wife also had to play her part on that first, dramatic night. It could be a delicate balancing act, according to the author of *Christianity and Sex Problems* (1906). On the one hand, husbands had to be aware that forced intercourse might make the wife repulsed by sex – and revulsion could easily develop into 'chronic frigidity'. But, on the other hand, wives had to be wary of the 'danger' that might be caused by 'tantalizing and straining to a harmful extent' their husbands' 'organs and constitution'.[25] William J. Robinson echoed this concern in *Woman: Her Sex and Love Life* (1917). In a section about husbands who 'tortured' their wives by demanding sexual intercourse against their 'marital feeling', he warned wives not to 'repel your husbands when they ask for sexual favors', adding 'at least do not repel them too often'.[26]

The central assumption in these turn-of-the-century discussions was that the two sexes experienced sexual pleasure in radically different ways. As psychiatrist Leopold Loewenfeld insisted in *On Conjugal Happiness* (1913), the new husband had to respect his wife's feelings if he was to remove the 'psychical obstacle' created by her high investment in virginity. 'Brutal insistence' on sex might lead to 'the most serious consequences to the mental state of the wife'. Indeed, Loewenfeld was surprised that the wife's 'first night' did not become 'the starting-point of hysteria' more frequently, since 'what takes place often amounts to nothing more or less than rape'.

In case the balance of power within the marital relationship was tipping too far toward the wife, however, Loewenfeld went on to argue that, while a 'man of fine feeling' would restrain himself once he realized that he was causing his wife pain, so too the wife had to be 'self-sacrificing enough not to expect her husband to completely abstain simply because intercourse causes her some discomfort'. A woman who regarded her virginity as a 'priceless treasure' was still obliged to learn how to give up this prize to her lawful spouse. Even if intercourse caused 'serious trouble' (haemorrhaging was mentioned), the wife should 'call in medical assistance' speedily 'so as to relieve her husband from protracted abstinence'. Submitting to her husband's 'wishes and needs' was important if the wife was to 'bind him enduringly to her'. Indeed, 'a refusal to grant it without valid reason' was 'not permissible'. 'Sensible and fine-feeling women who are devoted to their husbands', Loewenfeld concluded, would willingly submit to their spouse's demands 'even though sexual intercourse may give them little or no pleasure'.[27]

Loewenfeld was frank, if not brusque, about the pragmatic jostling between spouses in the bedroom. The Dutch sexologist Theodoor Hendrik Van de Velde took this one step further. His best-selling advice book *Ideal Marriage* (1928) was translated into English by the distinguished British sex reformer Stella Browne. Like Loewenfeld, Van de Velde believed that the body was like a machine that could be taught to perform efficiently. However, he placed greater emphasis on the unconscious and on the role of the husband as 'teacher'. Indeed, the binary of male-active and female-passive roles was particularly pronounced in his account. On the marriage night, Van de Velde advised, the husband had to recognize and respect his wife's anxieties, even if they were unconscious ones. This did not mean that the bridegroom should deal with his wife's fears with 'weak submission, sentimentality, or least of all, misplaced pity'. The happiness of both spouses depended on the husband showing 'delicate consideration' and 'technical proficiency' (Van de Velde did not indicate how the new husband was to gain the necessary know-how).

So how was the husband to respond if his wife met his sexual advances with 'defensive struggles, gestures of repulsion, or closed thighs'? How was such a wife to be 'wooed into compliance', Van de Velde asked. Should, for instance, the first intercourse be preceded by 'genital stimulation' or what is called 'foreplay' today? Absolutely *not*. For one thing, he explained, any pleasurable '*sensory* result' would 'be entirely cancelled by the [subsequent] pain of defloration'. More to the point, Van de Velde lectured, there were 'advantages in restricting her first coital experience to the removal of the hymenal barrier, and the opening of the sexual passage'. A

> more detailed activity of the bridegroom on this momentous occasion, an initiative that went beyond what was strictly necessary, might easily deeply offend the modesty of a more or less timid and quite inexperienced virgin bride. This should be avoided, for the psychic stresses and conflicts of the situation are in themselves great! And womanly modesty is in itself something so beautiful and precious – and so often disregarded by modern customs and costumes – that the husband should show it all possible reverence.

Van de Velde recommended that 'intensively erotic and definite stimulation' should be only 'sparingly applied' and complete nudity avoided. After all, 'the male member' would 'seem gigantic to her unaccustomed eyes' and would only 'terrify her and accentuate her unconscious psychic dread'.[28]

Loewenfeld and Van de Velde at least addressed female sexuality, albeit as a dread to be conquered in the interests of gratifying male sexual desire. For them the 'wrong' of marital rape was very different from the 'wrong' identified by their late-nineteenth-century predecessors. As we saw earlier, from the 1870s to the turn of the century marital rape was portrayed as an evil because of the dangers of unrestrained sex *for husbands*. For the sake of male health and well-being, husbands needed to consciously adopt the sexual standards of their wives. In contrast, by the time Loewenfeld and Van de Velde were writing, marital rape was harmful because it caused female 'frigidity'. This approach did acknowledge the sexual responsiveness of wives, even if it still implied that women's 'frigidity' was a problem because it threatened male sexual pleasure.

Despite these differences between the 1850s, when John Stuart Mill was writing, and the sexologists of the early decades of the twentieth century, both authoritative interventions into the privacy of the marital bed were based upon two assumptions. First, sex did not come as naturally to humans as it did to the birds and bees. It had to be taught. Husbands and wives had to possess both sexual and psychological knowledge if they were to successfully negotiate mutually agreeable bedroom activity. Second, while the sexual tensions portrayed as inevitable between husbands and wives could have been dealt with in different ways, there was general agreement that wives were more reluctant to have sex than their husbands. Thus there was always a risk that husbands would attempt to force intercourse. It was an assumption that remained intact until the sexual revolution of the 1960s.

The Marital Rape Exemption

As I have already shown, feminists had long been infuriated by the idea that sexual coercion within marriage was somehow exempted from the 'rape' designation. Nineteenth-century feminists argued for a definition of manliness that emphasized male self-restraint rather than sexual appetite. The truly 'pure, honest, noble, *manly*' husband would never 'demand sensual gratification, against the wishes of his wife', declared the author of *The Unwelcome Child* (1858).[29] The crucial point for many of these early feminists was that the marital rape exemption meant compulsory maternity for many women. In a time before reliable birth control it was imperative that a woman's 'no' was respected. Maternal mortality rates were high. Many women found themselves physically ruined for the rest of their lives after childbirth: prolapsed uteri, unsutured perineal tears and vaginal fistulas were a common and widely feared fate. At the very least, these feminists argued, women's health and the promotion of women within the public sphere depended upon discrediting the notion that husbands had unlimited access to their wives' bodies.

These early feminists were less interested in promoting legislative reform than in persuading individual men to change their behaviour. By the 1920s, however, even this type of feminist interest in marital rape had begun to recede. In part this was a result of the liberalization of divorce law. In the United Kingdom from 1923, wives no longer had to allege cruelty in order to get divorced. Simply proving adultery was sufficient, as it was already for husbands seeking divorce. This meant that wives were finding it legally easier to leave their marriages (although economic and social difficulties remained significant deterrents). In addition, feminists who used to be preoccupied with issues of violence began turning their attention elsewhere – effective birth control, equal wages and access to education increasingly commended their attention. It wasn't until the 1970s that feminists once again focused their energies on combating sexual violence inflicted by husbands.

Another reason why marital rape was discussed less in public fora between the 1920s and the 1970s was the increasing privatization of the home. The dramas of the First and Second World Wars raised anxieties about the 'brutalization' of returning servicemen by the violence of combat. Most commentators believed that wartime experiences had the opposite effect: veterans wished to retreat back into an increasingly private domesticity. Whether men had been brutalized or not, they needed to be re-established within the domestic sphere, as masters of their own homes. Suburbanization reinforced a particular ideal of the enclosed, tightly knit domestic unit. A new male domesticity emerged in which the home was increasingly portrayed as a haven from both the military and the market. The home was becoming an even more sacrosanct space, with the husband in a privileged position as protector of womankind.[30] Public acknowledgement of husbands as violators became suppressed.

When marital rape was discussed in this period, it was often to justify *retaining* a husband's legal exemption from prosecution. Thus the unnamed author of 'Rape and Battery Between Husband and Wife' in the *Stanford Law Review* in 1954 admitted that the legal assumption that marriage automatically and irreversibly implied consent to sexual intimacies violated commonsense understandings of marital duties, was contradictory and was manifestly unfair to wives. Nevertheless, the author pointed out that there were intractable problems in changing the law to allow husbands to be accused of rape. Was it not obvious that marital rape was less harmful to a woman than being raped by a stranger? Since the two parties had been 'very intimate' in the past, the 'possibilities of serious social, physical or mental harm' were much smaller. There was also the bugbear of providing robust proof. The 'mysteries of sexual relationships' had often baffled 'experienced judges as well as psychologists', the author lamented. Who had not observed the rapidity with which love was transformed into hatred? Could accusations of rape be prompted by considerations of property settlements? Any wife 'willing to prod the state into bringing a felony prosecution against her husband' was 'unlikely to recollect objectively', he insisted.

Furthermore, it was in society's interests that married couples stayed together. In an attempt at reconciliation, husbands might make sexual overtures to disgruntled wives. Why should they be discouraged from doing so? Indeed, unlike forcible rape between unmarried individuals, intercourse between married, albeit estranged, couples was to be encouraged on the premise that 'if passion still exists the marriage may have vitality'. For these reasons, the author concluded, rape remained 'a category ill-suited to marriage'.

What about 'battery' between spouses, the second part of this author's title? To prevent readers concluding that a husband might legitimately force his wife to have sex with him so long as he did not 'batter' her, the author was very clear: although 'criminal battery exists to redress invasions of bodily integrity', it was in the interests of practical policy that 'minor marital difficulties' be ignored. After all, he continued, like marital rape, proof of violence was difficult to ascertain. It 'seems more desirable to recognize that provocation is likely during the course of a marriage, and that resulting minor batteries should be kept out of the criminal courts, since prosecution would stifle the last prospects for a reconciliation'. And what about justice for the wife? She should appeal to the divorce court, rather than the criminal bench. The article concluded by reminding lawyers that 'resistance during preliminary love-making greatly increases the sexual pleasure of some women'.[31]

Defending the retention of the marital rape exemption for husbands was not uncommon in the 1950s. The author of 'Rape and Battery Between Husband and Wife' had framed his arguments in terms of procedural difficulties and the need to safeguard a particular understanding of power structures within marriage. Other legal commentators agreed on this need to defend the marital state, but added religious justifications as well. Writing in the early 1950s, Norval Morris (often described as 'the most influential American criminologist of his time')[32] and A. L. Turner reminded readers that in the eyes of the Church, marital intercourse was 'of the essence of marriage'. Indeed, the marriage service explicitly stated that 'it was ordained for a remedy against sin and to avoid fornication that such persons as have not the gift of continence might marry and keep themselves undefiled members of Christ's body'. The authors interpreted this to mean that intercourse was 'a privilege at least and perhaps a right and a duty inherent in the matrimonial state'. If a wife persisted in her refusal to allow sexual intercourse, they stated, 'the husband must choose between letting his wife's will prevail, thus wrecking the marriage' or forcing her to have sex 'without her consent'. They argued that it would be nothing less than 'intolerable' if the husband's response to his wife's refusal to engage in sexual intercourse was in any way influenced 'by the threat of criminal proceedings for rape'.

In this sense, according to these distinguished criminologists, the survival of the relationship should be valued more highly than the wife's desire not to have sex with her husband. The husband's immunity from rape charges stemmed from 'general policy considerations' which, however, were 'not easy to articulate'. Dragging a husband before the courts was a 'clumsy and dangerous mode of protecting the wife', they insisted. In case readers did not quite understand why this was important, they reiterated their view that the 'delicate fabric of human relationship involved in marriage might be jeopardized even by the threat of prosecution for rape'. Sexual intercourse – whether forced or not – was dubbed 'wooing': it was 'the best method of bringing to an end a quarrel'.[33]

Nonsense, exclaimed an increasingly vocal cluster of feminists in the 1970s. Forcing a woman to have sex was never going to 'end a quarrel'. Married or not, a woman's body belonged to one person: herself. The assumption that a husband had any control over his wife's body was ıe more example of patriarchal rule. The belief that a married vould feel less violated if her attacker was her husband was yet anoth... example of a 'disembodied assumption of impact – *the* violation not *her* violation'.[34]

Feminist attention shifted from the sexual aspect of the rape towards its foundation in regimes of power and domination of husbands over wives. Descriptions of their actions by rapist-husbands made this patently obvious, they observed. Thus, a thirty-eight-year-old college-educated businessman called Ross could be heard explaining why he raped his wife. 'I guess subconsciously I felt she was getting the better of me,' he admitted, arguing that

> It dawned on me to just throw her down and have her . . . which I did . . . I grabbed her by the arms and she put up resistance for literally fifteen seconds and then just resigned herself. There were no blows or anything like that. It was weird. I felt very animalistic, and I felt very powerful . . . I'm not proud of it, but, damn it, I walked around with a smile on my face for three days.

He continued by noting that 'You could say, I suppose, that I raped her. But I was reduced to a situation in the marriage where it was absolutely the only power I had over her'.[35]

Feminists also attacked marital rape for what it is: a not uncommon form of violent abuse. They were able to point to survey evidence revealing that between 8 and 14 per cent of wives claimed to have been raped at least once by their husbands. In contrast, less than 1 per cent of wives reported having been raped by someone other than their spouse.[36] Rape was a hidden form of assault.

Instead of discreetly passing over details of violence, anti-marital rape campaigners publicized them. Extremes of violence are often used in marital rape, including the use of broken glass and knives – so what possible reason could there be for courts to decree (as they did in a case in 1966) that because there 'had been a previous relationship', the wife's 'sense of violation' was 'not as strong as where the rape takes place on a stranger'?[37] On the contrary, these activists pointed out, the breach of trust made marital rape *especially* traumatizing. As one woman stammered after being raped by her husband,

> He raped me – he ripped off my pyjamas, he beat me up. I mean some scumbag down the street would do that to me. So to me it wasn't any

> different because I was married to him, it was rape . . . It emotionally hurt worse [than stranger rape]. I mean you can compartmentalize it as stranger rape – you were at the wrong place at the wrong time – you can manage to get over it differently. But here you're at home with your husband and you don't expect that. I was under constant terror even if he didn't do it.[38]

The distress caused by marital rape was an important weapon in the feminist arsenal. According to one study, 52 per cent of victims of marital rape suffered severe long-term effects, compared with 39 per cent of victims of stranger rape.[39] Diana H. Russell's dramatic exposé, bluntly entitled *Rape in Marriage* (1990), was able to show that victims of marital rape were harmed in similar ways to other victims of rape. The main difference was that wives suffered *additional* feelings of betrayal, inability to trust and isolation.[40] Contrary to myth, wives also sustained more severe physical injuries than did other rape victims.[41]

It was, nevertheless, difficult to persuade some wives to report sexual abuse by their husbands to the police. In 2000, of those women who withdrew their complaint of rape after making it to the police, over 42 per cent had made the complaint against their partner or former partner.[42] Within marriage, lack of money and access to alternative housing, in addition to emotional dependency and concerns over retaining access to children, meant that victims often felt unable to escape.

Although this feminist critique from the 1970s was immensely influential, greater awareness of the harm caused by rape within marriage did not necessarily translate into legislative reform. Many legal experts continued to adhere to the view that it was not appropriate to charge a husband with rape. As John Harman explained in an article published in the 1980s in the *Journal of Family Law*, marital rape 'hardly seems a fit object for redress by the complex, expensive, and grim machinery of police, courts, and prisons'.[43] Many ordinary citizens concurred. Thus a survey in 1982 of Texas residents found that 62 per cent were opposed to any change in the law that exempted husbands from rape charges brought by their wives, although there was speculation that opposition could be reduced if the penalties for rape were less severe.[44]

Given the dramatic liberalization of many aspects of family law and practice from the 1960s, why did so many people remain opposed to making married men accountable for sexually abusive acts against their wives? In the mid-1970s a radio debate in South Australia reviewed some of the main answers. The consultant psychiatrist David Barnes brought up one of the chief anxieties: fear of false accusations. 'Males and females can be sick, deluded, ill and have other reasons for making accusations of all forms of violence and brutality against their spouse,' he argued. As a compromise position, he suggested that accusing wives should be given 'some sort of pre-trial or pre-sentence examination'. Others repeated the claim that a wife's ability to accuse her husband of rape would threaten the entire institution of marriage. This was the point put forward by Robert Moore, the programme's interviewer. 'This discussion is as much about the institution of marriage as it is about rape,' he contended. 'To me, it's just inconceivable that a marriage . . . could survive a wife bringing a rape charge against her husband. And wouldn't a divorce just be more honest?' At this point an exasperated Susan Brownmiller (the renowned anti-rape activist) interrupted: 'Well, yes, except that there might also be a criminal proceeding because someone committed a criminal act.'[45]

The marital rape exemption was not only being debated on the popular airways. A robust justification of the marital rape exemption was published in the *New Law Journal* in 1991 by the internationally distinguished legal academic Glanville Williams. In the judgement of this legal don the question of the marital rape exemption should be addressed to 'a sensible married woman who is not a lawyer' rather than to 'dragons' (his term for feminist lawyers). Any 'sensible woman', he claimed, would scoff at attempts to prosecute husbands. Williams contended that he possessed sufficient empathy with female victims and that made his opinions matter. Fundamentally he believed that rape by a husband was less traumatic for the victim. 'Our warrior feminists,' he began,

> may object that only women can make this judgment, but some women, at least, do. My own interviewee asked: is the husband to be accounted a rapist because his stupid embraces caused his wife to miss her train that morning?

Fear of disgruntled wives was thus neatly collapsed into broader anxieties about 'working women'.

Why was Williams so hostile to prosecuting husbands? The charge of rape was 'too powerful (and even self-destructive) a weapon to be put into the wife's hands', he argued. Wives might accuse too hastily; they needed time if they were to show themselves capable of applying 'mature consideration' towards their husbands' behaviour. More importantly, rape was a crime all too easily committed. In Williams's words,

> We are speaking of a biological activity, strongly baited by nature, which is regularly and pleasurably performed on a consensual basis by mankind (to be quite clear, let me say 'humankind', an expression that I would not normally use). Occasionally some husband continues to exercise what he regards as his right when his wife refuses him, the refusal most probably resulting from the fact that the pair have had a tiff. What is wrong with his demand is not so much the act requested, but its timing, or the manner of the demand.

Williams believed that the 'fearsome stigma of rape' was 'too great a punishment for husbands who use their strength in these circumstances', although he willingly conceded that such a husband was 'a cad, an uncivilised bounder'.

So, if a wife found herself married to such a cad, what should she do? Williams agreed that she might choose to leave her rapist husband, even though 'various factors may temporarily impede this solution, particularly the problem of where she is to live, and how she is to finance the break-up and her own life afterwards'. Although Williams conceded that putting her husband behind bars 'may help her to rearrange her affairs', he insisted, nevertheless, that pursuing a conviction for rape was 'excessive for this purpose'.

Williams was also concerned with the sentencing implications of any charge of marital rape. He believed that courts should allow a 'previously settled relationship' as grounds for mitigating the harshness of any prison term. Instead of fearing that sentencing husbands for raping their wives would 'dilute' the severity of prison sentences given to stranger rapists, Williams was more concerned that 'hard sentences for stranger-rape may, and do, transfer into harsh sentences for husbands'. He fretted that

> the label of 'rape' itself biases the court (and commentators) towards severity. Not only judges but lawyers in general are much too ready to talk in terms of sentencing for terms of years, when a long sentence is not necessary for the future safety of the complainant. The extension of

> a term of severe condemnation like 'rape' will increase the possibility of this irrational reaction.

In other words, Williams was worried about a possible cross-infection between prison sentences handed out to stranger rapists and those handed out to husband rapists. To forestall such an outcome Williams proposed that the actions of husbands should be treated as 'common assault or other non-sexual offence'. In this way the cases could be dealt with in the Magistrates' rather than the Crown Court and the judge could hand down a fine or even issue a 'bind over' order. If the husband's actions deserved a custodial sentence, Williams expressed a hope that it would be 'reckoned in terms of days rather than years'.[46]

Williams was writing in Cambridge in 1991. It was no wonder he sounded beleaguered: the views he was espousing had been under sustained judicial attack for a couple of decades and, irrespective of the legal position, an increasing number of wives had begun taking their complaints of marital violation before the courts.[47]

I have already drawn attention to the feminist arguments against the marital rape exemption, but even within mainstream and conservative legal circles the profound injustice of exempting husbands from rape charges had been gathering support from the 1970s. Sir Matthew Hale's original articulation of the exemption in 1736 had been premised upon the idea that marriage was a contract that, once signed, could not be revoked. But, critics pointed out, if marriage was a contract, then it was a profoundly unusual one. The provisions were unwritten, the penalties unspecified. Consenting parties had no idea of the terms of the contract. Most pertinently, female contractors were not made aware that they were signing up for sexual intercourse on demand merely at the other signatory's whim. If such a clause was explicitly written into the marriage contract, how many women would be willing to sign? Furthermore, since rape was being defined primarily as an act of violence, not sex, the entire notion of a wife's 'consent' to it was hard to sustain.

The assumptions behind the marital rape exemption were increasingly regarded as profoundly distasteful and untenable in the context of modern gender relationships. In the late twentieth century, how was it possible to cling to the idea that a husband somehow owned his wife's body and therefore could not 'take by force' what he already 'owned by right'? The claim that, in marriage, 'two became one' was nothing more than a bad joke. As long ago as 1765 William Blackstone, the most famous of all jurists, had articulated this doctrine, asserting that husband and wife were 'one person in law: that is, the very being or legal existence of the woman is suspended during the marriage, or at least is incorporated and consolidated into that of the husband; under whose wing, protection and cover, she performs everything'.[48] In law this dogma (dubbed the 'unities theory') had gradually been replaced by the concept of 'separate spheres', which gave women rights within the domestic sphere. Most importantly, from 1839 in Mississippi (and then spreading to every other American jurisdiction within fifty years) and in Britain from the 1880s, a series of Married Women's Property Acts enabled wives to own property, enter contracts and sue independently of their husband. It made little sense to fence off the sexual sphere of marriage from this trend in property and contracts law.

Obviously, if a woman could divorce her husband, then surely she could revoke other parts of this so-called contract as well. The New Jersey Supreme Court put this point most powerfully in 1981. The 'implied consent rationale', it began, was 'offensive to our valued ideals of personal liberty'. If a woman could legally terminate the marriage 'contract', 'may she not also revoke a "term" of that contract, namely, consent to intercourse? Just as a husband has no right to imprison his wife because of her marriage vow to him . . . he has no right to force sexual relations upon her against her will.'[49]

A husband's right to enforce intercourse and the wife's duty to submit had always been limited, after all. As mentioned earlier, any wife could refuse her husband sexual intercourse if he had a venereal disease or if his demands were unreasonable. It made no sense to deprive a wife of the rights to refuse sexual intercourse for any other number of reasons too.

Other absurdities in the law cemented arguments for comprehensive reform. One of the most curious anomalies concerned the distinction between unlawful sexual acts and those that remained immune from prosecution. In the case of Kowalski in 1988, a husband who forced his wife to have oral sex with him and then raped her vaginally was convicted of indecent assault for the oral attack but was not legally liable for the vaginal rape. Kowalski appealed against conviction for indecent assault for forced fellatio on the grounds that when he was happily married to his wife fellatio had routinely been performed as a prelude to sexual intercourse *per vaginam*. It was, therefore, 'a permissible adjunct to the sexual intercourse *per vaginam* to which the wife had by her marriage consented'. Kowalski lost. The Appeal judge decreed that it was 'well settled' that a husband could not rape his wife but fellatio, although not unlawful, was 'not a practice to which parties give their consent by their marriage'. The judge continued:

> If, having married, they do consent to it [fellatio], then the act so performed is performed with consent and is not an assault. But such a consent once given, and even long continued, cannot relate back and attach itself to the marriage vows or to the marriage contract or to the married state. Actual consent to such an act of fellatio must then exist if the particular incident is not to be an assault.

In other words, the 'married state does not imply consent to fellatio' although it did imply consent to vaginal intercourse.[50] In other jurisdictions (such as Oklahoma in 1981) a husband could be charged with rape if he forcibly inserted a finger into the anus of his wife, but not if he inserted his penis into the anus or vagina of the same non-consenting spouse.[51]

Law reform campaigners also attacked the chief objections to the repeal of the marital rape exemption. The notion that wives might fantasize about being raped and then put up token resistance was mocked. Glanville Williams's assertion that some women might act on their rape fantasies, was simply an attempt to 'bait us women folk', one legal expert scornfully noted.[52] Equally, concerns about infringing family privacy were dismissed. After all, the law already did this in innumerable ways. And anyway why should the right to privacy of one spouse be allowed to override the right to protection of another? To those who argued that a husband might be vulnerable to false accusations, the reformers retorted that this was a problem in all areas of law: the legal process imposed scrupulous safeguards precisely for that reason. Making an accusation of rape remained highly stigmatized. The ordeal of having to defend such a claim in court strongly discouraged malicious allegations. More to the point, neither the risk of false accusations nor the difficulties of proof had ever been a justification for not criminalizing behaviour. As one court ruled in 1985, there was 'no other crime we can think of in which all of the victims are denied protection simply because someone might fabricate a charge'. More practically, in jurisdictions where marital rape was criminalized, there was no evidence that wives 'flooded the district attorneys with revenge filled trumped-up charges'.[53]

Finally, fears that criminalizing marital rape might devalue other rape charges had to be addressed directly. Some feminists (as well as anti-feminists) worried that jurists and members of the general public might underestimate the harmfulness of rape if husbands were being charged. Women Against Rape (WAR) waged a particularly effective attack on this assumption, not only pointing out that marital rape *was* as harmful as other forms of abuse, but also reminding critics that retaining the marital rape exemption cheapened the status of wives. 'Devaluing the wife who is raped devalues every rape survivor,' they declared.[54] Removing the marital rape exemption would not undermine marriage as an institution – all it challenged was marriage 'as an institution of rape'.[55] Furthermore, as others pointed out as well, if marriage was to be safeguarded, the best way to do this was to stamp out the practice of rape within the marital bond.[56] As members of the Protective Agency for Women and Children retorted as long ago as 1887 when accused of breaking up marriages, these were not 'true marriages' but 'a falsity and a sham'.[57] They attempted to persuade victims that 'the shame and scandal of these crimes lies in the fact, not the telling of it'.[58]

Very slowly these rape reformers had an impact. In America Nebraska was the first state to completely abolish the marital rape exemption in 1976. It rapidly spread to other states. By 1993 all states had abolished the exemption, although not in all circumstances. Thus, in some states, the wife still has to prove that she was living apart from her husband at the time of the rape or that he used violence against her. Furthermore, the penalties for raping one's wife remain often significantly lower than they are for non-spousal rape.[59]

In the United Kingdom the first domestic violence shelter was opened in England in 1971, but Scotland led the way in abolishing the marital rape exemption in 1989.[60] In contrast, in England and Wales the Criminal Law Revision Committee Report on Sexual Offences of 1984 concluded (by a narrow majority) that marital rape was less serious than non-consensual intercourse outside of marriage.[61] The English Law Commission dissented from the conclusions of the Criminal Law Committee Review. It sided with the minority opinion that 'a woman like a man was entitled on any particular occasion to decide whether or not to have sexual intercourse, outside or inside marriage'.[62] The English Law Commission's report *Rape Within Marriage* (1992)[63] stated that rape within marriage was as 'physically, emotionally, or psychological' disturbing for a woman as non-consensual intercourse with a stranger. In fact, it went on, 'the rape of a wife by her husband was particularly offensive in that it was an abuse of an act which has been or should have been his means of expressing love for his wife'.[64]

In 1992 the marital rape exemption was finally abolished throughout the UK. The effect of the repeal of the marital rape exemption was ambiguous. In the lead-up to its abolition *The Times* sported a headline predicting that a 'Wave of Prosecutions Will Follow'.[65] This did not happen. According to one study in 1996, of 450 reports of rape that year, the suspect was a husband in only twenty-two cases.[66] It remains the most difficult form of abuse to successfully prosecute.

These debates about raping husbands are predicated on the notion that a woman's body is property. This property is transferred to the husband on marriage, making it imperative that the husband 'uses it' in the interests of his own sexual health. According to this view, raping one's wife is wrong because of the way it hurts the man by draining him of vital energy. Commentators who accept the existence of an autonomous female sexuality can also hold that a wife should submit to her husband's each and every sexual demand on the grounds that sex will 'bind him enduringly to her', as Loewenfeld expresses it. The debates about whether husbands and wives are equal partners in sexual exchanges, or whether they possess separate sexual natures, fundamentally address the nature of gender relations within society more generally.

Paradoxically, the dramatic shifts towards greater female autonomy from the 1970s undercut some of the arguments against the abolition of the marital rape exemption. With widening access to divorce and increased employment opportunities for women, wives are exhorted to simply leave their abusive husbands, as opposed to dragging them before the courts. The abused wife found herself in a Catch-22 situation. On the one hand, modern assertions of female sexual agency carry the implication that abuse is somehow the wife's fault: she has failed to 'satisfy' her man. On the other hand, the law of consent is still framed according to an active male sexual subject who initiates sex. The wife is the sexual object, whose choices are limited to submitting or not. Counter-accusations in marital rape cases, in which the husband accuses the wife of sexually coercive actions, are not uncommon. In both cases the home remains a sacrosanct space. Incomplete abolition of the marital rape exemption for husbands has given the impression that the problem has been resolved. Only a handful of cases of marital rape have been successfully prosecuted. But, as a result of the legislation, further examination of violence within the home has been inhibited. Clearly, if we want to eradicate rape from the marital bedroom, legal reform is not enough.

CHAPTER TWELVE

The Prison

Haywood Patterson was an unlikely hero of the American left. On 25 March 1931, at the age of eighteen, this unemployed African-American was convicted of the rape of two women and sentenced to die in the electric chair. He finally regained his freedom in 1948, having served sixteen years for a crime that had not even taken place. [See photograph, below.]

His accusers were Victoria Price and Ruby Bates, two young white women travelling illegally on a train. Patterson and some other impoverished lads had hitched a ride on the same train. They were provoked into a fight with a group of white boys whom they duly threw off the

Haywood Patterson

train. In anger the white boys telegraphed ahead to the next station claiming to have witnessed a white woman being raped by a gang of black youths. When the train arrived at Paint Rock (Alabama), an angry crowd of armed men and women dragged Patterson and eight other young black men (one aged thirteen) off the train and imprisoned them. Price and Bates were intimidated into making rape accusations to escape being imprisoned themselves for prostitution and travelling illegally. All the accused men were convicted of rape at a trial in Scottsboro in Jackson County.

It was a *cause célèbre*. None of the young men was given proper legal representation and no evidence was produced that a crime had even been committed. Even more devastating for the case, one of the accusers eventually denied that any rape had taken place. On 5 January 1932 Ruby Bates wrote a letter to her boyfriend saying that it was

> a goddam lie about those Negroes jazzing me those policemen made me tell a lie . . . i was drunk at the time and did not know what i was doing i know it was wrong too let those Negroes die on account of me i hope you will believe my statement because it is gods truth i hope you will believe me i was jazzed but those white boys jazzed me i wish those Negroes are not Burnt on account of me it is those white boys fault.[1]

Bates stated under oath in court that no rape had taken place.

International pressure mounted on the courts to free the prisoners. The International Labor Defense, a legal defence organization with strong ties to the Communist Party, mobilized opinion. Eventually the United States Supreme Court ruled that the 'Scottsboro Boys', as Patterson and his fellow defendants came to be known, had been denied effective counsel. One by one they were released from prison. Patterson was one of the last to be freed – and not by a court of law. In 1948 Patterson slipped away from a work gang and went into hiding for a couple of years. When he was finally caught he was living in Michigan. The authorities in Alabama decided not to extradite him. The Scottsboro tragedy lived on long after the Supreme Court's ruling. The young men's misfortune was set to music by blues musician Leadbelly and *To Kill a Mockingbird* (novel, 1960; film, 1962) drew some of its inspiration from the trial.

In most accounts the story ends there. But it doesn't. Patterson's years in prison were violent. Although an early historian of the case claimed that Patterson was the only one of the Scottsboro Boys who 'adjusted' to prison life,[2] Patterson's autobiography exposes himself as a highly disagreeable figure. Rather than being an unambiguous victim of prejudice and privation, in prison Patterson became an aggressive 'wolf', preying sexually on other prisoners. From Patterson's point of view the choice was between being a 'man' or a 'gal-boy'. He described his initiation into the life of a wolf:

> I heard tell of the gal-boy life at Atmore. Gal-boy stuff went on at Kilby and at Birmingham jail too. All prisons all over, I guess, but I wasn't interested in it. I was a man who wanted women. But this was the main thing going on among the Atmore prisoners . . . They built 'covered wagons' or 'hunks' around the beds. That screened out what went on inside the bunks . . . I learned men were having men. Old guys, they called them wolves, they saw me looking at this stuff and thought I might be a gal-boy. One came up and propositioned me. I didn't like that none at all. I said, 'If any of that stuff goes on with me in on it I'll do all the f-ing myself. I been a man all my life.'

As Patterson quickly realized, he was being 'forced to be either a man or a gal-boy. They wouldn't hardly let you stay outside of this life. You had to prove you were a man or become a woman'.[3] In prison, to be a man meant to act a rapist.

The Problem

Rape inside prison is an open secret. It is unsparingly portrayed in films like *The Shawshank Redemption* (1984), with its graphic depiction of gang rape.[4] In other films – including *House Party* (1990), *Naked Gun 33⅓* (1994), and *Dirty Work* (1998) – the rape of inmates is presented in a comic manner.[5] Whether their story is portrayed as tragedy or comedy, men who transgress social mores can expect to be assaulted in turn. As late as 1994 half of Americans polled agreed that 'society accepts prison rape as part of the price criminals pay for their wrongdoing'.[6] [See cartoon, p. 332.] 'If you don't want to be involved,' prison guards abruptly asserted, 'you shouldn't get sent to prison in the first place.'[7] Criminals beware.

This tension between transgressor and victim is crucial in understanding the relative complacency with which prison rape has traditionally been regarded. On the one hand, many *victims* of prison predators had

'Sex offenders should be sent to prison in a prom dress', by J. D. Crowe, 2005

committed violent offences, including rape and sexual assault on girls and women, in the world outside the penitentiary. Retributive fantasies encourage the notion that these victims were finally getting their just deserts. On the other hand, some of the *perpetrators* of sexual abuse in prisons were bitter at being victimized by 'the system'. Patterson should not have been in prison in the first place. Powerless in the face of the force of the 'white justice system', he and others like him saw the sexual coercion of white inmates as a way of hitting back at symbols of oppression.

As Patterson recognized, the *fact* of sexual violence in prisons is well known, but its *extent* is generally hushed up. Indeed, Patterson's autobiography (published in 1950) was startling precisely because of the candid way he discussed coerced and non-coerced sex in American penitentiaries. The last time this had happened was in 1935, when prison governor and inspector Joseph F. Fishman published *Sex in Prison. Revealing Sex Conditions in American Prisons*. Although explicit (there was an attempt to censor the book under indecency legislation in Australia),[8] Fishman's book failed to incite extensive public debate. This reluctance to discuss rape in prison extended to the courts. According to one scholar, as late as 1969, there was not a single American legal decision mentioning sexual assault in prisons.[9]

On those rare occasions when the problem of coerced sex in prison was broached, it was placed in the context of presumed consensual homosexuality. Thus Marie E. Kopp, writing in the *Journal of the American Institute of Crime, Law, and Criminology* in 1937, admitted that it was 'well known' to psychiatrists and penologists that sex delinquency was 'inordinately high' in prisons and borstals. She claimed that the 'segregation of the sexes, the insufficient amount of physical work to dispose of superfluous energy, a lack of incentive to work and long hours of enforced idleness' made this form of 'delinquency' inevitable.[10] In the UK the Howard League for Penal Reform also focused on delinquency as opposed to sexual abuse. A questionnaire it sent to prisons in 1948 asked about the 'extent and effect of perverted relationships in prison'. The authors were anxious about the 'contamination of one prisoner by another', rather than violence.[11] Even evidence of extreme violence (which Patterson, for instance, recited with gusto) could be conceptualized as 'just sex', lacking a real victim. Even more strikingly, coercive techniques in prisons were sometimes dismissed as 'seduction'.[12]

In all such studies male aggressors in prison were dubbed 'situational homosexuals': their victims were simply women-substitutes. Patterson certainly understood his prison aggression in this context. As he commented after escaping from prison, he quickly reverted to 'women friends', having 'found my way back, and straightened out my sex nature. No more the gal-boy stuff.'[13] The author of 'Sex in Prison' (1951) expressed it more coyly, asserting that 'the adventitious and transient sex exchange between members of one sex' in prison does 'not constitute homosexuality any more than the single swallow makes the summer'.[14] The double entendre was probably intended.

This reluctance to acknowledge the violence and coercion accompanying many acts of sexual intercourse in detention centres came to an abrupt end in the 1960s. In part this greater willingness to discuss rape in prison was due to the increasing tendency to publicly discuss sexual issues in general. Feminism also made an impact by insisting that coercive sexual activities were no longer tolerable. Although the emphasis was on female victims, the feminist critique of masculine aggression could be easily imported into debates on male-on-male violence. Furthermore, protests against the Vietnam War encouraged people to speak out against 'the establishment', which was seen as including the police and prison authorities. Anti-Vietnam war protesters – many hailing from the middle classes – suddenly found themselves arrested and imprisoned: their experiences of incarceration proved profoundly disturbing. Two notable examples were Howard Levy and David Miller. Army doctor Levy had been court-martialled for refusing to train Special Forces troops, while David Miller had been sentenced for burning his draft card. They met in prison and later collaborated on a book about their experiences. *Going to Jail* (1970) included a spirited exposé of prison rape. Stephen Donaldson, Pentagon correspondent for the *Overseas Weekly*, also refused to remain silent about his prison traumas. Donaldson had been arrested for participating in a peaceful Quaker protest against the American bombing of Cambodia in 1973. Locked in a prison cell in Washington DC, he was viciously raped over sixty times by other inmates. Not only did he agree to speak publicly about the rapes, including being interviewed on the television show *Sixty Minutes*, he also established the organization Stop Prisoner Rape.[15]

Disquiet about prison rape grew within the justice system from the 1960s also. Alan J. Davis, Chief Assistant District Attorney of Philadelphia, was the first to admit that there was a crisis. In December 1968 he dramatically announced that sexual assaults were 'endemic' in Philadelphia's prisons and sheriffs' vans. 'Virtually every slightly-built young man committed by the courts,' Davis revealed, would be 'sexually approached within a day or two after his admission to prison.' Furthermore, many of these men would be 'repeatedly raped by gangs of inmates'.[16] Given Davis's position, his indictment of the justice system proved inflammatory.

How endemic is sexual violence in prisons? Numbers are uncertain. One thing seems clear, however: rape in prisons is particularly rife in America. British surveys uncovered significantly lower abuse rates – some even claimed that under 0.3 per cent of prisoners said they had experienced unwelcome sexual activity.[17] In startling contrast, estimates of sexual violence in American prisons came close to confirming Davis's 'endemic' label. According to the most reliable surveys, for every one hundred male prisoners held in American prisons, between five and nine had been sexually assaulted.[18] Depending on how the question was phrased, this figure could rocket to twenty-two prisoners assaulted for every one hundred incarcerated.[19] The exponential growth of the prison population in America in the last three decades of the twentieth century (in the 1980s alone there was a 150 per cent increase in the prison population) coincided with declining staffing levels and deteriorating prison accommodation. Furthermore, the much higher levels of acknowledged rape in American prisons is consistent with the increasing incidence of violence in American society in general. In 1994, for instance, for every million people in the general American population there were 392 reported rapes. In contrast, the figure was 98 per million for England and Wales.[20] America has one of the highest rates of heterosexual rape in the world. It is not implausible to suggest that men who rape other men in prisons are simply acting as they did in the outside world. In the absence of women, they turn their sexual aggression towards men.

Estimates about the extent of rape in prison are politically significant. Stephen Donaldson of Stop Prisoner Rape, extrapolating from the higher percentage of 22 per cent of prisoners being raped,[21] concludes that over 240,000 men are raped in American prisons every year. This is nearly twice the number of women recorded by the Bureau of Justice Statistics as being raped.[22] In case the message is still not clear, the author of an article in the *National Review* of 5 February 2001 spelt it out: 'male-on-male rape has become more common than male-on-female rape', he declared, demanding more political investment in male victims.[23] Cash and concern are distributed according to such estimates.

Yet the estimates of prison rape cannot bear the weight placed upon them. For instance, research purporting to show that 22 per cent of prisoners are raped actually refers to the percentage of inmates in Nebraska's prisons who 'experienced unwanted sexual contact'. That is hardly 'rape' *as defined by the legal system*. More to the point, that broad estimate should not be compared with the number of female rape victims recorded by the Bureau of Justice Statistics for one basic reason: few women ever have their rapes and sexual assaults recorded.

Despite these words of caution, it is important not to forget that only a small proportion of rapes carried out in prisons are reported as well. Like their female equivalents, male victims are reluctant to admit to having been abused. According to some estimates, between 60 and 70 per cent of sexual assaults in prisons are never reported to the staff.[24] Prisoners insist that the figure is even higher. In the early 1970s over a quarter of inmates at the Tennessee State Penitentiary believed that more than 90 per cent of rapes were never reported. As I argue below, it is not surprising that African-American prisoners are particularly reluctant to report abuse.[25] Even in cases where the rape is reported, the attrition rate for complaints is high. In an investigation of rape within the Philadelphia prison system in 1968, for instance, of the ninety-four rapes reported (and ignoring the vast number of victims who remained silent about their abuse), sixty-four were simply noted in the prison records, forty resulted in internal discipline procedures and only twenty-six were reported to the police.[26]

Furthermore, comparing male-on-male rape rates in prisons with male-on-female rape rates in civilian society ignores another group of victims: those incarcerated in women's prisons. Although this chapter is primarily about sexual assault on men,* it is important not to forget that prison rapists and their victims are not only men. Indeed, unlike men's prisons, where violent offenders are often kept separate from men serving terms for non-violent or petty crimes, in female prisons murderesses and other violent criminals share bunks with shoplifters. Potentially this makes women's prisons a particularly dangerous environment.[27] In the 1970s, Jane described being 'pursued' by another female prisoner. 'The bitch is repulsive. I'd as soon do it with a dog as that stud broad,' she ruminated. She continued, however, by saying that

> I keep getting these kites. She has treatened [sic] me, she hangs around my room, and she's got her hands all over my ass all day longer [sic]. Last night she gave me gum for my lock. Hey, I ain't got nothing against a good screw or even making it with the right broad but I'll barf if that bitch touches me. Problem is I'll get the shit kicked out of me or worse if I don't spread 'em in the next couple of days.[28]

In contrast with sexual coercion in men's prisons, which began attracting attention from the 1960s, there was almost no research on sexual violence within female prisons until more than thirty years later.[29] It was often assumed that sexual intimacies between female prisoners were based on affectionate (albeit 'perverted') ties. Thus the title of an article published in the *Journal of Abnormal Psychology* in 1913 addressed sex between female prisoners as 'A Perversion Not Uncommonly Noted'.[30] Indeed, a study of inmates in the Women's Federal Reformatory in West Virginia in the mid-1960s categorically stated that 86 per cent of the inmates had a lesbian experience while incarcerated but failed to address the question of coercion.[31]

When detailed research into violence in female institutions was undertaken, the results were surprising: levels of coerced sex were significant. In a study carried out in the early 1980s, one-tenth of 561 adolescent offenders in six correctional facilities for women had been sexually victimized.[32] Just over ten years later another study revealed that 7 per cent of female inmates in a small women's facility had been sexually coerced.[33] As I have repeatedly observed, statistical comparisons are difficult, but these levels of sexual victimization of female

*There is a more detailed discussion of female-on-female rapes in Chapter 8, 'Female Perpetrators; Male Victims'.

prisoners are lower than those experienced by their male counterparts. Among factors that may explain these lower levels of violence are the more violent nature of men's offending generally, the smaller populations crowded together in female prisons (enabling guards to control them more easily) and gender differences in the acceptability of sexual coercion. Nevertheless, this should not blind us to the fact that, in terms of the numbers of individuals affected, the level of sexual abuse in female prisons is significant.

Dynamics of Coercion

'Kid, we want your ass,' the coercer often tells a new prisoner, adding, 'You can either give it up or we'll take it. It's up to you. You can do it the easy way or the hard way.'[34] Getting a prisoner into debt over cigarettes or other valued commodities is another, more subtle approach. With steep interest rates, debts spiral upwards, leaving the victim with one choice: pay up now or 'grab your ankles'.[35]

In such dangerous environments sexual trade-offs may seem the best option for vulnerable men. In exchange for protection from a tougher or more experienced convict a prisoner might choose to provide sexual as well as other domestic favours. This type of contract may take two main forms. In the simplest version a 'ripper' would simply observe while other men harass a new inmate. The ripper would then offer protection in exchange for sex.[36] More deviously, older cons act out a cruel theatre of seduction. This was how nineteen-year-old Jeff was trapped. On his first night Jeff was thrown into a cell containing three other men. 'Hey, kid, you ever been in jail before?' one cellmate sympathetically enquired, following it up with some friendly small-talk. The following night, however, the same cellmate warned Jeff that the other guys 'wanted his ass' and intended 'taking it' that night. The old 'con' then presented Jeff with the choice:

> What are you going to do? Listen, kid, I can handle them. I can keep them off of you. But I have been in this hold for six weeks and I sure am horny. I sure could use some head. How about tonight after everyone is asleep? You take care of me – no one will know – and I'll look out for you while you're here.

As soon as Jeff 'copped some rod', however, the other inmates 'woke up' and demanded their share.[37]

Demands made by people such as Jeff's cellmate are not to be taken lightly. Whether or not victims resist, deliberate cruelty is commonplace. Claiming that it would improve a man's ability to give a good 'blowjob', teeth are frequently knocked out.[38] Gang rape is the norm. At the Tennessee State Penitentiary in the 1970s, for instance, more than two-thirds of inmates claimed that most rapes involved three or four perpetrators, and a significant 13 per cent believed that the average number of perpetrators at each rape was over five.[39] Like heterosexual rape within the domestic sphere, prison rapists were often able to force their victim to submit over a prolonged period. 'The prison setting, like the family setting, is a closed system,' explained the authors of *Men Behind Bars* (1982), noting that 'in both instances the victim is living in close proximity with the perpetrator'.[40] Unfortunately for the victims, heavily armed authorities enforce physical closeness between perpetrator and victim in prisons. This is sexual slavery monitored by the state.

Coerced sex tends to be less *physically* violent in female prisons. Women aggressors tend to employ different strategies in imposing their will. Female socialization prioritizes psychological over physical abuse, initially at least. Because women are accustomed to being sexually propositioned within civilian society, they are also much more likely to have developed strategies other than aggression for rejecting propositions. For instance, one young female prisoner interviewed in the late 1970s described how she evaded penetrative violence by meeting her aggressor halfway. She described encountering an older prisoner in the hall one evening. Nervously observing that the woman was carrying a bottle, this prisoner asked,

> 'What the hell you think you're going to do with that?'. She goes, 'Come on baby lady, let's see what you got under there'. So she starts to lift up my shirt and I push her away, only she laughs. Then she's coming at me again, only this time she's starting to take off her dress. No kidding. She ain't got anything on underneath. So here I am, standing in this goddamm corridor of this goddamm jail with a sex maniac with a root beer bottle coming at me in her hand. And she ain't kidding either . . . So I start pulling off my own dress real slowly and she starts to calm down. Like before, she looked like she could either split my face, shove that bottle up inside me or split my face open with it. But when she sees maybe I'm going to get it on with her, she kind of relaxes. So then I say, 'take it easy, okay, cause I'm on the rag'. I thought

> that would stop her, which it did, sort of. Only she says, 'Okay, I'll leave you alone, only let me suck your tits'. I figured, why not, the poor woman'd probably been in here a hundred years without seeing nobody half my age.[41]

Finally, prisoners of both sexes are vulnerable to attack by prison staff. Correctional officers carried out about a quarter of forced sexual encounters.[42] These officers had their own unique *modus operandi*. In particular assault was often conducted under the cover of strip and body-cavity searches. Prisoners claimed that these searches were used 'more for entertainment value than any real security measure'.[43] Women are frequently subjected to 'decrutching' (the forcible removal of drugs from a prisoner's vagina). Male prisoners' bodies, too, are vulnerable to penetration by guards. Derek Jansen, for instance, recalled a body-cavity search in which the guards

> told me that if you don't bend over and let this PA stick his finger in your ass to see if you've got hack-saw blades secreted in your anus, we'll do it by force. So the next thing you know, I've got a stun gun here . . . shocking me . . . just because I'm not going to bend over and spread my ass cheeks for you . . . So of course, in the end they went ahead and had the PA do his rectal exam. No contraband. They knew that to begin with.

According to Jansen, guards use this search technique 'against the most rebellious' prisoners, saying, in effect, that 'we're gonna degrade you to where you don't want to break the rules'.[44]

Power

Glaring inequalities in power leave many inmates with the feeling that they have little option but to submit silently to whatever indignities are inflicted upon them by guards or fellow inmates. Complaining or otherwise protesting often causes the violence to escalate. In the words of one man who was repeatedly raped by his cellmate, 'I guess I was a coward but I let him do what he wanted. I cannot tell you how ashamed I felt of myself but always when I was on the verge of telling, the thought of that stiletto would come to me and I would keep my mouth shut.'[45] Acquiring a reputation for being a 'snitch' was exceedingly imprudent. In one report,

> a quiet girl was severely kicked in the stomach and the breast by five other inmates, evidently because, after first encouraging them, she would not submit to homosexual threats. None of the officers (guards) saw what happened, as it occurred in a bedroom, but when she told the officer in the next shift, they attempted to beat her again – right in the presence of the officer.[46]

As one inspector of Federal Prisons lamented, in reality prisons were 'governed under the surface by a clique of the toughest and most depraved characters'. As a consequence, any prisoner 'who runs and tells the officers of an attempted assault on him by another prisoner places himself not only in a disagreeable and uncomfortable position, but actually jeopardizes himself to such an extent that he may be badly hurt or even killed'.[47] To be labelled a 'snitch' or 'snitch jacket' was to be marked for murder.[48]

Moreover, protesting to the authorities rarely had the desired effect. Correctional staff regarded any complaints against their own as reflecting badly on their professionalism. A universe of deprivations could be imposed, including being 'held back from being cut loose' from prison, grumbled one prisoner.[49] Even complaining about fellow inmates put the victim at risk of being thrown into the 'hole', alongside his tormenters. In such a context amnesia about the perpetrators' identity could be the safest option.[50]

More to the point, complaining is a waste of time because prisoners are rarely believed. One prisoner expressed this dilemma in poetry:

> Once an ex-con told me i was pretty,
> he said that if i were in prison i'd be somebody's woman,
> i'd have to obey him and be faithful to him,
> if i got caught screwing with someone else,
> i'd be slit with a knife or a razor blade,
> slit until the blood from my faggot ass
> met the blood from my throat,
> bled until the redness became a poem
> and then a song,
> until a mute nation heard
> but they haven't heard and sometimes
> i realize they can't hear at all.[51]

In the words of Judy Jacobs, who had been sentenced to two years in the York County Jail in rural Pennsylvania for the assault and battery of a man, 'you can't tell the cops, 'cause its just your word against hers . . . and you're both inmates, so your word doesn't mean nothing. You just end up going to Clinton [solitary confinement] or getting set back with the parole board.'[52] She even had difficulty mentioning the sexual abuse to her husband. In her words,

> I'm just so embarrassed and ashamed about everything. My husband comes up here and sees all these studs and he says, 'Judy, have you been messing around?' What can I tell him? I've been slapped so many times up here because I wouldn't participate. If you fight back, you're crunched.[53]

As prisoners like Judy Jackson recognized, both victims and aggressors were convicted criminals: prison officials disbelieved both. Unless a victim could proffer evidence of extreme physical injury, consent was assumed. Merely claiming to have been 'coerced' was an insufficient basis for complaint, even if the aggressor threatened to spread word around the prison that an inmate was a snitch.

In fact, the situation is far worse. Official complicity in prisoner abuse is widespread. At prisons like Holmesburg (Pennsylvania) sexual corruption was a highly regulated trade. In exchange for money or information, guards would allow certain prisoners to choose sexual partners from new or otherwise desirable inmates.[54] As one imprisoned rapist explained, 'the general run of guards are very low class morons and they consider these things all a joke. Cases of [forced] sodomy are things to talk over and laugh about over their glass of moonshine.'[55] The violent films *Up Close and Personal* (1996) and *Animal Factory* (2000) were both based on Holmesburg.

Furthermore, prisoners who failed to prevent sexual attack were invariably cast as complicit in their own victimization. Smaller, weaker or 'effeminate' victims were regarded as inviting rape. Simply 'allowing' the abuse was in itself proof that the victim was not really 'a man', effectively displacing blame for the attack from the aggressor and on to the victim. Thus, in the early 1980s, when one correctional officer was asked whether it was 'a very common occurrence for young straight boys to be turned out, or forced to be punks', he replied: 'That just depends on the institution and it depends on the person.' In other words, it was the responsibility of the victim to fight off aggressors.

Although possessing a weapon within prison was a serious felony and harshly punished (often by transfer of the offender to a maximum-security prison), this officer went on to insist that 'If the guy can fight and is willing to get down, then nine times out of ten he won't get raped. It's all a matter of physical stature and looks. The guy has to be willing to get a pipe or shank and defend himself . . . It's either fight or fuck.'[56]

The process of becoming inured to failure to protect victims was linked to distorted views about homosexuality. In a study conducted in 2000 a quarter of correctional officers believed that if an inmate had previously engaged in consensual sex he laid himself open to being raped on other occasions. Between 12 and 17 per cent of officers believed that some inmates deserved to be raped because they behaved or dressed in a feminine manner. In the face of such attitudes, incarcerated homosexuals found themselves in an impossible situation. Many correctional officers believed that homosexual prisoners 'get what they deserve' if they are raped.[57] An employee at the Dade County Rape Treatment Center (Florida) admitted that if a prisoner cried rape the counsellor should ask ('as diplomatically as possible') whether he was a homosexual.[58] Homosexuals were assumed to be permanently in a state of consent.

Prison officials believed that they have good reasons for turning a blind eye to coerced sex. Some claimed, rather disingenuously, that allowing a degree of coercion was beneficial for the victim, especially if the perpetrator was able to subsequently protect the more vulnerable prisoner from attacks by other (presumably more brutish) aggressors. Other officers were more concerned with saving their own skin. Threatening prisoners with being sent to cells or prison areas notorious for sexual violence was an effective means of controlling offenders. As Haywood Patterson argued in *Scottsboro Boy* (1950), homosexual rape in prison was encouraged by the prison authorities because it

> helped them to control the men. Especially the tough ones they called devils. They believed that if a devil had a gal-boy he would be quiet. He would be a good worker and he wouldn't kill guards and prisoners and try to escape. He would be like a settled married man . . . The guards, they even matched up gal-boys with wolves. They liked watching these goings on.[59]

Howard Levy and David Miller (the two men who were imprisoned for political activism) agreed. Prison administrators allowed the 'homosexual vigilante aura' to continue because it served their interests. 'When the prison officials place a young prisoner, political or not, in the jungle,' they alleged,

> they are saying in effect, 'Go ahead men, see what you can do with him'. It may not serve the administration's purpose to have a young prisoner actually assaulted but the threat of rape does serve its purpose. It induces all inmates, especially the younger, less apathetic ones, to cooperate, to get out of the jungle and stay out. Finally, preoccupation with their sexual frustration acts to divert the prisoners from confronting the enemy – the prison administration. It plays havoc with inmate solidarity, because some inmates are forced to prey upon other inmates.[60]

An investigation carried out by the *Los Angeles Times* in California's Corcoran State Prison went further, alleging that guards 'sometimes sent troublesome prisoners to live with one man, who raped inmates in return for favors from prison staff'.[61] Because convicts feared one another more than the prison staff, their energies were spent fighting among themselves instead of attacking the guards. Aggression was diverted.

Racial Tensions

A strong racial element permeates the arguments about the use of fear of rape to control prisoners. In the words of the mother of a prisoner who had been raped in prison, the prison administrators 'want to keep the black gangs quiet . . . They know they'll be in an uproar if they don't get something to release the sex drive, and usually it's young, non-violent inmates of a different race'.[62]

Such attitudes hark back to notions of the 'nigger rapist' and feed into stereotypes about the violent sexuality of African-American men. Nevertheless, a disproportionate proportion of aggressors are African-Americans and a disproportionate proportion of victims are white. According to a variety of studies undertaken in America during the 1990s, around 62 per cent of the prison population were white, yet they made up 78 per cent of the victims of sexual assault in prisons. In contrast, one-third of the prison population were African-American, but they made up only 10 per cent of victims.[63] Both black and white assailants predominantly targeted white victims (82 per cent of black assailants and 88 per cent of white assailants attacked white prisoners).[64] In some studies researchers were unable to find a single example of a white perpetrator and a black victim.[65] Furthermore, white prisoners were raped more frequently and more severely than black prisoners.

Reasons for this racial differentiation are hotly debated. Prison officials often base their explanations on the superior physical prowess of black and Chicano prisoners. Put bluntly, white prisoners are just not up to the mark. In the words of a correctional officer with nine years' experience in prisons, black prisoners

> do tend to be the aggressors. I think it's because of the physical size and power of the blacks. Most of them work out and are big, and as a group they appear to be more threatening and intimidating, whereas the whites are just a bunch of scuzzy bikers, and the Mexicans tends to stick more to their own race.[66]

Although this argument is unpersuasive, recently white supremacist groups in American prisons have used it to excuse their obsessive attention to muscular development. Bodybuilding, they claim, is a way of warning off black gang violence.

More politically astute explanations for the black-aggressor/white-victim dichotomy draw attention to power struggles both within and outside the prison system. Male African-American prisoners find themselves in a position where they can take revenge upon one symbol of their oppression: they may be unable to hit back at the predominately white guards, but white fellow prisoners prove an adequate substitute.[67] 'To subdue another is an affirmation of strength and power', one commentator observed in 1976: when that 'other' is white and 'when he is humiliated by being reduced to the status of punk, the act may be particularly gratifying'.[68] As one black aggressor succinctly quipped, 'now it's their turn'.[69] 'It's getting even I guess,' another black prisoner explained, adding that 'You guys (whites) [sic] been cutting our balls off ever since we been in this country. Punking whites is just one way of getting even.'[70] Black-on-white rape in prison is not simply a case of having 'hard rocks', observed an astute prisoner; it is

> a way for the black man to get back at the white man. It's one way he can assert his manhood. Anything white, even a defenceless punk, is

> part of what the black man hates. It's a part of what he's had to fight all his life just to survive, just to have a hole to sleep in and some garbage to eat . . . It's a new ego thing. He can show he's a man by making the white guy into a girl.[71]

This is a powerful explanation of black-on-white rape in prison, but it does not explain why even prisons with very little overt racial tension experience similar proportions of black-on-white rapes.[72] Explanations emphasizing racial conflict are therefore supplemented by an analysis of the differing strategies adopted by racial groups to deal with the threat of rape. Within the institutional framework of prisons black and Chicano prisoners are much more liable to take care of their own, protecting their vulnerable youngsters from sexual predators. As a consequence, white inmates find themselves reluctant to sexually abuse black or Chicano inmates out of fear of retaliation from their victims' racial cohort.[73] In contrast, white prisoners are less able to call on a community for protection. As Peter L. Nacci and Thomas R. Kane explained in 'Inmate Sexual Aggression' (1984),

> The prevalence of black assailants is accounted for by the fact that blacks were more likely to be involved in gang rapes. This pattern . . . warrants the inference that black and white aggressors employ different strategies of coercive power; that is, in potentially volatile situations blacks are more likely to coalesce, mounting strength in numbers.[74]

These different strategies help explain the different locations of rape as identified by prisoners. Black prisoners generally claim that assaults take place in cellblocks or other relatively private locations, while white prisoners complain about being most at risk in dining halls, auditoriums and chapels.[75] Assault is closely linked to conflicting perceptions of safety in public and private spaces.

In fact, faced with 'potentially volatile situations', white prisoners not only fail to show racial solidarity with other white prisoners but they deliberately exploit the fears of other vulnerable white prisoners to their own sexual advantage. More experienced white prisoners would attempt to strike a deal with frightened youngsters, offering protection from black aggressors in return for sexual 'favours'. One white aggressor spelt out his technique as involving patiently waiting 'until it looks like they're done with him', then 'I come on like a knight in shining armour, I take him under my wing and promise to keep the others away. After what he's been through it ain't nothing for him to take care of me and maybe a couple of others.'[76]

Paradoxically, prison reform may have contributed to rising levels of interracial sexual abuse. According to sociologist Leo Carroll, who spent fifteen months as a participant observer in a maximum-security prison in an eastern US state in the early 1970s, humanitarian interventions into prison life had contradictory effects. These interventions did improve material conditions and reduce incidents of sadistic punishments. However, an unintended consequence was to diminish the attractions of prison solidarity for *white* inmates. According to Carroll, the white prison population became increasingly stratified according to wealth: those prisoners who could afford various luxuries (such as mattresses, desks and food items) bought them, leaving poorer prisoners with a sense of resentment, if not bitterness. Frequent visits by family members and friends, combined with access to the media (prisoners with money could have televisions in their cells), made white inmates more receptive to influences outside the prison walls. 'Old cons' lost some of their influence. In effect, white prisoners lost any need for community. They became depoliticized.

Although prison reform dramatically changed prison life for black prisoners too, the negative impact of the changes was mitigated by the development of a sense of community through soul music and Black Power. Carroll argues that soul, by celebrating Black American culture, extolled 'perseverance in the face of oppression and acceptance of a life over which one has little control', while Black Power encouraged prisoners to 'mobilize black resources in the pursuit of control over their own social, economic, and political institutions'. Together, they proved a potent unifying force. Practically all black prisoners joined the Afro-American Society, for instance. By recognizing both their history as victims of racism and by positioning themselves as capable of transcending this role within the context of a worldwide revolutionary movement, black prisoners conceived of themselves as *political* prisoners. These ties of solidarity served to reduce intra-racial sexual violence.[77]

Such a politics of solidarity was not only barred to white prisoners; additionally, it was employed by African-American prisoners to abuse whites. Political activists Levy and Miller, for instance, warned about 'the manner by which white political prisoners related to the black-liberation struggle', warning other left-leaning inmates against engaging in revolutionary struggle within prison walls. In their words,

> White political prisoners tend to be sympathetic to that struggle and on occasion, a black aggressive homosexual can use the white political prisoner's sympathy as an inroad to a homosexual relationship. This is especially likely to occur when naïveté outstrips clear thinking . . . It is dangerous . . . If a young male prisoner is seen fraternizing with black inmates, and especially if he is seen talking with well-known black homosexuals, the majority of white inmates is preconditioned to believe the worst. As a matter of fact, some black inmates will themselves interpret what may essentially be an inexperienced liberal attitude as being an overture for protection. If one flaunts his pretentious liberal attitudes, he will only get himself in trouble; in fact, black inmates couldn't care less about eating with him.

According to them, the 'pretentious liberal' would most likely be approached by a 'brother' with the words, 'I hear you're a nigger lover, prove it.'[78]

All these racial arguments face a serious difficulty. The 'frustration hypothesis' – the claim that black prisoners rape their white counterparts because of the frustrations of oppression both within and without the penal complex – fails to differentiate between black prisoners. Perpetrators of sexual violence and their victims are all maligned: all black men from the ghetto are rapists.

Masculinity

The high proportion of inter-racial rape is only one area where sexual abuse in prison diverges from that in the outside world. Rape means something different to prison perpetrators than it does to their free brothers. As the Chief Assistant District Attorney of Philadelphia observed in 1968, sexual aggressors in prison tended to be

> members of a subculture that has found most nonsexual avenues of asserting their masculinity closed to them. To them, job success, raising a family, and achieving the respect of other men socially have been largely beyond reach. Only sexual and physical prowess stands between them and a feeling of emasculation.

As a consequence, imprisonment 'knock[ed] from under them whatever props to their masculinity they may have had'. They responded by exaggeratedly asserting their sexual potency.[79] The prison context places such a premium on aggression that even feigning courtesy or affection is rare, if not downright dangerous. Expressions of masculinity became a zero-sum game: it was a question of 'take or be taken'. Admittedly, the aggression of male society from which many prisoners emerged had been imported from the 'free world' to the prison. However, in prisoner's adaptation to the new circumstances of incarceration, public displays of aggression took on a terrifyingly new intensity.[80]

Furthermore, aggressive behaviour brings significant rewards within prison. While prisoners generally despise men convicted of rape in civilian society, the man who rapes fellow inmates places himself at the pinnacle of prison society. 'If you raped someone it was like a feather in your cap,' boasted one prisoner.[81] The rapist of prisoners commands respect, not disdain.

Indeed, the prison rapist is the epitome of manliness. While male *victims* of sexual abuse find themselves diminished as men, the man 'strong enough' to rape other men is the embodiment of a superior heterosexuality. This was why raping an unwilling young man was much more gratifying than having sex with a willing 'homosexual sissy'.[82] In the words of a commentator in 1976, aggressors were 'concerned not with the definition of the act, but only with the labelling of the actors, including themselves'. Their victims were 'queer' or 'girls'. As one violent prison rapist explained when questioned about his actions, 'He didn't even try to fight with me. The first time that I told him to stop hollering, he just gave in. Like a girl – first she's got to say no, and then she says yes, or she just lets you without saying anything. So I figure he must have really liked it.'[83]

In contrast with the feminized victim, rapists portrayed themselves as acting like real men, acting on irrepressible sexual urges as a 'temporary expedient'. They would leave prison with 'their heterosexuality untouched, their masculinity undiminished'.[84] Aggressors believed that it was important to 'clear out your tubes every once in a while'[85]: once these men were out of prison, women once again were the 'appropriate' target for their sexual needs. As one aggressor responded incredulously when asked about his sexuality outside of prison, 'Why would I want a fairy, when I can get a broad?'[86]

Whether these aggressors are attacking women in the 'free world' or men behind bars, the suffering experienced by victims is acute.*

*Chapter 8, 'Female Perpetrators; Male Victims', discusses the rape of non-incarcerated men. Some of the examples of suffering mentioned here involve these men.

'Almost fifteen years after my brutalization, I am still traumatized emotionally, physically and even socially,' confessed Tom Cahill, who had been repeatedly gang-raped while serving time for civil disobedience during the Vietnam War. He described how 'emotionally, the clock stopped for me' on 14 October 1968, when he was raped in Bexar County Jail (Texas). In his words,

> Few days have gone by since that time that I haven't experienced at least a few moments of shame and self-disgust and the wish for death . . . Despite much that has been published about rape in recent years because this violent crime is epidemic, many of us rape victims still feel it is expected of us to resist to the death or kill ourselves afterwards. At the very least, many of us feel, we are an embarrassment to society.

Cahill went on to speak of the absolute sense of loneliness and isolation that he felt afterwards. He sought refuge in drugs. His marriage collapsed. In addition to 'sexual dysfunction', he experienced an 'inability to express my emotions clearly, dependency, frequent situational depression, negativity, inappropriate guilt, a clinging to the past, fear of intimacy, feeling of powerlessness, and misdirected anger'. Recovery took a painfully long time.[87]

Like Cahill, many male victims felt diminished as men. 'We're going to take your manhood', 'You'll have to give up some face' and 'We're gonna make a girl of you', rapists incessantly reminded their victims.[88] Within closed institutions such as prisons or military barracks, the raped inmate became permanently marked as a victim, regularly targeted by other predators. In the words of one imprisoned rapist in the 1960s, 'When a boy was once perverted he was everybody's punk . . . A punk will be a punk as long as anyone knows that he had once capitulated.'[89] Inevitably, such victims were permanently labelled homosexual, by guards as well as other prisoners.[90] They were 'automatically considered inferior' and would be 'held in the same degraded and subservient position as are women outside of prison', observed two former prisoners.[91]

Long-term consequences of rape included loss of sexual desire and depression.[92] Many ended up trying to 'prove' their masculinity through violent 'acting-out', sexual promiscuity and general aggression.[93] Others sought relief in suicide.[94] A prisoner serving time for an assault while drunk witnessed three rapes while incarcerated. 'You know, it's unbelievable,' he stammered, adding, 'You can hear the guy hollering and no one doing nothing about it. And you know it could have been you.' One of the victims was transferred to the cell next to him. 'I could actually hear the guy crying,' he recalled. That victim hanged himself while another 'slashed his wrists . . . he couldn't let his girlfriend know that'.[95] Even the families of victims might want the whole incident 'hushed' in an attempt to 'avoid the shame and dishonor they believed would follow such a complaint'.[96]

Prevention

From the late-1960s the extent of sexual violence in prisons was increasingly seen as scandalous. Soaring incarceration levels in the United States put a growing number of young men at risk. Voters and lobbying groups started placing pressure on politicians to guarantee their safety. New buzzwords such as 'human rights' could even be heard within prison walls. Prisoners became less deferential and more willing to speak out about their abuses. Although prison administrators and guards continued to manipulate fears of rape as a mechanism of social control, excessive displays of violence within the confines of prisons turned out to be just too disruptive. Sexual threats frequently served as motives for stabbings, burnings and even murder, as Haywood Patterson discovered to his great distress (he was nearly killed in prison).

But what could prisoners do to combat rape? Self-help was their first recourse. Cultivating aggressive mannerisms was obviously a priority for new convicts.[97] In *Going to Jail* (1970) Levy and Miller provided first-time prisoners with practical advice on how they should handle themselves. In an environment characterized by 'exaggerated masculinity', they warned, anything slightly effeminate 'stands out immediately'. Long hair, for instance, was particularly unwise. Face to face with an aggressor, a prisoner should respond 'forcefully and decisively'. In their words,

> Curt, even hostile, remarks are in order. 'No, man. You must be crazy'. 'Get out of my face'. 'You can try whatever you want if you want your head busted'. If possible, one may be able to turn the situation around by making a joke; a joke helps the other guy save face. That is, it doesn't put him in the position, necessarily, of having to respond to a counter-threat or else back down. At the same time, a good joke gives the impression that one is not as naïve as he looks and that he

> would fight. One might smile and say, 'Sure, man, you can have all the ass you want after I stick my dick in your cakes. Tit for tat, right?'[98]

At worst, it was advisable to 'fight it out'.[99] Prisoners had to show that they were 'willing to get a pipe or shank and defend himself'.[100] A performance of hyper-masculinity was necessary in order to survive incarceration unmolested.

But should men be expected to fight in defence of their sexual integrity because they were convicted of a crime? Various institutional mechanisms exist for dealing with the risk of rape within prisons. Strange as it may sound, certain jurisdictions from 1969 accepted a 'specific threat of death, forcible sexual assault or substantial bodily injury in the immediate future' as a legitimate defence for escaping prison. Conditions were set high. Not only did the escapee have to prove that the threat was imminent, but he or she should also have a clean record (no history of 'frivolous complaints', for instance) and be able to prove that other avenues of complaint were closed. Furthermore, on escaping, the prisoner had to report immediately to the prison authorities. Prisoners who took this route to escape rape met with mixed responses in the courts.[101]

More typically, the prison system adapted its modes of social control in order to prevent rape. These institutional responses were in line with the increasingly more punitive response to crime and criminals. Although ostensibly concerned with restraining hyper-aggressive sexual predators, they primarily targeted vulnerable prisoners, ensuring that levels of fear remained high. Prisoners had to remain vigilant at all times. Responsibility for sexual violation was individualized; wider schemes, such as those of prisoners' rights, were sidelined.

The main ways in which prison authorities attempted to reduce the risk of rape were protective custody, the classification and careful placement of prisoners within cells, conjugal visits and increased surveillance. In their attempts to separate victims from perpetrators, protective segregation came into effect only once an attack had taken place. In reality, the victim found himself further victimized since his freedom of movement was severely curtailed, canteen and recreational privileges were lost, and his rights to attend school, job training and mental health programmes were withdrawn.[102]

Attempting to prevent attack might be seen as a more effective approach. Many prisons established schemes under which prisoners were screened and classified as being at risk of being abused or becoming an abuser. Consenting homosexuals and sex offenders were isolated in separate cellblocks, for instance, or aggressive offenders separated from white-collar criminals. The success of screening was limited. Sorting procedures were extremely crude, often doing little more than separating men by age, culture, body build and lifestyle. Homosexuals were often removed from the general prison population. This not only stigmatized gay men, but also wrongly implied that homosexuals were aggressors and that sex *within* the segregated homosexual group could automatically be considered consensual. Furthermore, many screening programmes targeted African-Americans as aggressors, thus exacerbating racial segregation (and racial tensions) within prisons.

More to the point, screening inmates was based on the mistaken belief that prison rapes are essentially about meeting sexual needs. This view underpinned another popular response to prison rape: the instigation of conjugal visits or 'home furlough' programmes. The Mississippi State Penitentiary in Sunflower County is the world's largest penal farm system. It was also one of the first prisons to introduce conjugal visits. Initially the scheme faced spirited opposition. Opponents claimed that allowing such visits would be 'wholly unrealistic in American culture' and placed undue emphasis upon the 'physical satisfactions of sex'. Rather than having a rehabilitative effect, the visits would actually heighten tension within prison, critics objected. According to this view, the most disruptive prisoners tended to be unmarried, violent and included a high proportion of 'sex deviants'. Only a few prisoners could produce a marriage certificate or prove that they were in a long-term common-law relationship. Many aggressive prisoners were too young to have established partners; others were too violent to be safely allowed out of the prison in home furlough programmes. As a consequence, this approach targeted precisely those men least likely to become 'wolves' in the first place.

Critics of conjugal visits were only half right. Staff at the Mississippi State Penitentiary praised the scheme for reducing homosexuality and preserving marriages, but its effectiveness was probably due more to the way it was used as a mechanism for social control. In other words, prisoners were better behaved, not because the visits caused some of those dangerous seminal fluids to seep away but because prisoners recognized that any infraction of the rules would result in the abolition of privileges.[103] In fact, from the 1960s to the 1980s, conjugal visits were much more concerned with eliminating what was euphemistically called 'situational homosexuality' rather than tackling the more urgent issue of institutionalized sexual brutality.

Finally, an assortment of responses to rape targeted the prison environment. The most important was the introduction of more effective systems of surveillance. Institutional blind spots, such as showers, storage areas, stairways, holding tanks and transportation vans were identified as risky places that required better policing. A debate also developed about the relative merits of single cells. This debate has not been resolved, with some officials arguing that prison overcrowding facilitates rape, and others countering that bedding a number of prisoners in each cell inhibits sexual violence because of the lack of privacy. Bizarrely, some experts exhort prison administrators to employ more female guards, so that male prisoners would be exposed to female presence.[104] Not only do such proposals place female employees at risk of rape, they also ignore the fact that female guards are known to sexually assault male prisoners. The assumption that women are a civilizing presence has little merit.

Such piecemeal responses to prison rape finally exasperated the judiciary. In the 1970s some judges decided that sexual assault was 'a greater punishment for the crime than this court could legally or morally impose', and dismissed indictments as a result.[105] Sexual assault should not be part of the punishment imposed by sentencing, they insisted: prison administrators were not free to 'let the state of nature take its course'.[106]

Such judicial reactions were in line with protests by prisoners themselves. Prisoners began bringing tort suits against correctional officers, as well as state and federal governments, for failing to prevent their violation. In 1979, for instance, Thomas Stokes was awarded $380,000 in compensation and punitive damages after bringing a case against the Sheriff and his deputy in Louisiana. Stokes had been raped in jail while awaiting court. The court decided that the Sheriff and his deputy had a 'constitutionally rooted obligation not to detain [Stokes] in a manner which made it likely he would be beaten and sexually assaulted'.[107]

Prisoners also started raising constitutional claims based on the violation of their civil rights. The Fourth Amendment, with its guarantees of privacy and personal integrity, was used in female prisons to prohibit male guards from carrying out strip searches and intrusive surveillance of prisoners.[108] The Due Process clause of the Fifth or Fourteenth Amendments was also applied.

Even more significantly, since the 1970s prisoners have brought claims based on the Eighth Amendment's right to be free from cruel and unusual punishment. The crucial decision involved Dee Farmer, a twenty-one-year-old man-to-woman transsexual who had been incarcerated in the high-security Terre Haute prison (Indianapolis) for credit-card fraud. Farmer's feminine appearance had been bolstered by breast implants and hormone oestrogen treatments. Nevertheless, she was sent to an all-male prison. On 1 April 1989 a prisoner seriously assaulted and raped her at knifepoint. Farmer immediately filed a complaint against officials for failing to protect her when they knew that her 'feminine appearance' put her at serious risk of sexual assault.

The case reached the Supreme Court. In Farmer v. Brennan (1994) the Supreme Court established the doctrine of 'deliberate indifference' by prison officials as the legal standard for Eighth Amendment claims.[109] It was an important ruling: inmates no longer had to prove that officers failed to act 'believing that harm actually would befall an inmate', but only that they failed to act 'despite his knowledge of a substantial risk of serious harm'.[110] Previously it had been relatively easy to demonstrate that a prisoner was at serious risk of harm, but not that the prison officials acted with 'deliberate indifference' in allowing this risk. After the Farmer decision awards rose dramatically. For instance, in Butler v. Bowd in 1992, four inmates who had been repeatedly raped were awarded damages of only one dollar; four years later, in Mathie v. Fries, the prisoner was awarded $250,000 in compensatory damages and $500,000 in punitive damages.[111] The financial costs of sexual brutality for prison administrators provided significant incentives for improving staffing levels and explicitly tackling sexual brutality.

Notwithstanding the difficulties of using the Eighth Amendment successfully (it can be invoked only after conviction and prisoners do not possess a constitutional right to a free attorney), prisoners and their families proved tenacious in establishing anti-rape lobbying groups. These ranged from small, local organizations such as the Illinois-based Mothers Against Prison Rape to the nationwide Prisoners Against Rape, which was founded by William Fuller and Larry Cannon in Lorton Prison in Virginia in the early 1970s, and Stop Prisoner Rape, set up in 1980 by a former prisoner, Stephen Donaldson.[112] The Safer Society Press, set up in 1964, also provides advice to prison administrators. More importantly, it distributes tapes aimed at educating prisoners about rape, since it believes that it was 'the prisoners who tolerate sexual assaults, fail to protect their peers, and fail to protect themselves'. Rape would only be eradicated by educating and empowering prisoners.

Many of these anti-rape prison groups proved controversial. Prisoners Against Rape, for instance, was strongly opposed to the therapeutic movement. One of its press statements, they declared that

> We are NOT a group therapy group; we are NOT a therapy session. WE struggled for 15 (fifthteen) months from 9 september 1973 until 27 december, 1974 (WITH THE HELP OF OUR COMMUNITY SUPPORTERS TO BE RECOGNIZED by the d. c. department of corrections as a SELF HELP GROUP . . . and certainly NOT as a therapy session. The psychological services center conducts therapy sessions . . . Our discussions concern the POLITICAL education and re-education of the victim, the rapist and this rape culture of male domination, male role, and male BULLSHIT ideas and dogmas.[113]

The Safer Society Press was braver in bucking institutional mores when it advised inmates to attempt to persuade perpetrators to engage in oral rather than anal sex (in order to reduce the likelihood of AIDS) and to use makeshift condoms out of gloves or plastic bags.[114] Men Against Sexism (MAS), established in Walla Walla Prison (Washington State) in the late 1970s, followed an even more revolutionary agenda that mixed feminism with gay rights. Although it fought for the provision of 'safe cells' for prisoners who were at risk of being abused, the project was tarnished when its members attempted an armed outbreak from the prison.

Finally, in recent years public pressure to improve safety within prisons has had some impact on Congress. On 3 September 2004 President Bush signed the Prison Rape Elimination Act. This Act tackled the issue of prison rape directly by authorizing a research programme to study the extent and effects of prison rape, establishing a panel to review the data and introducing procedures by which prisoners could complain and have these complaints heard. Financial help was given to state and local governments, as well as to prisons, to invest in programmes to eliminate prison rape and effectively prosecute abuses that came to light. A National Prison Rape Reduction Commission was created to make proposals for detecting, preventing, reducing and prosecuting prison rape. As Eli Lehrer, one of its chief proponents, explained, the Act was 'a perfect complement to [President Bush's] compassionate conservative agenda'.[115] The Act was primarily a conservative and evangelical Act, rejecting more radical proposals such as expanding prisoners' rights.

The extent of male-on-male rape in American prisons supports at least one central feminist tenet: the aggressiveness of masculinity. After all, the twinning of sex and aggression is not unique to prison life; it is forged outside prison walls. This male belligerence is exacerbated within closed and brutalizing institutions such as prisons. As one researcher argues, male-on-male rape in prisons is 'the expression of inter-male alienation at its nadir, its governing principle and a master allegory for inter-male relations in general'. The prison ambience merely exposes 'certain realities about male intersubjectivity that are repressed in the free world'.[116] William Fuller, one of the founders of Prisoners Against Rape, agrees, quipping that rape is 'as American as applepie. Our whole culture set-up is rape.' Men 'are programmed from the cradle to rape'.[117] It is a conclusion I shall challenge in the concluding chapter.

Until recently male-on-male rape has been sidelined, as has rape in male boarding schools.[118] The victims of assaults I discuss in this chapter are themselves convicted of crime. Before their incarceration many had committed violent offences, including rape and sexual assault of women and children. These male rape victims threaten to undermine certain feminist arguments according to which rape is a crime against a uniquely victimized class, women. One response is to suggest that men raped in prison actually become 'social females'.* From the perpetrator's point of view there is a partial truth to this observation. For aggressors rape is consistent with 'straight' behaviour. The male rapist of other men is not defined by his sexual acts. Because he forces a man to engage in sex, he is not gay. However, the humiliated victims are humiliated as men, not women. Indeed, it is precisely the ability to humiliate a fellow man that bestows status on the rapist. In the crucible of violence, everyone is at risk. Men do not receive special protection.

*There is further discussion of this issue in Chapter 2, 'Rape Myths'.

CHAPTER THIRTEEN

The Military

In modern conflicts rape reminds us that waging war is more than simply engaging in mechanical slaughter. The penis actually does become a weapon. After the occupation of Japan at the end of the war, for instance, in just ten days between 30 August and 10 September 1945, 1336 rapes were committed by Allied soldiers in the Kanagawa prefecture alone.[1] According to a former Army Reserve sergeant who had access to the files of the British Commonwealth Occupation Force (BCOF), the files read as a tale of 'raping, looting, and pillaging'. 'As far as acts of sexual depravity go,' he concluded,

> it's all there in the BCOF files. They were not all attesting to rape, but many, many, many were rape . . . We're talking about stories of you and I going down-town tonight. Going into a brothel, and perhaps being charged five cents too much for a glass of beer. So we go back to the camp, grab 30 of our mates and go wreck the brothel, burn it, [bash] the staff and rape the ones that we don't like. And then get a slap over the wrists for it.[2]

In particular there was a wave of brutal rapes in the city of Hiroshima, occupied at that time by the BCOF, consisting of New Zealand, Australian and Indian soldiers under British command. In the words of a Japanese prostitute talking about soldiers who had landed at Kure, the port of Hiroshima, in November 1945:

> Most of the people in Kure stayed inside their houses, and pretended

> they knew nothing about the rape by occupation forces. The Australian soldiers were the worst. They dragged young women into their jeeps, took them to the mountain, and then raped them. I heard them screaming for help nearby every night.[3]

For such actions the Australian troops earned the disreputable name 'Yabanjin' or 'barbarians'.

Allan S. Clifton, interpreter and member of the intelligence force serving in Japan, witnessed the reaction of Japanese medical personnel after a Japanese nurse had been raped by twenty Australian soldiers. 'So, we are barbarians, and you are civilized and this is your way of life that you fought against us to preserve,' he inferred from their looks of reproach. After all, throughout the Far East, military tribunals were court-martialling Japanese servicemen for similar crimes. The raped nurse was 'not a soldier', Clifton recalled, adding that she 'had no part in the war. Besides the war is over.' He admitted that, at first, he felt able to respond to Japanese critics. 'This is not the act of a typical Australian,' he imagined telling them. 'Brutes' could be 'found among all peoples, in all crimes. It is a question of proportions. There were so many more of them in your army.' But, as the rapes mounted up, Clifton became less convinced by his own rationalization.[4]

The mass rapes of these Japanese women only came to the attention of the authorities when they were considered to threaten the image of 'democracy' that the occupation forces were attempting to encourage. Their response, however, was to simply exchange one form of sexual exploitation for another. In the words of the same Japanese prostitute:

> A policeman from Hiroshima police station came to me, and asked me to work as a prostitute for the Australians – he wanted me and other prostitutes to act as a sort of 'fire-breaker', so that young women wouldn't get raped. We agreed to do this, and contributed greatly.[5]

As a result of these acts, the euphemistically named 'Recreation and Amusement Association' was set up to cater for the sexual needs of the occupying forces. Governors and police chiefs in all prefectorates were instructed to procure women for a nationwide system of brothels.

Back in Australia the commission of sexual atrocities was being denied as late as the 1990s. When a report on the rapes of 1945 was published in *The Age* in September 1993, uproar followed. The national president of the British Commonwealth Occupation Forces Council angrily insisted that Australian troops 'did not need to rape in Japan because they could have had a Japanese prostitute "for a pack of cigarettes".' The Victorian president of the Returned Services League was equally stunned by what he regarded as an attack on the nation's finest manhood. He claimed that Australian soldiers had behaved in 'a very decent manner'. To suggest otherwise was 'an outrage and a damned lie', he scolded. The only explanation, he believed, was that the accounts of rape were part of a conspiracy, seeking to 'square off, to make it look even, for the abominable atrocities committed by the Japanese'.[6] Both men interpreted the accounts of mass rape in Japan as an attack on Australian 'mateship': but what did it say about Australian national identity, if mateship meant that soldiers turned a blind eye to atrocities committed by their 'mates'? The 'Aussie' male's protective stance towards weaker women was under attack. The rapes exposed something truly despotic in the Australian myth.

Prevalence

Wartime rape is often portrayed as inevitable. Some anthropologists have even suggested that the frequency of rape in a particular society can be predicted by looking at that society's propensity to engage in battle. As one researcher concluded, a 'war-like culture alone' could predict whether men in that society were prone to rape women.[7]

Others went further. War *is* rape, insisted some feminists. Mary Daly, author of *Gyn/Ecology: The Metaethics of Radical Feminism* (1978), argued that the 'War State's essential identity' was a 'State of Rapism'. Military invasions were nothing more than 'elaborations upon the theme of rape/gynocide'. Indeed, according to Daly, rape was the dirty bounty shared by men on every side of the conflict: it was 'the secret bond that binds the warriors together, energizing them'.[8] Ignoring the fundamental problem of why men might choose to risk life and limb in combat if their real objective was unrestrained rape, the pervasiveness and carnivalesque nature of rape in wartime often gives the impression that military practices are inextricably entwined with sexual violence.

Historically, a direct causal relationship between military combat and sexual violence seems plausible. From the American Civil War of the 1860s onwards, the closer a conflict came to resemble 'total war' – that is, a conflict fought by citizen soldiers with no clear distinction between home front and combat zone – the greater was the likelihood of brutality, including the rape of enemy women. The bitterest conflicts of the twentieth century have provided clear examples of this propensity. John Horne and Alan Kramer's *German Atrocities, 1914. A History of Denial* (2001), for instance, meticulously documented the rape by German soldiers of women in Belgium during the First World War.[9] The mass rape of Chinese woman by invading Japanese troops in Nanking (1937) and of German women by Soviet soldiers (1945) generated additional insights into this correlation, as do the recent explosions of sexual violation during the conflicts in Bosnia and Herzegovina, Peru, Rwanda, Bangladesh, Cambodia, Cyprus, Haiti, Liberia, Somalia and Uganda, to name just a few.

There has been a tendency, however, to ignore or downplay the fact that British, American and Australian troops have also periodically engaged in orgies of sexual violence. In particular it has been difficult for many commentators to admit to rapes carried out by 'our side' during the two world wars.[10] Certain forms of combat during those conflicts did not facilitate the rape of enemy women: men confined to naval ships or trenches, for instance, lacked access to the requisite female victims. When Allied forces were engaged in heavy fighting – as in the period between the D-Day landings at Normandy in June to late-July 1944 – rape rates were also low. Such a situation could change extremely rapidly, however. This was the case in France between August and September 1944 and in Germany during March and April 1945, when fighting was much lighter and extensive contact was established between the troops and the newly liberated towns.[11] After the Allied forces landed in Normandy, for instance, French women found that the risk of rape remained high: it was simply the ethnic origin of the rapists that changed. According to the official history of the Office of the Judge Advocate General for the European Theatre of Operations:

> The French people welcomed their liberators, often giving them drink to show their appreciation . . . The people were grateful, but they had little or no protection. Many soldiers had the notion that French women were both attractive and free with their love. At any rate, whatever the operative factors, the number of violent sex crimes enormously increased with the arrival of our troops in France.

Because the 'invading soldiers came fully armed', the 'use of firearms was common in perpetrating the offense', the official history noted.[12] As a consequence, a minister in General de Gaulle's military cabinet urged that strong representations be made to General Eisenhower. 'If the Americans cannot bring American women for the needs of their men,' the minister pleaded, 'at least let them respect French women.'[13]

Sexual violence spread westward with the troops. In April 1945 the Judge Advocate in Europe revealed that he had to deal with around 500 rape cases involving American soldiers each week.[14] In the words of an American intelligence officer who witnessed the occupation of the German city of Krefeld, the 'behaviour of our troops, I regret to say, was nothing to brag about'. Although he placed some of the blame on the fact that soldiers proved particularly adept in finding (and consuming) 'cases of cognac and barrels of wine', he did admit that the 'tendency among the naïve or the malicious to think that only Russians loot and rape' had been severely dented. 'After battle, soldiers of every country are pretty much the same,' this intelligence officer was forced to conclude. The 'warriors of Democracy were no more virtuous than the troops of Communism were reported to be', he lamented.[15] There were 971 court-martial convictions for rape in the American forces between January 1942 and June 1947, at the conclusion of which seventy soldiers were executed.[16] The crisis could not be blamed on indiscipline within the military more generally. As one researcher concluded after analysing the American statistics during the Second World War, '[m]ilitary rape rates in the combat theatre . . . climbed to several times civilian rates, while military rates of other violent crimes were roughly equivalent to civilian rates'.[17] In other words, sexual violence was the *preferred* form of aggression.

Women are not the only sexual victims of war. The current wars in Afghanistan and Iraq have cut through the rhetoric focusing exclusively on female vulnerability. Most notoriously, in prisons like Abu Ghraib male as well as female prisoners were attacked by both male and female military personnel. Again this is not new to wars of the twenty-first century. It is impossible to know how many men were sexually abused by British, American and Australian troops in past conflicts. The evidence is piecemeal and anecdotal. We do, however, have accounts of the mutilation of male sexual organs after death. During the Second World War, for instance, Eugene B. (Sledgehammer) Sledge of the First Marine Division recalled being on patrol on Okinawa. 'I saw Mac take great pains to position himself and his carbine near a Japanese corpse,' he began:

> After getting just the right angle, Mac took careful aim and squeezed off a couple of rounds. The dead Japanese lay on his back with his trousers pulled down to his knees. Mac was trying very carefully to blast the head off the corpse's penis. He succeeded. As he exulted over his aim, I turned away in disgust. Mac was a decent, clean-cut man.[18]

In Vietnam, too, the male body and genitals were signalled out for particular abuse. Specialist 5, Harold 'Light Bulb' Bryant, a combat engineer with the 1st Cavalry Division, recalled an occasion after a firefight when 'this guy – one of the white guys – cut off the VC's dick and stuck it in his mouth as a reminder that the 1st Cavs had been through there. And he left the ace of spaces on the body.'[19]

More frequently male prisoners of war found themselves vulnerable to rape and other forms of sexual abuse during questioning and as part of interrogation techniques. An unnamed man from the 1st Air Cavalry Division in Vietnam admitted 'brutality done to people's testicles and stuff like that'. He explained that 'If you are looking for information, you seek out the most sensitive areas of their body. If you are out in the field, you basically want to degrade them more. And attacking their sexual organs would be more degrading than their arms or legs.'[20] Or, as an American POW interrogator admitted after describing using a twelve-volt jeep battery to torture the genitals of prisoners (who would 'jump and scream'), his job 'don't win hearts and minds'.[21]

Sexual torture was more common in some units than others. The culture of guerrilla and counter-revolutionary groups explicitly led them to present themselves as containing the toughest, the most lawless and the most aggressively masculine combatants. Men in such bodies frequently worked alone or in small cohesive groups relatively independently of main command structures. Inter-group pride and intense dependency meant that any atrocities that did occur were less liable to be reported. Raping or killing civilians sent out a warning to the guerrillas (and people suspected of helping them) that these units were indomitable. It was 'really a very good tactic if you stop to think about it', retorted one officer in 1969 when asked his opinion about the My Lai atrocity. 'If you scare people enough they will keep away from you,' he continued, quickly adding, 'Aw, I'm not saying that I approve of the tactic . . . I think it's an *effective* tactic.'[22]

Furthermore, rape and sexual abuse did not only take place in or near the war zones. Once sexual abuse against the enemy had been normalized, it soon spread to one's own side. Civilians around military bases or in areas where servicemen spent their free time were at risk. In the words of an official Second World War report into sexual violence in Queensland (Australia), the 'large floating population of [American] servicemen removed from the inhibitory effect of their own home environment and living under conditions wherein their sexual impulses are likely to be abnormally stimulated' was 'perhaps wholly' responsible for a surge in sexual assaults.[23] In Britain, too, during both world wars there was immense concern that wartime society was experiencing an epidemic of sexual crimes, including rape.[24] Although some historians have tended to ignore the coercive aspects of sex on the home front (with one historian of Britain during the Second World War writing that sex was 'one of the few freely available wartime pleasures'),[25] there was an increase in sexual attacks carried out by members of the armed forces as well as by civilian men.[26] Some evacuated children ended up being abused by the strangers with whom they lodged.[27] Whatever the level of the problem, the arrival of American soldiers on British soil augmented fear of rape with anxieties about racial miscegenation.[28]

Female members of the armed forces were also at risk from their male comrades.[29][See cartoon, below.] In one study of 558 American women who had served in Vietnam and subsequently elsewhere, half had experienced sexual violence during their military service. Thirty per cent of them said they had been raped. The researchers were struck by the fact that of the servicewomen who had served *before* the Vietnam War, only 3 per cent reported sexual violence, suggesting that there had

'Air Force Academy Rapes', by Mike Keefe, 2003

been a dramatic increase in sexual violence against American servicewomen at the time of the war in Vietnam.[30] This is not an anomaly of the past. The 1991 Tailhook scandal and revelations in 1993 of systematic sexual harassment of cadets at the US Air Force Academy were never properly dealt with. In 2003 the US Air Force admitted that nearly 70 per cent of female cadets reported that they had been sexually harassed and nearly 20 per cent sexually assaulted. Furthermore, the Academy punished women who had the guts to report their rapes.[31]

Finally, servicemen also raped fellow servicemen. During the Vietnam War, Steve Spund had gone 'absent without leave' from the Marines. He had returned home but his father had turned him into the military police. Spund described what happened next:

> They took me to the Naval Brig and I started to get worked over by the Marine guards. You'd be stripped of all your clothing, they take your unmentionables and put them through the bars and hit them or stretch them or choke you until you're white, or out of air. They usually tried to do things that would not leave bruises or blood.[32]

Spund's treatment was partly in retaliation for having disgraced the corps. More commonly, sexual abuse between members of the armed forces was dubbed 'hazing' and was understood in terms of male bonding. In the early 1980s P. F. Goyer and H. C. Eddleman, for instance, documented male sexual assault in the Navy and Marine Corps, uncovering widespread abuses including 'blanket parties' (a naked recruit would be wrapped in a blanket and sexually assaulted by the others) and 'greasings' (heavy machinery oil would be rubbed over the body of a recruit and a flexible tube inserted in his anus).[33] Servicemen were extremely reluctant to report such instances. The perils of 'ratting' on one's comrades included further assault, ostracism or discharge from the service.

Complicity

What conditions helped to increase incidents of rape? A main contributory factor was the widespread acceptance of sexual abuse both among members of the military and in the broader civilian communities. Servicemen and military authorities frequently responded to evidence of rape and sexual assaults with a tolerant shrug. Officers tended to simply accept that atrocities, including sexual atrocities, would take place. Referring to atrocities generally, one colonel admitted to two chaplains during the First World War that he had 'seen my own men commit atrocities, and should expect to see it again. You can't stimulate and let loose the animal in man and then expect to be able to cage it up again at a moment's notice.'[34] These chaplains described a discussion they had with an eighteen-year-old private who had found killing a German soldier so thrilling that he had been unable to stop firing rounds into his corpse ('I was so excited I couldn't stop,' he told them). Considering this comment, the chaplains concluded that the young soldier had 'lost control of himself': the 'sport' of 'shedding human blood' had incited 'bloodlust'. 'In a trifling way', they concluded, what the young soldier had experienced was 'the force in human nature which may make a soldier of any nationality bayonet an old man or rape a woman'.[35]

Such glosses on sexual aggression were repeated during the Second World War. As one British doctor admitted, he 'could understand a man overmastered by desire raping a woman' but he 'could not understand any man being so low and vicious as deliberately to make use of any anti-conceptional method'.[36] In wartime rape was 'to be expected'. General George S. Patton predicted during the Second World War that 'there would unquestionably be some raping', but he went on to argue that it should be harshly punished.[37] This language was also used by J. Glenn Gray in *The Warriors* (1959), in which he argued that there was 'enough of the rapist in every man to give him insight into the grossest manifestations of sexual passion. Hence it is presumptuous of any of us to scorn the practitioners of this lowest kind of passion as beings with whom we have no kinship.' He believed that 'this kind of love' was 'intimately associated with the impersonal violence of war'. Ares (the God of War) and Aphrodite (the God of Sex) 'attract one another as true mates', he argued. Consequently, '[c]opulation under such circumstances is an act of aggression; the girl is the victim and her conquest the victor's triumph. Preliminary resistance on her part always increases his satisfaction, since victory is more intoxicating the harder the winning may be.'[38] Indeed, according to an article in the *American Journal of Nursing* (1953), rape was an expression of 'pent-up aggressive feelings' and 'it may be more satisfactory . . . to have soldiers express their resentment and hostility by forcible rape against a conquered people than to turn the same feelings toward their officers'.[39]

Another way of explaining this callousness was to attribute it to poor leadership. As Michael McCusker of the 1st Marine Division in Vietnam reported after describing a horrific gang rape:

> The man who led the platoon, or the squad, was actually a private. The squad leader was a sergeant but he was a useless person and he let the private take over his squad. Later he said he took no part in the raid. It was against his morals. So instead of telling his squad not to do it, because they wouldn't listen to him anyway, the sergeant went into another side of the village and just sat and stared bleakly at the ground, feeling sorry for himself. But at any rate, they raped the girls, and then, the last man to make love to her, shot her in the head.[40]

By blaming the act of sexual violence on poor leadership, responsibility could be removed from the individual perpetrators. Indeed, by calling the gang rape 'making love', even the victim was portrayed as partly complicit in her own violation.

This cavalier attitude suggests that sexual violence in wartime had turned into what Mikhail Bakhtin called 'authorized transgression'.[41] So long as knowledge about sexual violence remained confined to the victims and the military community, very little was done. As Scott Camil of the 1st Marine Division in Vietnam admitted immediately before describing the way fellow soldiers shoved an entrenching tool into the vagina of a female sniper they had captured, the 'main thing was that if an operation was covered by the press there were certain things we weren't supposed to do, but if there was no press there, it was okay'.[42] Too great a frequency of violations might result in a mild reprimand. For instance, a Marine named Ed Treratola described how his unit would slip into a village, kidnap a woman and gang-rape her. Depending on their mood, they either freed her afterwards or killed her. This might occur every night, Treratola admitted, and 'the villagers complained'. When that occurred, 'the brass would say, "Well, look, cool it for a little while", you know, "at least let it happen with little more time in between."' 'But we were never discouraged,' he added.[43] Military authorities officially disapproved of rape and pillage, but 'turned a blind eye' to such antics, accepting them as necessary for effective combat performance when the time came.

Given the ubiquitous nature of rape accusations in the context of the Vietnam War, it is not surprising that according to some servicemen sexual violence was surreptitiously promoted in military training camps. This occurred at two levels. First, military training camps were hyper-masculine environments, in which every feminine trait was routinely denigrated. 'Hey diddle diddle, straight up the middle,' soldiers would chant, referring both to the frontal assault so glorified by elite troops and sexual activity.[44] 'From the moment one arrives, the drill instructors begin a torrent of misogynistic and anti-individualistic abuse,' recalled one recruit from the US Marine Corp Boot Camp. He continued by observing that the

> good things are manly and collective; the despicable are feminine and individual. Virtually every sentence, every description, every lesson embodies this sexual duality, and the female anatomy provides a rich field of metaphor for every degradation. When you want to create a solidary [sic] group of male killers, that is what you do, you kill the women in them. That is the lesson of the Marines. And it works.

The recruit went on to argue that even after leaving the camp, soldiers continued to treat women as 'desirable only in the circuit of tension and release which is the most essential form of male erotic experiences'.[45]

At another level instructors themselves sometimes promoted sexual violence. Numerous servicemen admitted being told by their instructors that 'we could rape the women' and taught how to strip women prisoners, 'spread them open' and 'drive pointed sticks or bayonets into their vaginas' afterwards.[46] Twenty-year-old Chuck Onan recalled that troops training alongside him in the Marine Corps Special Forces 'liked the idea' of torturing, raping and killing prisoners: 'Many volunteered to go to Vietnam. The sergeants made it seem attractive – in a sick way, you know – you'll get a chance to kill and all this.' The fact that Marines were allowed to rape women was 'an inducement to encourage Marines to volunteer for Vietnam'.[47] According to one veteran from Vietnam, infantry training for the Marine Corps included a class on interrogating POWs and villagers about

> where they hide things. They stress over and over that a woman has more available places to hide things like maps or anything than a male. So it took about twenty minutes to cover where to search a male suspect, and about an hour on a female. It was like everyone was getting into it pretty heavy like, you know, wishful-thinking, you know.[48]

Wishful thinking or not, it translated into performance in the field. As another vet admitted, 'When we went through the villages and searched people the woman would have their clothes taken off and the men would use their penises to probe them to make sure they didn't have anything hidden anywhere; and this was raping but it was done as searching.'[49]

Indeed, threatening rape was regarded as an acceptable way to get information from prisoners of war and civilians. Don Dzagulanes, an interrogator with the Americal Division in Southern I Corps described one technique, which combined misogyny with racist assumptions. In his words,

> Like I said, most of the prisoners we had were women. It wasn't uncommon to have a mother and daughter coming in the same group of prisoners. I don't know why, I can't understand it, but we had a rarity in our unit. We had a black interrogator, which is really uncommon. There aren't too many black people in military intelligence. So we found out that by threatening a woman with having the black interrogator rape her, would usually make them talk.

Fortunately for the women, the black interrogator was 'a pacifist, he never did anything. He didn't even want to interrogate.'[50]

Raping servicemen were right not to fear punishment. Despite the fact that rape was a crime according to international law and was punishable by death or imprisonment under Articles of both the British and American military codes, acts of rape were rarely reported and the accused were seldom convicted. Marines who gang-raped and murdered 'a Viet Cong whore' were simply given 'a light slap on the wrist'.[51] Military priorities were strikingly exposed when this reaction was compared with the sentences handed out to servicemen in the peace movement. For instance, David Miller served twenty-two months in a federal prison for burning his draft card and Dr Howard Levy served two years for refusing to teach medical techniques to Green Berets because he believed that they would use such techniques to harm rather than heal.[52] Whether on the grounds of troop morale, or because of fears that news of raping would reflect negatively on their reputation as leaders of a disciplined body of men, senior officers often refused to act upon (and even deliberately covered up) cases of rape. This was the case with British soldiers in Italy during the Second World War. When two women in Lübeck identified the two British soldiers who had raped them and stolen their bicycles, the colonel told a military policeman to tell the women that he 'had seen the two soldiers all the afternoon and it couldn't have been the ones', despite the fact that the stolen bicycles were next to the field where these men were found. When the women insisted, the colonel

> told me to tell the women that they were mistaken. He said the two soldiers were going on leave in the morning and that he had signed their passes, and as far as he was concerned they would be going on leave. I told them there was nothing they could do, and of course the Colonel knew it was them. They were very upset. I advised them to take their bikes and go home. They went away in tears. Sgt. Smith didn't think much of the outcome. He was disgusted.[53]

As one historian coolly put it, 'American military law governing the handling of rape by military personnel appears to be comparable to civilian law in its substantive aspects, but possibly less stringent than civilian law in its procedural requirements and actual implementation.'[54] This was a more academic rendition of the words of one First World War 'Footslogger': 'The men I was with were rough with women, boasted of their conquests, many of whom [sic] were actually raped, but there were no prosecutions to my knowledge,' he remarked.[55]

The oppressive omnipresence of violence made individual men believe that nothing could be done to prevent them. There was no use in protesting or 'ratting on' your mates. Thus Ed Murphy, rifleman in the 198th Infantry Brigade, Americal Division, recalled that his platoon leader was a Mormon minister, who had shown himself to be a 'pretty well high-character man' when he first arrived in Vietnam. Before long, however,

> he was condoning everything that was going on because it was part of a policy. Nobody told you that it's wrong. This hell changed him around. And he would condone rapes. Not that he would do them, but he would just turn his head to them because who was he in a mass military policy.[56]

As another soldier put it, he was unsure how he would have reacted if his comrades began raping a woman. 'I don't think I would have taken part in it,' he noted, 'but I also don't think I would have tried to stop it.' After all, attempting to stop the rape would have 'been encouraging your own sudden death. These are the guys who get in the fire fights with you. It would have been too easy to get blown away.'[57] Soldiers who had been at My Lai feared being 'fragged' if they reported the atrocity.[58] Private First Class Michael Bernhardt had refused to take part in the massacre at My Lai but did not report it, deciding that 'it was dangerous enough just fighting the acknowledged enemy'.[59] Greg Olsen had been there, too, but was not prepared to talk about what had occurred to anyone in authority. He claimed to be unaware of any 'avenue to do it', yet his real concern was that 'you certainly had second thoughts about taking that kind of stand . . . You got to remember that everybody there has a gun . . . It's nice to face your accuser, but not when he's got a gun in his hands.'[60]

Many civilians, too, were prepared to simply shrug off evidence of abuse by soldiers. On 3 March 1977, for instance, a judge in Norwich (England) passed a three-year prison sentence on Thomas Holdsworth, a nineteen-year-old guardsman who, in attempting to rape seventeen-year-old Carol Maggs, had caused her serious internal injuries and broken her ribs. Maggs had been unable to work for four months and continued to suffer severe psychological stress. However, in June the Court of Appeal reduced the sentence to a suspended sentence of six months. Justice Roskill told the guardsman that 'the best thing you can do now is to go back to your unit and serve your country'. Justice Wien justified the decision by saying that 'we have a man of previous good character whose Army career would be completely destroyed if this sentence were to stand'. He also observed that 'Miss Maggs would probably have been less severely injured had she submitted to rape', thus suggesting that refusing to be raped was a kind of contributory negligence.[61]

In more recent years the risk of rape has been raised during debates about allowing female soldiers a combat role in war. The danger was acknowledged as coming not only from the enemy, but also from men on their own side. In the words of an American infantryman interviewed in the 1990s,

> In a situation where times are hard – less food, no showers, road marching, with 70-100 lbs ruck on your back, and [you] don't know when the next supply shipment will be in, the male soldier will start thinking of sex and the female soldiers may be raped or something.[62]

Interviewing infantrymen in the 1990s, Laura L. Miller was struck by the frequency with which male soldiers expressed this threat. They were not willing to admit that *they* would rape their fellow soldiers, but insisted that their male comrades might. 'Now I don't have a problem with women [soldiers],' one infantryman declared 'but some of these guys, I know them and they're animals. They won't hesitate to take what they want or let a woman get killed to get her out of the way.' Miller observed that the threat of rape was expressed 'in a tone of concern for women's safety' but the 'underlying function of these stories' was intimidation: women entering male domains just might get what they deserved.[63]

To victims the odds of their rapist being punished in any way seemed extremely low. In Oceanside (California), a small seaside town next to Camp Pendleton Marine Corps Base, the number of rapes and rape allegations in the 1970s was startling. Women's organizations in the area claimed to have 1837 cases of women alleging rape. These victims

> reported that their alleged Marine Rapists told them that they (the Marines) [sic] would be protected – presumably by the Marine Corps. They also claimed that a woman would be investigated by the Attorney General's Office (others said the Department of Justice and the F. B. I.) if she were to sign a criminal complaint charging Rape.[64]

In the unlikely event of a soldier accused of sexual abuse being brought before a court martial, the chances of conviction were minuscule. Outside of military circles it is often not known that the 'good soldier' defence offered a significant degree of immunity from conviction. A defendant with long service and high rank could claim evidence of good military character that was incompatible with accusation of sexual abuse. Traits such as obedience, leadership, courage and combat effectiveness were assumed to be proof that a man lacked the 'propensity' to sexual misconduct. This defence was highly biased in favour of soldiers who could produce a lengthy dossier of assignments and evaluations, thus giving a significant advantage to high-ranking white officers in comparison with African-American or other minority servicemen.

Servicewomen brave enough to bring charges of sexual abuse found that they had broken the code of 'comradeship', an act fatal for any future reintegration within the unit. In nearly every case the complainant would be of a lower rank than the man she was accusing. In the performative setting of a court martial, where participants wear uniforms displaying clear signs of rank and honours (and since the most highly esteemed honours were linked to combat experience, female victims were by definition excluded from possessing them), the accuser would inevitably appear less reliable. In addition, her lower status would generally mean that she lacked the documentary evidence to provide her own 'good soldier' defence.[65] In the words of Specialist 4 Arthur E. 'Gene' Woodley, Jr., combat paratrooper with the 5th Special Forces Group, who had witnessed a number of rapes committed by men under his command, 'You think no crime is a crime durin' war, 'specially when you get away with it.'[66]

Justifications

Rape may not have been regarded as a particularly heinous crime in wartime, but the proliferation of excuses and justifications for sexual violence suggests that a considerable amount of shame and guilt are associated with the practice. A number of arguments are used by servicemen to excuse sexual violence: first, life is dangerous, making aggression the only way to survive; second, women 'owed' a debt to servicemen and wanted 'it' anyway; third, male sexual needs must be met; and, finally, male fears led to rage.

The first of these arguments was extremely popular among men who had seen combat. Life at the front was dangerous; consent impossible to define. Indeed, in this dangerous world scenario aggression was regarded as the only way to survive psychologically. As Roland Littlewood, an anthropologist and psychiatrist employed by University College London, explained it: 'Soldiers themselves view sexual relations as countering battle anxiety.' After all, he went on, war was 'an unusual biosocial situation' and sexual activity reduces anxiety and confers a sense of necessary autonomy in conflictual and overwhelming situations'.[67] In other words, sexual violence was blamed on post-battle anxiety.

A Freud-inspired version of this defence insists not only that combat anxieties necessitate a coercive sexual outlet, but that there is an intrinsic relationship between killing and violent sex. Perhaps no one put this argument more starkly than William Manchester in *Goodbye, Darkness* (1981), his memoir of war in the Pacific theatre. After a terrifying battle Manchester describes how the 'Whore of Death' appeared before him. Although he admitted that she was 'the most improbable of sex objects' (her flesh was covered with sores), he was seduced. Why? The important thing for Manchester was that the shell which 'had wiped out my squad had barely missed me'. For him it was axiomatic that 'so close a call with death' would be 'followed by eroticism'. He believed that it was 'characteristic of some creatures that they are often very productive before their death and, in some cases, appear to die in a frenzy of reproductive activity. Desire is the sequel to danger.' The 'soiled Whore of Death' winked at him and he 'became semihard'.

> She was an enchantress in an old tale whom men have loved to their destruction. She wouldn't sigh or swoon or feign affection . . . Her coarse, blurred, sepulchral voice, just audible, rasped obscenities and spoke of the bargain she proposed to strike in the language she had used for a thousand years of warfare. The key words were *lust* and *blood* and *death* . . . Abruptly she hoisted her skirt to her hips and spread her legs. My pulse was hammering, my sexual craving almost overwhelming. That was my moment of maximum temptation. For the first and only time in my life I understood rape. I have never been more ready.[68]

It is no coincidence that Manchester's vision was of a battlefield whore, as opposed to another female figure. A second justification for rape in wartime was the view that women were sluts anyway. In peacetime, evidence that a woman drinks alcohol or wears a short skirt is routinely seen as proof of low sexual standards; in wartime, such 'indicators' proffered unquestioned proof that the woman deserved molestation. Lieutenant Colonel W. B. Murgatroyd, prosecutor in a war crimes court in Italy in 1945, recalled having to provide legal advice to a 'horried' [sic] case involving the rape by three men of a twenty-one-year old, convent-educated woman. Murgatroyd admitted that the three men had forcibly dragged the woman to their billets where they gang-raped her and 'exposed her to unmentionable indignities, involving a piece of wood and a bar of soap'. He explained away their activities, however, by explaining that 'the accused were drunk, had got hold of this girl (possibly thinking she was on the streets)'.[69]

In wartime, this argument goes, the boundary between forced and consensual sex crumbles, and resistance by the woman is routinely conceptualized as a form of foreplay. American servicemen in Germany were known to boast that the 'German soldiers fought for six years, the German women for only five minutes'.[70] Women would 'consent' to sexual intercourse, fearful that any sign of resistance would lead to something worse. Courtship is conceived of as 'different' in wartime. It is an attitude that permeates relationships between the sexes. Thus, in his unpublished memoir 'The One Who Didn't Get

Away', J. H. Witte, a recently released POW in Germany, writes about giving some chocolate to a German widow. In his words,

> The widow invited me to walk alongside her; I found out that her husband had copped his lot at Stalingrad, that she hadn't had any dick for a long time, although she didn't put it quite as bluntly as that. We came to her house on the outskirts of the town and she invited me in which she could hardly have refused to do considering the nosh that I had given her.[71]

Even observers sympathetic to the victims' viewpoint registered a silent acquiescence. As Allan S. Clifton, interpreter and Intelligence officer, explained:

> In the immediate post-war period in Japan, because of economic hardship and semi-starvation, young and physically desirable women offered themselves at street corners or railway stations in exchange for almost anything that was edible or capable of conversion into food. For this reason, if for no other consideration, any condemnation of criminal assault was impossible.[72]

When food, shelter and life itself depended upon sexual congress, the liberal emphasis on free and informed consent in deciding issues of rape is of lesser or no importance for many people.

The third reason given for the sexual abuse of women in wartime was male sexual needs. In the words of one historian writing about sexual violence during the American Civil War, the presumed male requirement to engage in sexual intercourse was one reason why wartime rapes were seen as 'not directly threatening to the state, except, of course, when committed by slaves against "respectable" white women'.[73] The premise of this argument was that the male sex drive requires an 'outlet' and that rape is an inevitable consequence of the brutalization of war. In the words of George Ryley Scott, writing in 1940, in wartime, there

> is always a reversion to primeval savagery . . . The majority of cases of rape, however, are not performed by sadists. They are performed by ordinary human beings suffering from sex hunger, who, owing to one cause or another, cannot satisfy their passions by intercourse with their wives, their lovers, or prostitutes.[74]

These sexual needs were most frequently linked to myths about the animalistic inheritance of humankind. War saw 'mankind' revert to the 'beasts'. This was the language used by the American soldier in Vietnam as he struggled to make sense of the gang-rape of an adolescent Vietnamese woman whose question ('Why are you doing this to me?') I quoted at the very start of this book. 'It was just like an animal pack,' he recalled. After all the men had raped the young woman, they killed her and then mutilated her body. The unnamed soldier continued:

> That's what the hatred, the frustration was. After we raped her, took her cherry from her, after we shot her in the head, you understand what I'm saying, we literally start stomping [on] her body. And everybody was laughing about it. It's like seeing the lions around a just-killed zebra. You see them in these animal pictures, *Wild Kingdom* or something. The whole pride comes around and they start feasting on the body.[75]

This was not only brutality, but something 'natural' – something you might see on a beautifully shot wildlife documentary on TV.

However, the most common reason given for rape in wartime drew attention not to male power and solidarity but male fears and vulnerabilities. An unnamed soldier who had seen service in Vietnam recalled that his comrades were really 'getting into' instruction about how they could search women. It 'seems to me', he mused, that

> the philosophy over there is like somehow or another we're more afraid of females than we are of males, because, I don't know why, but the females was always like you never knew where you stood, so you went overboard in your job with her in all your daily actions. You doubled whatever you would do for a male.

Fears that Vietnamese women were actually the 'fiercesty fighters' made men anxious. They 'didn't want to be embarrassed by getting our asses kicked by a bunch of females', he concluded his analysis of wartime rape.[76] In a war in which women could be combatants, manliness demanded particularly vigilant policing.

This soldier's comment is insightful, even though he applied it only in limited situations (that is, conflicts in which women fought). But male fears of women more generally often motivated sexually abusive actions.

Another side to this explanation involves the claim that sexual violence arises out of servicemen's need for male comradeship. Soldiers were encouraged to bond with one another; individuality was subordinated. Group acts of rape served to reduce the individual's sense of responsibility for his actions. There was also an element of resistance against the structure of command. Panicky about rumours that the military were trying to dampen down sexual desire (most commonly, in the British context, by spiking the tea) and resentful of the rigid discipline structure, privates excused sexual violence by framing it in terms of 'hitting back' at the establishment by proving their plebeian virility.

Gang rape was seen as essential in the process of bonding men together *as men*. This trait is common in gang rapes in civilian contexts, too, particularly in fraternity rapes: the perpetrators are effectively competing with one another to show superior strength and virility. An audience is necessary for the act. Oliver Stone's film *Platoon* (1986) portrayed this cinematically when Chris Taylor (Charlie Sheen) stumbled across some American soldiers raping a Vietnamese woman. When he tried to stop them the rapists jeered, 'What are you, a homosexual, Taylor?'[77] Manliness was constantly negotiated through acts of sexual performance. Specialist 4 Arthur E. 'Gene' Woodley, Jr. put it most directly when explaining why he did not prevent the men under his command from raping women: 'I was in charge of a group of animals, and I had to be the biggest animal there. I allowed things to happen. I had learned not to care. And I didn't care,' he admitted.[78] Or, as another man who participated in the rape and killing of a Vietnamese woman explained, he was 'afraid of being ridiculed.' He was particularly terrified of being derided as 'queer' and 'chicken' – so he followed his comrades in raping the woman.[79]

The need to bond with one's fellow soldiers does not explain, however, the excesses of violence that accompany many wartime rapes. It was not enough to simply rape: soldiers often mutilated and tortured. To understand this, I think we need to acknowledge two things. Two factors are of help in explaining this excessive brutality. First, the importance of the group in these rapes. I have already hinted at this factor. In their book *German Atrocities, 1914. A History of Denial* (2001) John Horne and Alan Kramer observed that wartime rape was a 'three-way relationship – between the perpetrator, victim, and the victim's male compatriots'.[80] They could just as easily have argued that rape is a 'four-way relationship', since one of the startling differences between rape in peacetime and rape in war is the much greater prevalence of group rapes in war. A radically higher proportion of wartime rapes involve a group of men rather than a solitary offender. As other research has shown in non-military contexts, the greater the number of perpetrators involved in a rape, the greater the chances of extreme violence.[81] A similar dynamic operates in wartime. In 1936 Arthur N. Fox observed that rape was a rare occurrence in civilian society because of the 'suppression of these tendencies by society and hence their repression in the individual'. In wartime, however, there was a 'diffusion of instincts and homosexuality and sadism come forth with the crash of sublimations'. He continued, stating that during armed conflict

> ravishing is consummated by groups of men and then through the women, a group of men vicariously satisfy homosexual desires as well as the sadism associated with oral and anal release. Even today, groups of youth will occasionally assault one girl in this manner, and yet were each to be entirely alone with a girl he would find himself relatively impotent out of fear of the girl and lack of desire in himself.[82]

In 1969 G. D. Woods extended this argument, employing concepts derived from group psychology. Multiple rape, he observed, is a

> group activity . . . mutual goading forces individuals to behave more extremely than they otherwise would do . . . the leader tends to become the repository and epitome of the qualities highly valued in the group. In order to demonstrate their membership of the group, all members must behave in such a way as to positively affirm these highly valued qualities, but the leader must do so even more positively than the other members of the group.

According to Woods, the need to either gain or maintain prestige within groups explained why pack rapes often involved acts of 'gratuitous and extravagant defilement'. He continued:

> It should be remembered that this pattern of group or gang formation is a very widespread one, and perfectly natural. Whether there is such a thing as a 'group instinct' is contentious but certainly the formation of 'gangs' occurs at all levels of human society. For adolescents to form gangs involves basically the same process and need as, for example, for professional adults to form restrictive social clubs, and usually nothing more sinister.[83]

In the words of child psychologist Bruno Bettelheim, writing in 1968, in a gang a 'single act of unpremeditated intensity' enabled the members to 'at once establish a sense of their own existence and forcefully impress this now valid existence on others'.[84]

The second explanation for the extremes of torture in wartime rapes draws attention to the environment of extreme violence in which soldiers are immersed. Ripping up bodies, torture and abuse are not only accepted in wartime, they are often required by the highest authorities. In war aggression is not only a legitimate way to gain compliance, it is also undertaken long after any notion of 'compliance' has been discarded, as witnessed by acts of violence against the bodies of dead enemies and against the Japanese women after the surrender, as I discussed at the beginning of this chapter. These acts gave servicemen a sense of exhilarating power. They made them feel omnipotent. As one unnamed American soldier in Vietnam explained, he experienced

> a sense of power. A sense of destruction. See now, in the United States a person is babied. He's told what to do . . . But in the Nam you realised that you had the power to take a life. You had the power to rape a woman and nobody could say nothing to you. That godlike feeling you had was in the field . . . It was like I was a god. I could take a life, I could screw a woman.[85]

Finally, it is easier to sexually abuse and torture the enemy in campaigns where the enemy is regarded as racially and culturally foreign and inferior. Racist discourse meant that women were not really seen as human. As one Marine said after describing particularly sadistic rapes of Vietnamese women, '[i]t wasn't like they were humans. We were conditioned to believe that this was for the good of the nation, the good of our country, and that anything we did was okay.'[86]

In other theatres of war, where the enemy was regarded as 'closer to us', servicemen were more willing to pay women for sexual services as opposed to raping them. As one Vietnam veteran put it,

> You take a group of men and put them in a place where there are no round-eyed women. They are in an all-male environment. Let's face it. Nature is nature. There are women available. Those women are of another culture, another color, another society. You don't want a prostitute. You've got an M-16. What do you need to pay for a lady for? You

> go down to the village and you take what you want . . . Being in that kind of environment, you give a guy a gun and strange things happen. A gun is power. To some people carrying a gun constantly was like having a hard on.[87]

These three distorted attitudes about sex and violence were present in civilian society, too,[88] but became particularly strong in wartime. Indeed, wartime rape may be thought of as over-determined. Factors facilitating other forms of atrocity facilitate rape.[89] Uniforms provided anonymity. Weapons were freely available, as were 'disinhibitory' drugs and alcohol. Potential victims dehumanized; perpetrators de-individualized. The dichotomy between 'me' and 'them' becomes so wide that 'they' are a different species. The penis is explicitly coded as a weapon. In the words of the familiar chant:

> This is my weapon [hoisting his gun over his head]
> This is my gun [grabbing his crotch]
> This is for fighting,
> This is for fun.

Telling Rape Stories

The narrative of sexual violence carried out by British and American servicemen has tended to be written out of history. This refusal to translate private memory into public commemoration or widely shared war narratives is most evident when confronting experiences of *meting out* violence upon others.

This is hardly surprising. Sexual transgressions were even more taboo than state-legitimated killing in combat situations. In both cases the narrator of 'I was there' experiences a difficulty in unequivocally separating off the trauma of *feeling threatened* from the fact of *threatening*. In wartime the two often coexisted in time. Even servicemen who did not carry out atrocities might feel guilty. As one Vietnam veteran put it in 1994, war was

> a crime I have committed. Rape, mass murder, torture, the burning of homes, and the killing of prisoners are not. Yet I have known decent and courageous men who did these things, men for whom I would take serious risks. It has taken me twenty years to work out my feelings of guilt for loving them.[90]

'Survivor's guilt' has been directed not only at comrades, but also at the violated enemy, female as well as male. In the nightmares and narratives of combatants, trangressive acts do not differentiate between different sections of humanity, no matter how frantically officers and military instructors attempted to inculcate ideas that dehumanized the enemy.

The experiences of Americans and Australians during the Vietnam War and, more recently, in Iraq, disrupted public reticence about sexual abuse in war. A narrative of violence, and particularly sexual violence, brutally burst into the public arena during the Vietnam War. Interestingly, this was most effective when carried out by groups of veterans, such as the Vietnam Veterans Against the War movement and the Winter Soldier Investigation.[91] Here legitimate groups insisted upon telling their stories, creating a collective narrative that circled in a fixated fashion around My Lai-type incidents. After 1975 nearly all combat films portrayed a platoon in a My Lai-type situation.[92] Grade-B Vietnam films almost universally figured a veteran as a 'psychotic, axe-wielding rapist'. As one commentator quipped, 'The demented-vet portrait has become so casual, so commonplace, that one pictures the children of Vietnam veterans shivering beneath their blankets and wondering if Daddy will come in with a goodnight kiss or a Black & Decker chain saw.'[93]

The post-1975 'new memory' of war films graphically portrayed acts of rape, pillage and murder in the context of a celebration of survival-against-horrific-odds and comradeship. There was little if any discussion of the 'cause' of these atrocities, and viewers were left with the 'private motivations and goals of the individual soldier'.[94] This dramatic shift in the commemoration of the Vietnam War did not have an equivalent in Britain, despite the (arguably) similar experiences faced by service personnel in Korea.

The celebration of individual courage against overwhelming odds was only one way in which rape stories in wartime were stripped of political context. The other way was through the normalization of atrocities, presented as an inevitable – indeed, necessary for survival – aspect of warfare. As one British NCO insisted, after defending general acts of atrocity carried out by his men: there was no 'law' higher than the knowledges and instincts possessed by the fighting man. If anyone disagreed, he advised them to 'Get yourself to the sharp end, against an enemy like the Japanese . . . let me know how you get on.'[95]

The emphasis on psychological mechanisms of survival were often integrated into these arguments. For instance, a major article in the

1977 edition of the *International Journal of Offender Therapy and Comparative Criminology* insisted that soldiers who raped and then murdered their victims were acting within norms shared by their peer group. According to the author,

> the soldier rapist-murderer . . . does not appear as a helpless neurotic plagued by uncontrollable urges to defend against incestuous wishes. His actions are rational, flexible with the circumstances, supported by his peers, deliberately executed, and thus show all the typical traits of 'normal' behaviour – aggressive behaviour, though.

The crucial difference, the author insisted, was to distinguish between 'normal' soldier rapists and abnormal ones. 'Those forms of rape which are not culturally, societally, supported in which the rapist becomes truly deviant from the norms of his reference group,' the author suggested, were insane or criminal rapes: the rest were just 'normal rapes'.[96]

A similar reasoning has been used in studies about wartime sexuality more generally. Thus in 1975 Gavin Hart, a registrar at the First Australian Field Hospital in Vietnam, published his research entitled 'Sex Behavior in a War Environment'. Hart's research was based on interviews with 718 Australian men who had seen active service. He noted that over 10 per cent of the men had 'suffered penile trauma' on one occasion during their military service and 5 per cent had done so more than once. The cause of penile trauma? According to Hart, it was due to the refusal of some women to consent to certain sexual acts. In his words,

> [f]ailure [of the women] to indulge in fellatio at this stage often proved traumatic. Not infrequently, refusal caused the angry prostitute to violently wrench the erect penis causing severe preputial tears. A further cause of penile trauma was the strong desire of many soldiers, coupled with the unacceptance [sic] of prostitutes, to experience intraoral ejaculation . . . At the onset of orgasm the soldier firmly held the girl's head in close contact with his penis and, in retaliation, the girl forcefully bit the penis to effect release.

Forced sex is presented as a natural aspect of wartime sexuality. The 'unacceptance' of women to engage in particular acts was, in itself, unacceptable. Hart does mention sexual ethics: 'History continually relates how ethical and moral codes change radically under conditions of war. These altered standards together with absence from homeland and family, and ethical codes they represent, are conditions which favor promiscuity.'[97] The forced sexual acts carried out by soldiers are placed in the context of 'promiscuity'. Ethics is firmly located as an attitude of 'homeland and family'.

For many historians, too, rape is presented as a natural outcome of men's sexual needs. The notorious ideas of evolutionary psychologists, such as Randy Thornhill and Craig T. Palmer in A *Natural History of Rape: Biological Bases of Sexual Coercion* (2000),* convinced some historians.[98] In a 1997 issue of the *Journal of Military History*, for instance, Phillip S. Meilinger speculated on the evolutionary origins of human violence. Drawing on the work of Richard Wrangham and Dale Peterson concerning what they designated 'rape' among the great apes, Meilinger noted that there seemed to be no 'rational reason' for these acts of sexual aggression: the male chimps had plenty of food, there was no shortage of female chimps and they were not threatened in any way. The only explanation was the importance placed upon male pride and honour. 'Male chimps raid, fight, rape and murder to display their manhood,' Meilinger asserted, adding that chimps raped other chimps 'in response to slights or a lack of respect from others; they do it for the honour of being recognized as dominant'. He continued: 'The implication of this premise is apparent: if man's nearest relative kills over matters of honor, then perhaps we have *inherited* that same affliction. In short, we may make war not for reasons of policy, but out of the dictates of biology.'[99] According to such an approach, rape is a biological inheritance from the beasts. The author also engaged in a curious sleight of hand, conflating war and rape.

It is not an uncommon conflation. Many historians of warfare assume a natural link between the two. Women are set outside of culture, becoming merely the 'bounty' of war. Thus, in *Of Arms and Men: A History of War, Weapons and Aggression* (1989), Robert L. O'Connell distinguished ancient warfare from hunting, and then drew a parallel with modern combat. In his words,

> rather than serving as the equivalent of the hunt (an activity in which female predators frequently participate), warfare preserved the intraspecific role of the female as prize and object of combat. If nothing

*Their views are critiqued in Chapter 4, 'Rapacious Bodies'.

else, this helps to account for the aura of sexuality which has hung about war and weapons throughout history, serving as both a thematic equipoise to its ruthlessness and an indication of the complexity of the subject and the motives behind it.[100]

The 'aura of sexuality' associated with war was most blatantly displayed in Dave Grossman's book *On Killing* (1995). In what was otherwise a fairly straightforward account of military socialization, the shift to a highly sexualized prose is significant. In Grossman's words,

> Thrusting the sexual appendage (the penis) [sic] deep into the body of the victims can be perversely linked to thrusting the killing appendage (a bayonet or knife) deep into the body of the victim. This process can be seen in pornographic movies in which the sexual act is twisted, such that the male ejaculates – or 'shoots his wad' – into a female's face. The grip of a firer on the pistol grip of a gun is much like the grip on an erect penis, and holding the penis in this fashion while ejaculating into the victim's face is at some level an act of domination and symbolic destruction. The culmination of this intertwining of sex and death can be seen in snuff films, in which a victim is raped and then murdered on film.

Grossman went on to argue that the 'force of darkness and destruction within us' is always engaged in a struggle with 'a force of light and love for our fellow man'. The 'link between sex and war' is represented in mythology in the marriage between Ares and Aphrodite, through which 'Harmonia is born'.[101]

Finally, not only are war and sex collapsed into each other; the woman-victim is also erased from these rituals of violence. Commentators frequently insist that rapes in wartime are primarily concerned with aggression against a *male* enemy. Gillian Mezey, for instance, defined rape in wartime as 'an attack on the male adversary' and Stéphane Audoin-Rouzeau even went so far as to call wartime rape a particularly 'masculine trauma'. The wartime rapist became the 'witness of his own impotence', Audoin-Rouzeau quipped.[102] Other historians referred to the rape of 'the enemy's women', implying that women were simply the property of men, perpetuating the notion that in wartime women are merely pawns in the struggles between male nations. Of course, in many conflicts perpetrators of sexual violence raped women in order to hit back at the male population. This was particularly the case in conflicts in the former Yugoslavia.[103] It can be seen in comments by a soldier in Vietnam that his comrades treated female prisoners more harshly because it made 'a lasting impression on some guy – some "zip" – that's watching his daughter worked over. So we have a better opportunity of keeping him in line by working her over.'[104] But to state that rape is, in the words of two historians, an act of 'aggression and humiliation of the enemy through an attack on his women' is to erase the woman from the nation and to efface her trauma.[105]

Indeed, it is striking that servicemen who engaged in rapes and murder saw themselves, and were often portrayed in the media, as *casualties* of war, not as aggressors. The invention of Post-Traumatic Stress Disorder (PTSD) allowed men who had participated in atrocities to portray themselves as victims of trauma. The sex crimes prosecutor Alice Vachss was particularly incensed by this assumption, arguing that it

> is one thing to use Vietnam vet syndrome to explain a shoot-out with the police, where there is at least some correlation between the wartime behavior and the crimes. But to say that [a man] raped because he had flashbacks of Vietnam was a fundamentally offensive idea. Implicit was the concept that he was raping a Vietnamese woman (and that it was O.K.) but when he got back over here he couldn't adjust to it being culturally unacceptable to rape Americans – like some rap video where the targets of sexual violence always seem to be Asian women.[106]

Instead of being perpetrators of sexual violence, PTSD enabled sexual abusers to portray themselves as victims. The 'trauma' of being perpetrators of violence, including sexual violence, had made them 'ill'. It was the 'retaliatory pleasures of an aggressor who perceives himself as victim'.[107]

Contemporary War Crimes

Concern about sexual violence in wartime was muted after the Second World War. Rape and sexual violence were not explicitly mentioned in the Nuremberg Charter. Rape was referred to indirectly, but no specific prosecutions for rape were initiated. This changed as a result of the conflict in the former Yugoslavia and the genocide in Rwanda, when mass rapes galvanized the international community into addressing the issue in the context of torture and war crimes.[108] In those conflicts sexual violence included rape, sexual assault, sexual mutilation, forced impregnation and forced pregnancy, forced prostitution and forced cohabitation or marriage. In 2001 rape was recognized as a crime against humanity for the first time by both the Statute of the International Criminal Tribunal for the former Yugoslavia and the Statute of the International Criminal Tribunal for Rwanda. In the words of Debra Bergoffen, writing in *Hypatia* in 2003, by

> identifying rape, like torture, as a crime against humanity, the ruling affirms the principle of embodied subjectivity. It goes beyond past rulings on torture, however, in attending to the sexual realities of embodiment and in insisting that violating a *woman's* sexual integrity is a crime against humanity, 'the second most serious category of international war crimes after genocide'.[109]

A woman's capacity, or lack of capacity, became the determining element, instead of the degree of violence inflicted or pain experienced.

Recent attempts to make rape into a war crime have profoundly important implications,[110] especially in the way they treat rape not as a crime of passion or a crime against honour or dignity, but as a crime against humanity or as an element of genocide. However, it is doubtful whether it will affect most of the rapes I have dissected in this chapter. War crimes require that the sex-related violence takes place on a mass scale or is part of an orchestrated policy. Designating rape as a crime against humanity or genocide would not have helped prosecute most acts of violation carried out in wartime.

Despite its frequency, it is important to emphasize that rape is not inevitable either in the armed forces or during wartime. Indeed, some conditions of military life and lifestyle reduce the likelihood of sexual violence, at least against women. High levels of surveillance might inhibit opportunities for abuse. During periods of heavy fighting, concerns about basic survival might actually reduce the incidence of rape orgies.[111] It is even more important to recognize that military units operating in nearly identical environs display very different tendencies to act in sexually aggressive ways. In other words, rape is avoidable. The view that it *is* an inescapable element of modern warfare has encouraged passive responses to its occurrence. When anyone shrugs and mouths clichés such as 'war is an atrocity so atrocities will take place', we should beware.

What the experience of rape in twentieth-century wartime did reveal, however, is the fact that patently 'normal' men – conscripts, even – were capable of raping, given certain circumstances. War is one occasion when rape scripts diverge from the individualist canon of legal and psychiatric practice and enter fully into everyday mass culture. The prevalence of rape in military institutions and during war challenges generally accepted conceptions of 'the rapist'. Ideas about pathological acts or behaviour must be jettisoned. Male sexual aggression became part of a wider social malaise.[112] Instead of an emphasis on individual psychological states, there was a shift to social, material and political forces that facilitate sexual violence. Not only was violence increasingly sexualized as we move from the 'Great' War to the 'Good' One, but sex was increasingly located at the core of violence. To put it another way, in the course of the twentieth century violence was increasingly sexualized. The growing popularity of Freudian languages encouraged this coupling of narrative orchestrations of battle and boudoir. Unlike evolutionary or crowd theories (popular in the pre-1940s period), Freud licensed an explicit connection between two instincts of Eros and Thanatos.[113]

In the present century's wars in Afghanistan and Iraq, sexual violence has become so accepted and commonplace that participants keenly photographed themselves taking part. Issues of consent (when food, shelter and life itself depended upon sexual congress, the liberal emphasis on 'consent' was demoted), appropriateness (in particular the age of the victim) and privacy (the number of witnesses or participants to sexual acts) proved remarkably flexible, and, by and large, were cognitively 'set apart' from peacetime conduct. There is no doubt that barriers to certain forms of sexual contact and abuse were relaxed in startling ways in the course of war.[114] But such relaxation of the rules against sexual violence is not inevitable. I will return to this theme in the last chapter.

SECTION SIX

Law

You watch him
Pulpited in the dock, preaching repentance
While the two professionals in fancy dress
Manoeuvre formally to score off him or catch him.
But grief has her conventions –
The opaque mask of misery will confess
Nothing, nor plead moving extenuations.
But you who crowd the court-room, will you never be called
To witness for the defence?

CECIL DAY LEWIS, 'SEX-CRIME'.[1]

CHAPTER FOURTEEN

Getting Away with Rape

Writing this chapter made me angry. One statistic does it: in the UK today only 5 per cent of rapes reported to the police ever end in a conviction.

Given the huge proportion of rapes that are never even reported to the police in the first place, this is damning evidence that something is terribly wrong. The proportion of reported rapes that end in a conviction is 3 per cent or less in Warwickshire, Gloucestershire, Essex and Avon and Somerset. It is only more than 10 per cent in Cleveland, Cumbria, South Wales and South Yorkshire, reaching a peak of just under 13 per cent in Gwent.[2] [See map, p. 390.] In the European context such high attrition rates are unique to the UK. Austria and Denmark, for instance, have prosecution rates more than 50 per cent higher than those in Britain. In Finland, Germany, Hungary and Iceland a majority of prosecutions result in convictions. In fact, only Ireland has a lower conviction rate than Britain.[3] Furthermore, this attrition rate is getting worse. In 1977 one in three reported rapes resulted in a conviction. By 1985 this was 24 per cent or one in four and it was only one in ten by 1996.[4] Today it is one in twenty. Men who actually end up standing in the dock accused of rape, unlawful sexual intercourse and indecent assault are acquitted in 39 per cent of cases. The national average for *all* criminal cases discontinued in the magistrates' courts is 13 per cent. If we exclude those prisoners who plead guilty, the acquittal rate is over 70 per cent.[5] A vast array of American data comes to similar conclusions.[6] Rapists who end up being convicted in a court of law must regard themselves as exceptionally unlucky.

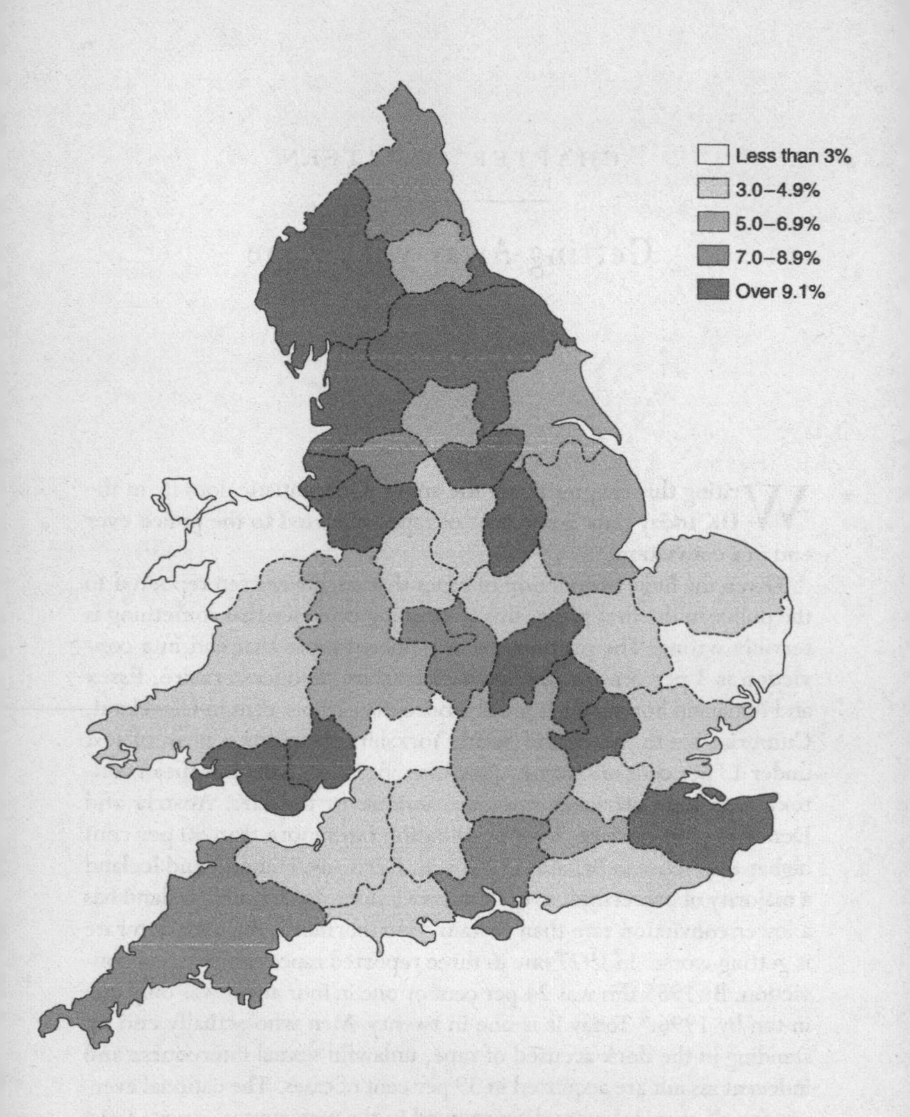

The percentage of reported rapes that end in a conviction in England and Wales, 2002

Source: Liz Kelly, Jo Lovett and Linda Regan, *A Gap or a Chasm? Attrition in Reported Rape Cases: A Home Office Research Study*, 2005

False Accusations

Could there be a simple reason for such high (and worsening) attrition rates? Some superficial analyses seem to dismiss its importance by attributing it to the dramatic escalation in the number of rapes and sexual assaults being reported to the police in recent decades. It is true that accusations of abuse have risen radically. In Britain between 1985 and 2003, for instance, rapes reported to the police increased from 1842 to 12,293. But no one can seriously suggest that the accused persons in 95 per cent of these reported cases are innocent. Or can they?

Unfortunately, many people still believe that women are prone to lie about being raped. This mistaken belief, which I discussed in detail in Chapter 2, 'Rape Myths', influences the way the legal system processes rape cases and prejudices perceptions of victims from the moment they report being raped to the time they give evidence in court. Most notoriously, until recent years the myth of false accusations was encoded at the very heart of law. The most obvious illustration of this process is the 'cautionary instruction', introduced into common law by Lord Chief Justice Matthew Hale in the seventeenth century. The cautionary instruction entails the judge informing the jury that rape is a charge easily made by the accuser and yet difficult for any defendant to disprove. Typically trial judges are instructed to say something like (the example is taken from California, where it was first introduced in 1856):

> A charge such as that made against the defendant in this case is one which is easily made and, once made, difficult to defend against, even if the person accused is innocent. Therefore, the law requires that you examine the testimony of the female person named in the information with caution.[7]

Until the 1980s judges routinely issued such instructions to juries in ordinary rape cases. Not surprisingly, jurors interpreted the instruction as suggesting that they needed to scrutinize the testimony of rape victims particularly rigorously. Was 'something wrong' with the victim's account? As has been demonstrated during mock trials, jurors who heard the cautionary instruction were much more likely to acquit the defendant than jurors who had not been instructed.[8]

But the context within which Hale formulated his instruction was exceptional. His judgement had been made during a trial in which the victim was a mentally incompetent infant. The legal system within which Hale worked when he issued his instruction in the seventeenth century was fundamentally different from the one facing defendants from the nineteenth century and later. In Hale's time criminals were not presumed innocent, proof beyond reasonable doubt was not required and notions of due process were shaky. The accused did not have the right to counsel or the right to testify under oath; he could not subpoena witnesses. This all changed from the nineteenth century. In particular the UK Prisoner's Counsel Act of 1836 not only gave defendants a right to professional counsel, but also allowed this counsel to address the jury directly. The effect was dramatic: professional counsel was able to lecture jurors, belligerently cross-examine rape victims and witnesses and cite favourable precedents.[9] Their professional language and standing played well with juries, and their willingness to question the victim's character could be devastating to the prosecution. Indeed, Martin Wiener, one of the most distinguished historians of crime, has persuasively argued that the increasing attention paid to the 'character' of women making rape accusations was primarily due to the expanded role given to defence counsel.[10]

Even if we dismiss the blatant misogyny behind the cautionary instruction, it is still important to ask the question: are men actually at risk of being falsely accused of rape? In the nineteenth and early twentieth centuries the most bandied-about estimate was that there were twelve false accusations to every 'true' one. In other words, 92 per cent of rape allegations were malicious.[11] Some commentators were willing to lower this to 80 per cent,[12] while still others swore that the proportion of false accusations had to be closer to 99 per cent.[13] The one exception to this bias against women alleging rape was when white women in reconstructionist and post-reconstructionist Southern states of America accused black men of rape. In such situations the trope of male innocence and female guilt was reversed.

From the 1970s onwards it was common for the police to profess that one in every five women reporting rape was making an unfounded claim.[14] Male fears alone cannot account for these high estimates. In a study of a large police department in Texas, one researcher found that male rape investigators believed that 12 per cent of rape cases they investigated were false – but female investigators were even more disbelieving, claiming that 40 per cent of their cases involved fabrications. Below I will be looking at some of the reasons why policemen and policewomen might believe inflated 'guestimates' of the number of women falsely crying rape. Clearly, however, one explanation may be the effect of reportage in the mass media. Rare cases of false allegations are big media events. The most commonly cited example is the tragic Gary Dotson case, in which Cathleen Crowell Webb withdrew her accusation of rape years after her alleged attacker had been imprisoned. This was the only reported case of a recantation in the decade after 1978 yet continues to be cited as though such injustices are commonplace.[15]

In contrast with inflated guesses, robust examinations of rape cases actually reveal low levels of deception. Some investigations have shown that the percentage of false accusations in rape cases is no larger than that for other felonies, and probably does not exceed 2–3 per cent of all rape charges.[16] The US Uniform Crime Report found higher levels, claiming that 8 per cent of forcible rapes between 1991 and 1997 were 'unfounded'. Because of particularly difficult problems of evidence in rape cases, this was higher than the 2 per cent of cases designated 'unfounded' in aggravated assault, robbery, arson, and property crimes.[17] Nevertheless, it is important to emphasize that just because the police decree a rape charge 'unfounded', this does not mean it is 'false'. Police often designate a case 'unfounded' because they don't think there is enough evidence to take the case to court, too much time has elapsed between the alleged attack and the victim reporting it, the victim's previous sexual conduct was not exemplary or the race of the victim and her attacker makes the police downgrade the seriousness of the attack.

The most reliable statistics on the extent of false accusations comes from a major UK Home Office research project in 2000–3. Initially the researchers concluded that 9 per cent of reported rape accusations were false. However, on closer analysis this percentage dropped dramatically. They found that many of the cases listed as 'no evidence of assault' were the result of someone other than the victim making the accusation. In other words, a policeman or passer-by might see a woman distressed or drunk, with her clothes ripped, and report it as a suspected rape. However, when the woman was able to provide an account for what happened, it proved that no rape had taken place. In other instances a woman regained consciousness in a public place or at home and, unable to recall what happened, worried about whether she might have been assaulted. The woman approached the police not in order to claim rape, but to see if any crime had been committed. Once such cases had been eliminated from the study, only 3 per cent of allegations should have been categorized as false.[18]

Indeed, contrary to the notion that men are at risk of being falsely accused, it is much more common for actual rapists to get away with their actions. A range of studies shows that between half and four-fifths of rapes are never reported to the police in the first place.[19] Other estimates are more gloomy. One survey of 1007 women in eleven UK cities found that a startling 91 per cent of women failed to report their abuse,[20] while the Rape Crisis Federation of England and Wales found that only 12 per cent of the 50,000 women who contacted their services in 1998 reported the crime of rape to the police.[21]

Furthermore, rape is not an easy charge to make. The stigma attached to any person claiming to have been raped is significant and in the (unlikely) event of trial, the victim faces an ordeal that is often described as approaching a 'second assault'. At the very least, rape trials resemble 'degradation ceremonies' for the victim, in which she is 'denounced and her motives questioned' in front of many witnesses.[22] Unlike other criminal trials, the rape victim becomes the focus of attention. Her life is placed under intense scrutiny. Jurors prove exceptionally reluctant to find a man guilty of rape unless there are aggravating circumstances.[23] And female jurors are frequently more distrustful than male ones.

Attrition

There are four points at which the identification and prosecution of rapists fails: victims choose not to report the assault; the police decide not to register the complaint or the Crown Prosecution Service drops the case; the rapist is not identified; the accused is acquitted at trial.

Only a small proportion of women report their rape. Fear of not being believed, concerns about re-victimization, anxiety about being judged in turn and the discomfort of the interrogation and the medical examination are some of the factors responsible for failure to complain. Victims also admit that they are often uncertain whether a crime has actually been committed. Reprisals, especially if the offender is a partner or ex-partner, are common.

Although these fears are largely justified, they do not affect all victims to the same degree. Confident, articulate, white women are in a stronger position to make claims and insist that they are taken seriously, as are women with a supportive family, partners or friends. In contrast, stigmatized groups within society, such as prostitutes and the poor, are most reluctant to report their rape, believing (often correctly) that they

The Overall Attrition Process for Rape Cases[24] *1996*
(actual proportions) $n = 483$

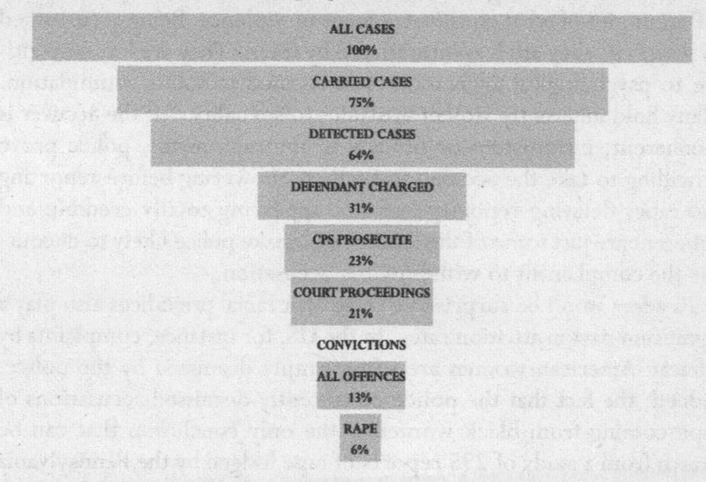

will be reproached for lying and that their sexual history will be widely broadcast.[25] There is even evidence that women perceived as being 'plain' or 'obese' are less likely to be believed when they cry rape, and are therefore less keen to report.[26] Women from ethnic minorities face great difficulties in reporting their abuse. In one study of eighty-eight women from ethnic minorities who sought help from the Haven Centre (a dedicated sexual assault referral service) between May 2000 and July 2001, only four were willing to have the police involved.[27]

Once a victim has gone to the police, however, a significant proportion of complaints are not taken seriously or followed up by the police. According to the Home Office in 1996, of all cases reported to the police, a quarter are not carried forward.[28] In contrast, only 3 per cent of *all* crimes are designated 'no crimes'.[29] Indeed, in many jurisdictions police are expected to 'unfound', 'clear' or 'no crime' a certain proportion of cases. Politicians, the Crown Prosecution Service and the courts all place immense pressure on the police to improve clear-up rates. As a consequence, if the police do not believe that there is a high chance of a successful prosecution, they attempt to persuade the complainant to drop the case. Often they have been able to do this by emphasizing (and even exaggerating) the ordeal of the trial.

In recent years there have been vast improvements in police education concerning sexual abuse, but many police officers remain deeply unsympathetic and distrustful of rape victims. Because the police are accustomed to working in an innately violent context, many have a very different idea of what constitutes force or violence. Being accustomed to weapons, they are less intimidated by them. They are less susceptible to psychological aggression; less attuned to subtle intimidation. Many hold inherently violent attitudes to sexuality.[30] If the accuser is incoherent, inconsistent or fits any of the rape myths, police prove unwilling to take the accusation further. Showering before reporting the rape, delaying reportage or not appearing totally credible and coherent are just some of the factors that make police likely to encourage the complainant to withdraw her accusation.

Readers won't be surprised to hear that racial prejudices also play a significant part in attrition rates. In the US, for instance, complaints by African-American women are often simply dismissed by the police. Indeed, the fact that the police consistently dismissed accusations of rape coming from black women is the only conclusion that can be drawn from a study of 295 reports of rape lodged by the Pennsylvania Police Department between 1 July and 7 December 1966. When both the accuser and accused were black, the police summarily decreed that 22 per cent of the rape claims were 'unfounded'. This was nearly twice the percentage deemed to be unfounded when both protagonists were white or where the accuser and accused were of different race (12 and 14 per cent respectively). Police lacked confidence in 'the veracity of black complainants' and adhered to the belief that black women were innately promiscuous.[31] Although the typical rape victim was precisely a young, poor black woman, because African-American women were assumed to be sexually voracious, they were placed outside the category of human capable of suffering sexual violation.

The problem is not simply a police culture infused with suspicion towards women claiming to have been raped. In 2002 the UK Crown Prosecution Service Inspectorate catalogued a vast range of problems with rape investigations. It admitted that, although the 'treatment afforded to rape victims throughout the investigative process is key to the prospects of securing a conviction', in reality there was a shortage of specialist staff available to receive rape victims. The 'environment into which a victim is taken is not always conducive to securing the confidence of the victim'. Indeed, waiting areas were 'of poor quality' and victims often had to wait for hours before being seen by staff. Although courts and jurors paid increasing attention to forensic evidence, many police stations did not have the facilities or procedures in place to enable forensic analysis. In fact, forensic medical examiners were generally only given 'on the job' training. Victims frequently had no choice of whether they were examined by a male or a female doctor. The recording and processing of cases was inconsistent; the preparation of cases for court sloppy.[32] How quickly could these basic flaws be remedied? Three years later, in February 2005, the Home Office still found it necessary to recommend that in the future complainants should be 'treated in a respectful and compassionate manner, by a skilled professional'. The attitude of policemen should shift from 'scepticism focusing on discreditability [sic]' to one of serious investigation, they blandly asserted.[33]

So, the police took 75 per cent of rape accusations forward, but they detected a suspect in only 65 per cent of cases. The suspect was actually charged, however, in fewer than one-third of cases. Even more worryingly, the Crown Prosecution Service agreed to prosecute in less than a quarter of instances and the case went to court in one-fifth of cases.

Once the accused were in court, a range of problems led to less than 6 per cent of men being convicted. Not surprisingly, sloppiness by the police in processing evidence was one significant reason for this low rate, but equally important is the fact that the 'rape myths' I analysed in Chapter 2, 'Rape Myths' and Chapter 3, '"No" Means "Yes"' are shared not only by the police and legal profession, but by jurors as well. In other words, the general public (or those called for jury service) have a conception about what constitutes 'rape' or 'sexual assault' that is much narrower than that decreed by law. To take one obvious example, the chances of a conviction against someone with whom a woman has had a previous relationship is exceptionally unlikely. As one experienced barrister admitted a few years ago,

> I feel very strongly about this. I feel very strongly that it's a great waste of public money to prosecute the ex-husband rape or the ex-boyfriend of rape unless there is extreme violence involved or it's part of some campaign of harassment. I have had to prosecute an awful lot of cases where people have still been sort of seeing each other after having a relationship, where he wants it and she doesn't and it happens. Well she says it was a rape and probably, yes, it really was. But frankly does it matter?[34]

It does. Such attitudes hark back to a time when, in legal terms, a woman could not be raped by her husband. It is also to appeal to a world in which women did not routinely have sex before marriage and, if a woman did, she married the man quickly afterwards and was 'faithful'.

Furthermore, jurors, defence counsel and judges not only expect a much higher level of resistance than required by law, they also require a greater degree of consistency in rape testimonies than they require from victims of other violent crimes. The fact that many victims naturally attempt to present their accounts in such a way as to counter rape myths (by understating the amount they drank, for instance), serves to simply spear the entire testimony as false. Discrepancies between what the victim told the police compared with what she told the doctor are also routinely mentioned. In their attempt to impose an internal logic or narrative coherence to their experience, victims often change their story. Both victims and jurors attempt to fit the story into their expectations of what rape 'really is like', but these expectations are drawn from television, newspaper report, and other sources. The problem is not that talk of rape has been silenced, but that it has been taken over by non-victims and has become ubiquitous. Through a multitude of cultural productions, jurors believe that they know what rape 'looks like', and disbelieve other scenarios. The '*CSI* effect' is strong: since jurors are rarely presented with decisive forensic evidence, which they expect, the rape story further loses veracity. 'Rape' has not been silenced: it is just that its narrative is only rarely told by rape victims, who are forced to tailor their courtroom account to strip it of its emotional dimensions and unique form within her embodied history.

Finally, for the complainant, the trial is a unique occasion in which her gender performance is most scrutinized. Every mannerism becomes crucial. Her clothes, hairstyle, posture, accent and tone of voice all take on immense significance. The woman is reduced to her body: what she was wearing, how she walked and her sexual attractiveness. Consent is inferred through the female victim's body, rather than the male perpetrator's actions. In this reduction of the woman to her body, she is diminished as not a full person under law and, indeed, within society. Few women are able to bear the burden of performance.

This becomes even more difficult in the face of interrogation in which the accused routinely frames his account in a passive voice, thus attributing agency and thus responsibility to the accuser. This is a particularly effective linguistic device. The defence asks why the alleged victim acted in particular ways. Why did she accept the drink? Why did she dance in a particular way? Why didn't she scream? Any action that the accuser failed to take is seen as bestowing responsibility. In contrast, the accused is rendered passive, merely a prop in the rape narrative.

New Punitiveness

There have been two main responses to the rising number of rape complaints and the falling proportion of successful prosecutions. As regards the first of these problems, there have been calls to 'get tough'. In the 1990s Alice Vachss, former head of the New York Special Victims Unit, was unequivocal in stating that rapists had been getting an easy time in the legal system. 'Rapism', she insisted, resembled an epidemic, but since there was no known cure for rapists, 'quarantine' was the only solution. People 'spend too much time trying to "understand" rapists from a treatment point of point', she complained, while they actually should be studying rapists 'from a combat point of view'. Understanding the enemy was worthwhile only if it helped to 'capture' them and 'put them down for the count'.[35] Three-quarters of a century earlier an unnamed journalist had expressed it just as bluntly, arguing that crimes against women were 'the work of that sort of utter beast who can be controlled only by fear'. If 'animals of that type' were allowed to imagine that the law was too feeble 'to prevent or even to avenge' their acts, then much more 'dastardly violence' was sure to follow.[36]

In response to the dramatic increase in sexual violence at the end of the twentieth century, a more punitive imperative crept into law enforcement. Initially this was part of a shift away from an individual-rights-based framework of justice to one concerned with the application of actuarial procedures in assessing the dangerousness of criminals and in managing risk-segregated populations. Treatment was jettisoned in exchange for 'tougher' penalties, increased employment of technologies of surveillance and community notification.

The 'new criminology' of the 1990s onwards focused on more punitive responses to sexual crimes. There was even a resurrection of arguments supporting corporal punishment, albeit given a modern 'spin' by appealing to uniform standards of efficiency, measurability and consistency.[37] Thus, in the mid-1990s, Whitney Wiedeman argued in the *American Journal of Criminal Law* for the use of electric shocks to punish offenders since shocks were 'more easily quantified and qualified as to the degree of punishment'. If that form of punishment was not sufficiently 'visible and visceral', then he proposed using 'some sort of whipping machine to assure greater uniformity in application'.[38]

Part of the reason Wiedeman argued for the return to corporal punishment for sex offenders was because of concern about the financial burden of incarceration. The USA had become one of the most carceral societies in the world and these prisons were not only exceptionally violent (rape and torture within maxi-units is routine) but were also grossly overcrowded. 'Two Strikes' or 'Three Strikes, And You Are Out' legislation proved popular with the American public and consequently legislators – but it also filled prisons to overflowing.[39] Prison terms were also being lengthened. For instance, in 1995 the legislature in Iowa summarily doubled the maximum term of incarceration for people convicted of more than one sexual offence.[40] Special laws were passed to increase the amount of time repeat offenders would have to spend in prison, as in Missouri's Repeat Sex Offender Statute of 1996. In the frenzy of legislators to outdo one another in being 'tough' on sex crimes, two facts tended to be ignored. First, the majority of defendants sentenced under 'Two Strikes' or 'Three Strikes' legislation were non-violent and, second, funding for increased levels of imprisonment was being taken from social programmes designed to prevent sex crimes from occurring in the first place.[41]

Increasingly punitive regimes also encourage the adoption of new technologies of control, including the use of the polygraph to predict future behaviour (and thus enable law-enforcement agencies to arrest and imprison people without returning them to court)[42] and electronic monitoring using radio frequencies or global positioning satellite systems. Under the UK 1998 Crime and Disorder Act, for instance, anyone cautioned or convicted of a sexual offence could have their movements restricted if their behaviour subsequently attracted suspicion.[43] All US jurisdictions introduced similar forms of monitoring.

By focusing on the disordered body of criminality, polygraphs and electronic tagging represented the blunter side of surveillance. From the 1990s many legal jurisdictions began imposing more free-floating forms of control. Responsibility for policing shifted away from law-enforcement agencies towards a vaguely defined entity called 'the community'. Although the registration of sex offenders has a long history – in California, for instance, registration started in 1947[44] – the best known was 'Megan's Law', named after seven-year-old Megan Kanka, who was raped and strangled by a convicted sex offender in Hamilton, New Jersey, in 1994. 'Megan's Law' permitted, among other things, the names and addresses of sex offenders to be published.

It was based on a number of assumptions, including that sex offenders would inevitably reoffend, that their crimes normally escalate and that if families knew that former sex offenders were in their midst they could take steps to protect their children. Within two years thirty-five states and the federal government had passed similar kinds of legislation requiring community notification of sex criminals and forty-nine states had sex-offender registration laws.[45] Typically these laws ended indeterminate sentencing (forcing judges to impose heavy penalties), established post-release supervision for all violent felony offenders and allowed the establishment of a national database at the FBI to track the whereabouts and movements of certain convicted sex offenders. They also required that information about sex offenders be disclosed to the public.

It was not simply an American phenomenon. In Britain the government passed the Sex Offender Act of 1997. Under this Act any person convicted of or cautioned for a sexual offence had to register with the police, who were allowed to inform local schoolteachers, employers and other members of the community of their whereabouts. Many of the offences committed by men under this legislation were not physically violent; extremely violent criminals (armed robbers or drug dealers, for instance) were not subjected to the same restrictions. Although protests against the legislation were raised on the grounds that it was a form of 'additional punishment' and violated rights to privacy, the Acts had widespread community support. American surveys consistently show between 79 and 82 per cent support.[46]

These laws allowed the authorities to disclose the names, addresses and crimes of offenders to the local communities they lived in.[47] It was a classic example of legislation driven by grassroots lobbying by bereaved parents. Children's names were attached to the laws, as in the Jacob Wetterling Crimes Against Children and Sexually Violent Offender Registration Act (1994), the Pam Lychner Sexual Offender Tracking and Identification Act (1996) and New York State's Jenna's Law (1998). It is significant that these 'named laws' reinforced the notion that 'innocent victims' were white and middle-class. The rape and murder of African-American or native-American children never became part of this legislative fanfare. Although it would have been politically impossible to identify the 'good victims' explicitly as white and middle-class, the ubiquitous publication of the girls' photographs performed the same function. In this way it was a form of symbolic violence, giving (in the words of social theorist Pierre Bourdieu) 'an action or a discourse the form which is recognised as suitable, legitimate, approved, that is, a form of the kind that allows the open production, in public view, of a wish or a practice that, if presented in any other way, would be unacceptable'.

By showing ostentatious respect for proper ways of 'doing things', force could be 'fully exercised while disguising its true nature as force'. In such a way a particular practice (such as honouring a white, middle-class 'good victim' with a named law while ignoring her underprivileged black counterpart) could gain 'recognition, approval and acceptance by dint of the fact that it can present itself under the appearance of universality – that of reason or morality'.[48]

The 'new punitive' approach to sex crimes is deeply flawed. Does increasing penalties for rape discourage potential criminals from acting against the law? Does it reduce the likelihood of recidivism among ex-convicts? The answer to these two questions is invariably 'no'.[49] Harry Mills, a serial exhibitionist, is fairly typical. Like most offenders, he always believed he would never get caught. He admitted that imprisonment 'puts me out of harm's way for a while', but

> apart from that aspect of it I can't see it does much good really. It certainly doesn't alter my character or disposition in any way, and if there's anything in the idea of deterrence, I should think that's long lost any relevance it might possibly have had. I don't even consider it now; I don't think 'Oh I might go to prison' or worry about being caught. It never comes into it, when I'm walking about such thoughts no longer even enter my head.[50]

Sexual abusers are rarely put off. Many stranger rapes take place almost as an afterthought – in the context of a burglary, for instance. More to the point, perpetrators don't conceive of their actions as abusive (so don't feel at risk) and, when they do, they believe that they are invulnerable anyway. *Other* men get caught; *they* won't.

Paradoxically, increasing penal penalties for rape may actually lead to a *reduction* of convictions for sexual abuse, as juries and judges choose to acquit defendants rather than impose punishments they believe are too harsh. Moreover, the best research on penal practices suggests that increasing punishments for individual perpetrators is only marginally (if at all) effective as a deterrent. The only convicts guaranteed not to reoffend are those killed, but even the most hardened pro-capital punishment advocates baulk at the prospect of executing most sex offenders. Sadistic stranger rapists, particularly if black and poor, could be shunted towards the electric chair, but they were scarcely representative of rapists, let alone sexual abusers generally.

We also need to take the protection of civil liberties seriously. The preventative state threatens these liberties. In the words of one analyst in the *Journal of Criminal Law and Criminology* in 1999,

> all free societies . . . must decide whether and to what extent those they fear are to be accorded liberties. This dilemma is surely evident with respect to sexual offenders who, although they have paid their debt to society as a result of incarceration, remain the subject of profound fear and disdain.

Compulsory community notification, the author went on, 'resembles methods of social control last employed in the American West of the mid-1880s', except that in the twenty-first century we have 'unwanted posters'.[51]

The cost of giving in to the moral panic about sexual abuse by imposing increasingly punitive punishments and modes of surveillance on offenders is high. After all, one of the main effects of 'notification' is increased vigilantism and hate crimes. Sex offenders are driven further underground and therefore away from established systems of support, either familial or institutional. Resentful, frustrated and rendered even less capable of reintegrating into society, these men are actually *more* likely to reoffend. Furthermore, notification gives a false sense of security. After all, family members sexually abuse children much more frequently than do tagged strangers. Unfortunately, with the current 'War on Terror' eroding the civil liberties of *all* citizens, and not just those deemed to have forfeited their rights by sexually abusing others, the boundary between what a state can do to 'them' and to 'us' has further crumbled. Now that torture and 'extraordinary rendition' have become an everyday part of American and British statecraft, punitive responses to current 'folk devils' such as terrorists and rapists does not look like diminishing.

Rape Reform: 'Rape as Assault'

The alternative approach to the sex-crime crisis is to reform the laws. These have taken two main forms. First, there has been the expansion of the concept of rape and sexual assault. I have discussed these shifts throughout this book. The exemption of husbands from rape accusations by their wives has been substantially (although not totally) removed. Date and acquaintance rape has become a legal reality. Women can be accused of raping men. Parts of the body deemed 'violable' by law have expanded. Second, rules of evidence have been reformed. Judges no longer issue a warning to jurors about the need for corroboration. They also don't need to issue the 'cautionary instruction'. Limits have been placed upon the accuser cross-examining the victim. 'Rape shield laws' have at least countered the legal assumption according to which women with prior sexual experience are fair game for sexual predators. When victims give evidence, the courts can be cleared of the public. In many jurisdictions, there are provisions for giving evidence via television or behind screens.

These rape law reforms have been analysed in detail in many texts. But most agree that these adjustments have failed. Rape shield laws are a good example of a reform that has had less impact in practice than hoped. The shield was introduced to encourage victims to report their crimes and to shift emphasis from the victim's behaviour to that of the perpetrator. Nevertheless, conviction rates did not improve substantially and little evidence exists that victims have become less terrified by the prospect of reporting and prosecuting the crime. Furthermore, a considerable degree of discretion is allowed to the police, prosecutors, and judges in deciding whether the alleged victim is even entitled to be 'shielded'. Alternative ways of bringing forth evidence of the victim's previous sexual relationship with the defendant are routinely exploited by defence counsel and, even more to the point, has been accepted by the British courts as a result of the introduction of the Human Rights Act 1998. Indeed, the 'rape shield' law was neutralised by the House of Lords in 2001 as a violation of the human rights of the accused (R v. A, 2001). The Law Lords found that this protection of the victim violated the right to fair trial of the accused under the European Convention of Human Rights and the Human Rights Act and rendered the protection inoperable.

These criticisms are not intended to deny that incremental reforms have been important. At the very least they have limited the damage caused to women in the course of the trial. Nevertheless, as the statistics at the start of this chapter show, the chances of a successful conviction are disgracefully low. Unless there is evidence of physical violence, rape remains tolerated before the law. Judges, jurors and law-enforcement officers still have no idea where the boundary between 'bad sex' and rape lies.

In recent years there have been calls for a more radical reform of rape law. In Chapter 1 I introduced some feminists who contend that rape is an act of power or aggression, not a sexual act. In some circles this insight has been used to argue that the law needs to eradicate rape legislation altogether. Instead acts that previously would have been prosecuted as rape should henceforth be prosecuted as assault.

Philosopher Michel Foucault persuasively made the case for radical change. He proposed that seeing rape as a *sexual* attack, as opposed to a form of assault, was to 'shore up the apparatus of repression, infusing sex with repressive power'.[52] Answering questions posed to him by a French commission concerned with the reform of the penal code, Foucault contended that 'sexuality can in no circumstances be the object of punishment'. When a legal system 'punishes rape one should be punishing physical violence and nothing but that'. Rape was 'nothing more than an act of aggression . . . there is no difference, in principle, between sticking one's fist into someone's face or one's penis into their sex'. Admitting that there were problems in asserting that rape was not more serious than a punch in the face, Foucault argued that

> sexuality as such, in the body, has a preponderant place, the sexual organ isn't like a hand, hair, or a nose. It therefore has to be protected, surrounded, invested in any case with legislation that isn't that pertaining to the rest of the body . . . [But it] isn't a matter of sexuality, it's the physical violence that would be punished, without bringing in the fact that sexuality was involved.[53]

This argument was consistent with Foucault's position under which sexuality was a regulatory technique employed by power to produce pliant and productive bodies.

There are important pragmatic grounds for being sympathetic to such a view. Because many men simply equate intercourse with pleasure, assertions that rape is assault both unpicks rape from sex but also (by associating it with an act men *are* likely to fear, that is, assault) enables men to empathize with victims. Most obviously, such a change in the law would benefit (some) victims. This basic fact has often been acknowledged, and not only by radical legal scholars. In 1974, for instance, D. Chipp, Australian Federal Liberal MP, observed that if rape was charged as assault 'you would see a lot more rapists charged in court. Girls could stand up to grilling to prove assault where the distressing and humiliating questions dragged up in an attempt to disprove rape would not be asked.'[54]

Some feminists, too, have argued for a gender-free, non-activity-specific law of rape in order to cut through insinuations of female culpability in their own victimization. It is important to recall that 'victim precipitation' (as I discussed in Chapter 3, '"No" Means "Yes"'), lives on today, and not only among men. An ICM poll in October 2005 found that one in every three *women* believe that women who acted flirtatiously are partially or totally responsible if they end up being raped and one in four *women* believe that women who wear sexy clothes are also partially or totally responsible if they are raped.[55] Self-restraint is doing the job of masking tape. Labelling rape as a form of assault might cause such attitudes to change.

The Foucauldian project of unpicking sex from regimes of institutional power is also highly attractive for another reason. There is a point in the argument that classifying rape as a sexual offence rather than assault creates woman as less than a full person. Her vagina is separated from her Self; she becomes a 'wounded space', as opposed to a full human subject. As Foucault also shows in his introduction to *The History of Sexuality*, the 'institutional incitement to speak about [sex]' actually constitutes a determination of the 'agents of power' to transform sexuality as something to be managed or policed. Sex becomes 'an issue, and a public issue no less; a whole web of discourses, special knowledges, analyses, and injunctions settled upon it'. The 'truth of sex' is sustained by networks of power.[56]

Nevertheless, in my view, the objections to the removal of 'sex' from 'rape' greatly outweigh any judicial advantages or theoretical niceties. Feminist philosophers such as Ann J. Cahill have presented the most important challenges to such a change. Cahill argues that rape is 'instrumental in the construction of the distinctly feminine body'. Women's bodies are 'produced within a context which, because of a hierarchy based on sex, marks them disproportionately and gender-specifically as weak, hostile, and responsible for the danger which constantly threatens them'. The horror of rape is precisely due to the 'constitutive element of a power discourse which produces her body as violable, weak, and alien to her subjectivity'. From this perspective, proposing to change the legal definition of rape (labelling it 'assault') is naïve. Rape is 'not reducible to legislation or the procedures of the criminal justice system. Indeed, to believe that such a change would have the desired result is to accept the legal realm as a highly privileged source of power with determinative effects.' Why should Foucault want to punish only one component (the assault) of rape? Why privilege violence over rape's 'role as an enforcement of a set of patriarchal, misogynist values'? Why is 'an attack with a penis distinct from an attack with any other body part?' Cahill asked, replying:

> precisely because the attack with the penis is the danger which is at the basis of the specifics of feminine bodily comportment. To desexualize the act of rape, to consider it legally only as any other assault, would be to obfuscate – not to weaken! – its role in the production of the sexual hierarchy through the inscription of individual bodies. Rather than resisting the insistent process of sexualization which Foucault describes and decries, it would in fact support the equally insistent process of sexual hierarchization which places women's bodies at such daily risk.

Foucault's proposal to remove the 'sex' from 'rape' serves only the interests of masculine sexuality.[57]

Cahill presents an extremely persuasive case. There are additional reasons to be wary about unpicking sex from rape, however. As I have discussed earlier, rape is discursively produced. What constitutes the 'sex' part of the definition has dramatically changed over time. Distinguishing between sex and power simply fails to acknowledge that both concepts have a history. Indeed, because the intimate relationship between notions of the self and sexuality simply did not exist until the eighteenth century (and then were not fully integrated into everyday concepts until well into the nineteenth century), any definition that posits rape as equivalent to assault makes a great deal more sense in that earlier period than it does today. In other words, an argument can be made that rape has *increasingly* become a sexual attack. For the nineteenth-century working woman the affront of rape was less to her sexual identity (let alone 'sexuality') and more to her class or respectability. This historical change will be discussed in greater detail in the last chapter.

For the purposes of the present argument, it is sufficient to observe that the sexualization of rape is a modern phenomenon – and has entered fully into rape narratives produced by rapists. In nineteenth-century narratives, for instance, when there was ambivalence about whether women were *capable* of sexual pleasure, rapists almost never attempted to demand a simulation of gratification. The fetishism of the orgasm came much later into rape discourses. Indeed, at precisely that historical moment when feminists were insisting that 'rape is about power not sex', rapists became most vocal in arguing that rape was about sex. It is the modern-day rapist who is much more likely to search for evidence of 'involuntary pleasure' in the female body. Lacking the visual evidence of pleasure (indeed, being confronted with visual evidence of pain) the rapist often either eroticizes that pain or gives primacy to the spoken word, savagely compelling a bogus recital of 'wanting it too'. In both, the rapist insists on the power of the word in evoking the 'little death'.

From the standpoint of modern subjectivities – strongly tied into notions of sexual identity – the separation of 'sex' from 'rape' would constitute a denial of the lived experience of many victims and perpetrators. As always, I have no sympathy for any definition of rape that ignores the experience of its victims: so long as rape victims continue to experience rape as different from non-sexual assault, it must be seen as such.

Rapists, too, choose a particular act of violence over other acts in full recognition of the cultural meaning assigned to that choice. Rapists confirm and extend their fragile subjectivity through a genitally orientated attack. They *choose* this particular way to oppress another person. It is not possible to pretend that, in dominant discourses of sexuality, the genitals are invested with the same significance as the fist. To reiterate, this is not to imply that genital contact *as such* is automatically sexual; but it has been labelled as sexual in a vast array of cultural productions within modern Western societies. The sexed body is constructed in these discursive mechanisms of power.

On a more prosaic level the assertion that rape is 'about' power not sex imposes a rigid, monolithic framework on an exceptionally diverse set of acts and actors. Acquaintance rape and stranger rape, paedophilia and gerophilia, prison buggery and marital assault cannot all be understood within a single category of motivation. And whose experience are we to prioritize in choosing between rape and power? Some victims identify their violation as an act of domination by the perpetrator – but others experience it in terms they characterize as primarily sexual. Most see it as a 'bit of each'. The sadism endured by the victim can be experienced as sexually exhilarating by the perpetrator. The meaning the victim assigns to the attack and the harm it causes may be influenced by perceptions of sexuality and domination, but responsibility for the act never budges from the perpetrator.

Feminist and Foucauldian discussions of 'power' do not restrict themselves to physical violence. But their proposal that rape should be treated as assault will make it much harder to bring many sexual abusers before a judge. Many rapists – especially those who know their victim – employ a series of tactics to engage in sexual intercourse with a woman before resorting to force. They bribe her, buy her too many alcoholic drinks or drugs, falsely promise love or threaten to break off the relationship and 'take the kids'. Aggression may accompany rape; but it is often a tactical weapon once other options have been exhausted, as opposed to an objective in itself.[58] Often men just don't 'see' the violence in many forms of coercion. If there is no wound, where is the hurt?

There are also definitional difficulties with the 'power not sex' dichotomy. What would be needed to decide whether an act was motivated by 'sex' rather than 'power'? In many surveys of rapists' motivations there seems to be an assumption that if a perpetrator had a consensual sexual partner (a wife or girlfriend), then by definition he had no 'need' for sex, making the attack something else than serving sexual needs.[59] It is common for sociologists to distinguish between power, anger and sex rapes. But might not all three motivations coexist? Might the driving force for the rape shift in the course of any single attack? Indeed, why should we exclude a host of completely different motivations, as in studies that show that rapists often characterize the pleasure of rape in terms of excitement and risk-taking rather than either sex or domination?[60] Motivations for rape vary immensely and by a constantly multiplying set of criteria. After all, it is no coincidence that, according to the *OED*, the word 'rapist' was first used in 1883, in an article in the *National Police Gazette*, in connection with 'nigger rapist'. Race cannot be effaced.[61] Age, generation, personality, peer group, political stance and ideology all impinge on the composition of abusive discourses. As I will be arguing in the next chapter, doesn't the 'sex versus power' dichotomy simply shore up some of those other binaries that have got us into trouble in the first place: male aggressor and female victim, for instance?

It is difficult, further, to see how changing the language of the law will automatically increase conviction rates. Won't labelling the act of rape a form of assault simply take away the social stigma associated with the word 'rape'? Unlike incarcerated rapists, men in prison on assault charges may actually be glorified by their peers. If rape myths remain intact, even radical fiddling with legislation won't make any difference for victims.

Rape is a central way in which power operates within our society. The problem of rape rests at every level of society and law. Punitive responses to convicted rapists allow a host of actual rapists free to operate within society. Widening surveillance targets the victims as much as their abusers. And it makes women scared. Rape reforms address neither the broader acceptance of rape myths (and thus allow juries to acquit with impunity) and fail to acknowledge that the law not only attempts to remedy injustices; it actually creates oppression. It does this by positing the legal subject as an autonomous, rational individual outside of her or his social, economic or political context. The notion of 'inflicting harm' is biased towards physical assault or property rights (of a husband over his wife's sexual body, for instance). The term 'consent' is never defined. Indeed, because of the legal assumption that the male acts (proposes or attempts sex), while the female simply reacts (by uttering a 'yes' or 'no'), the very notion of consent situates woman as subordinate. This differential construction of male and female subjects is exacerbated by the Cartesian distinction of mind-body upon which the law is based. As I implied in Chapter 3, the gendered dimension of the mind-body split results in legal decisions in which the *mens rea* (mental responsibility) in conjunction with the *actus reus* (conduct) of the male perpetrator overrides the integrity of the *corpus delicti* (body of crime) of the woman victim. As Nicola Lacey, eminent feminist legal scholar, has shown in her *Unspeakable Subjects* (1998), the law is coded masculine through and through.[62] It is male interests masquerading as human interests. No piecemeal reforms will be able to change this fact.

SECTION SEVEN

Resistance

Accomplices,
All of you, now – though now is still too late –
Bring on the missing evidence! Reveal the coiled
Venom, the curse that needs
Only a touch to be articulate.

CECIL DAY LEWIS, 'SEX-CRIME'.[1]

CHAPTER FIFTEEN

Violence, Politics, Erotics

Rapists are given an inordinate amount of attention in our society. Our interest in perpetrators of sexual violence arises out of a need to forge a bifurcated image of the world neatly divided into 'them' and 'us'. This black-and-white ethics obscures both the banality of evil that rapists embody and the fact that the seemingly 'unrestrained tyrannical desire' of abusers is always contested. In focusing on the horror sexual abusers inspire, it is easy to be deaf to the cries of their victims: why are *you* doing this to *me*?

In this book rapists and sexual abusers have bombarded you and me with rationalizations and justifications for their cruelty. Criminologists, jurists, psychologists, and sociologists have attempted to 'make sense' of sexual violence but, as I have shown, their efforts have been crucial to the process of constructing not only 'the sex offender' but sexuality itself. 'Normal' and 'abnormal' sexual practices have changed dramatically in historical time. Rape and other sexual abuses have uniformly been conceived as extreme wrongs, but the boundaries between these practices and 'bad sex' have not remained constant. White, elite, heterosexual men have monopolized definitions of sexual abuse, effectively masking the full range of human (particularly female) suffering. We have been exposed to a universe of excuses for sexual brutality. Should we despair?

Masculinity and the Rapacious Penis

It is easy to portray masculinity as steeped in the poison of latent and tangible sexual violence. Feminist theorist Catharine MacKinnon is generally paraded out to represent the extreme form of male-bashing. 'What do men want?' she asks. According to her, the answer to this question can be found in pornography. Men want

> women bound, women battered, women tortured, women humiliated, women degraded and defiled, women killed. Or, to be fair to the soft core, women sexually available, have-able, there for them, wanting to be taken and used, with perhaps just a little light bondage . . . Perhaps gender must be maintained as a social hierarchy so that men will be able to get erections; or, part of the male interest in keeping women down lies in the fact that it gets men up.[2]

The author of *The Americanization of Sex* (1988) was equally despondent. 'Not every man is a rapist,' he admitted, before immediately adding, 'But if we were to say that every man in our society is a potential rapist, that might not be so far afield.' According to this author, modern Western culture encourages a tendency to 'link sex with coercion'. The 'difference between rape and normal male sexual aggression' is 'basically one of degree'.[3] It was a view in line with the comment by Sharon Deevey in 'Such a Nice Girl' (1975) that 'every fuck is a rape even if it feels nice'.[4] Many activists in the anti-rape movements share such views. Their struggles in the front line of the sex wars give credibility to their pessimist assessment that Eros and Thanatos may be entwined and have a masculine gender.

Some historians of sexual violence are similarly disheartened. Thus Jane Caputi in *The Age of Sex Crime* (1987) put it bluntly when she urged readers not to be fooled by intimations that the rapist-murderer is 'despised', 'tabooed' and 'reviled' by 'patriarchal culture'. The superficially negative stereotypes applied to aggression are hypocritical, she argues, since the violent male is actually society's 'ultimate man'. He is Western culture's 'subliminal hero, the inevitable enactment of phallocracy's most fundamental conceptions of manhood and godhood'. In modern patriarchy, she persists, sexual violence against women is 'secretly desired, approved, institutionalized, and ultimately mandated. That *secretly* is key.'[5] Lawrence Kramer agrees, arguing in *After the Lovedeath: Sexual Violence and the Making of Culture* (1997) that 'modern western culture both promotes and rationalises violence against women'. Indeed, he continued, the 'tendency to sexual violence seems lodged in the very core of ordinary subjectivity like a bone in the throat'.[6] Most famously, Susan Brownmiller concurred, noting in her influential polemic *Against Our Will* (1975) that early man's

> discovery that his genitalia could serve as a weapon to generate fear must rank as one of the most important discoveries of prehistoric times, along with the use of fire and the first crude stone axe. From prehistoric times to the present, I believe, rape has played a critical function. It is nothing more or less than a conscious process of intimidation by which *all* men keep *all* women in a state of fear.[7]

MacKinnon advises people to 'compare victims' reports of rape with women's reports of sex. They look a lot alike.'[8] Similar rhetorical claims on the universal tendency of men to be sexually aggressive have been repeated in many of the texts I have analysed here.

We should not be tempted, however, by apocalyptic fantasies or simplistic slogans. The popular aphorism that 'all men are either rapists, rape-fantasists, or beneficiaries of a rape-culture' has become damaging for modern feminism. Despite Caputi's warnings against being duped by patriarchal society's repudiation of sexual violence, it is more plausible to argue that sexually aggressive men in modern Western society actually enervate male power. Rapists are not patriarchy's 'storm troopers', but its inadequate spawn. As a fifty-three-year-old rapist of three young girls whimpered in the 1950s, 'Now I'm all gone – going back like before I was nineteen – bashful, afraid, no sex, getting old, and going back [to prison].'[9]

Moreover, sexual predators don't only threaten and undermine the power of individual men. They corrode the category 'man' and its (imaginary) phallic edifice. In the modern period compulsory heterosexuality, marriage vows and the gendered division of labour have been particularly effective ways of controlling women. Although fear of rape has enabled men to assume the mantle of benevolent protectors while further confining 'their' womenfolk to domestic and other purportedly safe spheres, fear is a particularly blunt instrument of domination. The actions of men on the streets, intimidating, harassing and assaulting women, jeopardize the bastion of mature masculinity. Domesticated rapists (husband-rapists, for instance) subvert and threaten masculine governance, in part because they incite female resistance by exposing the brutal force beneath patriarchy's caress.

There are other problems with the notion that 'all men' have a tendency (whether innate or learnt) to engage in sexual violence: the accusation has rarely ever been hurled at *all* men. Throughout this book I have shown that the slogan 'all men are potentially rapists' has often been given a racist twist. African-American men, for instance, have been conceived of as being plagued by 'irresistible, and animal-like urges'. From the immensely popular film *The Birth of a Nation* (1915) to the obsession with the O. J. Simpson and Mike Tyson trials, black men have been portrayed as naturally rapacious. This vicious stereotype has even been used to *defend* African-American men from rape accusations, as in the trial of former heavyweight boxing champion Mike Tyson for the rape of Desiree Washington in 1991. Tyson's defence team emphasized Tyson's reputation as a 'sex-obsessed black athlete'. They also appealed to the corresponding stereotype of the sexually abandoned black woman. As one analyst of the trial pointed out, the defendant's legal team told the jury, in effect, that

> Tyson is your worse nightmare – a vulgar, socially inept, sex-obsessed black athlete. And any woman who would voluntarily enter a hotel suite with him must have known what she was getting into. In other words, both principals were animals – the black man for the crudity of his sexual demands, the black woman for eagerly acceding to them.[10]

Elsewhere in this book I have shown that other male minorities have been singled out as especially prone to violate woman: adolescent thugs, impoverished men, male immigrants and men viewed as unattractive have been most frequently stigmatized, while white professionals and middle-class husbands have been let off the hook.

Arguing that sexually aggressive men in modern Western society may enfeeble patriarchal power should not lead us to ignore the existence of an heroic tradition of rape – particularly in art of the Renaissance (although not earlier),[11] as well as in the contemporary glorification of hyper-masculinity in cinema and key sections of youth culture. Nor is it to underestimate the degree to which rape is trivialized and condoned in some aspects of popular culture. This book is packed with examples.

It is also vital to draw a distinction between competing masculinities within modern culture. Violence is assessed differently in various communities; its sexual manifestations are less stigmatizing in some contexts, even if rapacious tendencies and sexually aggressive acts almost always incite some degree of shame, embarrassment and guilt. Indeed, the stigma attached to being branded a rapist lies behind many misogynistic attempts to restrict that label to incidents involving sadistic stranger rape.

As I have already mentioned, even within the criminal fraternity, the disgrace attached to a (civilian)* rapist is palpable. Murderers might boast of their exploits; rapists rarely. The warden of Green Haven Correctional Facility in New York State was blunt. Rapists 'are not respected inside the prison', he lectured, adding, 'We got all the hard rocks here. Guys who hold up banks, shoot cops – macho types. They're respected, but not rapists.'[12] The capacity for physical violence is highly rated as a masculine trait within penal institutions, but demonstrations of *sexual* violence against women and children let slip that the man is weak and despicable. 'Skinners' (as such prisoners are called) risked being sexually assaulted in turn.[13] By damaging the myth that men have a responsibility for protecting weaker women (especially female 'chattels', that is, their daughters, sisters, girlfriends and wives), the rapist threatens the myth upon which modern manliness is constructed. He is the failed man, the person deficient in sex. His 'success' is due to 'brute force and not personal appeal', scoffed the authors of an article in *Issues in Criminology* in the early 1970s.[14] This argument was repeated in a slightly different form by the author of *Crime and Criminals* three-quarters of a century earlier. Drawing on his experience in the New York City Asylums for the Insane, this author concluded that the typical rapist was 'reticent, bashful, not interested in the common sports of boyhood. Lewd conversation always disgusted him. He evinced a great desire to be cured of his weakness as he is anxious "to become a man yet".'[15] Manliness is precisely the trait rapists lack and, perhaps equally importantly, are *seen to* lack.

This may help explain why so many perpetrators of sexual violence are keen to portray themselves as wounded, incomplete men. As one rapist stammered, 'It's different from anything else I've ever done. I feel more guilt about this. It's not consistent with me. When I talk about it, it's like being assaulted myself . . . I feel like I wasn't being myself'.[16] Whatever we might think about the self-serving nature of applying psychiatric diagnosis such as Post-Traumatic Stress Disorder on men who engaged in orgies of rape and murder in wartime, it at least acknowledges the 'disorder' of aggression.

*In Chapter 12, 'The Prison', I argued that the man who raped other men *in prison* could reap significant rewards.

There are other reasons for destabilizing the purported intrinsic link between adult manliness and aggression. Most obviously, it ascribes too much power to an allegedly rapacious penis. This dangerous inverted phallic worship can be criticized from two perspectives: the first addresses the supposed relationship between aggressivity and the penis in the context of empirical studies of sexual performance in rape; the second emphasizes the theoretical inadequacies in its conception of the male sexed body.

Empirical studies consistently show that an extremely large proportion of rapes are 'attempted', not 'completed'. The targeted victim fights or frightens the man off. I will be discussing the importance of resistance to victimization later. Nevertheless, even without effective resistance, the sexual body of the perpetrator frequently fails to fulfil its own set objective. For instance, over one-third of men convicted for sexual assault and sent to the Massachusetts Center for the Diagnosis and Treatment of Sexually Dangerous Persons suffered some kind of sexual dysfunction during the attack. Impotence (16 per cent of these criminals) and retarded ejaculation (15 per cent) were particularly common. This is likely to be a conservative estimate since dysfunction was inapplicable in one-fifth of the cases (because the victim successfully resisted, penetration was not attempted, or the assault was interrupted). Only a quarter of the rapists reported *no* physiological dysfunction during their rape. None of the offenders reported similar dysfunction in their consensual sexual relationships. Since most rapists are not caught, the authors decided to question *victims* about their attackers' sexual responses. According to victims' reports, fewer than half the aggressors managed to ejaculate.[17] Of course, the assumptions behind such statistics are problematic. Particularly troubling is the way the researchers consistently assume that 'good sex' for men means erection, ejaculation and orgasm. Despite this flawed assumption, these findings underscore the fact that sexual pleasure is not an inevitable outcome for the rapist, although anticipation of orgasm may have been one of the motivating factors.

As I have implicitly shown, the harm and suffering of rape is not caused solely by penile penetration, but by the confrontation with the aggressor's entire body – teeth, nails, belly. Assailants insist on kissing, playing with breasts, massaging, masturbating, peeing, displaying pornography, pulling hair, burning with cigarettes, cutting with knives and so on. As already discussed in Chapter 8, the penis is a deeply flawed instrument of domination. Penile rape is a highly unstable form of torture, both as performance (erectile dysfunction is common) and as strategy, peeling back the genteel camouflage masking vicious power relations.

There is other evidence, moreover, to suggest that men who sexually abuse women experience less pleasure from (both coerced and consensual) intercourse than non-abusive men. In the 1960s the sociologist Eugene Kanin studied a random sample of 400 full-time undergraduate males at a large, co-educational university in the Midwest. On the basis of their own descriptions of dating behaviour, he divided students into two categories: non-aggressive and 'offensively aggressive' men. To be placed in the second group, the man had to admit that he had made 'a forceful attempt for intercourse' that he perceived to be 'disagreeable and offensive to the girl involved'. In addition, he had to 'indicate that the female responded to his aggressive conduct with offended reactions', such as fighting, crying, screaming or pleading.

Because of his interest in the purported link between frustration and aggression, Kanin asked whether 'offensively aggressive men' were more likely to be sexually frustrated because of a 'lack of legitimate sexual outlets'. His findings confounded the hypothesis. Sexually aggressive men had significantly more sexual encounters than their non-aggressive counterparts. In addition, they were more persistent in seeking out new sexual conquests and were much more likely to use a range of techniques aimed at securing intercourse (including attempting to get the woman drunk and falsely professing love). This finding made Kanin question one of his basic assumptions. 'Up to this point,' he admitted, he had assumed that 'the absence of heterosexual encounters can be translated into sexual frustration. However, to experience frustration, one must first aspire for the elusive goal.' In contrast with the non-aggressive males who seemed quite content and satisfied with their sexual experiences, the 'erotically more successful males' (as Kanin bizarrely dubbed the 'offensively aggressive men') were discontented. Over half of the men in the aggressive category said that they were dissatisfied with their sex lives, in contrast with less than one-third of the non-aggressive males. In other words, those men who both experienced sexual intercourse most frequently and who had shown a willingness to use 'offensively aggressive' tactics to achieve intercourse were the least satisfied sexually.

The reason for this paradox, according to Kanin, lay in the differing sexual aspirations of the two groups. Sexual aggressives were more likely to be involved in groups (such as fraternities) that emphasized and rewarded sexual activity. Nearly a quarter of aggressive men reported that their friends pressured each other 'a great deal' or 'considerably' to seek sexual experiences, compared with only 6 per cent of non-aggressive men. The 'stigma' of virginity was also much stronger among men in the aggressive group. In other words, sexually aggressive men were least sexually contented because they were 'undergoing the experience of relative deprivation'. They were 'dissatisfied only by virtue of their high aspiration'. It is noteworthy that Kanin does not investigate the other possibility – that men who have sex only with eager women might be experiencing more emotional and erotic satisfaction because they *actually were* getting 'better sex'.[18]

In Kanin's random sample the young men who acted aggressively tended to be profoundly unhappy with their sex lives. More importantly, the fiction of a universal male sexual belligerence is theoretically unsupportable. As feminist theorist Sharon Marcus perceptively observed, taking 'male violence or female vulnerability as the first and last instances in any explanation of rape is to make the identities of rapist and raped pre-exist the rape itself'.[19]

The claim that the rapist is inescapably male is theoretically problematic for two reasons. First, it ignores sexual violence carried out by women and according to notionally feminine precepts. I have discussed this in Chapter 8, 'Female Perpetrators; Male Victims'. Second, it forges an immutable link between the male sex organ and violence, thus constructing the penis exclusively as a weapon, devoid of grace. This fallacy – sometimes referred to as the 'loaded gun' presentation of the penis – is widely held. It appears time and again in media representations of male sexuality. In the toe-curling comic film *There's Something About Mary* (1998), for instance, the character Don berates Ted about his dating rituals. 'You choke the chicken before any big date don't you?' he asked. 'Tell me you spank the monkey before any big date. Oh my God, he doesn't flog the dolphin before a big date. Are you *crazy*? That's like going out there with a loaded gun.' Ted responds by exclaiming, 'Holy shit, I've been going out with a loaded gun.' Even in serious scholarship, such as in the book *Stopping Rape* (1985), readers are told that 'a phallus is a substitute gun'.[20] In many representations the man is presented as possessing a dangerous weapon, his penis, which must be defused before encountering a woman. The male sexual organ is assumed to be voraciously and aggressively needy, easily bypassing the brain. Once aroused, it is an uncontrollable force. Contrary to the commonly heard cliché that, according to dualistic ways of thinking, Man represents 'Culture' while Woman is 'Nature', manliness is more frequently identified with primitiveness.

In my view this way of conceiving of the male sex organ is simplistic and much too negative. Not only does it fail to address sexual pleasure involving the male body, but it bestows too much authority in that appendage. Contrary to assertions that the penis (often misnamed the phallus) is the primary site for the realization of patriarchal and misogynistic power, it is, in fact, a hesitant and unstable organ, presenting an 'indeterminate set of possibilities'.[21] After all, the genital revolution of male adolescence, unanticipated hormonal surges and erectile diffidence exposes the male body as an anxious instrument and container of agency and identity. In that sexed body, the clichéd relation between male sexuality and power patently crumbles.

Feminism and Female Suffering

What about the other side to the purported link between aggressive sexuality and manliness? If, as Sharon Marcus observed, the identity of the rapist is portrayed as though it pre-exists any act of aggression, so too the identity of the rap*ed* is often portrayed as pre-existing any violation. If Man becomes an amorphous threat, free-floating, signifying danger, then Woman is (always) scared. Before His body, She quakes. As I emphasized earlier in this book, the female body is often portrayed as already, and always, violated. Before any penetration (consensual or not) the woman's body 'precipitates' attack. By virtue of being female, the woman is already 'victim', the wounded, suffering, gendered subject. She is defined in relation to 'it', the penis.

In this sense the words 'fear' and 'rape' have become intimately connected. As a result, many commentators – only some of whom are feminists – have argued that the whole *point* of rape for men as a class is to create dread in women as a class. 'Poor, helpless woman!' lamented a Kansas lawyer in 1901. The 'monstrous crime' of rape, he excitedly proclaimed, pursues women

> like a nightmare. It is an ever present peril to every woman in the land. Must she shun every alley and fly from every bush lest lascivious eyes be on her and unbridled, brutal passion block her way? Of all the hobgoblins abroad in the night, in fact or fancy, or in song or story, there is none so hideous as the stealthy form of the lecherous brute that leaps forth out of the darkness and drags defenceless woman to her ruin.[22]

Half a century later more detached statisticians set out to quantify women's fear. Innumerable surveys have been conducted. A recent UK poll revealed that nearly one-third of women claimed to be personally afraid of being raped.[23] This fear can be traced back in time. A 1949 poll in Philadelphia found that 90 per cent of women and half of men were afraid to walk in the street at night.[24] From the 1960s onwards the fear of crime generally, and of sex crimes in particular, also showed sustained and pronounced increase. Indecent assault was ranked as 'the worst crime', according to a large random poll of adults in England and Wales in 1960. It was regarded as more dreadful than cruelty against children or planning murder for money.[25] Later surveys came to similar conclusions. In the mid-1980s a survey of 1236 women in London revealed that more than half were often or sometimes frightened when they went out alone in daytime and three-quarters were uneasy, frightened or very frightened when going out alone at night. Startlingly, 81 per cent were 'sometimes or often' frightened even when at home alone in the daytime.[26] Not surprisingly, perhaps, this is a particularly female fear. According to a study in 1995, 72 per cent of women feared for their safety after dark, compared with only 27 per cent of men.[27] Another American survey, conducted two years later, found that over half of women changed their behaviour because of fear of violence, compared with only a quarter of men.[28] These fears were linked to dread of crime more generally, which was also rising from the late 1960s.[29] As fear of all types of crime rose, so too did women's specific fear of sexual crime. Ironically, women are actually *less* at risk of being assaulted than men, but because rape is believed to accompany all other face-to-face crimes, female fear is greater. In such a way rape becomes the 'master offence', generating free-floating fear relating to crime more generally. It is an ambient fear, a low-level but constant unease.

It must be added, however, that it is wrong to speak of *women's* overwhelming fear of rape, as though both levels of fear and responses to it do not differ by race, class, generation, ideological orientation and a host of other characteristics. After all, in most surveys the 'woman' being spoken about was white and middle-class. Their fears were often linked to anxieties about miscegenation and racial 'others'. Even rape education courses, such as the extremely popular 'Model Mugging' self-defence programmes of the 1970s and 1980s, employed examples of rape that played to the prejudices of white women. Their rape scenarios often assumed that the predominately white, middle-class and educated women on these courses would be 'immediately suspicious when they encounter a man of color on the street but not when they enter a fraternity party at a private university'.[30] In contrast, many ethnic minority women found that speaking about fear of violence from men within their own community fed racist prejudices and became a form of self-harm. For these women the terror caused by the threat of rape could be significantly less than their trepidation of increasing the police presence on their streets. Finally, for female shift-workers or those required to work at night, fear is an emotional luxury too expensive to indulge.

Keeping these differences in mind, it is nevertheless true that a powerful rhetoric has emphasized the vulnerability of women to male sexual violence in recent decades. Time and again, radical critiques of women's 'lot' stress that rape is 'indigenous, not exceptional, to women's social condition' and 'every female from nine months to ninety years is at risk'.[31]

Although it is certainly not the intention (see the poster 'Dead Men Don't Rape', below), this emphasis on female vulnerability draws attention away from female resilience. As I mentioned earlier, women resist rape – often successfully. Indeed, faced with danger, resistance is the most effective strategy, dramatically reducing the risk of actually being raped. In the late 1970s, for instance, a national US victimization survey of 22,000 women found that when the potential victim screamed, ran away or reasoned with the attacker, four out of five

Poster in the collection of Jane Ellen Swift, Sydney

rape attempts were not completed. In contrast, two-thirds of the women who did not attempt to resist were raped.[32] Other researchers concluded that employing more than one form of self-defence (screaming as well as fighting) was the most effective way of reducing the risk of being raped. They also found that the 'strategy often encouraged by the police' (that is, crying and pleading) was 'rarely effective on its own'.[33]

In response to critics who claimed that women who resisted rape were more likely to be injured, researchers found that the correlation between degree of resistance and injuries existed only because victims resist more strongly *when* they are being injured. Thus a couple of Canadian scholars in the 1980s examined a sample of 136 police reports of rape, coding for injury that was incurred after the rapists' initial attempts to subdue the woman. They concluded that 'resistance, whether precipitated by injury or not, was associated with a lower probability for subsequent injury'.[34]

A few years later the UCLA researchers Sarah Ullman and Raymond Knight examined 274 rape victims, finding that 85 per cent of the women who physically resisted did so in response to the perpetrator's violence. The remaining 15 per cent physically resisted in response to verbal aggression. Those women who resisted physically in response to physical attack were more likely to avoid rape than those who did not. In addition, the 'potential for physical injury was no greater for these women [who physically resisted] than for those who used other resistance strategies or who offered no resistance'. In other words, 'the correlation between physical resistance and injury of the woman' was the 'result of the initial level of the offender's violence'. Rapists inflicted the same level of injury irrespective of the way their victim responded. Threats made by aggressors were used to gain control of the victim and were often not carried through. It was the 'offender's aggression, and *not* the victim's resistance' that was 'responsible for physical injury'. Like previous researchers, they found that pleading and crying might actually *increase* the likelihood that the rape was completed (although not the severity of any injuries) because it encouraged the rapist to see himself as powerful and in control. It confirmed the rapist's view of how a woman should act. The most effective resistance strategy was to fight and scream, a strategy used by only 22 per cent of women, while 56 per cent of victims used the least effective strategy of begging and pleading. Finally, they found that women who resisted also coped better with the emotional aftermath of the attempted or completed rape. They felt less self-blame.[35] Unfortunately, some studies on the effectiveness of female resistance have been used as part of misogynistic arguments against women who fail to ward off attack, implying that they were somehow complicit in their own victimization.

Belittling the propensity of women to resist rape (whether, in hindsight, they employed the most 'effective' strategy or not) is only one problem with the emphasis on pervasive female passivity. It also constructs woman as the suffering subject outside of time and culture. Yet psychological trauma has *not* always been seen as the dominant effect of rape. Responses to painful, frightening sexual violation are culturally constructed. For many working-class women in nineteenth-century Britain and America, for instance, the harm of sexual abuse was located less in her psychological 'self' and more in her social and economic standing. The rapist endangered the nineteenth-century woman by attempting to undermine her class position, earning power or respectability. Early accounts made much more of the pain of defloration and ejaculation ('leaving wet') than do accounts today. Sexual attack then was less a matter of offence to sexual identity than an affront to a woman's ability to support herself. As a consequence, women placed emphasis on physical injury and the threat of pregnancy. The abuser was 'spoiling' or 'ruining' a female victim's gendered social position.[36]

In contrast, by the twentieth century the consequences of rape were no longer seen as 'a question of debauchery but of the shattering of identity, an incurable wound to which the victim seems doomed', in the words of Georges Vigarello's perceptive analysis of rape in France.[37] Rape had become an attack upon a woman's sexual identity, creating a 'psychic wound', a 'violation of the self', since a person's identity was much more likely to be defined in terms of sexuality. This intense focus on the body as marker of identity and as a locus of truth is a profoundly modern conception.

This tying of sexual acts more tightly into notions of the self and identity had other effects, too. Most notably it broadened accepted definitions of rape to include forced sexual encounters between spouses and acquaintances. As sex became linked increasingly to psychological events, shifting away from genitals and reproduction, the 'wrong' of date rape and marital rape acquired much greater significance. These were attacks not simply on the body but on the very integrity of the self.

This is obviously not to deny that female rape victims in the earlier period experienced intense psychological distress. However, the languages of the time made them express their agony more easily in terms of physical and economic ruin as opposed to psychic damage. This conception of the female body was echoed in forensic texts of the time. Nineteenth-century accounts employed the language of insanity and of the disordered body in order to discuss the aftermath of rape. In the influential textbook *Medical Jurisprudence, Forensic Medicine, and Toxicology* (1894), for instance, the authors agreed that the 'effect upon the health and mind of the [rape] victim may be disastrous', even though they located the 'disaster' in the topography of the body rather than any psychic space. In their words, convulsions were a common aftermath, as was

> a delirium in which the man and the whole scene pass again through the sufferer's disordered brain. Despair over the loss of her fair name and chastity may end in melancholia, in turn changing to suicidal mania. The shock to the system is sufficient to ruin forever the health in some cases and hurry the woman to an early grave. Hysteria, chorea, epilepsy even, are in the train of consequent nervous disorders. An attempt at violation is often the drop which makes the glass overflow.[38]

In these conceptualizations rape was seen less as a matter of identity or 'inner trauma'. It concerned the destruction of the women's mental equilibrium resulting from the loss of 'fair name and chastity'. While modern trauma narratives imply that a non-traumatic prior self exists that is ruptured by the assault, from the perspective of the 1890s the women's body was already infected with insanity, which sexual violation quickened (the 'drop which makes the glass overflow'). This is a world away from the languages employed in the twentieth century, in which psychoanalytical understandings of the relationship between body and mind are dominant.

This historically inflected balance between social ('external') and psychological ('internal') trauma resulting from sexual violation has had a major impact upon feminist strategy. Earlier generations of feminists were keen to portray women as resilient in the face of sexual violence.[39] The threat of sexual violence was to be fought through comprehensive intervention in social structures. Social purity and temperance campaigns of the late nineteenth century, for instance, hoped to encourage male continence and end male brutality towards women. These first-wave feminists placed great faith in the ballot and legal reform. [See cartoon, below.] As one activist engaged in a campaign to raise the age of consent observed in 1886,

> As to leaving the reform desired entirely to the men, we have left it entirely to them for three hundred years, for this disgrace to our civilization dates back to the common law of England, but the advancement of society has not caused legislation on this point to advance one iota . . . We think three hundred years is long enough to wait the tardy action of the men who make our laws.[40]

Cover of the *White Ribbon Ensign*, the journal of the Women's Christian Temperance Union, October 1911

Or, as temperance leader Frances Willard put it more succinctly, 'Men alone will never gain the courage thus to legislate against other men.'[41] For these feminists 'Votes for Women' would empower women, forcing politicians to take heed. Similarly, expanding the right to divorce would enable wives to escape their abusive husbands. As 1860s feminists such as Elizabeth Cady Stanton and Susan B. Anthony urged, crimes against women were due to male sexual privilege and men treating women as property. Divorce rights would mean that a woman's 'no' would really mean 'no'. Even as late as the 1960s feminists were prone to argue that rape was 'not the worst thing that could happen to a woman'.[42]

Second-wave feminists from the 1970s onwards were also passionately engrossed in similar kinds of reforms. In particular, as I discussed in the previous chapter, they fought successfully to reform rape law by introducing degrees of rape and limiting the admissibility of evidence of a victim's sexual past ('rape shield laws'). Broadening definitions of rape and sexual abuse to include forms that victims identified as abusive (date and marital rape, for instance) would not have happened without their incessant lobbying.

In the 1970s and 1980s, however, one influential feminist strand about rape moved decisively towards a trauma model and the notion of women's pervasive victimization. In Sharon Marcus's words, 'female vulnerability' came to 'pre-exist the rape itself'. Some feminist therapists went so far as to argue that *all* women were suffering from Post-Traumatic Stress Disorder or 'insidious trauma'. As one feminist argued, 'No one has *yet* beaten or raped me, or torn me from my home or taken my job or threatened my life. That is not to say that no one even will.' Every woman was a sufferer from PTSD brought on by the stress of knowing that 'they may be raped at any time and by anyone'.[43]

The claim that all women are in the thrall of mental illness is clearly absurd, and risks discounting the pain of women who suffer from the traumatic aftermath of actual abuse. Nevertheless, part of the attraction of this model is the way it turns certain taken-for-granted (male) precepts upside down. Rather than repudiating the cultural construction of male as reason and female as emotion, second-wave feminists reversed the respective *status* allotted to reason and emotion. Joining a well-known critique of modernity, they argued that the historical rise of 'reason' did not lead to the triumph of objective and universal truth, but became a tool for a particular type of domination.[44] In contrast, these activists insisted, emotions should be revered; feelings possessed a unique 'truth'. Unconscious forces and the 'inner self' came to the forefront. While still passionately committed to building up women's power and resisting oppressive male institutions, these feminists drew attention to female emotional and psychic fragility in the face of injurious social structures. Femininity became defined as 'victimhood'. Unhappiness with subjugation was privatized and consigned to psychic depths. The concept of victim as the revelatory voice of experience naturalizes and individualizes the experience of sexual violence.

This response was sound in the context of its time. It was developed within a dominant culture that refused to admit that certain types of sexual violence were wrong, let alone profoundly offensive. As I have shown throughout this book, feminists were addressing a society in which victims of sexual violence were routinely belittled in the courts, mass media and everyday encounters. Misogyny was habitual. When these feminists employed the term 'victim' to refer to women, they were engaged in a robust confrontation of patriarchal institutions and customs. By emphasizing the devastating effects of power structures on women's emotional and psychological development, they ignited a revolution.

Crucially, while the emphasis on trauma was a retreat to the 'inner world' of individual women, these feminists expounded their critique of patriarchy from the relative security of resilient communities of like-minded women. The emergence of trauma rhetoric was, ironically, immensely powerful in the construction of the *active* female subject. According to this approach, the mere disclosure of trauma became reformative. The performance of 'trauma speech' itself took on a redemptive character, transforming passive victims into active survivors.[45] Particularly when it involved the recovery of previously 'forgotten' memories of child abuse, 'breaking silence' became a central strategy of empowerment among women who had experienced sexual abuse. This emphasis upon women's pervasive victimization was simply one plank in the mission of raising feminist consciousness. In that particular context it could be empowering. The insistence on female victimization was articulated within supportive communities of angry, assertive women.

Paradoxically, however, the very success of second-wave feminism created difficulties for the next generation of feminists, who used their newfound freedoms (albeit still partial) to forge even more individualistic paths to power and self-fulfilment. In recent years the narratives of female victimization have become disengaged from earlier assertions of collective female agency. Against the persistence of male violence and its destructive effects, many women retain the subject position of victimhood, but in a context where the supportive community has largely fragmented. Feminist camaraderie vanished. Rape certainly did not.

Feminist theorist Carine M. Mardorossian has convincingly developed this argument. In 'Toward a New Feminist Theory of Rape' (2002) she points out that feminism in the 1970s and 1980s stressed women's victimization but in a context that both created and glorified political agency. For this generation of feminists, being a victim of sexual violence 'did not mean being incapacitated and powerless'.

Rather, it meant becoming 'a determined and angry (although not pathologically resentful) agent of change'. These women demonstrated, protested and organized themselves in order to more effectively attain radical change within society. They defined agency in terms of political responses to powerlessness – attending conscious-raising groups, supporting other victims and protesting in the streets.

In contrast, Mardorossian argues, more recent debates about the victimization of women have become depoliticized. Non-victims embraced the discourse. Rape victims are no longer supported by informal communities, but are dealt with by professional agencies, which Mardorossian characterizes as the contemporary equivalent of nineteenth-century charity workers. The meaning of 'agency' is watered down – it no longer means mobilization, resistance and protest, but includes emotional responses that range from laughing to becoming depressed or suicidal, to crying or even 'remaining silent'. In this way 'passivity itself' became a 'defence mechanism'. In contrast to second-wave feminism, in which the victims showed that they were 'more than the sum of their traumatic experiences, that they had the ability to act and organize even as they were dealing with the psychic effects of rape', in more recent years victims are represented 'as irremediably and unidirectionally shaped by the traumatic experience of rape and hence incapable of dealing with anything but their own inner turmoil'. Even labels such as 'survivor' serve to construct an identity based on 'a before' and 'an after' attack, thus forcing victims of sexual violence to (yet again) define themselves in terms of the actions of the perpetrator. Victimization becomes an inner turmoil rather than 'an external reality imposed on someone'. Rape speaks to a woman's 'inner self' as opposed to a 'criminal act'. Indeed, 'real victims' are increasingly distinguished from 'angry feminists', whose fury at pervasive inequality and misogyny is increasingly portrayed as pathological.[46]

Talk of female victimization leads to further difficulties. As Rachel Hall argues in '"It Can Happen to You": Rape Prevention in the Age of Risk Management' (2004), for many feminists the link between woman and victim was important in 'motivating us to continue our struggle'. Nevertheless, it also revived the 'old cultural feminist belief that women are morally superior to men'. The concept that women are victims was co-opted by conservative political forces and used to 'sanction the authority of the law, the necessity of order and protection, the mythical moral clarity of an absolute distinction between good and bad men'. The female victim

> justifies endless interventions into women's lives . . . all in the name of protecting them . . . She makes men feel needed, necessary, and important. She justifies heterosexual family and marriage, not to mention racial segregation. She makes overprotective fathers seem cute and affectionate as they limit their daughters' freedom.[47]

Still other critics point out that the emphasis placed upon the redemptive potential of confessional speech is equally problematic. Although survivor testimony could be liberating, it is not necessarily so. As feminists Linda Alcoff and Laura Gray argue in 'Survivor Discourse: Transgression or Recuperation?' (1993),

> when breaking the silence is taken up as the necessary route to recovery or as a privileged political tactic, it becomes a coercive imperative on survivors to confess, to recount our assaults, to give details, and even to do so publicly. Our refusal to comply might then be read as weakness of will or as re-enacted victimization.

But might it not also be the case, they continued, that 'survival itself sometimes necessitates a refusal to recount or even a refusal to disclose and deal with the assault or abuse'? Disclosure could be more emotionally, financially and physically damning to women than silence.[48] In other words, confessional discourse requires the adoption and framing of the experience along rigid lines shaped by legal doctrines or moralistic codes, which may not be in keeping with an individual woman's process of self-creation.

Finally, the trauma narrative once again demands that potential victims ('every female from nine months to ninety years')[49] act to prevent their own victimization, even though such an interpretation is strongly resisted by practically all feminists. Actual victims are expected to take responsibility for healing themselves, primarily through speech acts. As a consequence, women's bodies could be collapsed once again into 'rape space', mere 'embodiments of risk'.[50]

Of course, this assumption is not unique to late-twentieth-century discourses. The insistence that women are responsible for ensuring that men did not rape them was mainstream throughout the period I have discussed in this book. As 'social hygienists' Jacob and Rosamond Goldberg lectured in their *Girls on City Streets. A Study of 1400 Cases of Rape* (1935), parents had to ensure that their daughters were 'warned' against men and 'properly taught' how to 'avoid and . . . defend themselves against sex suggestions and assaults'. The dangers facing daughters were presented as inevitable. In the Goldbergs' text they were passively depicted as 'pitfalls which awaited them'. Girls who failed to deflect these 'perils' might be 'administered a severe beating' by their parents. In contrast, the Goldbergs' discussion of the responsibilities of boys and men *not* to rape was characterized by brevity: the section entitled 'The Guilty Males' was only one paragraph long in a book of 384 pages.[51] The author of a letter to the editor of the *British Medical Journal* in 1946 was particularly tongue-in-cheek about it. Assuming, he quipped, that women were to be allowed to 'continue going freely about in the streets', then

> not a few serious thinkers will be considering a possible need for the compulsory *veiling of women*, such as happened at the time of the rise of Islam. Indeed, so long as the leaders of civilization remain unaware of how to promote self control in the individual the Moslem solution may prove the only alternative to wholesale compulsory sterilization of the male.[52]

This assumption that male sexual aggression is a given and the only remedy therefore is female awareness was rife throughout the period. Even law-enforcement agencies – supposedly engaged in catching and prosecuting the 'bad guys' – promoted the belief. In a fairly typical

Ladies
YOU CAN
PROTECT
YOURSELF

Pamphlet from the 1970s, published by the City of Hickory Police Department, North Carolina

example, the City of Hickory Police Department in North Carolina in the mid-1970s issued a pamphlet for women concerning rape. [See image, p. 432.] It began: 'How can a woman avoid being attacked at night on the street? The simplest and best answer is don't be alone.' It continued by informing women that if they 'must be out at night, have your husband drive you or ride with a friend'. Self-defence measures were positively discouraged. 'When walking alone carrying a pistol, knife or tear-gas pen may not help,' the leaflet asserted, because 'nothing is more dangerous than a firearm in the hands of a nervous, inexperienced woman. If you miss, the attacker may use the weapon on you.'[53] The only solution for women was to avoid putting themselves in situations that might be risky. For many women (and men), this meant a reassertion of male power, including a recommitment to rigid social divisions of labour, with women relegated to the domestic sphere. Women needed to learn to rely upon their male protectors.

It was an attitude forcefully repudiated by second-wave feminists, with their self-defence classes and insistence on female agency in fighting off attackers. [See cartoon, below.] Until recently, they lamented, many young women reached adulthood without the most

"What did you learn
in school today?"

From Sydney Rape Crisis Collective, *Handbook for Rape Crisis Centres*

basic physical skills needed to ward off attack.[54] Physical education was insufficient, though. Self-defence classes also had to tackle the psychological inhibitions many (if not most) women had about fighting back. In particular women needed to repudiate notions of 'correct' female behaviour, such as the emphasis on female empathy which encouraged women to see their attackers as possessing low esteem and needing love (as the author of *How to Say No to a Rapist and Survive* (1975) actually encouraged).[55] In contrast, feminist-led classes impressed upon women the need to overcome feelings of politeness and timidity in protection of their own bodies.

These powerful feminist initiatives focusing on female empowerment were taking place within a hostile ideological environment in which responsibility for social problems *generally* was moving away from the state toward a neo-liberal and conservative emphasis on individual risk management. The environment, health issues, and crime were increasingly portrayed as being the responsibility of individuals, as opposed to something that could be tackled through state and welfare provisions. As Rachel Hall expressed it, within the schema of 'risk management',

> a woman's body, or more precisely, her sexual anatomy, becomes one risk factor among others. She is addressed by prevention discourses not exactly as less than a subject; rather, it is that her subjectivity momentarily collapses into her sexual anatomy. In other words, rape prevention, as a practice of risk assessment, encourages the metonymic treatment of women as 'rape space'.[56]

Thus in rape discourse as well as in crime talk more generally, emphasis on dangerousness (male danger) gradually shifted into a notion of risk (female vulnerability). Women were (yet again) urged to take responsibility for their own abuse. In a turn of phrase reminiscent of Foucault, Mardorossian accurately identified this as 'a new form of panopticism, an interiorized and individualized system of surveillance by which every woman becomes her own overseer'.[57]

At times when public expenditure on transport and services were in rapid decline, this renewed emphasis on individual measures to counter crime was significant. The site of intervention was no longer the male perpetrator, but the female victim. Structures of surveillance and, especially, female attention to *self*-policing increased dramatically. The problem was neatly repositioned away from cultures of male aggression towards individual, 'imprudent' women. In a context where feminism was losing its communal vibrancy, such incitements to female fear served only to encourage a restatement of paternalism for an age of individual free choice.

A minority of feminists proposed an alternative to these dispiriting developments. Instead of relying on patriarchal paternalism, (some) women should take on the mantle of (matriarchal) protection, they argued. This has led one strand of the contemporary feminist movement towards a more regulatory feminist politics. Andrea Dworkin and Catharine MacKinnon, for example, call for a curtailment of free speech and for stricter policing and regulation of sexual images that are not sanctioned by *their* sexual imaginary.[58] Such approaches jettison emancipatory agendas of plurality and solidarity by invoking the State as the arbiter of sexual legitimacy. No matter how much such feminists want to distance themselves from their neo-conservative bedfellows, their policies are effortlessly co-opted by a disciplining power which boasts of a long history in anti-female institutions. Their proposals are completely in tune with the repressive politics of late-twentieth- and early-twenty-first-century political administrations in Britain and America. In the name of 'protection' a new regulatory regime could be trained on the body (particularly the subordinate bodies of women, gays and transsexuals, as well as those bodies not represented as fully 'human subjects', such as the poor, prisoners, immigrants and asylum seekers). Such negative politics leaves no room for female initiatives save the paradox of purchasing freedom by investing in deadbolt locks and re-enacting revenge fantasies like those in the film *I Spit on your Grave* or *Baise Moi*.[59]

The negative politics of atomized fear (insisting that women police their own behaviour) as well as the neo-conservative feminist politics of state regulation (with its insistence that women willingly give over their freedoms to other, allegedly better informed, women and state institutions) are just two defensive mechanisms open to women. They are *particular* strategies in the creation of female subjectivities, and thankfully they have been rejected by the larger and more inclusive feminist community. Instead of fear and state-imposed regulation, many feminists stress the need to speak to pleasure. As feminist theorist Lois Pineau noted, 'sensuality is a source of delight, and teasing is playful and inspires wit'. 'What a relief to learn,' she exclaimed, 'that it is not sexual provocativeness, but its enemies, that constitute a danger to the world.'[60] A feminism that emphasizes vulnerability and seeks only to alleviate female unhappiness is a poor theory indeed. But the crucial question remains: what, then, should be done about rape?

Towards a Male Erotics

Rape is a crisis of manliness; its eradication is a matter for men – for a radically different conception of agency and masculinity. Although female offenders can easily be found, and they seem to be on the increase, rape remains primarily a problem associated with degraded masculinities. In the previous chapter I argued for the urgent need to reform the legal system so that more rapists are identified, convicted and punished for their crimes but, in the final analysis, political attempts to reduce and finally eliminate sexual aggression must start with the main perpetrators.

This is not to return to simplistic accusations against 'men'. To reiterate: sexual aggression is not innate to masculine identity. Instinct theorists and evolutionary psychologists fail to convince me that there is something 'natural' about men's violence. If rape is primarily 'about' male biology or an evolutionary inheritance, then why does it vary so greatly over geographical space and historical time? Much more convincingly, social theorists and feminists expose the innumerable ways in which environmental pressures and ideological structures create men who sexually abuse others. These cultural forces inscribe or 'impose upon' men a violent, aggressive conception of masculinity. More compellingly, they provide a dominant narrative from which people choose, in acts of self-creation, justifications for sexual violence and the guilt that accompanies it. Anthropological studies take this 'social constructivist' position even further by revealing that rape is extremely low in some societies. Most famously, Peggy Reeves Sanday's research on rape-free societies shows that discourses favourable to rape are not present in all cultures.[61] Societies characterized by sexual equality, peacefulness and high levels of female economic power tend to have relatively low levels of rape. Sexual abusers *learn* and teach themselves how to act as sexual abusers within specific historical communities. Ignoring the existence of those societies in which sexual violence is rare simply naturalizes the Western practice and experience of rape.

This process of making rape seem 'normal' is not only predicated upon a narrow Western construction of humanity; it is also infused with a profoundly hostile misunderstanding of masculinity and a distorted notion of male desire. As many teachers discover, young men respond angrily to any anti-rape counsellor who implies that 'all men' are rapists: they seek loving, affectionate relationships, these men honestly profess. The erotics of virile subjectivity, in which men are expected to relate to the world through ideas of ownership, control and domination, simply does not resemble what most men acknowledge as their desire, whether or not they succeed in acting according to those feelings.

Two main ways of tackling rape by addressing the 'problem of men' have been proposed. The first is to dramatically increase the cost of sexual violence for individual male perpetrators or for men as a class. In the previous chapter I argued that increasing punitive responses towards individual convicted rapists has been ineffective, if not counterproductive.

An alternative view argues that it makes sense to increase the cost of rape for *all* men, perpetrators or not. In his powerfully argued *Rape: A Philosophical Investigation* (1996) Keith Burgess-Jackson proposes imposing a special tax on men, the revenue of which could be invested in female protection and male programmes of sex education. Curfews could be imposed on men living in communities with high levels of violence. Men might even be 'required to participate in study groups or consciousness-raising sessions as a condition of receiving certain privileges, such as drinking alcoholic beverages or driving a motor vehicle'.[62] At the very least such proposals will make men less rape-supportive. They will be incensed rather than simply ill at ease when other men act wrongly.

Although such proposals are superficially attractive in the context of schemes of redistributive justice, their emphasis on coercion and punitive regulation will cause much disquiet, especially in liberal and left-wing circles. Appealing to an ever-increasing regulatory state apparatus to 'cure' social malaise is dangerous. It may also be counter-productive. Surveying, regulating and punishing 'all men' for the actions of some men will increase levels of resentment against women. It wrongly stigmatizes loving men.

Others (including myself) propose tackling the 'problem of men' in more positive ways. A politics of masculinity that focuses upon a man's body as a site of pleasure (for him and others), as opposed to an instrument of oppression and pain, demands a renewed focus on male comportment, imaginary and agency. For these commentators the male body serves as the locus for the social construction of masculinity. People discover sex: they learn its performance. They are taught to be aroused, or not. They are told in words, deeds and gestures what is forbidden. John Stoltenberg makes a similar observation when he insists that people born with penises are not *born* male: they *become* men. According to him, in a society 'predicated on the notion that there are two "opposite" and "complementary" sexes', the idea of a unified male sex

> not only makes sense, it *becomes* sense; the very idea of a male sexual identity produces sensation, produces the meaning of sensation, becomes the meaning of how one's body feels. The sense and the sensing of a male sexual identity is at once mental and physical, at once public and personal.

In other words, men 'grow up aspiring to feel and act unambiguously male, longing to belong to the sex that is male and daring', rather than belonging 'to the sex that is not'. One way this process takes place is through the creation of the male sexed body or what Stoltenberg calls 'erection learning'. Before 'becoming' a man, young boys experience erections in a vast number of contexts, including while riding a bike, talking in public and playing sports. They gradually learn which sensations are deemed 'appropriate' to erections, that is, hierarchical, heterosexual, genital, penetratively orientated interactions with certain types of women. Boys gradually 'learn to cancel out and deny erotic sensations that are not specifically linked to what they think a real man is supposed to feel', in favour of 'an aggressive and controlling and violative mode'.[63] They *learn* that to be 'sexed' means to have a penis that is forceful, invasive and always eager for 'action'.

There is a distressing conflation of penetration and violation in Stoltenberg's account, but it is not necessary to his argument. As feminist Ellen Willis noted, it is just as vital not to 'glorify diffuse, romantic, non-genitally orientated sensuality as the sole criterion that sex is "erotic", female, and good', as it is not to 'stigmatize powerful, assertive desires for genital gratification as "pornographic", male, and bad'.[64] Unlike phallic masculinity, which represents a turning away from a complex model of pleasure, 'good sex' takes many forms.[65] While no one denies that embracing a phallic mode of sexuality gives benefits to men (it can* confer social power), there are also costs. The

*It does not *always* confer social power. In various periods of history we can see how displays of phallic masculinity (in African-Americans, for instance) can be dangerous for them.

price is heavy. In 'Destructive Boundary Erotics and Refigurations of the Heterosexual Male Body' (1995), for instance, Catherine Waldby laments the 'deeroticization' of most of the male body, its 'refusal of pleasure, or an anxiety in pleasure in order not to surrender power'. 'To defend the sovereign ego,' she continues, 'the rest of the body is drained of erotic potential in favour of its localization in the penis, taken to be the phallus' little representative.'[66]

This is one reason why distinguished theorists of masculinity as different as Jeff Hearn and R. W. Connell have argued that it is in the interests of men as well as women to embrace an emancipatory praxis. Like me, they stress that the male-oppressive system eventually poisons the lives of everyone. Retreating from a harmful system will enable men to love and be loved in more fulfilling ways.[67]

This 'good sex' model is always in a process of negotiation, of course. Translated into the language of the philosopher Judith Butler, bodily performances are reiterative: by acts of repetition, the sexed body emerges.[68] In this book I have emphasized the power of narrative, rhetoric and habit in fashioning gender norms. Gendered stereotypes repeatedly performed invest sex with its dominant meanings. But these iterative performances can be subverted. Performances of gender don't simply constrain; they provide subjects with ways to 'tinker' with culture, subverting norms, redefining identities and exploiting pleasures. Sexuality and identities become malleable things indeed.

I have shown how people create themselves through drawing from a range of available narratives. Rapists become subjects in the process of narrating major events in their lives according to specific languages and tropes. Many of the narrativizing practices that frame their performance have been shown to be violent. Rapists and their allies have been concerned with distinguishing between 'bodies that matter' and 'other' bodies (black female bodies for white men; married women's bodies for their husbands; 'disordered' female bodies for controlled ones). But such violence is not inevitable. Just as second-generation feminists insisted that women needed to unite to overturn oppressive power relations, it is now time for men to do the same. Rape prevention must be re-politicized as an issue for men. Within a masculinist society men, too, are harmed every time one of their brothers abuses some other person. Men are not the all-powerful figures of Catharine MacKinnon's imagination,[69] and therefore must struggle for a more equitable world. It was a fact recognized by that defiant Black Power leader Eldridge Cleaver. He had defended raping black women on the grounds that he was refining his 'technique and *modus operandi*' for his future sprees against white women (and then justified raping white women on the grounds that it was an 'insurrectionist act' against white oppression). However, Cleaver later admitted to feeling shame. 'After I returned to prison,' he confessed,

> I took a long look at myself, and for the first time in my life, admitted that I was wrong, that I had gone astray – astray not so much from the white man's law as from being human, civilized – for I could not approve the act of rape. Even though I had some insight into my own motivations, I did not feel justified. I had lost my self-respect. My pride as a man dissolved and my whole fragile moral structure seemed to collapse, completely shattered. That is why I started to write. To save myself.[70]

Of course, as I have repeated time and again in this book, although discourse is always artificial, mutable and performative, it takes place within historical time and geographical place. It is easy to overestimate the subversive nature of texts. Subversion, the philosopher Susan Bordo writes, is 'contextual, historical, and above all, social. No matter how exacting the destabilizing potential of the text, bodily or otherwise, whether those texts are subversive or recuperative or both or neither cannot be determined in abstraction from actual social practice.'[71] Social practice occurs through choices made by subjects within time and place.

When looking back into the past, sometimes all we have is the violence of rhetoric. But, I want to reiterate, it is a rhetoric that can be pinned down, exposed as historically contingent and unstable. The world of narrative and rhetoric is not static: we can imagine and enact new ways of seeing, speaking, ways of being. As one literary critic explained, we can read backwards

> from what seems natural, obvious, self-evident, or universal in order to show that these things have their history, their reasons for being the way they are, their effects on what follows from them and that the starting point is not a (natural) given but a (cultural) construct, usually blind to itself.[72]

In other words, the narratives and rites involved in attempting to reduce another person to an undifferentiated body, a body-in-pain, are embedded in humdrum practices, everyday knowledges. Demystifying the category of the rapist makes sexual violence seem no longer inevitable. It also opens up another possibility of resistance. Steeped in notions of trauma and seduced by apocalyptic fantasies, it is easy to forget that the seemingly unrestrained brutality of abusers is always contested – 'Why are you doing this to me?' the rape victim asked at the beginning of this book, insisting on a here-and-now, a me-and-you, instead of an ahistorical narrative based on supposedly biological and psychological constants. Terror is always local. To universalize it (as in the 'all men are rapists, rape fantasists, or beneficiaries of a rape culture') is to remove the specifics of individual histories and the possibilities of acting otherwise. It is to situate sexual torture in the realm of moral edification. The traumatiz*ing* subject is a knowing being with a range of knowledges, emotions, desires and needs open to him or her: by uncovering its multiple voices, we make it imaginatively accessible and politically contestable. By revealing the specificities of the past, we can imagine a future in which sexual violence has been placed outside the threshold of the human.

Notes

CHAPTER ONE: SEXED BODIES

1 Cecil Day Lewis, 'Sex-Crime', *Selected Poems* (Harmondsworth, 1951), 38–40.
2 Unnamed soldier interviewed in Mark Baker, *Nam. The Vietnam War in the Words of the Men and Women Who Fought There* (London, 1981), 149–50. The book has come under attack in recent years because of the author's inability to name all the interviewees and evidence that some of those interviewed were lying about their war experience.
3 Jean Améry, *At the Mind's Limits* (London, 1999), 28 and 40.
4 There are innumerable examples, but a typical one is Adriene Sere, 'Man and the History of Rape', at http://www.saidit.org/archives/mar00/mar_article2.html.
5 L. Anderson, 'Boyz N St John's', *National Review*, 26 August 1991, 22; Mara Keire, 'The Vice Trust: A Reinterpretation of the White Slavery Scare in the United States, 1907–1917', *Journal of Social History* (2001), 5–41.
6 Jacob A. Goldberg and Rosamond W. Goldberg, *Girls on City Streets. A Study of 1400 Cases of Rape* (New York, 1935), 265.
7 Michael W. Agopian, Duncan Chappell and Gilbert Geis, 'Interracial Rape in a North American City: An Analysis of 63 Cases', in Terence P. Thornberry and Edward Sagarin (eds.), *Images of Crime: Offenders and Victims* (New York, 1972), 92.
8 Cited in Judith Lewis Herman, 'Considering Sex Offenders: A Model of Addiction', *Signs: Journal of Women in Culture and Society*, 13.4 (Summer 1988), 705.
9 Eric Reitan, 'Rape as an Essentially Contested Concept', *Hypatia*, 16.2 (Spring 2001), 43–66.
10 In Scotland there was a law against incest dating from 1567.
11 This changed only in 1975 with the publication of Suzanne M. Sgro's article 'Sexual Molestation of Children: The Last Frontier in Child Abuse', *Children Today*, 4 (May–June 1977). It was popularized by Ellen Weber, 'Incest: Sexual Abuse Begins at Home', *Ms*, 5 (April 1977). The best discussion can be found in Ian Hacking, 'The Making and Molding of Child Abuse', *Critical Inquiry*, 17.2 (Winter 1991), 274–5.
12 This book is concerned primarily (although not exclusively) with adults.
13 Jeanne L. Schroeder, 'Catharine's Wheel: MacKinnon's Pornography Analysis as a Return to Traditional Christian Sexual Theory', *New York Law School Law Review*, 38 (1993), 237 and 249.
14 Ann J. Cahill, *Rethinking Rape* (Ithaca, 2001), 101–2.
15 Michel Foucault, *The History of Sexuality. Volume 1: An Introduction*, trans. Robert Hurley (London, 1978), 43.
16 Pamela Haag, *Consent: Sexual Rights and the Transformation of American Culture* (Ithaca, 1999), 181.
17 See Susan Brownmiller, *Against Our Will: Men, Women, and Rape* (New York, 1975).

18 Ruth Seifert, 'The Second Front. The Logic of Sexual Violence in Wars', *Women's Studies International Forum*, 19.1/2 (1996), 36.
19 Alice Vachss, *Sex Crimes* (New York, 1993), 78.
20 Katharine Whitehorn, 'Rape: Fact and Fantasy', *The Bulletin* (31 August 1974), 30.
21 Catharine A. MacKinnon, 'Sexuality, Pornography, and Method: Pleasure Under Patriarchy', *Ethics*, 99.2 (January 1989), 323.
22 D. Gelman and K. Springen, 'The Mind of the Rapist', *Newsweek* (23 July 1990), 50.
23 Eileen Berrington and Helen Jones, 'Reality vs. Myth: Constructions of Women's Insecurity', *Feminist Media Studies*, 2.3 (2002), 211–12.
24 Roberta Culbertson, 'Embodied Memory, Transcendence, and Telling: Recounting Trauma, Reestablishing the Self', *New Literary History*, 26 (1995), 179. She is writing about victims of sexual violation.
25 A. Nicholas Groth, Ann Wolbert Burgess and Lynda Lytle Holmstrom, 'Rape: Power, Anger, and Sexuality', *American Journal of Psychiatry*, 134.11 (November 1977), 1241.
26 Michael W. Agopian, Duncan Chappell and Gilbert Geis, 'Interracial Rape in a North American City: An Analysis of 63 Cases', in Terence P. Thornberry and Edward Sagarin (eds.), *Images of Crime: Offenders and Victims* (New York, 1972), 98.
27 Louise A. Jackson, *Child Sexual Abuse in Victorian England* (London, 2000), 41.
28 For an extended analysis, see Robert M. O'Brien, 'UCR Violent Crime Rates, 1958–2000: Recorded and Offender-Generated Trends', *Social Science Research*, 32.3 (September 2003), 499–518.
29 D. G. Kilpatrick, C. N. Edmunds and A. K. Seymour, *Rape in America: A Report to the Nation* (Arlington, VA, 1992).
30 Lawrence A. Greenfeld, *Sex Offences and Offenders: An Analysis of Data on Rape and Sexual Assault* (Washington, DC, 1997).
31 Gallup Poll, Questionnaire 'Crime' qn46G, 29 August–3 September 2000, sample size 1012.
32 For example, see Linda Gordon, *Heroes of their Own Lives. The Politics and History of Family Violence, Boston, 1880–1960* (New York, 1988); Louise A. Jackson, *Childhood Sexual Abuse in Victorian England* (London, 2000); Philip Jenkins, *Moral Panic: Changing Concepts of the Child Molester in Modern America* (New Haven, 1998).
33 Liz Kelly, Jo Lovett and Linda Regan, *A Gap or a Chasm? Attrition in Reported Rape Cases: A Home Office Research Study* (London, 2005), x.
34 Lee Ellis, *Theories of Rape. Inquiries into the Causes of Sexual Aggression* (New York, 1989), 3.
35 Eugene J. Kanin, 'An Examination of Sexual Aggression as a Response to Sexual Frustration', *Journal of Marriage and the Family*, 29.3 (August 1967), 428–33; Mary P. Koss and Cheryl J. Oros, 'Sexual Experiences Survey: A Research Instrument Investigating Sexual Aggression and Victimization', *Journal of Consulting and Clinical Psychology*, 50 (1982), 455–7.
36 B. Lott, M. E. Reilly and D. R. Howard, 'Sexual Assault and Harassment: A Campus Community Case Study', *Journal of Women in Culture and Society*, 8 (1982), 296–319.
37 Neil M. Malamuth, 'Rape Proclivity Amongst Males', *Journal of Social Issues*, 37.4 (1981), 138–57.
38 Mary P. Koss, T. E. Dinero, C. A. Seibel and S. L. Cox, 'Strangers and Acquaintance Rape: Are There Differences in the Victim's Experience?', *Psychology of Women Quarterly*, 12 (1988), 1–24, and Mary P. Koss, Christine A. Gidycz and Nadine Wisniewski, 'The Scope of Rape: Incidence and Prevalence of Sexual

Aggression and Victimization in a National Sample of Higher Education Students', *Journal of Consulting and Clinical Psychology*, 55 (1987), 168.

CHAPTER TWO: RAPE MYTHS

1 Cecil Day Lewis, 'Sex-Crime', *Selected Poems* (Harmondsworth, 1951), 38–40.
2 Harriet Stump, 'Metropolitan Police Examinations', 1881, in National Archives (UK) CRIM 1/12/7.
3 Roland Barthes, *Mythologies*, trans. Annette Lavers (New York, 1972), 131 and 143.
4 Horatio R. Storer, 'The Law of Rape', *The Quarterly Journal of Psychological Medicine and Medical Jurisprudence*, ii (1868), 55.
5 Michael Ryan, *A Manual of Medical Jurisprudence* (London, 1831), 183.
6 John Leeson, 'To the Editor of The Times', *The Times*, 8 June 1835, 3, and 15 June 1835, 3. Gurney Williams also argued that it was impossible to rape a girl under the age of seven years ('unless there has first been mutilation by some instrument'): 'Rape in Children and Young Girls. Based on the Personal Investigation of Several Hundred Cases of Rape and of Over Fourteen Thousand Vaginal Examinations', *International Clinics*, 2.1 (1913), 256 and 259.
7 Rudolph Aug. Witthaus and Tracy C. Becker, *Medical Jurisprudence, Forensic Medicine, and Toxicology* (New York, 1894), 436–7 and 447–8. The case was reported in the *Medical Times and Gazette*, 23–4 April 1853.
8 Gurney Williams, 'Rape in Children and Young Girls. Based on the Personal Investigation of Several Hundred Cases of Rape and of Over Fourteen Thousand Vaginal Examinations', *International Clinics*, 2.1 (1913), 256 and 259.
9 Sydney Smith, *Forensic Medicine. A Text-Book for Students and Practitioners* (London, 1925), 221.
10 Charles Graham Grant, *Practical Forensic Medicine. A Police-Surgeon's Emergency Guide*, 3rd edn. (London, 1924), 46.
11 F. Lee Bailey and Henry Rothblatt, *Crimes of Violence: Rape and Other Sex Crimes* (Rochester, NY, 1973), 277–8.
12 William Adrian Bonger, *Criminality and Economic Conditions*, trans. Henry P. Horton (Boston, 1916), 617–18.
13 J. Dixon Mann, *Forensic Medicine and Toxicology*, 2nd edn., revised and enlarged (London, 1898), 102.
14 Sydney Smith, *Forensic Medicine. A Text-Book for Students and Practitioners* (London, 1925), 221.
15 Hugo Paul, *Cry Rape: Anatomy of the Rapist*, intro. by Jean-Paul St. Marc (New York, 1967), 12.
16 E. J. Hodgens, I. H. McFadyen, R. J. Failla and F. M. Daly, 'The Offence of Rape in Victoria', *Australian and New Zealand Journal of Criminology*, 5 (December 1972), 227.
17 Katharine Whitehorn, 'Rape: Fact and Fantasy', *The Bulletin*, 31 August 1974, 33.
18 'Whatever May Be the General Value', *The Times*, 16 July 1866.
19 Gurney Williams, 'Rape in Children and Young Girls. Based on the Personal Investigation of Several Hundred Cases of Rape and of Over Fourteen Thousand Vaginal Examinations', *International Clinics*, 2.1 (1913), 258–9.
20 Hugo Paul, *Cry Rape: Anatomy of the Rapist*, intro. by Jean-Paul St. Marc (New York, 1967), 101 and 104–5.
21 J. W. Roworth (pseudonym of Edward Casey), 'The Misfit Soldier', 49, Imperial War Museum archives: parts of this memoir were republished in my (ed.), *The Misfit Soldier* (Cork, 1999).

22 'The First Report of the Irish Poor Law Commissioners', *The Times*, 15 January 1836, 2.
23 Michael Ryan, *A Manual of Medical Jurisprudence* (London, 1831), 188.
24 Dr J. Y. Simpson, 'Clinical Lectures on the Diseases of Women', *Medical Times and Gazette*, 16 April 1859, 384.
25 For an excellent discussion, see Louise A. Jackson, *Child Sexual Abuse in Victorian England* (London, 2000), 75–6.
26 H. S. Holden, 'The Laboratory Aspects of Sexual Crime', *British Journal of Venereal Diseases*, xxiv.2 (June 1948), 68.
27 J. Dixon Mann, *Forensic Medicine and Toxicology*, 2nd edn., revised and enlarged (London, 1898), 107.
28 H. Aubrey Husband, *The Students' Hand-Book of Forensic Medicine and Medical Police*, 4th edn. (Edinburgh, 1883), 117.
29 Editorial, 'False Accusation of Rape', *The Alienist and Neurologist*, 22 (1901), 575–6.
30 Gurney Williams, 'Rape in Children and Young Girls. Based on the Personal Investigation of Several Hundred Cases of Rape and of Over Fourteen Thousand Vaginal Examinations', *International Clinics*, 2.1 (1913), 247.
31 May St. John Cosgrave, 'Medical Examination in Alleged Sexual Offences', *The Forensic Science Society Journal*, 3.2 (March 1924), 97.
32 Dr Letitia Fairfield commenting on Dr Holden's paper, in H. S. Holden, 'The Laboratory Aspects of Sexual Crime', *British Journal of Venereal Diseases*, xxiv.2 (June 1948), 70.
33 Philip Piker, 'A Psychologist Looks at Sex Offenses', *Journal of Social Hygiene*, 33 (1947), 397.
34 Alfred C. Kinsey, Wardell B. Pomeroy and Clyde E. Martin, *Sexual Behavior in the Human Male* (Philadelphia, 1948), 238.
35 James Holledge, *Sex and the Australian Teenager* (London, 1964), 8–9.
36 For example, see S. V. Clevenger, *Medical Jurisprudence of Insanity or Forensic Psychiatry*, vol. 2 (New York, 1898), 1032.
37 J. Sanderson Christison, *Crime and Criminals* (Chicago: The W. T. Keener Co., 1897), 47.
38 Lucy Ozarin, 'Bernard Sachs: 50 Year APA Member', *Psychiatric News*, 38.2 (17 January 2003), 48.
39 B. Sachs, 'Insanity and Crime', in Allan McLane Hamilton and Lawrence Godkin (eds.), *A System of Legal Medicine*, vol. 2, 2nd ed. (New York, 1900), 210–11.
40 George F. Butler, 'Hysteria', *The Alienist and Neurologist*, xxxii.3 (August 1911), 394.
41 William J. Robinson, *America's Sex and Marriage Problems. Based on Thirty Years Practice and Study* (New York, 1928), 307–9, 315, 323 and 329.
42 Florence Clothier, 'Psychological Implications of Unmarried Parenthood', *American Journal of Orthopsychiatry*, xiii.3 (July 1943), 542–43.
43 Narcyz Lukianowicz, 'Imaginary Sexual Partner. Visual Masturbatory Fantasies', *Archives of General Psychology*, 3 (October 1960), 434.
44 James G. Kiernan, 'Hysterical Mimicry of Dramatic Crimes', *The Alienist and Neurologist*, xxxii (1911), 108.
45 Hugo Paul, *Cry Rape: Anatomy of the Rapist*, intro. by Jean-Paul St. Marc (New York, 1967), 68–77.
46 Arthur N. Foxe, *Crime and Sexual Development. Movement and Fixation of the Libido in Criminotic Individuals* (New York, 1936), 63.
47 Arthur F. Schiff, 'Examination and Treatment of the Male Rape Victim', *Southern Medical Journal*, 73.11 (November 1980), 1499. In the Dade County Rape Treatment Center, he examined prisoners claiming to have been raped.

48 Home Office, 'The Criminal Injuries Compensation Scheme, 2001' (London, 2001), 30–52, can be found online at https://www.cica.gov.uk.

49 'What Price Rape', unidentified newspaper clipping, hand-dated 1977, in Margaret Beadman's 'Papers', Australian National Library MSS 5876.

50 It is important to note that around 9–10 per cent of memory claims were made either before or without the involvement of therapy: G. H. Gudjonsson, 'Accusations by Adults of Childhood Sexual Abuse: A Survey of the Members of the British False Memory Society', *Applied Cognitive Psychology*, 11 (1997), 3–18, and F. A. Goodyear-Smith, T. M. Laidlaw and R. G. Large, 'Surveying Families Accused of Childhood Sexual Abuse: A Comparison of British and New Zealand Results', *Applied Cognitive Psychology*, 9 (1997), 31–4.

51 Elizabeth F. Loftus, 'Remembering Dangerously', in Robert A. Baker (ed.), *Child Sexual Abuse and False Memory Syndrome* (Amherst, 1998), 31 and 46.

52 K. S. Pope, 'Memory Abuse and Science: Questioning Claims About the False Memory Syndrome Epidemic', *American Psychologist*, 51 (1996), 957.

53 D. Stephen Lindsay and J. Don Read, '"Memory Work" and Recovered Memories of Childhood Sexual Abuse: Scientific Evidence and Public, Professional, and Personal Issues', *Psychology, Public Policy, and Law*, 1 (1995), 850.

54 Council of Scientific Affairs, 'Council Report: Scientific Status of Refreshing Recollection by the Use of Hypnosis', *Journal of the American Medical Association*, 253 (1985), 1918–22, and Educational Council of the Canadian Psychiatric Association, 'Position Statement: Adult Recovered Memories of Childhood Sexual Abuse', *Canadian Journal of Psychiatry*, 41 (1996), 305.

55 For summaries of the vast literature, see Wendy J. Kisch, 'From the Couch to the Bench: How Should the Legal System Respond to Recovered Memories of Childhood Sexual Abuse?', *American University Journal of Gender and the Law*, 5 (1996–7), 207–46; Richard A. Leo, 'The Social and Legal Construction of Repressed Memory', *Law and Social Inquiry* (1998), 653–92; Mark Pendergrast, *Victims of Memory: Incest Accusations and Shattered Lives* (Hinsburg, VT, 1995); Douglas R. Richmond, 'Bad Science: Repressed and Recovered Memories of Childhood Sexual Abuse', *University of Kansas Law Review*, 44 (1995–6), 517–66.

56 For instance, see Christina Bannon, 'Recovered Memories of Childhood Sexual Abuse: Should the Courts Get Involved When Mental Health Professionals Disagree?', *Arizona State Law Journal*, 26 (1994), 835–56; Elizabeth F. Loftus, *Eyewitness Testimony* (Cambridge, MA, 1979); Elizabeth Loftus and Katherine Ketcham, *The Myth of Repressed Memory: False Memories and Allegations of Sexual Abuse* (New York, 1994); Elizabeth Loftus, 'When a Lie Becomes Memory's Truth: Memory Distortion After Exposure to Misinformation', *Current Directions in Psychological Science*, 1 (August 1992), 120–3; Richard Ofshe and Ethan Watters, *Making Monsters: False Memories, Psychotherapy, and Sexual Hysteria* (New York, 1994).

57 Ellen Bass and Laura Davis, *The Courage to Heal: A Guide for Women Survivors of Child Sexual Abuse* (New York, 1988), 20–1 and 148. There were hundreds of such books, but also see Kristin A. Kunzman, *The Healing Way: Adult Recovery from Childhood Sexual Abuse* (San Francisco, 1990).

58 K. S. Pope, 'Memory Abuse and Science: Questioning Claims About the False Memory Syndrome Epidemic', *American Psychologist*, 51 (1996), 957.

59 Carol Tavris, *The Mismeasure of Woman: Why Women are not the Better Sex, the Inferior Sex, or the Opposite Sex* (New York, 1992), 320. Also see Michael G. Kenny, 'The Recovered Memory Controversy: An Anthropologist's View', *Journal of Psychiatry and the Law*, 23 (1995), 437–60.

60 Janice Haaken, *Pillar of Salt: Gender, Memory, and the Perils of Looking Back* (London, 1998).

61 Janice Haaken, 'The Recovery of Memory, Fantasy, and Desire: Feminist Approaches to Sexual Abuse and Psychic Trauma', *Signs: Journal of Women in Culture and Society*, 21.4 (Summer 1996), 1088. Also see Janice Haaken, 'Sexual Abuse, Recovered Memory, and Therapeutic Practice: A Feminist-Psychoanalytic Perspective', *Social Text*, 40 (Autumn 1994), 115–45.

62 Carol Tavris, 'Beware the Incest-Survivor Machine', *New York Times Book Review*, 3 January 1993.

63 Beryl Satter, 'The Sexual Abuse Paradigm in Historical Perspective: Passivity and Emotion in Mid-Twentieth-Century America', *The Journal of the History of Sexuality*, 12.3 (July 2003), 452.

64 James Cronin, 'False Memory', *Z Magazine* (April 1994), 37.

65 G. D. Woods, 'Some Aspects of Pack Rape in Sydney', *Australian and New Zealand Journal of Criminology*, 2.2 (June 1969), 107–15. Part of his statement is reproduced (without citation) in Law Reform Commissioner, *Rape Prosecutions (Court Procedures and Rules of Evidence)*, working paper no. 4 (Melbourne, 1976), 20. For similar discussions about the class differentials in the acceptability of aggression, also see Allison Davis, 'Socialization and Adolescent Personality', in Theodore M. Newcomb and Eugene L. Hartley, *Readings in Social Psychology* (New York, 1947), 139–50, and Kaare Svalastoga, 'Rape and Social Structure', *Pacific Sociological Review* (Spring 1962), 51.

66 William J. Robinson, *America's Sex and Marriage Problems. Based on Thirty Years Practice and Study* (New York, 1928), 330.

67 Randy Thornhill and Craig Palmer, *A Natural History of Rape: Biological Bases of Sexual Coercion* (Cambridge, MA, 2000), 89–90.

68 Ann Landers, 'A Male's Theory on Date Rape', *San Francisco Examiner*, 4 August 1991, C-2.

69 Damian Warburton, 'The Rape of a Label. Why It Would be Wrong to Follow Canada in Having a Single Offence of Unlawful Sexual Assault', *Journal of Criminal Law*, 68 (2004), 539.

70 For a summary of the literature, see Mary E. Craig, 'Coercive Sexuality in Dating Relationships: A Situational Model', *Clinical Psychology Review*, 10 (1990), 395–423.

71 Clifford Kirkpatrick and Eugene Kanin, 'Male Sex Aggression on a University Campus', *American Sociological Review*, xxii (February 1957), 52–8.

72 Eugene J. Kanin, 'Male Aggression in Dating-Courtship Relations', *The American Journal of Sociology*, 63 (1957), 197.

73 For instance, see James Makepeace, 'Courtship Violence Among College Students', *Family Relations*, 30 (1981), 97–102; Jan E. Stets and Debra A. Henderson, 'Contextual Factors Surrounding Conflict Resolution While Dating: Results from a National Study', *Family Relations*, 40 (1991), 29–36; Gordon E. Barnes, Leonard Greenwood and Reena Sommer, 'Courtship Violence in a Canadian Sample of Male College Students', *Family Relations*, 40 (1991), 37–44.

74 Neil M. Malamuth and James V. P. Check, 'Sex Role Stereotyping and Reactions to Depictions of Stranger versus Acquaintance Rape', *Journal of Personality and Social Psychology*, 45 (1983), 344–56.

75 Mary P. Koss and C. Oros, 'Sexual Experiences Survey: A Research Instrument Investigating Sexual Aggression and Victimization', *Journal of Consulting and Clinical Psychology*, 50 (1982), 455–7.

76 Paula Lundberg-Love and Robert Geffner, 'Date Rape: Prevalence, Risk Factors,

and a Proposed Model', in Maureen A. Pirog-Good and Jan E. Stets (eds.), *Violence in Dating Relationships. Emerging Social Issues* (New York, 1989), 173.

77 Mary E. Craig, 'Coercive Sexuality in Dating Relationships: A Situational Model', *Clinical Psychology Review*, 10 (1990), 416. This was the work of Craig and S. C. Kalichman.

78 'Teens Express Themselves', *South Carolina State Newspaper*, 3 May 1988, 2a, cited in Mary E. Craig, 'Coercive Sexuality in Dating Relationships: A Situational Model', *Clinical Psychology Review*, 10 (1990), 416.

79 Eugene J. Kanin, 'Male Aggression in Dating-Courtship Relations', *The American Journal of Sociology*, 63 (1957), 197–204.

80 Kurt Weis and Sandra S. Borges, 'Victimology and Rape: The Case of the Legitimate Victim', *Issues in Criminology*, 8.2 (1973), 71–115.

81 Eugene J. Kanin, 'Date Rape: Unofficial Criminals and Victims', *Victimology: An International Journal*, 9 (1984), 101.

82 W. H. George and G. A. Marlatt, 'The Effects of Alcohol and Anger on Interest in Violence, Erotica, and Deviance', *Journal of Abnormal Psychology*, 95 (1986), 150–8. Also see L. Crowe and W. George, 'Alcohol and Human Sexuality: Review and Integration', *Psychological Bulletin*, 105 (1989), 374–86.

83 Both quotes are from Lynne Henderson, 'Rape and Responsibility', *Law and Philosophy*, 11.1/2 (1992), 160.

84 Keith Burgess-Jackson, *Rape: A Philosophical Investigation* (Aldershot, 1996), 31–2. This is the best exposition on the wrongs of date and acquaintance rape.

85 Keith Soothill, 'The Changing Face of Rape?', *British Journal of Criminology*, 31.4 (Autumn 1991), 388–9.

86 Jessica Harris and Sharon Grace, *A Question of Evidence? Investigating and Prosecuting Rape in the 1990s* (London, 1999), ix.

87 For the best discussion, see Allen Feldman, 'Memory Theatres, Virtual Witnessing, and the Trauma-Aesthetic', *Biography*, 27.1 (Winter 2004), 186.

88 For a discussion of this point in relation to sex killers, see Maria Tatar, *Lustmord. Sexual Murder in Weimar Germany* (Princeton, 1985), 54.

89 D. Lisak and S. Roth, 'Motives and Psychodynamics of Self-Reported, Unincarcerated Rapists', *American Journal of Orthopsychiatry*, 60 (1990), 268.

CHAPTER THREE: 'NO' MEANS 'YES"

1 H. L. A. Hart, *Punishment and Responsibility. Essays in the Philosophy of Law* (Oxford, 1968), 114.

2 See Mark Thornton, 'Rape and Mens Rea', *Canadian Journal of Philosophy*, supplementary volume 8 (1982), 119–46.

3 Lord Hailsham cited in Toni Pickard, 'Culpable Mistakes and Rape: Relating Mens Rea to the Crime', *The University of Toronto Law Journal*, 30.1 (Winter 1980), 90.

4 Dolly F. Alexander, 'Twenty Years of *Morgan*: Criticism of the Subjectivist View of *Mens Rea* and Rape in Great Britain', *Pace International Law Review*, 7 (1995), 233. This article provides the best critique.

5 Dann Byrne, 'The Imagery of Sex', in John Money and Herman Musaph (eds.), *Handbook of Sexology* (Amsterdam, 1977), 340; Claude Crépault and Marcel Couture, 'Men's Erotic Fantasies', *Archives of Sexual Behavior*, 9.6 (1980), 565; Lester A. Kirkendall and Leslie G. McBride, 'Preadolescent and Adolescent Imagery and Sexual Fantasies: Beliefs and Experiences', in M. E. Perry (ed.), *Handbook of Sexology, Vol. 7: Childhood and Adolescent Sexology* (Amsterdam, 1990).

6 Neil Malamuth, 'Aggression Against Women: Cultural and Individual Causes', in

Malamuth and Edward Donnerstein (eds.), *Pornography and Sexual Aggression* (New York, 1984).

7 Onesipherous W. Bartley, *A Treatise on Forensic Medicine or Medical Jurisprudence* (Bristol, 1815), 43.

8 J. Clifford Edgar and Jas. C. Johnson, 'Medico-Legal Consideration of Rape', in R. A. Witthaus and Tracy C. Becker (eds.), *Medical Jurisprudence, Forensic Medicine, and Toxicology*, vol. 2 (New York, 1894), 445; J. Dixon Mann, *Forensic Medicine and Toxicology*, 2nd edn. (London, 1898), 102; Michael Ryan, *A Manual of Medical Jurisprudence* (London, 1831), 190.

9 H. Aubrey Husband, *The Students' Hand-Book of Forensic Medicine and Medical Police*, 4th edn. (Edinburgh, 1883), 121, and Charles Gilbert Chaddock, 'Sexual Crimes', in Allen McLane Hamilton and Lawrence Godkin (eds.), *A System of Legal Medicine*, vol. 2, 2nd edn. (New York, 1900), 540.

10 J. Dixon Mann, *Forensic Medicine and Toxicology*, 2nd edn. (London, 1898), 96.

11 Rev. Dr Edgar of Belfast in a lecture in London in 1841, quoted in William Logan, *The Great Social Evil. Its Causes, Extent, Results, and Remedies* (London, 1871), 147.

12 For an example of drinks being spiked in order to rape a woman, see Jacob A. Goldberg and Rosamond W. Goldberg, *Girls on City Streets. A Study of 1400 Cases of Rape* (New York, 1935), 141.

13 'Outrage', *The Times*, 7 September 1877, 8.

14 Francis W. Newman, *Remedies for the Great Social Evil with Special Reference to Recent Laws Delusively Called Contagious Diseases Acts*, first pub. 1884 (London, 1889), 7.

15 For examples, see J. P. Payne, 'The Criminal Use of Chloroform', *Anaesthesia*, 53 (1998), 688–9.

16 Emily Finch and Vanessa E. Munro, 'Juror Stereotypes and Blame Attribution in Rape Cases Involving Intoxicants', *British Journal of Criminology*, 45 (2005), 27.

17 For more information, see http://www.roofie.com. Also see Sally Weale, 'Glass War: It's a Woman's Worst Nightmare and a Rapist's Ultimate Fantasy – and All It Takes Is One Spiked Drink', *The Guardian*, 20 June 2000, 6.

18 Rod Liddle, 'Dirty Work in the Moral Maze', *Times Online*, 2 April 2006, http://www.timesonline.co.uk/tol/comment/columnists/rod_liddle/article701147.ece, accessed 12 May 2006.

19 J. Snow, 'Further Remarks on the Employment of Chloroform by Thieves', *London Medical Gazette*, xlv (1850), 834–5.

20 'Police', *The Times*, 15 January 1850, 7, and 'Police', *The Times*, 1 February 1850, 7.

21 J. P. Payne, 'The Criminal Use of Chloroform', *Anaesthesia*, 53 (1998), 686.

22 Terence De Vere White, *The Parents of Oscar Wilde. Sir William and Lady Wilde* (London, 1967), 153.

23 Eric Lambert, *Mad and With Much Heart. A Life of the Parents of Oscar Wilde* (London, 1967), 108 and 119.

24 'Charge of Rape Under Chloroform', *British Medical Journal*, 17 November 1877, 708–9. Also see 'Trial of a French Dentist for Rape', *British Medical Journal*, 31 August 1878, 326–7, he was also acquitted.

25 Dudley Wilmot Buxton, *Anaesthetics. Their Uses and Administration* (London, 1888), 149–50. Also see S. V. Clevenger, *Medical Jurisprudence of Insanity or Forensic Psychiatry*, vol. 2 (New York, 1898), 673, and J. Dixon Mann, *Forensic Medicine and Toxicology*, 2nd edn. (London, 1898), 99.

26 Dudley Wilmot Buxton, *Anaesthetics. Their Uses and Administration* (London, 1888), 150–1.

27 J. Dixon Mann, *Forensic Medicine and Toxicology*, 2nd edn. (London, 1898), 100. Also see

Charles Gilbert Chaddock, 'Sexual Crimes', in Allen McLane Hamilton and Lawrence Godkin (eds.), *A System of Legal Medicine*, vol. 2, 2nd edn. (New York, 1900), 541.

28 Stephen Rogers, 'Can Chloroform Be Used to Facilitate Robbery?', *The Journal of Psychological Medicine*, v (1871), 751–69. The case was reported in J. Snow, 'Further Remarks on the Employment of Chloroform by Thieves', *London Medical Gazette*, xlv (1850), 834–35.

29 The use of hypnosis to rape a woman can even be seen in films, such as *Infidelity* (1917).

30 This was debated in relation to two men accused of homosexual rape: see Jonathan Venn, 'Misuse of Hypnosis in Sexual Contexts: Two Case Reports', *The International Journal of Clinical and Experimental Hypnosis*, xxxvi.1 (1988), 12–18.

31 This school was generally known as the School of Nancy and included such luminaries as Bernheim, Liébeault, Liégeois and Beaunis.

32 Hippolyte M. Bernheim, *New Studies in Hypnotism*, trans. Richard S. Sandor, first pub. 1891 (New York, 1980), 102–20.

33 Clark Bell, 'Hypnotism in the Criminal Courts', *The Medico-Legal Journal*, xiii.4 (1896), 354.

34 Campbell Perry, 'Hypnotic Coercion and Compliance to it: A Review of Evidence Presented in a Legal Case', *The International Journal of Clinical and Experimental Hypnosis*, xxvii.3 (1979), 189. This school was commonly known as the School of Paris and included Charcot, Brouardel and Gilles de la Tourette.

35 W. Xavier Suddeth, 'Hypnotism and Crime', *The Medico-Legal Journal*, xiii.3 (1895), 253–4.

36 Charles Gilbert Chaddock, 'Sexual Crimes', in Allen McLane Hamilton and Lawrence Godkin (eds.), *A System of Legal Medicine*, vol. 2, 2nd edn. (New York, 1900), 541–2.

37 'Resolution', in *International Journal of Clinical and Experimental Hypnosis*, 27 (1979), 452–3.

38 Horatio R. Storer, 'The Law of Rape', *The Quarterly Journal of Psychological Medicine and Medical Jurisprudence*, ii (1868), 58.

39 Ralph Slovenko, 'A Panoramic View: Sexual Behavior and the Law', in Slovenko (ed.), *Sexual Behavior and the Law* (Springfield, IL, 1965), 51.

40 'Forcible and Statutory Rape: An Exploration of the Operation and Objectives of the Consent Standard', *The Yale Law Journal*, 55 (1952–3), 66.

41 Walter Braun, *The Cruel and the Meek. Aspects of Sadism and Masochism. Being Pages from a Sexologist's Notebook* (New York, 1967), 8.

42 Hugo Paul, *Cry Rape: Anatomy of the Rapist*, intro. by Jean-Paul St. Marc (New York, 1967), 105.

43 'The Disappointed Old Maid', 1903, described in Sharon R. Ullman, *Sex Seen: The Emergence of Modern Sexuality in America* (Berkeley, CA, 1997), 21–2.

44 Sigmund Freud, 'Letters to Fliess', 1897, in Peter Gay (ed.), *The Freud Reader* (London, 1995), 112.

45 Sigmund Freud, *The Psychopathology of Everyday Life*, trans. A. A. Brill (London, 1914), 202–3.

46 Helene Deutsch, *The Psychology of Women: A Psychoanalytic Interpretation* (New York, 1944).

47 Horatio R. Storer, 'The Law of Rape', *The Quarterly Journal of Psychological Medicine and Medical Jurisprudence*, ii (1868), 58.

48 For a discussion of the impact of such ideas in divorce cases, see Robert L. Griswold, 'Law, Sex, Cruelty, and Divorce in Victorian America, 1840–1900', *American Quarterly*, 38.5 (Winter 1986), 734.

49 Hans von Hentig, 'Interaction of Perpetrator and Victim', *Journal of Criminal Law and Criminal Behavior*, 31 (1940), 305.

50 George Devereux, 'The Awarding of a Penis as a Compensation for Rape. A Demonstration of the Clinical Relevance of the Psycho-Analytic Study of Cultural Data', *International Journal of Psycho-Analysis*, xxxviii.vi (November–December 1957), 400.

51 Ralph Slovenko, 'A Panoramic View: Sexual Behavior and the Law', in his (ed.), *Sexual Behavior and the Law* (Springfield, IL, 1965), 52. Also see Lee Ellis, *Theories of Rape: Inquiries into the Causes of Sexual Aggression* (New York, 1989), 634.

52 Seymour Halleck, 'The Therapeutic Encounter', in H. L. P. Resnik and Marvin E. Wolfgang (eds.), *Sexual Behaviors. Social, Clinical, and Legal Aspects* (Boston, 1972), 191–2. Also see Warren S. Wille, 'Case Study of a Rapist', *Journal of Social Therapy and Corrective Psychiatry*, 7.1 (1961), 19.

53 Vincent Riccio and Bill Slocum, *All the Way Down. The Violent Underworld of Street Gangs* (New York, 1962), 106–7. Also see Ross Barber, 'An Investigation into Rape and Attempted Rape Cases in Queensland', *Australian and New Zealand Journal of Criminology* 6.4 (December 1973), 229.

54 'Forcible and Statutory Rape: An Exploration of the Operation and Objectives of the Consent Standard', *The Yale Law Journal*, 55 (1952–3), 66–9.

55 David Abrahamsen, *The Psychology of Crime* (New York, 1960), 161.

56 M. Factor, 'A Woman's Psychological Reaction to Attempted Rape', *Psychiatric Quarterly*, 23 (1954), 243–4.

57 *National Commission on the Causes and Prevention of Violence, The Offender and His Victim* (1969), cited in Virginia A. Sadock, 'Special Areas of Interest', in Harold I. Kaplan and Benjamin J. Sadock (eds.), *Comprehensive Textbook of Psychiatry. IV*, 4th edn. (Baltimore, 1985), 1092.

58 'A No-Good Girl of 15½', *The Times*, 23 November 1960, 16. In this case the alleged rapist had his sentence of six months' imprisonment exchanged for a £50 fine on the grounds that this respectable Jamaican had been 'led astray by the girl'.

59 Gilbert Geis and Duncan Chappell, 'Forcible Rape by Multiple Offenders', *Abstracts on Criminology and Penology*, 11.4 (July/August 1971), 434.

60 Commentary by Charles R. Haymen on Menachim Amir's 'Sociocultural Factors in Forcible Rape', in Leonard Gross (ed.), *Sexual Behavior. Current Issue. An Interdisciplinary Perspective* (New York, 1974), 185.

61 Ross Barber, 'An Investigation into Rape and Attempted Rape Cases in Queensland', *Australian and New Zealand Journal of Criminology*, 6.4 (December 1973), 228.

62 Eileen Andray, 'Abortion', letter to the editor, *The Times*, 13 July 1965, 13.

63 Sheldon H. Kardener, 'Rape Fantasies', *Journal of Religion and Health*, 14.1 (1975), 55.

64 For a discussion, see Peter W. Bardaglio, 'Rape and the Law in the Old South: "Calculated to Excite Indignation in Every Heart"', *The Journal of Southern History*, 60.4 (November 1994), 756.

65 Saidiya Hartman, 'Seduction and the Ruses of Power', *Callaloo*, 19.2 (1996), 539.

66 Thomas Read Rootes Cobb, *Inquiry into the Law of Negro Slavery. To Which is Prefaced, An Historical Sketch of Slavery* (Philadelphia, 1858), 83, 90 and 99.

67 Catherine Clinton, '"With a Whip in His Hand": Rape, Memory, and African-American Women', in Geneviève Fabre and Robert O'Meally (eds.), *History and Memory in African-American Culture* (Oxford, 1994), 207.

68 Gurney Williams, 'Rape in Children and Young Girls. Based on the Personal Investigation of Several Hundred Cases of Rape and of Over Fourteen Thousand Vaginal Examinations', *International Clinics*, 2.1 (1913), 246. He also believed the same was true of African-American boys and men.

69 Dallas v. State, 79 So. 690 (Fla. 1918), quoted in Jennifer Wriggins, 'Rape, Racism, and the Law', *Harvard Women's Law Journal*, 6 (1983), 121. Also see 'Prisoners Against Rape: Trying to Unlock Myths and Images', *The Washington Post*, 16 June 1975, B3.

70 Rosalyn Terborg-Penn, 'Woman Suffrage: "First Because We are Women and Second Because We are Colored Women"', *Truth. Newsletter of the Association of Black Women Historians* (April 1985), 9.

71 Jennifer Temkin, 'Prosecuting and Defending Rape: Perspectives from the Bar', *Journal of Law and Society*, 27.2 (June 2000), 232–3.

72 H. Aubrey Husband, *The Students' Hand-Book of Forensic Medicine and Medical Police*, 4th edn. (Edinburgh, 1883), 114.

73 Undated clip from the magazine's archive, *Slam*, cited in R. Amy Elman, 'Disability Pornography. The Fetishization of Women's Vulnerabilities', *Violence Against Women*, 3.3 (June 1997), 259.

74 Hugo Paul, *Cry Rape: Anatomy of the Rapist*, intro. by Jean-Paul St. Marc (New York, 1967), 13.

75 Jane Brook, 'Sexual Abuse and People with Intellectual Disabilities', *Social Work Review*, 9.3 (1997), 16–17.

76 *The Times*, 7 November 1885, 7.

77 J. Clifford Edgar and Jas. C. Johnson, 'Medico-Legal Consideration of Rape', in R. A. Witthaus and Tracy C. Becker (eds.), *Medical Jurisprudence, Forensic Medicine and Toxicology*, vol. 2 (New York, 1894), 420.

78 Later changed to Awareness.

79 David Abrahamsen, *Crime and the Human Mind* (London, 1945), 199.

80 Michelle Oberman, 'Turning Girls into Women: Re-Evaluating Modern Statutory Rape Law', *Journal of Criminal Law and Criminology*, 85.1 (Summer 1994), 27.

81 Justice Brennan in Michael M. v. Sonoma County Superior Court, 450 US 464, 470 (1981), p.493, cited in Rigel Oliveri, 'Statutory Rape Law and Enforcement in the Wake of Welfare Reform', *Stanford Law Review*, 52.2 (January 2000), 468.

82 Mike Males and Kenneth S. Y. Chew, 'The Ages of Fathers in California Adolescent Births', *American Journal of Public Health*, 86 (1996), 565–7.

83 David J. Landry and Jacqueline Dorroch Forrest, 'How Old are US Fathers?', *Family Planning Perspectives*, 27 (1995), 159–60.

84 Rigel Oliveri, 'Statutory Rape Law and Enforcement in the Wake of Welfare Reform', *Stanford Law Review*, 52.2 (January 2000), 475–7. I am indebted to her for this analysis.

85 Jack Doyle, Executive, Monroe County (New York), in Jon R. Sorensen, 'Pataki Welfare Reform Seeks to Reduce Illegitimate Births', *Buffalo News*, 10 November 1996, A1.

86 State of Kansas, Colleen Hermesmann v. Shane Seyer, 5 March 1993: http://www.nas.com/c4m/rape_case.html.

87 Miriam H. Ruttenberg, 'A Feminist Critique of Mandatory Arrest: An Analysis of Race and Gender in Domestic Violence Policy', *American University Journal of Gender and Law*, 2 (1994), 171 and 185, and Patricia Donovan, 'Can Statutory Rape Laws be Effective in Preventing Adolescent Pregnancy?', *Family Planning Perspective*, 29 (1997), 30–3.

88 Graham Hughes, 'The Crime of Incest', *The Journal of Criminal Law, Criminology, and Police Science*, 55 (1964), 323.

89 There were other extremely heated debates, such as the nineteenth-century argument about whether a man could marry (and thus have sexual intercourse with) the sister of his deceased wife: see Nancy F. Anderson, 'The "Marriage with a Deceased

Wife's Sister Bill" Controversy: Incest Anxiety and the Defense of Family Purity in Victorian England', *The Journal of British Studies*, 21.2 (Spring 1982), 67–86.

90 In 2000 the age of consent for both heterosexual and homosexual couples became sixteen in England, Wales and Scotland and seventeen in Northern Ireland.

91 Ilene Seidman and Susan Vickers, 'The Second Wave: An Agenda for the Next Thirty Years of Rape Law Reform', *Suffolk University Law Reform*, 38 (2004–5), 489.

92 Stephen Schulhofer, 'The Gender Question in Criminal Law', in Ellen Frankel Paul, Fred D. Miller and Jeffrey Paul (eds.), *Crime, Culpability, and Remedy* (Oxford, 1990), 133.

93 Ruth Hall and Lisa Longstaff, 'Defining Consent', *New Law Journal*, 147 (1997), 840.

CHAPTER FOUR: RAPACIOUS BODIES

1 Cecil Day Lewis, 'Sex-Crime', *Selected Poems* (Harmondsworth, 1951), 38–40.

2 Arne Svenson, *Prisoners* (New York, 1997), 119–20. Spelling as in original.

3 Henry Havelock Ellis, *The Criminal*, first pub. 1890 (London, 1914), 80–1, 92–3, 101–2, 111–12.

4 Henri Colin, 'Mental and Physical State of Criminals Convicted of Sexual Crime', *The Alienist and Neurologist*, xix (1898), 659–60. The term 'stigmata of degeneracy' was also used to describe a rapist in Louis E. Bisch, 'The Police Psychopathic Laboratory', *Journal of the American Institute of Criminal Law and Criminology*, 7.1 (May 1916), 85.

5 Martin W. Barr, 'The Criminal Irresponsible', *The Alienist and Neurologist*, xxx (1909), 611–12 and 617.

6 Henri Colin, 'Mental and Physical State of Criminals Convicted of Sexual Crime', *The Alienist and Neurologist*, xix (1898), 659–60.

7 Henry Alexander Davidson, *Forensic Psychiatry* (New York, 1952), 109.

8 Allan McLane Hamilton, 'Insanity in Medico-Legal Bearings', in Hamilton and Lawrence Godkin (eds.), *A System of Legal Medicine*, vol. 2, 2nd edn. (New York, 1900), 51. The term 'reverse evolution' is mine, not Hamilton's.

9 Bertram Pollens, *The Sex Criminal* (London, 1939), 153–4.

10 George E. Dawson, 'Psychic Rudiments and Morality', *The American Journal of Psychology*, 11.2 (January 1900), 193 and 203.

11 A. Lucas, 'Convicted of Criminal Assault', 1928, in National Archives of Australia A1/15 1933/2453: 'Revolting Attack on Australian Mother. Mediterranean Moron Gets Seven Years' Gaol. Brutal and Degenerate', [Brisbane] *Truth*, 30 September 1928.

12 William McDougall, *An Introduction to Social Psychology*, first pub. 1908 (Bristol, 1998), 29.

13 For a discussion, see my *An Intimate History of Killing: Face-to-Face Killing in Twentieth Century History* (London, 1999). It is important to note that women were not regarded as possessing the same configuration of the 'pugnacious instinct'. For the feminine version, also see my book.

14 William Adrian Bonger, *Criminality and Economic Conditions*, trans. Henry P. Horton (Boston, 1916), 612 and 617–20. Also see Clarence Seward Darrow, *Crime: Its Cause and Treatment* (London, 1920), 88, and Horatio R. Storer, 'The Law of Rape', *The Quarterly Journal of Psychological Medicine and Medical Jurisprudence*, ii (New York, 1868), 49.

15 Clarence Seward Darrow, *Crime: Its Cause and Treatment* (London, 1920), 88–9.

16 Clarence Seward Darrow, *Crime: Its Cause and Treatment* (London, 1920), 88.

17 'Flogging as Legal Punishment in England', *Albany Law Journal*, 57 (1898), 105.

Also see John L. Wharton, 'To the Editor of The Times. The Corporal Punishment Bill', *The Times*, 27 March 1900, 10.

18 Charles B. Lore, quoted in Clark Bell, 'Corporal Punishment for Crime', *The Medico-Legal Journal*, xvii.1 (1899), 81.

19 Hon. Simeon E. Baldwin, 'Corporal Punishments for Crime', *The Medico-Legal Journal*, xvii.1 (1899), 66–7, 71, 278 and 376, and Simeon E. Baldwin's, 'Whipping and Castration as Punishments for Crime', *The Yale Law Journal*, 8.9 (June 1899), 278, 376 and 382.

20 Lucius H. Perkins, 'Corporal Punishment for Crime', *The American Lawyer*, 9 (1901), 277–9. Spelling as in original.

21 For instance, see *The Times*, 29 August 1846, 6, and *The Times*, 12 May 1886, 4.

22 For an extended discussion, see Martha Elizabeth Hodes, *White Women, Black Men: Illicit Sex in the Nineteenth-Century South* (New Haven, 1997); Diane Miller Sommerville, 'The Rape Myth in the Old South Reconsidered', *Journal of Southern History*, lxi (August 1995), 481–518.

23 William Reynolds, 'The Remedy for Lynch Law', *The Yale Law Journal*, 7 (20 October 1897–June 1898), 20.

24 *Lynchings and What they Mean. General Findings of the Southern Commission on the Study of Lynching* (Atlanta, 1931), 19.

25 William Reynolds, 'The Remedy for Lynch Law', *The Yale Law Journal*, 7 (20 October 1897–June 1898), 21.

26 Sims v. Balkcom, 220 Ga. 7, 13 S. E. 2d. 766, 769 (1964).

27 'The Crime of Rape', *The Afro-American Ledger*, 3 August 1907, 4.

28 Haywood Patterson and Earl Conrad, *Scottsboro Boy* (London, 1950), 24.

29 Lisa Lindquist Dorr, 'Black-On-White Rape and Retribution in Twentieth-Century Virginia: "Men, Even Negroes, Must Have Some Protection"', *The Journal of Southern History*, 66.4 (November 2000), 718–19.

30 Luther Z. Rosser, 'Illegal Enforcement of Criminal Law', *American Bar Association Journal*, 7 (1921), 519–24.

31 'Study of Judge Lynch', *The Afro-American*, 16 May 1903, 4.

32 F. E. Daniel, 'Should Insane Criminals or Sexual Perverts be Allowed to Procreate?' *The Medico-Legal Journal*, xi.3 (December 1893), 282–3.

33 Walter White, *Rope and Faggot: A Biography of Judge Lynch*, first pub. 1929 (New York, 1969), 8–11, 56.

34 [Tampa] *Daily Times*, 30 January 1934, and [Tampa] *Morning Tribune*, 1 February 1934.

35 [Tampa] *Morning Tribune*, 1 February 1934.

36 There was controversy over the abolition of the death penalty for rape. See 'There is a Bill', *The Times*, 18 July 1840, 5; 'The First Report of the Irish Poor Law Commissioners', *The Times*, 15 January 1836, 2; 'The Crude, Precipitate and Blundering Measures', *The Times*, 19 June 1841, 4.

37 Simeon E. Baldwin, 'Whipping and Castration as Punishments for Crime' *The Yale Law Journal*, 8.9 (June 1899), 380.

38 State v. Petit, La. 1016, 44 So. 849 (1907).

39 Oliver Hill quoted in Eric W. Rise, *The Martinsville Seven: Race, Rape, and Capital Punishment* (Charlottesville, VA, 1995), 3.

40 Peter W. Bardaglio, 'Rape and the Law in the Old South: "Calculated to Excite Indignation in Every Heart"', *Journal of Southern History*, 60.4 (November 1994), 756.

41 Virginia Code of 1860, ch. 200, no.1. This racial difference was eradicated in 1866.

42 For instance, see Peter W. Bardaglio, 'Rape and the Law in the Old South: "Calculated to Excite Indignation in Every Heart"', *Journal of Southern History*, 60.4 (November 1994), 751.
43 McQuirter v. State, cited in Jennifer Wriggins, 'Rape, Racism, and the Law', *Harvard Women's Law Journal*, 6 (1983), 111.
44 Donald H. Partington, 'The Incidence of the Death Penalty for Rape in Virginia', *Washington and Lee Law Review*, 22 (1965), 43. Also see Donal E. J. MacNamara and Edward Sagarin, *Sex, Crime, and the Law* (New York, 1977); Frank E. Hartung, 'Trends in the Use of Capital Punishment', *Annals of American Academy of Political and Social Science*, 284 (1952), 8–19; Haywood Burns, 'Can a Black Man Get a Fair Trial in this Country?', *New York Times Magazine*, 12 July 1970, 5.
45 Hampton v. Commonwealth, 190 Va. 531, 554, 58 S.E.2d. 288, 298 (1960), cited in Donald H. Partington, 'The Incidence of the Death Penalty for Rape in Virginia', *Washington and Lee Law Review*, 22 (1965), 62.
46 Donald H. Partington, 'The Incidence of the Death Penalty for Rape in Virginia', *Washington and Lee Law Review*, 22 (1965), 62.
47 Elmer H. Johnson, 'Selective Factors in Capital Punishment', *Social Forces*, 36 (1957–8), 165–9.
48 Donald H. Partington, 'The Incidence of the Death Penalty for Rape in Virginia', *Washington and Lee Law Review*, 22 (1965), 52–3. The total number imposed was 444. Also see Phyllis L. Crocker, 'Crossing the Line: Rape-Murder and the Death Penalty', *Ohio Northern University Law Review*, 26 (2000) 701.
49 Marvin E. Wolfgang and Marc Riedel, 'Rape, Racial Discrimination and the Death Penalty', in Hugo Adam Bedau and Chester M. Pierce (eds.), *Capital Punishment in the United States* (New York, 1976), 109–14. Also see Marvin E. Wolfgang, 'Racial Discrimination in the Death Sentence for Rape', in William J. Bowers, *Executions in America* (Lexington, MA, 1974), 116.
50 Lisa Lindquist Dorr, 'Black-On-White Rape and Retribution in Twentieth-Century Virginia: "Men, Even Negroes, Must Have Some Protection"', *The Journal of Southern History*, 66.4 (November 2000), 714–15.
51 Harper Lee, *To Kill a Mockingbird* (London, 1960), 266.
52 'The Crime of Rape', *The Afro-American Ledger*, 3 August 1907, 4.
53 *The Afro-American Ledger*, 19 December 1904, 4.
54 Kimberle Crenshaw, 'Mapping the Margins: Intersectionality, Identity Politics, and Violence Against Women of Color', *Stanford Law Review*, 43.6 (July 1991), 1269.
55 Gary D. LaFree, 'The Effect of Social Stratification by Race on Official Reactions to Rape', *American Sociological Review*, 45.5 (October 1980), 844 and 847–52.
56 Gerrit S. Miller, 'The Primate Basis of Human Sexual Behavior', *The Quarterly Review of Biology*, vi.4 (December 1931), 380–403.
57 Richard Wrangham and Dale Peterson, *Demonic Males: Apes and the Origins of Human Violence* (Boston, 1996).
58 David Barash, *Sociobiology: The Whisperings Within* (New York, 1979), 53–5.
59 The notion that violence was a 'biologically male-linked trait' even started appearing in historical accounts: see Martin J. Wiener, *Men of Blood. Violence, Manliness and Criminal Justice in Victorian England* (Cambridge, 2004), 1–2, 201 and 290.
60 Randy Thornhill and Craig Palmer, *A Natural History of Rape: Biological Bases of Sexual Coercion* (Cambridge, MA, 2000).
61 Donald Symons, *The Evolution of Human Sexuality* (Oxford, 1979), 253.
62 Satoshi Kanazawa and Mary C. Still, 'Why Men Commit Crimes (And Why They Desist)', *Sociological Theory*, 18.3 (November 2000), 440.

63 For example, see S. B. Hrdy and G. C. Williams, 'Behavioral Biology and the Double Standard', in S. K. Wasser (ed.), *Social Behaviors of Female Vertebrates* (New York, 1983), 3–17; Jacquelyn W. White and Robin M. Kowalski, 'Deconstructing the Myth of the Nonaggressive Woman. A Feminist Analysis', *Psychology of Women Quarterly*, 18 (1994), 487–508.

64 Susan Sperling, 'Baboons with Briefcases: Feminism, Functionalism, and Sociobiology on the Evolution of Primate Gender', *Signs: Journal of Women in Culture and Society*, 17.1 (Autumn 1991), 4.

65 Cheryl Hanna, 'Bad Girls and Good Sports: Some Reflections on Violent Female Juvenile Delinquents, Title IX & the Promise of Girl Power', *Hastings Constitutional Law Quarterly*, 27 (1999–2000), 671.

66 Anne Campbell, *Men, Women, and Aggression* (New York, 1993).

67 Jerry A. Coyne, 'Of Vice and Men: A Case Study in Evolutionary Psychology', in Cheryl Brown Travis (ed.), *Evolution, Gender, and Rape* (Cambridge, MA, 2003), 183, checked the footnotes and found misrepresentations of other scholars' work.

68 For the best discussion of the book, from a range of perspectives (not all totally hostile), see Cheryl Brown Travis (ed.), *Evolution, Gender, and Rape* (Cambridge, MA, 2003). Also see Hilary Rose, 'Debating Rape', *The Lancet*, 357 (2001), 727–8; Hilary Rose and Steven Rose (eds.), *Alas, Poor Darwin. Arguments Against Evolutionary Psychology* (London, 2000); Elisabeth A. Lloyd, 'Science Gone Astray: Evolution and Rape', *Michigan Law Review*, 99.6 (2001), 1536–59.

69 Jerry A. Coyne, 'Of Vice and Men: A Case Study in Evolutionary Psychology', in Cheryl Brown Travis (ed.), *Evolution, Gender, and Rape* (Cambridge, MA, 2003), 179.

70 Cheryl Brown Travis, 'Talking Evolution and Selling Difference', in her (ed.), *Evolution, Gender, and Rape* (Cambridge, MA, 2003), 6.

71 Jerry A. Coyne, 'Of Vice and Men: A Case Study in Evolutionary Psychology', in Cheryl Brown Travis (ed.), *Evolution, Gender, and Rape* (Cambridge, MA, 2003), 176.

72 A notorious example is Owen D. Jones, 'Sex, Culture, and the Biology of Rape: Toward Explanation and Prevention', *California Law Review*, 87.4 (July 1999), 827–941 in which the author dismisses all evidence against evolutionary theory as outside the parameters of that theory.

73 Roxanne Lieb, Vernon Quinsey and Lucy Berliner, 'Sexual Predators and Social Policy', *Crime and Justice*, 23 (1998), 47.

74 Pauline B. Bart, 'Theories of Rape: Inquiries into the Causes of Sexual Aggression', *Contemporary Sociology*, 20.2 (March 1991), 268.

75 Horatio R. Storer, 'The Law of Rape', *The Quarterly Journal of Psychological Medicine and Medical Jurisprudence*, ii (New York, 1868), 62–3.

76 Sarnoff A. Mednick, 'Biological Factors in Crime Causation: The Reactions of Social Scientists', in Mednick, Terrie E. Moffitt and Susan A. Stack (eds.), *The Causes of Crime: New Biological Approaches*, 1 (1987), 2. Also see Susan Horan, 'The XYY Supermale and the Criminal Justice System: A Square Peg in a Round Hole', *Loyola Los Angeles Law Review*, 25 (1992), 1343–76; P. Jacobs et al., 'Aggressive Behavior, Mental Abnormality and the XYY Male', *Nature*, 208 (1965), 1351–2; H. Witkin et al., 'Criminality in XYY and XXV Men', *Science* (1983), 547–55. For a summary of the critique of this position, see Deborah W. Dennon, 'Gender, Crime, and the Criminal Law Defenses', *Journal of Criminal Law and Criminology*, 85.1 (Summer 1994), 127–8.

77 Randy Thornhill and Craig Palmer, *A Natural History of Rape: Biological Bases of Sexual Coercion* (Cambridge, MA, 2000), 154, 179 and 181.

78 Jerry A. Coyne, 'Of Vice and Men: A Case Study in Evolutionary Psychology', in Cheryl Brown Travis (ed.), *Evolution, Gender, and Rape* (Cambridge, MA, 2003), 185.
79 Wilhelm Stekel, *Auto-Erotism*, trans. James S. Van Tesllaar (London, 1951), quoted in Narcyz Lukianowicz, 'Imaginary Sexual Partner', *Archives of General Psychiatry*, 3 (October 1960), 429.
80 'Facts First', letter to the editor from Thomas Moore, *The Times*, 3 February 1961, 11, writing from the House of Commons. Also see Ross Barber, 'An Investigation into Rape and Attempted Rape Cases in Queensland', *Australian and New Zealand Journal of Criminology* 6.4 (December 1973), 173.
81 David Rueben, *Everything You Always Wanted to Know About Sex But Were Afraid to Ask* (New York, 1969), 248–9.
82 Murray A. Straus, 'Sexual Inequality, Cultural Norms, and Wife-Beating', in Emilio C. Viano (ed.), *Victims and Society* (Washington, DC, 1976), 543–59.

CHAPTER FIVE: BRUTALIZING ENVIRONMENTS

1 'Amos', quoted in Les Sussman and Sally Bordwell, *The Rapist File* (New York, 1981), 67–75.
2 Iain McCalman, *Radical Underworlds: Prophets, Revolutionaries, and Pornographers in London, 1795–1840* (Oxford, 1987).
3 William T. Stead, 'The Maiden Tribute of Modern Babylon', *Pall Mall Gazette*, 6 July 1885, 3 and 5. The full text can be found at http://www.attackingthedevil.co.uk/pmg/tribute/mt1.php.
4 For instance, see George Kibbe Turner, 'Daughters of the Poor', *McClure's Magazine*, xxxiv (1909), 57–8. For a discussion, see Egal Feldman, 'Prostitution, the Alien Woman, and the Progressive Imagination, 1910–15', *American Quarterly*, 19.2 (Summer 1967), 192–206.
5 Lucius H. Perkins, 'Corporal Punishment for Crime', *The American Lawyer*, 9 (1901), 274.
6 'A Southern Lawyer', 'Remedies for Lynch Law', *Sewanee Review*, 8 (January 1900), 3.
7 It is one of the most common themes in film: also see *Her Debt of Honor* (1916) and *The Border Raiders* (1918).
8 17 December 1874, quoted in Richard Altick, *Victorian Studies in Scarlet* (London, 1972), 295.
9 'National Society for the Prevention of Cruelty to Children, Scottish Branch report for the Year 1901. Moray, Nairn and Banffshire' (Edinburgh, 1901), 9–10, in the Glasgow Caledonian University Special Collection.
10 'National Society for the Prevention of Cruelty to Children. Scottish Branch. Report for the Year 1902. Edinburgh Committee' (Edinburgh, 1902), 38–9, in the Glasgow Caledonian University Special Collection.
11 Gustav Aschaffenburg, *Crime and Its Repression* (London, 1913), 117–18.
12 David Abrahamsen, *The Psychology of Crime* (New York, 1960), 158; Menachem Amir, 'Forcible Rape', *Federal Probation*, xxxi.1 (March 1967), 53; Richard T. Rada, 'Alcoholism and Forcible Rape', *American Journal of Psychiatry*, 132.4 (April 1975), 444.
13 Martin J. Wiener, *Men of Blood. Violence, Manliness and Criminal Justice in Victorian England* (Cambridge, 2004), 268–9.
14 Frances E. Willard, cited in Brian Donovan, *White Slave Crusades. Race, Gender, and Anti-Vice Activism, 1887–1917* (Urbana, 2006), 49.
15 Rev. F. M. Lehman with Rev. N. K. Clarkson, *The White Slave Hell; or, With Christ at Midnight in the Slums of Chicago* (Boston, 1910), 127.

16 Gurney Williams, 'Rape in Children and in Young Girls', *International Clinics* 23 (1913), 245. Also see J. V. Stevenson, *The Punishment and Prevention of Crime* (Glasgow, 1908), 3.
17 'Incest', Superintendent of Executive Branch of the Metropolitan Police, 1 July 1908, National Archives (London) MEPOL2/1260.
18 Albert Warren Stearns, *The Personality of Criminals* (Boston, 1931), 83–4.
19 Narcyz Lukianowicz, 'Incest', *British Journal of Psychiatry*, 120 (1972), 301–13.
20 Max Hodann, *History of Modern Morals*, trans. Stella Brown (London, 1937), 70.
21 'Sexual Offences Against Young Persons', *The Howard Journal*, ii.4 (1926), 49–50.
22 Marie E. Kopp, 'Surgical Treatment as Sex Crime Prevention Measure', *Journal of Law, Criminology, and Police Science*, 28 (1937–8), 696. She also says this distinguishes female sex criminals as well, but is referring to prostitutes.
23 Jacob A. Goldberg and Rosamond W. Goldberg, *Girls on City Streets. A Study of 1400 Cases of Rape* (New York, 1935), 187.
24 Havelock Ellis was discussed earlier. This was also the view of Dr T. D. Crothers, 'Sexual Crimes by Inebriates', *The Alienist and Neurologist*, xvii (1896), 187.
25 W. Norwood East, 'Observations on Exhibitionism', *The Lancet*, 23 August 1924, 373–4.
26 W. Norwood East, 'Sexual Offenders', *The Journal of Nervous and Mental Disease*, 103.6 (June 1946), 636–7.
27 W. Calder, 'The Sexual Offender: A Prison Medical Officer's Viewpoint', *The British Journal of Delinquency*, vi.1 (July 1955), 28.
28 W. H. George and G. A. Marlatt, 'The Effects of Alcohol and Anger on Interest in Violence, Erotica, and Deviance', *Journal of Abnormal Psychology*, 95 (1986), 150–8.
29 Clifford R. Shaw in collaboration with Maurice E. Moore, *The Natural History of a Delinquent Career* (New York, 1968), 8, 23, 229 and 232–3.
30 Professor Ernest W. Burgess, 'Discussion', in Clifford R. Shaw in collaboration with Maurice E. Moore, *The Natural History of a Delinquent Career* (New York, 1968), 238.
31 G. D. Woods, 'Some Aspects of Pack Rape in Sydney', *Australian and New Zealand Journal of Criminology*, 2.2 (June 1969), 105–19.
32 Ross Barber, 'An Investigation into Rape and Attempted Rape Cases in Queensland', *Australian and New Zealand Journal of Criminology*, 6.4 (December 1973), 228.
33 For an interesting example which does not explicitly mention rape however, see Earl R. Moses, 'Community Factors in Negro Delinquency', *The Journal of Negro Education*, 5.2 (April 1936), 220–9.
34 Menachem Amir (1971), 44, cited in James L. LeBeau, 'Rape and Racial Patterns', in Sol Chaneles (ed.), *Gender Issues, Sex Offenses, and Criminal Justice: Current Trends* (New York, 1984), 126. For excellent discussions (which introduce some subtlety), see James L. LeBeau, 'Rape and Racial Patterns', in Sol Chaneles (ed.), *Gender Issues, Sex Offenses, and Criminal Justice: Current Trends* (New York, 1984), 125–48, and Scott J. South and Richard B. Felson, 'The Racial Patterning of Rape', *Social Forces*, 69.1 (September 1990), 71–93.
35 Daniel E. J. MacNamara and Edward Sagarin, *Sex, Crime, and the Law* (New York, 1977), 52.
36 Menachem Amir, 'Sociocultural Factors in Forcible Rape', in Leonard Gross (ed.), *Sexual Behavior. Current Issues. An Interdisciplinary Perspective* (New York, 1974), 183.
37 Professor Ernest W. Burgess, 'Discussion', in Clifford R. Shaw in collaboration with Maurice E. Moore, *The Natural History of a Delinquent Career* (New York, 1968), 237. Also see Renet Bachman, Raymond Paternoster and Sally Ward, 'The

Rationality of Sexual Offending: Testing a Deterrence/Rational Choice Conception of Sexual Assault', *Law and Society Review*, 26.2 (1992), 344.

38 Eldridge Cleaver, *Soul on Ice* (New York, 1968), 14.

39 John Dollard, Leonard W. Doob, Neal E. Miller, O. H. Mowrer and Robert R. Sears, *Frustration and Aggression* (New Haven, 1939), 28–39; Leonard Berkowitz, 'The Frustration-Aggression Hypothesis Revisited', in Berkowitz (ed.), *Roots of Aggression: A Re-Examination of the Frustration-Aggression Hypothesis* (New York, 1969); Leonard Berkowitz, 'Situational Influences on Aggression', in Jo Groebel and Robert A. Hinde (eds.), *Aggression and War. Their Biological and Social Bases* (Cambridge, 1989), 91–100.

40 J. P. Scott, *Aggression* (Chicago, 1958), 35.

41 Lynn A. Curtis, *Violence, Race, and Culture* (Lexington, MA, 1975), 78–9.

42 Lewis Yablonsky, *The Violent Gang* (New York, 1962), 199.

43 G. D. Woods, 'Some Aspects of Pack Rape in Sydney', *Australian and New Zealand Journal of Criminology*, 2.2 (June 1969), 114–15.

44 T. C. N. Gibbens, C. Way and K. L. Soothill, 'Behavioural Types of Rape' *British Journal of Psychiatry*, 130 (1977), 35.

45 Lewis J. Doshay and George W. Henry, *The Boy Sex Offender and His Later Career* (Montclair, NJ, 1969), 166–7.

46 John L. Gillin, 'Social Background of Sex Offenders and Murderers', *Marriage Hygiene*, 1.3 (February 1935), 227–9.

47 Warren S. Wille, 'Case Study of a Rapist', *Journal of Social Therapy and Corrective Psychiatry*, 7.1 (1961), 10–21.

48 Philip Piker, 'A Psychiatrist Looks at Sex Offenses', *Journal of Social Hygiene*, 33 (1947), 392–3 and 395.

49 Renatus Hartogs, 'Discipline in the Early Life of Sex-Delinquents and Sex-Criminals', *The Nervous Child*, 9.2 (1951), 167–72.

50 David Abrahamsen, *The Psychology of Crime* (New York, 1960), 157–8.

51 Renatus Hartogs, 'Discipline in the Early Life of Sex-Delinquents and Sex-Criminals', *The Nervous Child*, 9.2 (1951), 167–72.

52 W. L. Marshall, 'Intimacy, Loneliness, and Sexual Offenders', *Behavioral Research and Therapy*, 27.5 (1989), 492–8. The chief proponent of attachment theory was John Bowlby, *Attachment and Loss* (London, 1969).

53 Warren S. Wille, 'Case Study of a Rapist', *Journal of Social Therapy and Corrective Psychiatry*, 7.1 (1961), 10–21.

54 For examples where Oedipal conflicts *are* asserted, see Murray L. Cohen, Ralph Garofalo, Richard Boucher and Theoharis Seghorn, 'The Psychology of Rapists', *Seminars in Psychiatry*, 3.3 (August 1971), 315–17, and Emanuel F. Hammer, 'A Psychoanalytic Hypothesis Concerning Sex Offenders. A Study by Clinical Psychologic Techniques', *Journal of Clinical and Experimental Psychopathology*, xviii.2 (June 1957), 180–3.

55 A. Nicholas Groth, 'The Adolescent Sexual Offender and His Prey', *International Journal of Offender Therapy and Contemporary Criminology*, 21.3 (1977), 253–4.

56 Chaplain H. Rex Lewy, speaking in Frederick P. Zuspan, 'Alleged Rape: An Invitational Symposium', *The Journal of Reproductive Medicine*, 12.4 (April 1974), 150. It is a view repeated in many popular crime texts: see Carlton Smith, *Hunting Evil* (New York, 2000), viii, for instance.

57 D. J. West, C. Roy and Florence L. Nichols, *Understanding Sexual Attacks: A Study Based Upon a Group of Rapists Undergoing Psychotherapy* (London, 1978), xiv.

58 D. J. West, C. Roy and Florence L. Nichols, *Understanding Sexual Attacks: A Study Based Upon a Group of Rapists Undergoing Psychotherapy* (London, 1978), 33.

59 bell hooks, *Outlaw Culture. Resisting Representations* (London, 1994), 110.
60 Roy Porter, 'Rape', in Sylvana Tomaselli and Roy Porter (eds.), *Rape. An Historical and Critical Enquiry* (Oxford, 1986), 222.
61 Alan Soble, *Pornography: Marxism, Feminism, and the Future of Sexuality* (New Haven, 1986), 81. Also see Diana Russell, 'On Pornography', *Chrysalis*, 4 (1977), 12.
62 For an excellent discussion, see Jane E. Larson, '"Even a Worm will Turn at Last": Rape Reform in Late Nineteenth Century America', *Yale Journal of Law and Humanities*, 9 (1997), 1–71.
63 Allan Griswold Johnson, 'On the Prevalence of Rape in the United States', *Signs: Journal of Women in Culture and Society*, 6.1 (Autumn 1980), 146.
64 Florence Rush, 'The Sexual Abuse of Children: A Feminist Point of View', in Noreen Connell and Cassandra Wilson (eds.), *Rape: The First Sourcebook for Women* (New York, 1974), 74–5.
65 Susan Brownmiller, *Against Our Will: Men, Women, and Rape* (New York, 1975). The analogy to race is taken from a radio interview and represents a view slightly modified from that of her book: see the transcript of the Monday Conference, 'Men, Women and Violence – The Politics of Rape', ABC programme broadcast on 15 November 1976, in Ann Summers, 'Papers', National Library of Australia, MS 7073, file 86.
66 J. V. Stevenson, *The Punishment and Prevention of Crime* (Glasgow, 1908), 10.
67 Hon. Austin H. MacCormick, 'New York's Present Problem', *Mental Hygiene*, xxii.1 (January 1938), 4.
68 J. Edgar Hoover, cited in Frederick Whiting, '"The Strange Particularity of the Lover's Preference": Pedophilia, Pornography, and the Anatomy of Monstrosity in *Lolita*', *American Literature*, 70.4 (December 1998), 849. Also see Henry A. Davidson, *Forensic Psychiatry* (New York, 1952), 109; Marie E. Kopp, 'Surgical Treatment as Sex Crime Prevention Measure', *Journal of Law, Criminology, and Police Science*, 28 (1937–8), 694; Mr A. Schroeder, Magistrate of the Perth Children's Court, quoted in *The West Australian*, 25 March 1938, cutting in 'Prohibited Publications (General) Crime Magazines', 1938, in National Archives of Australia A425/122 1938; 'Sexual Offences Against Children', letter to the editor from Robert Thompson of Pinner, Middlesex, *British Medical Journal*, 24 June 1961, 1832–3.
69 Linda Williams, 'Power, Pleasure, and Perversion: Sadomasochistic Film Pornography', *Representations*, 27 (Summer 1989), 47.
70 Robin Morgan first coined this phrase in 'Theory and Practice: Pornography and Rape' (1974). It is reprinted in her *Going Too Far: the Personal Chronicle of a Feminist* (New York, 1977), 165–6.
71 Ellen Willis, 'Feminism, Moralism, and Pornography', in Ann Snitow, Christine Stansell and Sharon Thompson (eds.), *Powers of Desire: The Politics of Sexuality* (London, 1983), 87.
72 Norman Podhoretz, 'Rape in Feminist Eyes', *Commentary*, 92.4 (October 1991), 29–35, and Norman Podhoretz, 'Rape and the Feminists', *Commentary*, 93 (1992), 6–7. Also see Helen Reynolds, *Cops and Dollars. The Economics of Criminal Law and Justice* (Springfield, IL, 1981), 161.
73 Cited in Laura X, 'A Brief Series of Anecdotes About the Backlash Experienced by Those of Us Working on Marital and Date Rape', *Journal of Sex Research*, 31.2 (1994), 152. Also see Neil Gilbert, 'The Wrong Response to Rape', *Wall Street Journal* (29 June 1993), A18.
74 Katie Roiphe, *The Morning After: Sex, Fear, and Feminism on Campus* (Boston, 1993).
75 Michael Novak, 'Against our Will', *Commentary*, 61.2 (February 1976), 90.

76 Gerald Schoenewolf, 'The Feminist Myth About Sexual Abuse', *The Journal of Psychohistory*, 18.3 (Winter 1991), 331–42. He practises psychoanalytical psychotherapy in New York and is the author of (among other books) *The Art of Hating* (Northvale, 1991) and *Sexual Animosity Between Men and Women* (Northvale, 1989).
77 Michael J. Goldstein, 'Exposure to Erotic Stimuli and Sexual Deviance', *Journal of Social Issues*, 29.3 (1973), 197–219.
78 Jay Carr, 'John Waters', *Boston Globe*, 10 April 1994, cited in Maria Tatar, *Lustmord. Sexual Murder in Weimar Germany* (Princeton, 1985), 176.
79 Allan S. Clifton, *Time of Fallen Blossoms* (London, 1950), 143.
80 Roy Porter, 'Rape', in Sylvana Tomaselli and Roy Porter (eds.), *Rape. An Historical and Critical Enquiry* (Oxford, 1986), 235.
81 Camille Paglia, *Sexual Personae: Art and Decadence from Nefertiti to Emily Dickinson* (New York, 1991); Katie Roiphe, *The Morning After: Sex, Fear, and Feminism on Campus* (Boston, 1993); Christine Hoff Sommers, *Who Stole Feminism? How Women Have Betrayed Women* (New York, 1994).

CHAPTER SIX: THE KNIFE (AND OTHER INVASIVE THERAPIES)

1 Dr Donaldson, 'Gateshead Co. Borough. Operation on Mentally Defective Patients in Poor Law Hospital', 8 August 1930, in National Archives (UK) MH79/291; minute to Sir George Newman from Hugh A. Macewen, 12 August 1930, in National Archives (UK) MH79/211; Dr Donaldson, 'Gateshead Co. Borough. Operation on Mentally Defective Patients in Poor Law Hospital', 8 August 1930, in National Archives (UK) MH79/211; 'Sterilisation and Castration of Boys at Gateshead Poor Law Institution', in National Archives (UK) MH79/291.
2 Marie E. Kopp, 'Surgical Treatment as Sex Crime Prevention Measure', *Journal of Law, Criminology, and Police Science*, 28 (1937–8), 698.
3 Allison C. Carey, 'Gender and Compulsory Sterilization Programs in America: 1907–1950', *Journal of Historical Sociology*, 11.1 (March 1998), 74.
4 R. C. Ellinwood, 'Vasectomy', *California State Medical Journal*, 2 (1904), 60–2, and Harry Sharp, 'The Severing of the Vasa Deferentia and its Relation to the Neuropsychopathic Constitution', *New York Medical Journal* (1902), 411–14.
5 Joel D. Hunter, 'Sterilization of Criminals', *The Journal of the American Institute of Criminal Law and Criminology*, 5 (May 1914 to March 1915), 519.
6 Allison C. Carey, 'Gender and Compulsory Sterilization Programs in America: 1907–1950', *Journal of Historical Sociology*, 11.1 (March 1998), 99.
7 State v. Feilen, 70 Wash. 65, 126 Pac. 75 (1912), in http://www.mrsc.org/mc/courts/WashReports/070WashReport/070WashReport0065.htm.
8 Harry Hamilton Laughlin, *Eugenical Sterilization in the United States* (Chicago, 1922), 292.
9 'Sterilization of Criminals', *The Yale Law Journal*, 23.4 (February 1914), 367.
10 'Iowa Vasectomy Law Held Invalid', *The Virginia Law Register*, 20.9 (January 1915), 712.
11 Charles A. Boston, 'A Protest Against Laws Authorizing the Sterilization of Criminals and Imbeciles', *Journal of the American Institute of Criminal Law and Criminology*, 4.3 (1913), 328, 331, 334, 339–41, 348, 355. Also see Bertram Pollens, *The Sex Criminal* (London, 1939), 177.
12 Clarence J. Ruddy, 'Compulsory Sterilization: Unwarranted Extension of the Powers of Government', *The Notre Dame Lawyer*, III.1 (October 1927), 5.
13 Cited in Clarence J. Ruddy, 'Compulsory Sterilization: Unwarranted Extension of the Powers of Government', *The Notre Dame Lawyer*, III.1 (October 1927), 5.

14 Dr B. M. Ricketts cited in Joel D. Hunter, 'Sterilization of Criminals', *The Journal of the American Institute of Criminal Law and Criminology*, 5 (May 1914 to March 1915), 525.
15 'Sterilization of Criminals', *The Yale Law Journal*, 23.4 (February 1914), 365.
16 Georg K. Stürp, 'Castration: the Total Treatment', in H. L. R. Resnik and Marvin E. Wolfgang (eds.), *Sexual Behaviors. Social, Clinical, and Legal Aspects* (Boston, 1972), 374.
17 Marie E. Kopp, 'Surgical Treatment as Sex Crime Prevention Measure', *Journal of Law, Criminology, and Police Science,* 28 (1937–8), 693.
18 Lucius H. Perkins, 'Corporal Punishment for Crime', *The American Lawyer*, 9 (1901), 277.
19 F. E. Daniel, 'Should Insane Criminals or Sexual Perverts be Allowed to Procreate?' *The Medico-Legal Journal*, xi.3 (December 1893), 275–92. It was reprinted in F. E. Daniel, 'Castration of Sexual Perverts', *Texas Medical Journal,* 27 (April 1912), 369–85.
20 F. E. Daniel, 'Editorial', *Texas Medical Journal*, 22 (1907), 347.
21 Hon. Simeon E. Baldwin, 'Corporal Punishments for Crime', *The Medico-Legal Journal*, xvii.1 (1899), 70.
22 Letters to the editor, 'Penalties for Sexual Offenders', *British Medical Journal*, 15 September 1951, 672–3.
23 R. E. Hemphill, 'A Case of Genital Self-Mutilation', *The British Journal of Medical Psychology*, xxiv (1951), 291. Also see '"Castrate Me!" Pleads Rapist Who Wants to Go Free . . . But No Doctor Will Do It', *Verdict* (May 1976), 46.
24 Warren S. Wille, 'Case Study of a Rapist: An Analysis of the Causation of Criminal Behavior', *Journal of Social Therapy*, 7.1 (1961), 14.
25 Linda E. Weinberger, Shoba Sreenivasan, Thomas Garrick and Hadley Osran, 'The Impact of Surgical Castration on Sexual Recidivism Risk Amongst Sexually Violent Predatory Offenders', *Journal of the American Academy of Psychiatry and Law*, 33.1 (2005).
26 Heidi Hansen and Lise Lykke-Olesen, 'Treatment of Dangerous Sexual Offenders in Denmark', *The Journal of Forensic Psychiatry*, 8.1 (May 1997), 195–6.
27 Gene G. Abel, Edward B. Blanchard and Judith V. Becker, 'Psychological Treatment of Rapists', in Marcio J. Walker and Stanley L. Brodsky (eds.), *Sexual Assault. The Victim and the Rapist* (Lexington, MA, 1976), 108.
28 F. E. Daniel, 'Should Insane Criminals or Sexual Perverts be Allowed to Procreate?' *The Medico-Legal Journal*, xi.3 (December 1893), 288. It was reprinted in F. E. Daniel, 'Castration of Sexual Perverts', *Texas Medical Journal,* 27 (April 1912), 369–85.
29 Louis Le Maire, 'Danish Experiences Regarding the Castration of Sexual Offenders', *The Journal of Criminal Law, Criminology, and Police Science*, 47 (1956–7), 298–9.
30 'Sexual Offences Against Children', *British Medical Journal*, 12 March 1966, 626.
31 Louis Le Maire, 'Danish Experiences Regarding the Castration of Sexual Offenders', *The Journal of Criminal Law, Criminology, and Police Science*, 47 (1956–7), 297.
32 F. E. Daniel, 'Should Insane Criminals or Sexual Perverts be Allowed to Procreate?' *The Medico-Legal Journal*, xi.3 (December 1893), 284–5. It was reprinted in F. E. Daniel, 'Castration of Sexual Perverts', *Texas Medical Journal,* 27 (April 1912), 369–85.
33 L. B. Liebster, 'Protection Against Sexual Offences', letter to the editor, *British Medical Journal*, 19 September 1946, 313.

34 Marie E. Kopp, 'Surgical Treatment as Sex Crime Prevention Measure', *Journal of Law, Criminology, and Police Science,* 28 (1937–8), 706.
35 Dr L. H. Field, 'Castration After Sex Crimes Urged', *The Times*, 19 April 1975, 3.
36 'Current Topics', *Albany Law Journal*, 36.27 (1887–8), 521.
37 Clifford Allen, 'Protection Against Sexual Offenders', letter to the editor, *British Medical Journal*, 21 September 1946, 441, and J. A. Fletcher, 'Letter to the Editor', *British Medical Journal*, 21 September 1946, 442.
38 Marie E. Kopp, 'Surgical Treatment as Sex Crime Prevention Measure', *Journal of Law, Criminology, and Police Science,* 28 (1937–8), 697.
39 Georg K. Stürp, 'Castration: the Total Treatment', in H. L. R. Resnik and Marvin E. Wolfgang (eds.), *Sexual Behaviors. Social, Clinical, and Legal Aspects* (Boston, 1972), 375.
40 Paul Wilburn Tappan, 'Treatment of the Sex Offender in Denmark', *The American Journal of Psychiatry*, 108 (September–October 1951), 245.
41 'Rapists Plea Against Castration', *The Times*, 3 December 1983, 5; 'Rapist Says Yes to Castration Sentence', *The Times*, 9 December 1983, 8; '"Castration" Plea by Sex Offender Rejected', *The Times*, 9 February 1984, 2.
42 Allison C. Carey, 'Gender and Compulsory Sterilization Programs in America: 1907–1950', *Journal of Historical Sociology*, 11.1 (March 1998), 99.
43 Georg K. Stürp, 'Castration: the Total Treatment', in H. L. R. Resnik and Marvin E. Wolfgang (eds.), *Sexual Behaviors. Social, Clinical, and Legal Aspects* (Boston, 1972), 363.
44 'Penal Castration in Germany', *The Times*, 12 November 1934, 13.
45 Paul Wilburn Tappan, 'Treatment of the Sex Offender in Denmark', *The American Journal of Psychiatry*, 108 (September–October 1951), 248.
46 F. L. Golla and R. Sessions Hodge, 'Hormone Treatment of the Sexual Offender', *The Lancet*, 11 June 1949, 1006.
47 John Sanderson Christison, *Crime and Criminals* (Chicago, 1897), 45.
48 'Danish Treatment of Psychopaths', *The Lancet*, 24 June 1950, 1162. The wives of these castrated men were described as not being overly concerned about the absence or infrequency of sexual intercourse with their husbands: they were 'often divorced women who have had . . . more than enough of sex with their previous husbands', *The Lancet* blandly observed.
49 Heidi Hansen and Lise Lykke-Olesen, 'Treatment of Dangerous Sexual Offenders in Denmark', *The Journal of Forensic Psychiatry*, 8.1 (May 1997), 196.
50 N. Heim, 'Sexual Behavior of Castrated Sex Offenders', *Archives of Sexual Behavior*, 10.1 (1981), 11–19.
51 Alfred Charles Kinsey made this argument in 'Castration of Sex Offenders', *British Medical Journal*, 9 April 1955, 897.
52 John Bremer, *Asexualization: A Follow-Up Study of 244 Cases* (Oslo, 1958), 318.
53 The literature is discussed in Linda E. Weinberger, Shoba Sreenivasan, Thomas Garrick and Hadley Osran, 'The Impact of Surgical Castration on Sexual Recidivism Risk Amongst Sexually Violent Predatory Offenders', *Journal of the American Academy of Psychiatry and Law*, 33.1 (2005), 16.
54 Richard Laur, *The Psychology of Rape* (North Hollywood: Challenge Publications, 1966), 157, referring to a patient in 1946.
55 'Rapists Plea Against Castration', *The Times*, 3 December 1983, 5; 'Rapist Says Yes to Castration Sentence', *The Times*, 9 December 1983, 8; '"Castration" Plea by Sex Offender Rejected', *The Times*, 9 February 1984, 2.
56 John MacDonald and Wilson Bradford, 'The Treatment of Sexual Deviation Using a Pharmacological Approach', *Journal of Sex Research* (August 2000), 3.

57 F. L. Golla and R. Sessions Hodge, 'Hormone Treatment of the Sexual Offender', *The Lancet*, 11 June 1949, 1006. Also see 'Treatment of Sex Offenders', *British Medical Journal*, 24 April 1954, 981.
58 F. L. Golla and R. Sessions Hodge, 'Hormone Treatment of the Sexual Offender', *The Lancet*, 11 June 1949, 1006; Charles W. Dunn, 'Hormone Treatment of the Sexual Offender', *The Lancet*, 30 July 1949, 217–18.
59 Charles William Dunn, 'Stilboestrol-Induced Gynecomastia in the Male', *Journal of the American Medical Association*, 28 December 1940, 2263–4.
60 John Money, 'The Therapeutic Use of Androgen-Depleting Hormone', in H. L. P. Resnik and Marvin E. Wolfgang (eds.), *Sexual Behaviors. Social, Clinical, and Legal Aspects* (Boston, 1972), 351.
61 Gregory K. Lehne, 'Treatment of Sex Offenders with Medroxyprogesterone Acetate', in J. M. A. Sitsen (ed.), *Handbook of Sexology, Vol. VI. The Pharmacology and Endocrinology of Sexual Function* (Amsterdam, 1988), 516.
62 John Money, 'The Therapeutic Use of Androgen-Depleting Hormone', in H. L. P. Resnik and Marvin E. Wolfgang (eds.), *Sexual Behaviors. Social, Clinical, and Legal Aspects* (Boston, 1972), 351 and 354–5.
63 F. Neumann and J. Kalmuss, *Hormonal Treatment of Sexual Deviations* (Berlin, 1991), 22.
64 Alan J. Cooper, A. A. A. Ismail, A. L. Phanjoo and D. L. Love, 'Antiandrogen (Cyproterone Acetate) Therapy in Deviant Hypersexuality', *British Journal of Psychiatry*, 120 (1972), 59–63. The other case studies they discussed concerned homosexuals.
65 John MacDonald and Wilson Bradford, 'The Treatment of Sexual Deviation Using a Pharmacological Approach', *Journal of Sex Research* (August 2000), 5–6.
66 John MacDonald and Wilson Bradford, 'The Treatment of Sexual Deviation Using a Pharmacological Approach', *Journal of Sex Research* (August 2000), 8. Note that they say this is a controversial idea.
67 Eva W. C. Chow and Alberto L. Choy, 'Clinical Characteristics and Treatment Response to SSRI in a Female Pedophile', *Archives of Sexual Behavior*, 31.2 (April 2002), 211–15.
68 A. Nicholas Groth, *Men Who Rape. The Psychology of the Offender* (New York, 1979), 216.
69 A. Nicholas Groth, *Men Who Rape. The Psychology of the Offender* (New York, 1979), 216; Ursula Laschet, 'Antiandrogen in the Treatment of Sex Offenders: Mode of Action and Therapeutic Outcome', in Joseph Zubin and John Money (eds.), *Contemporary Sexual Behavior: Critical Issues in the 1970s* (Baltimore, 1973), 317; F. Neumann and J. Kalmuss, *Hormonal Treatment of Sexual Deviations* (Berlin, 1991), 22.
70 Heidi Hansen and Lise Lykke-Olesen, 'Treatment of Dangerous Sexual Offenders in Denmark', *The Journal of Forensic Psychiatry*, 8.1 (May 1997), 198.
71 Gregory K. Lehne, 'Treatment of Sex Offenders with Medroxyprogesterone Acetate', in J. M. A. Sitsen (ed.), *Handbook of Sexology, Vol. VI. The Pharmacology and Endocrinology of Sexual Function* (Amsterdam, 1988), 516. Also see L. H. Field and Mark Williams, 'The Hormonal Treatment of Sexual Offenders', *Medicine, Science, and the Law*, 10.1 (January 1970), 28–9.
72 Richard T. Rada, D. R. Laws and Robert Kellner, 'Plasma Testosterone Levels in the Rapist', *Psychosomatic Medicine*, 38.4 (July–August 1976), 257 and 263.
73 Richard T. Rada, 'Plasma Androgens and the Sex Offender', *Bulletin of the American Academy of Psychiatry and Law*, 8 (1981), 456–64, and J. M. Bradford and D. McLean, 'Sexual Offenders, Violence and Testosterone: A Clinical Study', *Canadian Journal of Psychiatry*, 29 (1984), 335–43; R. A. Lang, Pierre Flor-Henry

and Roy R. Frenzel, 'Sex Hormone Profiles in Pedophiles and Incestuous Men', *Annals of Sex Research*, 3.1 (1990), 60.

74 P. D. Gurnani and M. Dwyer, 'Serum Testosterone Levels in Sex Offenders', *Journal of Offender Counseling, Services, and Rehabilitation*, 11 (1986), 39–45.

75 F. L. Golla and R. Sessions Hodge, 'Hormone Treatment of the Sexual Offender', *The Lancet*, 11 June 1949, 1006; Charles W. Dunn, 'Hormone Treatment of the Sexual Offender', *The Lancet*, 30 July 1949, 217–18.

76 'Breasts Amputated After Prisoners' Sex Treatment', *The Times*, 16 November 1978, 4.

77 See L. H. Field and Mark Williams, 'The Hormonal Treatment of Sexual Offenders', *Medicine, Science, and the Law*, 10.1 (January 1970), 29–30.

78 See L. H. Field and Mark Williams, 'The Hormonal Treatment of Sexual Offenders', *Medicine, Science, and the Law*, 10.1 (January 1970), 29–30.

79 Spalding Larry Helm, 'Florida's 1997 Chemical Castration Law', *Florida State University Law Review*, 117 (1998), 132–3.

80 'Castration of Sex Offenders', *British Medical Journal*, 9 April 1955, 897.

81 See L. H. Field and Mark Williams, 'The Hormonal Treatment of Sexual Offenders', *Medicine, Science, and the Law*, 10.1 (January 1970), 29.

82 Langevin's research of 1979, cited in R. Langevin, P. Wright and L. Handy, 'What Treatment Do Sex Offenders Want?', *Annals of Sex Research*, 1.3 (1988), 367.

83 W. Norwood East, 'Sexual Offenders', *The Journal of Nervous and Mental Disease*, 103.6 (June 1946), 637.

84 Karl M. Bowman, 'Psychiatric Aspects of the Problem', *Mental Hygiene*, xxii.1 (January 1938), 17, and Paul Wilburn Tappan, 'Treatment of the Sex Offender in Denmark', *The American Journal of Psychiatry*, 108 (September–October 1951), 245 and 248.

85 Steven S. Kan, 'Corporal Punishments and Optimal Incapacitation', *The Journal of Legal Studies*, 1 (January 1996), 129–30.

86 Some examples of using psychosurgery to treat sex offenders may be found in Domenico Caparole and Deryl F. Hamann, 'Sexual Psychopathy – A Legal Labyrinth of Medicine, Morals, and Mythology', *Nebraska Law Review*, 36 (1957), 342–3; G. Diechmann and R. Hassler, 'Treatment of Sexual Violence by Stereotaxic Hypothalamotomy', in W. H. Sweet, S. Obrador and J. G. Martin-Rodriguez (eds.), *Neurosurgical Treatment in Psychiatry, Pain, and Epilepsy* (Baltimore, 1977), 451–62; H. Orthner, D. Müller and F. Roeder, 'Stereotaxic Psychosurgery: Techniques and Results Since 1955', in E. Hitchcock, L. Laitinen and K. Vaernet (eds.), *Psychosurgery* (Springfield, IL, 1972), 377–90; Arthur Weider (ed.), *Contributions Towards Medical Psychology* (London, 1953), 422.

87 Vernon Herschel Mark and Frank Raymond Ervin, *Violence and the Brain* (New York, 1970), vii and 127–8. For other discussions of the nature of the brain of rapists and paedophiles, see Percy Wright, Jose Nobrega and Ron Langevin, 'Brain Density and Symmetry in Pedophilic and Sexually Aggressive Offenders', *Annals of Sex Research*, 3.3 (1990), 320, and Adrian Raine, *The Psychopathology of Crime: Criminal Behavior as a Clinical Disorder* (San Diego, 1993), 151.

88 'Treatment of Sex Offenders', *British Medical Journal* (24 April 1954): 981.

89 Roy G. Spece, 'Conditioning and Other Technologies Used to "Treat?", "Rehabilitate?", "Demolish?" Prisoners and Mental Patients', *Southern California Law Review*, 45.2 (1972), 633. See the image of him operating in http://my.dmci.net/~casey/experiments.htm.

90 Roy G. Spece, 'Conditioning and Other Technologies Used to "Treat?", "Rehabilitate?", "Demolish?" Prisoners and Mental Patients', *Southern California Law Review*, 45.2 (1972), 633.

91 Yong Kie Kim and W. Umbach, 'Combined Stereotactic Lesions for Treatment of Behaviour Disorders and Severe Pain', in Lauri Laitinen and Kenneth Livingston (eds.), *Surgical Approaches in Psychiatry* (Lancaster, 1973), 188.
92 Milton Greenblatt, 'Psychosurgery: A Review of Recent Literature', in Greenblatt, Robert Arnot and Harry C. Solomon (eds.), *Studies in Lobotomy* (London, 1951), 39.
93 Dr M. Hunter Brown, quoted in S. L. Chorover, *From Genesis to Genocide: The Meaning of Human Nature and the Power of Behavior Control* (Cambridge, MA, 1979). The cost factor was also argued by F. Raeder, H. Orthner and Dieter Müller, 'The Stereotaxic Treatment of Pedophilic Homosexuality and Other Sexual Deviations', in Edward Hitchcock, L. Laitinen and Kjeld Vaernet (eds.), *Psychosurgery* (Springfield, IL, 1972), 109.
94 Ronald Lloyd and Stanley Williamson, *Born to Trouble. Portrait of a Psychopath* (Plymouth, 1968), 145–6 and 150.
95 Ronald Lloyd and Stanley Williamson, *Born to Trouble. Portrait of a Psychopath* (Plymouth, 1968), 150.
96 F. Raeder, H. Orthner and Dieter Müller, 'The Stereotaxic Treatment of Pedophilic Homosexuality and Other Sexual Deviations', in Edward Hitchcock, L. Laitinen and Kjeld Vaernet (eds.), *Psychosurgery* (Springfield, IL, 1972), 87, 98–9 and 108–9.
97 Walter Jackson Freeman and James Winston Watts, *Psychosurgery: Intelligence, Emotion and Social Behavior Following Prefrontal Lobotomy for Mental Disorders* (Springfield, IL, 1942), 129–30.
98 Stanley David Porteus, *A Psychologist of Sorts. The Autobiography and Publications of the Inventor of the Porteus Maze Test* (Palo Alto, CA, 1969), 196. He was referring primarily to electro-shock treatments but his critique was also relevant to other treatments.
99 Robert L. Sadoff, *Forensic Psychiatry: A Practical Guide for Lawyers and Psychiatrists* (Springfield, IL, 1975), 76.
100 Milton Greenblatt, 'Psychosurgery: A Review of Recent Literature', in Greenblatt, Robert Arnot and Harry C. Solomon (eds.), *Studies in Lobotomy* (London, 1951), 21.
101 Mark A. J. O'Callaghan and Douglas Carroll, *Psychosurgery: A Scientific Analysis* (Lancaster, 1982), 287. Also see I. Rieber and V. Sigusch, 'Psychosurgery on Sex Offenders and Sexual "Deviants" in West Germany', *Archives of Sexual Behavior*, 8.6 (November 1979), 523–7.
102 Herbert L. Packer, *The Limits of the Criminal Sanction* (Stanford, 1969), 57–8.
103 Richard Delgado, 'Organic Rehabilitation and Criminal Punishment', in Elliott S. Valenstein (ed.), *The Psychosurgery Debate. Scientific, Legal, and Ethical Perspectives* (San Francisco, 1980), 523. Also see Richard Delgado, 'Organically Induced Behavioral Change in Correctional Institutions: Release Decisions and the "New Man" Phenomenon', *Southern California Law Review*, 50 (1977), 215–70.
104 Michael H. Shapiro, 'Legislating the Control of Behavior Control: Autonomy and the Coercive Use of Organic Therapies', *Southern California Law Review*, 237 (1974), 337; Richard Delgado, 'Organically Induced Behavioral Change in Correctional Institutions: Release Decisions and the "New Man" Phenomenon', *Southern California Law Review*, 50 (1977), 216; Roy G. Spece, 'Conditioning and Other Technologies Used to "Treat?", "Rehabilitate?", "Demolish?" Prisoners and Mental Patients', *Southern California Law Review*, 45.2 (1972), 647.
105 John B. Watson, *Behaviorism* (London, 1925), 125–9.
106 Virginia Greendlinger and Dann Byrne, 'Coercive Sexual Fantasies of College

Men as Predictors of Self-Reported Likelihood to Rape and Overt Sexual Aggression', *The Journal of Sex Research*, 23.1 (February 1987), 3 and 7–8. Also see Gene G. Abel, David H. Barlow, Edward Blanchard and Donald Guild, 'The Components of Rapists' Sexual Arousal', *Archives of General Psychiatry*, 34 (August 1977), 895–903, and R. J. McGuire, J. M. Carlisle and B. G. Young, 'Sexual Deviations as Conditioned Behaviour: A Hypothesis', *Behaviour Research and Therapy. An International Multi-Disciplinary Journal*, 2 (1965), 186.

107 Kevin J. Epps, 'Treating Adolescent Sex Offenders in Secure Conditions: The Experience at Glenthorne Centre', *Journal of Adolescence*, 17.2 (1994), 118.

108 Gene G. Abel and Edward B. Blanchard, 'The Measurement and Generation of Sexual Arousal in Male Sexual Deviates', in Michael Hersen, Richard M. Eisler and Peter M. Miller (eds.), *Progress in Behavior Modification. Volume 2* (New York, 1976), 101ff.

109 Alan Hyde, *Bodies of Law* (Princeton, 1997), 173–4.

110 Walter T. Simon and Peter G. W. Schouten, 'Problems in Sexual Preference Testing in Child Sexual Abuse Cases. A Legal and Community Perspective', *Journal of Interpersonal Violence*, 7.4 (December 1992), 503.

111 Alan J. Cooper, S. Swaminath, D. Baxter and C. Poulin, 'A Female Sex Offender with Multiple Paraphilias: A Psychologic Physiologic (Laboratory Sexual Arousal) and Endocrine Case Study', *Canadian Journal of Psychiatry*, 35 (May 1990), 336.

112 W. L. Marshall, 'The Modification of Sexual Fantasies: A Combined Treatment Approach to the Reduction of Deviant Sexual Behavior', *Behavioral Research and Therapy*, 11 (1973), 558.

113 Isaac M. Marks, *Living With Fear: Understanding and Coping with Anxiety* (London, 1978).

114 Barry M. Maletzky, '"Assisted" Covert Sensitization in the Treatment of Exhibitionism', *Journal of Consulting and Clinical Psychology*, 42.1 (1974), 34–9.

115 Roy G. Spece, 'Conditioning and Other Technologies Used to "Treat?", "Rehabilitate?", "Demolish?" Prisoners and Mental Patients', *Southern California Law Review*, 45.2 (1972), 635–9.

116 Robert J. Kohlenberg, 'Treatment of a Homosexual Pedophiliac Using In Vivo Desensitization', *Journal of Abnormal Psychology*, 83.2 (1974), 192–5. Reorientating homosexual paedophiles to seek arousal with adult men, as opposed to adult women, was controversial: see G. C. Davison and G. T. Wilson, 'Goals and Strategies in Behavioral Treatment of Homosexual Pedophilia: Comments on a Case Study', *Journal of Abnormal Psychology*, 83.2 (1974), 196–7. Also see G. C. Davison and G. T. Wilson, 'Attitudes of Behavior Therapists toward Homosexuality', *Behavior Therapy*, 4 (1973), 686–96.

117 Keith Hawton, 'Behavioural Approaches to the Management of Sexual Deviations', *The British Journal of Psychiatry*, 143 (1983), 248–50; W. L. Marshall, 'The Modification of Sexual Fantasies: A Combined Treatment Approach to the Reduction of Deviant Sexual Behavior', *Behavioral Research and Therapy*, 11 (1973), 559.

118 Gene G. Abel, Edward B. Blanchard and Judith V. Becker, 'Psychological Treatment of Rapists', in Marcio J. Walker and Stanley L. Brodsky (eds.), *Sexual Assault. The Victim and the Rapist* (Lexington, MA, 1976), 106–7.

119 Gene G. Abel and Edward B. Blanchard, 'The Measurement and Generation of Sexual Arousal in Male Sexual Deviates', in Michael Hersen, Richard M. Eisler and Peter M. Miller (eds.), *Progress in Behavior Modification. Volume 2* (New York, 1976), 111.

120 A. Nicholas Groth, *Men Who Rape. The Psychology of the Offender* (New York, 1979),

219. For problems (such as faking it) in relying on physiological tests, see W. L. Marshall and A. Eccles, 'Issues in Clinical Practice with Sex Offenders', *Journal of Interpersonal Violence*, 6.1 (March 1991), 69.

121 Samuel H. Pillsbury, 'Crimes Against the Heart. Recognizing the Wrongs of Forced Sex', *Loyola of Los Angeles Law Review*, 35 (2001–2), 918.

122 'Psychological Treatment of Rapists', in M. Walker and S. Brodsky (eds.), *Sexual Assault: The Victim and the Rapist* (Lexington, MA, 1976) and Robin Burgess, Robert Jewitt, James Sandham and Barbara L. Hudson, 'Working with Sex Offenders: A Social Skills Training Group', *British Journal of Social Work*, 10.2 (Summer 1980), 133.

123 Kurt Freund, 'Courtship Disorder: Is this Hypothesis Valid?', *Annals of the New York Academy of Sciences*, 528 (1988), 172–82, and Kurt Freund, H. Scher and S. Hucker, 'The Courtship Disorders', *Archives of Sexual Behavior*, 12 (1983), 369–79. Also see David Crawford, 'Problems for the Assessment and Treatment of Sexual Offenders in Closed Institutions: And Some Solutions', in D. A. Black (ed.), *BPS London Conference: University College London, 18–19 December 1980. Symposium: Broadmoor Psychological Department's 21st Birthday* (London, 1982), 39, and Ronald Blackburn, 'On the Relevance of the Concept of the Psychopath', in D. A. Black (ed.), *BPS London Conference: University College London, 18–19 December 1980. Symposium: Broadmoor Psychological Department's 21st Birthday* (London, 1982), 12.

124 A. Nicholas Groth, *Men Who Rape. The Psychology of the Offender* (New York, 1979), 217–18.

125 Gene G. Abel, E. B. Blanchard and J. V. Becket, 'Psychological Treatment of Rapists', in M. Walker and S. Brodsky (eds.), *Sexual Assault: The Victim and the Rapist* (Lexington, MA, 1976), 103–4.

126 For a critical summary of the literature, see Gordon C. Nagayama Hall, 'Prediction of Sexual Aggression', *Clinical Psychology Review* 10 (1990), 234–5.

127 Gene G. Abel, E. B. Blanchard and J. V. Becket, 'Psychological Treatment of Rapists', in M. Walker and S. Brodsky (eds.), *Sexual Assault: The Victim and the Rapist* (Lexington, MA, 1976), 102–3.

128 Gene G. Abel, E. B. Blanchard and J. V. Becket, 'Psychological Treatment of Rapists', in M. Walker and S. Brodsky (eds.), *Sexual Assault: The Victim and the Rapist* (Lexington, MA, 1976), 106.

129 Michael T. Dreznick, 'Heterosocial Competence of Rapists and Child Molesters: A Meta-Analysis', *Journal of Sex Research*, May 2003, in http://www.findarticles.com/p/articles/mi_m2372/is_2_40/ai_105518219/pg_7, and C. L. Muehlenhard and P. L. Falcon, 'Men's Heterosocial Skill and Attitudes Toward Women as Predictors of Verbal Sexual Coercion and Forceful Rape, *Sex Roles*, 23 (1990), 241–60.

130 Edward de Grazia, 'The Distinction of Being Mad', *University of Chicago Law Review*, 22 (1954–5), 352–3.

131 R. Langevin, P. Wright and L. Handy, 'What Treatment Do Sex Offenders Want?', *Annals of Sex Research*, 1.3 (1988).

132 'Credo' of Prisoners Against Rape, n.d. [mid-1970s], in Margaret Beadman, 'Papers', National Library of Australia, MS 5876.

CHAPTER SEVEN: THE COUCH (AND OTHER INTERIOR THERAPIES)

1 Caryl Whittier Chessman, *Cell 2455 Death Row* (New York, 1954), 346, and Caryl Whittier Chessman, *Trial by Ordeal* (Englewood Cliffs, 1956), 151–4.

2 Chessman's other books were *The Face of Justice* (Englewood Cliffs, 1957) and *The Kid was a Killer* (London, 1960). He also wrote innumerable articles.

3 David Stainrook Booth, 'Erotomania. A Case Study of Exhibitionism – A Medico-Legal Study', *The Alienist and Neurologist*, xxvi (1905), 1.
4 The rule has been followed in many Commonwealth countries and parts of the USA, but not Scotland.
5 M'Naghten Case, 8 Eng. Rep. 718, 722–3 (1843).
6 For example, see the critique by Francis Wharton, *A Monograph on Mental Unsoundness* (Philadelphia, 1855), 45 and 60. For the best discussion, see Janet A. Tighe, 'Francis Wharton and the Nineteenth-Century Insanity Defense: The Origins of a Reform Tradition', *American Journal of Legal History*, 27 (1983), 223–53.
7 James Cowles Prichard, *A Treatise on Insanity, and Other Disorders Affecting the Mind* (London, 1835), 6.
8 Henry Havelock Ellis, *The Criminal*, first pub. 1890 (London, 1914), 286–7.
9 Robert M. Ireland, 'Insanity and the Unwritten Law', *American Journal of Legal History*, 32 (1988).
10 B. Sachs, 'Insanity and Crime', in Allan McLane Hamilton and Lawrence Godkin (eds.), *A System of Legal Medicine*, vol. 2 (New York, 1900), 200–2.
11 Francis Wharton, *A Treatise on Mental Unsoundness*, 3rd edn. (Philadelphia, 1873), 284–8, 330 and 753–70.
12 Sigmund Freud, *Three Essays on the Theory of Sexuality* first pub. 1905, trans. James Strachey (London, 1949).
13 A. Hyatt Williams, 'The Psychopathology and Treatment of Sexual Murderers', in Ismond Rosen (ed.), *The Pathology and Treatment of Sexual Deviance. A Methodological Approach* (London, 1964), 351.
14 Benjamin Karpman, *The Sexual Offender and his Offenses. Etiology, Pathology, Psychodynamics and Treatment* (New York, 1954), 94.
15 Benjamin Karpman, *The Sexual Offender and his Offenses. Etiology, Pathology, Psychodynamics and Treatment* (New York, 1954), 482.
16 'Washington, D.C., Considers Sex Offenses. How One Community Undertook to Tell its Citizens the Facts about Sex Crimes and Criminals, and What May be Done to Deal Effectively with Such Problems', *Journal of Social Hygiene*, 36 (1950), 243–8. For a refutation of Karpman's idea that sex offenders were neurotics, see 'The Sexual Psychopath. A Symposium', *The Journal of Criminal Law, Criminology, and Police Science*, 43 (1952–3), 595–6.
17 Benjamin Karpman, *The Sexual Offender and his Offenses. Etiology, Pathology, Psychodynamics and Treatment* (New York, 1954), 47 and 100.
18 Benjamin Karpman, 'Felonious Assault Revealed as a Symptom of Abnormal Sexuality. A Contribution to the Psychogenesis of Psychopathic Behavior', *Journal of Criminal Law and Criminology*, 37 (1946–7), 193–5.
19 Nathan Roth, 'Factors in the Motivation of Sex Offenders', *The Journal of Criminal Law, Criminology, and Police Science*, 42 (1951–2), 624 and 632.
20 Philip Piker, 'A Psychiatrist Looks at Sex Offenses', *Journal of Social Hygiene*, 33 (1947), 392–3 and 395.
21 Otto Fenichel, *The Psychoanalytic Theory of Neurosis* (London, 1946), 354–8.
22 Emanuel F. Hammer, 'A Psychoanalytic Hypothesis Concerning Sex Offenders. A Study by Clinical Psychologic Techniques', *Journal of Clinical and Experimental Psychopathology*, xviii.2 (June 1957), 177–83. Also see H. Lindner, 'The Blacky Pictures Test: A Study of Sexual Offenders and Non-Sexual Offenders', *Journal of Projective Techniques*, 17 (1953), 79–84.
23 Emanuel F. Hammer, 'A Psychoanalytic Hypothesis Concerning Sex Offenders. A Study by Clinical Psychologic Techniques', *Journal of Clinical and Experimental Psychopathology*, xviii.2 (June 1957), 177–83.

24 Emanuel F. Hammer, 'A Comparison of H-T-P's of Rapists and Pedophiles: III. The "Dead" Tree as an Index of Psychopathology', *Journal of Clinical Psychology*, xi.1 (January 1955), 67–9.
25 Benjamin Karpman, *The Sexual Offender and his Offenses. Etiology, Pathology, Psychodynamics and Treatment* (New York, 1954), 44. Also see J. H. Fitch, 'Men Convicted of Sexual Offences Against Children. A Descriptive Follow-Up Study', *British Journal of Criminology*, 3 (1962–3), 29–30, and F. A. Musacchio speaking at 'The Sexual Psychopath. A Symposium', *Journal of Criminal Law, Criminology, and Police Science*, 43 (1952–3), 592.
26 Bertram Pollens, *The Sex Criminal* (London, 1939), 38–9.
27 Oscar B. Markey, 'A Study of Aggressive Sex Misbehavior in Adolescents Brought to Juvenile Court', *The American Journal of Orthopsychiatry*, xx (1950), 719.
28 George E. Gardner, 'The Community and the Aggressive Child. The Aggressive and Destructive Impulses in the Sex Offender', *Mental Hygiene*, xxxiv.1 (January 1950), 47–55.
29 T. W. Adorno, *The Authoritarian Personality* (New York, 1950).
30 Gary Fisher and Ephraim Fivlin, 'Psychological Needs of Rapists', *British Journal of Criminology*, 11.2 (April 1971), 183.
31 Helen Silving, 'Psychoanalysis and the Criminal Law', *The Journal of Criminal Law, Criminology, and Police Science*, 51 (1960), 23.
32 R. P. Snaith and S. A. Collins, 'Five Exhibitionists and a Method of Treatment', *British Journal of Psychiatry*, 138 (1981), 126. Also see Seymour J. Epstein and Paul L. Deyoub, 'Hypnotherapeutic Control of Exhibitionism: A Brief Communication', *The International Journal of Clinical and Experimental Hypnosis*, xxxi.2 (1983), 63–6; P. D. Rope, 'The Use of Hypnosis in Exhibitionism', in J. Lassner (ed.), *Hypnosis and Psychosomatic Medicine* (New York, 1967), 276–83; G. G. Richie, 'The Use of Hypnosis in a Case of Exhibitionism', in *Psychotherapy: Theory, Research and Practice*, 5 (1968), 40–3; William M. Polk, 'Treatment of Exhibitionism in a 38-Year Old Male by Hypnotic Assisted Covert Sensitization', *International Journal of Clinical and Experimental Hypnosis*, xxxi.3 (1983), 132–8.
33 R. P. Snaith and S. A. Collins, 'Five Exhibitionists and a Method of Treatment', *British Journal of Psychiatry*, 138 (1981), 130.
34 For a description, see John J. Landers, 'Group Therapy in HM Prison, Wormwood Scrubs', *The Howard Journal*, ix.4 (1957), 333.
35 Ralph Brancale, Alfred Vuocolo and William E. Prendergast, 'The New Jersey Program for Sex Offenders', in H. L. P. Resnik and Marvin E. Wolfgang (eds.), *Sexual Behaviors. Social, Clinical, and Legal Aspects* (Boston, 1972), 343–5.
36 Julian L. Woodward, 'Changing Ideas on Mental Illness and Its Treatment', *American Sociological Review*, 16.4 (August 1951), 445. This was a survey commissioned by both the *Collier's* Magazine and the City of Louisville on the subject of mental health. They questioned a random sample of 3971 residents aged eighteen years or over.
37 BBC, Audience Research Department, 'A Report on Some Audience Research Enquiries Connected with the Television Series "Crime"', January 1961, 16, in Modern Records Centre, University of Warwick, MSS 16B/5/2/3.
38 'Freud as "Biggest Success Since Jesus Christ"', *The Times*, 14 June 1963, 7.
39 'Psychiatric Prison in North Bucks', *The Times*, 3 July 1954, 4.
40 'Psychiatric Prison Stone-Laying', *The Times*, 2 July 1960, 3.
41 Wilfred Johnson interviewed in Tony Parker, *The Twisting Lane. Some Sex Offenders* (London, 1970), 56–7.
42 Questionnaire signed by D. Ivanbey [illegible], 'The Howard League for Penal

Reform. Questionnaire on Mental Health in Prison', 1948, in Modern Records Centre, University of Warwick, MSS 16c/3/MH/7. Quote from 'Any further observations'. Emphasis in original.

43 'Treatment of Sex Offenders', *The Lancet*, 31 December 1949, 1239.

44 Hon. Austin H. MacCormick, 'New York's Present Problem', *Mental Hygiene*, xxii.1 (January 1938), 7–8.

45 Manfred S. Guttmacher and Henry Weihofen, *Psychiatry and the Law* (New York, 1952), 113.

46 See the criticisms of the judge in Frank T. Field, 'Papers, 1962–63', in National Archives of Australia, series A432, item 1963/2200.

47 Art Gordon and Frank J. Porporino, 'Managing the Treatment of Sex Offenders: A Canadian Perspective', May 1990, in http://www.csc-scc.gc.ca/text/rsrch/briefs/b5/b05e_e.shtml.

48 Donald Shaskan, 'One Hundred Sex Offenders', *American Journal of Orthopsychiatry*, ix (1939), 566.

49 Albert Ellis and Ralph Brancale, *The Psychology of Sex Offenders* (Springfield, IL, 1956), 37. Also see Paul Schewe and William O'Donohue, 'Rape Prevention: Methodological Problems and New Directions', *Clinical Psychiatry Review*, 13 (1993), 667–72, and Lucy W. Taylor, 'The Role of Offender Profiling in Classifying Rapists: Implications for Counselling', *Counselling Psychology Quarterly*, 6 (1993), 334.

50 Mary P. Koss, 'Hidden Rape: Sexual Aggression and Victimization in a National Sample of Students in Higher Education', in Ann Wolbert Burgess (ed.), *Rape and Sexual Assault*, 2 (New York, 1988), 11.

51 Mary P. Koss and Cheryl J. Oros, 'Sexual Experiences Survey: A Research Instrument Investigating Sexual Aggression and Victimization', *Journal of Consulting and Clinical Psychology*, 50 (1982), 455–7.

52 An example is given in Nicholas Broughton and Paul Chesterman, 'Malingered Psychosis', *The Journal of Forensic Psychiatry*, 12.2 (September 2001), 411–15.

53 J. Miller Leavy, a deputy district attorney from Los Angeles, in Thomas J. Meyers, 'The Psychiatric Examination', *Journal of Criminal Law, Criminology, and Police Science*, 54 (1963), 431.

54 J. Miller Leavy, a deputy district attorney from Los Angeles, in Thomas J. Meyers, 'The Psychiatric Examination', *Journal of Criminal Law, Criminology, and Police Science*, 54 (1963), 431.

55 Walter T. Simon and Peter G. W. Schouten, 'Problems in Sexual Preference Testing in Child Sexual Abuse Cases. A Legal and Community Perspective', *Journal of Interpersonal Violence*, 78.4 (December 1992), 509. Also see W. L. Marshall and A. Eccles, 'Issues in Clinical Practice with Sex Offenders', *Journal of Interpersonal Violence*, 6.1 (March 1991), 69.

56 John MacDonald and Wilson Bradford, 'The Treatment of Sexual Deviation Using a Pharmacological Approach', *Journal of Sex Research* (August 2000), 14.

57 Gene G. Abel, Candice Osborn, David Anthony and Peter Gardos, 'Current Treatments of Paraphiliacs', *Annual Review of Sex Research*, iii (1992), 270–9.

58 Harry Mills interviewed in Tony Parker, *The Twisting Lane. Some Sex Offenders* (London, 1969), 164–5.

59 Gene G. Abel, Candice Osborn, David Anthony and Peter Gardos, 'Current Treatments of Paraphiliacs', *Annual Review of Sex Research*, iii (1993), 270–9.

60 R. Langevin, P, Wright and L. Handy, 'What Treatment Do Sex Offenders Want?', *Annals of Sex Research*, 1.3 (1988), 367.

61 W. Calder, 'The Sexual Offender. A Prison Medical Officer's Viewpoint', *The British Journal of Delinquency*, vi.1 (July 1955), 34–5.

62 L. H. Field and Mark Williams, 'The Hormonal Treatment of Sexual Offenders', *Medicine, Science, and the Law*, 10.1 (January 1970), 29.
63 A. Nicholas Groth, *Men Who Rape. The Psychology of the Offender* (New York, 1979), 216–17.
64 Joseph J. Peters, James M. Pedigo, Joseph Stey and James J. McKenna, 'Group Psychotherapy of the Sex Offender', *Federal Probation* (September 1968), 42.
65 Asher Pacht, Seymour L. Halleck and John C. Ehrmann, 'Diagnosis and Treatment of the Sexual Offender: A Nine-Year Study', *The American Journal of Psychiatry*, 118.9 (March 1962), 806.
66 Walter Russell Deathe, 'Transcript of his Appeal', 1962, National Archives of Australia B4747.
67 Joseph J. Peters, James M. Pedigo, Joseph Stey and James J. McKenna, 'Group Psychotherapy of the Sex Offender', *Federal Probation* (September 1968), 42.
68 Herman M. Adler, 'Biological and Pathological Aspects of Behavior Disorders', *The American Journal of Psychiatry*, vii (November 1927), 513–14.
69 Seymour Halleck, 'The Therapeutic Encounter', in H. L. P. Resnik and Marvin E. Wolfgang (eds.), *Sexual Behaviors. Social, Clinical, and Legal Aspects* (Boston, 1972), 196.
70 Gwen Adshead and Gillian Mezey, 'Ethical Issues in the Psychotherapeutic Treatment of Paedophiles: Whose Side are You On?', *Journal of Forensic Psychiatry*, 4.2 (1993), 364.
71 Seymour Halleck, 'The Therapeutic Encounter', in H. L. P. Resnik and Marvin E. Wolfgang (eds.), *Sexual Behaviors. Social, Clinical, and Legal Aspects* (Boston, 1972), 195.
72 David Crawford, 'Treatment Approaches with Pedophiles', in M. Cook and K. Howells (eds.), *Adult Sexual Interests in Children* (London, 1981), 181–2.
73 Gwen Adshead and Gillian Mezey, 'Ethical Issues in the Psychotherapeutic Treatment of Paedophiles: Whose Side are You On?', *Journal of Forensic Psychiatry*, 4.2 (1993), 362, and Keith Hawton, 'Behavioural Approaches to the Management of Sexual Deviations', *The British Journal of Psychiatry*, 143 (1983), 249.
74 John Bremer, *Asexualization: A Follow-Up Study of 244 Cases* (Oslo, 1958), 319.
75 Roy G. Spece, 'Conditioning and Other Technologies Used to "Treat?", "Rehabilitate?", "Demolish?" Prisoners and Mental Patients', *Southern California Law Review*, 45.2 (1972), 647.
76 Henry Alexander Davidson, *Forensic Psychiatry* (New York, 1952), 110.
77 Henry Alexander Davidson, *Forensic Psychiatry* (New York, 1952), 110–11.
78 Gregory K. Lehne, Adolescent Paraphilias', in M. E. Perry (ed.), *Handbook of Sexuality, Volume 7: Childhood and Adolescent Sexology* (Amsterdam, 1990), 387.
79 Alice Vachss, *Sex Crimes* (New York, 1993), 216.
80 Kathleen Maguire and Ann L. Pastore (eds.), *Sourcebook of Criminal Justice Statistics 1995* (Washington, DC, 1996).
81 Dr Groves B. Smith, Director of the Psychiatric Division of the Illinois Department of Safety, quoted in Lawrence T. Burick, 'An Analysis of the Illinois Sexually Dangerous Persons Act', *Journal of Criminal Law, Criminology, and Police Science*, 59 (1968), 257.
82 For a superb discussion, see Simon A. Cole, 'From the Sexual Psychopath Statute to "Megan's Law": Psychiatric Knowledge in the Diagnosis, Treatment, and Adjudication of Sex Criminals in New Jersey, 1949–1999', *Journal of the History of Medicine*, 55 (2000), 314. Also see p. 293.
83 Nathanial J. Pallone, 'Sadistic Criminal Aggression: Perspectives from Psychology, Criminology, Neuroscience', Louis B. Schlesinger (ed.), *Explorations in Clinical*

Psychopathology. Clinical Syndromes with Forensic Implications (Springfield, IL, 1996), 187–90.

84 'Credo' of Prisoners Against Rape, n.d. [mid-1970s], in Margaret Beadman, 'Papers', National Library of Australia, MS 5876.

85 www.geocities.com/HotSprings/Spa/5060/welcome.html; www.ncsac.org; groups.yahoo.com/group/sexualdeviates; www.sexualrecovery.org; www.sexualrecovery.com. All accessed on 12 March 2006.

86 See www.geocities.com/HotSprings/Spa/5060/welcome.html, accessed on 12 March 2006.

87 See www.sexualrecovery.org, accessed on 12 March 2006.

88 Janice M. Irvine, 'Regulated Passions: The Invention of Inhibited Sexual Desire and Sex Addiction', *Social Text*, 37 (Winter 1993), 218.

89 Philip Jenkins, *Moral Panic. Changing Concepts of the Child Molester in Modern America* (New Haven, 1998), 73 and 218.

90 Kaye-Lee Pantony and Paula J. Caplan, 'Delusional Dominating Personality Disorder: A Modest Proposal for Identifying Some Consequences of Rigid Masculine Socialization', *Canadian Psychology*, 32.2 (1991), 120–35, and Paula J. Caplan, 'How *Do* They Decide Who Is Normal? The Bizarre, But True, Tale of the DSM Process', *Canadian Psychology*, 32.2 (1991), 162–70.

91 'Freud as "Biggest Success Since Jesus Christ"', *The Times*, 14 June 1963, 7.

92 Russell George (not his real name) interviewed in Tony Parker, *The Twisting Lane. Some Sex Offenders* (London, 1969), 32–5.

93 Calvin M. Langton and W. L. Marshall, 'Cognition in Rapists. Theoretical Patterns by Typological Breakdown', *Aggression and Violent Behavior*, 6 (2001), 503–47.

94 Edward Dengrove, 'Behavior Therapy of the Sexual Disorders', *The Journal of Sex Research*, 3.1 (February 1967), 49.

CHAPTER EIGHT: FEMALE PERPETRATORS; MALE VICTIMS

1 Cecil Day Lewis, 'Sex-Crime', *Selected Poems* (Harmondsworth, 1951), 38–40.

2 Nori Samir Gunbar Al-Yasseri, statement reproduced in Mark Danner, *Torture and Truth. America, Abu Ghraib and the War on Terror* (London, 2005), 228–9. For further insights, see Deborah Staines (ed.), *Interrogating the War on Terror* (Newcastle, 2007).

3 Richard Goldstein, 'Bitch Bites Man!', in *Village Voice*, 10 May 2004, in http://www.villagevoice.com/generic/show_print.php?id=53375&page=goldstein2&issue.

4 John Barry, Michael Hirsch and Michael Isikoff, 'The Roots of Torture', *Newsweek*, 24 May 2004, 28.

5 Quoted in 'Notebook', *The New Republic*, 24 May 2004, 11.

6 See http://badgas.co.uk/lynndie/.

7 Jill Elaine Hasday, 'Contest and Consent: A Legal History of Marital Rape', *California Law Review*, 88 (2000), 1495 (US Justice's Department National Incident-Based Reporting System) and Art A. O'Connor, 'Female Sex Offenders', *British Journal of Psychiatry*, 150 (1987), 615 (UK Home Office statistics).

8 This is the figure for 1991: *Bureau of Justice Statistics*, 1992.

9 Bureau of Justice Statistics, US Department of Justice, NCJ 175688, *Women Offenders* (Washington, DC, 1999), 5.

10 Monica Pa, 'Towards a Feminist Theory of Violence', *University of Chicago Law School Roundtable*, 9 (2002), 46.

11 Cheryl Hanna, 'Bad Girls and Good Sports: Some Reflections on Violent Female Juvenile Delinquents, Title IX & the Promise of Girl Power', *Hastings Constitutional Law Quarterly*, 27 (1999–2000), 668.

12 For an example, see 'Unusual "Sex Crime" in New England', *The Journal of Sex Education*, 4.4 (February–March 1952), 176–7, re rape of Everitt F. Amaral on 11 May 1951 by three women.

13 'Forcible and Statutory Rape: An Exploration of the Operation and Objectives of the Consent Standard', *The Yale Law Journal*, 62 (1952–3), 70.

14 R. v. Ram and Ram (1893), Cox CC 609. Also see Jacob A. Goldberg and Rosamond W. Goldberg, *Girls on City Streets. A Study of 1400 Cases of Rape* (New York, 1935), 86.

15 Home Office, *Setting the Boundaries: Reforming the Law on Sex Offences* (London, 2000), 15. Also at http://www.lawbore.net/articles/setting-the-boundaries.pdf.

16 David Finkelhor, *Sexually Victimized Children* (New York, 1979), quoted in Arthur H. Green, 'Female Sex Offenders', in Jon A. Shaw (ed.), *Sexual Aggression* (Washington, DC, 1999), 195. Also see David Finkelhor, *Child Sexual Abuse: New Theory and Research* (New York, 1984), 171–77.

17 American Humane Association, *National Study on Child Neglect and Abuse Reporting* (Denver, 1981); 'National Center for Child Abuse and Neglect: Study Findings: National Study of Incidence and Severity of Child Abuse and Neglect', DHWW Pub. No. OHDS 81-30325 (Washington, DC, 1981), quoted in Arthur H. Green, 'Female Sex Offenders', in Jon A. Shaw (ed.), *Sexual Aggression* (Washington, DC, 1999), 195. For a similar estimate, see Marcia T. Turner and Tracey N. Turner, *Female Adolescent Sexual Abusers: An Exploratory Study of Mother-Daughter Dynamics with Implications for Treatment* (Brandon, VT, 1994), 11. For other estimates, see Davis and Leitenberg and Fehrenbach, in A. J. Cooper, S. Swaminath, D. Baxter and C. Poulin, 'A Female Sex Offender with Multiple Paraphilias: A Psychologic, Physiologic (Laboratory Sexual Arousal) and Endocrine Case Study', *Canadian Journal of Psychiatry*, 35 (1990), 334.

18 L. Timnick, 'The Times Poll: 20% in Survey Were Child Abuse Victims', *Los Angeles Times*, 25 August 1985, 1.

19 US Department of Health and Human Services Administration on Children, Youth, and Families, *Child Maltreatment 1998: Reports from the States to the National Child Abuse and Neglect Data Systems* (Washington, DC, 2000).

20 Paul J. Isley and David Gehrenbeck-Shim, 'Sexual Assault of Men in the Community', *Journal of Community Psychology*, 25.2 (1997), 161. This was based on a survey of 336 agencies.

21 G. S. Fritz, K. Stoll and N. N. Wagner, 'A Comparison of Male and Females Who were Sexually Molested as Children', *Journal of Sex Marital Therapy*, 7 (1981), 54–9, and M. P. Mendel, *The Male Survivor: The Impact of Sexual Abuse* (London, 1993).

22 Hugo Adrian Coxell, M. King, G. Mezey and D. Gordon, 'Lifetime Prevalence, Characteristics, and Associated Problems of Non-Consensual Sex in Men: Cross Sectional Survey', *British Medical Journal*, 318 (1999), 846.

23 Adrian W. Coxell, Michael B. King, Gillian C. Mezey and Philip Kell, 'Sexual Molestation of Men: Interviews with 224 Men Attending a Genitourinary Medicine Service', *International Journal of STD and AIDS*, 11.9 (2000), 575.

24 Michael Graubart Levin, 'Fight, Flee, Submit, Sue: Alternatives for Sexually Assaulted Prisoners', *Journal of Legal and Social Problems*, 18 (1983–5), 519: People v Lovercamp, 43 Cal. App 3d at 825; 118 Cal. Rptr. all 111 and 115.

25 Cindy Struckman-Johnson, 'Sexual Coercion Reported by Women in Three Midwestern Prisons', *Journal of Sex Research* (August 2002).

26 Judy Jacobs, quoted in Kitsi Burkhart, 'Women in Prison', in The Editors of

Ramparts Magazine and Frank Browning (eds.), *Prison Life. A Study of the Explosive Conditions in America's Prisons* (New York, 1972), 17.

27 Philip Wylie, *Generation of Vipers*, first pub. 1942 (New York, 1955), xii, 51–3 and 191–216.

28 Sheldon Kardener, 'Rape Fantasies', *Journal of Religion and Health*, 14 (1975), 50–7.

29 However the seriousness of the crime was diminished by the announcer in the promotional footage who intoned the words, 'She was born innocent, but that was fourteen years ago!'

30 Hugo Paul, *Cry Rape: Anatomy of the Rapist*, intro. by Jean-Paul St. Marc (New York, 1967), 10.

31 George Hewins, *The Dillen. Memories of a Man of Stratford-upon-Avon* (London, 1981), 82.

32 Moira Lines, *Victim of a Female Rapist* (London, 1971).

33 Dyanne Thorne, quoted by Lynn Rapaport, 'Holocaust Pornography: Profaning the Sacred in Ilsa, She-Wolf of the SS', *Shofar: An Interdisciplinary Journal of Jewish Studies*, 22.1 (2003), 65–6.

34 Sándor Ferenczi, 'Confusion of Tongues Between Adults and the Child', *Final Contributions to the Problems and Methods of Psycho-Analysis*, first pub. 1933 (New York, 1980), 162.

35 David Abrahamsen, *Crime and the Human Mind* (London, 1945), 42.

36 Cesare Lombroso and Guglielmo Ferrero, *The Female Offender* (np, 1895), 151.

37 William Bonger, *Criminality and Economic Conditions*, trans. Henry P. Horton (Boston, 1916), 60.

38 David Abrahamsen, *Crime and the Human Mind* (London, 1945), 42.

39 Frances Alice Kellor, 'Sex in Crime', *International Journal of Ethics*, 9.1 (October 1898), 74–85.

40 There are innumerable examples of this logic, but a typical one is Adriene Sere, 'Man and the History of Rape', at http://holysmoke.org/fem/fem0126.htm.

41 William T. Stead, 'The Maiden Tribute of Modern Babylon', *Pall Mall Gazette*, 6 July 1885. The full text can be found at http://www.attackingthedevil.co.uk/pmg/tribute/mt1.php.

42 Monica Pa, 'Towards a Feminist Theory of Violence', *University of Chicago Law School Roundtable*, 9 (2002), 50.

43 Hans Gross, *Criminal Psychology: A Manual for Judges, Practitioners, and Students* (Boston, 1912), 316.

44 Cesare Lombroso and Guglielmo Ferrero, *The Female Offender* (np, 1895), 152.

45 Richard Laur, *The Psychology of Rape* (New York, 1966), 122.

46 Isaac Baker Brown, *On the Curability of Certain Forms of Insanity, Epilepsy, Catalepsy and Hysteria in Females* (London, 1866), 70.

47 B. Sherwood-Dunn, 'Conservation of the Ovary', *Transactions of the American Association of Obstetricians and Gynecologists: Minutes of the Proceedings of the Tenth Annual Meeting, August 17–20*, x (1897), 227.

48 Thomas Spencer Wells, Alfred Hegar and Robert Battey, 'Castration in Nervous Diseases: A Symposium', *American Journal of Medical Science*, 92.10 (1886), 466.

49 Field, quoted in Horatio Storer, 'Obstinate Erotomania', *American Journal of Obstetrics and Diseases of Women and Children*, 1.4 (1869), 425.

50 A. J. Cooper, S. Swaminath, D. Baxter and C. Poulin, 'A Female Sex Offender with Multiple Paraphilias: A Psychologic, Physiologic (Laboratory Sexual Arousal) and Endocrine Case Study', *Canadian Journal of Psychiatry*, 35 (1990), 337.

51 Catherine F. Lewis and Charlotte R. Stanley, 'Women Accused of Sexual Offenses',

Behavioral Sciences and the Law, 18 (2000), 78–80. Faller found that only 7.5 per cent of his female offenders were psychiatrically disturbed, although half had some problems with substance abuse: K. C. Faller, 'Women Who Sexually Abuse Children', *Violence and Victims*, 2 (1987), 263–76.

52 Patricia Pearson, *When She Was Bad. How Women Get Away with Murder* (London, 1998), 57.

53 Richard Laur, *A Psychology of Rape* (New York, 1966), 125.

54 Richard Laur, *A Psychology of Rape* (New York, 1966), 125.

55 Cited in Thomas J. Cottle, 'Children in Jail', *Crime and Delinquency*, 25 (1979), 328–9.

56 Alice Vachss, *Sex Crimes* (New York, 1993), 205.

57 Sándor Ferenczi, 'Confusion of Tongues Between Adults and the Child', reprinted in *Contemporary Psychoanalysis*, 24 (1933), 196–206.

58 L. Shengold, 'Child Abuse and Deprivation: Soul Murder', *Journal of the American Psychoanalytic Association*, 27 (1979), 533–60.

59 Anna Freud, *The Ego and the Mechanisms of Defense* (London, 1937), 121–2.

60 A. J. Cooper, S. Swaminath, D. Baxter and C. Poulin, 'A Female Sex Offender with Multiple Paraphilias: A Psychologic, Physiologic (Laboratory Sexual Arousal) and Endocrine Case Study', *Canadian Journal of Psychiatry*, 35 (1990), 336–7.

61 Barbara Krahe, Eva Waizenhofer and Ingrid Moller, 'Women's Sexual Aggression Against Men: Prevalence and Predictors', *Sex Roles: A Journal of Research* (1 August 2003), n.p.

62 Arlene McCormack, Frances E. Rokkaus, Robert R. Hazelwood and Ann W. Burgess, 'An Exploration of Incest in the Childhood Development of Serial Rapists', *Journal of Family Violence*, 7.3 (1992), 220.

63 Adrien Katherine Wing, 'Violence and State Accountability: Critical Race Feminism', *Georgetown Journal of Gender and Law*, 1 (1999–2000), 103.

64 Joseph Mallia, 'Violence by Female Teens Growing at Alarming Rate', *Boston Herald*, 9 March 1997, 1, and Gini Sikes, *8 Ball Chicks: A Year in the Violent World of Girl Gangsters* (London, 1997), 101–2.

65 Gini Sikes, *8 Ball Chicks: A Year in the Violent World of Girl Gangsters* (London, 1997), 102.

66 Meda Chesney-Lind, 'Are Girls Closing the Gender Gap in Violence?', *Criminal Justice*, 16 (2001), 20.

67 W. L. Marshall, 'Intimacy, Loneliness and Sexual Offenders', *Behavioral Research and Therapy*, 27.5 (1989), 498–9.

68 J. Hindman, 'Research Disputes. Assumptions About Child Molesters', *National District Attorneys Association Bulletin*. 7 (1988), 1–3.

69 Judith Lewis Herman, 'Considering Sex Offenders: A Model of Addiction', *Signs: Journal of Women in Culture and Society*, 13.4 (Summer 1988), 704.

70 Catherine Gasquoine Hartley, *Sex Education and National Health* (London, 1920), 97–8.

71 For a summary of this literature, see Alana D. Grayson and Rayleen V. De Luca, 'Female Perpetrators of Child Sexual Abuse: A Review of the Clinical and Empirical Literature', *Aggression and Violent Behavior*, 4.1 (1999), 95, and Donna M. Vandiver and Jeffery T. Walker, 'Female Sex Offenders: An Overview and Analysis of 40 Cases', *Criminal Justice Review*, 27.2 (Autumn 2002), 290.

72 Marcia T. Turner and Tracey N. Turner, *Female Adolescent Sexual Abusers: An Explanatory Study of Mother-Daughter Dynamics with Implications for Treatment* (Brandon, VT, 1994), 7.

73 Quoted in Jane F. Gilgun, 'We Shared Something Special: The Moral Discourse of Incest Perpetrators', *Journal of Marriage and the Family*, 57.2 (May 1995), 271.

74 Art A. O'Connor, 'Female Sex Offenders', *British Journal of Psychiatry*, 150 (1987), 618.

75 Art A. O'Connor, 'Female Sex Offenders', *British Journal of Psychiatry*, 150 (1987), 615–20.
76 J. C. Solomon, 'Child Sexual Abuse by Family Members: A Radical Feminist Perspective', *Sex Roles: A Journal of Research*, 27 (1992), 473–85, and K. C. Faller, 'Women Who Sexually Abuse Children', *Violence and Victims*, 2 (1987), 263–76.
77 For instance, see David Finkelhor, *Child Sexual Abuse: New Theory and Research* (New York, 1984).
78 Carlton Smith, *Hunting Evil* (New York, 2000), xiii-xv, 119 and 268.
79 Catherine F. Lewis and Charlotte R. Stanley, 'Women Accused of Sexual Offenses', *Behavioral Sciences and the Law*, 18 (2000), 79.
80 Catherine F. Lewis and Charlotte R. Stanley, 'Women Accused of Sexual Offenses', *Behavioral Sciences and the Law*, 18 (2000), 79–80.
81 A. J. Cooper, S. Swaminath, D. Baxter and C. Poulin, 'A Female Sex Offender with Multiple Paraphilias: A Psychologic, Physiologic (Laboratory Sexual Arousal) and Endocrine Case Study', *Canadian Journal of Psychiatry*, 35 (1990), 334–7.
82 Monica Pa, 'Towards a Feminist Theory of Violence', *University of Chicago Law School Roundtable*, 9 (2002), 50.
83 Hugo Paul, *Cry Rape: Anatomy of the Rapist*, intro. by Jean-Paul St. Marc (New York, 1967), 100.
84 'Legal Definition of Rape Differs', *Virginian-Pilot*, 30 October 1975, in the papers of Margaret Beadman, National Library of Australia MS 5876.
85 Freda Adler, *Sisters in Crime: The Rise of the New Female Criminal* (New York, 1975), 93–5.
86 Bonnie Mann, 'How America Justifies Its War: A Modern/Postmodern Aesthetics of Masculinity and Sovereignty', *Hypatia*, 21.4 (Fall 2006), 159. Mann is writing from a feminist perspective and accepts that military women remain the 'lesser partner'.
87 Barbara Ehrenreich, 'Barbara Ehrenreich's Commencement Address at Barnard College', http://www.rockridgeinstitute.org/perspectives/becommencement.
88 Barbara Ehrenreich, 'Prison Abuse: Feminism's Assumptions Upended', *Los Angeles Times*, 16 May 2004, M1.
89 National Coalition for the Protection of Children and Families, 'Abu Ghraib: Lessons in S-xual Morality', http://www.nationalcoalition.org/culture/articles/ca050523.html.
90 Frank Rich, 'It was Porn That Made Them Do It', *New York Times*, 30 May 2004, AR1 and AR16.
91 Phyllis Schlafly, 'Equality for Women in our Army', *Eagle Forum*, 19 May 2004, in http://www.eagleforum.org/column/2004/may2004/04-05-19.html.
92 Monica Pa, 'Towards a Feminist Theory of Violence', *University of Chicago Law School Roundtable*, 9 (2002), 51.
93 Elaine Scarry, *The Body in Pain. The Making and Unmaking of the World* (New York, 1985), 59.
94 Monique Plaza, 'Our Costs and Their Benefits', trans. Wendy Harrison, *m/f*, 4 (1980), 31.
95 Marcia T. Turner and Tracey N. Turner, *Female Adolescent Sexual Abusers: An Explanatory Study of Mother-Daughter Dynamics with Implications for Treatment* (Brandon, VT, 1994), 8.
96 Richard Goldstein, 'Bitch Bites Man!', in *Village Voice*, 10 May 2004, in http://www.villagevoice.com/generic/show_print.php?id=53375&page=goldstein2&issue.
97 R. Mathews, J. K. Matthews and K. Speltz, *Female Sexual Offenders: An Exploratory*

Study (Orwell, VT, 1989) and J. K. Matthews, R. Mathews, and K. Speltz, 'Female Sexual Offenders: A Typology', in M. Q. Patton (ed.), *Family Sexual Abuse: Frontline Research and Evaluation* (Newbury Park, CA, 1991), 199–219.

98 Moira Gatens, *Imagining Bodies. Ethics, Power and Corporeality* (London, 1996), 33.

99 Unnamed man quoted in Jayne Walker, John Archer and Michelle Davies, 'Effects of Rape on Men: A Descriptive Analysis', *Archives of Sexual Behavior*, 34.1 (February 2005), 74.

100 Linda Williams, 'Power, Pleasure, and Perversion: Sadomasochistic Film Pornography', *Representations*, 27 (Summer 1989), 46–7.

101 In Britain, under the 1861 Offences Against the Person Act, indecent assaults upon women were differentiated from those upon men.

102 The Sexual Offences Act of 2003.

103 HM Crown Prosecution Service Inspectorate, *A Report on the Joint Inspection into the Investigation and Prosecution of Cases Involving Allegations of Rape* (London, April 2002), 35.

104 See Susan B. Sorenson, J. A. Stein, J. M. Siegel, J. M. Golding and M. A. Burnam, 'The Prevalence of Adult Sexual Assault: The Los Angeles Epidemiologic Catchment Area Project', *American Journal of Epidemiology*, 126.6 (1987), 1154–64 (found that 7 per cent of men had forced sex); Cindy Struckman-Johnson and David Struckman-Johnson, 'Acceptance of Male Rape Myths Among College Men and Women', *Sex Roles: A Journal of Research*, 27.3/4 (1992), 86. Philip M. Sarrel and William H. Masters, 'Sexual Molestation of Men by Women', *Archives of Sexual Behavior*, 11.2 (1982), 117–31 (found that 16 per cent of men had forced sex) cited in Cindy Struckman-Johnson, 'Forced Sex on Dates: It Happens to Men, Too', *The Journal of Sex Research*, 24 (1988), 237; Hugo Adrian Coxell, M. King, G. Mezey and D. Gordon, 'Lifetime Prevalence, Characteristics, and Associated Problems of Non-Consensual Sex in Men: Cross Sectional Survey', *British Medical Journal*, 318 (1999), 846 (found that 3 per cent of men had forced sex since the age of sixteen).

105 National Crime Victimization Survey, at http://www.albany.edu/sourcebook/1995/pdf/t49.pdf.

106 Liz Kelly, Jo Lovett and Linda Regan, *A Gap or a Chasm? Attrition in Reported Rape Cases: A Home Office Research Study* (London, 2005), 19.

107 F. C. Hickson, P. M. Davies, A. J. Hunt, P. Weatherburn, T. J. McManus and A. P. M. Coxon, 'Gay Men as Victims of Nonconsensual Sex', *Archives of Sexual Behaviour*, 23.3 (1994), 281–94. Also see Michael Scarce, *Male on Male Rape: The Hidden Toll of Stigma and Shame* (New York, 1997).

108 Fred Pelka, 'Raped: A Male Survivor Breaks His Silence', in Patricia Searles and Ronald J. Berger (eds.), *Rape and Society: Readings on the Problem of Sexual Assault* (Boulder, 1995), 251–2.

109 Michael Scarce, *Male on Male Rape: The Hidden Toll of Stigma and Shame* (New York, 1997).

110 There is a vast literature on this subject, but for an excellent start see Philip Jenkins, *Pedophiles and Priests: Anatomy of a Contemporary Crisis* (Oxford, 2001).

111 Louise A. Jackson, *Child Sexual Abuse in Victorian England* (London, 2000), 5.

112 'Age of Consent', *Union Signal*, 10 June 1886, 2, cited in Jane E. Larson, '"Even a Worm Will Turn at Last": Rape Reform in Late Nineteenth Century America', *Yale Journal of Law and Humanities*, 9 (1997), 58.

113 Charles Armstrong, 'Fiendish Attempt at Castration in the Human Subject', *The Dublin Quarterly Journal of Medical Science*, Liii (1 February 1859), 240–2.

114 Andrea Nelson and Pamela Oliver, 'Gender and the Construction of Consent in

Child-Adult Sexual Contact: Beyond Gender Neutrality and Male Monopoly', *Gender and Society*, 12.5 (October 1998), 555 and 573.

115 Claude Crépault and Marcel Couture, 'Men's Erotic Fantasies', *Archives of Sexual Behavior*, 9.6 (1980), 565, n. 94.

116 Carline White, 'I'm Male, 55 and Overweight. Why Rape Me?', *The Independent*, 20 August 1991, 15.

117 For discussions, see Michael Scarce, *Male on Male Rape: The Hidden Toll of Stigma and Shame* (New York, 1997) and Paul J. Isely and David Gehrenbeck-Shim, 'Sexual Assault of Men in the Community', *Journal of Community Psychology*, 25.2 (1997).

118 Lauren E. Duncan, 'Gender Role Socialization and Male-on-Male vs. Female-on-Male Child Sexual Abuse', *Sex Roles: A Journal of Research*, November 1998: on line at http://www.findarticles.com/p/articles/mi_m2294/is_9-10_39/ai_53857390/print.

119 Cited in Jayne Walker, John Archer and Michelle Davies, 'Effects of Rape on Men: A Descriptive Analysis', *Archives of Sexual Behavior*, 34.1 (February 2005), 70.

120 Jayne Walker, John Archer and Michelle Davies, 'Effects of Rape on Men: A Descriptive Analysis', *Archives of Sexual Behavior*, 34.1 (February 2005), 77.

121 Cindy Struckman-Johnson and David Struckman-Johnson, 'Acceptance of Male Rape Myths Among College Men and Women', *Sex Roles: A Journal of Research*, 27.3/4 (1992), 97. The female respondents had similar results although not as dramatic as the male respondents.

122 R. E. Smith, C. J. Pine and M. E. Hawley, 'Social Cognitions About Male Victims of Female Sexual Assault', *The Journal of Sex Research*, 24 (1988), 101–12.

123 Michael Scarce, *Male on Male Rape: The Hidden Toll of Stigma and Shame* (New York, 1997), 61.

124 Jayne Walker, John Archer and Michelle Davies, 'Effects of Rape on Men: A Descriptive Analysis', *Archives of Sexual Behavior*, 34.1 (February 2005), 76.

125 Michael King and Earnest Woollett, 'Sexually Assaulted Males: 115 Men Consulting a Counseling Service', *Archives of Sexual Behavior*, 26.6 (1997), 587, and Gillian C. Mezey and Michael B. King, quoted in Siegmund Fred Fuchs, 'Male Sexual Assault: Issues of Arousal and Consent', *Cleveland State Law Review*, 51 (2004), 99. It is common for men to ejaculate when being raped: see L. Rentoul and N. Appleboom (eds.), 'Understanding the Physiological Impact of Rape and Serious Sexual Assault of Men: A Literature Review', *Journal of Psychiatric and Mental Health Nursing*, 4 (1997), 267–74, and R. McMullen, *Male Rape: Breaking the Silence on the Last Taboo* (Boston, 1990). MacKinnon even suggests that female victims may experience orgasm during rape: Catharine A. MacKinnon, 'Sexuality, Pornography, and Method: "Pleasure Under Patriarchy"', *Ethics*, 99.2 (January 1989), 338.

126 Philip M. Sarrel and William H. Masters, 'Sexual Molestation of Men by Women', *Archives of Sexual Behavior*, 11 (1982).

127 Richard Laur, *A Psychology of Rape* (New York, 1966), 123.

128 See J. Bancroft, *Human Sexuality and its Problems* (Edinburgh, 1989), 128–30; John Bancroft, 'Psychophysiology of Sexual Dysfunction', in Marcel Dekker (ed.), *Handbook of Biological Psychiatry* (New York, 1980) 359–92; John Bancroft and A. Matthews, 'Autonomic Correlates of Penile Erection', *Journal of Psychosomatic Research*, 15 (1971), 159–67; Philip M. Sarrel and William H. Masters, 'Sexual Molestation of Men by Women', *Archives of Sexual Behavior*, 11 (1982), 117–29; R. Stoller, 'Sexual Excitement', *Archives of General Psychiatry*, 33 (1976), 899–909.

129 John Bancroft, 'Psychophysiology of Sexual Dysfunction', in H. Van Praag et. al (eds.), *Handbook of Biological Psychiatry*, vol. III (New York, 1980), 359.

130 Alan Hyde, *Bodies of Law* (Princeton, 1997).

131 Also see Walter S. DeKeseredy, 'Tactics of the Antifeminist Backlash Against Canadian National Women Abuse Surveys', *Violence Against Women. An International and Interdisciplinary Journal*, 5.11 (November 1999), 1260–1.

132 D. A. Donnelly and L. M. Williams, '"Honey, We Don't Do Men": Gender Stereotypes and the Provision of Services to Sexually Assaulted Males', *Journal of Interpersonal Violence*, 11.3 (1996), 447.

133 For instance, see http://www.fathermag.com/news/rape/rankin.shtml, accessed 12 March 2006.

134 For an example, see Murray A. Straus, 'Psychical Assaults by Wives: A Major Social Problem', in Richard Gelles and Donileen R. Loseke (eds.), *Current Controversies on Family Violence* (London, 1993), 83.

135 Lisa D. Brush, 'Philosophical and Political Issues in Research on Women's Violence and Aggression', *Sex Roles: A Journal of Research* (June 2005).

CHAPTER NINE: EXHIBITIONISTS

1 'Police v. J. Pettitt – Trial on Charge of Indecent Exposure', 1950, in the National Archives of Australia, A432/94 1950/2027. For another example, see Ronald G. W. Naylor, 'Letters to Victor Gollancz', 3 March 1962 and 1 January 1963, in the Modern Records Centre, University of Warwick MSS 157/3/H6/1.

2 As we shall see shortly, there has been a recent change.

3 House of Commons, MP John Patten's reply to question: http://www.publications.parliament.uk/pa/cm198889/cmhansrd/1989-10-26/Writtens-9.html.

4 Charles Lasègue, 'Les exhibitionnistes', *L'Union médicale*, 23 (1877), 709–14, and Richard von Krafft-Ebing, *Psychopathia Sexualis*, trans. Charles Gilbert Chaddock (London, 1893).

5 Described in Alex. K. Gigeroff, *Sexual Deviations in the Criminal Law. Homosexual, Exhibitionistic, and Pedophilic Offences in Canada* (Toronto, 1968), 51–2.

6 Cited in Marilyn Ruth Riley, 'Exhibitionism: A Psycho-Legal Perspective', *San Diego Law Review*, 16.5 (August 1979), 864.

7 Jeffrey C. Narvil, 'Revealing the Bare Uncertainties of Indecent Exposure', *Columbia Journal of Law and Social Problems*, 29 (1995–6), 99.

8 Alex J. Arieff and David B. Rotman, 'One Hundred Cases of Indecent Exposure', *The Journal of Nervous and Mental Disease*, 96.5 (November 1942); F. H. Taylor, 'Observations of Some Cases of Exhibitionism', *Journal of Mental Science*, 93 (1947), 631; Ivor H. Jones and Dorothy Frei, 'Exhibitionism – A Biological Hypothesis', *British Journal of Medical Psychology*, 52 (1979), 63.

9 W. Calder, 'The Sexual Offender: A Prison Medical Officer's Viewpoint', *The British Journal of Delinquency*, vi.1 (July 1955), 38.

10 F. H. Taylor, 'Observations on Some Cases of Exhibitionism', *Journal of Mental Science*, 93 (1947), 633.

11 Bertram Pollens, *The Sex Criminal* (London, 1939), 68.

12 Dr T. S. Davies, 'Cyproterone Acetate in Sexual Misbehaviour', *Medicine, Science and the Law*, 10.4 (October 1970), 237.

13 Benjamin Karpman, *The Sexual Offender and his Offenses: Etiology, Pathology and Treatment*, first pub. 1954 (Washington, DC, 1964), 169 and 172–3.

14 Marilyn Ruth Riley, 'Exhibitionism: A Psycho-Legal Perspective', *San Diego Law Review*, 16.5 (August 1979), 858.

15 Graham Rooth, 'Exhibitionism, Sexual Violence and Paedophilia', *British Journal of Psychiatry*, 122 (1973), 705.

16 D. J. Power, 'Sexual Deviation and Crime', *Medicine, Science and the Law*, 16.2 (1976), 116.

17 Bertram Pollens, *The Sex Criminal* (London, 1939), 26–7.
18 Benjamin Karpman, *The Sexual Offender and his Offenses: Etiology, Pathology and Treatment*, first pub. 1954 (Washington, DC, 1964), 169 and 172–3.
19 David Green, 'Adolescent Exhibitionists: Theory and Therapy', *Journal of Adolescence*, 10.1 (March 1987), 45. The mean age was nineteen years.
20 David Green, 'Adolescent Exhibitionists: Theory and Therapy', *Journal of Adolescence*, 10.1 (March 1987), 48.
21 National Council for Civil Liberties, *Vagrancy – An Archaic Law. A Memorandum of Evidence to the Home Office Working Party on Vagrancy and Street Offences* (London, 1975), 6.
22 J. J. Putnam, *Addresses on Psycho-Analysis* (London, 1921), quoted in W. Norwood East, 'Observations on Exhibitionism', *The Lancet*, 23 August 1924, 375.
23 Karl M. Bowman, 'Psychiatric Aspects of the Problem', *Mental Hygiene*, xxii.1 (January 1938), 14.
24 Also see David T. Maclay, 'The Diagnosis and Treatment of Compensatory Types of Indecent Exposure', *British Journal of Delinquency*, 3.1 (July 1952), 40. He did not draw attention to the gender aspect.
25 F. E. Frenkel, 'Sex-Crime and its Socio-Historical Background', *Journal of The History of Ideas*, xxv.3 (July–September 1964), 339.
26 David T. Maclay, 'The Diagnosis and Treatment of Compensatory Types of Indecent Exposure', *British Journal of Delinquency*, 3.1 (July 1952), 40.
27 Nathan King Rickles, *Exhibitionism* (Philadelphia, 1950), 1–2.
28 Dr Paul Garnier, 'Sexual Pervert Impulses and Obsessions', *The Alienist and Neurologist*, xxi (1900), 636–7.
29 Graham Rooth, 'Changes in the Conviction Rate for Indecent Exposure', *British Journal of Psychiatry*, 121 (1972), 89 and 93–4.
30 Charles Gilbert Chaddock, 'Sexual Crimes', in Allan McLane Hamilton and Lawrence Godkin (eds.), *A System of Legal Medicine*, vol. 2, second edn. (New York, 1900), 550.
31 Richard von Krafft-Ebing, *Psychopathia Sexualis*, trans. Charles Gilbert Chaddock (London, 1893). Also see Léon Henri Thoinot and Arthur W. Weysee, *Medicolegal Aspects of Moral Offenses* (Philadelphia, 1911); Dr Paul Garnier, 'Sexual Pervert Impulses and Obsessions', *The Alienist and Neurologist*, xxi (1900), 636; Nathan King Rickles, *Exhibitionism* (Philadelphia, 1950), 25.
32 W. Norwood East, 'Observations on Exhibitionism', *The Lancet*, 23 August 1924, 372.
33 Max Hodann, *History of Modern Morals*, trans. Stella Browne (London, 1937), 67.
34 Dr Paul Garnier, 'Sexual Pervert Impulses and Obsessions', *The Alienist and Neurologist*, xxi (1900), 636–7.
35 Allan McLane Hamilton, 'Insanity in Medico-Legal Bearings', in Hamilton and Lawrence Godkin (eds.), *A System of Legal Medicine*, vol. 2, 2nd ed. (New York, 1900), 50. Also see George E. Dawson, 'Psychic Rudiments and Morality', *The American Journal of Psychology*, 11.2 (January 1900), 211.
36 David S. Booth, 'Erotomania. A Case of Exhibitionism in a Medico-Legal Study', *The Alienist and Neurologist*, xxvi.1 (February 1905), 1–4.
37 C. H. Hughes, 'Morbid Exhibitionism', *The Alienist and Neurologist*, xxv (1904), 349–50.
38 H. Christoffel, 'Exhibitionism and Exhibitionists', *International Journal of Psychoanalysis*, xvii (1936), 321–45, and Nathan King Rickles, 'Exhibitionism', *The Journal of Nervous and Mental Disease*, 95 (1942), 11–17.
39 W. Norwood East, 'Observations on Exhibitionism', *The Lancet*, 23 August 1924, 372–4. He did believe, however, that that punishment might teach those exhibitionists

who gained sexual gratification through exposure to 'appreciate the value of reality, and the vanity of phantasy formation'.

40 Also see F. H. Taylor, 'Observations on Some Cases of Exhibitionism', *Journal of Mental Science*, 93 (1947), 636.

41 Martin W. Peck, 'Exhibitionism: Report of a Case', *The Psychoanalytic Review*, xi.2 (April 1924), 159–65. He also believed that senility might bring on exhibitionist tendencies again.

42 David T. Maclay, 'The Diagnosis and Treatment of Compensatory Types of Indecent Exposure', *British Journal of Delinquency*, 3.1 (July 1952), 35, 38 and 41–3. Maclay did admit that the *threat* of punishment if the individual reoffended might be effective.

43 F. H. Taylor, 'Observations on Some Cases of Exhibitionism', *Journal of Mental Science*, 93 (1947), 636.

44 David T. Maclay, 'The Diagnosis and Treatment of Compensatory Types of Indecent Exposure', *British Journal of Delinquency*, 3.1 (July 1952), 41.

45 F. H. Taylor, 'Observations on Some Cases of Exhibitionism', *Journal of Mental Science*, 93 (1947), 638. Some commentators claimed that people in 'primitive races' did engage in exhibitionism: see Frank S. Caprio, *Variations in Sexual Behavior. A Psychodynamic Study of Deviations in Various Expressions of Sexual Behavior* (New York, 1955), 221.

46 Alex J. Arieff and David B. Rotman, 'One Hundred Cases of Indecent Exposure', *The Journal of Nervous and Mental Disease*, 96.5 (November 1942), 524.

47 Manfred Guttmacher, *Sex Offenses* (New York, 1951), 205. Also see Manfred S. Guttmacher and Henry Weihofen, *Psychiatry and the Law* (New York, 1952), 114.

48 Manfred S. Guttmacher and Henry Weihofen, *Psychiatry and the Law* (New York, 1952), 114–15. Also see 'E. C. B., Jr.', 'Pedophilia, Exhibitionism, and Voyeurism: Legal Problems in the Deviant Society', *Georgia Law Review*, 4 (1969), 153.

49 Renatus Hartogs, 'Discipline in the Early Life of Sex-Delinquents and Sex-Criminals', *The Nervous Child*, 9.1 (1951), 170.

50 Otto Fenichel, *The Psychoanalytic Theory of Neurosis* (New York, 1945), 345–6.

51 D. J. Power, 'Sexual Deviation and Crime', *Medicine, Science and the Law*, 16.2 (1976), 116.

52 Nathan King Rickles, *Exhibitionism* (Philadelphia, 1950), 53–65, 79–85 and 105–9, and Nathan King Rickles, 'Exhibitionism', *The Journal of Nervous and Mental Disease*, 95.1 (January 1942), 12–15. Also see D. J. Power, 'Sexual Deviation and Crime', *Medicine, Science and the Law*, 16.2 (1976), 117, and Marilyn Ruth Riley, 'Exhibitionism: A Psycho-Legal Perspective', *San Diego Law Review*, 16.5 (August 1979), 855–6.

53 Thomas P. Hackett, 'The Psychotherapy of Exhibitionists in a Court Clinic Setting', *Seminars in Psychiatry*, 3.3 (August 1971), 297–306.

54 Arnold Veraa, 'Probation Officer Treatment for Exhibitionists', *Federal Probation*, 40 (1976), 55 and 58–9.

55 As one jurist put it, the 'fear of the chronic sex fiend running loose on the streets does not disturb the average legislator quite so much as the fear of a voter whose taxes have been raised': see 'E. C. B., Jr.', 'Pedophilia, Exhibitionism, and Voyeurism: Legal Problems in the Deviant Society', *Georgia Law Review*, 4 (1969), 160. This was one of the reasons why hypnosis was popular: R. P. Snaith and S. A. Collins, 'Five Exhibitionists and a Method of Treatment', *British Journal of Psychiatry*, 138 (1981), 130.

56 Manfred S. Guttmacher and Henry Weihofen, *Psychiatry and the Law* (New York, 1952), 114.

57 This was widely observed at the time: for instance, see Karl M. Bowman, 'The

Problem of the Sex Offender', *The American Journal of Psychiatry*, 108 (September–October 1951), 251.

58 Marc H. Hollender, C. Winston Brown and Howard B. Roback, 'Genital Exhibitionism in Women', *American Journal of Psychiatry*, 134.4 (April 1977), 436.

59 Marc H. Hollender, C. Winston Brown and Howard B. Roback, 'Genital Exhibitionism in Women', *American Journal of Psychiatry*, 134.4 (April 1977), 438.

60 Nathan King Rickles, *Exhibitionism* (Philadelphia, 1950), 49–50.

61 Nathan King Rickles, *Exhibitionism* (Philadelphia, 1950), 49–50.

62 Jeno Hárnik, 'The Various Developments Undergone by Narcissism in Men and Women', *International Journal of Psycho-Analysis*, 5 (1924), 66–9, 72 and 79.

63 Jeno Hárnik, 'The Various Developments Undergone by Narcissism in Men and Women', *International Journal of Psycho-Analysis*, 5 (1924), 73.

64 Otto Fenichel, *The Psychoanalytic Theory of Neurosis* (New York, 1945), 346. He is quoting Jeno Hárnik, but the source of the quote is not given. It is not from the 1924 article quoted above.

65 Otto Fenichel, *The Psychoanalytic Theory of Neurosis* (New York, 1945), 347. It is not at all clear if he is quoting someone here or not. Also see Sigmund Freud, 'Medusa's Head', in James Strachey (ed.), *The Standard Edition of the Complete Psychological Works of Sigmund Freud*, xviii (1940), first pub. 1922, and Sándor Ferenczi, 'Nakedness as a Means for Inspiring Terror', in Ferenczi (ed.), *Further Contributions to the Theory and Technique of Psycho-Analysis*, first pub. 1919 (London, 1950).

66 Stevenson Smith and Edwin Guthrie, 'Exhibitionism', *The Journal of Abnormal Psychology and Social Psychology*, xvii (1922–3), 206–8.

67 Jim Stevenson and Ivor H. Jones, 'Behavior Therapy Technique for Exhibitionism', *Archives of General Psychiatry*, 27 (December 1972), 839–41. Also see Arnold Veraa, 'Probation Officer Treatment for Exhibitionists', *Federal Probation*, 40 (1976), 54.

68 I. Wickramesekera, 'Aversive Behavior Rehearsal for Sexual Exhibitionism', *Behavior Therapy*, 7 (1976), 167–76.

69 Edward Dengrove, 'Behavior Therapy of the Sexual Disorders', *The Journal of Sex Research*, 3.1 (February 1967), 58–60.

70 Alex. K. Gigeroff, J. W. Mohr and R. E. Turner, 'Sex Offenders on Probation: The Exhibitionist', *Federal Probation*, 32 (1968), 20.

71 Nathan King Rickles, *Exhibitionism* (Philadelphia, 1950), 7.

72 Nathan King Rickles, *Exhibitionism* (Philadelphia, 1950), 7.

73 F. H. Taylor, 'Observations on Some Cases of Exhibitionism', *Journal of Mental Science*, 93 (1947), 636.

74 F. H. Taylor, 'Observations on Some Cases of Exhibitionism', *Journal of Mental Science*, 93 (1947), 636.

75 Anthony Storr, *Sexual Deviation* (Harmondsworth, 1964), 93.

76 Nathan King Rickles, *Exhibitionism* (Philadelphia, 1950), 57, cited in Marilyn Ruth Riley, 'Exhibitionism: A Psycho-Legal Perspective', *San Diego Law Review*, 16.5 (August 1979), 856.

CHAPTER TEN: SEXUAL PSYCHOPATHS

1 Charles Sam Green, 'This Man is Dangerous!', *True Detective*, March 1958, 24–9.

2 Harry L. Kozol, Murray I. Cohen and Ralph F. Garofalo, 'The Criminally Dangerous Sex Offender', *The New England Journal of Medicine*, 275.2 (14 July 1960), 79–84.

3 James Cowles Prichard, *A Treatise on Insanity, and Other Disorders Affecting the Mind* (London, 1835), 6.

4 W. Norwood East, 'Psychopathic Personality and Crime', *Journal of Mental Science*, xci (October 1945), 428.

5 Benjamin Karpman, *The Sexual Offender and his Offenses. Etiology, Pathology, Psychodynamics and Treatment*, 9th edn., first pub. 1954 (Washington, DC, 1964), 56.
6 Herman M. Adler, 'Biological and Pathological Aspects of Behavior Disorders', *The American Journal of Psychiatry*, vii (November 1927), 512.
7 Benjamin Karpman, *The Sexual Offender and his Offenses. Etiology, Pathology, Psychodynamics and Treatment*, 9th edn., first pub. 1954 (Washington, DC, 1964), 7.
8 Edward D. Hoedemaker, '"Irresistible Impulse" as a Defence in Criminal Law', *Washington Law Review*, 23.1 (February 1948), 1–7, and Dwight D. Palmer, 'Conscious Motives in Psychopathic Behavior', *Proceedings of the American Academy of Forensic Sciences* (1954), 146–9.
9 Hervey Milton Cleckley, *The Mask of Sanity. An Attempt to Reinterpret the So-Called Psychopathic Personality* (St Louis, 1941).
10 Harrison G. Gough, 'A Sociological Theory of Psychopathy', *American Journal of Sociology*, 53.5 (March 1948), 361.
11 Dr R. H. Bryant, 'The Constitutional Psychopathic Inferior. A Menace to Society and a Suggestion for the Disposition of Such Individuals', *The American Journal of Psychiatry*, lxxxiii (April 1927), 673.
12 George H. Mead, *Mind, Self and Society From the Standpoint of a Social Behaviorist* (Chicago, 1934).
13 W. Norwood East, 'Psychopathic Personality and Crime', *Journal of Mental Science*, xci (October 1945), 439–40.
14 D. K. Henderson, 'Psychopathic States', *The Journal of Mental Science*, lxxxxviii.373 (October 1942), 490.
15 Estelle B. Freedman, '"Uncontrollable Desires": The Response to the Sexual Psychopath, 1920–1960', *Journal of American History*, 74.1 (June 1987), 88.
16 Estelle B. Freedman, '"Uncontrollable Desires": The Response to the Sexual Psychopath, 1920–1960', *Journal of American History*, 74.1 (June 1987), 90.
17 For instance, see the film *The Lonely Sex* (1959).
18 J. Edgar Hoover, 'How Safe is Your Daughter?', *American Magazine*, 144 (July 1947), 32.
19 Donald Leon, 'Sexual Psychopathy as a "Defence" in California', *UCLA Intramural Law Review*, 1 (1952–3), 21.
20 David G. Wittels, 'What Can We Do About Sex Crimes', *Saturday Evening Post*, 11 December 1948, 30.
21 Samuel M. Fahr, 'Iowa's New Sexual Psychopath Law – An Experimental Noble in Purpose?', *Iowa Law Review*, 41 (1955–6), 526.
22 Lewis Yablonsky, *The Violent Gang* (New York, 1962), 198.
23 Benjamin Karpman, 'The Sexual Psychopath', *Journal of Criminal Law, Criminology, and Police Science*, 42 (1951), 191–2.
24 Elias S. Carson, 'The Concept of the Psychopath', *The American Journal of Orthopsychiatry*, xviii (1948), 306–7.
25 George Thompson, *Psychopathic Delinquent and the Criminal* (Springfield, IL, 1953), 12.
26 Robert Lindener, *Stone Walls and Men* (New York, 1946), 153.
27 Ralph D. Rabinovitch speaking at 'The Sexual Psychopath. A Symposium', *Journal of Criminal Law, Criminology, and Police Science*, 43 (1952–3), 617.
28 James J. Graham, 'What to Do With the Psychopath?', *Journal of Criminal Law, Criminology, and Police Science*, 53 (1962), 448.
29 Walter Bromberg, *Crime and the Mind. An Outline of Psychiatric Criminology* (Philadelphia, 1948), 86.
30 Benjamin Karpman, *The Sexual Offender and his Offenses. Etiology, Pathology, Psychodynamics and Treatment* (New York, 1954), 478–9.

31 Benjamin Karpman, 'The Sexual Psychopath', *Journal of Criminal Law, Criminology, and Police Science*, 42 (1951), 189–91 and 196.
32 Bertram Pollens, *The Sex Criminal* (London, 1939), 25.
33 T. C. N. Gibbens, 'Recent Trends in the Management of Psychopathic Offenders', *Journal of Delinquency*, 2.2 (October 1951), 108–9.
34 Andrew Horwitz, 'Sexual Psychopath Legislation: Is There Anywhere to Go But Backwards?', *University of Pittsburgh Law Review*, 57 (1995–6), 38.
35 These statistics come from the State of Washington, comparing 1965 with 1969 and 1970: George J. MacDonald and Robinson A. Williams, *Characteristics and Management of Committed Sexual Offenders in the State of Washington* (State of Washington, 1971).
36 George J. MacDonald and Robinson A. Williams, *Characteristics and Management of Committed Sexual Offenders in the State of Washington* (State of Washington, 1971), 1–2.
37 Donald R. Ravenscroft, 'An Examination of the Nebraska Statute Providing for Commitment and Treatment of Sexual Psychopaths', *Nebraska Law Review*, 29 (1949–50), 507–8.
38 R. William Rosenfeld, 'Commitment of Sexual Psychopaths in Ohio', *Western Reserve Law Review*, 2 (June 1950), 78.
39 George J. MacDonald and Robinson A. Williams, *Community Adjustment of Treated Sexual Offenders* (State of Washington, 1971), 3.
40 Edwin H. Sutherland, 'The Diffusion of Sexual Psychopath Laws', *American Journal of Sociology*, 56.2 (September 1950), 146.
41 T. C. N. Gibbens, 'Recent Trends in the Management of Psychopathic Offenders', *Journal of Delinquency*, 2.2 (October 1951), 104–5, and Roxanne Lieb, Vernon Quinsey and Lucy Berliner, 'Sexual Predators and Social Policy', *Crime and Justice*, 23 (1998), 63–5.
42 Paul W. Tappan, 'The Sexual Psychopath – A Civic-Social Responsibility', *The Journal of Social Hygiene*, 35 (1949), 355.
43 Karl M. Bowman and Milton Rose, 'A Criticism of Current Usage of the Term "Sexual Psychopath"', *American Journal of Psychiatry*, 109 (September 1952), 178. Also see Desmond Curran and Paul Mallinson, 'Psychopathic Personality', *Journal of Mental Science*, 90 (January 1944), 267.
44 Edwin Hardin Sutherland and Donald Ray Cressey, *Criminology*, 8th edn. (Philadelphia, 1970), 159–60.
45 Manfred S. Guttmacher and Henry Weihofen, *Psychiatry and the Law* (New York, 1952), 111.
46 *Royal Commission on the Criminal Law Relating to Criminal Sexual Psychopaths* (Ottawa, 1958), 15.
47 'Indiana Sexual Psychopath Statutes', *Indiana Law Journal*, 25 (1949–50), 194.
48 R. William Rosenfeld, 'Commitment of Sexual Psychopaths in Ohio', *Western Reserve Law Review*, 2 (June 1950), 70–1.
49 Cited in Murray L. Cohen, Ralph Garofalo, Richard Boucher and Theoharis Seghorn, 'The Psychology of Rapists', *Seminars in Psychiatry*, 3.3 (August 1971), 308.
50 Murray L. Cohen, Ralph Garofalo, Richard Boucher and Theoharis Seghorn, 'The Psychology of Rapists', *Seminars in Psychiatry*, 3.3 (August 1971), 308.
51 Murray L. Cohen, Ralph Garofalo, Richard Boucher and Theoharis Seghorn, 'The Psychology of Rapists', *Seminars in Psychiatry*, 3.3 (August 1971), 309.
52 Elias S. Cohen, 'Administration of the Criminal Sexual Psychopath Statute in Indiana', *Indiana Law Journal*_32.4 (Summer 1957) 461.

53 Domenico Caporale and Deryl F. Hamann, 'Sexual Psychopathy – A Legal Labyrinth of Medicine, Morals, and Mythology', *Nebraska Law Review*, 36 (1957), 337.
54 Sallyanne Payton, 'Disability Benefits for Sexual Psychopaths', *Stanford Law Review*, 20 (1967–8), 119–34.
55 Also see Anthony Granucci and Susan J. Granucci, 'Indiana's Sexual Psychopath Act in Operation', *Indiana Law Journal*, 44 (1969), 562, who pointed out that just because sexual psychopath laws were not a medical category, it did not mean it could not be a 'recognizable and justifiable legal category'.
56 Domenico Caparole and Deryl F. Hamann, 'Sexual Psychopathy – A Legal Labyrinth of Medicine, Morals, and Mythology', *Nebraska Law Review*, 36 (1957), 341.
57 William R. Foley, 'California's Sexual Psychopath – Criminal or Patient?', *University of San Francisco Law Review*, 1.2 (April 1967), 337.
58 William R. Foley, 'California's Sexual Psychopath – Criminal or Patient?', *University of San Francisco Law Review*, 1.2 (April 1967), 337.
59 Domenico Caparole and Deryl F. Hamann, 'Sexual Psychopathy – A Legal Labyrinth of Medicine, Morals, and Mythology', *Nebraska Law Review*, 36 (1957), 332.
60 Paul W. Tappan, 'The Sexual Psychopath – A Civic-Social Responsibility', *The Journal of Social Hygiene*, 35 (1949), 361–2. He is more optimistic.
61 Donald R. Ravenscroft, 'An Examination of the Nebraska Statute Providing for Commitment and Treatment of Sexual Psychopaths', *Nebraska Law Review*, 29 (1949–50), 511.
62 Murray L. Cohen, Ralph Garofalo, Richard Boucher and Theoharis Seghorn, 'The Psychology of Rapists', *Seminars in Psychiatry*, 3.3 (August 1971), 308.
63 Paul W. Tappan, 'The Sexual Psychopath – A Civic-Social Responsibility', *The Journal of Social Hygiene*, 35 (1949), 361–2. He is more optimistic.
64 'The Sexual Psychopath. A Symposium', *Journal of Criminal Law, Criminology, and Police Science*, 43 (1952–3), 596; Paul W. Tappan, 'The Sexual Psychopath – A Civic-Social Responsibility', *The Journal of Social Hygiene*, 35 (1949), 362.
65 Dr R. H. Bryant, 'The Constitutional Psychopathic Inferior. A Menace to Society and a Suggestion for the Disposition of Such Individuals', *The American Journal of Psychiatry*, lxxxiii (April 1927), 677–9.
66 Lawrence T. Burick, 'An Analysis of the Illinois Sexually Dangerous Persons Act', *The Journal of Criminal Law, Criminology, and Police Science*, 59 (1968), 255.
67 Ralph Brancale, Albert Ellis and Ruth R. Doorbar, 'Psychiatric and Psychological Investigations of Convicted Sex Offenders: A Summary Report', *The American Journal of Psychiatry*, 109 (July 1952), 17–18.
68 T. C. N. Gibbens, 'Recent Trends in the Management of Psychopathic Offenders', *Journal of Delinquency*, 2.2 (October 1951), 105–6.
69 Estelle B. Freedman, '"Uncontrollable Desires": The Response to the Sexual Psychopath, 1920–1960', *Journal of American History*, 74.1 (June 1987), 100 and 103.
70 T. C. N. Gibbens, 'Recent Trends in the Management of Psychopathic Offenders', *Journal of Delinquency*, 2.2 (October 1951), 106.
71 T. C. N. Gibbens, C. Way and K. L. Soothill, 'Behavioral Types of Rape', *British Journal of Psychiatry*, 130 (1977), 33.
72 Manfred Guttmacher and Henry Weihofen, 'Sex Offenses', *Journal of Criminal Law and Criminology*, 43 (1952–3), 171–2.
73 Sallyanne Payton, 'Disability Benefits for Sexual Psychopaths', *Stanford Law Review*, 20 (1967–8), 119–34.

74 Simon A. Cole, 'From the Sexual Psychopath Statute to "Megan's Law": Psychiatric Knowledge in the Diagnosis, Treatment, and Adjudication of Sex Criminals in New Jersey, 1949–1999', *Journal of the History of Medicine*, 55 (2000), 298.
75 Paul W. Tappan, 'Treatment of the Sex Offender', *The American Journal of Psychiatry*, 108 (September–October 1951), 241.
76 M. C. Slough and Tom L. Schwinn, 'The Sexual Psychopath', *The University of Kansas City Law Review*, 19 (1950–1), 138.
77 Domenico Caparole and Deryl F. Hamann, 'Sexual Psychopathy – A Legal Labyrinth of Medicine, Morals, and Mythology', *Nebraska Law Review*, 36 (1957), 325–6.
78 Seymour Halleck, 'The Therapeutic Encounter', in H. L. P. Resnik and Marvin E. Wolfgang (eds.), *Sexual Behaviors. Social, Clinical, and Legal Aspects* (Boston, 1972), 190.
79 George J. MacDonald and Robinson A. Williams, *Characteristics and Management of Committed Sexual Offenders in the State of Washington* (State of Washington, 1971), 9.
80 See Simon A. Cole, 'From the Sexual Psychopath Statute to "Megan's Law": Psychiatric Knowledge in the Diagnosis, Treatment, and Adjudication of Sex Criminals in New Jersey, 1949–1999', *Journal of the History of Medicine*, 55 (2000), 307–8.
81 Elias S. Cohen, 'Administration of the Criminal Sexual Psychopath Statute in Indiana', *Indiana Law Journal* 32.4 (Summer 1957), 455.
82 Albert Ellis, Ruth R. Doorbar and Robert Johnston III, 'Characteristics of Convicted Sex Offenders', *The Journal of Social Psychology*, 40 (1954), 10–11. Also see Ralph Brancale, Albert Ellis, and Ruth R. Doorbar, 'Psychiatric and Psychological Investigations of Convicted Sex Offenders: A Summary Report', *The American Journal of Psychiatry*, 109 (July 1952), 19.
83 Elias S. Cohen, 'Administration of the Criminal Sexual Psychopath Statute in Indiana', *Indiana Law Journal* 32.4 (Summer 1957), 455.
84 Stephen Robertson, 'Separating the Men from the Boys: Masculinity, Psychosexual Development, and Sex Crime in the United States, 1930s–1960s', *Journal of the History of Medicine and Allied Sciences*, 56.1 (2001), 5.
85 Donald Leon, 'Sexual Psychopathy as a "Defence" in California', *UCLA Intramural Law Review*, 1 (1952–3), 23.
86 Domenico Caparole and Deryl F. Hamann, 'Sexual Psychopathy – A Legal Labyrinth of Medicine, Morals, and Mythology', *Nebraska Law Review*, 36 (1957), 330.
87 Peter Sullivan, 'Commitment of Sexual Psychopaths and the Requirements of Procedural Due Process', *Fordham Law Review*, 44 (1976), 924.
88 Domenico Caparole and Deryl F. Hamann, 'Sexual Psychopathy – A Legal Labyrinth of Medicine, Morals, and Mythology', *Nebraska Law Review*, 36 (1957), 340.
89 Lawrence T. Burick, 'An Analysis of the Illinois Sexually Dangerous Persons Act', *The Journal of Criminal Law, Criminology, and Police Science*, 59 (1968), 259.
90 Andrew Horwitz, 'Sexual Psychopath Legislation: Is There Anywhere to Go But Backwards?', *University of Pittsburgh Law Review*, 57 (1995–6), 45–6.
91 Domenico Caparole and Deryl F. Hamann, 'Sexual Psychopathy – A Legal Labyrinth of Medicine, Morals, and Mythology', *Nebraska Law Review*, 36 (1957), 340.
92 Mark A. Small, 'The Legal Context of Mentally Disordered Sex Offender (MDSS) Treatment Programs', *Criminal Justice and Behavior*, 19.2 (June 1992), 130.
93 Lawrence T. Burick, 'An Analysis of the Illinois Sexually Dangerous Persons Act',

The Journal of Criminal Law, Criminology, and Police Science, 59 (1968), 256. Also see Mark A. Small, 'The Legal Context of Mentally Disordered Sex Offender (MDSS) Treatment Programs', *Criminal Justice and Behavior*, 19.2 (June 1992), 130.

94 Samuel M. Fahr, 'Iowa's New Sexual Psychopath Law – An Experimental Noble in Purpose?', *Iowa Law Review*, 41 (1955–6), 533 and 539.

95 *In re Maddox* (351 Mich. 358, 88 N. W. 2d 470 (1958), 474–5.

96 Edward de Grazia, 'The Distinction of Being Mad', *University of Chicago Law Review*, 22 (1954–5), 352–4.

97 Group for the Advancement of Psychiatry, *Psychiatry and Sex Psychopath Legislation: The 30s to the 80s* (New York, 1977), 840 and 935.

98 Vikki H. Sturgeon and John Taylor, 'Report of a Five-Year Follow-Up Study of Mentally Disordered Sex Offenders Released from Atascadero State Hospital in 1973', *Criminal Justice Journal*, 4 (1980), 31–63.

99 David Finkelhor, *Child Sexual Abuse. New Theory and Research* (New York, 1984), 1–2.

100 Jon Silverman and David Wilson, *Innocence Betrayed. Paedophilia, the Media and Society* (Cambridge, 2002), 22 analyzed interest in child sexual abuse in six leading British newspapers. See the title of Diana E. H. Russell and Rebecca M. Bolen's *The Epidemic of Rape and Child Abuse in the United States* (London, 2000).

101 Illinois, Kansas, California, Wisconsin, Minnesota, New Jersey, North Dakota and Arizona.

102 Andrew Horwitz, 'Sexual Psychopath Legislation: Is There Anywhere to Go But Backwards?', *University of Pittsburgh Law Review*, 57 (1995–6), 37.

103 E. Janus, 'Sexual Predator Commitment Laws: Lessons for Law and the Behavioral Sciences', *Behavioral Science and the Law*, 18 (2000), 10.

104 Quoted in Simon A. Cole, 'From the Sexual Psychopath Statute to "Megan's Law": Psychiatric Knowledge in the Diagnosis, Treatment, and Adjudication of Sex Criminals in New Jersey, 1949–1999', *Journal of the History of Medicine*, 55 (2000), 310–11.

105 Cited in Ralph Slovenko, *Psychiatry and Criminal Culpability* (New York, 1995) re. Petition of Andre Young, 122 Wash. 2d 1, 857 P.2d 989 (1993).

106 Quoted in Simon A. Cole, 'From the Sexual Psychopath Statute to "Megan's Law": Psychiatric Knowledge in the Diagnosis, Treatment, and Adjudication of Sex Criminals in New Jersey, 1949–1999', *Journal of the History of Medicine*, 55 (2000), 311.

107 Simon A. Cole, 'From the Sexual Psychopath Statute to "Megan's Law": Psychiatric Knowledge in the Diagnosis, Treatment, and Adjudication of Sex Criminals in New Jersey, 1949–1999', *Journal of the History of Medicine*, 55 (2000), 312.

108 Based on those committed to Nebraska hospitals: Domenico Caparole and Deryl F. Hamann, 'Sexual Psychopathy – A Legal Labyrinth of Medicine, Morals, and Mythology', *Nebraska Law Review*, 36 (1957), 340.

CHAPTER ELEVEN: THE HOME

1 Cecil Day Lewis, 'Sex-Crime', *Selected Poems* (Harmondsworth, 1951), 38–40.

2 Don James, *The Sexual Side of Life* (Derby, CT, 1957), 142–4.

3 Margaret Mitchell, *Gone with the Wind*, first pub. 1936 (London, 1973), 930.

4 Hale was also notorious for his role in witch-hunt trials.

5 Sir Matthew Hale, *Pleas of the Crown* (London, 1678), 628–9.

6 James Schouler, *A Treatise on the Law of Domestic Relations: Embracing Husband and Wife, Parent and Child, Guardian and Ward, and Master and Servant*, 4th edn., first pub. 1870 (Boston, 1889), 37.

7 This is convincingly argued by A. James Hammerton, *Cruelty and Companionship in Nineteenth-Century Married Life* (London, 1992), 108.
8 Sir Cresswell Cresswell's comment in N— v. N— (1862), cited in A. James Hammerton, *Cruelty and Companionship in Nineteenth-Century Married Life* (London, 1992), 109.
9 John Stuart Mill, 'The Subjection of Women', in Mill, *On Liberty. Representative Government. The Subjection of Women. Three Essays*, first pub. 1869 (London, 1912), 463 and 522.
10 Quoted in Robert L. Griswold, 'Law, Sex, Cruelty, and Divorce in Victorian America, 1840–1900', *American Quarterly*, 38.5 (Winter 1986), 733.
11 Paulina Wright Davis, *A History of the National Women's Rights Movement* (New York, 1871), 66.
12 John Harvey Kellogg, *Plain Facts for Old and Young* (Burlington, IA, 1884), 225–6.
13 Russell Thacher Trall, *Sexual Physiology: A Scientific and Popular Exposition of the Fundamental Problems in Sociology* (New York, 1866), xi.
14 John Cowan, *The Science of a New Life* (New York, 1869), 105.
15 George Henry Napheys, *The Transmission of Life. Counsels on the Nature and Hygiene of the Masculine Functions* (Toronto, 1884), 179–80.
16 Alice B. Stockham, *Tokology. A Book for Every Woman* (Chicago, 1889), 154.
17 John Tosh, *A Man's Place: Masculinity and the Middle-Class Home in Victorian England* (New Haven, 1999).
18 Robert L. Griswold, 'Law, Sex, Cruelty, and Divorce in Victorian America, 1840–1900', *American Quarterly*, 38.5 (Winter 1986), 722.
19 Margaret Marsh, 'Suburban Men and Masculine Domesticity, 1870–1915', *American Quarterly*, 40.2 (June 1988), 179–80.
20 Andrew Jackson Davis, *The Genesis and Ethics of Conjugal Love* (New York, 1874), 20 and 25–8.
21 Francis W. Newman, *Remedies for the Great Social Evil with Special Reference to Recent Laws Delusively Called Contagious Diseases Acts*, first pub. 1884 (London, 1889), 10–11.
22 Francis W. Newman, *Remedies for the Great Social Evil with Special Reference to Recent Laws Delusively Called Contagious Diseases Acts*, first pub. 1884 (London, 1889), 10–11.
23 Alice Mona Caird, *The Morality of Marriage, and Other Essays on the Status and Destiny of Women* (London, 1897), 105–6.
24 Nicholas Francis Cooke, *Satan in Society, By a Physician* (Cincinnati, 1871), 146.
25 Hugh Northcote, *Christianity and Sex Problems* (Philadelphia, 1906), 129.
26 William J. Robinson, *Woman: Her Sex and Love Life* (New York, 1917), 344.
27 Leopold Loewenfeld, *On Conjugal Happiness. Experiences, Reflections and Advice of a Medical Man*, 3rd edn., trans. Ronald E. S. Krohn (London, 1913), 200–1.
28 Theodoor Hendrik Van de Velde, *Ideal Marriage. Its Physiology and Technique*, first pub. in 1928, trans. Stella Browne (London, 1946), 228–31. Van de Velde was formerly director of the Gynaecological Clinic in Haarlem, Netherlands.
29 Henry Clarke Wright, *The Unwelcome Child; or, The Crime of an Undesigned and Undesired Maternity* (Boston, 1858), 182–4.
30 For a discussion, see my *Working-Class Cultures in Britain, 1890–1960: Gender, Class and Ethnicity* (London, 1994).
31 'Rape and Battery Between Husband and Wife', *Stanford Law Review*, 6 (1953–4), 719–28.
32 Michael Tonry, 'Obituary: Norval Morris', *Guardian Unlimited*, 9 April 2004. Contrary to Tonry's characterization, Morris was a New Zealander, not American, although he spent much of his career in Australia and America.

33 Norval Morris and A. L. Turner, 'Two Problems in the Law of Rape', *The University of Queensland Law Journal*, 2 (1952–3), 259–60.

34 Kate Warner, 'Sentencing in Cases of Marital Rape: Towards Changing the Male Imagination', *Legal Studies*, 20 (2000), 602.

35 David Finkelhor and Kersti Yllo, *License to Rape: Sexual Abuse of Wives* (New York, 1985), 66.

36 Diana H. Russell, *Rape in Marriage* (Indianapolis, 1990), xxii and 2. Also see David Finkelhor and Kersti Yllo, *License to Rape: Sexual Abuse of Wives* (New York, 1985), 6–7, which found that 10 per cent of women who were married said their husbands used force to have sex with them. According to another estimate, one in every seven married or formerly married women had been raped by their husband: Sarah M. Harless, 'From the Bedroom to the Courtroom: The Impact of Domestic Violence Law on Marital Rape Victims', *Rutgers Law Journal*, 35 (2003–4), 306. Also see Irene Hanson Frieze, 'Investigating the Causes and Consequences of Marital Rape', *Signs: Journal of Women in Culture and Society*, 8.3 (Spring 1983), 533–4. and Women Against Rape, 'The Rapist Who Pays the Rent', 140, *New Law Journal*, 16 November 1990, 1599.

37 Case of Thorne; 2 Cr App R (S), 1966, 246–7, cited in Kate Warner, 'Sentencing in Cases of Marital Rape: Towards Changing the Male Imagination', *Legal Studies*, 20 (2000), 600.

38 Cited in Myra J. Hird, *Engendering Violence. Heterosexual Interpersonal Violence from Childhood to Adulthood* (Aldershot, 2002), 72.

39 See Diana H. Russell, *Rape in Marriage* (Indianapolis, 1990), 192–3, and 'To Have and To Hold: the Marital Rape Exemption and the Fourteenth Amendment', *Harvard Law Review*, 99 (1985–6), 1262.

40 Diana H. Russell, *Rape in Marriage* (Indianapolis, 1990). Also see Jana L. Jasinski and Linda M. Williams, with David Finkelhor, *Partner Violence: A Comprehensive Review of the 20 Years of Research* (Thousand Oaks, 1998).

41 Liz Kelly, Jo Lovett and Linda Regan, *A Gap or a Chasm? Attrition in Reported Rape Cases: A Home Office Research Study* (London, 2005), 15; R. Bergen, 'Surviving Wife Rape: How Women Define and Cope with the Violence', *Violence Against Women*, 1.2 (1995), 117–38; P. Easteal, 'Rape in Marriage: Has the License Lapsed?', in Patricia Weiser Easteal (ed.), *Balancing the Scales: Rape, Law Reform, and Australian Culture* (Sydney, 1995); Patricia Weiser Easteal, 'Survivors of Sexual Assault: An Australian Survey', *International Journal of Sociology of Law*, 22 (1994), 337–8; A. Myhill and J. Allen, *Rape and Sexual Assault of Women: The Extent and Nature of the Problem – Findings from the British Crime Survey*, Home Office Research Study 237 (London, 2002); Diana H. Russell, *Rape in Marriage* (Indianapolis, 1990), 90 and 193.

42 HM Crown Prosecution Service Inspectorate, *A Report on the Joint Inspection into the Investigation and Prosecution of Cases Involving Allegations of Rape* (London, April 2002), 34.

43 John Harman, 'Consent, Harm, and Marital Rape', *Journal of Family Law*, 22 (1983–4), 40.

44 Charles R. Jeffords and R. Thomas Dull, 'Demographic Variations in Attitudes towards Marital Rape', *Journal of Marriage and the Family*, 44 (1982), 755–62, and Charles R. Jeffords, 'Prosecutorial Discretion in Cases of Marital Rape', *Victimology. An International Journal*, 9.4 (1984), 416.

45 *Monday Conference Transcript. Men, Women and Violence – The Politics of Rape* (Sydney, 1976), 22.

46 Glanville Williams, 'The Problem of Domestic Rape', *New Law Journal*, 141 (15

February 1991), 205, and 'The Problem of Domestic Rape', *New Law Journal*, 141 (22 February 1991), 246. Also see the witty responses by Celia Wells, 'Rape In Marriage', *New Law Journal*, 141 (1 March 1991), 276; Mrs Meyers, 'Rape in Marriage', *New Law Review*, 1 March 1991, 276; Helen Fenwick, 'Marital Rights or Partial Immunity?', *New Law Journal*, 142 (19 June 1992), 870. After the marital rape exemption was repealed, Williams wrote another article in *New Law Journal*, 142 (10 January 1992), 11.

47 Richard J. Gelles, 'Power, Sex, and Violence: The Case of Marital Rape', *The Family Coordinator*, 26.4 (October 1977), 339.

48 William Blackstone, *Commentaries on the Laws of England*, vol. I (Oxford, 1765), 430.

49 State v. Smith, 85 N.J. 193, 205, 426 A.2d 38, 44 (1981), cited in Sandra Ryder and Sheryl A. Kuzmenka, 'Legal Rape: The Marital Rape Exemption', *Journal of the Marshall Law Review*, 24 (1990–1), 403.

50 'Indecent Assault – The Scope of Marital Consent. R. v. Kowalski', *Journal of Criminal Law*, 53 (1989), 49–50.

51 For a discussion, see Larry Catá Backer, 'Raping Sodomy and Sodomizing Rape: A Morality Tale About the Transformation of Modern Sodomy Jurisprudence', *American Journal of Criminal Law*, 37 (1993–4), 101–2. This was only criminalized by an amendment in 1990, and then only if a divorce or separation petition was pending at the time of the incident. These limitations were removed in 1993.

52 Margaret Anderson, 'Domestic Rape', *New Law Journal*, 141 (15 March 1991), 336.

53 Warren v State, 255 Ga. At 155, 336 S.E.2d 221 at 225, cited in Sandra Ryder and Sheryl A. Kuzmenka, 'Legal Rape: The Martial Rape Exemption', *Journal of the Marshall Law Review*, 24 (1990–1), 405.

54 Women Against Rape, 'The Rapist Who Pays the Rent', 140, *New Law Journal*, 16 November 1990, 1599.

55 Women Against Rape, 'The Rapist Who Pays the Rent', 140, *New Law Journal*, 16 November 1990, 1599.

56 Tina Dempster, 'Consent and Marital Rape', *New Law Journal*, 140 (10 August 1990), 1149.

57 'First Annual Report of the Protective Agency for Women and Children, 1887', 10, in Elizabeth Pleck, 'Feminist Responses to Crimes Against Women, 1868–1896', *Signs: Journal of Women in Culture and Society*, 8.31 (1983), 466.

58 'First Annual Report of the Protective Agency for Women and Children, 1887', 11, in Elizabeth Pleck, 'Feminist Responses to Crimes Against Women, 1868–1896', *Signs: Journal of Women in Culture and Society*, 8.31 (1983), 465.

59 Sarah M. Harless, 'From the Bedroom to the Courtroom: The Impact of Domestic Violence Law on Marital Rape Victims', *Rutgers Law Journal*, 35 (2003–4), 331.

60 Stallard v. HM Advocate 1989 SCCR 248.

61 Fifteen Report of the Criminal Law Revision Committee Report on Sexual Offences, CMND 9213, 1984, para. 2.64.

62 English Law Commission working paper no. 116, paras 4.16-4.25 siding with para. 2.64 of the Fifteen Report of the Criminal Law Revision Committee Report on Sexual Offences, CMND 9213, 1984.

63 n. 205, 1992.

64 Law Commission, *Rape Within Marriage*, no. 205, 1992, para. 3.12.

65 *The Times*, 28 October 1991.

66 Jessica Harris and Sharon Grace, *A Question of Evidence? Investigating and Prosecuting Rape in the 1990s* (London, 1999), 6.

CHAPTER TWELVE: THE PRISON

1 Haywood Patterson and Earl Conrad, *Scottsboro Boy* (London, 1950), 269.
2 Dan T. Carter, *Scottsboro. A Tragedy of the American South* (Baton Rouge, 1969), 408.
3 Haywood Patterson and Earl Conrad, *Scottsboro Boy* (London, 1950), 91.
4 Other examples include *Poison* (1991), *American Me* (1992) and *American History X* (1998).
5 For examples of jokes about prison rape, see Bruce Jackson, 'Prison Folklore', *The Journal of American Folklore*, 78.310 (October–December 1965), 321.
6 Robert W. Dumond, 'The Impact and Recovery of Prison Rape', 13, in http://www.spr.org/pdf/Dumond.pdf.
7 Wayne S. Wooden and Jay Parker, *Men Behind Bars. Sexual Exploitation in Prison* (New York, 1982), 211.
8 Joseph F. Fishman, *Sex in Prison. Revealing Sex Conditions in American Prisons* (London, 1935) and 'Prohibited Publication. Sex in Prison', 1936, in National Archives of Australia A425/122 1935/11290. In the end, the Australian censorship board refused to censor it on the grounds that it was 'a serious work'.
9 According to Michael Graubart Levin, 'Fight, Flee, Submit, Sue: Alternatives for Sexually Assaulted Prisoners', *Journal of Legal and Social Problems*, 18 (1983–4), 507.
10 Marie E. Kopp, 'Surgical Treatment as Sex Crime Prevention Measure', *American Institute of Crime, Law, and Criminology*, 28 (1937–8), 694.
11 'The Howard League for Penal Reform. Questionnaire on Mental Health in Prison', 1948, in Modern Records Centre, University of Warwick, MSS 16c/3/MH//7.
12 For instance, see Gordon James Knowles, 'Male Prison Rape: A Search for Causation and Prevention', *The Howard Journal*, 38.3 (1999), 276.
13 Haywood Patterson and Earl Conrad, *Scottsboro Boy* (London, 1950), 256.
14 Robert M. Lindner, 'Sex in Prison', *Complex*, 6 (1951), 11–12.
15 For information on Donaldson, see http://www.nypl.org/research/chss/spe/rbk/faids/donaldson.pdf.
16 Alan J. Davis, 'Sexual Assaults in the Philadelphia Prison System and Sheriff's Vans', *Trans-Action*, December 1968, 9.
17 B. McGurk, R. Forde and A. Barnes, 'Sexual Victimisation Among 15-17-Year-Old Offenders in Prison', Occasional Paper No. 65 (London, 2000) and K. G. Power, I. Markova, A. Rowlands et al. 'Sexual Behaviour in Scottish Prisons', *British Medical Journal*, 302 (1991), 1507–8. For a slightly higher figure (2 per cent), see K. Edgar, I. O'Donnell and C. Martin, *Prison Violence: The Dynamics of Conflict, Fear and Power* (Cullompton, 2003).
18 For estimates, see Alan J. Davis, 'Sexual Assaults in the Philadelphia Prison System and Sheriff's Vans', *Trans-Action*, December 1968, and Wayne S. Wooden and Jay Parker, *Men Behind Bars. Sexual Exploitation in Prison* (New York, 1982), 99.
19 For lower estimates, see Peter L. Nacci and Thomas R. Kane, 'Inmate Sexual Aggression: Some Evolving Propositions, Empirical Findings, and Mitigating Counter-Forces', *Journal of Offender Counseling, Services, and Rehabilitation*, 9 (1984), 10–11. For higher estimates, see Wayne S. Wooden and Jay Parker, *Men Behind Bars. Sexual Exploitation in Prison* (New York, 1982).
20 United Nations, *Global Report on Crime and Justice* (New York, 1999), 286.
21 Taken from Cindy Struckman-Johnson and David Struckman-Johnson, 'Sexual Coercion as Reported by Women in Three Midwestern Prisons', *Journal of Sex Research* (August 2002), in http://findarticles.com/p/articles/mi_m2372/is_3_39/ai_94130318.

22 Eli Lehrer, 'Hell Behind Bars: The Crime that Dare Not Speak its Name', *National Review*, 5 February 2001, at http://www.heritage.org/Press/Commentary/ED020501.cfm.

23 Eli Lehrer, 'Hell Behind Bars: The Crime that Dare Not Speak its Name', *National Review*, 5 February 2001, at http://www.heritage.org/Press/Commentary/ED020501.cfm.

24 Peter L. Nacci and Thomas R. Kane, 'Inmate Sexual Aggression: Some Evolving Propositions, Empirical Findings, and Mitigating Counter-Forces', *Journal of Offender Counseling, Services, and Rehabilitation*, 9 (1984), 1–20.

25 David A. Jones, *The Health Risks of Imprisonment* (Lexington, MA, 1976), 156–7.

26 Alan J. Davis, 'Sexual Assaults in the Philadelphia Prison System', in Gagnon and Simon (eds.), *The Sexual Scene*, 2nd edn. (New Brunswick, 1973), 228.

27 Patricia Pearson, *When She was Bad: How Women Get Away with Murder* (London, 1997), 208.

28 Quoted in Kenneth Dimick, *Ladies in Waiting Behind Prison Walls* (Muncie, IN, 1979), 90.

29 Cindy Struckman-Johnson and David Struckman-Johnson, 'Sexual Coercion as Reported by Women in Three Midwestern Prisons', *Journal of Sex Research* (August 2002), in http://findarticles.com/p/articles/mi_m2372/is_3_39/ai_94130318.

30 Margaret Otis, 'A Perversion Not Uncommonly Noted', *Journal of Abnormal Psychology*, 8 (1913), 113–16.

31 Rose Giallombardo, *Society of Women: A Study of a Women's Prison* (New York, 1966).

32 C. Bartollas and C. M. Sieverdes, 'The Sexual Victim in a Coeducational Juvenile Correctional Institution', *The Prison Journal*, 58 (1983), 80–90, cited in Cindy Struckman-Johnson and David Struckman-Johnson, 'Sexual Coercion as Reported by Women in Three Midwestern Prisons', *Journal of Sex Research* (August 2002), in http://findarticles.com/p/articles/mi_m2372/is_3_39/ai_94130318.

33 Cindy J. Struckman-Johnson, David L. Struckman-Johnson, L. Rucker, K. Bumby and S. Donaldson, 'Sexual Coercion Reported by Men and Women in Prison', *The Journal of Sex Research*, 33 (1976), 67–76.

34 Wayne S. Wooden and Jay Parker, *Men Behind Bars. Sexual Exploitation in Prison* (New York, 1982), 103.

35 Clyde B. Vedder and Patricia G. King, *Problems of Homosexuality in Corrections* (Springfield, IL, 1967), 24.

36 Leo Carroll, 'Humanitarian Reform and Biracial Sexual Assault in a Maximum Security Prison', *Urban Life*, 5.4 (1977), 421.

37 Wayne S. Wooden and Jay Parker, *Men Behind Bars. Sexual Exploitation in Prison* (New York, 1982), 102–3.

38 Christopher D. Man and John P. Cronan, 'Forecasting Sexual Abuse in Prison: The Prison Subculture of Masculinity as a Backdrop for "Deliberate Indifference"', *The Journal of Criminal Law and Criminology*, 92.1 (2001), 161.

39 David A. Jones, *The Health Risks of Imprisonment* (Lexington, MA, 1976), 159.

40 Wayne S. Wooden and Jay Parker, *Men Behind Bars. Sexual Exploitation in Prison* (New York, 1982), 118.

41 Cited in Thomas J. Cottle, 'Children in Jail', *Crime and Delinquency*, 25 (1979), 328–9.

42 Cindy Struckman-Johnson and David Struckman-Johnson, 'Sexual Coercion Rates in Seven Midwestern Prison Facilities for Men', *The Prison Journal*, 80.4 (2000), 389. For a discussion of the risks faced by female prisoners, see Human Rights Watch, Women's Rights Project, *All Too Familiar: Sexual Abuse of Women in US State Prisons* (New York, 1966) and Cindy Struckman-Johnson and David Struckman-Johnson, 'Sexual Coercion as Reported by Women in Three Midwestern Prisons',

Journal of Sex Research (August 2002), in http://findarticles.com/p/articles/mi_m2372/is_3_39/ai_94130318.

43 Sarah Eschholz and Michael S. Vaughn, 2001, 'Police Sexual Violence and Rape Myths. Civil Liability Under Section 1983', *Journal of Criminal Justice*, 29 (2001), 389–90.

44 Quoted in Lorna A. Rhodes, *Total Confinement. Madness and Reason in the Maximum Security Prison* (Berkeley, CA, 2004), 70.

45 Unnamed prisoner quoted by Joseph F. Fishman, *Sex in Prison. Revealing Sex Conditions in American Prisons* (London, 1935), 98.

46 Cited in Gene Kassebaum, 'Sex in Prison', *Sexual Behavior*, 2 (January 1972), 39.

47 Joseph F. Fishman, *Sex in Prison. Revealing Sex Conditions in American Prisons* (London, 1935), 95–6. Also see Alan J. Davis, 'Sexual Assaults in the Philadelphia Prison System and Sheriff's Vans', *Trans-Action*, December 1968, 10.

48 Arthur Kaufman, 'Rape of Men in the Community', in Irving R. Stuart and Joanne G. Greer (eds.), *Victims of Sexual Aggression: Treatment of Children, Women and Men* (New York, 1984), 167. Also see Wayne S. Wooden and Jay Parker, *Men Behind Bars. Sexual Exploitation in Prison* (New York, 1982), 107.

49 Lee H. Bowker, *Prison Victimization* (New York, 1980), 43.

50 Alan J. Davis, 'Sexual Assaults in the Philadelphia Prison System and Sheriff's Vans', *Trans-Action*, December 1968, 10, and Wayne S. Wooden and Jay Parker, *Men Behind Bars. Sexual Exploitation in Prison* (New York, 1982), 118–19.

51 Tommi, 'The Rape Poem', cited in Daniel Burton Rose, 'The Anti-Exploits of Men Against Sexism, 1977–78', in Don Sabo, Terry A. Kupers and Willie London (eds.), *Prison Masculinities* (Philadelphia, 2001), 224.

52 Judy Jacobs, quoted in Kitsi Burkhart, 'Women in Prison', in The Editors of *Ramparts* Magazine and Frank Browning (eds.), *Prison Life. A Study of the Explosive Conditions in America's Prisons* (New York, 1972), 17.

53 Judy Jacobs, quoted in Kitsi Burkhart, 'Women in Prison', in The Editors of *Ramparts* Magazine and Frank Browning (eds.), *Prison Life. A Study of the Explosive Conditions in America's Prisons* (New York, 1972), 17.

54 Sol Chaneles, 'Preface', in Chaneles (ed.), *Gender Issues, Sex Offenses, and Criminal Justice: Current Trends* (New York, 1984), xiii.

55 Sidney Blotzman, quoted in Clifford R. Shaw in collaboration with Maurice E. Moore, *The National History of a Delinquent Career* (New York, 1968), 189.

56 Unnamed correctional officer in a medium security prison in California interviewed by Wayne S. Wooden and Jay Parker, *Men Behind Bars. Sexual Exploitation in Prison* (New York, 1982), 203.

57 Helen M. Eigenberg, 'Correctional Officers' Definitions of Rape in Male Prisons', *Journal of Criminal Justice*, 28.5 (September–October 2000).

58 Arthur F. Schiff, 'Examination and Treatment of the Male Rape Victim', *Southern Medical Journal*, 73.11 (November 1980), 1499. He had worked at the Dade County Rape Treatment Center in Miami.

59 Haywood Patterson and Earl Conrad, *Scottsboro Boy* (London, 1950), 92. Also see Anthony M. Scacco, 'Preface', in Scacco (ed.), *Male Rape. A Casebook of Sexual Aggression* (New York, 1982), vii.

60 Howard Levy and David Miller, *Going to Jail. The Political Prisoner* (New York, 1970), 153–4.

61 Eli Lehrer, 'Hell Behind Bars: The Crime that Dare Not Speak its Name', *National Review*, 5 February 2001, at http://www.heritage.org/Press/Commentary/ED020501.cfm.

62 Unnamed woman quoted by Eli Lehrer, 'Hell Behind Bars: The Crime that Dare

Not Speak its Name', *National Review*, 5 February 2001, at http://www.heritage.org/Press/Commentary/ED020501.cfm.

63 See Christopher D. Man and John P. Cronan, 'Forecasting Sexual Abuse in Prison: The Prison Subculture of Masculinity as a Backdrop for "Deliberate Indifference"', *The Journal of Criminal Law and Criminology*, 92.1 (2001), 161.

64 Peter L. Nacci and Thomas R. Kane, 'Inmate Sexual Aggression: Some Evolving Propositions, Empirical Findings, and Mitigating Counter-Forces', *Journal of Offender Counseling, Services, and Rehabilitation*, 9 (1984), 7–8.

65 Alan J. Davis, in Anthony M. Scacco (ed.), *Male Rape: A Casebook of Sexual Aggressions* (New York, 1982), 1982, 116.

66 Unnamed correctional officer quoted in Wayne S. Wooden and Jay Parker, *Men Behind Bars. Sexual Exploitation in Prison* (New York, 1982), 191–2.

67 Leo Carroll, 'Humanitarian Reform and Biracial Sexual Assault in a Maximum Security Prison', *Urban Life*, 5.4 (1977), 422, and Gordon James Knowles, 'Male Prison Rape: A Search for Causation and Prevention', *The Howard Journal*, 38.3 (1999), 275.

68 E. Sagarin, 'Prison Homosexuality and its Effects on Post-Prison Sexuality', *Psychiatry*, 39 (1976), 255.

69 Gordon James Knowles, 'Male Prison Rape: A Search for Causation and Prevention', *The Howard Journal*, 38.3 (1999), 276.

70 Leo Carroll, 'Humanitarian Reform and Biracial Sexual Assault in a Maximum Security Prison', *Urban Life*, 5.4 (1977), 422.

71 Leo Carroll, 'Humanitarian Reform and Biracial Sexual Assault in a Maximum Security Prison', *Urban Life*, 5.4 (1977), 422.

72 Peter L. Nacci and Thomas R. Kane, 'Inmate Sexual Aggression: Some Evolving Propositions, Empirical Findings, and Mitigating Counter-Forces', *Journal of Offender Counseling, Services, and Rehabilitation*, 9 (1984), 3 and 8.

73 Christopher D. Man and John P. Cronan, 'Forecasting Sexual Abuse in Prison: The Prison Subculture of Masculinity as a Backdrop for "Deliberate Indifference"', *The Journal of Criminal Law and Criminology*, 92.1 (2001), 2001, 160.

74 Peter L. Nacci and Thomas R. Kane, 'Inmate Sexual Aggression: Some Evolving Propositions, Empirical Findings, and Mitigating Counter-Forces', *Journal of Offender Counseling, Services, and Rehabilitation*, 9 (1984), 7–8.

75 Referring to the Tennessee State Penitentiary: David A. Jones, *The Health Risks of Imprisonment* (Lexington, MA, 1976), 159.

76 Leo Carroll, 'Humanitarian Reform and Biracial Sexual Assault in a Maximum Security Prison', *Urban Life*, 5.4 (1977), 433.

77 Leo Carroll, 'Humanitarian Reform and Biracial Sexual Assault in a Maximum Security Prison', *Urban Life*, 5.4 (1977), 428–32.

78 Howard Levy and David Miller, *Going to Jail. The Political Prisoner* (New York, 1970), 147.

79 Alan J. Davis, 'Sexual Assaults in the Philadelphia Prison System and Sheriff's Vans', *Trans-Action*, December 1968, 15.

80 For a discussion, see Howard Levy and David Miller, *Going to Jail. The Political Prisoner* (New York, 1970), 137–8.

81 'Prisoners Against Rape: Trying to Unlock the Myths and Images', *The Washington Post*, 16 June 1975, B3.

82 Gordon James Knowles, 'Male Prison Rape: A Search for Causation and Prevention', *The Howard Journal*, 38.3 (1999), 271.

83 E. Sagarin, 'Prison Homosexuality and its Effects on Post-Prison Sexuality', *Psychiatry*, 39 (1976), 251.

84 E. Sagarin, 'Prison Homosexuality and its Effects on Post-Prison Sexuality', *Psychiatry*, 39 (1976), 254.
85 Howard Levy and David Miller, *Going to Jail. The Political Prisoner* (New York, 1970), 140.
86 E. Sagarin, 'Prison Homosexuality and its Effects on Post-Prison Sexuality', *Psychiatry*, 39 (1976), 253.
87 Tom Cahill, 'Cruel and Unusual Punishment: Rape in Prison', *Victimology: An International Journal*, 9.1 (1984), 8–10.
88 Alan J. Davis, 'Sexual Assaults in the Philadelphia Prison System and Sheriff's Vans', *Trans-Action*, December 1968, 15.
89 Sidney Blotzman, quoted in Clifford R. Shaw in collaboration with Maurice E. Moore, *The National History of a Delinquent Career* (New York, 1968), 189–90.
90 Human Rights Watch, *No Escape: Male Rape in US Prisons*, 2001, in http://www.hrw.org/reports/2001/prison/report8.html#_1_50.
91 Howard Levy and David Miller, *Going to Jail. The Political Prisoner* (New York: Grove Press, 1970), 139–40.
92 P. F. Goyer and H. C. Eddleman, 'Same-Sex Rape of Nonincarcerated Men', *American Journal of Psychiatry*, 141.4 (1984), 576–9.
93 M. Lew, *Victims No Longer: Men Recovering from Incest and Other Sexual Child Abuse* (New York, 1988).
94 Kenneth Adams, 'Adjusting to Prison Life', in Michael Ronry (ed.), *Crime and Justice. A Review of Research*, vol. 16 (Chicago, 1992), 287–8, and Clemens Bartollas, Stuart J. Miller and Simon Dinitz, *Juvenile Victimization. The Institutional Paradox* (New York, 1976), 165.
95 Quoted in John Money and Carol Bohmer, 'Prison Sexology: Two Personal Accounts of Masturbation, Homosexuality, and Rape', *The Journal of Sex Research*, 16.3 (August 1980), 263.
96 Alan J. Davis, 'Sexual Assaults in the Philadelphia Prison System and Sheriff's Vans', *Trans-Action*, December 1968, 10.
97 Kenneth Adams, 'Adjusting to Prison Life', in Michael Ronry (ed.), *Crime and Justice. A Review of Research*, vol. 16 (Chicago, 1992), 287.
98 Howard Levy and David Miller, *Going to Jail. The Political Prisoner* (New York, 1970), 148 and 151.
99 Lee H. Bowker, *Prison Victimization* (New York, 1980), 13.
100 Wayne S. Wooden and Jay Parker, *Men Behind Bars. Sexual Exploitation in Prison* (New York, 1982), 203.
101 Michael Graubart Levin, 'Fight, Flee, Submit, Sue: Alternatives for Sexually Assaulted Prisoners', *Journal of Legal and Social Problems*, 18 (1983–4), 511. For the difficulties, see People v Lovercamp, 43 Cal. App 3d at 825; 118 Cal. Rptr. all 111 and 115.
102 Donald J. Cotton and A. Nicholas Groth, 'Inmate Rape: Prevention and Intervention', *Journal of Prison and Jail Health*, 2 (1982), 49. Also see Wayne S. Wooden and Jay Parker, *Men Behind Bars. Sexual Exploitation in Prison* (New York, 1982), 108.
103 Lee H. Bowker, *Prison Victimization* (New York, 1980), 12.
104 Azmy I. Ibrahim, 'Deviant Behavior in Men's Prisons', *Crime and Delinquency*, 20.1 (January 1974), 38–44.
105 As in a New York decision in 1983: see Michael Graubart Levin, 'Fight, Flee, Submit, Sue: Alternatives for Sexually Assaulted Prisoners', *Journal of Legal and Social Problems*, 18 (1983–4), 508.
106 Farmer, 114 S. Ct. at 1977.

107 Discussed in Michael Graubart Levin, 'Fight, Flee, Submit, Sue: Alternatives for Sexually Assaulted Prisoners', *Journal of Legal and Social Problems*, 18 (1983–4), 505–6.
108 Human Rights Watch, Women's Rights Project, *All Too Familiar: Sexual Abuse of Women in US State Prisons* (New York, 1966), 28–9.
109 Farmer v. Brennan, 511 US 825, 828 (1994).
110 Christopher D. Man and John P. Cronan, 'Forecasting Sexual Abuse in Prison: The Prison Subculture of Masculinity as a Backdrop for "Deliberate Indifference"', *The Journal of Criminal Law and Criminology*, 92.1 (2001), 135.
111 Butler v. Dowd, 979 F.2d 661, 664 (8th Cir. 1992); Mathie v. Fries, 935 F.Supp.1284, 1306 (E. D. N. Y. 1996).
112 See http://www.spr.org.
113 'Prisoners Against Rape', no date, in Margaret Beadman's Papers, in the National Library of Australia, MS. 5876. Punctuation, capitalization and spelling as in original.
114 Helen M. Eigenberg, 'Correctional Officers' Definitions of Rape in Male Prisons', *Journal of Criminal Justice*, 28.5 (September–October 2000). Note that the use of condoms has become problematical. If the victim could persuade his attacker to use a condom (even if only a home-made one since condoms were usually contraband), the chance that an inmate could report a rape was reduced even further. In some jurisdictions, the use of a condom suggests that the sexual intercourse was consensual rather than forced, thus placing the victim in a double bind situation. For a discussion, see Adam Starchild, 'Rape of Youth in Prisons and Juvenile Facilities', *The Journal of Psychohistory*, 18.2 (Fall 1990), 146.
115 James E. Robertson, 'Compassionate Conservatism and Prison Rape: The Prison Rape Elimination Act of 2003', *New England Journal on Crime and Civil Confinement*, 30 (2004), 15.
116 Sam Joshi, '"Watcha Gonna Do When They Cum All Over You?" What Police Themes in Male Erotic Video Reveal about (Leather)sexual Subjectivity', *Sexualities*, 6.3 (2003), 331.
117 'Prisoners Against Rape', *The Washington Post*, 16 June, no year, in the papers of Margaret Beadman, Australian National Library.
118 For an exception, see Alisdare Hickson, *The Poisoned Bowl. Sex, Repression and the Public School System* (London, 1995), 109 and 127–9.

CHAPTER THIRTEEN: THE MILITARY

1 Yuki Tanaka, 'Rape and War: The Japanese Experience', in Asian Center for Women's Human Rights (ed.), *Common Grounds, Violence Against Women in War and Armed Conflict Situations* (Quezon City, 1998), 174.
2 Bernard Carroll, in *The Age*, 25 September 1993, 3.
3 Cited in Susanne Davies, 'Women, War, and the Violence of History', in *Violence Against Women. An International and Interdisciplinary Journal*, 2.4 (December 1996), 361, and Yuki Tanaka, 'Rape and War: The Japanese Experience', in Asian Center for Women's Human Rights (ed.), *Common Grounds, Violence Against Women in War and Armed Conflict Situations* (Quezon City, 1998), 174. See 'Diggers Raped Japanese Women: Academic', *The Age*, 23 September 1993, 1.
4 Allan S. Clifton, *Time of Fallen Blossoms* (London, 1950), 141–4.
5 Cited in Susanne Davies, 'Women, War, and the Violence of History', in *Violence Against Women. An International and Interdisciplinary Journal*, 2.4 (December 1996), 361, and Yuki Tanaka, 'Rape and War: The Japanese Experience', in Asian Center for Women's Human Rights (ed.), *Common Grounds, Violence Against Women in War*

and Armed Conflict Situations (Quezon City, 1998), 174. Susanne Davies, 'Women, War, and the Violence of History', in *Violence Against Women. An International and Interdisciplinary Journal*, 2.4 (December 1996), footnotes the source as 'Diggers Raped Japanese Women: Academic', *The Age*, 23 September 1993, 1.

6 'Diggers Raped Japanese Women', *The Age*, 23 September 1993, 1, cited in Susanne Davies, 'Women, War, and the Violence of History', in *Violence Against Women. An International and Interdisciplinary Journal*, 2.4 (December 1996), 361.

7 Don Grubin, 'Sexual Offending: A Cross-Cultural Comparison', *Annual Review of Sex Research*, iii (1992), 208–9.

8 Mary Daly, *Gyn/Ecology: the Metaethics of Radical Feminism* (Boston, 1978), 38 and 357.

9 John Horne and Alan Kramer, *German Atrocities, 1914. A History of Denial* (New Haven, 2001).

10 In common parlance, 'our side' continues to exclude the Soviet Union, despite the fact that they were also part of 'the Allies'.

11 Madeline Morris, 'By Force of Arms: Rape, War, and Military Culture', *Duke Law Journal*, 45.4 (February 1996), 665–6.

12 The official history of the Office of the Judge Advocate General for the ETO, unpub. manuscript, cited in Madeline Morris, 'By Force of Arms: Rape, War, and Military Culture', *Duke Law Journal*, 45.4 (February 1996), 666–7.

13 Cited in John Costello, *Love, Sex and War. Changing Values 1939–45* (London, 1985), 142.

14 Perry Biddiscombe, 'Dangerous Liaisons: The Anti-Fraternization Movement in the US Occupation Zones of Germany and Austria, 1945–1948', *Journal of Social History*, 34.3 (2001), 633.

15 Cited in John Costello, *Love, Sex and War. Changing Values 1939–45* (London, 1985), 144.

16 Danise Aydelott, 'Mass Rape During War: Prosecuting Bosnian Rapists Under International Law', *Emory International Law Review*, 7 (1993), 591.

17 Madeline Morris, 'By Force of Arms: Rape, War, and Military Culture', *Duke Law Journal*, 45.4 (February 1996), 653.

18 Eugene B. (Sledgehammer) Sledge, interviewed in Studs Terkel, *'The Good War'. An Oral History of World War Two* (London, 1985), 63.

19 Specialist 5, Harold 'Light Bulb' Bryant, interviewed in Wallace Terry, *Bloods. An Oral History of the Vietnam War* (New York, 1984), 26.

20 Unnamed panellist from the 1st Air Cavalry Division, in *Winter Soldier Investigation. Testimony Given in Detroit, Michigan, on January 31, 1971, February 2, 1971*, in http://lists.villagr.virginia.edu/sixties/HTML_doc/Resources/Primary/Winter_Soldier/WS_entry.html, no page given. Also see the evidence from Steve Noetzel of the 5th Special Forces Group and Jon Drolshagen, a POW interrogator.

21 Steve Noetzel of the 5th Special Forces Group and a member of the psychological warfare civic action team, 'Vietnam Veterans Against the War', *The Winter Soldier Investigation. An Inquiry into American War Crimes* (Boston, 1972), 103–5.

22 Unnamed army officer, interviewed in December 1969, cited in Edward M. Opton, 'It Never Happened and Besides They Deserved It', in Nevitt Sanford and Craig Camstock (eds.), *Sanctions for Evil* (San Francisco, 1971), 65. My emphasis.

23 'Report of Committee of Inquiry Regarding Sexual Offences', *Queensland Parliamentary Papers 1944–1945*, 942–3, cited by Rosemary Campbell, *Heroes and Lovers. A Question of National Identity* (Sydney, 1989), 96.

24 See 'Combating Crime', *The Times*, 23 July 1946, 5, and 'A Problem Picture', *The Times*, 3 June 1948, 5.

25 John Costello, *Love, Sex and War. Changing Values 1939–45* (London, 1985), 9.

26 Nesta H. Wells, 'Sexual Offences as Seen by a Woman Police Surgeon', *British Medical Journal*, 6 December 1958, 1405–7.
27 For instance, see Mrs V. Shoulder, 'Childhood Days in Wartime Years', in Imperial War Museum (henceforth IWM) archives 96/26/1, 6.
28 See the Letter to the editor by 'Atkin', 'Americans and the Law', *The Times*, 3 August 1942, 5.
29 Madeline Morris, 'By Force of Arms: Rape, War, and Military Culture', *Duke Law Journal*, 45.4 (February 1996), 655–6.
30 Anne G. Sadler, Brenda M. Booth, Deanna Nielson and Bradley N. Doebbeling, 'Health-Related Consequences of Physical and Sexual Violence: Women in the Military', *Obstetrics and Gynecology*, 96.3 (September 2000), 473–4.
31 'Sex Abuse at US Air Force Academy', *Guardian*, 30 August 2003.
32 Steve Spund interviewed in Willa Seidenberg and William Short, *A Matter of Conscience. GI Resistance During the Vietnam War* (Andover, MA, 1991), 14.
33 P. F. Goyer and H. C. Eddleman, 'Same-Sex Rape of Nonincarcerated Men', *American Journal of Psychiatry*, 141.4 (1984), 576–9.
34 Unnamed colonel, quoted by Rev. T. W. Pym and Rev. Geoffrey Gordon, *Papers from Picardy by Two Chaplains* (London, 1917), 29–30.
35 Rev. T. W. Pym and Rev. Geoffrey Gordon, *Papers from Picardy by Two Chaplains* (London, 1917), 26 and 30.
36 Lesley A. Hall, '"Somehow Very Distasteful": Doctors, Men and Sexual Problems between the Wars', *Journal of Contemporary History*, 20.4 (October 1985), 570.
37 General George S. Patton, Jr., *War As I Knew It*, cited in Susan Brownmiller, *Against Our Will: Men, Women and Rape* (New York, 1975), 31.
38 J. Glenn Gray, *The Warriors* (New York, 1959), 66.
39 D. A. Bloch, 'Sex Crimes and Criminals', *American Journal of Nursing*, 53 (1953), 440–3, cited in Rochelle Semel Albin, 'Psychological Studies of Rape', *Signs: Journal of Women in Culture and Society*, 3.2 (Winter 1977), 425.
40 Michael McCusker of the 1st Marine Division, in 'Vietnam Veterans Against the War', *The Winter Soldier Investigation. An Inquiry into American War Crimes* (Boston, 1972), 29.
41 Mikhail Bakhtin, *Rabelais and His World*, trans. H. Iswolsky (Bloomington, 1985).
42 Sgt. Scott Camil of the 1st Marine Division, in 'Vietnam Veterans Against the War', *The Winter Soldier Investigation. An Inquiry into American War Crimes* (Boston, 1972), 13–14.
43 Ed Treratola, interviewed in Mark Lane, *Conversations with Americans* (New York, 1970), 96.
44 Philip Caputo, *A Rumor of War* (London, 1977), 15.
45 G. F. Gilder, *Sexual Suicide* (New York, 1973), 258–9.
46 For example, see the testimonies of Chuck Onan and Jimmy Roberson, interviewed in Mark Lane, *Conversations with Americans* (New York, 1970), 28 and 60, and Daniel Lang, *Casualties of War* (New York, 1969), 25–6.
47 Chuck Onan, interviewed in Mark Lane, *Conversations with Americans* (New York, 1970), 30.
48 Unnamed panellist, in *Winter Soldier Investigation. Testimony Given in Detroit, Michigan, on January 31, 1971, February 2, 1971*, in http://lists.villagr.virginia.edu/sixties/HTML_doc/Resources/Primary/Winter_Soldier/WS_entry.html, no page given.
49 Sgt. Scott Camil of the 1st Marine Division, in 'Vietnam Veterans Against the War', *The Winter Soldier Investigation. An Inquiry into American War Crimes* (Boston, 1972), 13.

50 Don Dzagulanes, with the Americal Division in Southern I Corps, 'Vietnam Veterans Against the War', *The Winter Soldier Investigation. An Inquiry into American War Crimes* (Boston, 1972), 119–20.
51 Sergeant Michael McCuster, in 'Vietnam Veterans Against the War', *The Winter Soldier Investigation. An Inquiry into American War Crimes* (Boston, 1972), 29. Also see the interview with Jerry Samuels, in Philip Scribner Balboni, 'Mylai was Not an Isolated Incident. What Every Vietnam Veteran Knows', *The New Republic*, 19 December 1970, 15.
52 For their experiences, see Howard Levy and David Miller, *Going to Jail. The Political Prisoner* (New York, 1970).
53 W. A. Blackman, 'Army Experience', IWM 99/85/1, 11.
54 Madeline Morris, 'By Force of Arms: Rape, War, and Military Culture', *Duke Law Journal*, 45.4 (February 1996), 681.
55 Charles Cain, 'The Footsloggers', in IWM PP/MCR/48, from the First World War.
56 Ed Murphy, E-4 Rifleman in the 198th Infantry Brigade, Americal Division, in 'Vietnam Veterans Against the War', *The Winter Soldier Investigation. An Inquiry into American War Crimes* (Boston, 1972), 47–8.
57 Unnamed soldier interviewed by Mark Baker, *Nam. The Vietnam War in the Words of the Men and Women Who Fought There* (London, 1981), 133.
58 Ronald Haeberle, quoted in Michael Bilton and Kevin Sims, *Four Hours in My Lai. A War Crime and its Aftermath* (London, 1992), 183.
59 Michael Bernhardt, quoted in a letter by Ron Ridenhour, in Joseph Goldstein, Burke Marshall and Jack Schwartz (eds.), *The Peers Commission Report* (New York, 1976), 37.
60 Greg Olsen, in Michael Bilton and Kevin Sims, *Four Hours in My Lai. A War Crime and its Aftermath* (London, 1992), 82.
61 'Contempt of Court', *The Times*, 21 June 1977, 15. *The Times* reporter was protesting against the decision.
62 Unnamed US infantryman interviewed by Laura L. Miller, 'Not Just Weapons of the Weak: Gender Harassment as a Form of Protest for Army Men', *Social Psychology Quarterly*, 60.1 (March 1997), 39.
63 Laura L. Miller, 'Not Just Weapons of the Weak: Gender Harassment as a Form of Protest for Army Men', *Social Psychology Quarterly*, 60.1 (March 1997), 39.
64 Margaret Beadman, 'Papers', paper entitled 'The Military and Rape', mid-1970s, 1–2, National Library of Australia MS 5876.
65 Elizabeth Lutes Hillman, 'The "Good Soldier" Defence: Character Evidence and Military Rank at Courts-Martial', *The Yale Law Journal*, 108.4 (January 1999), 879–911.
66 Specialist 4 Arthur E. 'Gene' Woodley, Jr., cited in Wallace Terry, *Bloods. An Oral History of the Vietnam War* (New York, 1984), 262.
67 Roland Littlewood, 'Military Rape', in *Anthropology Today*, 13.2 (April 1997), 12–13.
68 William Manchester, *Goodbye Darkness. A Memoir of the Pacific War* (Boston, 1980), 71–3.
69 Lieutenant Colonel W. B. Murgatroyd, 'War Crimes in Italy 1944–1945', in IWM 83/36/1.
70 Cited in Perry Biddiscombe, 'Dangerous Liaisons: The Anti-Fraternization Movement in the US Occupation Zones of Germany and Australia, 1945–1948', *Journal of Social History*, 34.3 (2001), 614.
71 J. H. Witte, 'The One that Didn't Get Away', 214, in IWM 87/12/1.

72 Allan S. Clifton, *Time of Fallen Blossoms* (London, 1950), 141–4.
73 Victoria Bynum, *Unruly Women. The Politics of Social and Sexual Control in the Old South* (Chapel Hill, 1992), 118.
74 George Ryley Scott, *Sex Problems and Dangers in War-Time. A Book of Practical Advice for Men and Women on the Fighting and Home Fronts* (London, 1940), 76–7.
75 Unnamed soldier interviewed in Mark Baker, *Nam. The Vietnam War in the Words of the Men and Women Who Fought There* (New York, 1981), 149–50.
76 Unnamed panellist, in *Winter Soldier Investigation. Testimony Given in Detroit, Michigan, on January 31, 1971, February 2, 1971*, in http://lists.villagr.virginia.edu/sixties/HTML_doc/Resources/Primary/Winter_Soldier/WS_entry.html, no page given.
77 Oliver Stone's *Platoon* (1986).
78 Specialist 4 Arthur E. 'Gene' Woodley, Jr., cited in Wallace Terry, *Bloods. An Oral History of the Vietnam War* (New York, 1984), 256.
79 Daniel Lang, *Casualties of War* (New York, 1969), 35. Also see George Ryan, in Murray Polner, *No Victory Parades. The Return of the Vietnam Veteran* (New York, 1971), 40.
80 John Horne and Alan Kramer, *German Atrocities, 1914. A History of Denial* (New Haven, 2001), 199.
81 Menachem Amir, 'Forcible Rape', *Federal Probation*, xxxi.1 (March 1967), 55.
82 Arthur N. Foxe, *Crime and Sexual Development. Movement and Fixation of the Libido in Criminotic Individuals* (New York, 1936), 61.
83 G. D. Woods, 'Some Aspects of Pack Rape in Sydney', *Australian and New Zealand Journal of Criminology*, 2.2 (June 1969), 113–14.
84 Bruno Bettelheim, 'Violence: A Neglected Mode of Behavior', in Shalom Endleman (ed.), *Violence in the Streets* (Chicago, 1968), 41–2.
85 Unnamed soldier interviewed by Mark Baker, *Nam. The Vietnam War in the Words of the Men and Women Who Fought There* (New York, 1981), 134.
86 Sgt. Scott Camil of the 1st Marine Division, in 'Vietnam Veterans Against the War', *The Winter Soldier Investigation. An Inquiry into American War Crimes* (Boston, 1972), 14.
87 Mark Baker, *Nam. The Vietnam War in the Words of the Men and Women Who Fought There* (New York, 1981), 206.
88 See Devon L. L. Polaschek and Tony Ward, 'The Implicit Theories of Potential Rapists. What Our Questionnaires Tell Us', *Aggression and Violent Behavior*, 7 (2002), 393ff.
89 See my *Face-to-Face Killing in Twentieth Century Warfare: Intimate History of Killing* (London, 1999)
90 William Crandell, 'What Did America Learn from the Winter Soldier Investigation?', *Viet Nam Generation*, 5 (March 1994), 3.
91 I suggest a number of reasons why this might be the case in my 'Remembering War', *Journal of Contemporary History*, 39.4 (2004), 473–85.
92 Richard Slotkin, 'Unit Pride: Ethnic Platoons and the Myths of American Nationality', *American Literary History* (2001), 491.
93 George Swiers, '"Demented Vets" and Other Myths. The Moral Obligation of Veterans', in Harrison E. Salisbury (ed.), *Vietnam Reconsidered. Lessons from a War* (New York, 1985), 198.
94 Frank J. Wetta and Martin A. Novelli, '"Now a Major Motion Picture": War Films and Hollywood's New Patriotism', *The Journal of Military History*, 67 (July 2003), 861.
95 George MacDonald Fraser, *Quartered Safe Out Here. A Recollection of the War in Burma* (London, 1992).

96 Martin Bauermeister, 'Women Victims and Their Assailants', *International Journal of Offender Therapy and Comparative Criminology*, 21.3 (1977), 245.
97 Gavin Hart, 'Sexual Behavior in a War Environment', *The Journal of Sex Research*, 11.3 (August 1975), 223.
98 Randy Thornhill and Craig T. Palmer, *A Natural History of Rape: Biological Bases of Sexual Coercion* (Cambridge, MA, 2000). Most unfortunately, these ideas have been embraced by Niall Ferguson in *The War of the World. History's Age of Hatred* (London, 2006).
99 Phillip S. Meilinger, 'Demonic Males: Apes and the Origins of Human Violence; War Before Civilization: The Myth of the Peaceful Savage; A History of Warfare', *The Journal of Military History*, 61.3 (July 1997), 599–600. Emphasis in original. This is a review essay of, among other works, Richard Wrangham and Dale Peterson's *Demonic Males: Apes and the Origins of Human Violence* (Boston, 1996).
100 Robert L. O'Connell, *Of Arms and Men: A History of War, Weapons and Aggression* (New York, 1989), 37.
101 Lieutenant Colonel Dave Grossman, *On Killing. The Psychological Cost of Learning to Kill in War and Society* (Boston, 1995), 137.
102 Quoted in John Horne and Alan Kramer, *German Atrocities, 1914. A History of Denial* (New Haven, 2001), 200.
103 Nicola Henry, Tony Ward and Matt Hirshberg, 'A Multifactorial Model of Wartime Rape', *Aggression and Violent Behavior*, 9.5 (August 2004), 535–62.
104 Unnamed panellist, in *Winter Soldier Investigation. Testimony Given in Detroit, Michigan, on January 31, 1971, February 2, 1971*, in http://lists.villagr.virginia.edu/sixties/HTML_doc/Resources/Primary/Winter_Soldier/WS_entry.html, no page given.
105 Richard B. Bidler and Adrien Katherine Wing, '[Review of] Mass Rape. The War Against Women in Bosnia-Herzegovina', *The American Journal of International Law*, 88.4 (October 1994), 850.
106 Alice Vachss, *Sex Crimes* (New York, 1993), 205.
107 Maria Tatar, *Lustmord. Sexual Murder in Weimar Germany* (Princeton, 1985), 182.
108 Judith G. Gardam and Michelle J. Jarvis, *Women, Armed Conflict and International Law* (The Hague, 2001), 12.
109 Debra Bergoffen, 'February 22, 2001: Toward a Politics of the Vulnerable Body', *Hypatia*, 18.1 (Winter 2003), 117.
110 For an excellent discussion, see Kirsten Campbell, 'Legal Memories: Sexual Assault Memory and International Humanitarian Law', *Signs: Journal of Women in Culture and Society*, 28.1 (Autumn 2002), 149–78.
111 G. Stuart Watts, 'Sex Problems of Soldiers on Service', *Marriage Hygiene*, 1.3 (February 1948), 170–1.
112 For a statement of this in the context of the war in the former Yugoslavia, see Gillian Mezey, 'Rape in War', *Journal of Forensic Psychiatry*, 5.3 (1994), 583–4.
113 Sigmund Freud, 'Why War', in Edwin I. Megargee and Jack E. Hokanson (eds.), *The Dynamics of Aggression. Individual, Group and International Analyses* (New York, 1970), 17, exchange in September 1932.
114 After completing the proofs for this book J. Robert Lilly's *Taken by Force. Rape and American GIs in Europe during World War II* (London, 2007) was published. I highly recommend it.

CHAPTER FOURTEEN: GETTING AWAY WITH RAPE

1 Cecil Day Lewis, 'Sex-Crime', *Selected Poems* (Harmondsworth, 1951), 38–40.
2 Liz Kelly, Jo Lovett and Linda Regan, *A Gap or a Chasm? Attrition in Reported Rape Cases: A Home Office Research Study* (London, 2005), 25 and 94–5. The statistics have been rounded up.

3 Liz Kelly, Jo Lovett and Linda Regan, *A Gap or a Chasm? Attrition in Reported Rape Cases: A Home Office Research Study* (London, 2005), 29
4 Jessica Harris and Sharon Grace, *A Question of Evidence? Investigating and Prosecuting Rape in the 1990s* (London, 1999), iii.
5 HM Crown Prosecution Service Inspectorate, *A Report on the Joint Inspection into the Investigation and Prosecution of Cases Involving Allegations of Rape* (London, 2002), 97–8. Also see Liz Kelly, Jo Lovett and Linda Regan, *A Gap or a Chasm? Attrition in Reported Rape Cases: A Home Office Research Study* (London, 2005), xi.
6 There is a vast literature, but see Gary D. LaFree, 'The Effect of Social Stratification by Race on Official Reactions to Rape', *American Sociological Review*, 45.5 (October 1980), 844 and 847–52 and Kenneth Polk, 'Rape Reform and Criminal Justice Processing', *Crime and Delinquency*, 31.2 (1985), 203.
7 This was the wording used in California, but other jurisdictions were very similar. In California, it was first introduced in 1856 (People v. Benson) to deal with rape cases in which the prosecutrix was a minor, her testimony uncorroborated, and the court viewed that evidence as improbable, but was extended over time to apply to a much wider range of sexual crimes, whether collaborated or not, probable or improbable, and the person making an accusation an adult. For a discussion, see 'Casenotes', *Fordham Urban Law Journal*, 4 (1975–76), 419–30 and Armand Arabian, 'The Cautionary Instruction in Sex Cases: A Lingering Insult', *Southwestern University Law Review*, 10 (1978), 585–616.
8 C. J. Oros and D. Elman, 'Impact of Judge's Instruction Upon Jurors' Decision: the "Cautionary Charge" in Rape Trials', *Representative Research in Social Psychology*, 10 (1979), 28–34 and Arthur W. Lyons and Joanne Regina, 'Mock Jurors' Behavior as a Function of Sex and Exposure to an Educational Videotape About Jury Duty', *Psychological Reports* (1986), 599.
9 Martin J. Wiener, *Men of Blood. Violence, Manliness, and Criminal Justice in Victorian England* (Cambridge, 2004), 84.
10 Martin J. Wiener, *Men of Blood. Violence, Manliness, and Criminal Justice in Victorian England* (Cambridge, 2004), 84.
11 J. Clifton Edgar and Jas. C. Johnson, 'Medico-Legal Consideration of Rape', in R. A. Witthaus and Tracy C. Becker (eds.), *Medical Jurisprudence, Forensic Medicine, and Toxicology*, vol. 2 (New York, 1894), 417; Cyril John Polson, *The Essentials of Forensic Medicine* (London, 1955), 360; W. Bathurst Woodman and Charles Meymott Tidy, *A Handy-Book of Forensic Medicine and Toxicology* (London, 1877), 728.
12 J. Sanderson Christison, *Crime and Criminals* (Chicago, 1897), 47.
13 William J. Robinson, *America's Sex and Marriage Problems. Based on Thirty Years Practice and Study* (New York, 1928), 307–8
14 Julie Taylor, 'Rape and Women's Credibility: Problems of Recantations and False Accusations Echoed in the Case of Cathleen Crowell Webb and Gary Dotson', *Harvard Women's Law Review*, 10 (1987), 90; Thomas W. McCahill, Linda C. Meyer and Arthur M. Fischman, *The Aftermath of Rape* (Lexington, MA, 1979), 98; Diana E. Russell, *Politics of Rape: The Victim's Perspective* (New York, 1974), 89; Law Reform Commission, *Rape Prosecutions (Court Procedures and Rules of Evidence)* working paper no. 4 (Melbourne, 1976), 17; Shirley Feldman-Summers and Gayle C. Palmer, 'Rape as Viewed by Judges, Prosecutors, and Police Officers', *Crime, Justice and Behavior*, 19 (1980), 36.
15 A. Thomas Morris, 'The Empirical, Historical, and Legal Case Against the Cautionary Instruction: A Call for Legislative Reform', *Duke Law Journal*, 1988.1 (February 1988), 164.
16 A. Thomas Morris, 'The Empirical, Historical, and Legal Case Against the

Cautionary Instruction: A Call for Legislative Reform', *Duke Law Journal*, 1988.1 (February 1988), 164–66 provides a measured analysis of the evidence.

17 US Department of Justice, *Uniform Crime Reports* (Washington, DC, 1997).

18 Liz Kelly, Jo Lovett, and Linda Regan, *A Gap or a Chasm? Attrition in Reported Rape Cases: A Home Office Research Study* (London, 2005), xi and 46–7

19 Elaine Hilberman, *The Rape Victim: A Project of the Committee on Women of the American Psychiatric Association* (New York, 1976), 9; Neil M. Malamuth and James V. P. Check, 'An Empirical Assessment of Some Feminist Hypotheses about Rape', *International Journal of Women's Studies*, 8 (1985), 414–23.

20 K. Painter, *Wife Rape, Marriage and Law: Survey Report, Key-Findings and Recommendation* (Manchester, 1991).

21 Cited in HM Crown Prosecution Service Inspectorate, *A Report on the Joint Inspection into the Investigation and Prosecution of Cases Involving Allegations of Rape* (London, 2002), 1.

22 Thomas W. McCahill, Linda C. Meyer and Arthur M. Fischman, *The Aftermath of Rape* (Lexington, MA, 1979), 224–25.

23 The Victim in a Forcible Rape Case: A Feminist View', *American Criminal Law Review*, 11 (1973), 344.

24 Jessica Harris and Sharon Grace, *A Question of Evidence? Investigating and Prosecuting Rape in the 1990s* (London, 1999), 43.

25 The belief that prostitutes were likely to be lying was not universal: see Jessica Harris and Sharon Grace, *A Question of Evidence? Investigating and Prosecuting Rape in the 1990s* (London, 1999), 39–40.

26 Julie Taylor, 'Rape and Women's Credibility: Problems of Recantations and False Accusations Echoed in the Case of Cathleen Crowell Webb and Gary Dotson', *Harvard Women's Law Review*, 10 (1987), 92–3. Also see Hubert S. Feild and Leigh B. Bienen, *Jurors and Rape: A Study in Psychology and Law* (Lexington, MA, 1980), 47 and 119 and Ronald Mazzella and Alan Feingold, 'The Effects of Physical Attractiveness, Race, Socioeconomic Status, and Gender of Defendants and Victims on Judgments of Mock Jurors: A Meta-Analysis', *Journal of Applied Psychology*, 24.15 (August 1994), 1315.

27 HM Crown Prosecution Service Inspectorate, *A Report on the Joint Inspection into the Investigation and Prosecution of Cases Involving Allegations of Rape* (London, 2002), 19.

28 Jessica Harris and Sharon Grace, *A Question of Evidence? Investigating and Prosecuting Rape in the 1990s* (London, 1999), 43.

29 Jeanne Gregory and Sue Lees, 'Attrition in Rape and Sexual Assault Cases', *The British Journal of Criminology*, 36.1 (Winter 1996), 3–4.

30 Eric R. Galton, 'Police Processing of Rape Complaints: A Case Study', *American Journal of Criminal Law*, 4 (1975–76), 15–30.

31 'Police Discretion and the Judgment that a Crime Has Been Committed', *University of Pennsylvania Law Review*, 117.2 (December 1968), 277 and 302–4.

32 HM Crown Prosecution Service Inspectorate, *A Report on the Joint Inspection into the Investigation and Prosecution of Cases Involving Allegations of Rape* (London, 2002), 7–11.

33 Liz Kelly, Jo Lovett, and Linda Regan, *A Gap or a Chasm? Attrition in Reported Rape Cases: A Home Office Research Study* (London, 2005), 84 and 89.

34 Jennifer Temkin, 'Prosecuting and Defending Rape: Perspectives from the Bar', *Journal of Law and Society*, 27.2 (June 2000), 226.

35 Alice Vachss, *Sex Crimes* (New York, 1993), 281.

36 Unnamed newspaper, quoted by Clifford R. Shaw in collaboration with Maurice E. Moore, *The Natural History of a Delinquent Career* (Chicago, 1931), 5.

37 For the best discussion, see Carolyn Strange, 'The Undercurrents of Penal Culture: Punishment of the Body in Mid-Twentieth Century Canada', *Law and History Review*, 19.2 (2001), 343–85.

38 Whitney S. Wiedeman, 'Don't Spare the Rod: A Proposed Return to Public Corporal Punishment of Criminals', *American Journal of Criminal Law*, 23 (1995–96), 660–62.

39 National Conference of State Legislatures, '"Three Strikes' Legislation Update", Denver: National Conference of State Legislatures', December 1996, quoted in Roxanne Lieb, Vernon Quinsey, and Lucy Berliner, 'Sexual Predators and Social Policy', *Crime and Justice*, 23 (1998), 70.

40 Roxanne Lieb, Vernon Quinsey, and Lucy Berliner, 'Sexual Predators and Social Policy', *Crime and Justice*, 23 (1998), 70.

41 US Department of Justice, *Three Strikes and You're Out: A Review of State Legislation* (Washington, DC, 1997).

42 Diane Patrick, Diane Pasini-Hill, Linda Jones, Sydney Cooley-Towell, and Kim English, *How is the Post-Conviction Polygraph Examination Used in Adult Sex Offender Management Activities?* (Denver, 2000), 22; Stan Abrams, 'The Use of the Polygraph with Sex Offenders', *Annals of Sex Research*, 4.3 (1991), 241, 251–61; Kim English, Suzanne Pullen, and Linda Jones, *How are Adult Felony Sex Offenders Managed on Probation and Parole? A National Survey*, (Denver, 1996); Barbara K. Schwartz, 'Overview of Rehabilitative Efforts in Understanding and Managing Sexually Coercive Behaviors', *Annals of the New York Academy of Sciences*, 989 (2003), 373–74.

43 UK Crime and Disorder Act 1998, in http://www.opsi.gov.uk/acts/acts1998/19980037.htm.

44 This is according to Elizabeth A. Pearson, 'Status and Latest Developments in Sex Offender Registration and Notification Laws', US Bureau of Justice (ed.), *National Conference on Sex Offenders Registries* (Washington, DC, 1998), 45.

45 Simon A. Cole, 'From the Sexual Psychopath Statute to "Megan's Law": Psychiatric Knowledge in the Diagnosis, Treatment, and Adjudication of Sex Criminals in New Jersey, 1949–1999', *Journal of the History of Medicine*, 55 (2000), 306. The exception was Massachusetts.

46 Dretha M. Phillips and Rochelle Troyano, *Community Notification as Viewed by Washington's Citizens* (Olympia, 1998) and Jane O. Hansen, 'Sexual Predators: Why Megan's Law is Not Enough', *Atlanta Journal-Constitution*, 10 June 1997, D11, quoted in Roxanne Lieb, Vernon Quinsey, and Lucy Berliner, 'Sexual Predators and Social Policy', *Crime and Justice*, 23 (1998), 73.

47 For a defence, see Deborah Coddington, *The Australian Paedophile and Sex Offender Index* (Sydney, 1997), 6–7 and *The [New Zealand] Paedophile and Sex Offender Index* (Auckland, 1996).

48 Pierre Bourdieu, *In Other Words: Essays Towards a Reflexive Sociology* (Cambridge, 1990), 84–5.

49 For early commentary, see Hon. Simeon E. Baldwin, 'Corporal Punishments for Crime', *The Medico-Legal Journal*, xvii.1 (1899), 64; Harry Elmer Barnes, 'Shall We Get Tough or Be Sensible in Facing the Increase of Crime?', *Federal Probation*, 23 (1959), 30; 'E. C. B. Jr.', 'Pedophilia, Exhibitionism, and Voyeurism: Legal Problems in the Deviant Society', *Georgia Law Review*, 4 (1969), 157; Barry Schwartz, 'The Effect in Philadelphia of Pennsylvania's Increased Penalties for Rape and Attempted Rape', *Journal of Criminal Law, Criminology, and Police Science*, 59 (1968), 509–15.

50 Harry Mills, interviewed in Tony Parker, *The Twisting Lane. Some Sex Offenders* (London, 1969), 165.

51 Wayne A. Logan, 'Liberty Interests in the Preventive State: Procedural Due Process and Sex Offender Community Notification Laws', *The Journal of Criminal Law and Criminology*, 89.4 (1999), 1225–226.
52 Monique Deveaux, 'Feminism and Empowerment: A Critical Reading of Foucault', *Feminist Studies*, 20.2 (Summer 1994), 236.
53 Michel Foucault, 'Confinement, Psychiatry, Prison', in L. D. Kritzman (ed.), *Politics, Philosophy, Culture: Interviews and Other Writings, 1977–1984*, trans. Alan Sheridan (New York, 1988), 200–202.
54 'Drop Rape as a Charge – Chipp', in *The Australian*, 23 November 1974, 7, in the papers of Mrs Margaret Beadman, Australian National Library.
55 'Sexual Abuse Poll', ICM and Amnesty International poll, February 2003, online at http://www.icmresearch.co.uk/reviews/2005/Amnesty%20International%20-20SexualAssault.htm, pp. 5 and 7, accessed 15 May 2006.
56 Michel Foucault, *The History of Sexuality. Volume 1: An Introduction*, trans. Robert Hurley (London, 1978), 17–35.
57 Ann J. Cahill, 'Foucault, Rape, and the Construction of the Feminine Body', *Hypatia*, 15.1 (Winter 2000), 43–63.
58 Lee Ellis, *Theories of Rape. Inquiries into the Causes of Sexual Aggression* (New York, 1989), 23.
59 A. Nicholas Groth, Ann Wolbert Burgess, and Lynda Lytle Holmstrom, 'Rape: Power, Anger, and Sexuality', *American Journal of Psychiatry*, 134 (1977), 1239 and Gene G. Abel, David H. Barlow, Edward Blanchard, and Donald Guild, 'The Components of Rapists' Sexual Arousal', *Archives of General Psychiatry*, 34 (August 1977), 895–903.
60 Diana Scully and Joseph Marolla, 'Convicted Rapists' Vocabulary of Motive: Excuses and Justifications', *Social Problems*, 31.5 (June 1984), 530–44; Lee Ellis, *Theories of Rape. Inquiries into the Causes of Sexual Aggression* (New York, 1989), 22.
61 As Susan Brownmiller does in *Against Our Will: Men, Women, and Rape* (New York, 1975).
62 Nicola Lacey, *Unspeakable Subjects. Feminist Essays in Legal and Social Theory* (Oxford, 1998).

CHAPTER FIFTEEN: VIOLENCE, POLITICS, EROTICS

1 Cecil Day Lewis, 'Sex-Crime', *Selected Poems* (Harmondsworth, 1951), 40.
2 Catharine A. MacKinnon, 'Sexuality, Pornography, and Method: "Pleasure Under Patriarchy"', *Ethics*, 99.2 (January 1989), 326–7 and 335.
3 Edwin M. Schur, *The Americanization of Sex* (Philadelphia, 1988), 178.
4 Sharon Deevey, 'Such a Nice Girl', in Nancy Myron and Charlotte Bunch (eds.), *Lesbianism and the Women's Movement* (Baltimore, 1975), 24.
5 Jane Caputi, *The Age of Sex Crime* (London, 1987), 62 and 120.
6 Lawrence Kramer, *After the Lovedeath: Sexual Violence and the Making of Culture* (Berkeley, CA, 1997), 1–2.
7 Susan Brownmiller, *Against Our Will: Men, Women, and Rape* (New York, 1975), 14–15.
8 Catharine A. MacKinnon, 'Sexuality, Pornography, and Method: "Pleasure Under Patriarchy"', *Ethics*, 99.2 (January 1989), 336.
9 David Abrahamsen, *The Psychology of Crime* (New York, 1960), 159–60.
10 Sonja Steptoe, 'A Damnable Defense', *Sports Illustrated*, 24 February 1992, 92, in Darci E. Burrell, 'Myth, Stereotype, and the Rape of Black Women', *UCLA Women's Law Journal*, 4 (1993), 89–91.

11 Diane Wolfthal, *Images of Rape: The 'Heroic' Tradition and its Alternatives* (Cambridge, 1999).

12 Warden Harris, quoted in Les Sussman and Sally Bordwell, *The Rapists File* (New York, 1981), 27. Also see George Clark, 'Horror at Candlelight Lodge', *True Detective*, 1.2 (1950), 7.

13 Christopher D. Man and John P. Cronan, 'Forecasting Sexual Abuse in Prison: The Prison Subculture of Masculinity as a Backdrop for "Deliberate Indifference"', *The Journal of Criminal Law and Criminology*, 92.1 (2001), 174. Also see the interview by imprisoned sex offender, Wilfred Johnson (not his real name), in Tony Parker, *The Twisting Lane. Some Sex Offenders* (London, 1969), 41–2.

14 Kurt Weis and Sandra S. Borges, 'Victimology and Rape: The Case of the Legitimate Victim', *Issues in Criminology*, 8.2 (Fall 1973), 86–7.

15 J. Sanderson Christison, *Crime and Criminals* (Chicago, 1897), 46.

16 Unnamed rapist quoted in Diana Scully and Joseph Marolla, 'Convicted Rapists' Vocabulary of Motive: Excuses and Justifications', *Social Problems*, 31.5 (June 1984), 541.

17 Nicholas A. Groth and Ann Wolbert Burgess, 'Sexual Dysfunction During Rape', *The New England Journal of Medicine* (6 October 1977), 764–6. In another study, 22 per cent of 108 serial rapists suffered from sexual dysfunction: see Janet Warren, Roland Reboussin, Robert R. Hazelwood, Natalie A. Gibbs, Susan L. Trumbetta and Andrea Cummings, 'Crime Scene Analysis and the Escalation of Violence in Serial Rape', *Forensic Science International*, 1000 (1999), 46.

18 Eugene J. Kanin, 'An Examination of Sexual Aggression as a Response to Sexual Frustration', *Journal of Marriage and the Family*, 29.3 (August 1967), 428–32.

19 Sharon Marcus, 'Fighting Bodies, Fighting Words: A Theory and Politics of Rape Prevention', in Judith Butler and Joan W. Scott (eds.), *Feminists Theorize the Political* (London, 1992), 391.

20 Pauline Bart and Patricia O'Brien, *Stopping Rape: Successful Career Strategies* (New York, 1985), 1.

21 This terminology has been adopted (and altered) from Ann J. Cahill's remarkable book *Rethinking Rape* (Ithaca, 2001), 13. She is referring to the body of the rape victim, but I wish to apply it to the body of the male perpetrator.

22 Lucius H. Perkins, 'Corporal Punishment for Crime', *The American Lawyer*, 9 (1901), 276–7.

23 'Crime Uncovered', ICM and *Guardian* poll, February 2003, online at http://www.icmresearch.co.uk/reviews/2003/observer-crime-uncovered-feb03.htm, p. 50, accessed 15 May 2006.

24 George Chauncey, Jr., 'The Postwar Sex Crime Panic', in William Graebner (ed.), *True Stories from the American Past* (New York, 1983), 163.

25 BBC, Audience Research Department, 'A Report on Some Audience Research Enquiries Connected with the Television Series "Crime"', January 1961, 15, in Modern Records Centre, University of Warwick, MSS 16/B/5/2/3. It was based on a random survey of 1184 adults from twenty-four towns and villages in England and Wales in May 1960.

26 R. E. Hall, *Ask Any Woman: A London Enquiry into Rape and Sexual Assault* (Bristol, 1985), 35–6 and 65. For a survey based on residents in Seattle, see Mark Warr, 'Fear of Rape Among Urban Women', *Social Problems*, 32.3 (February 1985), 238–50.

27 Julie A. Wright, 'Using the Female Perspective in Prosecuting Rape Cases', *Prosecutor*, 29 (1995), 21.

28 *Public Opinion About Crime: The Attitudes of Victims and Non-Victims in Selected Cities*

(Washington, DC, 1997), quoted in Esther I. Madriz, 'Images of Criminals and Victims: A Study on Women's Fear and Social Control', *Gender and Society*, 11.3 (June 1997), 11.

29 Richard Berke, 'Crime is Becoming Nation's Top Fear', *New York Times*, 23 January 1994, A-21; Hazel Erskine, 'The Polls: Fear of Violence and Crime', *Public Opinion Quarterly* (Spring 1974), 131; Esther I. Madriz, 'Images of Criminals and Victims: A Study on Women's Fear and Social Control', *Gender and Society*, 11.3 (June 1997), 3–6.

30 Shannon Jackson, 'Representing Rape: Model Mugging's Discourse and Embodied Performances', *The Drama Review*, 37.3 (Fall 1993), 127.

31 Catharine MacKinnon, *Toward a Feminist Theory of the State* (Cambridge, MA, 1989), 172; Catharine A. MacKinnon, 'Sexuality, Pornography, and Method: "Pleasure Under Patriarchy"', *Ethics*, 99.2 (January 1989), 340; Pauline Bart and Patricia O'Brien, *Stopping Rape: Successful Career Strategies* (New York, 1985), 1.

32 Patricia McDaniel, 'Self-Defense Training and Women's Fear of Crime', *Women's Studies International Forum*, 16.1 (1993), 38.

33 Pauline Bart and Patricia O'Brien, *Stopping Rape: Successful Career Strategies* (New York, 1985), 108–12.

34 Vernon Quinsey and Douglas Upfold, 'Rape Resistance and Victim Injury as a Function of Female Resistance Strategy', *Canadian Journal of Behavioural Sciences*, 17 (1985), 40–50.

35 Sarah E. Ullman and Raymond A. Knight, 'Fighting Back. Women's Resistance to Rape', *Journal of Interpersonal Violence*, 7.1 (March 1992), 31–43.

36 For the best discussion, see Marybeth Hamilton Arnold, '"The Life of a Citizen in the Hands of a Woman": Sexual Assault in New York City, 1790 to 1820', in Kathy Peiss and Christina Simmons (eds.), *Passion and Power. Sexuality in History* (Philadelphia, 1989), 35–56.

37 Georges Vigarello, *A History of Rape. Sexual Violence in France from the 16th to the 20th Century*, trans. Jean Birrell (Cambridge, 2001), 244.

38 J. Clifton Edgar and Jas. C. Johnson, 'Medico-Legal Consideration of Rape', in Rudolph Aug. Witthaus and Tracy C. Becker (eds.), *Medical Jurisprudence. Forensic Medicine and Toxicology*, vol. 2 (New York, 1894), 1894, 445–6.

39 This is argued by Beryl Satter, 'The Sexual Abuse Paradigm in Historical Perspective: Passivity and Emotion in Mid-Twentieth-Century America', *The Journal of the History of Sexuality*, 12.3 (July 2003), 451. Also see Pamela Haag, '"Putting Your Body on the Line": The Question of Violence, Victims, and the Legacies of Second-Wave Feminism', *Differences: A Journal of Feminist Cultural Studies*, 8.2 (Summer 1996), 23–67.

40 Frances E. Willard, 'President's Annual Address', *Minutes of the Twelfth Annual Meeting of the National WTCU* (30 October–3 November 1885), 74, cited in Jane E. Larson, '"Even a Worm will Turn at Last": Rape Reform in Late Nineteenth Century America', *Yale Journal of Law and Humanities*, 9 (1997), 42.

41 'Morality that is Immoral', *Union Signal*, 7 October 1886), 2, cited in Jane E. Larson, '"Even a Worm will Turn at Last": Rape Reform in Late Nineteenth Century America', *Yale Journal of Law and Humanities*, 9 (1997), 26.

42 Beryl Satter, 'The Sexual Abuse Paradigm in Historical Perspective: Passivity and Emotion in Mid-Twentieth-Century America', *The Journal of the History of Sexuality*, 12.3 (July 2003), 451.

43 Laura S. Brown, 'Not Outside the Range: One Feminist Perspective on Psychic Trauma', in Cathy Caruth (ed.), *Trauma: Explorations in Memory* (Baltimore, 1995), 107.

44 This is most cogently argued in recent years by Linda Nicolson, *The Play of Reason: From the Modern to the Postmodern* (New York, 1999).
45 For a sensitive analysis, see Linda Alcoff and Laura Gray, 'Survivor Discourse: Transgression or Recuperation?', *Signs: Journal of Women in Culture and Society*, 18.2 (Winter 1993), 260–90.
46 Carine M. Mardorossian, 'Toward a New Feminist Theory of Rape', *Signs: Journal of Women in Culture and Society*, 27.3 (Spring 2002), 743–75.
47 Rachel Hall, '"It Can Happen to You": Rape Prevention in the Age of Risk Management', *Hypatia*, 19.3 (2004), 12.
48 Linda Alcoff and Laura Gray, 'Survivor Discourse: Transgression or Recuperation?', *Signs: Journal of Women in Culture and Society*, 18.2 (Winter 1993), 281.
49 Pauline Bart and Patricia O'Brien, *Stopping Rape: Successful Career Strategies* (New York, 1985), 1.
50 Rachel Hall, '"It Can Happen to You": Rape Prevention in the Age of Risk Management', *Hypatia*, 19.3 (2004), 3.
51 Jacob A. Goldberg and Rosamond W. Goldberg, *Girls on City Streets. A Study of 1400 Cases of Rape* (New York, 1935), 25, 161, 188 and 280.
52 A. J. Brock, 'Letter to the Editor', *British Medical Journal*, 21 September 1946, 442.
53 City of Hickory Police Department, 'Ladies You Can Protect Yourself', mid 1970s, in Margaret Beadman, 'Papers', in Australian National Library MSS 5876.
54 For the best analysis, see Marion Iris Young, *Throwing Like a Girl and Other Essays in Feminist Philosophy and Social Theory* (Bloomington, 1990).
55 Frederic Storaska, *How to Say No to a Rapist and Survive* (New York, 1975).
56 Rachel Hall, '"It Can Happen to You": Rape Prevention in the Age of Risk Management', *Hypatia*, 19.3 (2004), 2.
57 Carine M. Mardorossian, 'Toward a New Feminist Theory of Rape', *Signs: Journal of Women in Culture and Society*, 27.3 (Spring 2002), 757.
58 Catharine A. MacKinnon and Andrea Dworkin (eds.), *In Harm's Way. The Pornography Civil Rights Hearings* (Cambridge, MA, 1997) and Catharine A. MacKinnon and Andrea Dworkin, *Pornography and Civil Rights: A New Day for Women's Equality* (Minneapolis, 1988).
59 Drucilla Cornell famously dubbed MacKinnon's views the 'politics of revenge': *Beyond Accommodation. Ethical Feminism, Deconstruction, and the Law* (London, 1991), 11.
60 Lois Pineau, 'Date Rape: A Feminist Analysis', *Law and Philosophy*, 8.2 (August 1989), 233.
61 Peggy Reeves Sanday, 'The Socio-Cultural Context of Rape: A Cross-Cultural Study', *Journal of Social Issues*, 37 (1981), 5–27, and Peggy Reeves Sanday, 'Rape-Free versus Rape-Prone: How Culture makes a Difference', in Cheryl Brown Travis (ed.), *Evolution, Gender, and Rape* (Cambridge, MA, 2003), 337–62. Also see Gwen J. Broude and Sarah J. Greene, 'Cross-Cultural Codes on Twenty Sexual Attitudes and Practices', *Ethnology*, 15.4 (1976), 409–30, and Maria-Barbara Watson-Franke, 'A World in Which Women Move Freely Without Fear of Men. An Anthropological Perspective on Rape', *Women's Studies International Forum*, 25.6 (2002), 599–606.
62 Keith Burgess-Jackson, *Rape: A Philosophical Investigation* (Aldershot, 1996), 192.
63 John Stoltenberg, *Refusing to be a Man: Essays on Sex and Justice*, rev. edn. (London, 2000), 27 and 45–9. Note that I find Stoltenberg's repressive views about pornography (his partner was Andrea Dworkin) unhelpful. For an impassioned critique of Stoltenberg, see Scott Tucker, 'Gender, Fucking, and Utopia: An Essay in Response to John Stoltenberg's *Refusing to be a Man*', *Social Text*, 27 (1990), 3–34.

64 Ellen Willis, quoted in Scott Tucker, 'Gender, Fucking, and Utopia: An Essay in Response to John Stoltenberg's *Refusing to be a Man*', *Social Text*, 27 (1990), 16.
65 For one, controversial discussion, see Lois Pineau, 'Date Rape: A Feminist Analysis', 8.2, *Law and Philosophy* (1989), 217–43.
66 Catherine Waldby, 'Destructive Boundary Erotics and Refigurations of the Heterosexual Male Body', in Elizabeth Grosz and Elspeth Probyn (eds.), *Sexy Bodies. The Strange Carnalities of Feminism* (London, 1995), 271.
67 See the insightful analyses of R. W. Connell, *Gender and Power: Society, The Person, and Sexual Politics* (Cambridge, 19987), xiii and Jeff Hearn, *The Gender of Oppression: Men, Masculinity, and the Critique of Marxism* (Brighton, 1987), 185.
68 Judith Butler, *Bodies That Matter: On the Discursive Limits of 'Sex'* (New York, 1993).
69 For a subtle analysis, see Jeanne L. Schroeder, 'Catharine's Wheel: MacKinnon's Pornography Analysis as a Return to Traditional Christian Sexual Theory', *New York Law School Law Review*, 38 (1993), 237.
70 Eldridge Cleaver, *Soul on Ice* (New York, 1968), 15 and 26.
71 Susan Bordo, *Twilight Zones. The Hidden Life of Cultural Images from Plato to O. J.* (Berkeley, CA, 1997), 186.
72 Barbara Johnson, translator's intro. to Jacques Derrida, *Dissemination* (Chicago, 1981), xv.

Bibliography

ARCHIVAL SOURCES

National Archives of Australia

Deathe, Walter Russell, 'Transcript of his Appeal', 1962
Field, Frank T., 'Papers, 1962–63'
Lucas, A, 'Convicted of Criminal Assault', 1928
'Police v. J. Pettitt – Trail on Charge of Indecent Exposure', 1950
'Prohibited Publications'
Prosser, Sydney Walter, 'File of Papers, 1914–1916'

National Library of Australia

Beadman, Margaret, 'Papers'
Summers, Ann, 'Papers'

Glasgow Caledonian University Special Collection

National Society for the Prevention of Cruelty to Children, 'Papers and Reports'

Imperial War Museum Archive (London)

Blackman, W. A., 'Army Experience'
Cain, Charles, 'The Footsloggers'
Casey, Edward [J. W. Roworth], 'The Misfit Soldier'
Dixon, R. G., 'The Wheels of Darkness'
Murgatroyd, Lieutenant-Colonel W. B., 'War Crimes in Italy 1944–1945'
Shoulder, Mrs V., 'Childhood Days in Wartime Years'
Witte, J. H., 'The One that Didn't Get Away'

Modern Records Centre (Warwick)

BBC, Audience Research Department, 'A Report on Some Audience Research Enquiries Connected with the Television Series *Crime*', January 1961
The Howard League for Penal Reform, 'Papers'
Gollancz, Victor, 'Papers'

National Archives (London)

Metropolitan Police files
Ministry of Health files
Criminal files

ARTICLES AND CHAPTERS IN BOOKS

Abel, Gene G., David H. Barlow, Edward Blanchard and Donald Guild, 'The Components of Rapists' Sexual Arousal', *Archives of General Psychiatry*, 34, August 1977

Abel, Gene G. and Edward B. Blanchard, 'The Measurement and Generation of Sexual Arousal in Male Sexual Deviates', in Michael Hersen, Richard M. Eisler and Peter M. Miller (eds.), *Progress in Behavior Modification. Volume 2*, Academic Press, 1976

Abel, Gene G., Edward B. Blanchard and Judith V. Becker, 'Psychological Treatment of Rapists', in Marcia J. Walker and Stanley L. Brodsky (eds.), *Sexual Assault. The Victim and the Rapist*, Lexington Books, 1976

Abel, Gene G., Candice Osborn, David Anthony and Peter Gardos, 'Current Treatments of Paraphiliacs', *Annual Review of Sex Research*, iii, 1992

Abrams, Stan, 'The Use of the Polygraph with Sex Offenders', *Annals of Sex Research*, 4.3, 1991

Adams, Kenneth, 'Adjusting to Prison Life', in Michael Tonry (ed.), *Crime and Justice. A Review of Research*, vol. 16, University of Chicago Press, 1992

Adler, Herman M., 'Biological and Pathological Aspects of Behavior Disorders', *The American Journal of Psychiatry*, vii, November 1927

Adshead, Gwen and Gillian Mezey, 'Ethical Issues in the Psychotherapeutic Treatment of Paedophiles: Whose Side are You On?', *Journal of Forensic Psychiatry*, 4.2, 1993

Agopian, Michael W., Duncan Chappell and Gilbert Geis, 'Interracial Rape in a North American City: An Analysis of 63 Cases', in Terence P. Thornberry and Edward Sagarin (eds.), *Images of Crime: Offenders and Victims*, Praeger Publishers, 1972

Albin, Rochelle Semmel, 'Psychological Studies of Rape', *Signs: Journal of Women in Culture and Society*, 3.2, Winter 1977

Alcoff, Linda and Laura Gray, 'Survivor Discourse: Transgression or Recuperation?', *Signs: Journal of Women in Culture and Society*, 18.2, Winter 1993

Alexander, Dolly F., 'Twenty Years of *Morgan*: Criticism of the Subjectivist View of *Mens Rea* and Rape in Great Britain', *Pace International Law Review*, 7, 1995

Amir, Menachem, 'Forcible Rape', *Federal Probation*, xxxi.1, March 1967

Amir, Menachem, 'Sociocultural Factors in Forcible Rape', in Leonard Gross (ed.), *Sexual Behavior. Current Issues. An Interdisciplinary Perspective*, Spectrum Publications, 1974

Anderson, L., 'Boyz N St John's', *National Review*, 26 August 1991

Anderson, Margaret, 'Domestic Rape', *New Law Journal*, 141, 15 March 1991

Anderson, Nancy F., 'The "Marriage with a Deceased Wife's Sister Bill" Controversy: Incest Anxiety and the Defense of Family Purity in Victorian England', *The Journal of British Studies*, 21.2, Spring 1982

Arabian, Armand, 'The Cautionary Instruction in Sex Cases: A Lingering Insult', *Southwestern University Law Review*, 10, 1978

Arieff, Alex J. and David B. Rotman, 'One Hundred Cases of Indecent Exposure', *The Journal of Nervous and Mental Disease*, 96.5, November 1942

Armstrong, Charles, 'Fiendish Attempt at Castration in the Human Subject', *The Dublin Quarterly Journal of Medical Science*, liii, 1 February 1859

Arnold, Marybeth Hamilton, '"The Life of a Citizen in the Hands of a Woman": Sexual Assault in New York City, 1790 to 1820', in Kathy Peiss and Christina Simmons (eds.), *Passion and Power. Sexuality in History*, Temple University Press, 1989

Aydelott, Danise, 'Mass Rape During War: Prosecuting Bosnian Rapists Under International Law', *Emory International Law Review*, 7, 1993

Bachman, Ronet, Raymond Paternoster and Sally Ward, 'The Rationality of Sexual Offending: Testing a Deterrence/Rational Choice Conception of Sexual Assault', *Law and Society Review*, 26.2, 1992

Backer, Larry Catá, 'Raping Sodomy and Sodomizing Rape: A Morality Tale About the

Transformation of Modern Sodomy Jurisprudence', *American Journal of Criminal Law*, 37, 1993–94

Baker, Katharine K., 'Once a Rapist? Motivationary Evidence and Relevancy in Rape Law', *Harvard Law Review*, 110.3, January 1997

Balboni, Philip Scribner, 'Mylai was Not an Isolated Incident. What Every Vietnam Veteran Knows', *The New Republic*, 19 December 1970

Baldwin, Simeon E., 'Corporal Punishments for Crime', *The Medico-Legal Journal*, xvii.1, 1899

Baldwin, Simeon E., 'Whipping and Castration as Punishments for Crime', *The Yale Law Journal*, 8.9, June 1899

Bancroft, John, 'Psychophysiology of Sexual Dysfunction', in Marcel Dekker (ed.), *Handbook of Biological Psychiatry*, Praag, 1980

Bancroft, John and A. Matthews, 'Autonomic Correlates of Penile Erection', *Journal of Psychosomatic Research*, 15, 1971

Bannon, Christina, 'Recovered Memories of Childhood Sexual Abuse: Should the Courts Get Involved When Mental Health Professionals Disagree?', *Arizona State Law Journal*, 26, 1994

Barber, Ross, 'An Investigation into Rape and Attempted Rape Cases in Queensland', *Australian and New Zealand Journal of Criminology*, 6.4, December 1973

Bardaglio, Peter W., 'Rape and the Law in the Old South: "Calculated to Excite Indignation in Every Heart"', *Journal of Southern History*, 60.4, November 1994

Barnes, Gordon E., Leonard Greenwood and Reena Sommer, 'Courtship Violence in a Canadian Sample of Male College Students', *Family Relations*, 40, 1991

Barnes, Harry Elmer, 'Shall we get Tough or Be Sensible in Facing the Increase of Crime?', *Federal Probation*, 23, 1959

Barr, Martin W., 'The Criminal Irresponsible', *The Alienist and Neurologist*, xxx, 1909

Barry, John, Michael Hirsch and Michael Isikoff, 'The Roots of Torture', *Newsweek*, 24 May 2004

Bart, Pauline B., 'Theories of Rape: Inquiries into the Causes of Sexual Aggression', *Contemporary Sociology*, 20.2, March 1991

Bartholomew, Allen Austin, Kerry L. Milte and Frank Galbally, 'Homosexual Necrophilia', *Medicine, Science, Law*, 18.1, 1978

Bartollas, C. and C. M. Sieverdes, 'The Sexual Victim in a Coeducational Juvenile Correctional Institution', *The Prison Journal*, 58, 1983

Bauermeister, Martin, 'Women Victims and Their Assailants', *International Journal of Offender Therapy and Comparative Criminology*, 21.3, 1977

Bell, Clark, 'Corporal Punishment for Crime', *The Medico-Legal Journal*, xvii.1, 1899

Bell, Clark, 'Hypnotism in the Criminal Courts', *The Medico-Legal Journal*, xiii.4, 1896

Bergen, R., 'Surviving Wife Rape: How Women Define and Cope with the Violence', *Violence Against Women. An International and Interdisciplinary Journal*, 1.2, 1995

Bergoffen, Debra, 'February 22, 2001: Toward a Politics of the Vulnerable Body', *Hypatia*, 18.1, Winter 2003

Berke, Richard, 'Crime is Becoming Nation's Top Fear', *New York Times*, 23 January 1994

Berkowitz, Leonard, 'The Frustration–Aggression Hypothesis Revisited', in Berkowitz (ed.), *Roots of Aggression: A Re-Examination of the Frustration–Aggression Hypothesis*, Atherton Press, 1969

Berkowitz, Leonard, 'Situational Influences on Aggression', in Jo Groebel and Robert A. Hinde (eds.), *Aggression and War. Their Biological and Social Bases*, Cambridge University Press, 1989

Berrington, Eileen and Helen Jones, 'Reality vs. Myth: Constructions of Women's Insecurity', *Feminist Media Studies*, 2.3, 2002

Bettelheim, Bruno, 'Violence: A Neglected Mode of Behavior', in Shalom Endleman (ed.), *Violence in the Streets*, Quadrangle Books, 1968

Biddiscombe, Perry, 'Dangerous Liaisons: The Anti-Fraternization Movement in the US Occupation Zones of Germany and Austria, 1945–1948', *Journal of Social History*, 34.3, 2001

Bilder, Richard B. and Adrien Katherine Wing, '[Review of] Mass Rape. The War Against Women in Bosnia-Herzegovina', *The American Journal of International Law*, 88.4, October 1994

Bisch, Louis E., 'The Police Psychopathic Laboratory', *Journal of the American Institute of Criminal Law and Criminology*, 7.1, May 1916

Blackburn, Ronald, 'On the Relevance of the Concept of the Psychopath', in D. A. Black (ed.), *BPS London Conference: University College London, 18–19 December 1980. Symposium: Broadmoor Psychological Department's 21st Birthday*, British Psychological Society, 1982

Bloch, D. A., 'Sex Crimes and Criminals', *American Journal of Nursing*, 53, 1953

Booth, David Stainrook, 'Erotomania. A Case Study of Exhibitionism – A Medico-Legal Study', *The Alienist and Neurologist*, xxvi, 1905

Boston, Charles A., 'A Protest Against Laws Authorizing the Sterilization of Criminals and Imbeciles', *Journal of the American Institute of Criminal Law and Criminology*, 4.3, 1913

Bourke, Joanna, 'Remembering War', *Journal of Contemporary History*, 39.4, 2004

Bowman, Karl M., 'The Problem of the Sex Offender', *The American Journal of Psychiatry*, 108, September–October 1951

Bowman, Karl M., 'Psychiatric Aspects of the Problem', *Mental Hygiene*, xxii.1, January 1938

Bowman, Karl M. and Milton Rose, 'A Criticism of Current Usage of the Term "Sexual Psychopath"', *American Journal of Psychiatry*, 109, September 1952

Bradford, J. M. and D. McLean, 'Sexual Offenders, Violence and Testosterone: A Clinical Study', *Canadian Journal of Psychiatry*, 29, 1984

Brancale, Ralph, Albert Ellis and Ruth R. Doorbar, 'Psychiatric and Psychological Investigations of Convicted Sex Offenders: A Summary Report', *The American Journal of Psychiatry*, 109, July 1952

Brancale, Ralph, Alfred Vuocolo and William E. Prendergast, 'The New Jersey Program for Sex Offenders', in H. L. P. Resnik and Marvin E. Wolfgang (eds.), *Sexual Behaviors. Social, Clinical, and Legal Aspects*, Little, Brown and Co., 1972

Brook, Jane, 'Sexual Abuse and People with Intellectual Disabilities', *Social Work Review*, 9.3, 1997

Broude, Gwen J. and Sarah J. Greene, 'Cross-Cultural Codes on Twenty Sexual Attitudes and Practices', *Ethnology*, 15.4, 1976

Broughton, Nicholas and Paul Chesterman, 'Malingered Psychosis', *The Journal of Forensic Psychiatry*, 12.2, September 2001

Brown, Laura S., 'Not Outside the Range: One Feminist Perspective on Psychic Trauma', in Cathy Caruth (ed.), *Trauma: Explorations in Memory*, The Johns Hopkins University Press, 1995

Brush, Lisa D., 'Philosophical and Political Issues in Research on Women's Violence and Aggression', *Sex Roles: A Journal of Research*, June 2005

Bryant, Dr R. H., 'The Constitutional Psychopathic Inferior. A Menace to Society and a Suggestion for the Disposition of Such Individuals', *The American Journal of Psychiatry*, lxxxiii, April 1927

Burgess, Robin, Robert Jewitt, James Sandham and Barbara L. Hudson, 'Working with Sex Offenders: A Social Skills Training Group', *British Journal of Social Work*, 10.2, Summer 1980

Burick, Lawrence T., 'An Analysis of the Illinois Sexually Dangerous Persons Act', *The Journal of Criminal Law, Criminology, and Police Science*, 59, 1968

Burkhart, Kitsi, 'Women in Prison', in The Editors of *Ramparts* Magazine and Frank Browning (eds.), *Prison Life. A Study of the Explosive Conditions in America's Prisons*, Harper Colophon Books, 1972

Burns, Haywood, 'Can a Black Man Get a Fair Trial in this Country?', *New York Times Magazine*, 12 July 1970

Burrell, Darci E., 'Myth, Stereotype, and the Rape of Black Women', *UCLA Women's Law Journal*, 4, 1993

Butler, George F., 'Hysteria', *The Alienist and Neurologist*, xxxii.3, August 1911

Byrne, Donn, 'The Imagery of Sex', in John Money and Herman Musaph (eds.), *Handbook of Sexology*, Excerpta Medica, 1977

Cahill, Ann J., 'Foucault, Rape, and the Construction of the Feminine Body', *Hypatia*, 15.1, Winter 2000

Cahill, Tom, 'Cruel and Unusual Punishment: Rape in Prison', *Victimology: An International Journal*, 9.1, 1984

Calder, W., 'The Sexual Offender: A Prison Medical Officer's Viewpoint', *The British Journal of Delinquency*, vi.1, July 1955

Campbell, Kirsten, 'Legal Memories: Sexual Assault Memory and International Humanitarian Law', *Signs: Journal of Women in Culture and Society*, 28.1, Autumn 2002

Caplan, Paula J., 'How *Do* They Decide Who Is Normal? The Bizarre, But True, Tale of the DSM Process', *Canadian Psychology*, 32.2, 1991

Caporale, Domenico and Deryl F. Hamann, 'Sexual Psychopathy – A Legal Labyrinth of Medicine, Morals, and Mythology', *Nebraska Law Review*, 36, 1957

Carey, Allison C., 'Gender and Compulsory Sterilization Programs in America: 1907–1950', *Journal of Historical Sociology*, 11.1, March 1998

Carroll, Leo, 'Humanitarian Reform and Biracial Sexual Assault in a Maximum Security Prison', *Urban Life*, 5.4, 1977

Carson, Elias S., 'The Concept of the Psychopath', *The American Journal of Orthopsychiatry*, xviii, 1948

'Casenotes', *Fordham Urban Law Journal*, 4 (1975–6), 419–30

'"Castrate Me!" Pleads Rapist Who Wants to Go Free . . . But No Doctor Will Do It', *Verdict*, May 1976

Chaddock, Charles Gilbert, 'Sexual Crimes', in Allen McLane Hamilton and Lawrence Godkin (eds.), *A System of Legal Medicine*, vol. 2, 2nd edn., E. B. Treat and Co., 1900

Chauncey, Jr., George, 'The Postwar Sex Crime Panic', in William Graebner (ed.), *True Stories from the American Past*, McGraw-Hill, Inc., 1983

Chesney-Lind, Meda, 'Are Girls Closing the Gender Gap in Violence?', *Criminal Justice*, 16, 2001

Chow, Eva W. C. and Alberto L. Choy, 'Clinical Characteristics and Treatment Response to SSRI in a Female Pedophile', *Archives of Sexual Behavior*, 31.2, April 2002

Christoffel, H., 'Exhibitionism and Exhibitionists', *International Journal of Psychoanalysis*, xvii, 1936

Clark, George, 'Horror at Candlelight Lodge', *True Detective*, 1.2, 1950

Clinton, Catherine, '"With a Whip in His Hand": Rape, Memory, and African-American Women', in Geneviève Fabre and Robert O'Meally (eds.), *History and Memory in African-American Culture*, Oxford University Press, 1994

Clothier, Florence, 'Psychological Implications of Unmarried Parenthood', *American Journal of Orthopsychiatry*, xiii.3, July 1943

Cohen, Elias S., 'Administration of the Criminal Sexual Psychopath Statute in Indiana', *Indiana Law Journal*, 32.4, Summer 1957
Cohen, Murray L., Ralph Garofalo, Richard Boucher and Theoharis Seghorn, 'The Psychology of Rapists', *Seminars in Psychiatry*, 3.3, August 1971
Cole, Simon A., 'From the Sexual Psychopath Statute to "Megan's Law": Psychiatric Knowledge in the Diagnosis, Treatment, and Adjudication of Sex Criminals in New Jersey, 1949–1999', *Journal of the History of Medicine*, 55, 2000
Colin, Henri, 'Mental and Physical State of Criminals Convicted of Sexual Crime', *The Alienist and Neurologist*, xix, 1898
Cooper, Alan J., A. A. A. Ismail, A. L. Phanjoo and D. L. Love, 'Antiandrogen (Cyproterone Acetate) Therapy in Deviant Hypersexuality', *British Journal of Psychiatry*, 120, 1972
Cooper, Alan J., S. Swaminath, D. Baxter and C. Poulin, 'A Female Sex Offender with Multiple Paraphilias: A Psychologic Physiologic (Laboratory Sexual Arousal) and Endocrine Case Study', *Canadian Journal of Psychiatry*, 35, May 1990
Cosgrave, May St. John, 'Medical Examination in Alleged Sexual Offences', *The Forensic Science Society Journal*, 3.2, March 1924
Cottle, Thomas J., 'Children in Jail', *Crime and Delinquency*, 25, 1979
Cotton, Donald J. and A. Nicholas Groth, 'Inmate Rape: Prevention and Intervention', *Journal of Prison and Jail Health*, 2, 1982
Council of Scientific Affairs, 'Council Report: Scientific Status of Refreshing Recollection by the Use of Hypnosis', *Journal of the American Medical Association*, 253, 1985
Coxell, Adrian W., M. King, G. Mezey and D. Gordon, 'Lifetime Prevalence, Characteristics, and Associated Problems of Non-Consensual Sex in Men: Cross Sectional Survey', *British Medical Journal*, 318, 1999
Coxell, Adrian W., Michael B. King, Gillian C. Mezey and Philip Kell, 'Sexual Molestation of Men: Interviews with 224 Men Attending a Genitourinary Medicine Service', *International Journal of STD and AIDS*, 11.9, 2000
Coyne, Jerry A., 'Of Vice and Men: A Case Study in Evolutionary Psychology', in Cheryl Brown Travis (ed.), *Evolution, Gender, and Rape*, The MIT Press, 2003
Craig, Mary E., 'Coercive Sexuality in Dating Relationships: A Situational Model', *Clinical Psychology Review*, 10, 1990
Crandell, William, 'What Did America Learn from the Winter Soldier Investigation?', *Viet Nam Generation*, 5, March 1994
Crawford, David, 'Problems for the Assessment and Treatment of Sexual Offenders in Closed Institutions: And Some Solutions', in D. A. Black (ed.), *BPS London Conference: University College London, 18–19 December 1980. Symposium: Broadmoor Psychological Department's 21st Birthday*, British Psychological Society, 1982
Crawford, David, 'Treatment Approaches with Pedophiles', in M. Cook and K. Howells (eds.), *Adult Sexual Interests in Children*, Academic Press, 1981
Crenshaw, Kimberle, 'Mapping the Margins: Intersectionality, Identity Politics, and Violence Against Women of Color', *Stanford Law Review*, 43.6, July 1991
Crépault, Claude and Marcel Couture, 'Men's Erotic Fantasies', *Archives of Sexual Behavior*, 9.6, 1980
'The Crime of Rape', *The Afro-American Ledger*, 3 August 1907
Crocker, Phyllis L., 'Crossing the Line: Rape-Murder and the Death Penalty', *Ohio Northern University Law Review*, 26, 2000
Cronin, James, 'False Memory', *Z Magazine*, April 1994
Crothers, Dr T. D., 'Sexual Crimes by Inebriates', *The Alienist and Neurologist*, xvii, 1896

Crowe, L. and W. George, 'Alcohol and Human Sexuality: Review and Integration', *Psychological Bulletin*, 105, 1989
Culbertson, Roberta, 'Embodied Memory, Transcendence, and Telling: Recounting Trauma, Reestablishing the Self', *New Literary History*, 26, 1995
Curran, Desmond and Paul Mallinson, 'Psychopathic Personality', *Journal of Mental Science*, 90, January 1944
'Current Topics', *Albany Law Journal*, 36.27 (1887–8)
Daniel, F. E., 'Castration of Sexual Perverts', *Texas Medical Journal*, 27, April 1912
Daniel, F. E., 'Editorial', *Texas Medical Journal*, 22, 1907
Daniel, F. E., 'Should Insane Criminals or Sexual Perverts be Allowed to Procreate?', *The Medico-Legal Journal*, xi.3, December 1893
Davies, Susanne, 'Women, War, and the Violence of History', *Violence Against Women. An International and Interdisciplinary Journal*, 2.4, December 1996
Davies, Dr T. S., 'Cyproterone Acetate in Sexual Misbehaviour', *Medicine, Science and the Law*, 10.4, October 1970
Davis, Alan J., 'Sexual Assaults in the Philadelphia Prison System', in John H. Gagnon and William Simon (eds.), *The Sexual Scene*, 2nd edn., Transaction Books, 1973
Davis, Alan J., 'Sexual Assaults in the Philadelphia Prison System and Sheriff's Vans', *Trans-Action*, December 1968
Davis, Allison, 'Socialization and Adolescent Personality', in Theodore M. Newcomb and Eugene L. Hartley (eds.), *Readings in Social Psychology*, Society for the Study of Social Issues, 1947
Davison, G. C. and G. T. Wilson, 'Attitudes of Behavior Therapists toward Homosexuality', *Behavior Therapy*, 4, 1973
Davison, G. C. and G. T. Wilson, 'Goals and Strategies in Behavioral Treatment of Homosexual Pedophilia: Comments on a Case Study', *Journal of Abnormal Psychology*, 83.2, 1974
Dawson, George E., 'Psychic Rudiments and Morality', *The American Journal of Psychology*, 11.2, January 1900
Deevey, Sharon, 'Such a Nice Girl', in Nancy Myron and Charlotte Bunch (eds.), *Lesbianism and the Women's Movement*, Diana Press, 1975
de Grazia, Edward, 'The Distinction of Being Mad', *University of Chicago Law Review*, 22, 1954–5
DeKeseredy, Walter S., 'Tactics of the Antifeminist Backlash Against Canadian National Women Abuse Surveys', *Violence Against Women. An International and Interdisciplinary Journal*, 5.11, November 1999
Delgado, Richard, 'Organic Rehabilitation and Criminal Punishment', in Elliott S. Valenstein (ed.), *The Psychosurgery Debate. Scientific, Legal, and Ethical Perspectives*, W. H. Freeman and Co., 1980
Delgado, Richard, 'Organically Induced Behavioral Change in Correctional Institutions: Release Decisions and the "New Man" Phenomenon', *Southern California Law Review*, 50, 1977
Dempster, Tina, 'Consent and Marital Rape', *New Law Journal*, 140, 10 August 1990
Dengrove, Edward, 'Behavior Therapy of the Sexual Disorders', *The Journal of Sex Research*, 3.1, February 1967
Denno, Deborah W., 'Gender, Crime, and the Criminal Law Defenses', *The Journal of Criminal Law and Criminology*, 85.1, Summer 1994
Deveaux, Monique, 'Feminism and Empowerment: A Critical Reading of Foucault', *Feminist Studies*, 20.2, Summer 1994
Devereux, George, 'The Awarding of a Penis as a Compensation for Rape. A Demonstration of the Clinical Relevance of the Psycho-Analytic Study of Cultural

Data', *International Journal of Psycho-Analysis*, xxxviii.vi, November–December 1957

Dieckmann, G. and R. Hassler, 'Treatment of Sexual Violence by Stereotaxic Hypothalamotomy', in W. H. Sweet, S. Obrador and J. G. Martin-Rodriguez (eds.), *Neurosurgical Treatment in Psychiatry, Pain, and Epilepsy*, University Park Press, 1977

Donnelly, D. A. and S. Kenyon, '"Honey, We Don't Do Men": Gender Stereotypes and the Provision of Services to Sexually Assaulted Males', *Journal of Interpersonal Violence*, 11.3, 1996

Donovan, Patricia, 'Can Statutory Rape Laws be Effective in Preventing Adolescent Pregnancy?', *Family Planning Perspective*, 29, 1997

Dorr, Lisa Lindquist, 'Black-On-White Rape and Retribution in Twentieth-Century Virginia: "Men, Even Negroes, Must Have Some Protection"', *The Journal of Southern History*, 66.4, November 2000

Dreznick, Michael T., 'Heterosocial Competence of Rapists and Child Molesters: A Meta-Analysis', *Journal of Sex Research*, May 2003

Duncan, Lauren E., 'Gender Role Socialization and Male-on-Male vs. Female-on-Male Child Sexual Abuse', *Sex Roles: A Journal of Research*, November 1998

Dunn, Charles W., 'Hormone Treatment of the Sexual Offender', *The Lancet*, 30 July 1949

Dunn, Charles William, 'Stilboestrol-Induced Gynecomastia in the Male', *Journal of the American Medical Association*, 28 December 1940

East, W. Norwood, 'Observations on Exhibitionism', *The Lancet*, 23 August 1924

East, W. Norwood, 'Psychopathic Personality and Crime', *Journal of Mental Science*, xci, October 1945

East, W. Norwood, 'Sexual Offenders', *The Journal of Nervous and Mental Disease*, 103.6, June 1946

Easteal, Patricia Weiser, 'Rape in Marriage: Has the License Lapsed?', in Easteal (ed.), *Balancing the Scales: Rape, Law Reform, and Australian Culture*, Federation Press, 1995

Easteal, Patricia Weiser, 'Survivors of Sexual Assault: An Australian Survey', *International Journal of Sociology of Law*, 22, 1994

'E. C. B. Jr', 'Pedophilia, Exhibitionism, and Voyeurism: Legal Problems in the Deviant Society', *Georgia Law Review*, 4, 1969

Edgar, J. Clifton and Jas. C. Johnson, 'Medico-Legal Consideration of Rape', in R. A. Witthaus and Tracy C. Becker (eds.), *Medical Jurisprudence, Forensic Medicine, and Toxicology*, vol. 2, William Wood and Co., 1894

Educational Council of the Canadian Psychiatric Association, 'Position Statement: Adult Recovered Memories of Childhood Sexual Abuse', *Canadian Journal of Psychiatry*, 41, 1996

Ehrenreich, Barbara, 'Prison Abuse: Feminism's Assumptions Upended', *Los Angeles Times*, 16 May 2004

Eigenberg, Helen M., 'Correctional Officers' Definitions of Rape in Male Prisons', *Journal of Criminal Justice*, 28.5, September–October 2000

Ellinwood, R. C., 'Vasectomy', *California State Medical Journal*, 2, 1904

Ellis, Albert, Ruth R. Doorbar and Robert Johnston III, 'Characteristics of Convicted Sex Offenders', *The Journal of Social Psychology*, 40, 1954

Elman, R. Amy, 'Disability Pornography. The Fetishization of Women's Vulnerabilities', *Violence Against Women*, 3.3, June 1997

Epps, Kevin J., 'Treating Adolescent Sex Offenders in Secure Conditions: The Experience at Glenthorne Centre', *Journal of Adolescence*, 17.2, 1994

Epstein, Seymour J. and Paul L. Deyoub, 'Hypnotherapeutic Control of Exhibitionism: A Brief Communication', *The International Journal of Clinical and Experimental Hypnosis*, xxxi.2, 1983

Erskine, Hazel, 'The Polls: Fear of Violence and Crime', *Public Opinion Quarterly*, Spring 1974

Eschholz, Sarah and Michael S. Vaughn, 'Police Sexual Violence and Rape Myths. Civil Liability Under Section 1983', *Journal of Criminal Justice*, 29, 2001

Factor, M., 'A Woman's Psychological Reaction to Attempted Rape', *Psychiatric Quarterly*, 23, 1954

Fahr, Samuel M., 'Iowa's New Sexual Psychopath Law – An Experimental Noble in Purpose?', *Iowa Law Review*, 41, 1955–6

Faller, K. C., 'Women Who Sexually Abuse Children', *Violence and Victims*, 2, 1987

'False Accusation of Rape', *The Alienist and Neurologist*, 22, 1901

Feldman, Allen, 'Memory Theatres, Virtual Witnessing, and the Trauma-Aesthetic', *Biography*, 27.1, Winter 2004

Feldman, Egal, 'Prostitution, the Alien Woman, and the Progressive Imagination, 1910–15', *American Quarterly*, 19.2, Summer 1967

Feldman-Summers, Shirley and Gayle C. Palmer, 'Rape as Viewed by Judges, Prosecutors, and Police Officers', *Crime, Justice and Behavior*, 19, 1980

Fenwick, Helen, 'Marital Rights or Partial Immunity?', *New Law Journal*, 142, 19 June 1992

Ferenczi, Sándor, 'Confusion of Tongues Between Adults and the Child', *Final Contributions to the Problems and Methods of Psycho-Analysis*, first pub. 1933, Brunner Mazel, 1980

Ferenczi, Sándor, 'Nakedness as a Means for Inspiring Terror', in Ferenczi (ed.), *Further Contributions to the Theory and Technique of Psycho-Analysis*, first pub. 1919, Hogarth Press, 1950

Field, L. H. and Mark Williams, 'The Hormonal Treatment of Sexual Offenders', *Medicine, Science, and the Law*, 10.1, January 1970

Finch, Emily and Vanessa E. Munro, 'Juror Stereotypes and Blame Attribution in Rape Cases Involving Intoxicants', *British Journal of Criminology*, 45, 2005

Fisher, Gary and Ephraim Rivlin, 'Psychological Needs of Rapists', *British Journal of Criminology*, 11.2, April 1971

Fitch, J. H., 'Men Convicted of Sexual Offences Against Children. A Descriptive Follow-Up Study', *British Journal of Criminology*, 3, 1962–3

Fleming, Annaliese Flynn, 'Louisiana's Newest Capital Crime: The Death Penalty for Child Rape', *The Journal of Criminal Law and Criminology*, 89, 1998–9

'Flogging as Legal Punishment in England', *Albany Law Journal*, 57, 1898

Foley, William R., 'California's Sexual Psychopath – Criminal or Patient?', *University of San Francisco Law Review*, 1.2, April 1967

'Forcible and Statutory Rape: An Exploration of the Operation and Objectives of the Consent Standard', *The Yale Law Journal*, 55, 1952–3

Foucault, Michel, 'Confinement, Psychiatry, Prison', in L. D. Kritzman (ed.), *Politics, Philosophy, Culture: Interviews and Other Writings, 1977–1984*, trans. Alan Sheridan, Routledge, 1988

Freedman, Estelle B., '"Uncontrollable Desires": The Response to the Sexual Psychopath, 1920–1960', *Journal of American History*, 74.1, June 1987

Frenkel, F. E., 'Sex-Crime and its Socio-Historical Background', *Journal of The History of Ideas*, xxv.3, July–September 1964

Freud, Sigmund, 'Letters to Fliess', 1897, in Peter Gay (ed.), *The Freud Reader*, Vintage, 1995

Freud, Sigmund, 'Medusa's Head', in James Strachey (ed.), *The Standard Edition of the Complete Psychological Works of Sigmund Freud*, xviii (1940), first pub. 1922

Freud, Sigmund, 'Why War', in Edwin I. Megargee and Jack E. Hokanson (eds.), *The*

Dynamics of Aggression. Individual, Group and International Analyses, Harper and Row, 1970

Freund, Kurt, 'Courtship Disorder: Is this Hypothesis Valid?', *Annals of the New York Academy of Sciences*, 528, 1988

Freund, Kurt, H. Scher and S. Hucker, 'The Courtship Disorders', *Archives of Sexual Behavior*, 12, 1983

Frieze, Irene Hanson, 'Investigating the Causes and Consequences of Marital Rape', *Signs: Journal of Women in Culture and Society*, 8.3, Spring 1983

Fritz, G. S., K. Stoll and N. N. Wagner, 'A Comparison of Male and Females Who were Sexually Molested as Children', *Journal of Sex and Marital Therapy*, 7, 1981

Fuchs, Siegmund Fred, 'Male Sexual Assault: Issues of Arousal and Consent', *Cleveland State Law Review*, 51, 2004

Gallup Poll, Questionnaire 'Crime' qn46G, 29 August–3 September 2000

Galton, Eric R., 'Police Processing of Rape Complaints: A Case Study', *American Journal of Criminal Law*, 4, 1975–6

Gardner, George E., 'The Community and the Aggressive Child. The Aggressive and Destructive Impulses in the Sex Offender', *Mental Hygiene*, xxxiv.1, January 1950

Garnier, Dr Paul, 'Sexual Pervert Impulses and Obsessions', *The Alienist and Neurologist*, xxi, 1900

Geis, Gilbert and Duncan Chappell, 'Forcible Rape by Multiple Offenders', *Abstracts on Criminology and Penology*, 11.4, July/August 1971

Gelles, Richard J., 'Power, Sex, and Violence: The Case of Marital Rape', *The Family Coordinator*, 26.4, October 1977

Gelman, D. and K. Springen, 'The Mind of the Rapist', *Newsweek*, 23 July 1990

George, W. H. and G. A. Marlatt, 'The Effects of Alcohol and Anger on Interest in Violence, Erotica, and Deviance', *Journal of Abnormal Psychology*, 95 (1986)

Gibbens, T. C. N., 'Recent Trends in the Management of Psychopathic Offenders', *Journal of Delinquency*, 2.2, October 1951

Gibbens, T. C. N., C. Way and K. L. Soothill, 'Behavioural Types of Rape', *British Journal of Psychiatry*, 130, 1977

Gigeroff, Alex. K., J. W. Mohr and R. E. Turner, 'Sex Offenders on Probation: The Exhibitionist', *Federal Probation*, 32, 1968

Gilbert, Neil, 'The Wrong Response to Rape', *Wall Street Journal*, 29 June 1993

Gilgun, Jane F., 'We Shared Something Special: The Moral Discourse of Incest Perpetrators', *Journal of Marriage and the Family*, 57.2, May 1995

Gillin, John L., 'Social Background of Sex Offenders and Murderers', *Marriage Hygiene*, 1.3, February 1935

Glazer, Yale, 'Child Rapists Beware! The Death Penalty and Louisiana's Amended Aggravated Rape Statute', *American Journal of Criminal Law*, 25, 1997–8

Gleeson, Kate, 'From Centenary to the Olympics: Gang Rape in Sydney', *Current Issues in Criminal Justice*, 16, November 2004

Goldstein, Michael J., 'Exposure to Erotic Stimuli and Sexual Deviance', *Journal of Social Issues*, 29.3, 1973

Goldstein, Richard, 'Bitch Bites Man!', *Village Voice*, 10 May 2004

Golla, F. L. and R. Sessions Hodge, 'Hormone Treatment of the Sexual Offender', *The Lancet*, 11 June 1949

Goodyear-Smith, F. A., T. M. Laidlaw and R. G. Large, 'Surveying Families Accused of Childhood Sexual Abuse: A Comparison of British and New Zealand Results', *Applied Cognitive Psychology*, 9, 1997

Gough, Harrison G., 'A Sociological Theory of Psychopathy', *American Journal of Sociology*, 53.5, March 1948

Goyer, P. F. and H. C. Eddleman, 'Same-Sex Rape of Nonincarcerated Men', *American Journal of Psychiatry*, 141.4, 1984

Graham, James J., 'What to Do With the Psychopath?', *The Journal of Criminal Law, Criminology, and Police Science*, 53, 1962

Granucci, Anthony and Susan J. Granucci, 'Indiana's Sexual Psychopath Act in Operation', *Indiana Law Journal*, 44, 1969

Grayson, Alana D. and Rayleen V. De Luca, 'Female Perpetrators of Child Sexual Abuse: A Review of the Clinical and Empirical Literature', *Aggression and Violent Behavior*, 4.1, 1999

Green, Arthur H., 'Female Sex Offenders', in Jon A. Shaw (ed.), *Sexual Aggression*, American Psychiatric Press, 1999

Green, Charles Sam, 'This Man is Dangerous!', *True Detective*, March 1958

Green, David, 'Adolescent Exhibitionists: Theory and Therapy', *Journal of Adolescence*, 10.1, March 1987

Greenblatt, Milton, 'Psychosurgery: A Review of Recent Literature', in Greenblatt, Robert Arnot and Harry C. Solomon (eds.), *Studies in Lobotomy*, William Heinemann, 1951

Greendlinger, Virginia and Donn Byrne, 'Coercive Sexual Fantasies of College Men as Predictors of Self-Reported Likelihood to Rape and Overt Sexual Aggression', *The Journal of Sex Research*, 23.1, February 1987

Gregory, Jeanne and Sue Lees, 'Attrition in Rape and Sexual Assault Cases', *The British Journal of Criminology*, 36.1, Winter 1996

Griswold, Robert L., 'Law, Sex, Cruelty, and Divorce in Victorian America, 1840–1900', *American Quarterly*, 38.5, Winter 1986

Groth, A. Nicholas, 'The Adolescent Sexual Offender and His Prey', *International Journal of Offender Therapy and Contemporary Criminology*, 21.3, 1977

Groth, A. Nicholas, Ann Wolbert Burgess and Lynda Lytle Holmstrom, 'Rape: Power, Anger, and Sexuality', *American Journal of Psychiatry*, 134.11, November 1977

Groth, Nicholas A. and Ann Wolbert Burgess, 'Sexual Dysfunction During Rape', *The New England Journal of Medicine*, 6 October 1977

Grubin, Don, 'Sexual Offending: A Cross-Cultural Comparison', *Annual Review of Sex Research*, iii, 1992

Gudjonsson, G. H., 'Accusations by Adults of Childhood Sexual Abuse: A Survey of the Members of the British False Memory Society', *Applied Cognitive Psychology*, 11, 1997

Gurnani, P. D. and M. Dwyer, 'Serum Testosterone Levels in Sex Offenders', *Journal of Offender Counseling, Services, and Rehabilitation*, 11, 1986

Guttmacher, Manfred and Henry Weihofen, 'Sex Offenses', *The Journal of Criminal Law and Criminology*, 43, 1952–3

Haag, Pamela, '"Putting Your Body on the Line": The Question of Violence, Victims, and the Legacies of Second-Wave Feminism', *Differences: A Journal of Feminist Cultural Studies*, 8.2, Summer 1996

Haaken, Janice, 'The Recovery of Memory, Fantasy, and Desire: Feminist Approaches to Sexual Abuse and Psychic Trauma', *Signs: Journal of Women in Culture and Society*, 21.4, Summer 1996

Haaken, Janice, 'Sexual Abuse, Recovered Memory, and Therapeutic Practice: A Feminist-Psychoanalytic Perspective', *Social Text*, 40, Autumn 1994

Hackett, Thomas P., 'The Psychotherapy of Exhibitionists in a Court Clinic Setting', *Seminars in Psychiatry*, 3.3, August 1971

Hacking, Ian, 'The Making and Molding of Child Abuse', *Critical Inquiry*, 17.2, Winter 1991

Hall, Gordon C. Nagayama, 'Prediction of Sexual Aggression', *Clinical Psychology Review*, 10, 1990

Hall, Lesley A., '"Somehow Very Distasteful": Doctors, Men and Sexual Problems between the Wars', *Journal of Contemporary History*, 20.4, October 1985

Hall, Rachel, '"It Can Happen to You": Rape Prevention in the Age of Risk Management', *Hypatia*, 19.3, 2004

Hall, Ruth and Lisa Longstaff, 'Defining Consent', *New Law Journal*, 147, 1997

Halleck, Seymour, 'The Therapeutic Encounter', in H. L. P. Resnik and Marvin E. Wolfgang (eds.), *Sexual Behaviors. Social, Clinical, and Legal Aspects*, Little, Brown and Co., 1972

Hamilton, Allan McLane, 'Insanity in Medico-Legal Bearings', in Hamilton and Lawrence Godkin (eds.), *A System of Legal Medicine*, vol. 2, 2nd edn., E. B. Treat and Co., 1900

Hammer, Emanuel F., 'A Comparison of H-T-P's of Rapists and Pedophiles: III. The "Dead" Tree as an Index of Psychopathology', *Journal of Clinical Psychology*, xi.1, January 1955

Hammer, Emanuel F., 'A Psychoanalytic Hypothesis Concerning Sex Offenders. A Study by Clinical Psychologic Techniques', *Journal of Clinical and Experimental Psychopathology*, xviii.2, June 1957

Hanna, Cheryl, 'Bad Girls and Good Sports: Some Reflections on Violent Female Juvenile Delinquents, Title IX & the Promise of Girl Power', *Hastings Constitutional Law Quarterly*, 27, 1999–2000

Hansen, Heidi and Lise Lykke-Olesen, 'Treatment of Dangerous Sexual Offenders in Denmark', *The Journal of Forensic Psychiatry*, 8.1, May 1997

Hansen, Jane O., 'Sexual Predators: Why Megan's Law is Not Enough', *Atlanta Journal-Constitution*, 10 June 1997

Harless, Sarah M., 'From the Bedroom to the Courtroom: The Impact of Domestic Violence Law on Marital Rape Victims', *Rutgers Law Journal*, 35, 2003–4

Harman, John, 'Consent, Harm, and Marital Rape', *Journal of Family Law*, 22, 1983–4

Hárnik, Jenö, 'The Various Developments Undergone by Narcissism in Men and Women', *International Journal of Psycho-Analysis*, 5, 1924

Hart, Gavin, 'Sexual Behavior in a War Environment', *The Journal of Sex Research*, 11.3, August 1975

Hartogs, Renatus, 'Discipline in the Early Life of Sex-Delinquents and Sex-Criminals', *The Nervous Child*, 9.1, 1951

Hawton, Keith, 'Behavioural Approaches to the Management of Sexual Deviations', *The British Journal of Psychiatry*, 143, 1983

Heim, N., 'Sexual Behavior of Castrated Sex Offenders', *Archives of Sexual Behavior*, 10.1, 1981

Hemphill, R. E., 'A Case of Genital Self-Mutilation', *The British Journal of Medical Psychology*, xxiv, 1951

Hartman, Saidiya, 'Seduction and the Ruses of Power', *Callaloo*, 19.2, 1996

Hartogs, Renatus, 'Discipline in the Early Life of Sex-Delinquents and Sex-Criminals', *The Nervous Child*, 9.2, 1951

Hartung, Frank E., 'Trends in the Use of Capital Punishment', *Annals of American Academy of Political and Social Science*, 284, 1952

Hasday, Jill Elaine, 'Contest and Consent: A Legal History of Marital Rape', *California Law Review*, 88, 2000

Heisler, G., 'Ways to Deter Law Violators: Effects of Levels of Threat and Vicarious Punishment on Cheating', *Journal of Consulting and Clinical Psychology*, 42, 1974

Henderson, D. K., 'Psychopathic States', *The Journal of Mental Science*, lxxxxviii.373, October 1942

Henderson, Lynne, 'Rape and Responsibility', *Law and Philosophy*, 11.1/2, 1992

Henry, Nicola, Tony Ward and Matt Hirshberg, 'A Multifactorial Model of Wartime Rape', *Aggression and Violent Behavior*, 9.5, August 2004

Herman, Judith Lewis, 'Considering Sex Offenders: A Model of Addiction', *Signs: Journal of Women in Culture and Society*, 13.4, Summer 1988

Hickson, F. C., P. M. Davies, A. J. Hunt, P. Weatherburn, T. J. McManus and A. P. M. Coxon, 'Gay Men as Victims of Nonconsensual Sex', *Archives of Sexual Behaviour*, 23.3, 1994

Higgins, Michael, 'Is Capital Punishment for Killers Only?', *ABA Journal*, August 1997

Hillman, Elizabeth Lutes, 'The "Good Soldier" Defence: Character Evidence and Military Rank at Courts-Martial', *The Yale Law Journal*, 108.4, January 1999

Hindman, J., 'Research Disputes. Assumptions About Child Molesters', *National District Attorneys Association Bulletin*, 7, 1988

Hodgens, E. J., I. H. McFadyen, R. J. Failla and F. M. Dayly, 'The Offence of Rape in Victoria', *Australian and New Zealand Journal of Criminology*, 5, December 1972

Hoedemaker, Edward D., '"Irresistible Impulse" as a Defence in Criminal Law', *Washington Law Review*, 23.1, February 1948

Holden, H. S., 'The Laboratory Aspects of Sexual Crime', *British Journal of Venereal Diseases*, xxiv.2, June 1948

Hollender, Marc H., C. Winston Brown and Howard B. Roback, 'Genital Exhibitionism in Women', *American Journal of Psychiatry*, 134.4, April 1977

Home Office, 'The Criminal Injuries Compensation Scheme, 2001', Home Office, 1 April 2001

Hoover, J. Edgar, 'How Safe is Your Daughter?', *American Magazine*, 144, July 1947

Horan, Susan, 'The XYY Supermale and the Criminal Justice System: A Square Peg in a Round Hole', *Loyola Los Angeles Law Review*, 25, 1992

Horwitz, Andrew, 'Sexual Psychopath Legislation: Is There Anywhere to Go But Backwards?', *University of Pittsburgh Law Review*, 57, 1995–6

Hrdy, S. B. and G. C. Williams, 'Behavioral Biology and the Double Standard', in S. K. Wasser (ed.), *Social Behaviors of Female Vertebrates*, Academic Press, 1983

Hughes, C. H., 'Morbid Exhibitionism', *The Alienist and Neurologist*, xxv, 1904

Hughes, Graham, 'The Crime of Incest', *The Journal of Criminal Law, Criminology, and Police Science*, 55, 1964

Hunter, Joel D., 'Sterilization of Criminals', *The Journal of the American Institute of Criminal Law and Criminology*, 5, May 1914 to March 1915

Ibrahim, Azmy I., 'Deviant Behavior in Men's Prisons', *Crime and Delinquency*, 20.1, January 1974

'Indecent Assault – The Scope of Marital Consent. R. v. Kowalski', *Journal of Criminal Law*, 53, 1989

'Indiana Sexual Psychopath Statutes', *Indiana Law Journal*, 25, 1949–50

'Iowa Vasectomy Law Held Invalid', *The Virginia Law Register*, 20.9, January 1915

Ireland, Robert M., 'Insanity and the Unwritten Law', *American Journal of Legal History*, 32, 1988

Irvine, Janice M., 'Regulated Passions: The Invention of Inhibited Sexual Desire and Sex Addiction', *Social Text*, 37, Winter 1993

Isely, Paul J. and David Gehrenbeck-Shim, 'Sexual Assault of Men in the Community', *Journal of Community Psychology*, 25.2, 1997

Jackson, Bruce, 'Prison Folklore', *The Journal of American Folklore*, 78.310, October–December 1965

Jackson, Shannon, 'Representing Rape: Model Mugging's Discourse and Embodied Performances', *The Drama Review*, 37.3, Fall 1993

Jacobs, P., et al., 'Aggressive Behavior, Mental Abnormality and the XYY Male', *Nature*, 208, 1965

Janus, E., 'Sexual Predator Commitment Laws: Lessons for Law and the Behavioral Sciences', *Behavioral Science and the Law*, 18, 2000

Jeffords, Charles R., 'Prosecutorial Discretion in Cases of Marital Rape', *Victimology. An International Journal*, 9.4, 1984

Jeffords, Charles R. and R. Thomas Dull, 'Demographic Variations in Attitudes towards Marital Rape', *Journal of Marriage and the Family*, 44, 1982

Johnson, Allan Griswold, 'On the Prevalence of Rape in the United States', *Signs: Journal of Women in Culture and Society*, 6.1, Autumn 1980

Johnson, Elmer H., 'Selective Factors in Capital Punishment', *Social Forces*, 36, 1957–8

Jones, Ivor H. and Dorothy Frei, 'Exhibitionism – A Biological Hypothesis', *British Journal of Medical Psychology*, 52, 1979

Jones, Owen D., 'Sex, Culture, and the Biology of Rape: Toward Explanation and Prevention', *California Law Review*, 87.4, July 1999

Joshi, Sam, '"Watcha Gonna Do When They Cum All Over You?" What Police Themes in Male Erotic Video Reveal about (Leather)sexual Subjectivity', *Sexualities*, 6.3, 2003

Kan, Steven S., 'Corporal Punishments and Optimal Incapacitation', *The Journal of Legal Studies*, 1, January 1996

Kanazawa, Satoshi and Mary C. Still, 'Why Men Commit Crimes (And Why They Desist)', *Sociological Theory*, 18.3, November 2000

Kanin, Eugene J., 'Date Rape: Unofficial Criminals and Victims', *Victimology: An International Journal*, 9, 1984

Kanin, Eugene J., 'An Examination of Sexual Aggression as a Response to Sexual Frustration', *Journal of Marriage and the Family*, 29.3, August 1967

Kanin, Eugene J., 'Male Aggression in Dating-Courtship Relations', *The American Journal of Sociology*, 63, 1957

Kardener, Sheldon H., 'Rape Fantasies', *Journal of Religion and Health*, 14.1, 1975

Karpman, Benjamin, 'Felonious Assault Revealed as a Symptom of Abnormal Sexuality. A Contribution to the Psychogenesis of Psychopathic Behavior', *The Journal of Criminal Law and Criminology*, 37, 1946–7

Karpman, Benjamin, 'The Sexual Psychopath', *The Journal of Criminal Law, Criminology, and Police Science*, 42, 1951

Kassebaum, Gene, 'Sex in Prison', *Sexual Behavior*, 2, January 1972

Kaufman, Arthur, 'Rape of Men in the Community', in Irving R. Stuart and Joanne G. Greer (eds.), *Victims of Sexual Aggression: Treatment of Children, Women and Men*, Van Nostrand Reinhold Co., 1984

Keire, Mara, 'The Vice Trust: A Reinterpretation of the White Slavery Scare in the United States, 1907–1917', *Journal of Social History*, 2001

Kellor, Frances Alice, 'Sex in Crime', *International Journal of Ethics*, 9.1, October 1898

Kenny, Michael G., 'The Recovered Memory Controversy: An Anthropologist's View', *Journal of Psychiatry and the Law*, 23, 1995

Kerstetter, Wayne A., 'Gateway to Justice: Police and Prosecutorial Response to Sexual Assaults Against Women', *The Journal of Criminal Law and Criminology*, 81.2, 1990

Kiernan, James G., 'Hysterical Mimicry of Dramatic Crimes', *The Alienist and Neurologist*, xxxii, 1911

Kim, Yong Kie and W. Umbach, 'Combined Stereotactic Lesions for Treatment of Behaviour Disorders and Severe Pain', in Lauri Laitinen and Kenneth Livingston (eds.), *Surgical Approaches in Psychiatry*, MTO Press, 1973

King, Michael and Earnest Woollett, 'Sexually Assaulted Males: 115 Men Consulting a Counseling Service', *Archives of Sexual Behavior*, 26.6, 1997

Kirkendall, Lester A. and Leslie G. McBride, 'Preadolescent and Adolescent Imagery and Sexual Fantasies: Beliefs and Experiences', in M. E. Perry (ed.), *Handbook of Sexology, Vol. 7: Childhood and Adolescent Sexology*, Elsevier, 1990

Kirkpatrick, Clifford and Eugene Kanin, 'Male Sex Aggression on a University Campus', *American Sociological Review*, xxii, February 1957

Kisch, Wendy J., 'From the Couch to the Bench: How Should the Legal System Respond to Recovered Memories of Childhood Sexual Abuse?', *American University Journal of Gender and the Law*, 5, 1996–7

Knowles, Gordon James, 'Male Prison Rape: A Search for Causation and Prevention', *The Howard Journal*, 38.3, 1999

Kohlenberg, Robert J., 'Treatment of a Homosexual Pedophiliac Using In Vivo Desensitization', *Journal of Abnormal Psychology*, 83.2, 1974

Kopp, Marie E., 'Surgical Treatment as Sex Crime Prevention Measure', *Journal of Law, Criminology, and Police Science*, 28, 1937–8

Koss, Mary P., 'Hidden Rape: Sexual Aggression and Victimization in a National Sample of Students in Higher Education', in Ann Wolbert Burgess (ed.), *Rape and Sexual Assault II*, Garland Publishing, 1988

Koss, Mary P. and Cheryl J. Oros, 'Sexual Experiences Survey: A Research Instrument Investigating Sexual Aggression and Victimization', *Journal of Consulting and Clinical Psychology*, 50, 1982

Koss, Mary P., T. E. Dinero, C. A. Seibel and S. L. Cox, 'Strangers and Acquaintance Rape: Are There Differences in the Victim's Experience?', *Psychology of Women Quarterly*, 12, 1988

Koss, Mary P., Christine A. Gidycz and Nadine Wisniewski, 'The Scope of Rape: Incidence and Prevalence of Sexual Aggression and Victimization in a National Sample of Higher Education Students', *Journal of Consulting and Clinical Psychology*, 55, 1987

Kozol, Harry L., Murray I. Cohen and Ralph F. Garofalo, 'The Criminally Dangerous Sex Offender', *The New England Journal of Medicine*, 275.2, 14 July 1960

Krahé, Barbara, 'Women's Sexual Aggression Against Men: Prevalence and Predictors', *Sex Roles: A Journal of Research*, September 2003

LaFree, Gary D., 'The Effect of Social Stratification by Race on Official Reactions to Rape', *American Sociological Review*, 45.5, October 1980

Landers, Ann, 'A Male's Theory on Date Rape', *San Francisco Examiner*, 4 August 1991

Landers, John J., 'Group Therapy in H. M. Prison, Wormwood Scrubs', *The Howard Journal*, ix.4, 1957

Landry, David J. and Jacqueline Darroch Forrest, 'How Old are US Fathers?', *Family Planning Perspectives*, 27, 1995

Lang, R. A., Pierre Flor-Henry and Roy R. Frenzel, 'Sex Hormone Profiles in Pedophiles and Incestuous Men', *Annals of Sex Research*, 3.1, 1990

Langevin, R., P. Wright and L. Handy, 'What Treatment Do Sex Offenders Want?', *Annals of Sex Research*, 1.3, 1988

Langton, Calvin M. and W. L. Marshall, 'Cognition in Rapists. Theoretical Patterns by Typological Breakdown', *Aggression and Violent Behavior*, 6, 2001

Larson, Jane E., '"Even a Worm will Turn at Last": Rape Reform in Late Nineteenth Century America', *Yale Journal of Law and Humanities*, 9, 1997

Laschet, Ursula, 'Antiandrogen in the Treatment of Sex Offenders: Mode of Action and Therapeutic Outcome', in Joseph Zubin and John Money (eds.), *Contemporary Sexual Behavior: Critical Issues in the 1970s*, The Johns Hopkins University Press, 1973

Lasègue, Charles, 'Les exhibitionnistes', *L'Union médicale*, 23, 1877
Laura X, 'A Brief Series of Anecdotes About the Backlash Experienced by Those of Us Working on Marital and Date Rape', *Journal of Sex Research*, 31.2, 1994
LeBeau, James L., 'Rape and Racial Patterns', in Sol Chaneles (ed.), *Gender Issues, Sex Offenses, and Criminal Justice: Current Trends*, The Haworth Press, 1984
Lehrer, Eli, 'Hell Behind Bars: The Crime that Dare Not Speak its Name', *National Review*, 5 February 2001
Lehne, Gregory K., 'Adolescent Paraphilias', in M. E. Perry (ed.), *Handbook of Sexuality, Volume 7: Childhood and Adolescent Sexology*, Elsevier, 1990
Lehne, Gregory K., 'Treatment of Sex Offenders with Medroxyprogesterone Acetate', in J. M. A. Sitsen (ed.), *Handbook of Sexology, Vol. VI. The Pharmacology and Endocrinology of Sexual Function*, Elsevier, 1988
Le Maire, Louis, 'Danish Experiences Regarding the Castration of Sexual Offenders', *The Journal of Criminal Law and Criminology and Police Science*, 47, 1956–7
Leo, Richard A., 'The Social and Legal Construction of Repressed Memory', *Law and Social Inquiry*, 1998
Leon, Donald, 'Sexual Psychopathy as a "Defence" in California', *UCLA Intramural Law Review*, 1, 1952–3
Levin, Michael Graubart, 'Fight, Flee, Submit, Sue: Alternatives for Sexually Assaulted Prisoners', *Journal of Legal and Social Problems*, 18, 1983–5
Lewis, Catherine F. and Charlotte R. Stanley, 'Women Accused of Sexual Offenses', *Behavioral Sciences and the Law*, 18, 2000
Lewis, Cecil Day, 'Sex-Crime', *Selected Poems*, Penguin Books, 1951
Lieb, Roxanne, Vernon Quinsey and Lucy Berliner, 'Sexual Predators and Social Policy', *Crime and Justice*, 23, 1998
Lindner, H., 'The Blacky Pictures Test: A Study of Sexual Offenders and Non-Sexual Offenders', *Journal of Projective Techniques*, 17, 1953
Lindner, Robert M., 'Sex in Prison', *Complex*, 6, 1951
Lindsay, D. Stephen and J. Don Read, '"Memory Work" and Recovered Memories of Childhood Sexual Abuse: Scientific Evidence and Public, Professional, and Personal Issues', *Psychology, Public Policy, and Law*, 1, 1995
Lisak, D. and S. Roth, 'Motives and Psychodynamics of Self-Reported, Unincarcerated Rapists', *American Journal of Orthopsychiatry*, 60, 1990
Littlewood, Roland, 'Military Rape', *Anthropology Today*, 13.2, April 1997
Lloyd, Elisabeth A., 'Science Gone Astray: Evolution and Rape', *Michigan Law Review*, 99.6, 2001
Loftus, Elizabeth, 'When a Lie Becomes Memory's Truth: Memory Distortion After Exposure to Misinformation', *Current Directions in Psychological Science*, 1, August 1992
Loftus, Elizabeth F., 'Remembering Dangerously', in Robert A. Baker (ed.), *Child Sexual Abuse and False Memory Syndrome*, Prometheus Books, 1998
Logan, Wayne A., 'Liberty Interests in the Preventive State: Procedual Due Process and Sex Offender Community Notification Laws', *The Journal of Criminal Law and Criminology*, 89.4, 1999
Lott, B., M. E. Reilly and D. R. Howard, 'Sexual Assault and Harassment: A Campus Community Case Study', *Journal of Women in Culture and Society*, 8, 1982
Lukianowicz, Narcyz, 'Imaginary Sexual Partner', *Archives of General Psychiatry*, 3, October 1960
Lukianowicz, Narcyz, 'Incest', *British Journal of Psychiatry*, 120, 1972
Lundberg-Love, Paula and Robert Geffner, 'Date Rape: Prevalence, Risk Factors, and a Proposed Model', in Maureen A. Pirog-Good and Jan E. Stets (eds.), *Violence in Dating Relationships. Emerging Social Issues*, Praeger, 1989

Lyons, Arthur W. and Joanne Regina, 'Mock Jurors' Behavior as a Function of Sex and Exposure to an Educational Videotape About Jury Duty', *Psychological Reports*, 1986

Maclay, David T., 'The Diagnosis and Treatment of Compensatory Types of Indecent Exposure', *British Journal of Delinquency*, 3.1, July 1952

McCormack, Arlene, Frances E. Rokkaus, Robert R. Hazelwood and Ann W. Burgess, 'An Exploration of Incest in the Childhood Development of Serial Rapists', *Journal of Family Violence*, 7.3, 1992

MacCormick, Austin H., 'New York's Present Problem', *Mental Hygiene*, xxii.1, January 1938

McDaniel, Patricia, 'Self-Defense Training and Women's Fear of Crime', *Women's Studies International Forum*, 16.1, 1993

MacDonald, John and Wilson Bradford, 'The Treatment of Sexual Deviation Using a Pharmacological Approach', *Journal of Sex Research*, August 2000

McGuire, R. J., J. M. Carlisle and B. G. Young, 'Sexual Deviations as Conditioned Behaviour: A Hypothesis', *Behaviour Research and Therapy. An International Multi-Disciplinary Journal*, 2, 1965

McGurk, B., R. Forde and A. Barnes, 'Sexual Victimisation Among 15-17-Year-Old Offenders in Prison', Occasional Paper No. 65, Home Office Research, Development and Statistics Directorate, 2000

MacKinnon, Catharine A., 'Sexuality, Pornography, and Method: Pleasure Under Patriarchy', *Ethics*, 99.2, January 1989

McLaury, William M., 'Remarks on the Relation of Menstruation to the Sexual Functions', *American Journal of Obstetrics*, 1887

Maclay, David T., 'The Diagnosis and Treatment of Compensatory Types of Indecent Exposure', *British Journal of Delinquency*, 3.1, July 1952

Madriz, Esther I., 'Images of Criminals and Victims: A Study on Women's Fear and Social Control', *Gender and Society*, 11.3, June 1997

Makepeace, James, 'Courtship Violence Among College Students', *Family Relations*, 30, 1981

Malamuth, Neil M., 'Aggression Against Women: Cultural and Individual Causes', in Malamuth and Edward Donnerstein (eds.), *Pornography and Sexual Aggression*, Academic Press, 1984

Malamuth, Neil M., 'Rape Proclivity Amongst Males', *Journal of Social Issues*, 37.4, 1981

Malamuth, Neil M. and James V. P. Check, 'An Empirical Assessment of Some Feminist Hypotheses about Rape', *International Journal of Women's Studies*, 8, 1985

Malamuth, Neil M. and J. V. P. Check, 'Sex Role Stereotyping and Reactions to Depictions of Stranger Versus Acquaintance Rape', *Journal of Personality and Social Psychology*, 45, 1983

Males, Mike and Kenneth S. Y. Chew, 'The Ages of Fathers in California Adolescent Births', *American Journal of Public Health*, 86, 1996

Maletzky, Barry M., '"Assisted" Covert Sensitization in the Treatment of Exhibitionism', *Journal of Consulting and Clinical Psychology*, 42.1, 1974

Man, Christopher D. and John P. Cronan, 'Forecasting Sexual Abuse in Prison: The Prison Subculture of Masculinity as a Backdrop for "Deliberate Indifference"', *The Journal of Criminal Law and Criminology*, 92.1, 2001

Mann, Bonnie, 'How America Justifies Its War: A Modern/Postmodern Aesthetics of Masculinity and Sovereignty', *Hypatia*, 21.4, Fall 2006

Marcus, Sharon, 'Fighting Bodies, Fighting Words: A Theory and Politics of Rape Prevention', in Judith Butler and Joan W. Scott (eds.), *Feminists Theorize the Political*, Routledge, 1992

Mardorossian, Carine M., 'Toward a New Feminist Theory of Rape', *Signs: Journal of Women in Culture and Society*, 27.3, Spring 2002

Markey, Oscar B., 'A Study of Aggressive Sex Misbehavior in Adolescents Brought to Juvenile Court', *The American Journal of Orthopsychiatry*, xx, 1950

Marsh, Margaret, 'Suburban Men and Masculine Domesticity, 1870–1915', *American Quarterly*, 40.2, June 1988

Marshall, W. L., 'Intimacy, Loneliness, and Sexual Offenders', *Behavioral Research and Therapy*, 27.5, 1989

Marshall, W. L., 'The Modification of Sexual Fantasies: A Combined Treatment Approach to the Reduction of Deviant Sexual Behavior', *Behavioral Research and Therapy*, 11, 1973

Marshall, W. L. and A. Eccles, 'Issues in Clinical Practice with Sex Offenders', *Journal of Interpersonal Violence*, 6.1, March 1991

Matthews, J. K., R. Mathews and K. Speltz, 'Female Sexual Offenders: A Typology', in M. Q. Patton (ed.), *Family Sexual Abuse: Frontline Research and Evaluation*, Sage, 1991

Mazzella, Ronald and Alan Feingold, 'The Effects of Physical Attractiveness, Race, Socioeconomic Status, and Gender of Defendants and Victims on Judgments of Mock Jurors: A Meta-Analysis', *Journal of Applied Psychology*, 24.15, August 1994

Mednick, Sarnoff A., 'Biological Factors in Crime Causation: The Reactions of Social Scientists', in Mednick, Terrie E. Moffitt and Susan A. Stack (eds.), *The Causes of Crime: New Biological Approaches*, 1, 1987

Meilinger, Phillip S., 'Demonic Males: Apes and the Origins of Human Violence; War Before Civilization: The Myth of the Peaceful Savage; A History of Warfare', *The Journal of Military History*, 61.3, July 1997

Meyers, Mrs, 'Rape in Marriage', *New Law Review*, 1 March 1991

Meyers, Thomas J., 'The Psychiatric Examination', *The Journal of Criminal Law, Criminology, and Police Science*, 54, 1963

Mezey, Gillian, 'Rape in War', *Journal of Forensic Psychiatry*, 5.3, 1994

Mill, John Stuart, 'The Subjection of Women', in Mill, *On Liberty. Representative Government. The Subjection of Women. Three Essays*, first pub. 1869, Oxford University Press, 1912

Miller, Gerrit S., 'The Primate Basis of Human Sexual Behavior', *The Quarterly Review of Biology*, vi.4, December 1931

Miller, Laura L., 'Not Just Weapons of the Weak: Gender Harassment as a Form of Protest for Army Men', *Social Psychology Quarterly*, 60.1, March 1997

Money, John, 'The Therapeutic Use of Androgen-Depleting Hormone', in H. L. P. Resnik and Marvin E. Wolfgang (eds.), *Sexual Behaviors. Social, Clinical, and Legal Aspects*, Little, Brown and Co., 1972

Money, John and Carol Bohmer, 'Prison Sexology: Two Personal Accounts of Masturbation, Homosexuality, and Rape', *The Journal of Sex Research*, 16.3, August 1980

Morris, A. Thomas, 'The Empirical, Historical, and Legal Case Against the Cautionary Instruction: A Call for Legislative Reform', *Duke Law Journal*, 1988.1, February 1988

Morris, Madeline, 'By Force of Arms: Rape, War, and Military Culture', *Duke Law Journal*, 45.4, February 1996

Morris, Norval and A. L. Turner, 'Two Problems in the Law of Rape', *The University of Queensland Law Journal*, 2, 1952–3

Morrison, W. D., 'Corporal Punishment', *Law Magazine and Review: A Quarterly Review of Jurisprudence*, fifth series, 25, 1899–1900

Moses, Earl R., 'Community Factors in Negro Delinquency', *The Journal of Negro Education*, 5.2, April 1936

Muehlenhard, C. L. and P. L. Falcon, 'Men's Heterosocial Skill and Attitudes Toward Women as Predictors of Verbal Sexual Coercion and Forceful Rape', *Sex Roles*, 23, 1990

Nacci, Peter L. and Thomas R. Kane, 'Inmate Sexual Aggression: Some Evolving Propositions, Empirical Findings, and Mitigating Counter-Forces', *Journal of Offender Counseling, Services, and Rehabilitation*, 9, 1984

Narvil, Jeffrey C., 'Revealing the Bare Uncertainties of Indecent Exposure', *Columbia Journal of Law and Social Problems*, 29, 1995–6

Nelson, Andrea and Pamela Oliver, 'Gender and the Construction of Consent in Child-Adult Sexual Contact: Beyond Gender Neutrality and Male Monopoly', *Gender and Society*, 12.5, October 1998

'Notebook', *The New Republic*, 24 May 2004

Novak, Michael, 'Against our Will', *Commentary*, 61.2, February 1976

Oberman, Michelle, 'Turning Girls into Women: Re-Evaluating Modern Statutory Rape Law', *The Journal of Criminal Law and Criminology*, 85.1, Summer 1994

O'Brien, Robert M., 'UCR Violent Crime Rates, 1958–2000: Recorded and Offender-Generated Trends', *Social Science Research*, 32.3, September 2003

O'Connor, Art A., 'Female Sex Offenders', *British Journal of Psychiatry*, 150, 1987

Oliveri, Rigel, 'Statutory Rape Law and Enforcement in the Wake of Welfare Reform', *Stanford Law Review*, 52.2, January 2000

Opton, Edward M., 'It Never Happened and Besides They Deserved It', in Nevitt Sanford and Craig Camstock (eds.), *Sanctions for Evil*, Jossy-Bass, 1971

Oros, C. J. and D. Elman, 'Impact of Judge's Instruction Upon Jurors' Decision: the "Cautionary Charge" in Rape Trials', *Representative Research in Social Psychology*, 10, 1979

Orthner, H., D. Müller and F. Roeder, 'Stereotaxic Psychosurgery: Techniques and Results Since 1955', in E. Hitchcock, L. Laitinen and K. Vaernet (eds.), *Psychosurgery*, Charles C. Thomas, 1972

Otis, Margaret, 'A Perversion Not Uncommonly Noted', *Journal of Abnormal Psychology*, 8, 1913

Ozarin, Lucy, 'Bernard Sachs: 50 Year APA Member', *Psychiatric News*, 38.2, 17 January 2003

Pa, Monica, 'Towards a Feminist Theory of Violence', *University of Chicago Law School Roundtable*, 9, 2002

Pacht, Asher, Seymour L. Halleck and John C. Ehrmann, 'Diagnosis and Treatment of the Sexual Offender: A Nine-Year Study', *The American Journal of Psychiatry*, 118.9, March 1962

Pallone, Nathanial J., 'Sadistic Criminal Aggression: Perspectives from Psychology, Criminology, Neuroscience', Louis B. Schlesinger (ed.), *Explorations in Clinical Psychopathology. Clinical Syndromes with Forensic Implications*, Charles C. Thomas, 1996

Palmer, Dwight D., 'Conscious Motives in Psychopathic Behavior', *Proceedings of the American Academy of Forensic Sciences*, 1954

Pantony, Kaye-Lee and Paula J. Caplan, 'Delusional Dominating Personality Disorder: A Modest Proposal for Identifying Some Consequences of Rigid Masculine Socialization', *Canadian Psychology*, 32.2, 1991

Partington, Donald H., 'The Incidence of the Death Penalty for Rape in Virginia', *Washington and Lee Law Review*, 22, 1965

Payne, J. P., 'The Criminal Use of Chloroform', *Anaesthesia*, 53, 1998

Payton, Sallyanne, 'Disability Benefits for Sexual Psychopaths', *Stanford Law Review*, 20, 1967–8

Pearson, Elizabeth A., 'Status and Latest Developments in Sex Offender Registration and

Notification Laws', US Bureau of Justice (ed.), *National Conference on Sex Offenders Registries*, US Bureau of Justice, 1998

Peck, Martin W., 'Exhibitionism: Report of a Case', *The Psychoanalytic Review*, xi.2, April 1924

Pelka, Fred, 'Raped: A Male Survivor Breaks His Silence', in Patricia Searles and Ronald J. Berger (eds.), *Rape and Society: Readings on the Problem of Sexual Assault*, Westview Press, 1995

Perkins, Lucius H., 'Corporal Punishment for Crime', *The American Lawyer*, 9, 1901

Perry, Campbell, 'Hypnotic Coercion and Compliance to it: A Review of Evidence Presented in a Legal Case', *The International Journal of Clinical and Experimental Hypnosis*, xxvii.3, 1979

Peters, Joseph J., James M. Pedigo, Joseph Stey and James J. McKenna, 'Group Psychotherapy of the Sex Offender', *Federal Probation*, September 1968

Pickard, Toni, 'Culpable Mistakes and Rape: Relating Mens Rea to the Crime', *The University of Toronto Law Journal*, 30.1, Winter 1980

Piker, Philip, 'A Psychiatrist Looks at Sex Offenses', *Journal of Social Hygiene*, 33, 1947

Pillsbury, Samuel H., 'Crimes Against the Heart. Recognizing the Wrongs of Forced Sex', *Loyola of Los Angeles Law Review*, 35, 2001–2

Pineau, Lois, 'Date Rape: A Feminist Analysis', *Law and Philosophy*, 8.2, August 1989

Plaza, Monique, 'Our Costs and Their Benefits', trans. Wendy Harrison, *m/f*, 4, 1980

Pleck, Elizabeth, 'Feminist Responses to Crimes Against Women, 1868–1896', *Signs: Journal of Women in Culture and Society*, 8.31, 1983

Podhoretz, Norman, 'Rape and the Feminists', *Commentary*, 93, 1992

Podhoretz, Norman, 'Rape in Feminist Eyes', *Commentary*, 92, 1991

Polaschek, Devon L. L. and Tony Ward, 'The Implicit Theories of Potential Rapists. What Our Questionnaires Tell Us', *Aggression and Violent Behavior*, 7, 2002

'Police Discretion and the Judgment that a Crime Has Been Committed', *University of Pennsylvania Law Review*, 117.2, December 1968

Polk, Kenneth, 'Rape Reform and Criminal Justice Processing', *Crime and Delinquency*, 31.2, 1985

Polk, William M., 'Treatment of Exhibitionism in a 38-Year Old Male by Hypnotic Assisted Covert Sensitization', *International Journal of Clinical and Experimental Hypnosis*, xxxi.3, 1983

Pope, K. S., 'Memory Abuse and Science: Questioning Claims About the False Memory Syndrome Epidemic', *American Psychologist*, 51, 1996

Porter, Roy, 'Rape', in Sylvana Tomaselli and Roy Porter (eds.), *Rape. An Historical and Critical Enquiry*, Basil Blackwell, 1986

Power, D. J., 'Sexual Deviation and Crime', *Medicine, Science and the Law*, 16.2, 1976

Power, K. G., I. Markova, A. Rowlands et al. 'Sexual Behaviour in Scottish Prisons', *British Medical Journal*, 302, 1991

'Prisoners Against Rape: Trying to Unlock the Myths and Images', *The Washington Post*, 16 June 1975

'The Problem of Domestic Rape', *New Law Journal*, 141, 22 February 1991

'Psychological Treatment of Rapists', in M. Walker and S. Brodsky (eds.), *Sexual Assault: The Victim and the Rapist*, Lexington Books, 1976

Quinsey, Vernon and Douglas Upfold, 'Rape Resistance and Victim Injury as a Function of Female Resistance Strategy', *Canadian Journal of Behavioural Sciences*, 17, 1985

Rada, Richard T., 'Alcoholism and Forcible Rape', *American Journal of Psychiatry*, 132.4, April 1975

Rada, Richard T., 'Plasma Androgens and the Sex Offender', *Bulletin of the American Academy of Psychiatry and Law*, 8, 1981

Rada, Richard T., D. R. Laws and Robert Kellner, 'Plasma Testosterone Levels in the Rapist', *Psychosomatic Medicine*, 38.4, July–August 1976

Raeder, F., H. Orthner and Dieter Müller, 'The Stereotaxic Treatment of Pedophilic Homosexuality and Other Sexual Deviations', in Edward Hitchcock, L. Laitinen and Kjeld Vaernet (eds.), *Psychosurgery*, Charles C. Thomas, 1972

Rapaport, Lynn, 'Holocaust Pornography: Profaning the Sacred in *Ilsa, She-Wolf of the SS*', *Shofar: An Interdisciplinary Journal of Jewish Studies*, 22.1, 2003

'Rape and Battery Between Husband and Wife', *Stanford Law Review*, 6, 1953–4

Ravenscroft, Donald R., 'An Examination of the Nebraska Statute Providing for Commitment and Treatment of Sexual Psychopaths', *Nebraska Law Review*, 29, 1949–50

Reitan, Eric, 'Rape as an Essentially Contested Concept', *Hypatia*, 16.2, Spring 2001

Rentoul, L. and N. Appleboom (eds.), 'Understanding the Physiological Impact of Rape and Serious Sexual Assault of Men: A Literature Review', *Journal of Psychiatric and Mental Health Nursing*, 4, 1997

'Resolution', *International Journal of Clinical and Experimental Hypnosis*, 27, 1979

Reynolds, William, 'The Remedy for Lynch Law', *The Yale Law Journal*, 7, 20 October 1897–June 1898

Rich, Frank, 'It was Porn That Made Them Do It', *New York Times*, 30 May 2004

Richie, G. G., 'The Use of Hypnosis in a Case of Exhibitionism', *Psychotherapy: Theory, Research and Practice*, 5, 1968

Richmond, Douglas R., 'Bad Science: Repressed and Recovered Memories of Childhood Sexual Abuse', *University of Kansas Law Review*, 44, 1995–6

Rickles, Nathan King, 'Exhibitionism', *The Journal of Nervous and Mental Disease*, 95.1, January 1942

Rieber, I. and V. Sigusch, 'Psychosurgery on Sex Offenders and Sexual "Deviants" in West Germany', *Archives of Sexual Behavior*, 8.6, November 1979

Riley, Marilyn Ruth, 'Exhibitionism: A Psycho-Legal Perspective', *San Diego Law Review*, 16.5, August 1979

Robertson, James E., 'Compassionate Conservatism and Prison Rape: The Prison Rape Elimination Act of 2003', *New England Journal on Crime and Civil Confinement*, 30, 2004

Robertson, Stephen, 'Separating the Men from the Boys: Masculinity, Psychosexual Development, and Sex Crime in the United States', *Journal of the History of Medicine*, 56, January 2001

Rogers, Stephen, 'Can Chloroform Be Used to Facilitate Robbery?', *The Journal of Psychological Medicine*, v, 1871

Rooth, Graham, 'Changes in the Conviction Rate for Indecent Exposure', *British Journal of Psychiatry*, 121, 1972

Rooth, Graham, 'Exhibitionism, Sexual Violence and Paedophilia', *British Journal of Psychiatry*, 122, 1973

Rope, P. D., 'The Use of Hypnosis in Exhibitionism', in J. Lassner (ed.), *Hypnosis and Psychosomatic Medicine*, Springer-Verlag, 1967

Rose, Daniel Burton, 'The Anti-Exploits of Men Against Sexism, 1977–78', in Don Sabo, Terry A. Kupers and Willie London (eds.), *Prison Masculinities*, Temple University Press, 2001

Rose, Hilary, 'Debating Rape', *The Lancet*, 357, 2001

Rosenfeld, R. William, 'Commitment of Sexual Psychopaths in Ohio', *Western Reserve Law Review*, 2, June 1950

Rosser, Luther Z., 'Illegal Enforcement of Criminal Law', *American Bar Association Journal*, 7, 1921

Roth, Nathan, 'Factors in the Motivation of Sex Offenders', *The Journal of Criminal Law, Criminology, and Police Science*, 42, 1951–2

Ruddy, Clarence J., 'Compulsory Sterilization: Unwarranted Extension of the Powers of Government', *The Notre Dame Lawyer*, III.1, October 1927

Rush, Florence, 'The Sexual Abuse of Children: A Feminist Point of View', in Noreen Connell and Cassandra Wilson (eds.), *Rape: The First Sourcebook for Women*, New American Library, 1974

Russell, Diana, 'On Pornography', *Chrysalis*, 4, 1977

Ruttenberg, Miriam H., 'A Feminist Critique of Mandatory Arrest: An Analysis of Race and Gender in Domestic Violence Policy', *American University Journal of Gender and Law*, 2, 1994

Ryder, Sandra and Sheryl A. Kuzmenka, 'Legal Rape: The Martial Rape Exemption', *Journal of the Marshall Law Review*, 24, 1990–1

Sachs, B., 'Insanity and Crime', in Allan McLare Hamilton and Lawrence Godkin (eds.), *A System of Legal Medicine*, vol. 2, 2nd edn., E. B. Treat and Co., 1900

Sadler, Anne G., Brenda M. Booth, Deanna Nielson and Bradley N. Doebbeling, 'Health-Related Consequences of Physical and Sexual Violence: Women in the Military', *Obstetrics and Gynecology*, 96.3, September 2000

Sadock, Virginia A., 'Special Areas of Interest', in Harold I. Kaplan and Benjamin J. Sadock (eds.), *Comprehensive Textbook of Psychiatry. IV*, 4th edn., Williams and Wilkins, 1985

Sagarin, E., 'Prison Homosexuality and its Effects on Post-Prison Sexuality', *Psychiatry*, 39, 1976

Salmon, The Hon Mr Justice, 'Crimes of Violence. An Address to the Cambridge Law Society', *Cambridge Law Journal*, 1960

Sanday, Peggy Reeves, 'Rape-Free versus Rape-Prone: How Culture makes a Difference', in Cheryl Brown Travis (ed.), *Evolution, Gender, and Rape*, The MIT Press, 2003

Sanday, Peggy Reeves, 'The Socio-Cultural Context of Rape: A Cross-Cultural Study', *Journal of Social Issues*, 37, 1981

Satter, Beryl, 'The Sexual Abuse Paradigm in Historical Perspective: Passivity and Emotion in Mid-Twentieth-Century America', *The Journal of the History of Sexuality*, 12.3, July 2003

Schewe, Paul and William O'Donohue, 'Rape Prevention: Methodological Problems and New Directions', *Clinical Psychiatry Review*, 13, 1993

Schiff, Arthur F., 'Examination and Treatment of the Male Rape Victim', *Southern Medical Journal*, 73.11, November 1980

Schiff, A. F., 'Statistical Features of Rape', *Journal of Forensic Science*, 14.1, 1969

Schoenewolf, Gerald, 'The Feminist Myth About Sexual Abuse', *The Journal of Psychohistory*, 18.3, Winter 1991

Schroeder, Jeanne L., 'Catharine's Wheel: MacKinnon's Pornography Analysis as a Return to Traditional Christian Sexual Theory', *New York Law School Law Review*, 38, 1993

Schulhofer, Stephen, 'The Gender Question in Criminal Law', in Ellen Frankel Paul, Fred D. Miller and Jeffrey Paul (eds.), *Crime, Culpability, and Remedy*, Basil Blackwell, 1990

Schwartz, Barbara K., 'Overview of Rehabilitative Efforts in Understanding and Managing Sexually Coercive Behaviors', *Annals of the New York Academy of Sciences*, 989, 2003

Schwartz, Barry, 'The Effect in Philadelphia of Pennsylvania's Increased Penalties for Rape and Attempted Rape', *The Journal of Criminal Law, Criminology, and Police Science*, 59, 1968

Scully, Diana and Joseph Marolla, 'Convicted Rapists' Vocabulary of Motive: Excuses and Justifications', *Social Problems*, 31.5, June 1984

Seidman, Ilene and Susan Vickers, 'The Second Wave: An Agenda for the Next Thirty Years of Rape Law Reform', *Suffolk University Law Reform*, 38, 2004–5

Seifert, Ruth, 'The Second Front. The Logic of Sexual Violence in Wars', *Women's Studies International Forum*, 19.1/2, 1996

'Sexual Offences Against Young Persons', *The Howard Journal*, ii.4, 1926

'The Sexual Psychopath. A Symposium', *The Journal of Criminal Law and Criminology and Police Science*, 43, 1952–3

Sgro, Suzanne M., 'Sexual Molestation of Children: The Last Frontier in Child Abuse', *Children Today*, 4, May–June 1977

Shapiro, Michael H., 'Legislating the Control of Behavior Control: Autonomy and the Coercive Use of Organic Therapies', *Southern California Law Review*, 237, 1974

Sharp, Harry, 'The Severing of the Vasa Deferentia and its Relation to the Neuropsychopathic Constitution', *New York Medical Journal*, 1902

Shaskan, Donald, 'One Hundred Sex Offenders', *American Journal of Orthopsychiatry*, ix, 1939

Shengold, L., 'Child Abuse and Deprivation: Soul Murder', *Journal of the American Psychoanalytic Association*, 27, 1979

Sherwood-Dunn, B., 'Conservation of the Ovary', *Transactions of the American Association of Obstetricians and Gynecologists: Minutes of the Proceedings of the Tenth Annual Meeting, August 17–20*, x, 1897

Silving, Helen, 'Psychoanalysis and the Criminal Law', *The Journal of Criminal Law, Criminology, and Police Science*, 51, 1960

Simon, Walter T. and Peter G. W. Schouten, 'Problems in Sexual Preference Testing in Child Sexual Abuse Cases. A Legal and Community Perspective', *Journal of Interpersonal Violence*, 7.4, December 1992

Simpson, Dr J. Y., 'Clinical Lectures on the Diseases of Women', *Medical Times and Gazette*, 16 April 1859

Slotkin, Richard, 'Unit Pride: Ethnic Platoons and the Myths of American Nationality', *American Literary History*, 2001

Slough, M. C. and Tom L. Schwinn, 'The Sexual Psychopath', *The University of Kansas City Law Review*, 19, 1950–1

Slovenko, Ralph, 'A Panoramic View: Sexual Behavior and the Law', in Slovenko (ed.), *Sexual Behavior and the Law*, Charles C. Thomas, 1965

Small, Mark A., 'The Legal Context of Mentally Disordered Sex Offender (MDSS) Treatment Programs', *Criminal Justice and Behavior*, 19.2, June 1992

Smith, R. E., C. J. Pine and M. E. Hawley, 'Social Cognitions About Male Victims of Female Sexual Assault', *The Journal of Sex Research*, 24, 1988

Smith, Stevenson and Edwin Guthrie, 'Exhibitionism', *The Journal of Abnormal Psychology and Social Psychology*, xvii, 1922–23

Snaith, R. P. and S. A. Collins, 'Five Exhibitionists and a Method of Treatment', *British Journal of Psychiatry*, 138, 1981

Snow, J., 'Further Remarks on the Employment of Chloroform by Thieves', *London Medical Gazette*, xlv, 1850

Solomon, J. C., 'Child Sexual Abuse by Family Members: A Radical Feminist Perspective', *Sex Roles: A Journal of Research*, 27, 1992

Sommerville, Diane Miller, 'The Rape Myth in the Old South Reconsidered', *Journal of Southern History*, lxi, August 1995

Soothill, Keith, 'The Changing Face of Rape?', *British Journal of Criminology*, 31.4, Autumn 1991

Sorenson, Susan B., J. A. Stein, J. M. Siegel, J. M. Golding and M. A. Burnam, 'The Prevalence of Adult Sexual Assault: The Los Angeles Epidemiologic Catchment Area Project', *American Journal of Epidemiology*, 126.6, 1987

Sorrel, Philip M. and William H. Masters, 'Sexual Molestation of Men by Women', *Archives of Sexual Behavior*, 11.2, 1982
South, Scott J. and Richard B. Felson, 'The Racial Patterning of Rape', *Social Forces*, 69.1, September 1990
'A Southern Lawyer', 'Remedies for Lynch Law', *Sewanee Review*, 8, January 1900
Spalding Helm, Larry, 'Florida's 1997 Chemical Castration Law', *Florida State University Law Review*, 117, 1998
Spece, Roy G., 'Conditioning and Other Technologies Used to "Treat?", "Rehabilitate?", "Demolish?" Prisoners and Mental Patients', *Southern California Law Review*, 45.2, 1972
Sperling, Susan, 'Baboons with Briefcases: Feminism, Functionalism, and Sociobiology on the Evolution of Primate Gender', *Signs: Journal of Women in Culture and Society*, 17.1, Autumn 1991
Starchild, Adam, 'Rape of Youth in Prisons and Juvenile Facilities', *The Journal of Psychohistory*, 18.2, Fall 1990
Stead, William T., 'The Maiden Tribute of Modern Babylon', *Pall Mall Gazette*, 6 July 1885
Steptoe, Sonja, 'A Damnable Defense', *Sports Illustrated*, 24 February 1992
'Sterilization of Criminals', *The Yale Law Journal*, 23.4, February 1914
Stets, Jan E. and Debra A. Henderson, 'Contextual Factors Surrounding Conflict Resolution While Dating: Results from a National Study', *Family Relations*, 40, 1991
Stevenson, Jim and Ivor H. Jones, 'Behavior Therapy Technique for Exhibitionism', *Archives of General Psychiatry*, 27, December 1972
Stoller, R., 'Sexual Excitement', *Archives of General Psychiatry*, 33, 1976
Storer, Horatio R., 'The Law of Rape', *The Quarterly Journal of Psychological Medicine and Medical Jurisprudence*, ii, D. Appleton and Co., 1868
Storer, Horatio R., 'Obstinate Erotomania', *American Journal of Obstetrics and Diseases of Women and Children*, 1.4, 1869
Strange, Carolyn, 'The Undercurrents of Penal Culture: Punishment of the Body in Mid-Twentieth Century Canada', *Law and History Review*, 19.2, 2001
Straus, Murray A., 'Psychical Assaults by Wives: A Major Social Problem', in Richard Gelles and Donileen R. Loseke (eds.), *Current Controversies on Family Violence*, Sage, 1993
Straus, Murray A., 'Sexual Inequality, Cultural Norms, and Wife-Beating', in Emilio C. Viano (ed.), *Victims and Society*, Visage Press, 1976
Struckman-Johnson, Cindy, 'Forced Sex on Dates: It Happens to Men, Too', *The Journal of Sex Research*, 24, 1988
Struckman-Johnson, Cindy and David Struckman-Johnson, 'Acceptance of Male Rape Myths Among College Men and Women', *Sex Roles: A Journal of Research*, 27.3/4, 1992
Struckman-Johnson, Cindy and David Struckman-Johnson, 'Sexual Coercion Rates in Seven Midwestern Prison Facilities for Men', *The Prison Journal*, 80.4, December 2000
Struckman-Johnson, Cindy J., David L. Struckman-Johnson, L. Rucker, K. Bumby and S. Donaldson, 'Sexual Coercion Reported by Men and Women in Prison', *The Journal of Sex Research*, 33, 1976
'Study of Judge Lynch', *The Afro-American*, 16 May 1903
Sturgeon, Vikki H. and John Taylor, 'Report of a Five-Year Follow-Up Study of Mentally Disordered Sex Offenders Released from Atascadero State Hospital in 1973', *Criminal Justice Journal*, 4, 1980

Stürp, Georg K., 'Castration: the Total Treatment', in H. L. R. Resnik and Marvin E. Wolfgang (eds.), *Sexual Behaviors. Social, Clinical, and Legal Aspects*, Little, Brown and Co., 1972

Suddeth, W. Xavier, 'Hypnotism and Crime', *The Medico-Legal Journal*, xiii.3, 1895

Sullivan, Peter, 'Commitment of Sexual Psychopaths and the Requirements of Procedural Due Process', *Fordham Law Review*, 44, 1976

Sutherland, Edwin H., 'The Diffusion of Sexual Psychopath Laws', *American Journal of Sociology*, 56.2, September 1950

Svalastoga, Kaare, 'Rape and Social Structure', *Pacific Sociological Review*, Spring 1962

Swiers, George, '"Demented Vets" and Other Myths. The Moral Obligation of Veterans', in Harrison E. Salisbury (ed.), *Vietnam Reconsidered. Lessons from a War*, Harper and Row, 1985

Tanaka, Yuki, 'Rape and War: The Japanese Experience', in Asian Center for Women's Human Rights (ed.), *Common Grounds, Violence Against Women in War and Armed Conflict Situations*, ASCENT, 1998

Tappan, Paul W., 'The Sexual Psychopath – A Civic-Social Responsibility', *The Journal of Social Hygiene*, 35, 1949

Tappan, Paul Wilburn, 'Treatment of the Sex Offender in Denmark', *The American Journal of Psychiatry*, 108, September–October 1951

Tavris, Carol, 'Beware the Incest-Survivor Machine', *New York Times Book Review*, 3 January 1993

Taylor, F. H., 'Observations of Some Cases of Exhibitionism', *Journal of Mental Science*, 93, 1947

Taylor, Julie, 'Rape and Women's Credibility: Problems of Recantations and False Accusations Echoed in the Case of Cathleen Crowell Webb and Gary Dotson', *Harvard Women's Law Review*, 10, 1987

Taylor, Lucy W., 'The Role of Offender Profiling in Classifying Rapists: Implications for Counselling', *Counselling Psychology Quarterly*, 6, 1993

Temkin, Jennifer, 'Prosecuting and Defending Rape: Perspectives from the Bar', *Journal of Law and Society*, 27.2, June 2000

Terborg-Penn, Rosalyn, 'Woman Suffrage: "First Because We are Women and Second Because We are Colored Women"', *Truth. Newsletter of the Association of Black Women Historians*, April 1985

Thornton, Mark, 'Rape and Mens Rea', *Canadian Journal of Philosophy*, supplementary volume 8, 1982

Tighe, Janet A., 'Francis Wharton and the Nineteenth-Century Insanity Defense: The Origins of a Reform Tradition', *American Journal of Legal History*, 27, 1983

'To Have and To Hold: the Marital Rape Exemption and the Fourteenth Amendment', *Harvard Law Review*, 99, 1985–6

Travis, Cheryl Brown, 'Talking Evolution and Selling Difference', in Travis (ed.), *Evolution, Gender, and Rape*, The MIT Press, 2003

Tucker, Scott, 'Gender, Fucking, and Utopia: An Essay in Response to John Stoltenberg's *Refusing to be a Man*', *Social Text*, 27, 1990

Turner, George Kibbe, 'Daughters of the Poor', *McClure's Magazine*, xxxiv, 1909

Ullman, Sarah E. and Raymond A. Knight, 'Fighting Back. Women's Resistance to Rape', *Journal of Interpersonal Violence*, 7.1, March 1992

'Unusual "Sex Crime" in New England', *The Journal of Sex Education*, 4.4, February–March 1952

Vandiver, Donna M. and Jeffery T. Walker, 'Female Sex Offenders: An Overview and Analysis of 40 Cases', *Criminal Justice Review*, 27.2, Autumn 2002

Venn, Jonathan, 'Misuse of Hypnosis in Sexual Contexts: Two Case Reports', *The International Journal of Clinical and Experimental Hypnosis*, xxxvi.1, 1988

Veraa, Arnold, 'Probation Officer Treatment for Exhibitionists', *Federal Probation*, 40, 1976

'The Victim in a Forcible Rape Case: A Feminist View', *American Criminal Law Review*, 11, 1973

von Hentig, Hans, 'Interaction of Perpetrator and Victim', *The Journal of Criminal Law and Criminal Behavior*, 31, 1940

Waldby, Catherine, 'Destructive Boundary Erotics and Refigurations of the Heterosexual Male Body', in Elizabeth Grosz and Elspeth Probyn (eds.), *Sexy Bodies. The Strange Carnalities of Feminism*, Routledge, 1995

Walker, Jayne, John Archer and Michelle Davies, 'Effects of Rape on Men: A Descriptive Analysis', *Archives of Sexual Behavior*, 34.1, February 2005

Warburton, Damian, 'The Rape of a Label. Why It Would be Wrong to Follow Canada in Having a Single Offence of Unlawful Sexual Assault', *Journal of Criminal Law*, 68, 2004

Warner, Kate, 'Sentencing in Cases of Marital Rape: Towards Changing the Male Imagination', *Legal Studies*, 20, 2000

Warr, Mark, 'Fear of Rape Among Urban Women', *Social Problems*, 32.3, February 1985

Warren, Janet, Roland Reboussin, Robert R. Hazelwood, Natalie A. Gibbs, Susan L. Trumbetta and Andrea Cummings, 'Crime Scene Analysis and the Escalation of Violence in Serial Rape', *Forensic Science International*, 1000, 1999

'Washington, D.C., Considers Sex Offenses. How One Community Undertook to Tell its Citizens the Facts about Sex Crimes and Criminals, and What May be Done to Deal Effectively with Such Problems', *Journal of Social Hygiene*, 36, 1950

Watson-Franke, Maria-Barbara, 'A World in Which Women Move Freely Without Fear of Men. An Anthropological Perspective on Rape', *Women's Studies International Forum*, 25.6, 2002

Watts, G. Stuart, 'Sex Problems of Soldiers on Service', *Marriage Hygiene*, 1.3, February 1948

Weber, Ellen, 'Incest: Sexual Abuse Begins at Home', *Ms*, 5, April 1977

Weinberger, Linda E., Shoba Sreenivasan, Thomas Garrick and Hadley Osran, 'The Impact of Surgical Castration on Sexual Recidivism Risk Amongst Sexually Violent Predatory Offenders', *Journal of the American Academy of Psychiatry and Law*, 33.1, 2005

Weis, Kurt and Sandra S. Borges, 'Victimology and Rape: The Case of the Legitimate Victim', *Issues in Criminology*, 8.2, 1973

Weitzman, L., 'Legal Regulation of Marriage: Tradition and Change', *California Law Review*, 62, 1974

Wells, Celia, 'Rape In Marriage', *New Law Journal*, 141, 1 March 1991

Wells, Nesta H., 'Sexual Offences as Seen by a Woman Police Surgeon', *British Medical Journal*, 6 December 1958

Wells, Thomas Spencer, Alfred Hegar and Robert Battey, 'Castration in Nervous Diseases: A Symposium', *American Journal of Medical Science*, 92.10, 1886

Wetta, Frank J. and Martin A. Novelli, '"Now a Major Motion Picture": War Films and Hollywood's New Patriotism', *The Journal of Military History*, 67, July 2003

'The Whipping Post and Its Deterrent Effect', *The Medico-Legal Journal*, xviii.4, March 1901

White, Jacquelyn W. and Robin M. Kowalski, 'Deconstructing the Myth of the Nonaggressive Woman. A Feminist Analysis', *Psychology of Women Quarterly*, 18, 1994

Whitehorn, Katharine, 'Rape: Fact and Fantasy', *The Bulletin*, 31 August 1974

Whiting, Frederick, '"The Strange Particularity of the Lover's Preference": Pedophilia, Pornography, and the Anatomy of Monstrosity in *Lolita*', *American Literature*, 70.4, December 1998

Wickramesekera, I., 'Aversive Behavior Rehearsal for Sexual Exhibitionism', *Behavior Therapy*, 7, 1976

Wiedeman, Whitney S., 'Don't Spare the Rod: A Proposed Return to Public Corporal Punishment of Criminals', *American Journal of Criminal Law*, 23, 1995–6

Wille, Warren S., 'Case Study of a Rapist', *Journal of Social Therapy and Corrective Psychiatry*, 7.1, 1961

Williams, A. Hyatt, 'The Psychopathology and Treatment of Sexual Murderers', in Ismond Rosen (ed.), *The Pathology and Treatment of Sexual Deviance. A Methodological Approach*, Oxford University Press, 1964

Williams, Glanville, 'The Problem of Domestic Rape', *New Law Journal*, 141, 15 February 1991

Williams, Gurney, 'Rape in Children and Young Girls. Based on the Personal Investigation of Several Hundred Cases of Rape and of Over Fourteen Thousand Vaginal Examinations', *International Clinics*, 2.1, 1913

Williams, Linda, 'Power, Pleasure, and Perversion: Sadomasochistic Film Pornography', *Representations*, 27, Summer 1989

Willis, Ellen, 'Feminism, Moralism, and Pornography', in Ann Snitow, Christine Stansell and Sharon Thompson (eds.), *Powers of Desire: The Politics of Sexuality*, Virago Press, 1983

Wing, Adrien Katherine, 'Violence and State Accountability: Critical Race Feminism', *Georgetown Journal of Gender and Law*, 1, 1999–2000

Witkin, H., et al., 'Criminality in XYY and XXV Men', *Science*, 1983

Wittels, David G., 'What Can We Do About Sex Crimes', *Saturday Evening Post*, 11 December 1948

Wolfgang, Marvin E. and Marc Riedel, 'Rape, Racial Discrimination and the Death Penalty', in Hugo Adam Bedau and Chester M. Pierce (eds.), *Capital Punishment in the United States*, AMS Press, 1976

Wolfgang, Marvin E., 'Racial Discrimination in the Death Sentence for Rape', in William J. Bowers, *Executions in America*, Lexington Books, 1974

Women Against Rape, 'The Rapist Who Pays the Rent', *New Law Journal*, 140, 16 November 1990

Woods, G. D., 'Some Aspects of Pack Rape in Sydney', *Australian and New Zealand Journal of Criminology*, 2.2, June 1969

Woodward, Julian L., 'Changing Ideas on Mental Illness and Its Treatment', *American Sociological Review*, 16.4, August 1951

Wriggins, Jennifer, 'Rape, Racism, and the Law', *Harvard Women's Law Journal*, 6, 1983

Wright, Julie A., 'Using the Female Perspective in Prosecuting Rape Cases', *Prosecutor*, 29, 1995

Wright, Percy, Jose Nobrega and Ron Langevin, 'Brain Density and Symmetry in Pedophilic and Sexually Aggressive Offenders', *Annals of Sex Research*, 3.3, 1990

Zuspan, Frederick P., 'Alleged Rape: An Invitational Symposium', *The Journal of Reproductive Medicine*, 12.4, April 1974

BOOKS

Abrahamsen, David, *The Psychology of Crime*, Columbia University Press, 1960
Adler, Freda, *Sisters in Crime: The Rise of the New Female Criminal*, McGraw-Hill, 1975
Adorno, T. W., *The Authoritarian Personality*, Harper and Brothers, 1950
Altick, Richard, *Victorian Studies in Scarlet*, Dent, 1972
American Humane Association, *National Study on Child Neglect and Abuse Reporting*, American Humane Association, 1981
Améry, Jean, *At the Mind's Limits*, Granta, 1999
Aschaffenburg, Gustav, *Crime and Its Repression*, Heinemann, 1913
Bailey, F. Lee and Henry Rothblatt, *Crimes of Violence: Rape and Other Sex Crimes*, Lawyers Co-Operative Publishing Co., 1973
Baker, Mark, *Nam: The Vietnam War in the Words of the Men and Women Who Fought There*, Abacus, 1981
Bakhtin, Mikhail, *Rabelais and His World*, trans. H. Iswolsky, Indiana University Press, 1985
Bancroft, John, *Human Sexuality and its Problems*, Churchill Livingstone, 1989
Barash, David, *Sociobiology: The Whisperings Within*, Souvenir Press, 1979
Bart, Pauline and Patricia O'Brien, *Stopping Rape: Successful Career Strategies*, Pergamon, 1985
Barthes, Roland, *Mythologies*, trans. Annette Lavers, Hill and Wang, 1972
Bartley, Onesipherous W., *A Treatise on Forensic Medicine or Medical Jurisprudence*, Barry and Son, 1815
Bartollas, Clemens, Stuart J. Miller and Simon Dinitz, *Juvenile Victimization. The Institutional Paradox*, John Wiley and Sons, 1976
Bass, Ellen and Laura Davis, *The Courage to Heal: A Guide for Women Survivors of Child Sexual Abuse*, Cedar, 1988
Bernheim, Hippolyte M., *New Studies in Hypnotism*, trans. Richard S. Sandor, first pub. 1891, International Universities Press, 1980
Bilton, Michael and Kevin Sims, *Four Hours in My Lai. A War Crime and its Aftermath*, Viking, 1992
Blackstone, William, *Commentaries on the Laws of England*, vol. I, Clarendon Press, 1765
Bonger, William Adrian, *Criminality and Economic Conditions*, trans. Henry P. Horton, Little, Brown and Co., 1916
Bordo, Susan, *The Male Body: A New Look at Men in Public and in Private*, Farrar, Straus, and Giroux, 1999
Bordo, Susan, *Twilight Zones. The Hidden Life of Cultural Images from Plato to O. J.*, University of California Press, 1997
Bourdieu, Pierre, *In Other Words: Essays Towards a Reflexive Sociology*, Polity Press, 1990
Bourke, Joanna, *Dismembering the Male: Men's Bodies, Britain, and the Great War*, Reaktion, 1996
Bourke, Joanna, *An Intimate History of Killing: Face-to-Face Killing in Twentieth Century History*, Granta, 1999
Bourke, Joanna (ed.), *The Misfit Soldier*, Cork University Press, 1999
Bourke, Joanna, *Working-Class Cultures in Britain, 1890–1960: Gender, Class and Ethnicity*, Routledge, 1994
Bowker, Lee H., *Prison Victimization*, Elsevier, 1980
Bowlby, John, *Attachment and Loss*, Hogarth Press, 1969
Braun, Walter, *The Cruel and the Meek. Aspects of Sadism and Masochism. Being Pages from a Sexologist's Notebook*, Lyle Stuart, 1967
Bremer, John, *Asexualization: A Follow-Up Study of 244 Cases*, Oslo University Press, 1958

Bromberg, Walter, *Crime and the Mind. An Outline of Psychiatric Criminology*, J. B. Lippincott Co., 1948
Brown, Isaac Baker, *On the Curability of Certain Forms of Insanity, Epilepsy, Catalepsy, and Hysteria in Females,* Robert Harwicke, 1866
Brownmiller, Susan, *Against Our Will: Men, Women, and Rape*, Ballantine Books, 1975
Bureau of Justice Statistics, US Department of Justice, *Women Offenders*, NCJ 175688, Bureau of Justice Statistics, US Department of Justice, 1999
Burgess-Jackson, Keith, *Rape: A Philosophical Investigation*, Dartmouth Publishing Co., 1996
Butler, Judith, *Bodies That Matter: On the Discursive Limits of 'Sex'*, Routledge, 1993
Buxton, Dudley Wilmot, *Anaesthetics. Their Uses and Administration*, H. K. Lewis, 1888
Bynum, Victoria, *Unruly Women. The Politics of Social and Sexual Control in the Old South*, The University of North Carolina Press, 1992
Cahill, Ann J., *Rethinking Rape*, Cornell University Press, 2001
Caird, Alice Mona, *The Morality of Marriage, and Other Essays on the Status and Destiny of Women*, George Redway, 1897
Campbell, Anne, *Men, Women, and Aggression*, Basic Books, 1993
Campbell, Rosemary, *Heroes and Lovers. A Question of National Identity*, Allen and Unwin, 1989
Canada, Royal Commission on the Criminal Law Relating to Criminal Sexual Psychopaths, *Report of the Royal Commission on the Criminal Law Relating to Sexual Psychopaths*, Queen's Printer, 1958
Caprio, Frank S., *Variations in Sexual Behavior. A Psychodynamic Study of Deviations in Various Expressions of Sexual Behavior*, The Citadel Press, 1955
Caputi, Jane, *The Age of Sex Crime*, The Women's Press, 1987
Caputo, Philip, *A Rumor of War*, Macmillan, 1977
Carter, Dan T., *Scottsboro. A Tragedy of the American South*, Louisiana State University Press, 1969
Chaneles, Sol (ed.), *Gender Issues, Sex Offenses, and Criminal Justice: Current Trends*, The Haworth Press, 1984
Chessman, Caryl Whittier, *Cell 2455 Death Row*, Prentice-Hall, 1954
Chessman, Caryl Whittier, *The Face of Justice*, Prentice-Hall, 1957
Chessman, Caryl Whittier, *The Kid was a Killer*, F. Muller, 1960
Chessman, Caryl Whittier, *Trial by Ordeal*, Prentice-Hall, 1956
Chorover, S. L., *From Genesis to Genocide: The Meaning of Human Nature and the Power of Behavior Control*, The MIT Press, 1979
Christison, John Sanderson, *Crime and Criminals*, The W. T. Keener Co., 1897
Cleaver, Eldridge, *Soul on Ice*, McGraw-Hill, 1968
Cleckley, Hervey Milton, *The Mask of Sanity. An Attempt to Reinterpret the So-Called Psychopathic Personality*, C. V. Moshy Co., 1941
Clevenger, S. V., *Medical Jurisprudence of Insanity or Forensic Psychiatry*, vol. 2, The Lawyers' Co-Operative Publishing Co., 1898
Clifton, Allan S., *Time of Fallen Blossoms*, Cassell, 1950
Cobb, Thomas Read Rootes, *Inquiry into the Law of Negro Slavery. To Which is Prefaced, An Historical Sketch of Slavery*, T. & J. W. Johnson & Co., 1858
Coddington, Deborah, *The Australian Paedophile and Sex Offender Index*, The Mount View Trust, 1997
Coddington, Deborah, *The [New Zealand] Paedophile and Sex Offender Index*, Alister Taylor Publishers, 1996
Connell, R. W., *Gender and Power: Society, The Person, and Sexual Politics*, Polity, 1987
Cooke, Nicholas Francis, *Satan in Society, By a Physician*, C. F. Vent, 1871

Cornell, Drucilla, *Beyond Accommodation. Ethical Feminism, Deconstruction, and the Law*, Routledge, 1991
Costello, John, *Love, Sex and War. Changing Values 1939–45*, Collins, 1985
Cowan, John, *The Science of a New Life*, Cowan and Co., 1869
Curtis, Lynn A., *Violence, Race, and Culture*, Lexington Books, 1975
Daly, Mary, *Gyn/Ecology: the Metaethics of Radical Feminism*, The Beacon Press, 1978
Danner, Mark, *Torture and Truth. America, Abu Ghraib and the War on Terror*, Granta Books, 2005
Darrow, Clarence Seward, *Crime: Its Cause and Treatment*, George G. Harrap, 1920
Davidson, Henry Alexander, *Forensic Psychiatry*, Ronald Press, 1952
Davis, Andrew Jackson, *The Genesis and Ethics of Conjugal Love*, A. J. Davis and Co., 1874
Davis, Paulina Wright, *A History of the National Women's Rights Movement*, Journeyman Printers Cooperative, 1871
Derrida, Jacques, *Dissemination*, University of Chicago Press, 1981
Deutsch, Helene, *The Psychology of Women: A Psychoanalytic Interpretation*, Grune and Stratton, 1944
de Velde, Theodoor Hendrik Van, *Ideal Marriage. Its Physiology and Technique*, first pub. 1928, trans. Stella Browne, William Heinemann, 1946
Dimick, Kenneth, *Ladies in Waiting Behind Prison Walls*, Accelerated Development Inc., 1979
Dollard, John, Leonard W. Doob, Neal E. Miller, O. H. Mowrer and Robert R. Sears, *Frustration and Aggression*, Yale University Press, 1939
Donovan, Brian, *White Slave Crusades. Race, Gender, and Anti-Vice Activism, 1887–1917*, University of Illinois Press, 2006
Doshay, Lewis J. and George W. Henry, *The Boy Sex Offender and His Later Career*, Patterson Smith, 1969
Edgar, K., I. O'Donnell and C. Martin, *Prison Violence: The Dynamics of Conflict, Fear and Power*, Willan, 2003
Ellis, Albert and Ralph Brancale, *The Psychology of Sex Offenders*, Charles C. Thomas, 1956
Ellis, Henry Havelock, *The Criminal*, first pub. 1890, n.p., 1914
Ellis, Lee, *Theories of Rape. Inquiries into the Causes of Sexual Aggression*, Hemisphere Publishing, 1989
English, Kim, Suzanne Pullen and Linda Jones, *How are Adult Felony Sex Offenders Managed on Probation and Parole? A National Survey*, Colorado Department of Public Safety, 1996
Feild, Hubert S. and Leigh B. Bienen, *Jurors and Rape: A Study in Psychology and Law*, Lexington Books, 1980
Fenichel, Otto, *The Psychoanalytic Theory of Neurosis*, Kegan Paul, Trench, Tribner and Co., 1946
Fenichel, Otto, *The Psychoanalytic Theory of Neurosis*, Norton, 1945
Ferguson, Niall, *The War of the World. History's Age of Hatred*, Allen Lane, 2006
Finkelhor, David, *Child Sexual Abuse: New Theory and Research*, Free Press, 1984
Finkelhor, David, *Sexually Victimized Children*, Free Press, 1979
Finkelhor, David and Kersti Yllo, *License to Rape: Sexual Abuse of Wives*, Henry Holt & Co., 1985
Fishman, Joseph F., *Sex in Prison. Revealing Sex Conditions in American Prisons*, John Lane, 1935
Foucault, Michel, *The History of Sexuality. Volume 1: An Introduction*, trans. Robert Hurley, Allen Lane, 1978
Foucault, Michel, *The History of Sexuality. Volume 1. An Introduction*, trans. Robert Hurley, Penguin, 1990

Foxe, Arthur N., *Crime and Sexual Development. Movement and Fixation of the Libido in Criminotic Individuals*, The Monograph Editions, 1936

Fraser, George MacDonald, *Quartered Safe Out Here. A Recollection of the War in Burma*, Harvill, 1992

Freeman, Walter Jackson and James Winston Watts, *Psychosurgery: Intelligence, Emotion and Social Behavior Following Prefrontal Lobotomy for Mental Disorders*, Charles C. Thomas, 1942

Freud, Anna, *The Ego and the Mechanisms of Defense*, Hogarth Press, 1937

Freud, Sigmund, *The Psychopathology of Everyday Life*, trans. A. A. Brill, T. Fisher Unwin, 1914

Freud, Sigmund, *Three Essays on the Theory of Sexuality* first pub. 1905, trans. James Strachey, Imago Publishing Co., 1949

Gardam, Judith G. and Michelle J. Jarvis, *Women, Armed Conflict and International Law*, Kluwer Law International, 2001

Gatens, Moira, *Imagining Bodies. Ethics, Power and Corporeality*, Routledge, 1996

Giallombardo, Rose, *Society of Women: A Study of a Women's Prison*, John Wiley and Sons, 1966

Gigeroff, Alex. K., *Sexual Deviations in the Criminal Law. Homosexual, Exhibitionistic, and Pedophilic Offences in Canada*, University of Toronto Press, 1968

Gilder, G. F., *Sexual Suicide*, Quadrangle Books, 1973

Goldberg, Jacob A. and Rosamond W. Goldberg, *Girls on City Streets. A Study of 1400 Cases of Rape*, American Social Hygiene Association, 1935

Goldstein, Joseph, Burke Marshall and Jack Schwartz (eds.), *The Peers Commission Report*, Free Press, 1976

Gordon, Linda, *Heroes of their Own Lives. The Politics and History of Family Violence, Boston, 1880–1960*, Viking, 1988

Grant, Charles Graham, *Practical Forensic Medicine. A Police-Surgeon's Emergency Guide*, 3rd edn., H. K. Lewis and Co., 1924

Gray, J. Glenn, *The Warriors*, Harcourt, Brace and Company, 1959

Greenfeld, Lawrence A., *Sex Offences and Offenders: An Analysis of Data on Rape and Sexual Assault*, US Department of Justice, Bureau of Judicial Statistics, 1997

Gross, Hans, *Criminal Psychology: A Manual for Judges, Practitioners, and Students*, Little, Brown and Co., 1912

Gross, Leonard (ed.), *Sexual Behavior. Current Issue. An Interdisciplinary Perspective*, Spectrum Publications, 1974

Grossman, Lieutenant Colonel Dave, *On Killing. The Psychological Cost of Learning to Kill in War and Society*, Little, Brown and Co., 1995

Groth, A. Nicholas, *Men Who Rape. The Psychology of the Offender*, Plenum Press, 1979

Group for the Advancement of Psychiatry, *Psychiatry and Sex Psychopath Legislation: The 30s to the 80s*, Mental Health Materials Center, 1977

Guttmacher, Manfred, *Sex Offenses*, W. W. Norton, 1951

Guttmacher, Manfred S. and Henry Weihofen, *Psychiatry and the Law*, W. W. Norton and Co., 1952

Haag, Pamela, *Consent: Sexual Rights and the Transformation of American Culture*, Cornell University Press, 1999

Haaken, Janice, *Pillar of Salt: Gender, Memory, and the Perils of Looking Back*, Free Association, 1998

Hale, Sir Matthew, *Pleas of the Crown*, Richard Tonson, 1678

Hall, R. E., *Ask Any Woman: A London Enquiry into Rape and Sexual Assault*, Falling Wall Press, 1985

Hammerton, A. James, *Cruelty and Companionship in Nineteenth-Century Married Life*, Routledge, 1992

Harris, Jessica and Sharon Grace, *A Question of Evidence? Investigating and Prosecuting Rape in the 1990s*, Home Office Research Study 196, 1999

Hart, H. L. A., *Punishment and Responsibility. Essays in the Philosophy of Law*, Clarendon Press, 1968

Hartley, Catherine Gasquoine, *Sex Education and National Health*, Leonard Parsons, 1920

Hearn, Jeff, *The Gender of Oppression: Men, Masculinity, and the Critique of Marxism*, Wheatsheaf, 1987

Hewins, George, *The Dillen. Memories of a Man of Stratford-upon-Avon*, Elm Tree, 1981

Hickson, Alisdare, *The Poisoned Bowl. Sex, Repression and the Public School System*, Constable, 1995

Hilberman, Elaine, *The Rape Victim: A Project of the Committee on Women of the American Psychiatric Association*, Basic Books, 1976

Hird, Myra J., *Engendering Violence. Heterosexual Interpersonal Violence from Childhood to Adulthood*, Ashgate Publishing Ltd., 2002

H. M. Crown Prosecution Service Inspectorate, *A Report on the Joint Inspection into the Investigation and Prosecution of Cases Involving Allegations of Rape*, in H. M. Crown Prosecution Service Inspectorate, April 2002

Hodann, Max, *History of Modern Morals*, trans. Stella Brown, William Heinemann, 1937

Hodes, Martha Elizabeth, *White Women, Black Men: Illicit Sex in the Nineteenth-Century South*, Yale University Press, 1997

Holledge, James, *Sex and the Australian Teenager*, Horwitz Publications, 1964

Home Office, Communications Directorate, *Setting the Boundaries: Reforming the Law on Sex Offences*, Home Office, 2000

hooks, bell, *Outlaw Culture. Resisting Representations*, Routledge, 1994

Horne, John and Alan Kramer, *German Atrocities, 1914. A History of Denial*, Yale University Press, 2001

Human Rights Watch, Women's Rights Project, *All Too Familiar: Sexual Abuse of Women in US State Prisons*, Human Rights Watch, 1966

Hursch, Carolyn J., *The Trouble with Rape*, Nelson-Hall, 1977

Husband, H. Aubrey, *The Students' Hand-Book of Forensic Medicine and Medical Police*, 4th edn., E. & S. Livingstone, 1883

Hyde, Alan, *Bodies of Law*, Princeton University Press, 1997

Jackson, Louise A., *Child Sexual Abuse in Victorian England*, Routledge, 2000

James, Don, *The Sexual Side of Life*, Monarch Books, 1957

Jasinski, J. L. and L. M. Williams, *Partner Violence: A Comprehensive Review of the 20 Years of Research*, Sage, 1998

Jenkins, Philip, *Moral Panic: Changing Concepts of the Child Molester in Modern America*, Yale University Press, 1998

Jenkins, Philip, *Pedophiles and Priests: Anatomy of a Contemporary Crisis*, Oxford University Press, 2001

Jones, David A., *The Health Risks of Imprisonment*, Lexington Books, 1976

Karpman, Benjamin, *The Sexual Offender and his Offenses. Etiology, Pathology, Psychodynamics and Treatment*, Julian Press, 1954

Karpman, Benjamin, *The Sexual Offender and his Offenses: Etiology, Pathology and Treatment*, first pub. 1954, Julian Press, 1964

Kellogg, John Harvey, *Plain Facts for Old and Young*, I. F. Senger, 1884

Kelly, Liz, Jo Lovett and Linda Regan, *A Gap or a Chasm? Attrition in Reported Rape Cases*, Home Office Research Study 293, Home Office Research, Development and Statistics Directorate, 2005

Kilpatrick, D. G., C. N. Edmunds and A. K. Seymour, *Rape in America: A Report to the Nation*, National Victim Center, 1992

Kinsey, Alfred C., Wardell B. Pomeroy and Clyde E. Martin, *Sexual Behavior in the Human Male*, W. B. Saunders Co., 1948

Kramer, Lawrence, *After the Lovedeath: Sexual Violence and the Making of Culture*, University of California Press, 1997

Kunzman, Kristin A., *The Healing Way: Adult Recovery from Childhood Sexual Abuse*, Harper and Row, 1990

Lacey, Nicola, *Unspeakable Subjects. Feminist Essays in Legal and Social Theory*, Hart, 1998

Lambert, Eric, *Mad and With Much Heart. A Life of the Parents of Oscar Wilde*, Frederick Muller, 1967

Lane, Mark, *Conversations with Americans*, Simon and Schuster, 1970

Laughlin, Harry Hamilton, *Eugenical Sterilization in the United States*, Psychopathic Laboratory of the Municipal Court of Chicago, 1922

Laur, Richard, *The Psychology of Rape*, Challenge Publications, 1966

Law Reform Commission, *Rape Prosecutions (Court Procedures and Rules of Evidence)*, working paper no. 4, Law Reform Commission, 1976

Lee, Harper, *To Kill a Mockingbird*, Heinemann, 1960

Lehman, Rev. F. M. with Rev. N. K. Clarkson, *The White Slave Hell; or, With Christ at Midnight in the Slums of Chicago*, The Christian Witness Co., 1910

Levine, Sylvia and Joseph Koenig (eds.), *Why Men Rape. Interviews with Convicted Rapists*, A Star Book, 1982

Levy, Howard and David Miller, *Going to Jail. The Political Prisoner*, Grove Press, 1970

Lew, M., *Victims No Longer: Men Recovering from Incest and Other Sexual Child Abuse*, Harper Collins Publishers, 1988

Lilly, J. Robert, *Taken by Force. Rape and American GIs in Europe during World War II*

Lindener, Robert, *Stone Walls and Men*, Odyssey Press, 1946, Palgrave Macmillan, 2007

Lines, Moira, *Victim of a Female Rapist*, Sexa Ltd., 1971

Lloyd, Ronald and Stanley Williamson, *Born to Trouble. Portrait of a Psychopath*, The Bowering Press, 1968

Loewenfeld, Leopold, *On Conjugal Happiness. Experiences, Reflections and Advice of a Medical Man*, 3rd edn., trans. Ronald E. S. Krohn, John Bale, Sons and Dannielsson, 1913

Loftus, Elizabeth F., *Eyewitness Testimony*, Harvard University Press, 1979

Loftus, Elizabeth and Katherine Ketcham, *The Myth of Repressed Memory: False Memories and Allegations of Sexual Abuse*, St. Martin's, 1994

Logan, William, *The Great Social Evil. Its Causes, Extent, Results, and Remedies*, Hodder and Stoughton, 1871

Lombroso, Cesare and Guglielmo Ferrero, *The Female Offender*, np, 1895

Lynchings and What they Mean. General Findings of the Southern Commission on the Study of Lynching, Atlanta: Southern Committee on the Study of Lynching, 1931

McCahill, Thomas W., Linda C. Meyer and Arther M. Fischman, *The Aftermath of Rape*, Heath, 1979

McCalman, Iain, *Radical Underworlds: Prophets, Revolutionaries, and Pornographers in London, 1795–1840*, Oxford University Press, 1987

MacDonald, George J. and Robinson A. Williams, *Characteristics and Management of Committed Sexual Offenders in the State of Washington*, Department of Social Health Services, Western State Hospital, 1971

McDougall, William, *An Introduction to Social Psychology*, first pub. 1908, Thoemmes Press, 1998

MacKinnon, Catharine, *Toward a Feminist Theory of the State*, Harvard University Press, 1989

MacKinnon, Catharine A. and Andrea Dworkin (eds.), *In Harm's Way. The Pornography Civil Rights Hearings*, Harvard University Press, 1997

MacKinnon, Catharine A. and Andrea Dworkin, *Pornography and Civil Rights: A New Day for Women's Equality*, Organizing Against Pornography, 1988

McMullen, R., *Male Rape: Breaking the Silence on the Last Taboo*, GMP Publishers Ltd., 1990

MacNamara, Daniel E. J. and Edward Sagarin, *Sex, Crime, and the Law*, The Free Press, 1977

Maguire, Kathleen and Ann L. Pastore (eds.), *Sourcebook of Criminal Justice Statistics 1995*, Department of Justice, 1996

Manchester, William, *Goodbye Darkness. A Memoir of the Pacific War*, Little, Brown and Co., 1980

Mann, J. Dixon, *Forensic Medicine and Toxicology*, 2nd edn., revised and enlarged, Charles Griffith and Co., 1898

Mark, Vernon Herschel and Frank Raymond Ervin, *Violence and the Brain*, Harper and Row, 1970

Marks, Isaac M., *Living With Fear: Understanding and Coping with Anxiety*, McGraw-Hill, 1978

Mathews, R., J. K. Matthews and K. Speltz, *Female Sexual Offenders: An Exploratory Study*, Safer Society Press, 1989

Mead, George H., *Mind, Self and Society From the Standpoint of a Social Behaviorist*, University of Chicago Press, 1934

Mendel, M. P., *The Male Survivor: The Impact of Sexual Abuse*, Sage, 1993

Mitchell, Margaret, *Gone With the Wind*, first pub. 1936, Avon Books, 1973

Monday Conference Transcript. Men, Women and Violence – The Politics of Rape, Australian Broadcasting Commission, 1976

Morgan, Robin, *Going Too Far: the Personal Chronicle of a Feminist*, Random House, 1977

Myhill, A. and J. Allen, *Rape and Sexual Assault of Women: The Extent and Nature of the Problem – Findings from the British Crime Survey*, Home Office Research Study 237, Home Office Research, Development and Statistics Directorate, 2002

Napheys, George Henry, *The Transmission of Life. Counsels on the Nature and Hygiene of the Masculine Functions*, J. S. Robertson, 1884

National Council for Civil Liberties, *Vagrancy – An Archaic Law. A Memorandum of Evidence to the Home Office Working Party on Vagrancy and Street Offences*, NCCL, 1975

Neumann, F. and J. Kalmuss, *Hormonal Treatment of Sexual Deviations*, Verlag, 1991

Newman, Francis W., *Remedies for the Great Social Evil with Special Reference to Recent Laws Delusively Called Contagious Diseases Acts*, first pub. 1884, Reform Union, 1889

Nicolson, Linda, *The Play of Reason: From the Modern to the Postmodern*, Cornell University Press, 1999

Northcote, Hugh, *Christianity and Sex Problems*, F. A. David Co., 1906

O'Callaghan, Mark A. J. and Douglas Carroll, *Psychosurgery: A Scientific Analysis*, The MIT Press, 1982

O'Connell, Robert L., *Of Arms and Men: A History of War, Weapons and Aggression*, Oxford University Press, 1989

Ofshe, Richard and Ethan Watters, *Making Monsters: False Memories, Psychotherapy, and Sexual Hysteria*, Charles Scribner, 1994

Packer, Herbert L., *The Limits of the Criminal Sanction*, Stanford University Press, 1969

Painter, K., *Wife Rape, Marriage and Law: Survey Report, Key-Findings and Recommendation*, University of Manchester, Department of Social Policy and Social Work, 1991

Paglia, Camille, *Sexual Personae: Art and Decadence from Nefertiti to Emily Dickinson*, Vintage, 1991

Parker, Tony, *The Twisting Lane. Some Sex Offenders*, Panther, 1970

Patrick, Diane, Diane Pasini-Hill, Linda Jones, Sydney Cooley-Towell and Kim English, *How is the Post-Conviction Polygraph Examination Used in Adult Sex Offender Management Activities?*, Colorado Department of Public Safety, December 2000

Patterson, Haywood and Earl Conrad, *Scottsboro Boy*, Victor Gollancz, 1950

Paul, Hugo, *Cry Rape: Anatomy of the Rapist*, intro. by Jean-Paul St. Marc, Dalhousie Press, 1967

Pearson, Patricia, *When She Was Bad: How Women Get Away with Murder*, Virago Press, 1997

Pendergrast, Mark, *Victims of Memory: Incest Accusations and Shattered Lives*, Upper Access Books, 1995

Pernick, Martin S., *A Calculus of Suffering. Pain, Professionalism, and Anesthesia in Nineteenth Century America*, Columbia University Press, 1985

Phillips, Dretha M. and Rochelle Troyano, *Community Notification as Viewed by Washington's Citizens*, Washington State Institute for Public Policy, 1998

Pollens, Bertram, *The Sex Criminal*, Putnam, 1939

Polner, Murray, *No Victory Parades. The Return of the Vietnam Veteran*, Holt, Rinehard and Winston, 1971

Polson, Cyril John, *The Essentials of Forensic Medicine*, English Universities Press, 1955

Porteus, Stanley David, *A Psychologist of Sorts. The Autobiography and Publications of the Inventor of the Porteus Maze Test*, Pacific Books, 1969

Prichard, James Cowles, *A Treatise on Insanity, and Other Disorders Affecting the Mind*, Sherwood, Gilbert, and Piper, 1835

Putnam, J. J., *Addresses on Psycho-Analysis*, International Psycho-Analytical Press, 1921

Pym, Rev. T. W. and Rev. Geoffrey Gordon, *Papers from Picardy by Two Chaplains*, Constable and Company, 1917

Raine, Adrian, *The Psychopathology of Crime: Criminal Behavior as a Clinical Disorder*, Academic Press, 1993

Reynolds, Helen, *Cops and Dollars. The Economics of Criminal Law and Justice*, Charles C. Thomas, 1981

Rhodes, Lorna A., *Total Confinement. Madness and Reason in the Maximum Security Prison*, University of California Press, 2004

Riccio, Vincent and Bill Slocum, *All the Way Down. The Violent Underworld of Street Gangs*, Simon and Schuster, 1962

Rickles, Nathan King, *Exhibitionism*, J. B. Lippincott, 1950

Rise, Eric W., *The Martinsville Seven: Race, Rape, and Capital Punishment*, University of Virginia Press, 1995

Robinson, William J., *America's Sex and Marriage Problems. Based on Thirty Years Practice and Study*, Eugenics Publishing Co., 1928

Robinson, William J., *Sexual Problems of To-Day*, 6th edn., first pub. 1912, The Critic and Guide Co., 1916

Robinson, William J., *Woman: Her Sex and Love Life*, The Critic and Guide Co., 1917

Roiphe, Katie, *The Morning After: Sex, Fear, and Feminism on Campus*, Little, Brown and Co., 1993

Rose, Hilary and Steven Rose (eds.), *Alas, Poor Darwin. Arguments Against Evolutionary Psychology*, Jonathan Cape, 2000

Rueben, David, *Everything You Always Wanted to Know About Sex But Were Afraid to Ask*, D. McKay, 1969

Russell, Diana E. H., *The Politics of Rape: The Victim's Perspective*, Stein and Day, 1984

Russell, Diana E. H. and Rebecca M. Bolen, *The Epidemic of Rape and Child Abuse in the United States*, Sage, 2000

Russell, Diana H., *Rape in Marriage*, Indiana University Press, 1990

Ryan, Michael, *A Manual of Medical Jurisprudence*, Renshaw and Rush, 1831

Sadoff, Robert L., *Forensic Psychiatry: A Practical Guide for Lawyers and Psychiatrists*, Thomas, 1975
Scacco, Anthony M. (ed.), *Male Rape. A Casebook of Sexual Aggression*, AMS Press, 1982
Scarce, Michael, *Male on Male Rape: The Hidden Toll of Stigma and Shame*, Plenum Press, 1997
Scarry, Elaine, *The Body in Pain. The Making and Unmaking of the World*, Oxford University Press, 1985
Schoenewolf, Gerald, *The Art of Hating*, Aronson, 1991
Schoenewolf, Gerald, *Sexual Animosity Between Men and Women*, Aronson, 1989
Schouler, James, *A Treatise on the Law of Domestic Relations: Embracing Husband and Wife, Parent and Child, Guardian and Ward, and Master and Servant*, 4th edn., Little, Brown and Co., 1889
Schur, Edwin M., *The Americanization of Sex*, Temple University Press, 1988
Scott, George Ryley, *Sex Problems and Dangers in War-Time. A Book of Practical Advice for Men and Women on the Fighting and Home Fronts*, T. Werner Laurie, 1940
Scott, J. P., *Aggression*, University of Chicago Press, 1958
Seidenberg, Willa and William Short, *A Matter of Conscience. GI Resistance During the Vietnam War*, Addison Gallery of American Art, 1991
Segal, Lynne, *Slow Motion. Changing Masculinities; Changing Men*, 3rd edn., Palgrave Macmillan, 2007
Shaw, Clifford R. in collaboration with Maurice E. Moore, *The Natural History of a Delinquent Career*, Greenwood Press, 1968
Sikes, Gini, *8 Ball Chicks: A Year in the Violent World of Girl Gangsters*, Anchor, 1997
Silverman, Jon and David Wilson, *Innocence Betrayed. Paedophilia, the Media and Society*, Polity, 2002
Slovenko, Ralph, *Psychiatry and Criminal Culpability*, John Wiley and Sons, 1995
Smith, Carlton, *Hunting Evil*, St. Martin's Paperbacks, 2000
Smith, Sydney, *Forensic Medicine. A Text-Book for Students and Practitioners*, J. & A. Churchill, 1925
Soble, Alan, *Pornography: Marxism, Feminism, and the Future of Sexuality*, Yale University Press, 1986
Sommers, Christine Hoff, *Who Stole Feminism? How Women Have Betrayed Women*, Simon and Schuster, 1994
Staines, Deborah, *Interrogating the War on Terror*, Cambridge Scholars Publishing, 2007
Stearns, Albert Warren, *The Personality of Criminals*, The Beacon Press, 1931
Stekel, Wilhelm, *Auto-Eroticism*, trans. James S. Van Tesllaar, Peter Nevill, 1951
Stevenson, J. V., *The Punishment and Prevention of Crime*, Royal Philosophical Society of Glasgow, 1908
Stockham, Alice B., *Tokology. A Book for Every Woman*, The Author, 1889
Stoltenberg, John, *Refusing to be a Man: Essays on Sex and Justice*, rev. edn., UCL Press, 2000
Storaska, Frederic, *How to Say No to a Rapist and Survive*, Random House, 1975
Storr, Anthony, *Sexual Deviation*, Penguin, 1964
Sussman, Les and Sally Bordwell, *The Rapist File*, Chelsea House, 1981
Sutherland, Edwin Hardin and Donald Ray Cressey, *Criminology*, 8th edn., J. B. Lippincott Co., 1970
Svenson, Arne, *Prisoners*, Blast Books, 1997
Symons, Donald, *The Evolution of Human Sexuality*, Oxford University Press, 1979
Tatar, Maria, *Lustmord. Sexual Murder in Weimar Germany*, Princeton University Press, 1985
Tavris, Carol, *The Mismeasure of Woman: Why Women are not the Better Sex, the Inferior Sex, or the Opposite Sex*, Simon and Schuster, 1992

Terkel, Studs, *'The Good War'. An Oral History of World War Two*, Hamilton, 1985
Terry, Wallace, *Bloods. An Oral History of the Vietnam War*, Random House, 1984
Thoinot, Léon Henri and Arthur W. Weysee, *Medicolegal Aspects of Moral Offenses*, F. A. Davis Co., 1911
Thompson, George, *Psychopathic Delinquent and the Criminal*, Charles C. Thomas, 1953
Thornhill, Randy and Craig Palmer, *A Natural History of Rape: Biological Bases of Sexual Coercion*, The MIT Press, 2000
Tosh, John, *A Man's Place: Masculinity and the Middle-Class Home in Victorian England*, Yale University Press, 1999
Trall, Russell Thacher, *Sexual Physiology: A Scientific and Popular Exposition of the Fundamental Problems in Sociology*, n.p., 1866
Travis, Cheryl Brown (ed.), *Evolution, Gender, and Rape*, The MIT Press, 2003
Turner, Marcia T. and Tracey N. Turner, *Female Adolescent Sexual Abusers: An Exploratory Study of Mother-Daughter Dynamics with Implications for Treatment*, The Safer Society Press, 1994
Ullman, Sharon R., *Sex Seen: The Emergence of Modern Sexuality in America*, University of California Press, 1997
United Nations, *Global Report on Crime and Justice*, Oxford University Press, 1999
US Department of Health and Human Services Administration on Children, Youth, and Families, *Child Maltreatment 1998: Reports from the States to the National Child Abuse and Neglect Data Systems*, USGPO, 2000
US Department of Justice, *Three Strikes and You're Out: A Review of State Legislation*, US Department of Justice, 1997
US Department of Justice, *Uniform Crime Reports*, US Department of Justice, 1997
Vachss, Alice, *Sex Crimes*, Random House, 1993
Vedder, Clyde B. and Patricia G. King, *Problems of Homosexuality in Corrections*, Charles C. Thomas, 1967
Vietnam Veterans Against the War, *The Winter Soldier Investigation. An Inquiry into American War Crimes*, Beacon Press, 1972
Vigarello, Georges, *A History of Rape. Sexual Violence in France from the 16th to the 20th Century*, trans. Jean Birrell, Cambridge University Press, 2001
von Krafft-Ebing, Richard, *Psychopathia Sexualis*, trans. Charles Gilbert Chaddock, F. J. Rebman, 1893
Watson, John B., *Behaviorism*, Kegan Paul, 1925
Weider, Arthur (ed.), *Contributions Towards Medical Psychology*, Ronald Press, 1953
Weihofen, Henry, *The Urge to Punish: New Approaches to the Problem of Mental Irresponsibility for Crime*, Victor Gollancz, 1957
Weiss, Carl and David James Friar, *Terror in the Prisons: Homosexual Rape and Why Society Condones It*, 1974
West, D. J., C. Roy and Florence L. Nichols, *Understanding Sexual Attacks: A Study Based Upon a Group of Rapists Undergoing Psychotherapy*, Heinemann Educational, 1978
Wharton, Francis, *A Monograph on Mental Unsoundness*, Kay and Brother, 1855
Wharton, Francis, *A Treatise on Mental Unsoundness*, 3rd edn., n.p., 1873
White, Walter, *Rope and Faggot: A Biography of Judge Lynch*, first pub. 1929, Alfred A. Knopf, 1969
White, Terence De Vere, *The Parents of Oscar Wilde. Sir William and Lady Wilde*, Hodder and Stoughton, 1967
Wiener, Martin J., *Men of Blood. Violence, Manliness and Criminal Justice in Victorian England*, Cambridge University Press, 2004
Witthaus, Rudolp Aug. and Tracy C. B. Becker, *Medical Jurisprudence, Forensic Medicine, and Toxicology*, W. Wood and Co., 1894

Wolfthal, Diane, *Images of Rape: The 'Heroic' Tradition and its Alternatives*, Cambridge University Press, 1999

Wooden, Wayne S. and Jay Parker, *Men Behind Bars. Sexual Exploitation in Prison*, Plenum Press, 1982

Woodman, W. Bathurst and Charles Meymott Tidy, *A Handy-Book of Forensic Medicine and Toxicology*, J. & A. Churchill, 1877

Wrangham, Richard and Dale Peterson, *Demonic Males: Apes and the Origins of Human Violence*, Houghton Mifflin, 1996

Wright, Henry C., *The Unwelcome Child* (1858)

Wylie, Philip, *Generation of Vipers*, first pub. 1942 (New York, 1955)

Yablonsky, Lewis, *The Violent Gang*, The Macmillan Co., 1962

Young, Marion Iris, *Throwing Like a Girl and Other Essays in Feminist Philosophy and Social Theory*, Indiana University Press, 1990

WEBSITES

Dumond, Robert D., 'The Impact and Recovery of Prison Rape', at http://www.spr.org/pdf/Dumond.pdf

Ehrenreich, Barbara, 'Barbara Ehrenreich's Commencement Address at Barnard College', http://www.rockridgeinstitute.org/perspectives/becommencement

Gordon, Art and Frank J. Porporino, 'Managing the Treatment of Sex Offenders: A Canadian Perspective', May 1990, in http://www.csc-scc.gc.ca/text/rsrch/briefs/b5/b05e_e.shtml

Human Rights Watch, *No Escape: Male Rape in US Prisons*, 2001, in http://www.hrw.org/reports/2001/prison/report8.html#_1_50

National Coalition for the Protection of Children and Families, 'Abu Ghraib: Lessons in S-xual Morality', http://www.nationalcoalition.org/culture/articles/ca050523.html

Schlafly, Phyllis, 'Equality for Women in our Army', *Eagle Forum*, 19 May 2004, in http://www.eagleforum.org/column/2004/may2004/04-05-19.html

Sere, Adriene, 'Man and the History of Rape', at http://www.saidit.org/archives/mar00/mar_article2.html

'Winter Soldier Investigation. 'Testimony Given in Detroit, Michigan, on January 31, 1971, February 2, 1971', at http://lists.villagr.virginia.edu/sixties/HTML_doc/Resources/Primary/Winter_Soldier/WS_entry.html

NEWSPAPERS AND PERIODICALS

The Afro-American Ledger, 1904

The Age, 1993

Boston Herald, 1997

British Medical Journal, 1800–1999

Buffalo News, 1996

[Tampa] *Daily Times*, 1934

The Fayetteville Observer, 1955

The Guardian, 1800–2006

The Independent, 1991

The Lancet, 1800–1999

Leeds Mercury, 1860

Los Angeles Times, 1985

Monmouthshire Merlin, 1829

[Tampa] *Morning Tribune*, 1934

Sydney Morning Herald, 1887

The Times, 1800–2006

[Brisbane] *Truth*, 1928
The Washington Post, 1975
The West Australian, 1938

FILMS

American History X (1998)
American Me (1992)
Animal Factory (2000)
The Birth of a Nation (1915)
The Border Raiders (1918)
Born Innocent (1974)
A Child's Cry (1986)
Curtains (1983)
Dirty Work (1998)
The Disappointed Old Maid (1899)
Fallen Angel (1981)
Forty Days and Forty Nights (2002)
Gone With the Wind (1939)
The Graduate (1967)
Her Debt of Honor (1916)
House Party (1990)
I Spit on your Grave (1978)
Infidelity (1917)
Jaded (1996)
Little Big Man (1970)
The Lonely Sex (1959)
The Naked Gun 33⅓ (1994)
Nightmare on Elm Street (1984)
Platoon (1986)
Poison (1991)
The Shawshank Redemption (1984)
Something About Amelia (1984)
The Summer of '42 (1971)
There's Something About Mary (1998)
To Kill a Mockingbird (1962)
Up Close and Personal (1996)
Wedding Crashers (2005)
When a Bough Breaks (1986)

Index

Picture Credits

112 P. Johnsgard

141 Political Cartoons

180 AP/Press Association

182 Courtesy of the University of Southern California, on behalf of the USC Specialized Libraries and Archival Collections

211 Political Cartoons

232 Gregory Urgquiaga, *The Contra Costa Times*

241 Political Cartoons

307 Mary Evans Picture Library

329 Alabama State Archives/Montgomery Archives

332 Political Cartoons

363 Political Cartoons